PROGRESSIVES AND RADICALS IN
ENGLISH EDUCATION

1750–1970

Also by W. A. C. Stewart

THE EDUCATIONAL INNOVATORS 1750–1880
(*with W. P. McCann*)

THE EDUCATIONAL INNOVATORS 1889–1967

PROGRESSIVES AND RADICALS IN ENGLISH EDUCATION

1750–1970

W. A. C. STEWART

AUGUSTUS M. KELLEY · Publishers
New Jersey 1972

© W. A. C. Stewart 1972

Published in the United States by
Augustus M. Kelley · Publishers
Clifton, New Jersey 07012

Library of Congress Catalog Card Number 72—77862
Standard Book Number 0 678 07015 6

Printed in Great Britain by
RICHARD CLAY (THE CHAUCER PRESS), LTD.,
Bungay, Suffolk

TO E.E.S.

Contents

Preface and Acknowledgements ... ix
Introduction ... xi

PART ONE: 1750–1850

1 *The Eighteenth Century: Experiment and Enlightenment* ... 3
  1 Early Experiments: William Gilpin and David Manson ... 3
  2 Rousseau and English Education in the Late Eighteenth Century ... 12
  3 David Williams and the Laurence Street Academy ... 22

2 *The Industrial Revolution and After* ... 33
  4 Robert Owen and the New Lanark Schools ... 33
  5 The Followers of Owen: Working-class Educators and Utopians ... 42
  6 The Hills and Hazelwood School ... 54
  7 King's Somborne School ... 67

3 *Continental Influences* ... 75
  8 Pestalozzi, Fellenberg, and English Education ... 75
  9 Kay-Shuttleworth and the Continental Reformers ... 85

4 *Some General Themes* ... 91
  10 Labour and Education: 1780–1850 ... 91
  11 Rewards and Punishments: 1780–1850 ... 94

5 *Epilogue: 1750–1850* ... 100

PART TWO: 1850–1880

6 *The Royal Commissions and After* ... 103
  12 New Influences and the Intelligentsia ... 103
  13 Henry Morley and Johannes and Bertha Ronge ... 110
  14 Barbara Bodichon and Portman Hall ... 113
  15 The International School ... 118
  16 William Ellis and the Birkbeck Schools ... 125

7 *Epilogue: 1850–1880* ... 132

PART THREE: 1889–1970

8	*The Growth of School: 1889–1898*		143
	17 Abbotsholme		144
	18 Bedales		149
	19 Clayesmore		153
	20 King Alfred's		162
9	*Merging into Educational Radicalism: 1898–1918*		173
	21 Quaker Schools		174
	22 Badminton		184
	23 Theosophical Schools		188
10	*New Schools and Europe: 1890–1918*		202
11	*Preface to the Post-War Surgence*		213
	24 Maria Montessori		213
	25 Homer Lane		221
12	*The Post-War Surgence: The Twenties*		232
	26 Beginnings of the New Psychology: Bembridge, Rendcomb		232
13	*The Post-War Surgence: The Twenties*		246
	27 The Wave of the New Psychology: Summerhill, the Malting House		246
14	*The Post-War Surgence: The Twenties*		262
	28 The New Communities: Dartington and Beacon Hill		262
15	*The Post-War Surgence: The Twenties*		287
	29 Rudolf Steiner and Anthroposophy		287
16	*The Slackening Tide: Bryanston*		303
17	*The Slackening Tide: The Thirties and Gordonstoun*		317
18	*The Second World War: Wennington*		345
19	*The International Movement in Progressive Education*		353
20	*Three Headmasters: Cecil Reddie and Abbotsholme*		378
21	*Three Headmasters: J. H. Badley and Bedales*		402
22	*Three Headmasters: A. S. Neill and Summerhill*		415
23	*Some Facts, Figures, and Interpretations*		435
24	*Conclusion*		465
	Bibliography		487
	Index		509

Preface and Acknowledgements

IN THE present century schools have come into existence to express particular beliefs about education and by these assertions to voice criticism of and opposition to certain educational principles and practices. A good deal has been written about individual schools or educational experiments but no thorough study has been made of unorthodoxy in English education, and when beginning on such an inquiry one needs to find reasonable justification for choosing a starting-point as well as for the criteria by which to select the innovators who are to be considered.

It is common to say that identifiably modern ideas in education may be traced to Rousseau, especially to the influence of *Émile*, published in 1762. While the claim has substance, evidence exists to show that there were innovators in British educational theory and practice before 1762, and it is these who provide me with a starting-point. So I shall start at 1750. The full presentation of the earlier period is found in the first of the two-volume study on which this book is based.[1] For help in that study with the full treatment of the period 1750–1880 I am indebted to my collaborator Dr. W. P. McCann. In this book, however, most of the emphasis is on the twentieth century and so there has been a great deal of replanning and rewriting and necessary bringing up to date. I have been able to benefit from advice and comment given on the earlier volumes.

I hope the present book will be of interest to students of education, to serving teachers, to historians, and to all who are interested in social and educational change. My acknowledgements to the Leverhulme Trust and to all those who helped to shape the longer study are made in the earlier volumes. For the typing and careful presentation of the bibliography and manuscript of this book I am greatly indebted to Mrs. Rachel Mussell and Miss Jane Oakes.

W.A.C.S.

Keele 1970

[1] W. A. C. Stewart and W. P. McCann, *The Educational Innovators 1750–1880* (vol. i, Macmillan, 1967); W. A. C. Stewart, *The Educational Innovators 1889–1967* (vol. ii, Macmillan, 1968).

Introduction

I

THE PRESENT pattern of compulsory schooling in England is now a century old, and an immense increase in educational provision took place in the last quarter of the last century. To bring about such expansion some degree of control and standardization was inevitable, and there seems to have been a broad consensus on how children should be treated and how they should be taught. Children as pupils were supposed to be dependent upon the authority of the adult. Knowledge was organized as material to be taught and learned, and the learner had to match himself against what the teacher (or the examiner) required and to prepare himself accordingly. Schools were instruments of induction for the young and of supremacy for the adults, while the induction itself was in morals, obedience, and piety as well as in the three R's or more sophisticated subjects. These are the sketch-lines of the average, orthodox view on schools in the period 1750–1870, leaving out of account the quality of education given or the degree of devotion or neglect shown by teachers or pupils. Evidence exists, however, of unorthodox theory and practice over the same period, minority opinion that merits attention.

Some people who have had ideas and theories about dealing with children and the kinds of knowledge that are important have started schools to practise what they preach, and there are plenty of examples of teacher-innovators in the pages that follow. Others have interested themselves in unorthodoxy in education by writing about it, often as part of a larger social or philosophical analysis; it was so with Locke, with Rousseau, and with Owen. There are also those who backed new schools with money as sympathizers while not themselves originating the ideas or taking an active part in the day-to-day conduct of affairs.

Before we can talk of unorthodoxy in education there have to be enough schools to have established a prevailing mood and practice, an orthodoxy, and while I could take this a long way back, I shall start at 1750 before the dramatic expansion of education in the nineteenth century and a few years before the publication of *Émile*. I could consider theorists, philanthropists, and practitioners expressing unorthodox ideas about education, but for the most part I shall examine only those principles that reached a sufficient degree of definiteness to be worked out in a school. Yet I do not list every unorthodox school in the country throughout the period, for this is not a commentary of that kind. It is my intention to consider unorthodox principles of substance, with evidence from schools to support the argument, and the coverage will be almost entirely in England. However, no analysis of this kind can entirely ignore Germany, Switzerland, and France, but these are mentioned mainly in connection with the work of Froebel, Pestalozzi, Fellenberg, and Rousseau in the earlier period. In the twentieth century, besides the countries mentioned above, the main source for foreign reference is, of course, the United States of America, where Dewey, Helen Parkhurst, Kilpatrick, and others made so notable a contribution. But still the main emphasis in this book is on England.

I use the terms 'progressive', 'experimental', and 'radical' almost interchangeably, but where stricter definition is involved I have used some variant of the term 'innovating' as this represents a more accurately neutral description of much of the educational practice, however radical the theory sometimes was, and it must be admitted at once that what was thought to be a deviation in 1800 is likely to be much less so in 1850 or 1900 or 1970.

II

Where, then, will educational innovation in schools be seen sufficiently clearly? Obviously in the area of knowledge, and this means predominantly in the curriculum, both in the range and content of subject-matter and in the consideration given to children's individual differences, particularly in the subjects taught to them and the methods of learning encouraged. If, in addition, a school pays heed to the aptitudes and interests of the pupils before prescribing a programme of studies, this can be another unusual feature, and so too with personal relationships, especially those between teachers and pupils.

Introduction

This will appear particularly clearly in the forms of authority and discipline and punishment. Unorthodox teaching methods are another index of innovation.

The schools included here, then, have to be markedly original in their approach to what is taught and how it is taught; in their recognition of the pupil as initiator and the teacher as guide rather than authoritarian; in their concern for the humane organization of the school community to these ends. Some schools exemplify reform, but were not really regarded as radical; Rugby under Arnold, Shrewsbury under Butler, and Marlborough under Dancy would be three good examples of these. None of them at any time ran a serious risk of being separated from the public schools but instead modified and reformed the system from within rather than breaking through into being a quite different kind of school. Mack, speaking of Hazelwood, founded by the brothers Hill early in the nineteenth century and one of the schools considered later in this book, makes this point clear:

> [Hazelwood's] ideas were too new and its break with the past too abrupt to appeal to most upper-class Englishmen so long as a more moderate substitute could be found. Middle-class attachment to the Hills' doctrine was predicated on despair of such a substitute. But at the end of the twenties Arnold provided a solution of the moral problem which did not necessitate destruction of the [public] schools or involve a thorough-going liberalism, and thus it was Arnold and not the Hills who has lived as England's great educator.[1]

The norms Hazelwood assumed, both for the society for which it was educating and for the methods of education practised in the school, were implicitly and explicitly different from those of the public schools, even the reformed public schools. Summerhill and Abbotsholme in the twentieth century are in the same category as Hazelwood, although the norms are utterly different.

Education and schools are, admittedly, part of a wider and deeper panorama of ideas and institutions. However, the focus

[1] E. C. Mack, *Public Schools and British Opinion, 1780–1860* (London, 1938), pp. 168–9.

in this book is on the working out in practice of unorthodox educational ideas, and the linking social and economic themes arise from these.

Part One

1750–1850

1 The Eighteenth Century: Experiment and Enlightenment

1 EARLY EXPERIMENTS: WILLIAM GILPIN AND DAVID MANSON

THE WORK of at least two educationalists, begun as early as the 1750s, foreshadowed some of the experiments usually ascribed to the new school of educationalists inspired by Rousseau. These pioneers were William Gilpin of Cheam School and David Manson of Belfast. Unknown to each other, they made some highly original reforms in school discipline, organization, and teaching method. Their innovations were the expression of a critical attitude to traditional forms of education, but neither Gilpin nor Manson was influenced by Continental theorists. They did not consciously start a movement, yet they were the pioneers in the whole progressive tradition in England. It is to William Gilpin that I turn first of all.

WILLIAM GILPIN OF CHEAM SCHOOL

William Gilpin, who became headmaster of Cheam School in Surrey in 1752, was the first English schoolmaster decisively to break with the public-school traditions of fagging, corporal punishment, and the supremacy of classical studies. Much of his work was a reaction against the moral atmosphere and authoritarian regime of these schools. He also believed that the work of public schools could be more closely related to society, or, more accurately, to that section of society to which his pupils would eventually belong. Many of his pupils he expected to become 'landholders, tradesmen and public officers',[1]

---
[1] 'An Account of the Rev. Mr. Gilpin', in W. Gilpin, *Memoirs of Dr. Richard Gilpin* (London, 1879), p. 127.

and he was not averse from introducing commercial principles and practice into the school curriculum. 'I consider my school,' he wrote, 'in the light of something between a school to qualify for business, and the public school, in which classical learning only is attended to.'[2]

Gilpin, far more conscious than most schoolmasters of his time of the importance of early childhood in the formation of character, was not content to pass over the bullying by older boys of the younger as 'schoolboys' tricks'; he believed that such practices, together with arbitrary discipline exercised by the masters, could lead to a permanently hardened cast of mind and might be the 'foundation for knavery' in later life.[3]

With this critical assessment of the public schools in mind, Gilpin was determined to reform the organization at Cheam as soon as he was able. He had started teaching there, as an assistant usher, in 1750, and became principal of Cheam in 1752.[4] His first 'new scheme', as he called it, was to frame a code of laws for the whole school, with specific punishments for each transgression. These laws were publicly read at stated times before the whole school, and also strictly observed by Gilpin himself. Punishments were, however, carried out by the principal, but a safeguard was added in that if he carried out the punishment more severely than the law enjoined, he would listen to complaints, and if a sufficient number of 'good witnesses' appeared, then he would recompense the boy who had suffered. In doubtful cases which the existing law did not sufficiently cover, or where the offence was not sufficiently proved, a jury of twelve boys were empanelled to decide upon the case.[5]

These innovations, which foreshadow later schemes of self-government instituted by David Williams and the Hill family, were not justified on any of the theoretical or psychological grounds familiar to later educationalists. Gilpin merely hoped that by associating his pupils with the maintenance of school discipline he would accomplish two things – impress on the

[2] Cited in C. P. Barbier, 'Gilpin, Master of Cheam', *Glasgow Herald*, 14 Sept. 1957.
[3] Gilpin, *Memoirs*, p. 128.
[4] W. D. Templeman, *The Life and Work of William Gilpin* (Urbana, Ill., 1939), pp. 58–9.
[5] Gilpin, *Memoirs*, p. 123.

boys' minds 'an early love of order, law and liberty', and make corporal punishment virtually unnecessary. The latter was, in fact, administered only in extreme cases, for 'vice or obstinate idleness'.

The main punishments were fines and imprisonment. The latter consisted of confinement to the dining-room on holiday afternoons. Fines were deducted from the boys' weekly allowance, and an account of them was kept by a secretary in books that were always open to inspection. The money was spent on books or sports equipment. About £5 of the money accruing from fines, however, was spent twice a year on bread for the poor. This had a moral purpose, for Gilpin hoped that it would have a good effect on the future conduct of the boys. Instead of a powerful group of older boys, and a dependent mass of younger pupils, he sought to substitute a corporate consciousness, based on the acceptance of moral laws, under which each boy was equally and personally responsible to the community as a whole. With the normal run of boys Gilpin was nearly always successful and a good example of his method was his treatment of the country rambles on holiday afternoons. When the boys returned from vacation, they were given the option of promising never to go out of bounds without leave. Those who made the promise were allowed, on written application to the principal, to go for country walks on leave, provided they agreed not to enter any house and to return by a stated time. Those who went out of bounds after promising not to were punished far more severely than those who committed the same offence without having given the undertaking.[6]

Some of Gilpin's innovations were designed to reproduce in microcosm certain aspects of the outside world that his pupils might experience when they left school. Boys were allowed to keep small shops, in which trade was done in gingerbread, cakes, apples, and similar commodities, but this concession to Mammon was modified by the medieval Christian practice of the just price. A legalized scale of profit per article was laid down, and any violation of this meant that the individual concerned was not allowed to continue in business.

Another strictly regulated introduction to economics was by

[6] Ibid., pp. 125-6.

means of the cultivation of garden plots. Templeman, in his biography of Gilpin, represents the introduction of gardening to the curriculum as a pioneering attempt that anticipated similar efforts in the mid-nineteenth century by almost a hundred years.[7] Gilpin probably had a different aim in view, and an introduction to economics was very likely as much in his mind as the value of gardening. The borders of the playground were divided into some thirty strips of soil, on which the boys tried to grow melons, cucumbers, onions, and other vegetables for domestic consumption. The cultivation was mainly in the hands of the older boys, who used the younger ones as assistants, and it was the custom of the former, when they left school, to bequeath the plots to their assistants by means of a will.

If Gilpin's notions of commercial practice had a somewhat feudal ring, his attitude to study and learning was decidedly modern. It seemed to Gilpin a waste of time to learn a dead language with critical exactness, to give precise attention to the significance of each word and expression, or to compose verses in it. In fact, he bluntly informed parents that if they wanted their sons to achieve critical exactness in Greek and Latin, then his school was not for them. It was of much more use to his pupils to learn their own language with accuracy than to study a dead one. He concentrated on getting his pupils to keep at a translation until they had mastered the sense of it, translating and re-translating several times if necessary.[8] At all times he tried to give them 'a delicacy of taste and a feeling of the beauties of the authors'.[9]

The curriculum at Cheam was reasonably wide and included, in addition to Greek and Latin, English, arithmetic, geography, religious instruction, drawing, and dancing. The boys played football and cricket, went riding and rambling, and also had a large range of extra-curricular activities — drama, indoor hobbies, the keeping of pets, and, as we have seen, the running of miniature shops and gardens. Geography was apparently taught in part by fitting together pieces of a jigsaw map of Britain, and in 1765 a pupil wrote to his parents

[7] Templeman, *William Gilpin*, p. 67.
[8] Gilpin, *Memoirs*, p. 132.
[9] 'Biographical Sketch of the late Rev. W. Gilpin', in Rev. Richard Warner, *Miscellanies* (Bath, 2 vols., 1819), ii, p. 155.

Early Experiments: Gilpin and Manson

complaining that he had lost Flintshire and asking for a replacement.[10]

According to a contemporary biographer, Gilpin had 'a commanding person, dignified manners and a deep sonorous voice'.[11] His person could strike his pupils with terror at times, but Gilpin was renowned for his absolute fairness and integrity, and there can be no doubt of the respect the boys had for him. Many of his pupils kept in touch with him when they had left school. They visited him and sent him letters from all over the world. Several of his pupils became eminent in public life, and at the turn of the century Cheam's old boys included a prime minister, a lord chancellor of Ireland, two secretaries of the Treasury, and one at the War Office.[12]

Gilpin retired from Cheam in 1777, having achieved his ambition of saving £10,000,[13] a remarkable result in view of the moderate fees he charged – £25 a year, with an additional £5 or £6 for extras in school equipment.[14] Colonel William Mitford offered Gilpin the living of Boldre on the edge of the New Forest in Hampshire. In April 1777 he became, and remained for the rest of his life, vicar of Boldre, in a parish of wretched and poverty-stricken forest dwellers.

Gilpin made heroic and largely successful efforts to civilize his parishioners. To this end he founded two schools of industry, one for boys and one for girls.[15] He gave most of his time to drawing, however, and made a second reputation as a topographer, developing a landscape style that had considerable influence on English taste for the two following generations.[16] He died in 1804 in his eightieth year.

[10] [C. P. Barbier], 'Submerged by Dr. Syntax: William Gilpin of Cheam', *Times Educational Supplement*, no. 2226, 17 Jan. 1958, p. 67 (hereafter *T.E.S.*).

[11] 'W.H.G.', *A Memoir of the Late Rev. William Gilpin, M.A.* (Lymington, 1851), p. 17. According to Templeman (*William Gilpin*, p. 13), 'W.H.G.' were the initials of W. Henry Grove of Lymington.

[12] [Barbier], *T.E.S.*

[13] Warner, *Miscellanies*, ii, p. 157.

[14] Sir H. C. M. Lambert, 'A Cheam School Bill in 1766', *Surrey Archaeological Transactions*, xxv (1924), pp. 80–4.

[15] Templeman, *William Gilpin*, pp. 194 ff.

[16] C. P. Barbier, *William Gilpin, His Drawings, Teaching and Theory of the Picturesque* (Oxford, 1963).

DAVID MANSON AND THE BELFAST PLAY SCHOOL

Very different from William Gilpin was the mercurial Irishman David Manson, brewer, inventor, and schoolmaster. His school, which opened in 1752 and ran for some forty years, was one of the first to modify the normal school routine by combining lessons with play and amusement and devising a system of pupil self-government based on a complex gradation of rank. His elaborate series of rewards and punishments, and his rejection of corporal punishment in an age when its use was almost universal, predated by nearly seventy years a similar system used by the Hills in Hazelwood School. In addition, his organization of one scholar teaching another anticipated the monitorial system of Bell and Lancaster. Manson's reputation, which was extremely high in his home town of Belfast and throughout Ireland in his lifetime, never spread very widely in England, although his name was known in Scottish educational circles in the early nineteenth century.

Manson's early education and training were in the tradition of the hedge school, that peculiar form of educational self-help which arose in Ireland in the period following the penal code of William III. Forbidden to teach in school in the normal way, schoolmasters took their pupils under a hedge or bank and gave them lessons in the open air. In the later eighteenth century, when the laws were less strictly enforced, the schools might be taught in a barn, cabin, or other building, but they retained the name of hedge school.[17]

Manson was born in Cairncastle, Co. Antrim, in 1726, and started work as a farmer's boy.[18] His quickness and intelligence attracted the attention of a neighbouring clergyman, who took charge of his education. It was common in Ireland, at that time and for long after, for intelligent peasant boys to rise to the position of schoolmaster with the help of well-disposed scholars and the support of their families. Manson qualified as a teacher and began teaching in his home parish as a hedge schoolmaster. His first school was in a cowshed, but his subsequent work, in different parts of the country, was less re-

[17] P. J. Dowling, *The Hedge Schools of Ireland* (Dublin, n.d.), pp. 1, 45–6.
[18] J. J. Marshall, 'David Manson, Schoolmaster in Belfast', *Ulster Journal of Archaeology*, xiv (1908), p. 59.

stricted. For a short while he gave up teaching in Ireland in order to follow the more profitable occupation of tutoring sailors in Liverpool in mathematical navigation at a fee of 6d. an hour.

In 1752 his mother's illness and his own approaching marriage caused him to return to Belfast and, in the same year, he opened a brewery. Shortly afterwards, however, he started an evening school at his house, where he taught grammar, reading, and spelling, and the number of his scholars eventually rose to twenty. After the success of his evening school, Manson established a day school and in 1760 he added a boarding-school. In 1752 entry was restricted to pupils who were completely without education. Later on he took in pupils who had found difficulties at other schools, or, as he put it, had been 'accustomed to the rod, and who had contracted an aversion to reading'. The organization of the school was based upon Manson's own estimation of the character of children and his belief in their need for freedom. He took issue with Locke over the latter's contention that a child's obstinacy justified punishment by the master. Manson argued that the child was a free individual who had the right to be given a choice of actions rather than be forced to accept a positive command from the teacher. Manson was, however, a great believer in 'shaming', much practised by the Quakers and later by Joseph Lancaster. A crying child, for instance, might be exposed to ridicule by the teacher or mimicked by his companions until he stopped:

> The method, then, to make them easy under a state of discipline is to convince them that they are free; that they act from choice, not compulsion.[19]

Side by side with his reforms in the matter of punishment Manson introduced what used to be called the play-way method of teaching reading and spelling. His scheme bears a close resemblance to that advocated by Comenius, the great seventeenth-century Bohemian educational reformer. He had suggested making lessons more interesting and more closely related to life by the introduction of games based on farming,

---

[19] Manson, *New Pocket Dictionary*, quoted in W. J. McCallister, *The Growth of Freedom in Education* (London, 1931, p. 332).

medicine, war, politics, and so on, and the granting of titles of rank to the most deserving:

> Further in order to encourage them, the mock titles of doctor, licentiate, or student of medicine, may be given to those who make the greatest progress.[20]

The first activity of the morning in Manson's school was the division of the children into ranks on the strength of their performance in repeating a passage of prose that they had been given to learn the previous evening. The amount to be learned however, was entirely the choice of the child. The children in the school were thus sorted into a simplified version of feudal social relationships, with the best children forming an élite that Manson termed the Royal Society. Tickets were given with the proviso that the recipients maintained good behaviour and did not fall below a certain standard in spelling. The 'king' and 'queen' received two tickets each, and there was a great incentive to collect these tickets, for they could be exchanged for valuable prizes, at the rate of ten tickets for a half-guinea medal. Noisy behaviour or bad spelling, however, always meant the loss of tickets already gained. Manson's prodigality in the matter of prizes was held to be one of the causes that led to his removal to smaller premises in Co. Donegal in 1782. He seems to have kept solvent, however, by profits from his brewing business, which he continued to run and to advertise side by side with his school.[21]

To return to the schoolroom. The children were arranged in seats according to their rank, with the king and queen at the head and the tenants between the undertenants and landlords, and proceeded, in Manson's words, to 'rehearse each other the back lessons of the Grammar'. Each correct line said by a landlord counted as £1 of rent due by the tenant, and each line correctly recited by a tenant counted as £1 paid. The object of the whole exercise, of course, was for the members of

---

[20] J. A. Comenius, *The Great Didactic*, trans. M. W. Keatinge (London, 1896), p. 331.

[21] In an advertisement of May 1782 he advertised: 'For sale, in barrels and half barrels, fine beer of his own manufacture, which he hopes will be found equal, if not superior to the famous Burton ale in strength and flavour': cited in Marshall, in *Ulster Journal of Archaeology*, xiv, p. 69.

the Royal Society to claim as much rent as possible from the tenants and for the latter, together with the undertenants, to keep out of debt.

At the end of each week there was a general reorganization. If a child had kept the office of king or queen for a week he or she was given a guinea medal, and had the privilege of calling a parliament after school on Saturday, at which arrears of rent were dealt with; those in arrears could pay for their discharge, but those who had nothing to give that was acceptable to their landlords had to plead poverty with their feet uncovered and their arrears were discharged 'out of the fund of toys, which were taken from those who used them at improper seasons'. The way was thus clear for new accounts to be opened the following week.

The whole process seems excessively complicated, but would probably have been clearer in the middle of the eighteenth century, when feudal rank and obligations were much more familiar to children than they are today.

Manson also introduced the practice of teaching by means of cards. In his day card-playing was an almost universal amusement, and taking advantage of this he furnished his pupils with packs of cards similar to playing cards, on which were printed elementary lessons in reading, spelling, and arithmetic, which the children studied as a form of play. This particular project gained great fame; according to one of his biographers, 'David Manson's cards were long known in Belfast.'[22]

Manson's incentive ability was not confined to the schoolroom. In 1760 he constructed a velocipede, an early form of bicycle, which he leased out to subscribers for use in the mornings and evenings on payment of half a guinea. He gave his pupils free rides on the velocipede as a reward for merit. He invented an improved spinning machine, based on the principle of a spinning wheel which, turned by one man, set in motion twenty spindles. His greatest invention, however, was a 'flying machine', which remained at the model stage. By means of this machine, he claimed, people would be able to 'raise themselves above the tops of the houses, and thus enjoy a most delightful prospect'.

Apart from his talent for invention, Manson took a great

[22] Ibid., p. 66.

interest in social reform. The condition of the handloom weavers attracted his attention and he wrote a book to show that their work need not be done in unhealthy conditions in crowded towns but might be carried on just as well in the pure air of the countryside, in conjunction with a small farm. The book gave detailed instructions on farming techniques and designs for improved dwellings.[23] Manson wrote two very popular textbooks, a dictionary and a spelling book, and his school continued with great success until the last years of his life, when his health failed; he died on 2 March 1792.

The dynamic of Manson's and Gilpin's work had been a reaction against the educational constrictions of their day – authoritarianism, corporal punishment, the traditional curriculum, and the prevailing attitude that education was a dismal experience, to be enforced by the rod. They based their reforms not on theories but on the way in which a sensible, humane teacher would try to build up good and friendly relationships with children. Their outlook owed nothing to the Enlightenment and they lived before the effects of the Industrial Revolution had influenced educational thought and practice; some of their schemes have a curiously archaic air. Nevertheless, they anticipated several aspects of the work of more sophisticated and far more famous successors. William Gilpin and David Manson left no disciples, founded no school of thought, nor did they propound any general theory of education. Those who came after them in the field of educational innovation found their inspiration not from them but in Continental theory.

2 ROUSSEAU AND ENGLISH EDUCATION IN THE LATE EIGHTEENTH CENTURY

FEW books have had a greater immediate effect on English educational thought than Rousseau's *Émile*. An English translation first appeared in 1762, in the same year as the French publication. Two further translations appeared in 1763, and the success was great and immediate. This was partly due to

[23] Ibid., p. 68.

the emotional appeal of the book, to its 'sensibility', a quality greatly prized in the eighteenth century and which was an essential part of the popularity of all Rousseau's works.[1] The main appeal of *Émile*, however, lay in its repudiation of dogmas that were thought to fetter human development. William Godwin, a critical admirer, believed that '*Émile* is upon the whole to be regarded as the principal reservoir of philosophical truth as yet existing in the world'.[2] Between the 1760s and 1790s there was, in fact, an outbreak of Rousseaumania in England. 'Parties are formed for the destruction and defence of his fame,' wrote David Williams, one of his most judicious followers.[3] As late as the 1790s, the young Wordsworth and Coleridge moved in a circle of enthusiastic Rousseauphiles, including Charles Lamb, William Hazlitt, and the remarkable Thomas Poole, a Somerset farmer, self-taught in Latin and French, experimental stock-breeder, founder of a local school, and a supporter of the French Revolution.[4] A number of educational novels, with *Émile* as their model, celebrated in various forms the supremacy of 'natural' over artificial education; they included Henry Brooke's enormously long *The Fool of Quality* (1766), David Williams's *History of Philo and Amelia* (1774), Maria Edgeworth's unfinished *Harry and Lucy* (1778), a translation of Madame de Genlis's *Adèle et Théodore* (1783), and the most famous of all, Thomas Day's *Sandford and Merton* (1783-9).

This last near-novel tells the story of the re-education of Tommy Merton, a spoilt, selfish child, corrupted by luxury and idleness. His salvation is brought about by his tutor, Mr. Barlow, and Henry Sandford, a country-bred child of nature. Tommy undergoes a variety of testing experiences, in most of which Day's hatred of aristocratic values, his predilection for bodily hardihood and Sermon on the Mount ethics, and his

---

[1] J. H. Warner, 'The Basis of J. J. Rousseau's Contemporaneous Reputation in England', *Modern Language Notes*, vol. lv, no. 4 (Apr. 1940), pp. 270–80.

[2] W. Godwin, *An Enquiry Concerning Political Justice, and its Influence on General Virtue and Happiness* (London, 2 vols., 1793), ii, p. 504 n. See also [W. Godwin], *An Account of the Seminary ... at Epsom in Surrey for the Instruction of Twelve Pupils ...* (London, 1783), p. 4.

[3] D. Williams, *Lectures on Education* (London, 3 vols., 1789), i, pp. 110–11 (hereafter *Lectures*).

[4] E. Légouis, *The Early Life of William Wordsworth*, trans. J. W. Matthews (London, 1897), pp. 56, 365–6.

belief that education should be both useful and elevating, are evident.

Sandford and Merton exemplified the tendency for radicals and reformers who were influenced by Rousseau to focus their interest upon the second book of *Émile*, in which Rousseau's ideal of 'negative education', the physical development of the pupil in natural surroundings, without the benefit of formal lessons, was brilliantly and passionately set out.

David Williams confirmed that many attempts were made to educate children as noble savages.[5] He described one child of nature of his acquaintance who, at the age of thirteen, slept on the floor, spoke 'a jargon he had formed out of the several dialects of the family', could not read or write, and appeared to Williams as 'a little emaciated figure; his countenance betraying marks of premature decay, or depraved passions; his teeth discoloured, and his hearing almost gone'. Rousseau himself, declared Williams, would have made 'some dreadful exclamation' at the sight.[6]

Richard Lovell Edgeworth, an Irish landowner, educated at Oxford, friend of scientists and industrialists, and ceaseless experimenter in mechanical and educational projects, attempted to bring up his son, Richard Lovell, on an intelligent assessment of the principles of the second book of *Émile*. Between the ages of three and eight the boy led a hardy open-air life, becoming 'bold, free, fearless, generous' and considered by all as very clever. He even passed the critical scrutiny of Rousseau himself, with whom he had a long conversation when Edgeworth visited Paris in 1777. But Edgeworth found in him what seemed to be a flaw: the boy refused to obey anyone but his father. Edgeworth considered the experiment a failure and packed the boy off to boarding-school. He felt the result was partly due to errors in Rousseau's theory, about which he thereafter became less enthusiastic; but he also admitted his own failure to superintend the boy in the way necessary to make the experiment a success.[7]

During the last part of the eighteenth and the early part of the nineteenth century, these ideas had a widespread influence

[5] Williams, *Lectures*, i, p. 185.
[6] Ibid., iii, pp. 5–6.
[7] R. L. Edgeworth, *Memoirs* (London, 2 vols., 1820), i, pp. 177–9.

on the upbringing of children. Williams, writing in 1789, maintained that recent alterations and improvements in the management of children and in the discipline of schools had been principally due to the eloquence of Rousseau,[8] and Mrs. Gaskell believed that the new ideas had spread widely to all classes of society.[9] No fewer than thirteen editions of *Sandford and Merton* had been published by 1823. The didactic element of Day's story inspired a number of moral tales for children in which there was a move away from an appreciation of 'natural' education towards a concern with botanizing and moralizing. Mrs. Trimmer, for instance, wrote a number of stories in which her child heroes collected flowers and grasses, compared and analysed and recorded, while a moralizing parent or tutor was always on hand with lessons on the marvels of God's handiwork and the need for piety and good behaviour.[10] This was not the ideal of Rousseau, whose Émile at twelve years of age was healthy and confident, with a free and open manner, untroubled by books or learning.[11]

What were the leading ideas of Rousseau's *Émile*? Its originality lay in the fact that it was the first comprehensive attempt to describe a system of education according to nature. The key idea of the book was the possibility of preserving the original perfect nature of the child by means of the careful control of his education and environment, based upon an analysis of the different physical and psychological stages through which he passed from birth to maturity.

Rousseau divided the educative process into four periods, corresponding to the stages of a child's life. 'Every age, every station in life,' he maintained, 'has a perfection, a ripeness of its own.'[12] The first was the period of infancy, from birth to about two years of age, during which the child began to learn to walk and talk and during which he should be free from unnatural restraint. The second period was that of childhood, lasting from two to twelve years, described in the second book

---

[8] Williams, *Lectures*, ii, p. 8.
[9] E. C. Gaskell, *The Life of Charlotte Brontë* (London, 2 vols., 1857), i, p. 49.
[10] Cf. Mrs. Sarah Trimmer, *An Easy Introduction to the Knowledge of Nature, and Reading the Holy Scriptures* (London, 1780).
[11] J. J. Rousseau, *Émile*, trans. Barbara Foxley (London, 1961), p. 124.
[12] Ibid., p. 122.

of *Émile*. Here Rousseau diverged most from contemporary practice and won for himself the extremes of support and opposition. He argued that this stage should be a time of unrestricted play in natural surroundings, free from intellectual pursuits and external restraint, leaving the child to develop his five senses as he wished. Action should spring from necessity and not from obedience, for the supreme good was not authority but freedom: 'That man is truly free who desires what he is able to perform, and does what he desires. This is my fundamental maxim. Apply it to childhood, and all the rules of education spring from it.'[13] The child should receive no formal academic training, but should be left to make the most of a happy time that would never return: 'the education of the earliest years should be merely negative', maintained Rousseau. 'It consists, not in teaching virtue or truth, but in preserving the heart from vice and the spirit from error.'[14] This conception of education was only possible if one maintained the fundamental goodness of the child, and Rousseau's expressed belief in this clashed with equally fundamental eighteenth-century orthodoxies concerning the nature of children, and was the chief cause of the vituperation he received from the church and the establishment:

> Let us lay it down as an incontrovertible rule that the first impulses of nature are always right; there is no original sin in the human heart....[15]

The third period, the pre-adolescent period from twelve to fifteen years, was the age of intelligence for which the previous stage had prepared. The child's appetite for knowledge was now to be whetted through the medium of his present interest and his realization of the useful. Science, geography, and handicraft were among the subjects now to be taken up.

The type of education described in the first three books of *Émile* was specifically designed to free the child from corrupting passions and second-hand opinions, whether emanating from books or from society. His acquaintance would be with the objects of the material world, and necessity and utility would form the spur to discovery. The aim was a child who was

[13] Ibid., p. 48.   [14] Ibid., p. 57.   [15] Ibid., p. 56.

'self-regarding' in the best sense of the term, who was prepared for the next stage of education, his introduction to the moral and social order.

The years after fifteen formed a bridge between childhood and manhood, when the child's moral and social development became the chief concern of his tutor, and to this end the relevance of history, metaphysics, religion, physical training, and sexual knowledge was discussed. Finally, for *Émile* was cast in the form of a novel, came the preparation for marriage, the wedding of Émile and Sophie, and devotion to a life of civic virtue.

These, in brief, are the main points of a work that was destined to change the thinking of whole generations of teachers and to affect educational practice throughout Western Europe. It is often said that Rousseau was the first to put the child firmly in the centre of the educational stage. But he did more than this. In a sense education had always been child-centred, but the child had been seen as an object to be operated upon by adults, and made to conform to their rules and methods in order to fit into adult society. Rousseau regarded children as human beings, restored a belief in their essential goodness, and directed attention to the necessity of closely examining their nature and adapting education accordingly. Rousseau's injunction to tutors in the preface of *Émile*, 'Begin thus by making a more careful study of your scholars, for it is clear that you know nothing about them',[16] set the tone for the whole work.

Rousseau's educational views were a product of his discontent with society as a whole. *Émile* was the spearhead of a protest against the stifling formality and elaborate insincerity of the *grand siècle*, a conscious reaction against the artificial child beloved of society families of the time. Taine, the French critic and historian, has painted a remarkable picture of these manikins, the 'embroidered, gilded, dressed up, powdered little gentlemen, decked with sword and sash, carrying the chapeau under the arm, bowing, presenting the hand, rehearsing fine attitudes before a mirror . . .'.[17]

Critics of this conception of life and manners were strongly

[16] Ibid., pp. 1–2.
[17] H. A. Taine, *The Ancient Regime*, trans. J. Durand (London, 1876), p. 273.

attracted to an ideal of a simpler and more natural existence which travel and exploration were making popular. The appeal of *Émile* was strengthened by the cult of the noble savage that flourished in the 1770s and 1780s, fed by romantic accounts of the discoveries of the islands of the South Pacific. Commerson's account of Tahiti, and Hawkesworth's *Voyages*, describing Cook's discovery of Polynesia, were two of the many accounts of the ideal natural man that impressed critics of the civilized life.[18] However, Voltaire, in *L'Ingénu*, dared to suggest that a real noble savage might not be well received in civilized France.

In England it was among those concerned with problems of science, industry, public health, education, and philosophical speculation that the ideas of Rousseau found their most receptive audience. The philosophical societies, the majority of whose members stood outside the social, religious, and political establishment, were the focus of the new critical and scientific spirit. Among those associated with the societies were several of the educationalists mentioned earlier in the chapter. Day and Edgeworth, for instance, were among the Lichfield group who attended meetings of the Birmingham Lunar Society, whose members included the engineers Matthew Boulton and James Watt, as well as Joseph Priestley, Josiah Wedgwood, and Erasmus Darwin, grandfather of Charles. In Manchester a similar group called themselves the Literary and Philosophical Society, whose leading member was Dr. Thomas Percival, pioneer of public-health reform, author of *A Father's Advice to his Daughters*, and a friend of the young Robert Owen. In Liverpool William Roscoe, described as 'banker, politician, poet, historian, and art collector', was connected with the Lunar Society and also with William Godwin, Mary Wollstonecraft, and other London radicals.[19]

There were international links as well. Edgeworth, Williams, and Darwin had met Rousseau himself, and Percival was a friend of Diderot and Voltaire. David Williams associated with French and German intellectuals, and was a leading

---

[18] For an account of the cult of the noble savage, see H. N. Fairchild, *The Noble Savage* (New York, 1928); C. B. Tinker, *Nature's Simple Plan* (Princeton, 1922).

[19] B. Simon, *Studies in the History of Education, 1780–1870* (London, 1960), pp. 17 ff.

member of the Club of 13 which flourished in the 1770s and 1780s. The members of this body supported the American cause in the War of Independence and corresponded with Franklin and Jefferson; Thomas Day was another member, and Priestley and Edgeworth were closely associated with the club.[20] The doctrines of Rousseau could not but find a ready reception in such circles.

The impact of *Émile* in English intellectual circles and the rise of a group of followers alarmed orthodox educationalists who supported the Anglican public-school and university tradition, and many sprang to its defence. Vicesimus Knox and John Brown were among the most representative of the defenders of established educational practice. Brown, vicar of Newcastle upon Tyne, man of letters, and critic of the manners and morals of the day, embodied his views in three sermons on education published in 1764.[21] The fact that they were published within two years of the first translation of *Émile* is an indirect tribute to Rousseau's influence on England.

In opposition to Rousseau, Brown accepted as axiomatic the natural depravity of youth. The child was naturally evil, and if he was not taught virtue he would inevitably turn to vice: 'the condition of human nature inevitably leads him to acquire that which is destructive of it.'[22] To counteract this, Brown advocated a long training in the formation of virtuous habits and the eradication of evil passions.[23] The object was to produce good citizens, and to this end Brown was willing to push his doctrines to extremes:

> even to shackle the mind (if you so please to speak) with salutary prejudices, such as may create a conformity of thought and action with the established principles on which his native society is built.[24]

Brown did not consider childhood to be an early stage of development having its own special characteristics in the progress

---

[20] N. Hans, 'Franklin, Jefferson, and the English Radicals at the End of the Eighteenth Century', *Proceedings of the American Philosophical Society*, vol. 98, no. 6 (1954).
[21] J. Brown, *Sermons on Various Subjects* (London, 1764).
[22] Ibid., sermon i, p. 12.
[23] Ibid., p. 7; sermons ii and iii, *passim*.
[24] Ibid., sermon i, pp. 16–17.

towards a full personality; to him, children were incipient adults with unregulated passions.

A similar view of child nature was taken by Vicesimus Knox, who succeeded his father as headmaster of Tonbridge School while still in his twenties, and whose celebrated defence of classical learning, *Liberal Education*, was published in 1781, before his thirtieth birthday. The book went through nine editions in the following eight years. Knox, described as 'a strenuous supporter of the establishment',[25] wrote as a practical man in opposition to the schemes of Rousseau and the visionaries, and defended 'the ancient system of education, which consists of a classical discipline' precisely because it was coming under attack.[26] The arguments that Knox used have in essentials become the standard defence: the classics make for the 'enlargement, refinement and embellishment of the mind', they have a meliorative effect on the character, and are the best preparation for every liberal pursuit.[27] Hard study of the grammar, followed by the learning of passages by heart, would strengthen the character, but should this fail to stifle 'the vicious propensities of human nature', then corporal punishment should be administered in addition.[28]

John Wesley described *Émile* as 'the most empty, silly, injudicious thing that a self-conceited infidel wrote', and advocated more religion and stricter control of children, urging: 'Break their wills that you may save their soul.'[29] Hannah More, who also saw the enemy in the ideas of Rousseau and the French Enlightenment, consistently stressed the corruption and helplessness of human nature; the duty of tutors was not only to act upon this belief but also to convey it to young people, who, she lamented, 'are peculiarly disposed to turn away from it as a morose, unamiable and gloomy idea'.[30] The whole object of education, she considered, was to counteract the innate depravity of children:

---

[25] *Dictionary of National Biography.*
[26] V. Knox, *Liberal Education; or, A Practical Treatise on the Methods of Acquiring Useful and Polite Learning* (London, 1781), p. 3.
[27] Ibid., pp. 4, 9, 11–12.
[28] Ibid., pp. 21, 286, 290.
[29] A. H. Body, *John Wesley and Education* (London, 1936), pp. 19, 52.
[30] Hannah More, *Strictures on the Modern System of Female Education* (London, 2 vols., 1799), ii, p. 255.

Is it not a fundamental error to consider children as innocent beings, whose little weaknesses may perhaps want some correction, rather than as beings who bring into the world a corrupt nature and evil disposition, which it should be the great end of education to rectify?[31]

The whole approach to education as exemplified by these writers has been called the classical-Christian,[32] and it rests on four main propositions: that the child is evil by nature; that childhood is a preparation for adult life; that education must therefore consist of that which will be useful to the child when he becomes a man; and that the value of the subjects taught lies not in their intrinsic interest but in the moral and intellectual training they give.

The mark of the new school of educationalists was that they were prepared to overthrow these assumptions about childhood and child education and begin the study of education afresh on the basis of Rousseau's injunction to make the child and his nature the starting-point. Almost all the leading characteristics of the new school contradicted the classical-Christian presuppositions. The new theorists rejected the almost universal belief that the child was innately wicked, and stressed the desire for knowledge on the part of the child, which it was the function of the tutor to stimulate and direct. They believed in the value of natural virtues and behaviour, and the development of the child according to his own nature rather than in conformity with the artificial qualities demanded by adult society. The importance of interesting the pupil in the educational process was emphasized, with the stress on things rather than on words and memory work. Coercion and authority, of course, had little part to play in the structure of the new education. In the curriculum the emphasis was on the natural sciences rather than on the classical languages, and Christian doctrine did not figure largely in their schemes. 'She does not attack religion nor inveigh against it,' said a Baptist minister of Maria Edgeworth and her edu-

[31] Ibid., i, p. 64.
[32] A. A. Evans, 'The Impact of Rousseau on English Education', *Researches and Studies*, University of Leeds Institute of Education, no. ii (Jan. 1955), p. 19.

cational stories, 'but makes it appear unnecessary by exhibiting perfect virtue without it.'[33]

The views and activities of the new school represented, for the first time in modern English educational history, a decisive break with the prevailing ideas of education. Hence the true beginning of modern progressive education dates from the last quarter of the eighteenth century. Educational thought and practice became polarized round the classical-Christian and what could be called the natural-scientific standpoints. The former had the weight of social approval and established practice behind it and deep roots in the political and religious establishment, and it was a very long time before it was to be dislodged. However, there remained a noticeable shift of emphasis in the thinking of a significant minority of people towards a greater respect for the personality of the child and for his ability often to initiate his own learning as an ideal of education. This change of emphasis took place decisively in the period 1760–1800, but it did not establish itself in England until the nineteenth century, and then only rarely, as we shall see.

3 DAVID WILLIAMS AND THE LAURENCE STREET ACADEMY

DAVID WILLIAMS was a product of the British radical and Dissenting tradition, which was itself inspired by the ideals of the European Enlightenment. He was born in Glamorganshire in 1738, the son of a speculator in coal and iron mines. He was educated at Carmarthen Academy and intended for the Dissenting ministry, but on his own testimony he was unsuited by nature for the life of a pastor.[1] He bowed to family pressure, however, and was ordained in 1758, taking up his ministry at Frome in Somerset. Three years later he was invited to Exeter, where he remained for eight years, leaving after disagreements with his congregation to take charge of a Dissenting meeting-

---

[33] Cited in G. E. Hodgson, *Rationalist English Educators* (London, 1912), p. 162.

[1] *Annual Biography and Obituary for the Year 1818* (London, 1818), p. 18.

house in Highgate, London. In 1773 Williams gave up his ministry and decided to set up a school. To aid him in this enterprise he married a girl whom he had long known, took a house in Chelsea, and advertised for pupils.

Williams had little difficulty in finding pupils for his school in Laurence Street, and it was a success from the first. Most of the pupils were the sons of wealthy or aristocratic parents, and some pupils came to Williams from well-known public schools.[2] His fees were £100 a year, high for that time, but he could hardly ever make the school pay, mainly because he carried out his reforming ideas regardless of cost.[3]

Fundamentally Williams believed in education according to nature and stood four-square by Rousseau on this. He upheld the innate goodness of the child, his educability and perfectibility, and believed that the learning process originated in the impressions made by objects of the natural world upon the human senses. If a child were brought up according to his normal inclinations in natural surroundings, Williams maintained, he would grow up healthy and with a sound and active mind.[4] However, he was unwilling to follow Rousseau too far in the matter of natural education, recognizing that the object of education was to reconcile the claims of nature and the claims of society. Education, he wrote, was 'the art of forming a man on rational principles, and yet making him capable of entering into the community and becoming a useful and good citizen'.[5]

Williams was the first British educationalist to give Rousseau's educational theories searching criticism and to attempt to apply what he considered was valuable in them to the classroom situation. Williams's *Lectures on Education* submitted *Émile* to a thorough examination, and the verdict was on the whole a favourable one, but he could not tolerate Rousseau's tendency 'to speak of everything with passion', nor his 'vague theories and visionary systems'. The latter is perhaps Williams's main criticism of Rousseau. His own object, he declared, was to 'arrange and disentangle' Rousseau's principles,

[2] Williams, *Lectures*, i, pp. 165, 236, 260; ii, p. 128.
[3] Ibid., i, p. 232.
[4] Williams, *A Treatise on Education* (London, 1774), p. 24 (hereafter *Treatise*).
[5] Ibid., p. 15.

to bring them to the test of experience and to suggest improvements.[6]

Williams's main disagreement was with Rousseau's staging of child development. That a child should not extend his mental cultivation, develop the use of his reason or his passions, or embrace moral or religious principles between the ages of two and twelve seemed to Williams fanciful and absurd and in no way based upon observation. Because children were not properly employed in schools, argued Williams, it did not mean that they should be allowed to run about 'idly and at hazard', nor, if they grew up as 'prating impertinent puppets', should they be suffered to sink into 'the inattention and stupidity of brutes',[7] and here Williams obviously had in mind the failure already mentioned of attempts to rear children of nature.

Reason and imagination were not innate but ultimately the product of experience of the external world. The first desire of children, after food, was for acquaintance with external objects. Reason, in Williams's view, was the power of comparing objects or ideas of objects, and arose gradually in children during their early years, and one did not have to wait, as Rousseau would have it, until 'the moment when reason unfolds as the sun rises, at a given period'. On the contrary, Williams maintained, the first twelve years of a child's life was the time when he most desired and most easily assimilated knowledge. Williams believed that the tutor was concerned, in his own expressive phrase, with 'the management of curiosity'.[8] Each child was born with certain capacities, and it was the job of the teacher to lead children into employments and pursuits best suited to those capacities. In this way the teacher could judiciously aid nature. 'The instructions of nature,' wrote Williams, 'are by trial and experience; those of education by words, maxims and precepts.'[9] The basis of Williams's educational method was therefore to contrive incidents in which the effect of a line of conduct could be observed by the child as part of a group. Education became a process that began with the pupil's own situation, and the function of the tutor was not to impose principles by authority but to bring about situations

[6] *Lectures*, i, p. 112.   [7] Ibid., ii, pp. 306–7.
[8] Ibid., iii, p. 13.   [9] Ibid., i, p. 72.

in which the child could learn by means of his own experience. Received ideas, either from books or from the teacher, interfered with this process. Moral conduct depended on the correct perception of the world by the child himself on the basis of his own experience.

Politically, Williams was a radical, but he was no democrat in the modern sense. He believed that intellectual liberty based upon the use of reason was possible only for an educated élite and should not be extended to the mass of the people, who were actuated solely by habit. He further agreed with the view held by many of the radicals of his day that a state system of education would be an interference with political liberty.[10]

Williams tried to involve the pupils themselves in the creation of a code of conduct and in the reformation of those who did not abide by it. The basis of his system was a court, consisting entirely of pupils, headed by a magistrate who changed weekly. His institution of a court had much in common with Gilpin's system. Unlike Gilpin, however, Williams abolished corporal punishment entirely. His opposition to it lay not so much in its severity as in the fact that it was often the result of a chance reaction of the child's conduct upon the teacher's feelings, and could thus be arbitrary and brutal. He put in its place a kind of social contract, to which all subscribed, and by which a transgressor could be punished in accordance with 'equal laws, enacted by general consent, and executed with general approbation'. The great thing was that the boys themselves should habitually make and exercise the laws and thus experience and appreciate 'habits of regulated liberty and moral virtue'. Williams was consistent in submitting himself to the rulings of the court and not interfering in their decisions, relying upon experience to correct errors. At one point the court decided that discretion and responsibility for punishment should be entirely vested in Williams himself, but he successfully argued against this.

Williams's remedial methods were not confined to the operations of the court, but included work with boys whose education had been neglected or deficient, and with these he was often successful in an ingenious way. Williams rarely lost an opportunity to point out the moral consequence of any course

[10] Ibid., pp. 75 ff.; *Treatise*, p. 37.

of action, but his morality had nothing in common with conventional piety of the Hannah More type. The most important virtue he considered to be truth, which he defined as 'a disposition to represent to others the information and ideas that occur, exactly as they occur'.[11] In this he felt he had an example to set; every caller at the house was given an answer with scrupulous exactitude and Williams never allowed himself to be represented as 'out' when he was on the premises, no matter how busy he was. Only thus, he felt, could he convince his charges that he was in earnest about the practice of truth, for he realized that 'any ground of suspicion of my sincerity would have been instantly and fairly occupied by the majority'.[12] In addition to personal example, he tried various methods to cure lying when he found it. On one occasion he tackled a liar by secretly taking another boy into his confidence, getting him to fight and insult the first youth, and then disbelieving the liar's story when he came seeking help. Not content with this, he asked his confederate's help to cure the liar.[13] His pupils would carry their insistence upon truth at all times home with them in the holidays, frequently to the astonishment and indignation of their families and friends. As a result, the single-minded Williams found that complaints from parents 'poured on me'.[14]

Perhaps the most revolutionary step was Williams's abdication of the traditional role of teacher. As Williams believed that the purposes of a rational education were lost without rapport between teacher and pupils, he gradually gave up his position as a teacher and became a member of every class, receiving instruction in common with the pupils and going ahead of them merely in order to stimulate them to further efforts. In this way he found it easy to acquire the pupils' confidence, since he was no longer in a position of power or authority. In addition, he noticed that it kept his assistants up to the mark to find the principal of the academy a member of their classes.[15] Williams put a boy who could not read under the care and tuition of another boy, and was interested to find that he learned more rapidly than by any other method yet

[11] *Lectures*, i, p. 32.
[12] Ibid., p. 238.
[13] Ibid., pp. 226–9.
[14] Ibid., pp. 259–60; ii, pp. 14–15.
[15] Ibid., ii, pp. 310–11.

tried. From then on the whole school went over to 'reciprocal assistance', as Williams called the method, and although it differed in intention and organization from the later monitorial system of Bell and Lancaster, Williams's method was essentially the same in so far as boys taught boys. The assistants had to forgo their 'assumed dignity' and step down from their ranks of 'imagined consequence'.[16]

Williams's academy did not adhere to the common practice of having a fixed curriculum, with regular lessons at particular times of the day. In some ways Williams anticipated twentieth-century practice in the integration of subjects and the introduction of what is now called the project method. The pupils tackled an extremely wide range of subjects, including geography, history, languages (Greek, Latin, Italian, and French), natural history, mathematics, astronomy, moral and political philosophy, poetry and eloquence, and science, including the special study of chemistry.[17] Though no rigid division of subjects according to age was made, Williams felt that advanced science, chemistry, and the higher reaches of philosophy were better suited to the twelve to fifteen years age-group.

Williams dethroned the classics from first place in the curriculum and substituted the study of natural history. In this he directly followed Bacon, who, he pointed out, was the first to indicate the natural order of the sciences and to postpone until a later date subjects that were incomprehensible to young children.[18] Williams's view that natural history — 'the first pursuit of the human mind', as he called it — was peculiarly suited to the young had been stimulated by his experiences with a six-year-old child in the days before he opened the school. Both tutor and pupil had begun a study of the subject by gathering botanical specimens, and then took part in harvesting and gardening. After this they examined the furniture of the house, classified the wood involved in its making, then constructed their own. They searched for stones and ores, smelted them, and constructed metal objects. The classification and designation of the objects involved the need to practise drawing and arithmetic. The child made progress that astonished Williams; in his own young days, he confessed, he had 'waded in

[16] Ibid., pp. 127–31.   [17] Ibid., pp. 121–2.
[18] Ibid., p. 312.

wretchedness through volumes of arithmetic calculations' without comprehension.[19]

In his school Williams used natural history as a means of introducing the study of languages: specimens of flora were obtained from gardens to which they had access, and after the names and properties had been learned, the Greek, Latin, Italian, and French equivalents were obtained in that order. Williams employed native Greeks to teach Greek, and Jesuit novices to teach Latin, although he said he had a distaste for the alleged 'interference and intrigue' of Jesuit fathers.[20]

Williams's attitude to learning languages was utilitarian. 'The only possible use of learning languages,' he wrote, 'is to know what was written in them.'[21] This cut across the prevailing view, as put forward by Knox, for instance, that the study of Latin and Greek was useful in itself and its fruits of universal application. Certainly Williams had no objection to the Greek and Latin authors as such – he was steeped in a knowledge of them, and derived many of his educational ideas from them. But he understood that much of the classical heritage was beyond the grasp of children. He thought it was painful to hear young children discuss the thoughts of Socrates and Plato when they almost entirely lacked knowledge of men and the world.[22] However, Williams liked to use the classical authors as sources of guidance concerning points of law and morality in problems that cropped up in the investigations of his pupils.

Williams was always looking for new approaches in the presentation of subjects. Geography, for instance, was not introduced with astronomy, as Rousseau had advocated, but was taught by what we now call the concentric system, beginning with the survey of a house, then proceeding to a neighbourhood, a district, and so on. Williams's pupils made several excursions for this purpose, anticipating the method later used by the Hill brothers at Hazelwood. Once the boys had reached the stage of studying the oceans and the world they could proceed from a study of climatic variations to an examination of

[19] Ibid., i, pp. 133–40.   [20] Ibid., ii, pp. 122–4.
[21] *Treatise*, p. 124.
[22] D. Williams, *Lectures on the Universal Principles and Duties of Religion and Morality* (London, 2 vols., 1779), i, p. 195.

the solar system, and they made their own maps and globes and studied the construction of clocks.[23] But Williams's geography was largely human geography: the divisions of the earth were considered as habitations of man, in relationship one with the other, and this logically entailed the study of the history of mankind, beginning with an examination of the 'fabulous origin or settlement of men', and tracing their history from the banks of the Ganges and Euphrates all over the globe.[24] Geography, astronomy, and history thus became in effect a unified study of the history of man in his environment.

All these studies Williams considered suitable for boys up to the age of about twelve. Beyond that age there were facilities for the study of chemistry, hydrostatics, and the construction of air-pumps.[25] But the older boys were encouraged to go beyond mere investigations. A group of them studied the papers of the Royal Society, and finding some of them 'puerile, improbable and foolish', wrote a number of mock-serious questions to that body. For instance:

Q.1. The Transactions containing an account of its having rained mice in Iceland, we wish to know, whether they had any qualities or properties different from earthly mice – whether they had the same pilfering disposition, and the same predilection for cheese.[26]

The study of the Royal Society's *Transactions* was symptomatic of Williams's encouragement of older boys to examine primary sources. Despairing of finding suitable textbooks, he encouraged them to consult the French *Encyclopédie* and the transactions of several European philosophical societies. These were not to be read *seriatim*, but to be looked at only when required for information or for the construction of a particular machine. In this way boys of thirteen or fourteen read with avidity and understood, for instance, the principles on which heat and cold were measured 'as well as any philosophers in Europe'.[27]

Williams must have been the first modern schoolmaster to

[23] *Lectures*, iii, pp. 11–12, 22–5.
[24] Ibid., pp. 26–7.
[25] Ibid., pp. 28–32.
[26] Ibid., p. 35.
[27] Ibid., ii, pp. 316–17; iii, pp. 27–32.

teach political economy. Characteristically, he avoided presenting principles or systems because he believed in the empirical method of beginning with the boys' own situations and status and working from there. Nearly all his pupils came from wealthy or landed families,[28] and at first Williams found it difficult to give them a clear and accurate idea of property (for possession, he noted, did not lead to a clear understanding of claim and right), so he tried several experiments. He divided his annual income into equal portions for a month, a week, and a day, to show how best it could be used for the good of the school. This was after a disastrous attempt to put the whole household economy into the pupils' hands: the result was 'to render me poor and the young men avaricious'. We are not told what Mrs. Williams's reactions were.[29] Another experiment was to declare all the 'raw materials' of the household common property and to make the pupils' skill in converting them to use the only grounds of a claim upon them. Some naturally produced more than others and so could claim more raw material, but since their talents gave general enjoyment and did not result in subjecting others to their will, this did not matter. Thus the pupils were supposed to learn in practice the use of surplus production, 'the spring both of alienation and of social industry', in the fostering of the useful arts.[30] To counter the tendency to inequality produced by parents' 'indiscreet and enormous allowances of money' to some pupils, Williams contrived to make the boys give some of their money to charitable causes, and taught them not to expect gratitude, in keeping with his views that actions should be performed for moral and useful reasons and not under the stimulus of reward and punishment.[31]

Williams also gave his pupils some experience of what today we should call sociology. He asked his pupils to examine the rank of society from which they came, and to estimate their place in society and their prospects in the light of the school maxim 'Every idle man is a knave'. Classical authors were sifted to discover their attitudes to rank, honour, and riches, thereby to modify the attitude of boys to these properties. In fact

[28] Ibid., i, pp. 236, 260; ii, p. 128.
[29] Ibid., ii, pp. 265–7.
[30] Ibid., iii, pp. 77–81.
[31] Ibid., ii, pp. 157–8, 169–71.

Williams had to prevent some of the younger pupils from adopting too thoroughly the maxim) that 'goodness is the sister of poverty'. Some of the older pupils, in consequence of their studies, even changed their views on the prospects that their families envisaged for them.[32]

Religious teaching in Williams's academy was, in effect, the comparative study of world religions. Like most deists, Williams opposed both organized Christianity and atheism; to him the world was divided between 'the votaries of superstition' and 'those of a coarse contemptuous ... infidelity',[33] and he had, therefore, no desire to induce pupils to accept any one religion or to promote unbelief. His pupils, who included Anglicans and Dissenters, Catholics and Jews,[34] spent their time in 'tracing the pretensions of all sacred systems to their origin', and in critically examining 'ancient and modern miracles'. The estimate of each religion was left to the discrimination of the pupils.

In the study of history, economics, religion, and associated subjects, Williams confined himself to suggesting universal truths, in the light of which investigations might be carried out, or presenting questions for his pupils to try to answer. In this he was true to his belief that the role of the tutor was to guide and stimulate rather than to issue statements that he expected his pupils to accept unquestioningly.

Williams made the first and indeed the only consistent attempt to apply the basic principles of *Émile* to the education of a group of boys in a classroom situation. As early as the 1770s he raised nearly every problem that later generations of schoolteachers have had to meet, and he was a most enterprising and successful experimentalist whose great strength was his use of psychological theory. With Rousseau as a guide he tried to understand the psychology of the child by means of close observation, and to base his teaching upon his theories.

Later he set up a chapel in Margaret Street, Westminster, where he preached his universal religion, gaining a European reputation both for his ideas and his eloquence.[35] His views

---

[32] Ibid., iii, pp. 138–40.
[33] Ibid., ii, p. 22.   [34] Ibid., p. 46.
[35] T. Morris, *General View of the Life and Writings of the Rev. David Williams* (London, 1792), p. 13.

were influential in revolutionary France, where they contributed to the cult of the worship of Reason and the Supreme Being in 1793-4.[36] He was made a French citizen, and together with Joseph Priestley, Sir James Mackintosh, and other notable Englishmen he helped in the drawing up of a new constitution and undertook diplomatic missions. Williams was welcomed to discussions with French philosophers and politicians[37] and was also in touch with many noted German educationalists. His educational thinking, writing, and practice are an excellent example of the radical, rational, and humane temper of his mind, and they were of great importance.

[36] D. Williams, 'More Light on Franklin's Religious Ideas', *American Historical Review*, xliii (July 1938), pp. 803-13.
[37] David Williams's MS. autobiography entitled 'Incidents in My Life', *passim*.

2 The Industrial Revolution and After

4 ROBERT OWEN AND THE NEW LANARK SCHOOLS[1]

ROBERT OWEN'S life (1771–1858) covers the traditionally accepted time-span of the Industrial Revolution, and he accepted the existence and implications of industrial change. He was born fourteen years before his future father-in-law David Dale set up one of the first cotton-spinning mills in the British Isles at New Lanark, and died seven years after the Great Exhibition had proclaimed Britain's world industrial supremacy. Although Owen was aware of the attractions of the pre-industrial pastoral society,[2] he did not look back upon it with nostalgia but accepted the new industrial system as the one in which his life had to be lived. 'He was the first British writer who grasped the meaning of the Industrial Revolution,' wrote Max Beer in his introduction to Owen's autobiography,[3] and he was impressed by the possibilities for production of the new industrialism, and how its new sources of wealth might be used for the benefit of the people.[4] He realized that the character of the working class was being formed chiefly by circumstances arising from trade, manufactures, and commerce,[5] and could only be transformed by a change in society, a process in which education would play a crucial part.

The two major influences in Owen's early life were Manchester and Scotland. Through his acquaintance with Dr.

---

[1] This chapter owes a great deal to discussions with Professor J. F. C. Harrison. See also H. Silver, *The Concept of Popular Education* (London, 1965) and H. Silver (ed.), *Robert Owen on Education* (Cambridge, 1969).
[2] R. Owen, *Observations on the Effects of the Manufacturing System* (London, 1815), pp. 6–7.
[3] M. Beer, Introduction to *The Life of Robert Owen* (London, 1920), pp. v–vi.
[4] R. Owen, *Report to the County of Lanark of a Plan for Relieving Public Distress* (Glasgow, 1821), pp. 1–4.
[5] Owen, *Observations on the Effects of the Manufacturing System*, p. 5.

Percival, a leading Unitarian and member of the Manchester Literary and Philosophical Society, and others of like mind, the ideas of French philosophical and educational thought, which directed attention to the conscious control of the environment in the interests of humanity and the important role that education would play in this process,[6] became apparent to Owen, together with a practical realization of the part to be played by science and rational organization in the improvement of public welfare.

At New Lanark in Scotland he became 'on the most friendly terms with many of the professors of the Universities of Edinburgh and Glasgow', of whom he mentions two by name, Professors Jardine and Mylne. The Scottish university tradition, which included the influences of David Hume, Dugald Stewart, Adam Ferguson, and Adam Smith, was instinct with the values of reason and nature, a deistical view of the universe, and an empirical 'common-sense' approach to man and society.[7] Thus, during his early manhood, from the 1790s to the opening of the New Lanark schools in 1816, Owen's educational theories developed in harmony with the views of the Enlightenment and of those who advocated education according to nature, although until about 1812 he had admired the monitorial system of Lancaster and Bell. In 1814, while still giving Bell and Lancaster their due as innovators in the sphere of method, he now denounced 'this mockery of learning' which could render the mind of a child irrational for life.[8] The children of the working class, Owen now argued, should have not only the best manner but also, and far more important, the best matter of instruction. It was not enough now to teach children to know their place, to become docile and obedient; they must become rational and useful members of society. No longer were children, in Owen's mind, to be treated as the recipients of those values that the middle and upper classes thought were necessary for them if they were to know

---

[6] S. E. Ballinger, 'The Idea of Social Progress through Education in the French Enlightenment Period: Helvétius and Condorcet', *History of Education Journal*, x (1959), pp. 88–99.

[7] Gladys Bryson, *Man and Society: The Scottish Inquiry of the Eighteenth Century* (Princeton, 1945), *passim*.

[8] R. Owen, *A New View of Society: or, Essays on the Principles of the Formation of the Human Character* (London, 1813–14).

their place in society. It was a decisive break with the old philanthropic attitude to the education of the poor, the tradition in which Bell and Lancaster were firmly rooted, and its importance in the history of British education cannot be overestimated. For the first time the educational outlook that had inspired Edgeworth, Day, and Williams was applied not to upper- or middle-class children but to the children of the poor. Owen's educational principles could almost be summed up as Rousseauism applied to working-class children. He was the first to demonstrate that what later was called elementary education could be based upon affection, imagination, and the full realization of the potentialities of the child.

Owen increasingly liberated himself from the simplified view of the power of education and the environment to which he had subscribed in 1812, in which education 'wholly and solely' accounted for 'general bodily and mental differences', a view that was and sometimes still is mistaken for Owen's last word on the subject. He developed a more subtle conception of the powers of education in relation to the endowment of the child. He stressed the 'endless varieties' of children's aptitudes and the different propensities and qualities that gave individuality and distinctiveness to a person's character. Education, he pointed out in 1823, 'cannot make human beings all alike'; what it could do was to make everybody 'good, wise and happy'.[9]

If parental and social attention was essential in the early part of the child's life, it was no less necessary during his time at a school. Owen made it clear that the education that children would receive under his plan would be based upon the principles of Rousseau and Pestalozzi, whereas under the existing educational system 'the child goes, half-fed and half-clothed, to learn ... strange sounds, which convey no meaning to his mind'.[10] At New Lanark a totally different situation existed.

Childhood was the age of curiosity and children had an intense urge to examine every object around them. If, therefore, a child's attention was not arrested by the mode of tuition

[9] R. Owen, *Report of the Proceedings at the Several Public Meetings held in Dublin* (Dublin, 1823), pp. 71–2.
[10] Ibid., p. 77.

adopted, 'it is our duty to alter and amend our plan'. Children should be presented with 'simple and ... agreeable facts', and gradually introduced to others 'of a more complex nature'. From birth to the age of twelve, every child should be able to acquire 'a general knowledge of the earth, and of the animal, vegetable and mineral kingdoms – of the useful sciences, and of human nature and its past history' in addition to 'as much both of theory and practices in the arts and sciences, as will afford them full employment and agreeable recreation'.[11]

Strongly reminiscent of the work of David Williams and the new school of educationalists rather than directly of Rousseau, these principles were the ones on which the children of the operatives of New Lanark were educated. In an age when Andrew Bell, Sir Thomas Bernard of the Society for the Betterment of the Poor, Patrick Colquhoun, the economist, and others believed that the education of the poor should properly consist of the three R's together with religion and the formation of habits of order and submission suitable to their station in life,[12] Owen considered he was giving the New Lanark children an education according to nature that would produce 'full-formed men and women, physically and mentally, who would always think and act consistently and rationally'.[13]

When Owen arrived at New Lanark in 1800 to take over the direction of the mills from his father-in-law David Dale his views were still in process of formation, and though he very soon began to put in hand improvements in housing, health, and working conditions in the New Lanark community, he was not able to put into practice his theories on education until sixteen years later, in 1816. In education, as in the community experiments, Owen's starting-point was the situation and conditions he inherited from David Dale.

Dale's treatment of the five hundred or so pauper apprentices on whom the running of the mills depended would not recommend itself to later generations, but compared with fellow mill-owners north and south of the Tweed, his methods were unusually enlightened. Although Owen admitted that

[11] Ibid., pp. 79–81.   [12] Cf. below, pp. 91–3.
[13] R. Owen, *The Life of Robert Owen* (London, 2 vols., 1857), i, p. 134 (hereafter *Life*). Owen's autobiography is in two volumes, numbered 1 and 1A, but the narrative is entirely in vol. 1, the second volume containing reprints of various pamphlets and documents.

the children 'looked fresh, and, to a superficial observer, healthy in their countenances',[14] he assessed Dale's work as 'a very partial experiment', and argued that his kind intentions had been rendered almost nugatory by the fact that the whole scheme depended upon the children working eleven and a half hours a day in the mills. Owen, by refusing to employ any child before ten years of age and improving the conditions for adult workers in the village, put into practice educational projects far beyond any that had been envisaged at the time.

Owen's educational system at New Lanark consisted of three schools, graded according to age: children between two and six years of age attended the infant school, those from six to fourteen the day school, and older children and the adults went to evening classes.

The greatest attraction at New Lanark, and one that Owen himself was most interested in, was the infant school.[15] His first conception of this institution was merely the provision of a playground in which the children's minds might be properly directed towards co-operation and living together, which he felt was an essential part of the education of the young.[16] His first task was to find a suitable teacher, and he looked for a teacher who had the qualifications of love for and patience with the children, and, what was perhaps more important, was willing to follow Owen's instructions. His choice fell upon James Buchanan and, as an assistant, Molly Young, both working people from the village.

Buchanan has hardly received fair treatment in histories of education. To a great extent this is due to Owen's rather cavalier treatment of him in his autobiography, in which he stressed Buchanan's low standard of learning and lack of independent character.[17] Later writers have enlarged upon this, until Buchanan appears in Cullen's *Adventures in Socialism* as 'a quiet, simple-minded old weaver named Jamie Buchanan, who could scarcely read, write or spell',[18] but the publication of

[14] *Report from the Select Committee on the State of the Children Employed in the Manufactories of the United Kingdom*, P.P. (1816), iii, p. 20.
[15] *Life*, p. 138.
[16] [R. Owen], *A Statement Regarding the New Lanark Establishment* (Edinburgh, 1812), p. 13.
[17] *Life*, p. 139.
[18] A. Cullen, *Adventures in Socialism* (Glasgow, 1910), p. 49.

the *Buchanan Family Records* in 1923 enables a more accurate picture to be presented. At the opening of the infant schools in 1816 Buchanan was an ex-serviceman of the Scottish Militia, thirty-two years of age, and fully literate as his surviving diaries and letters show; indeed, his granddaughter claimed for him an education 'considerably above the average for the times'.[19] In November 1815, when he was entrusted by Owen with the future direction of the infant school, he wrote in his diary: 'I commenced my new era, and gave up the desire of becoming rich or great, content if my life would be useful.'[20]

Owen insisted that no corporal punishment, threats, or abusive terms were to be used; that teachers were to adopt a pleasant manner of speech and that they should teach the children to make each other happy. The pupils were not to be 'annoyed with books', but taught the uses and qualities of common things 'by familiar conversation', and, when their curiosity was aroused, to ask questions about them.[21]

Buchanan certainly tried to fulfil Owen's instructions in both the letter and the spirit. He began by making the children march round the room to the strains of the flute – then, like the Pied Piper, he led them through New Lanark village to the river, let them play on the banks of the Clyde, and then marched them back again. He also devised indoor amusements for the children, simple gymnastic movements, arm exercises, clapping their hands, to all of which the children counted in numbers. He conducted oral lessons on arithmetical tables, object lessons in which the children did most of the talking, and hymn-singing to the sound of the flute.[22] Buchanan, in fact, gave himself up to the new teaching so unreservedly that it is difficult to see why Owen repeatedly stated that Buchanan did not understand his system. Buchanan remained at New Lanark for nearly two years, when he left to take up an appointment as head of the first London infant school at Brewer's Green.

In the day school for older children Owen was not able to carry out his plans as he would have wished. According to his son Robert Dale Owen, if he had had a free hand he would

---

[19] [B. I. Buchanan], *Buchanan Family Records* (Cape Town, 1923), p. 1.
[20] Ibid., p. 2.
[21] *Life*, pp. 139, 140.
[22] [Buchanan], *Buchanan Family Records*, p. 3.

have allowed the children to spend their first seven or eight years in the practical study of natural history, geography, ancient and modern history, chemistry, and astronomy; in doing this they would be 'following the plans prescribed by nature'. Having thus acquired a practical knowledge of the objects of the natural world around him, only then would the child have been taught to read, to use and understand words, 'the artificial signs adopted to represent these objects'. With his background of practical knowledge, the child would then learn to read with increased interest, since knowledge of the language would open up new discoveries in subjects already familiar.[23] This scheme, however, had to be modified because of the parents' insistence on the children learning to read at an earlier age than eight.

The children learned the three R's, natural history, geography, and history. In addition there was religious instruction, dancing and singing, sewing for the girls, and marching for the boys. Above all, the atmosphere of the school was free from the severe discipline and sense of authority traditionally found in educational institutions, as every visitor testified. The teaching method was founded on Owen's philosophical and psychological theories. The children were led gradually, and with as full an explanation as they could comprehend, from fact to fact, gradually increasing in complexity; thus 'their powers of reflection and judgement may be habituated to draw accurate conclusions from the facts presented to them'.[24] A high place was given to the study of natural history: as with David Williams, it was considered to be 'almost the first knowledge of which Nature directs an infant to acquire'.[25]

It followed almost as a matter of course that all rewards and punishments were abolished. This was done on the grounds not only that they were unjust but that they tended to enhance deficiencies of character.[26] Even Miss Edgeworth's children's books, though read, were criticized because they contained 'too much of praise and blame'.[27] Following Rousseau, only the

---

[23] R. D. Owen, *An Outline of the System of Education at New Lanark* (Glasgow, 1824), pp. 34–5 (hereafter *Outline*).
[24] Owen, *Report to the County of Lanark*, pp. 43–4; *A New View of Society*, 'Essay Third', p. 25.
[25] *Outline*, p. 45.   [26] Ibid., pp. 9–10.
[27] Ibid., pp. 35–6.

'natural' rewards and punishments in the shape of the necessary consequences of an action were recognized, and standards of right and wrong were fixed in relation to the increase or decrease of happiness of the school community.[28] Owen wanted to get away from the authority and fear inherent in the traditional pupil-teacher relationship; to this end the New Lanark teachers had to be critical of themselves rather than of the children if a lesson did not go well, and they were expected never to overstep the boundary of kindly admonition when dealing with an offence.[29]

In his autobiography Owen made a list of the ten innovations that he had introduced into the education of young children. They were: the absence of corporal punishment; kindness on the part of the teachers; instruction in realities by means of conversation; the answering of questions in a 'kind and rational manner'; the abolition of fixed hours and the alternation of lessons and play; the introduction of music, dancing, and drill into the curriculum; excursions into the countryside; the attempt to train children to think and act rationally; and the placing of children in superior surroundings.[30] Though some of these had been anticipated by David Williams, the total picture is a powerful vindication of Owen's plans and of the methods of the advocates of education according to nature, and represents an astonishing innovation in the education of the working class.

Owen's schemes never had the complete backing of his partner William Allen, the Quaker philanthropist and chemist, who found it difficult to reconcile his principles with Owen's free-thinking on religion and libertarian views on children's amusements. In 1819 Allen and another Quaker partner, Joseph Foster, visited New Lanark to investigate allegations that the religious beliefs of the inhabitants were being undermined. Owen paid little attention at the time to what he called Allen's 'crude and prejudiced notions',[31] but Allen persisted in his opposition to what he considered damaging to religious belief, and to the music-making. Finally, in January 1824, the London partners – Allen, Foster, Michael Gibbs, and Charles Walker – made Owen sign an agreement on the reorganization

[28] Ibid., pp. 11–13.
[30] *Life*, pp. 232–3.
[29] Ibid., pp. 16, 25.
[31] Ibid., p. 236.

of the schools, whose terms covered the dismissal of many of the teachers, including the dancing master and Miss Whitwell, a London headmistress with Owenite leanings who had come to teach at New Lanark, and the appointment of a new master, John Daniel, at a salary of £150 a year, to teach on the Lancasterian system. If the parents wished their children to learn dancing, they would have to pay for it themselves. Weekly reading of the Scriptures and 'other religious exercise' was instituted, music and singing (except for instruction in psalmody) were abolished, and the wearing of kilts was banned. The one positive feature was Allen's insistence that lectures in chemistry, mechanics, experimental philosophy, and natural history were to be given twice a week.[32]

Owen rightly believed this document to be an unwarranted interference in his educational schemes, and resigned from active management of the establishment. Thus, after eight years, what MacNab called 'the most valuable establishment in education to be found in this or any other country'[33] came to an end. Owen's 'liberal modes of natural instruction' were replaced by the rote-learning of the Lancasterian system, which Allen, according to Owen, believed to be 'the perfection of education'.[34]

Four years later, in 1828, Matthew Davenport Hill, a founder of Hazelwood, the experimental school at Birmingham, visited New Lanark. He found the children 'more disorderly than I had expected', the master in 'a constant state of painful exertion', and in the habit of striking the children hard in order to maintain 'a very distant approach to silence'.[35] It was a sad transformation of the New Lanark scheme. The last footnote was added by George Jacob Holyoake, the Owenite and Co-operator. Fifty-three years after Owen's experiment had come to an end and nearly twenty years after Owen's own death, he saw in the New Lanark schoolhouse in 1877 the

---

[32] 'New Arrangements Respecting the Schools at New Lanark, Determined upon the 21st of January, 1824', in R. Owen, *The New Existence of Man Upon the Earth* (London, 1854), pt. v, app. A, pp. vii-ix.
[33] H. G. MacNab, M.D., *The New Views of Mr. Owen of Lanark Impartially Examined* (London, 1819), p. 224.
[34] *Life*, p. 235.
[35] R. and F. Davenport-Hill, *The Recorder of Birmingham: A Memoir of Matthew Davenport-Hill* (London, 1878), p. 88.

remains of the blackboard and canvas diagrams 'of immense dimensions ... well and brightly painted' lying ruined against the walls.[36]

5 THE FOLLOWERS OF OWEN: WORKING-CLASS EDUCATORS AND UTOPIANS

AFTER the end of Owen's connections with the New Lanark schools, his educational doctrines provided the inspiration for two quite separate movements, the working-class Co-operators and socialists of the 1830s and 1840s and a small group of independent middle-class philanthropists, among whom Robert Pemberton and John Minter Morgan were the most important. The former tended to stress the rational and scientific elements of Owenite education, the latter the utopian aspect of his theory.

In propagating his ideas, Owen had pointed out that co-operative communities might be set up by any section of the population in order to relieve themselves of the evils of their condition. It was the working class who responded to the suggestion, and from the early efforts of London printers, who in 1821 formed a 'Co-operative and Economic Society', the Owenite Co-operative movement grew until by 1830 there were some three hundred local societies, and two hundred more were opened in the next few years.

These early Co-operators were imbued with a zeal for education that would make each member an efficient producer, fit to assume the duties of the new society that they believed their efforts would bring about, and many of these Co-operative societies set up schools of their own to hasten this process.

I

OWENITE CO-OPERATIVE SCHOOLS

The Second Co-operative Congress in 1831 passed a resolution to set up schools 'for the formation of a superior physical, moral, and intellectual character for the children of Co-

---

[36] *The Times*, 13 Nov. 1877.

operatives'.[1] At the Third Congress, Robert Owen emphasized that these schools should not only give children the necessary education but also give to the subjects taught to them 'an entirely new character'.[2] According to Aubrey Black, whose researches have thrown much light on the early history of Co-operative education, nine societies, principally in the London and Manchester areas, set up schools in the twelve months following the Second Congress resolution.[3]

The creation of an atmosphere of love and trust in the classroom, and the substitution of practical and dynamic methods of teaching for rote-learning from books were, of course, the hallmarks of the Owenite pedagogy and there is evidence that informal methods were pursued in London and Salford. Much of the instruction was given orally, and often lessons took the form of conversations, although there were also lectures several times a week.[4] The schools also aimed, as did Owen's at New Lanark, to provide recreation in the form of music, dancing, and singing, to counterbalance similar attractions in the town where they were mixed up with the 'vicious habit of drinking intoxicating liquors, thereby seducing those who are betrayed by these allurements, to immoral practices and finally to their destruction'.[5]

An unusual feature of the school in Salford, judging by previously accepted Owenite standards, was the attempt made to bring the senior pupils (who did not necessarily include the oldest pupils) into the government of the school. The first or most advanced class had a vote on all the transactions of the school, and the other classes had a right to send petitions to the teachers in favour of any reform or in pursuance of any grievance. The Co-operative schools in London and Salford I have described, however, were essentially a product of the upsurge of Co-operation in the early 1830s, and this had lost its impetus long before the end of the decade.

[1] *Proceedings of the Second Co-operative Congress* (Birmingham, 1831), p. 24.
[2] *Proceedings of the Third Co-operative Congress* (London, 1832), p. 41.
[3] A. Black, 'Early Co-operative Education, 1830–36' (unpublished dissertation, University of Manchester, 1951), p. 17.
[4] *Crisis*, vol. iii, nos. 7 and 8, 19 Oct. 1833.
[5] Ibid.

II

THE RATIONAL SCHOOLS

The schools of the Co-operative societies were regarded mainly as a means whereby the ideals and methods of Co-operation might more speedily be achieved. There were several others which sprang from the missionary zeal of the Rational Religionists, a quasi-socialist body which flourished from 1839 to 1845, and whose schools were more numerous, better organized, and more effective than those of the Co-operators. As J. F. C. Harrison emphasizes, the Co-operative and tradeunion upsurge of the early 1830s was largely a political, economic, and social movement; that of the late 1830s and early 1840s was primarily a movement of ideas, which aroused the fear and horror of many respectable people, particularly of the clergy.[6]

The Universal Community Society of Rational Religionists was formed in May 1839 by the amalgamation of two existing Owenite bodies, the Association of All Classes and All Nations (founded 1835) and the National Community Friendly Society (founded 1837). The latter body had been registered under the Friendly Societies Acts, and as Owen's paper *Union* pointed out, 'the shield of the law was thereby thrown over the proceedings of the socialists'.[7] The Rational Religionists were therefore in a much stronger position than previous Owenite organizations.

The aim of the Rational Religionists was nothing less than the total reformation of society. Their programme included wealth for all, enlightened and non-coercive government, full employment, and universal education. The change to this state of society was to be accomplished peacefully, by a radical modification of public opinion. In this operation a high place was assigned to 'infant and other schools'.[8] The magnitude of the task might have daunted any other man than Owen, but armed with his own views on human nature and society, Owen convinced himself and his followers that the millennium was

---

[6] J. F. C. Harrison, *Learning and Living, 1790–1960* (London, 1961), p. 110.
[7] *Union*, vol. 9, no. 1, 1 Dec. 1842.
[8] *The Constitution and Laws of the Universal Community Society of Rational Religionists* (London, 1839), p. 17.

capable of realization. Education played an even more important part in the schemes of the Rational Religionists than it had done in those of the Co-operators: the universal community could only be brought about if young people were educated from an early age to become rational beings.[9]

The Rational Religionists were organized very much like a modern political party, with a central board of directors, chosen annually at Congress, together with officers, district boards, and travelling missionaries. Members paid dues of $1\frac{1}{2}d$. a week, and at one period at the beginning of the 1840s the movement had sixty-five branches in England and Scotland, with over three thousand members. It employed eighteen full-time missionaries and lecturers, and established Halls of Science in many of the larger towns.[10] This solid organizational framework made it much easier to establish stable and effective schools.

The 1840 Congress resolved that the branches of the Society should immediately set up day and Sunday Schools, to teach, in addition to 'the usual routine' of education, facts and general science.[11] During the next three or four years enormous efforts were made by the branches to carry this resolution into effect, and by 1842 there were nine day schools and twelve Sunday schools in operation.[12] These varied greatly in size and quality, but all attempted a wide curriculum, with attention to science teaching and the deliberate avoidance of religious instruction. A correspondent in the *New Moral World* stressed this important aspect of their work: a young man who taught in a branch Sunday school was, he wrote, 'effectually superseding the baneful institutions of the priesthood'.[13] The priesthood, not unnaturally, were in full cry against the 'infidel schools', as they had been against the Co-operative schools in the 1830s.

What peculiar features did these institutions possess that

[9] 'Report of the Leeds Congress of Rational Religionists', *New Moral World*, n.s., vol. i, no. 3, 18 July 1840.
[10] Mary Hennell, *An Outline of the Various Social Systems and Communities Which Have Been Founded on the Principle of Co-operation* (London, 1844), p. 173.
[11] *New Moral World*, n.s., vol. i, no. 3.
[12] Ibid., vol. iii, no. 47, 21 May 1842.
[13] Ibid., vol. vii, no. 83, 23 May 1840.

could arouse such opposition on the part of the clergy? The aims and organizations of a Rational school can be studied in detail in the prospectus of the Liverpool school, which was printed in full in E. T. Craig's newspaper, *Star in the East*.[14] The first meeting of the Liverpool Rational School Society took place on 21 July 1839, and its resolutions clearly indicated the Owenite strategy of attempting to found an alternative educational system for the working class. The opening statement of the prospectus began with the proposition that the great mass of the people were brought up in 'a lamentable state of ignorance', and this ignorance was the source of 'intemperance, vice and crime'. Existing schools for the poor, however, merely inculcated 'mysterious and unintelligible dogmas, creeds, and catechisms of faith', and since it was obvious that neither the government nor 'the priesthood' would provide a superior system (the reference was to the recent abandonment by Parliament of plans for an unsectarian normal school or training college), the people must 'unite, and determine to educate themselves'. After adopting this fighting statement the meeting then resolved to form the Society for the purpose of providing as many schools as were required and urged the setting up of similar schools 'in every part of this great empire'.

The rules for the conduct of the school were simple, and stressed punctuality, regular attendance, cleanness and neatness in dress and person, and the desirability of friendly behaviour on the part of the children. The hours were from 9 in the morning and from 2 to 5 in the afternoon, with half-day holidays on Thursday and Saturday afternoons. Every three months a 'Festival and Ball' would be held for 'the recreation and amusement of the children'. The curriculum was ambitious, far too ambitious for the resources available, and was announced as 'Reading, Writing, Arithmetic, Grammar, Geography, Astronomy, the use of the Globes, Mechanics, Mathematics, Architecture, Drawing, Painting, Music, Singing, Dancing, Natural History, Mineralogy, Chemistry, the Sciences of Human Nature, of Human Society, and of the Effects of External Circumstances upon Human Nature, of Politics ...'. A report in the *New Moral World* in November

[14] *Star in the East*, 17 Aug, 1839.

The Followers of Owen

1842 showed that of these subjects only the three R's, geography, astronomy, music, and dancing were then being taught.[15] The provision of school books, globes, pictures, philosophical apparatus, and a school library was planned. In the sphere of method, in an effort to break away from the rote-learning and the monitorial system of the average day school, the subjects were to be taught by means of 'practical experiments, object teaching, familiar conversation and oral instruction'. A similar adventurousness in curriculum and method characterized other Rational schools.

One of the most interesting aspects of these schools was the number that adopted the Pestalozzian method of teaching. The Ashton Sunday school in Lancashire and the Hyde day school adopted it,[16] as did the school at Yarmouth, which was conducted 'on the principles of object teaching, united with the best portions of the Pestalozzian system'.[17] George James Holyoake, later to become the elder statesman of the Co-operative movement, during his short stay as teacher at the Sheffield branch school, adopted as his method 'the idea of Pestalozzi as developed by Dr. Mayo at Cheam'.[18] According to Holyoake, one reason for the adoption of Pestalozzi's method by the Owenite schools was that it was 'tangible, practicable and of immediate application'.[19] On the other hand, the fact that it was considered an advanced and progressive method probably also had its appeal. However, a clear distinction was made between Pestalozzian methods and 'object teaching', despite their close identification brought about by the widespread popularity of the Mayos' work on object lessons. Object teaching in Owenite schools apparently was derived from the experience of the New Lanark schools, in which 'objects' normally meant botanical and geological specimens, maps, globes, and models. The importance accorded to these objects in the Rational schools sprang from the Owenite insistence that knowledge of the natural world was one of the means by which the mind could be freed from the preconceptions of existing society.

[15] *New Moral World*, n.s., vol. iv, no. 21, 19 Nov. 1842.
[16] Ibid., vol. iii, no. 23, Dec. 1841; no. 16, 16 Oct. 1841.
[17] Ibid., vol. i, no. 2, 11 July 1840.
[18] Letter to the *Sheffield Iris*, printed in *New Moral World*, n.s., vol. iii, no. 2, 10 July, 1841.
[19] Ibid.

Objects were fragments of the world of nature, and children's appreciation of them came through the senses, whereas books and teachers were a source of preconceptions. Hence the insistence of Owenite educationalists on placing 'facts' before children, on letting children make up their own minds, and hence also the distrust of textbooks and the importance placed on the interrogative method of teaching, based on knowledge gained by individual inquiry.

Some insight into the aims and methods of Owenite education is provided by the activities of John Ellis, one of the most capable and successful of the travelling schoolmasters of the early 1840s.[20] In September 1841 Ellis took charge of the day and evening schools of the Hyde branch in Cheshire; by the end of the year the day school had 110 pupils, and Ellis was trying to conduct it on Pestalozzian lines. The school was co-educational, for Ellis did not believe in relegating girls to sewing and knitting; in fact, he thought they should have preferential treatment in order to redress the usual bias against educating them. He would, he claimed, try to give an all-round physical, moral, and intellectual education, but would also suit the instruction to the capacity of the child. He would not teach words without ideas, nor present ideas that did not convey facts. His aim was to arouse 'the perceptive and reflective faculties' of children, 'to unbuild, to raise the superstructure of the mind'.

These theories were extremely advanced in the 1840s, and very few schoolmasters would have thought of conducting a working-class school of over a hundred children on these lines. Ellis's curriculum was also much in advance of the time, putting the emphasis on science and cutting out religious instruction. He also included a good deal of moral teaching, of a vaguely Owenite character – 'universal governmental principles' and 'universalism', as well as 'moral truths' from the Bible, the Koran, and Confucius – but he emphasized that he would be careful 'not to teach any kind of religion, whether constructed by Confucius or Jesus Christ'.

Ellis was not only a 'practical schoolmaster', as he described

---

[20] This account is based on reports printed ibid., vol. iii, no. 16, 16 Oct. 1841; no. 26, 25 Dec. 1841; no. 35, 26 Feb. 1842; no. 39, 26 Mar. 1842; no. 41, 9 Apr. 1842.

himself, but also a writer of textbooks. He wrote three: *Songs for Children*, *The Human Body Described*, and *Lessons on Objects*; the last named of these was an official textbook for use in Owenite schools, together with *Chambers's Educational Course*.[21] Ellis's book on anatomy was written in simple language; in fact, much of it was based on exercises on oral lessons written by children themselves. The book was divided into twenty-six lessons, each dealing with a different aspect of the subject – the skin, the muscular system, the bones, and so on.

It is unfortunate that Ellis's progressive experiment lasted no longer than a school year, but the closure of the school was due to desperate economic conditions in the town, not to internal failure. In April 1832 Ellis wrote despairingly to the *New Moral World*: 'Hyde is in ruins, misery is depicted on every countenance ... the people are going to America by sixty or more per week....' Many of his best scholars emigrated, and when his chief monitor left 'there was scarcely a dry cheek in the school'. Ellis was much affected by the breakup of his school, and it seems to have strengthened his determination to bring about a new order of society.

Most of the schools mentioned appear to have closed for one reason or another by about 1843; their decline paralleled that of the organization of the Rational Religionists, but during the three or four years of their heyday they had provided a kind of education far in advance of anything hitherto given to working-class children. Their special claim to distinction was that they were the only popular educational institutions of the nineteenth century that were specifically designed to produce a change in society by changing the character of the knowledge given to the individuals composing it, and through them influencing the society itself.

These schools exemplified the struggle between two differing concepts of working-class education which has persisted from the Mechanics' Institutes to the Workers' Educational Association and beyond – whether education should consist of 'knowledge', or whether it should be based on working-class ideology and social and economic factors. Though the Owenites took the latter position, they were not merely ideologists. Their position, as Ellis put it, was rather that the education

[21] Ibid., no. 47, 21 May 1842.

he gave (which contained little positive Owenite propaganda) would influence not only body and mind but also character, creating an aversion from 'irrational amusements' and 'ignorant company', developing the reason, and creating a desire for a rational system of society.[22] Whatever weaknesses may exist in this line of argument, it was at least one that was based on an analysis of social responsibility and social structure, and it was very much in advance of the current view that the three R's and the Bible, taught relentlessly and by rote, were properly the staple educational food of working-class children.

III

ROBERT PEMBERTON AND OTHERS

As the working-class disciples of Owen had taken from the master's principles their scientific and rational aspects, so the middle-class Owenites speculated upon the grand educational designs that might exist in their ideal colonies and commonwealths.

Robert Pemberton was born in 1787 and grew up in London as the adopted son of a Mrs. Southbrook. Blessed with a private income, he married in 1824 and spent his time travelling on the Continent.[23] Returning to England, he wrote educational treatises until in 1854, at the age of sixty-seven, he came across the works of Robert Owen and was immediately converted. 'I am perusing your works with intense interest,' he wrote to Owen, 'and I shall read them over and over again as long as I exist ... by what I have already read of your philosophy I at once perceive that you are the father of the true philosophy of the human mind....'[24] Three weeks later, with characteristic immodesty, he informed Owen that 'I find we are in perfect harmony and agreement in all the principal points of our investigation.'[25] He was rewarded by being greeted by Owen as 'a welcome co-adjutor'.

Pemberton's own investigations had been summed up in his first work, *The Attributes of the Soul from the Cradle,*

[22] Ibid., no. 16, 16 Oct., 1841.
[23] R. C. B. Pemberton, *Pemberton Pedigrees* (Bedford, 1923), chart 40.
[24] Pemberton to Owen, 2 Oct. 1854 (Owen correspondence).
[25] Pemberton to Owen, 21 Oct. 1854.

published in 1849. His views, rooted in the social philosophy of the Enlightenment, contained echoes of the theories of Rousseau, Pestalozzi, and Owen himself. He stressed the importance of the environment in education and of natural methods of teaching, the primacy of the senses in perception, the significance of the years of infancy, and distrust of formal teaching from books.[26]

The work that Pemberton considered to be most in harmony with the Owenite vision was *The Happy Colony*, published in 1854. Inspired by More's *Utopia*,[27] it was dedicated to 'the Workmen of Great Britain' and envisaged the founding of a classless society in New Zealand, financed by shilling subscriptions from working men. Its chief feature was an Elysian Academy, at which young people would spend the first twenty-one years of their life, acquiring, as part of an encyclopaedic education, no fewer than eight languages, which would fit them for free communication with the countries of the world.[28]

Having caught the interest of Owen, Pemberton soon became immersed in the millennial plans that occupied the last two years of Owen's life. Pemberton was also in correspondence with John Winter Morgan, who had written to express his admiration for *The Attributes of the Soul*, and enclosed a copy of his own *Christian Commonwealth*,[29] a similar utopian scheme, which, unlike those of Owen and Pemberton, had received the support of the church.[30] Pemberton also came to know Thomas Atkin, a civil engineer and disciple of Owen and another author of utopian plans for education, and in *An Address to the Bishops and Clergy* Pemberton linked Robert Owen, himself, and Thomas Atkins together as educational visionaries, whose labours in the mental kingdom would go far beyond the achievements of science.[31]

The high point of Pemberton's pubic endeavours to con-

[26] R. Pemberton, *The Attributes of the Soul from the Cradle* (London, 1849), *passim*.
[27] Pemberton to Owen, 21 Oct. 1854.
[28] R. Pemberton, *The Happy Colony* (London, 1854), *passim*, *An Address to the People, on the Necessity of Popular Education, in Conjunction with Emigration as a Remedy for All our Social Evils* (London, 1859), pp. 4–5, 9.
[29] Pemberton to Owen, 21 Oct. 1854.
[30] W. H. G. Armytage, *Heavens Below* (London, 1961), pp. 209 ff.
[31] R. Pemberton, *An Address to the Bishops and Clergy of All Denominations* (London, 1855), pp. 13–15.

C

vert the people to a higher conception of education was achieved at a meeting at St. Martin's Hall on 1 January 1855. This was convened by Robert Owen as an advertisement for his long-promised millennium, which would be inaugurated on 14 May of that year by an aggregate meeting in London of delegates from all governments, countries, religious sects, parties, and classes. The revolution would be brought about by peaceful means and with the consent of mankind, and it was the object of the meeting to discover and develop the actual means. A London newspaper described the proceedings as 'a host of visionary and impracticable schemes connected with political, social, educational and religious reforms'.[32] Owen and Pemberton appeared on the platform together and the latter actually read Owen's speech, in which Owen praised Pemberton's ideas on education as 'true, beautiful, and with himself perfectly original', though they had both come to the same fundamental conclusions. Pemberton in his turn praised Owen as 'a good and divine agent' employed by Providence 'for bringing about the perfection and happiness of man' and whose system was too beautiful for 'the uneducated priesthood and the uneducated gambling commercial world.'[33]

Pemberton gave an outline of his educational views and explained the details of his 'projected new city', the capital of the 'Happy Colony', a large drawing of which hung at the back of the platform. It consisted of a series of concentric circles which contained dwelling-houses, parks, gardens, and orchards. In the inner circle, in grounds covering fifty acres, was situated the academy, which was made up of four colleges with conservatories, workshops, swimming-pools, and riding-schools near by. On the ground geographical and astronomical maps were laid out and circular groves embodied the Muses and history.

After Pemberton had demonstrated his particular scheme a letter was read from James Silk Buckingham, former M.P. for Sheffield (1832–7), a seafarer, traveller, editor, and social reformer. A drop scene showing his model town was presented, a project similar to that of Pemberton except that it consisted

[32] *Lloyd's Weekly London Newspaper*, 7 Jan. 1855.
[33] *Robert Owen's Address, Delivered at the Meeting in St. Martin's Hall, Long Acre, London, on the 1 January, 1855* (London, 1855), p. 21.

of concentric squares rather than circles. Thomas Atkins then told the meeting about his model town, the chief feature of which was a model school 'for scientific, visual and practical education'. It consisted of a circular area, 60 feet in diameter, from which diverged, at the points of the compass, four corridors 150 feet long, 30 feet wide, and 30 feet high. The corridors forming the two arms of the cross were thus 360 feet long, the equivalent of the number of degrees from the earth's poles. Each corridor would contain specimens of the animal, vegetable, and mineral kingdoms classified according to the latitudes in which they were found. In addition, the model school would have an industrial department which would include a farm, garden, workshop, laboratory, and factory.[34]

The painted drop scenes of the millenarians of 1855 represented nothing more than the hopes of those who had despaired of changing the existing educational system and were seeking a short-cut to progress. They were too involved, too far beyond anything remotely possible at the time, despite Pemberton's brave hope of getting the British workman to finance his projects. Perhaps Pemberton sensed this, for within a few years, although still an admirer of Owen, he was beginning to doubt the possibilities of bringing about the ideal society by means of meetings, petitions, and propaganda, and thought Owen was 'out of his depth' in trying to create societies by philanthropic means.[35] Pemberton turned once more to exploring the importance of sound and speech in education. His experiments in language teaching, although intellectually arbitrary, were as concrete and workable as his previous utopian schemes had been visionary and impracticable, though both were interconnected and sprang from the same philosophical sources.

IV

The followers of Owen in educational experiments of the 1830s were working men trying to provide for themselves and their children a schooling and an outlook on life that would

[34] Ibid., pp. 26–8; cf. also 'Prospectus of the Industrial and Provident Moral Scientific, and Educational Association (Proposed by Thomas Atkins, Esq., C.E., Oxford)' (Owen correspondence).
[35] R. Pemberton, *The Science of Mind Formation* (London, 1858), pp. 72–3.

have an influence on other schools and arouse a working-class response to education for a changing society. The professional teaching skill, the organization of the schools, the necessary money, and the innovating zeal did not last, and this radical educational experiment, the only one started and maintained by working-class groups, died within ten years. The ventures of the Rational Religionists, maintained by an ethical zeal and a well-conceived organization, carried forward in the 1840s Owen's strategy of founding an educational alternative to the elementary schools of the Anglican and Free Church societies. But the organization of the religious bodies was stronger and rationalist socialism was a minority movement.

Utopians sprang from Owenism as from unorthodox religious groups, and Robert Pemberton's scheme for the 'Happy Colony' in New Zealand was like a number of other ideal schemes, some of which reached no further than written prospectuses and preliminary meetings. The 1850s and 1860s were the decades of the great Commissions, which evaluated the whole educational provision of the country, and by that time the energy of working-class innovation was spent.

6 THE HILLS AND HAZELWOOD SCHOOL[1]

I

I met in London several members of a very remarkable family, possessing, I think more practical ability, administrative and deliberative, than I have ever since found united in any one household; a family deserving well of their country, and every member of which has since made his mark, in one department or other; the Hills, formerly of Hazelwood, Birmingham.[2]

---

[1] See especially C. G. Hey's M.A. thesis, 'The History of Hazelwood School, Birmingham, and its Influence on Educational Developments in the Nine-Century' (Wales, 1954), which has provided a valuable survey of the subject although the view taken here is rather different.

[2] R. D. Owen, *Threading My Way* (London, 1874), pp. 307–8.

The Hills and Hazelwood School

ROBERT DALE OWEN'S assessment of Thomas Wright Hill and his five sons is borne out when we consider their careers. Matthew Davenport became Recorder of Birmingham and M.P. for Hull; Rowland is known to history as the originator of the Penny Post; Arthur was a well-known educationalist who became principal of Bruce Castle School; Frederic became inspector of prisons and secretary to the postmaster-general; and Edwin was a prominent inventor who became a high official in the Post Office. The first three sons, however, have also another claim to fame as the founders of one of the best known progressive schools of the nineteenth century, Hazelwood, and its extension, Bruce Castle, which Thomas de Quincey considered 'the most original experiment in Education which in this country at least has been attempted since ... the Edgeworths'.[3]

Hazelwood was the successor to Hill Top, a school that Thomas Wright Hill had founded in Birmingham at the beginning of the nineteenth century. Hill had settled in late eighteenth-century Birmingham, which he found congenial to his scientific and educational interests. After a strict upbringing and a good education at Kidderminster Grammar School, he had become successively a brass-founder, a charity-school teacher, a partner in a leather firm, and a works superintendent at Kidderminster. He opened Hill Top School in 1803, having bought it cheaply from his friend Thomas Clark, who left teaching to make his fortune manufacturing cotton machinery.[4]

Hill Top was really a trial run for a new type of school. In July 1819 the whole institution moved to Hazelwood in Edgbaston, occupying a building that had been specially designed by Rowland Hill, with a large schoolroom seating 250, which had a stage at one end, and with numerous classrooms, and a museum. In 1820 it was partly rebuilt and extended following a disastrous fire. The reconstructed school had several novel features: a built-in heating and ventilation system, an observation platform on the roof for astronomical observation and

[3] [T. de Quincey], 'Plans for the Instruction of Boys in Large Numbers', *London Magazine*, ix (1824), p. 410.
[4] J. L. Dobson, 'The Hill Family and Educational Change in the Nineteenth Century. I: Thomas Wright Hill and the School at Hill Top, Birmingham', *Durham Research Review*, no. 10 (Sept. 1959), pp. 261–3.

surveying operations, in addition to studies, a library, a reference library, a gymnasium, and a swimming-bath. It was after these extensions and reconstructions at Hazelwood that the school acquired its characteristic features: complete self-government by the boys, a mark system of reward and punishment of great complexity, a minutely ordered time-table, and attention to useful rather than classical knowledge in the curriculum.

Hazelwood was a school very much in the radical and utilitarian tradition. Thomas Wright Hill, as a friend of Joseph Priestley, was greatly influenced by the example of the eighteenth-century Dissenting academies with their emphasis on producing the cultured, self-reliant man of affairs. The most striking point about Hazelwood, however, was its resemblance to the Chrestomathic proposals of Jeremy Bentham, although the Hills denied that they had seen Bentham's treatise when they published the first edition of their book describing the Hazelwood system, *Public Education*.[5] Such views were a part of the climate of middle-class radical thought in the immediate post-Napoleonic periods and the systems of Bell and Lancaster, to whom Bentham admitted a debt, also had an influence on the arrangements of Hazelwood School.[6]

Hazelwood School at Edgbaston and its later extension at Bruce Castle at Tottenham near London, can best be understood in this context, for it gathered together the varied yearnings of the middle class for an education of their own as an alternative to the classical public school and developed them coherently to a highly idiosyncratic conclusion.

II

Most of our knowledge of Hazelwood comes from *Public Education*, first publised anonymously in 1819, with a revised and extended second edition in 1825. Much of it was composed by Matthew Davenport Hill with the assistance of Arthur Hill, but the credit for the details of the system is largely due to

[5] *Public Education: Plans for the Government and Liberal Instruction of Boys, in Large Numbers; as Practised at Hazelwood School* (London, 2nd ed., 1825), p. 185 n.
[6] J. Bentham, *Chrestomathia*, in J. Bowring (ed.), *The Works of Jeremy Bentham* (Edinburgh, 11 vols., 1838–43), viii, pp. 46 ff.

Rowland. *Public Education* was published partly as a justification for Hazelwood, partly as an advertisement for it. Although written in a plain, flat style, which hardly does justice to the exciting innovations in its pages, it was an epoch-making book showing a wide acquaintance with leading educators both living and dead, and examining carefully every aspect of the system.

The general object of the school was simple; it was to produce 'men of business'.[7] 'Business' was not understood in the narrow commercial or industrial sense, but seen as the capacity for practical administration in any walk of life. Arthur's son Birkbeck Hill told the Schools Inquiry Commission of 1868 that the main concern of Bruce Castle School was with 'the upper stratum of the middle classes'.[8] The schools produced, in fact, the kind of administrators and commercial intelligentsia that the Hill brothers, themselves products of the system, so well exemplified.

At Hazelwood and Bruce Castle the guiding principle of leadership was not fundamentally different from that in force at Arnold's Rugby: 'He who is to command, should first learn to obey.' Though Hazelwood boys were trained to be the directors, as the Hills termed it, they were also given experience as subordinates. Directors, the Hills believed, should have ascendancy over the minds of others, be able to estimate the qualities of those around them, be acquainted with the principle of the division of labour, but above all have a practical acquaintance with the science of evidence, and the operations of the school court provided ample opportunity for boys to familiarize themselves with that.[9] The duties were defined as 'punctual, intelligent, unhesitating obedience', which the arrangements of the school were in part designed to cultivate. However, other more positive virtues were not forgotten:

> The object which we have kept in view, in forming our system of government and instruction, is to render our pupils, in the highest degree, virtuous and intelligent men;

[7] *Public Education*, pp 315 ff.
[8] *Report of the Endowed Schools Inquiry Commission*, P.P. (1867–8), xxviii, p. 839.
[9] *Public Education*, pp. 324 ff.

and at the same time so to modify the education of each, as to enable him to pass with honour, success and happiness, through that path of life into which he will probably be thrown.[10]

The philosophical basis of the school affected the nineteen principles on which it was run. The attention given to each subject in the curriculum was measured, in true Benthamite fashion, by 'its effect on the welfare and happiness of the individual pursuing it, and of society at large', and each child was expected to concentrate upon those studies 'for which nature had best qualified him'.[11] A thorough grounding in the elements of each subject was emphasized, together with individual work, constant revision, and reasonable hope of reward, so that the pupil could advance steadily with 'moderate exertion'.[12] 'This plan,' says Arthur Hill, in a language more descriptive of a factory than a school, 'has all the advantages which a master and workman both obtain, in the man's being employed in *piece-work* instead of *day work*.'[13]

The Hills' insistence on punctuality was based on the belief that efficiency in the affairs of life depended on the exact disposition of time, and the knowledge that the only way to ensure approximate punctuality in later life was to insist upon absolute punctuality at school. The same approach was applied to the other twin bugbears of school life – attendance and silence. It was held that regular attendance, particularly at the first muster of each term, was beneficial to a boy's character and was therefore rewarded. The boys mostly entered into the spirit of the thing, and cases were known of boys walking twenty miles a day to be at the first muster on time.

The Hills maintained that it was impossible to maintain a medium between silence and noisiness for any length of time. When the boys were engaged in work or private study in the main schoolroom, and at mealtimes, the duty of preserving silence fell upon a boy called a silentiary, who wore slippers for silence and a hat to distinguish him from the other boys.

---

[10] [A. Hill], *Sketch of the System of Education, Moral and Intellectual, in Practice at the Schools of Bruce Castle, Tottenham, and Hazelwood, Near Birmingham* (London, 1833), p. 1.
[11] Ibid., p. 3.   [12] Ibid., pp. 3 ff.   [13] Ibid., p. 5.

The silentiary was paid a salary out of a fund made up from two sources – a tax on talkative boys and a subsidy paid by older pupils.

Delegation of responsibility to the pupils in this manner was an integral part of the Hazelwood system. A detailed account of the government of Hazelwood, and its system of rewards and punishments, is given in chapter 14 of *Public Education*. In outline the arrangements consisted of a School Committee, the supreme law-making body, and an elected jury court, presided over by a judge, which tried major offences against school discipline. Minor offences were dealt with by a magistrate, assisted by elected officials, and a number of executive officers assisted in the running of the school. Corporal punishment, public disgrace, and minor impositions were abolished, and their place was taken by a system in which misdemeanours were punished by the loss of marks, a token coinage that could be earned by good performance in academic work and school administration. Nearly all punishments were in the form of fines from the boy's personal stock of marks. Only in rare cases was solitary confinement imposed or boys deprived of their free time. Marks contributing to rank, which was a measure of the pupil's general standing in the school, and made up on a weekly and aggregate system. As the assessment of school work was made at intervals and varied from subject to subject, all boys had a chance to gain rank. A later innovation was the introduction of circles and guardians, the latter being senior boys who took charge of a circle or group of ten junior boys, and were responsible for their welfare, conduct, and general adaptation to the school routine. This idea was taken direct from the practice of Fellenberg's Institution, on the advice of Robert Dale Owen, a former pupil there.[14]

III

The academic aspect of Hazelwood School was in some degree more conventional than the organizational side. Nevertheless, there was a seriously thought-out procedure concerning curriculum and method that foreshadowed a great deal of what was considered progressive much later in the century. The Hills

[14] *Public Education*, pp. 370 ff.

never hesitated to take over and adapt the latest and most advanced teaching methods of their own day. In fact, they claimed little credit themselves for their methods, but stated they were merely an improvement on various techniques that had been current for years. The Hill brothers were familiar with the work of most of the leading educators of that time, and gave particular notice to the Edgeworths and Bell and Lancaster, but whatever they learned from others they transformed and improved and welded into a single working system.

The academic aim was so to dispose the available time and so to provide the greatest motivation for learning as to allow each boy to work to his maximum efficiency. This was ensured by means of punctuality, division into classes (by no means common in the 1820s), a complete bar on idleness, and clearly defined goals and objectives. The next step was to provide the necessary motivation for academic study. Here the Hills inverted the usual practice in schools, and relegated fear of punishment and hope of reward to the bottom of the scale as means of encouraging habits of learning, on the grounds that they were not only degrading but also inefficient. They did not completely abolish rewards and punishments in the academic sphere, but kept them to the minimum. Punishment had to be precise in its effect, and rewards were to be various and small, and adapted to the disposition of the pupil. Even 'gentle and temperate' emulation could be used.[15]

The Hills argued that the two most powerful stimuli to academic work were love of employment and love of knowledge, and of these the latter was undoubtedly the more powerful and permanent. Children could not be expected to work without some worth-while purpose or activity, and the Hills attached a great deal of importance to generating a love of knowledge in their pupils. Generally speaking, they relied on giving a perspective to relate the part to the whole, the usefulness of what was taught and its direct relationship to life outside school. They felt it was important that the planning and presentation of knowledge should be clear, vivid, and accurate, and related as much as possible to the senses, so they stressed first-hand experiences and practical illustration and frequently

[15] Ibid., p. 190.

used apparatus, models, maps, and documents.

Nevertheless, they also realized that it was essential to give each boy a personal stake in mastering a subject, and an experience of success. Nobody was likely to continue to make efforts that met only with disappointment and failure; therefore, every pupil should have an opportunity, continuously throughout his school life, of tasting the sweets of achievement. Given differences of preference and ability, they thought this was best done by ranking the school frequently according to subject or effort or behaviour, so that each boy had an opportunity to do well in something:

> Thus each boy, in his turn, attains rank and consideration in that branch of study wherein nature fitted him to excel, and where comparatively moderate efforts will ensure success. If this were all, if our plan merely served to carry each boy onwards in the path which nature had pointed out for him, we should consider a valuable point to have been gained; inasmuch as we hold single excellence in higher estimation than various mediocrity. But the cause continues to operate. The confidence that exertion will be followed by success, being established in his mind, will cheer him on in other departments of education.[16]

Another important feature of the system was the practice of voluntary labour. This was introduced to enable those duller boys who excelled at hard work to gain upon their more brilliant fellows, for voluntary labour was also paid in personal marks that contributed to rank. By working the printing-press, producing the school magazine, making models, doing etchings and paintings, studying music, modelling in clay, constructing machines, composing verses, and similar tasks, boys could contribute to their own position in the school as well as enjoying themselves at a hobby. Of course the able boys had benefit from this as well as the others.

The Hazelwood curriculum was a wide one, with a commercial basis. The subjects offered were: English, spelling, elocution, parsing, penmanship, shorthand, geography, history, mathematics (including arithmetic, algebra, geometry, trigo-

[16] Ibid., pp. 209–10.

nometry, and mensuration), French, Latin, Greek, gymnastics, drawing, and science. Predictably, the teaching varied, and a former pupil, William Sargant, recalled that the arithmetic teaching was 'amazing', the classics tuition 'defective', and that 'a good deal of time was wasted on shorthand'.[17]

Mathematics was a subject in which Thomas Wright Hill and Rowland Hill were particularly interested, and great pains were taken to make the subject interesting and comprehensible. The pupils did a great deal of basic number work by manipulating marbles and counters, with a step-by-step progression and attention to concrete problems. Much was made of the practice of mental arithmetic (for which there was a special set) and of 'mixed arithmetic', in which boys solved problems by their own methods in the shortest possible time – which was intended by the Hills to approximate to what would be the situation in later life.[18] In trigonometry practical surveying was done in the surrounding districts, for which special excursions were arranged.

The introduction of gymnastics and physical exercise into the curriculum was unusual for the period. In this the Hills admitted their debt to the Reverend Lant Carpenter, a Unitarian minister, whose *Principles of Education: Intellectual, Moral and Physical* had been published in 1820. In addition to cricket and Rugby, the boys had one hour per day of running, leaping, wrestling, vaulting, and spear-throwing, and there was also swimming in the school's own pool. An Athletics Committee gave prizes at the end of each session, but these were small and athletics and games were not allowed to take a superior place in the life of the school.[19]

In language teaching the Hills were undoubtedly pioneers. In their day, language teaching was a centre of great controversy and all sorts of systems abounded. Language teaching at Hazelwood had two guiding principles – that language is primarily for the transmission of meaning, and that language was not taught by means of grammar but grammar by means of familiarity with the language. The classical languages were

[17] W. L. Sargant, *Essays of a Birmingham Manufacturer* (London, 4 vols., 1869–72), ii, p. 189.
[18] *Public Education*, pp. 111 ff.
[19] Ibid., pp. 133–5.

included in the curriculum largely because the Hills considered that they formed the basis of modern culture. The English language itself, however, they regarded less and less as a 'subject' than as a means of communicating ideas, whose use underlay much of the organization and day-to-day work of the school. To the Hills, all teachers were teachers of English and much of the English work of the school was, therefore, incidental to voluntary labour, court and jury work, dramatic performances, the production of the magazine, and so on. Above all, they followed Maria Edgeworth's advice that in all forms of self-expression, but particularly in written work, there must be genuine motivation.

But the greatest curricular innovation of the Hills was undoubtedly the science course, which they introduced at Hazelwood and Bruce Castle in 1829. It has had little notice, possibly because no account of it appears in *Public Education*, which was published before the science studies began.

In 1829 the Hills engaged a brilliant young scientist and teacher, Edward Wedlake Brayley, the eldest son of the topographer and archaeologist of that name. Brayley's main aim was to demonstrate the utility of a knowledge of science as an integral part of a liberal education and to convince the parents that whatever their sons' future employment might be, a knowledge of science would be a positive advantage. Brayley's standpoint was essentially Baconian: he defined civilization as the stage in human development in which nature is known and controlled by man for the welfare and happiness of mankind. A knowledge of science, he argued, extends the intellectual range; it preserves the mind from the inroads of superstition; and, for good measure, it is a means of improving the arts and manufactures.

Hazelwood and Bruce Castle have a just claim to be considered the pioneers of the teaching of science in the nineteenth century. Only Mill Hill, one of the newer foundations, whose curriculum was not bound by ancient statute or tradition, and Bootham, a Quaker school in York founded in 1828, can be said to have preceded it, but the natural and experimental philosophy taught at Mill Hill in 1821 and Bootham in 1828 could not compare with the Hills' ambitious efforts. It was not until 1859 that Rugby built a science laboratory and lecture-room, and this was an isolated effort. The Schools Inquiry Commission Report of 1868 noted that science was taught in only a handful of the 128 schools examined and that for all practical purposes it was excluded from the education of the upper classes in England.[20]

The Hills' scientific course failed because of the opposition of the boys' parents. Despite Brayley's personal brilliance as a teacher, they were unconvinced that science had a useful place in commercial and general education. Brayley argued that even given the relatively small amount of time a boy spent at school, science would be a worth-while subject, more useful to those entering a business or commercial career than the study of dead languages. Substitution of science for the classics in the curriculum could not be made, however, without the parents' permission, which scarcely ever was given, and the science course had to be discontinued in the early 1830s, greatly to the disappointment of Rowland Hill, who gave up teaching very soon afterwards. At Mill Hill and Bootham, however, the more modest offerings were maintained and developed.

IV

Bruce Castle School was a branch of the parent school started in the summer of 1827 at Tottenham, North London. It was opened mainly because Hazelwood was not attracting pupils in the numbers for which the Hills had hoped: London, it was felt, would provide better opportunities for expansion than the Midlands. Hazelwood continued to exist side by side with Bruce Castle for six years and did not close until 1833,[21] after fourteen years in Edgbaston.

Initially Rowland Hill took charge of Bruce Castle, but in 1833 Arthur Hill took over the leadership, which he retained until 1868, when his son, George Birkbeck Hill, who had taught there for ten years, succeeded him. Under his rule as headmaster, the standard of scholarship was raised, but less

[20] D. M. Turner, *A History of Science Teaching in England* (London, 1927), pp. 89–91.
[21] J. L. Dobson, 'Bruce Castle School at Tottenham and the Hills' Part in the Work of the Society for the Diffusion of Useful Knowledge', *Durham Research Review*, no. 12 (Sept. 1961), p. 74.

attention was given to the detailed working of the original Hazelwood system, and from the evidence available it appears that Bruce Castle, during the years of Birkbeck Hill's stewardship, moved nearer to the usages of the average private boarding-school. Guardians were chosen by a process of indirect election at the beginning of each term, and apart from his general prefectorial role, each guardian had ten boys under his special care and management, and lots were drawn as to which guardian should have first choice of wards. The Masters' Conference, which had existed at Hazelwood, had somewhat more extensive duties at Bruce Castle. The general effect of the upgrading of the guardians' responsibility and the widening of the scope of the masters' weekly meetings was to tilt the balance of democracy away from the boys themselves towards the staff.

On the academic side there was also a move to more traditional processes. The number of subjects was reduced, classes were made larger, the opportunities for promotion from one class to another increased, a greater degree of specialization introduced, and formal examinations instituted. Languages increased in importance (Hill himself taught Latin and French and a Pole taught German), but the teaching of the natural sciences was abandoned. Birkbeck Hill's fastidious humanism contrasted strongly with his grandfather's scientific enthusiasms. Birkbeck's position, in fact, reflected not only a slackening of the original Hazelwood impetus, but also the different social and educational climate of the mid-Victorian years which helped to bring about the change.

In 1877 Birkbeck Hill gave up the leadership of Bruce Castle School because of ill-health, relinquishing the building to the Reverend William Almack, who continued to run the school until its final closure in 1891.[22] The connection of the Hill family with Hazelwood and Bruce Castle had lasted for fifty-eight years, and the two schools had the longest life of any progressive foundation of the nineteenth century.

What attracted attention to the Hazelwood system was its modernity, its sense of being not only up to date but ahead of its time. It represented a conscious departure from Renaissance and Enlightenment educational ideals, and seems

[22] Ibid., p. 79.

'modern' in a way that even the most advanced of previous schools do not. The values of the new industrial age were replacing or modifying the old order. Hazelwood was permeated from the very beginning with the utilitarian spirit, even in the smallest particulars. Some aspects of Hazelwood were among the first examples of what later became widespread practices in middle-class schools, for instance the introduction of sport and gymnastics, the imaginative use of natural methods of language teaching, and the comprehensive if short-lived science course. Individual work as a recognized part of the school curriculum, although it had been to some extent anticipated by David Williams, received wide currency at Hazelwood. In setting out to educate the middle classes the Hill brothers took note in their schools of the educational expectations of the new men, the industrialists and professional intelligentsia of the mid-Victorian age.

Where the public schools stressed etiquette, manners, 'good form', the mystique of the gentleman, Hazelwood supported the virtues of utility, efficiency, individual initiative, and rational self-reliance. Where public schools encouraged the amateur, the ideal of the leisured gentleman who did things for their own sake and not for economic motives and who tacitly accepted wealth as the means to the enjoyment of the good life, Hazelwood rewarded individual initiative with pecuniary gain and made clear that lack of application or irrational action would involve financial loss. Money, even though the coin was imitation, was literally the measure of virtue and progress at Hazelwood. The public school lived in an atmosphere that implied that social and political relations were bounded by an unwritten code of tradition and ethical restraints, whereas the life of a Hazelwood boy was bounded by a proliferation of explicit and printed laws, rules, and regulations, numbered and codified and operated throughout his waking hours.[23] The whole school organization, in fact, rested on the un-British foundation of a written constitution. As the Hazelwood system worked out in practice it appears at times to be the very opposite of the libertarian Rousseauist spirit that had inspired an earlier generation of educators. Its achieve-

[23] Cf. R. and F. Hill (eds.), *Laws of Hazelwood School* (London, 1827).

ment was not without cost to the individual boy, as William Sargant perceived:

> By juries and committees, by marks, and by appeals to a sense of honour, discipline was maintained. But this was done, I think, at too great a sacrifice: the thoughtlessness, the spring, the elation of childhood were taken from us; we were premature men ... the school was in truth a moral hotbed, which forced us into a precocious imitation of maturity....[24]

The Hills themselves had little doubt of their success, and they concluded *Public Education* with the assertion that they had created the Edgeworths' 'Utopian idea of a school', in which the pupils 'improve ... in the social virtues, without learning party spirit; and though they love their companions, they do not, therefore, combine together to treat their instructors as pedagogues and tyrants'.[25] If Bentham's influence was to be found at Hazelwood, so too were traces of the spirit of Rousseau and Pestalozzi, but mediated through the minds and the skill of the remarkable succession of the Hill family.

7 KING'S SOMBORNE SCHOOL

KING'S SOMBORNE SCHOOL was the creation of the Reverend Richard Dawes, dean of Hereford. Opened in 1842 as a village school in rural Hampshire, it was influenced by none of the domestic or Continental educational theories described elsewhere in these chapters, nor was it overtly a response to particular economic or social conditions. King's Somborne was simply an attempt at educational progress made by an original man in conditions that were daunting in the extreme. It was the first rural school seriously to attempt to raise educational standards above the acquisition of mere literacy, and the first to make a breach in the custom that different classes of the community should be educated in separate

---

[24] Sargant, *Essays of a Birmingham Manufacturer*, ii, p. 191.
[25] Cited in *Public Education*, p. 356.

schools. Dawes managed all this in the face of an almost total initial opposition to education by the local farmers.

For twenty years of his life Dawes was a Cambridge don, and might have remained so had he not been unexpectedly passed over for the mastership of his college. He was born in Yorkshire in 1793 and entered Trinity College, Cambridge, in 1813. Passing out fourth wrangler in 1817, he became fellow, mathematical tutor, and bursar of Downing College, and was ordained the following year.[1] 'In Dawes's time,' wrote the historian of the college, 'the Downing Combination Room acquired a social and convivial celebrity second to that of no other college in the University.'[2]

Dawes might have continued a pleasant and useful existence at Cambridge for the rest of his life but for the incident over the mastership. In 1836, when the mastership at Downing fell vacant, Dawes was a natural candidate. But 'a small external body of high-placed ecclesiastics', including the archbishops of Canterbury and York and the masters of St. John's and Clare, with whom the mastership was in gift, recalled that Dawes, with characteristic independence, had once voted for the admission of Dissenters to the university. Dawes lost the election, the master of Clare protesting that 'if Mr. Dawes had been his own brother he could not have given him his support'.[3]

All prospects of advancement in the university having ceased, Dawes married and took the college living of Tadlow with East Hartley, and in the following year Sir John Mill, a former pupil, gave him the rectory of King's Somborne in Hampshire.[4]

Thus Dawes found himself, at the age of forty-four, in one of the most backward rural districts in the country. King's Somborne was a parish of some 7,500 acres, lying in the Test Valley, with a population of 1,125.[5] The land was in the hands

---

[1] W. C. Henry, *A Biographical Notice of the Late Rev. Richard Dawes, M.A., Dean of Hereford* (London, 1867), pp. 5-6.
[2] H. W. Pettit Stevens, *Downing College* (London, 1899), p. 168.
[3] Henry, *Biographical Notice*, p. 10.
[4] Stevens, *Downing College*, p. 170.
[5] Rev. H. Moseley, 'Report for the Year 1847 on Schools Inspected in the Southern District', *Minutes of the Committee of Council on Education, 1847-8*, P.P. (1847-8), p. 180.

of five or six farmers, and the labourers existed on wages of between 6s. and 9s. a week, and in order to avoid starvation drew heavily on the poor-rate. The teachers were often barely literate and had usually failed at other callings, and their low pay reflected their low standards: 'It is but little they pay me, but then it is but little I teaches 'em,' admitted one honest old dame to an inspector.[6] Dawes quickly discovered the farmers' view of education: if the labourer was educated he would not work; it would invert the order of society by raising the labourer above his place; it would interfere with the workings of Divine Providence, for the labouring classes were never intended to know anything but the Bible; it was impossible because labourers were born with inferior intellect.[7] All dismally familiar prejudices, rooted deep not only in rural Hampshire.

Science, education, and administration were Dawes's main concerns, and his social outlook was hard-headed rather than pietistic. He had no illusions that acquaintance with the Scriptures necessarily resulted in improved morals,[8] and he was willing to allow that the heavy drinking and wild amusements of the totally uneducated might be due more to bad circumstances than to original sin.[9]

'The task I set myself,' wrote Dawes, 'was to make the schools so good that the parents might see that there was no question about the fact that their children were the better for attending them, and that the knowledge they were acquiring was in their [the parents'] estimation interesting and valuable.'[10] The 'comprehensive' basis of his own school was perhaps its most interesting feature. Dawes felt that this measure would not only encourage social cohesion in the countryside but also assist the finances of the school. Fees, and the length of time spent by a child at school, were adjusted to the class of the parent. Labourers paid 2d. a week for the first child and 1d. for the others.

[6] R. Dawes, *Suggestive Hints towards Improved Secular Instruction, Making it bear on Practical Life* (London, 6th. ed., 1953), p. xv.
[7] R. Dawes, *Observations on the Working of the Government Scheme of Education, and on School Inspection* (London, 1849), pp. 46–9.
[8] R. Dawes, *Suggestive Hints*, p. xiii.
[9] R. Dawes to Rev. J. Allen, *Minutes of the Committee of Council on Education, 1843–4*, P.P. (1845), xxxv, p. 306.
[10] R. Dawes, *Schools and Other Similar Institutions for the Industrial Classes* (London, 1853), p. 11.

Farmers and tradesmen paid 6s. a quarter if they lived in the parish and 10s. if they lived outside.[11] In addition it was expected that the children in the second group would remain at school a longer time. This would constitute the sole benefit they gained over the labourers' children, for both would receive the same education in the school. The appeal to the farmers and tradesmen was on the score of cheapness, because for £2 a year or less their children would receive an education hardly inferior to that of a boarding school that might charge twenty times that amount.

The capital expenditure on the school was provided by grants from the Committee of Council on Education, the National Society, the Diocesan Board at Winchester, and a contribution from Dawes himself.[12] It was provided with a master and mistress, a married couple, at a salary of £70 a year, together with a house and garden. In course of time a second master was added (a former pupil of the school, aged seventeen), four paid monitors, and after 1847 pupil-teachers were engaged.[13] In the early years, however, both Dawes and his wife taught in the classroom.[14]

At the opening of the school in October 1842 there were 38 children present. By 1850 this had grown to 219 children. Apart from the 52 children in the junior school, 55 pupils were the children of farmers and tradesmen and 112 the children of labourers.

There was much contention about school fees in the nineteenth century, but in the conditions of his parish in the 1840s Dawes took the view that free education would not appeal to the labourer, but would be seen as merely another aspect of the benevolence that consistently regarded the labourer as a pauper fit only for charity.[15] For the same reasons Dawes refused to provide school books free, and insisted that parents buy them for their children.

---

[11] R. Dawes, *Hints on an Improved and Self-Paying System of National Education, Suggested from the Working of the Village School of King's Somborne in Hampshire* (London, 5th ed., 1855).

[12] R. Dawes, *Schools for the Industrial Classes*, p. 4.

[13] Ibid., p. 7; *Hints on National Education*, p. 14.

[14] R. Dawes, *Effective Primary Instruction* (London, 1857), pp. 7–8; Stevens, *Downing College*, p. 17.

[15] R. Dawes, *Hints on National Education*, pp. 9–10.

Dawes immediately distinguished the teaching given in his school from the monitorial instruction in the three R's that was common in all but a few of the British and National village schools of the time. He sought to make the children think and reason rather than master facts, and he modified the usual curriculum in order to bring it closer to everyday life, and in particular to include a good deal of science. Above all he realized that children learned most rapidly and effectively when solving problems that related directly to their own experience. Most of these principles, in some form, we have noticed in the work of Gilpin, Manson, Williams, Owen, and the Hills.

For the children of King's Somborne, school life rapidly became both exciting and pleasurable. The whole of nature became their textbook. They roamed the fields to collect information, to discover on which side of their bodies sheep lay down, and to examine the differences in the teeth of various animals; they worked out the velocity of the wind by watching the shadows of clouds race across the sunlit meadows and the speed of sound by watching a distant woodman fell a tree and noting the lapse of time between the blow of his axe and the sound reaching their ears. They calculated the water pressure on the fish in local streams and found out the principles of the pop-guns they were accustomed to make from elder trees.[16]

In the classroom the same methods of observation and experiment were used, but apart from the inclusion of the sciences, the formal curriculum was not particularly wide. 'Few subjects well taught, rather than many ill-taught,' maintained Dawes, 'ought to be the maxim of the schoolmaster.'[17] He emphasized problem-solving and the relation of the most abstract subject to everyday life wherever this was possible.

Geography was taught with the aid of maps, a magnetic compass, and a globe, in addition to several models of the local features and landscape. The children were made familiar with neighbouring towns and villages and the geography of the local parish, relating their knowledge to maps and gradually extending it to the whole of England, and they also studied the commercial and economic life of the country. History was

[16] R. Dawes, *Suggestive Hints*, pp. 5–8, 73 ff.
[17] R. Dawes, *Effective Primary Instruction*, p. 12.

linked to local history and much use was made of local remains. The children learned that one of John of Gaunt's houses used to stand on the site of the school, and they could see for themselves the remains of the Roman road from Winton to Sarum, which ran through the parish. 'The great art in teaching children,' wrote Dawes, 'is not in talking only, but in practically illustrating what is taught,'[18] and he made full use of the opportunities that the sciences offered in carrying this out. The number of experiments and demonstrations in his *Suggestive Hints towards Improved Secular Instruction* and his booklet on *The Teaching of Common Things* would have kept a teacher going for years and would provide interesting lessons even today.

The sciences formed a large part of the curriculum and covered a very wide field. There were lessons in arithmetic, geometry, mechanics, physics, astronomy, chemistry, natural history, geology, and statistics. All of these were taught in a practical manner and, wherever possible, in relation to the crafts and commerce of the district. Elementary statistics was based on an examination of the census figures; from these the consumption per head of population was worked out, and combined with other commercial and manufacturing statistics.[19]

The idea of teaching science to village children, Dawes observed, was 'by many looked upon as visionary, by some as useless, and by others even as mischievous'.[20] One of the ways in which Dawes was able to gain acceptance for it was by linking chemistry to agriculture. The science of agriculture was beginning to excite attention in England in the 1840s. Dawes was friendly with the staff of the neighbouring Queenwood Agricultural College, and there was in fact a good deal of useful exchange between the school and the college; the principal visited the school from time to time, and two of the most promising boys worked in the college chemistry laboratory for two days a week.[21]

[18] R. Dawes, *Suggestive Hints*, pp. 27–36.
[19] Ibid., pp. 37–142, *passim*; W. H. Brookfield, 'General Report for the Year 1850', *Minutes of the Committee of Council, 1850–1*, P.P. (1851), xliv(2), p. 384. Cf. also N. Ball, 'Richard Dawes and the Teaching of Common Things', *Educational Review*, vol. 17, no. 1 (Nov. 1964), pp. 59–68.
[20] R. Dawes, *Suggestive Hints*, p. xi.
[21] R. Dawes, *Schools for the Industrial Classes*, p. 12.

Unlike some earlier educational innovators, Dawes was a believer in school books and paid a great deal of attention to their selection. Apart from Dawes's belief that the children and parents would place greater value on volumes that they had purchased themselves, the possession of books enabled the pupils to do lessons at home in the evening – a form of homework unprecedented in an elementary school of that date. The school also had a large lending library, which was well patronized; in 1845, for instance, 540 books were borrowed,[22] giving parents, in Dawes's words, 'new sources of happiness and of social comfort ... to which they have hitherto been strangers'.

King's Somborne School received a great deal of attention from the inspectors, no doubt because it was educationally so far in advance of other schools of its type. The most detailed report was made by the Reverend Henry Moseley, one of the most perceptive of the early inspectors. He pointed out that in school hygiene, reading, spelling, width of curriculum, attendance, and length of time spent at school, King's Somborne excelled all other schools of its type. The average attendance was 89 per cent, compared with the 66 per cent of other schools; 32 per cent of the pupils remained at school after the age of eleven years, compared with 23 per cent at other schools. As in the case of all successful and happy schools, the appearance and demeanour of the children spoke for itself. Significantly, the children created their own voluntary circles. A dozen of the older boys organized a voluntary chemistry class which met on Saturday mornings,[23] and many of the pupils kept journals in which observations on natural history at different seasons of the year were kept. Moseley also discovered that the width of the curriculum had a very beneficial effect on the children's powers of reading, for at one of his examinations 40 per cent of the children read with 'tolerable ease and correctness', whereas at other schools the percentage was under 17, despite the fact that at these schools scarcely anything but reading was taught.[24]

Dawes condemned the narrow aims and religious bias of

[22] R. Dawes, *Hints on National Education*, p. 35.
[23] R. Dawes, *Schools for the Industrial Classes*, p. 12.
[24] Moseley, *Minutes of the Committee of Council on Education*, P.P. (1847–8), p. 175.

the National Society, becoming one of the leaders of the progressive wing of the Society. He was a strong supporter of Kay-Shuttleworth and his efforts for state education, the policy of the Committee of Council, and the work of the inspectors.[25] He condemned the labours of the National Society as 'a national deception, retarding the cause of education rather than advancing it', and described the instruction given in many of their schools as 'absolutely valueless'.[26]

Dawes left King's Somborne in 1850 to become dean of Hereford, and remained there until his death in 1867, repairing the cathedral, speaking at educational and scientific meetings, and campaigning for the reform of educational charities and the opening of the lower ranks of the civil service to elementary-school children by competitive examination.[27] Although Dawes's work at King's Somborne continued to strike a response here and there it was not taken up on any serious scale and failed to inaugurate a new era of educational progress in the countryside. This must be attributed partly to Dawes's own independent and liberal views, and also to the fact that the very high standards reached at King's Somborne during Dawes's stewardship were extremely difficult for the average clergyman or schoolmaster of the time to attain. Dawes combined a first-rate scientific mind with a genius for making difficult concepts both simple and interesting, and few men of this calibre were to be found in rural villages in the mid-nineteenth century.

[25] R. Dawes, *Observations on the Government Scheme*, pp. 5–9, 32.
[26] R. Dawes, *Remarks Occasioned by the Present Crusade against the Educational Plans of the Committee of Council on Education* (London, 1850), pp. 4–11.
[27] Henry, *Biographical Notice, passim*; *Dictionary of National Biography*; *Gentleman's Magazine*, May 1867, pp. 674–5.

3 Continental Influences

8 PESTALOZZI, FELLENBERG, AND ENGLISH EDUCATION

THE SCHOOLS started by Robert Owen and his followers, together with Hazelwood and King's Somborne, can be regarded as largely native products, responses to the conditions in town and country occasioned by the massive changes to an industrialized England. Dawes and the Hills did not draw heavily on the Continental thinkers, although Owen owed more of a debt to them.

I

PESTALOZZI: HIS WORK AND INFLUENCE

In England Pestalozzi is often thought of as a brilliant but eccentric schoolmaster, unpractical in all the ordinary concerns of life, who invented object lessons and new ways of teaching arithmetic. From the first it was Pestalozzi's method rather than his social and philosophical outlook that interested English educationalists, although he was throughout his life a philosopher and man of affairs, deeply concerned with political, social, and educational conditions in Europe. He cared little for conventional prestige, however, and like his predecessor, Rousseau, and his successor, Froebel, lived a restless, unsettled life, trying several different occupations and rarely holding a post for more than a few years.

Pestalozzi was born in Zürich in 1746 of Italian lineage, a man thirty-four years younger than Rousseau and twenty-five years older than Robert Owen.[1] His father died when he was five years old and he was brought up by his mother and a family maidservant. In his late teens and early twenties he had become involved in the Helvetic Society, a group of young men inspired by the writings of the French Enlightenment,

[1] This account of Pestalozzi's life is based upon K. Silber, *Pestalozzi: The Man and His Work* (London, 1960), *passim.*

especially those of Montesquieu and Rousseau. The object of the Society was to work a renewal in Switzerland's morals on the ideals of asceticism, public duty, and 'natural life', and inspired by Rousseau, Pestalozzi repudiated both the law and the church for which he had been educated and looked to nature and the countryside. In 1767, at the age of twenty-one, he went to learn farming methods at Tschiffelli's experimental farm at Kirchberg in the canton of Berne, but his early ventures were disastrous. He turned to writing, attempting to write for the poor in a manner they would understand. He worked on philosophical, moral, and fictional themes, including *Leonard and Gertrude*, a novel of village life, didactic in tone and reforming in purpose. In 1799, when he was fifty-three, there came a turning-point when he took charge of a group of war orphans at Stanz, living as one of them and sharing their burdens. In his teaching he alternated manual work with the three R's, and strove to win over his pupils by kindness and love. After about six months, however, the progress of the war with France caused the abandonment of the project, and at the end of the year he started teaching at the infant school at Burgdorf. Encouraged by the progress that the children made, Pestalozzi opened an Institute of Education in Burgdorf Castle. In 1804 this community was transferred to Münchenbuchsee, and a year later he settled at Yverdon to realize his educational ideals in his middle and old age.

Pestalozzi's sympathy for the peasantry and his own remembrance of his mother's care convinced him that the clue to educational progress was to be found in those processes of learning exemplified by the peasant mother and her child. His teaching experience had convinced him that a beginning must be made by the reduction of a subject to its elements, which should then be presented in an orderly form proceeding from the simple to the more complex. Pestalozzi worked out the principles of his method in his book *How Gertrude Teaches Her Children*, published in 1801, which ranks with *Émile* as one of the most significant books in the whole history of education. The book had little direct connection with either Gertrude or her children, but was a series of twelve letters to his friend Gessner, in which he developed his psychological and educational theories.

Pestalozzi's starting-point was that all knowledge derived from sense impressions. He believed that a person's mind, when presented with a mass of confused objects, would attempt to discover three things:

1. How many, and what kind of objects are before him.
2. Their appearance, form, or outline.
3. Their names; how he may represent each of them by a sound or word.[2]

These three qualities, Pestalozzi believed, could be discovered in all objects, and thus he propounded his theory that all elementary instruction took place according to the threefold principle of counting, measuring, and naming, or as he expressed it, by means of the three concepts of Number, Form, and Language.

The fundamental power that underlay the operations of the mind relevant to the formation of concepts Pestalozzi called *Anschauung*, which may be translated as intuition or psychic energy. This ability of the human mind to form what Pestalozzi called 'distinct notions' from the first 'obscure impressions' by stages of 'definite impressions' and 'clear images', he believed existed in every human being, but it needed to be fostered and cultivated.

The teaching of the three R's and other subjects on these lines formed the basis of Pestalozzi's method, which was refined and extended by his numerous assistants at Yverdon and entered the classrooms of Europe.

II

THE EDUCATIONAL IDEAS OF FELLENBERG

In 1804, when Pestalozzi moved to Münchenbuchsee, he found himself neighbour to a like-minded educational theorist, Philipp Emanuel von Fellenberg, who had adopted and put into practice many of Pestalozzi's own principles on his estate at Hofwyl. Pestalozzi, impressed by Fellenberg's business sense and love of order, agreed to a merger of the two institutions, an

[2] J. H. Pestalozzi, *How Gertrude Teaches Her Children*, trans. L. E. Holland and F. C. Turner (London, 1894), p. 87.

arrangement that would allow him time to pursue his own theories. The venture, however, was not a success. Although the views of both were ultimately based on nature, their temperaments and methods were different. Fellenberg's 'adherence to convention where Pestalozzi was utterly spontaneous, his stress on class distinctions in contrast to Pestalozzi's convicion of men's equality, his disciplinarianism as opposed to Pestalozzi's belief in freedom for the children'[3] – all these made the venture a failure, and the two educators ultimately returned to their own ways.

Fellenberg, twenty-five years younger than Pestalozzi, was born in Berne in 1771 of a patrician family.[4] His father was a progressive, a follower of Rousseau and an advocate of educational reform on the lines of Pestalozzi. In his youth Fellenberg was a supporter of the American patriots Washington, Franklin, and Jefferson, and was sympathetic to the early ideals of the French Revolution. He travelled throughout Europe and visited Paris in 1794, where he became convinced that any political change must be preceded by a spiritual change, which could only be achieved by education. He was also interested in the ideas of the German philosophers Kant and Fichte, and hoped for a fusion of the enlightened political and social ideas of revolutionary France and the idealistic philosophy of the Germans. A further visit to France, however, disillusioned him, and he sought to solve the problems of society in his own way. He was distressed by the neglect of religion and morals, the selfishness and avarice of the Swiss aristocracy, and by the ignorance and torpor of the people. Only a spiritual change within human beings, based upon a simpler and purer way of life, would prevent social upheaval, and this way of life must centre upon an agricultural community where people could pursue an unsophisticated, pastoral, and religious existence. From such a community in his native canton of Berne ripples of regeneration would, he hoped, spread across Europe and the world.

Fellenberg was essentially an agriculturalist and throughout

---

[3] Silber, *Pestalozzi*, p. 152.
[4] This account of Fellenberg's life and work is based upon E. M. Gray, 'The Educational Work of Emanuel von Fellenberg (1771–1844)' (unpublished M.A. thesis, University of Belfast, 1952).

his life upheld the integral relationship between agriculture and education. On his estate at Hofwyl he founded a number of establishments in which he attempted to realize his aspirations. In the first forty years of the nineteenth century, five different institutions were founded: the Scientific Educational Institution for the Higher Social Classes (1806), the Poor School (1810), a girls' school (1823), an intermediate school (1830), and a nursery school (1831). The Institute and the Poor School were by far the most celebrated and, in their different ways, affected education throughout Western Europe, not least in Britain. The organization of these two schools exemplified Fellenberg's fundamental doctrine that apart from a minimum of elementary mental training, the range and content of education provided in any society should vary from class to class. Education for the higher social classes, for instance, should enable them to become honest, rational, and scientific agriculturalists, conscious of their duty to society and determined to improve social conditions. The peasantry, on the other hand, apart from basic moral and religious training, needed an education that would reconcile them to a life of simplicity, economy, and self-discipline. Denied any large portion of the world's goods, they were to be trained to the enjoyment of their own simple and undemanding existence, and their education, therefore, was to be adapted to the peasants' daily tasks and so designed that they would not need to seek satisfaction outside these.

The Institute for the Higher Classes attracted pupils from all over Europe and from as far afield as the Americas. It had at its fullest about a hundred pupils, nearly all from wealthy or aristocratic families, for whom were provided no fewer than thirty highly qualified teachers. The compulsory lessons were minimal but of a high quality, and a great deal of initiative was allowed to the pupils, though they were expected to utilize every hour of a long day. The curriculum was practically unlimited, ranging from languages and literature to science and philosophy, and it included a wide range of agricultural pursuits. Theories of the self-activity of the pupils, derived from Pestalozzi and Herbart, influenced the learning of natural history, geography, history, and other subjects. Student self-government was also encouraged and the Institute had a students' union with its own council and offices.

The scope, equipment, and facilities of the Institute were such as had never been seen in Europe before. It had in it elements of the public school, the university, and the military academy, and it instilled manly virtues in a manner that was almost a caricature of the methods and ideals of the English public school. Robert Dale Owen, Robert Owen's son, was a pupil there although Owen *père* differed so greatly in outlook, principle, and practice from Fellenberg, his exact contemporary.

The Poor School, at which vagrant children were trained to agricultural labour by a teacher of genius and transparent goodness named Jacob Wehrli, was, on the other hand, restricted in scope and curriculum. Eleven hours each day in summer and nine in winter were spent in agricultural and craft labour, and only an hour or two a day on the three R's, history and geography, drawing and music. As far as possible, the formal education was merged with, or made a function of, the agricultural work, as Wehrli, who lived and worked with the children, believed that an education based on agriculture was a unified process, which at all times helped to form the morality suitable for the peasant's station in life.[5]

It was, in fact, the practices of Wehrli and the Poor School that particularly attracted the attention of educators in England in the first thirty years of the century, a time when the education of the poor was the most important question of educational policy.[6] During the 1830s, with the growth of interest in agricultural schools in Britain, Fellenberg attracted a large circle of eminent correspondents, including Lady Byron, the poet's widow, Shelley's second wife Mary, Sir Walter Scott, Louisa Barwell, the children's authoress and writer of the anonymously published *Letters from Hofwyl*, and B. F.

---

[5] Eventually the Poor School became a semi-normal school, in which a number of boys trained for posts as teachers in rural schools. See Rev. M. C. Woodbridge, 'Sketches of Hofwyl', in *Letters from Hofwyl by a Parent, on the Educational Institutions of de Fellenberg* (London, 1842), appendix, pp. 324–5.

[6] Cf. J. Attersoll, *Translation of the Reports of M. le Comte de Capo D'Istria and M. Rengger upon the Principles and Progress of the Establishment of M. de Fellenberg at Hofwyl, Switzerland* (London, 1820), pp. 22–3, 35; Count Louis de Villevielle, *The Establishment of M. Emmanuel de Fellenberg at Hofwyl* (London, 1820), pp. 23, 24–5.

Duppa, the lawyer who became secretary of the Central Society of Education and later acted as Fellenberg's agent in Britain, popularizing his theories and suggesting a scale of charges for English pupils at Hofwyl.[7]

III

SOME EFFECTS OF PESTALOZZI AND FELLENBERG IN ENGLAND

A number of British people visited Pestalozzi at Yverdon or Fellenberg at Hofwyl and returned to found schools to apply the principles of the masters, or wrote books and pamphlets about their theory and practice. J. H. Synge and J. P. Greaves wrote about the two Continental educationalists, H. G. Wright founded a school on Pestalozzian lines called Alcott House at Ham Common, Surrey, but the best known was Cheam School, conducted 1826–46 by Dr. Charles Mayo, who had taught at Yverdon for three years, his sister Elizabeth Mayo, and a brilliant mathematics and science tutor, Charles Reiner. Mayo and his sister wrote about Pestalozzi's teaching method and applied it in *Lessons on Objects*, *Lessons on Shells*, and *Analysis of History*.

Mayo took from Pestalozzi the more obvious and superficial aspects of his theory – the religious and moral tone, the need for progression, development, and harmony, and the importance of a balance between moral, intellectual, and physical education. But Cheam was not a Pestalozzian school in any strict sense; it was an attempt to unite broad Pestalozzian principles with the practices of an Anglican public school. This gave the teaching methods more vitality than those in common use in similar schools, for Mayo had a genuine concern that existing teaching was too abstract, too mechanical, and had little relation to the world of children. It is difficult to say how far improved methods based on Pestalozzi's work gave Cheam its reputation for brilliance. Mayo was fortunate in having a highly intelligent group of pupils who in a number of cases later became eminent in academic, public, and military life.[8] Cheam was so popular in Mayo's time that in

[7] K. Guggisberg, *Philipp Emanuel von Fellenberg und sein Erziehungstaat* (Berne, 2 vols., 1953), ii, pp. 469, 471–3, 478.
[8] C. H. Mayo, *A Genealogical Account of the Mayo and Elton Families* (London, 2nd ed., 1908), p. 266 n.

order to enter it was necessary for boys' names to be put down immediately following their birth – or at least several years before starting at the school.

Much of the merit of the school came from Reiner's teaching of science. A subtler Pestalozzian and more brilliant teacher than Mayo, he gave to the school an unusual and unremarked distinction: though the name and fame of Pestalozzi gave Cheam a certain esoteric attraction, its more enduring strength lay in its pioneering work in the sciences.

Here, then, is a school that was near the borderline of the progressive, innovating group and the more imaginative wing of orthodoxy. However, in the thirties and forties of the last century the features described above were a great deal more original than they would have appeared in the second half of the century.

Ealing Grove, outside London, owed its foundation to the beneficence of Lady Byron and her interest in social and philanthropic works, to which she had turned in the later 1820s when recovering from the effects of the separation from her husband and his subsequent death at Missolonghi in 1824. Lady Byron's first interest was the Co-operative movement, to which she brought the over-zealous idealism of an aristocratic reformer and the advantages of a lady of means. She aided it with gifts, loans to Co-operative societies, and propaganda on behalf of its principles.[9] She was not, however, a follower of Robert Owen, had no faith in his environmental theories, and after meeting him saw in his character little beyond 'vanity and presumption'.[10] It was to Fellenberg that Lady Byron turned for confirmation and elaboration of her educational ideal. She had visited Hofwyl in 1828 in order to place two young cousins there,[11] and now that she had the founding of a school in mind, Fellenberg became her infallible guide and, according to Kay-Shuttleworth's biographer Frank Smith, 'the final authority in any matter of dispute'.[12]

[9] W. H. Brown, *Brighton's Co-operative Advance* (Manchester, n.d.), pp. 57–8.
[10] Ibid., p. 59.
[11] E. C. Mayne, *The Life and Letters of Anne Isabella, Lady Noel Byron* (London, 1929), p. 330.
[12] F. Smith, *The Life and Work of Sir James Kay-Shuttleworth* (London,

In many ways their background and outlook were similar. Both were patricians, both saw the solution to contemporary social problems in a form of education that would give a prominent place to the moral improvement of its charges. Lady Byron's educational principles were basically social and strongly affected by the unsettled state of society; this she traced to the French Revolution, an upheaval that appeared to her to have unleashed all that was vicious in human nature. This emphasis on moral catastrophe rather than on economic or social conditions as leading to popular discontents was characteristic. 'The moral depravity of men in their social relations,' she argued, was responsible for 'the tumults of the age'.[13] She looked in vain, however, to existing schools for the reformation of character or morals, concerned as they were with the mere technical aspects of instruction. Education needed a new direction over and above that of producing readers or mathematicians:

> There is a growing conviction that the great antidote to vice and crime, and therefore to political disturbances, is to be found in an improved moral education in the mass of the people.[14]

1923), p. 52. Her admiration for Fellenberg even expressed itself in verse in a sonnet composed in 1839:

> *To de Fellenberg – the Schoolmaster*
> Patrician! but whose lineage fades from mind,
> When thy life's nobler volume is unroll'd;
> When thou art known the friend of human kind,
> Truth's latent gems devoted to unfold
> And draw from Nature's mines the purest gold:
> The mountains – witnesses of ages past
> Remember not their shadows to have cast
> Over a Patriot so sublimely bold!
> Tho' not a war-note startled vale or lake,
> The heroic spirit of the land to wake,
> Thou, – once by dreamers of material glory fix'd,
> Wert rous'd by Childhood's holier appeal;
> And with thy Saviour's glowing love inspir'd
> Did'st for 'these little ones' prove all a
>   Martyr's zeal!

[13] [Lady Noel Byron], *What Fellenberg has Done for Education* (London, 1839), p. xi.
[14] Ibid., p. xxxiii.

The improved moral education would have rural labour as its core. To Fellenberg went the honour of first perceiving 'the bearing which the pursuits of agriculture might have upon the morals of mankind',[15] and Lady Byron hoped for an English Fellenberg. In default of this, however, there was work for her to do on the lines laid down by the master, and in this spirit she opened Ealing Grove School in 1834.

Though the school was founded and financed by Lady Byron, the initial organization and day-to-day running of it was in the hands of E. T. Craig, a thoughtful and original educationalist. His intellectual interests ranged from Owenism, phrenology, and mesmerism to the advocacy of longevity through physical exercise, clean air, and vegetarianism. Apprenticed early in life as a fustian-cutter, he had, when young, witnessed the Peterloo massacre and watched Luddites marched to their execution in Lancaster. He became a keen Co-operator and founded an Owenite society in Manchester and took over the editorship of the *Lancashire and Yorkshire Co-operator* in 1831. With the decline of Co-operation in Manchester in the early 1830s, Craig left England and took a post as superintendent of the agricultural colony at Ralahine in Ireland, founded by the wealthy Owenite J. S. Vandeleur. It was here that Craig was able to organize some remarkably effective and original educational experiments, the results of which he later introduced into Ealing Grove School. Craig's curriculum reflected both his own interests and the working-class Owenite's faith in useful and scientific knowledge. Craig's views on the importance of labour in education seem, however, to have been his own, and to have owed nothing to Fellenberg. They arose from a working-class faith in the importance of labour and a dissatisfaction with the kind of instruction being given in contemporary British and National schools. The educational system, he argued, needed a reassessment of the importance of the work of the wealth-producer; labour should be viewed 'not as a disgrace, but as the honourable means of health and independence'.[16] Craig's discoveries harmonized well with the practical aims of Lady Byron, and although his fundamental outlook was very different from hers, he was an

---

[15] Ibid., p. 24.
[16] *Co-operative News*, 5 Oct. 1878.

appropriate choice as the principal of her school. However, his own independent and important discoveries deserve recognition on their merits.

Although it was essentially an attempt in educational terms to face up to the turbulent social problem of the early 1830s, Ealing Grove School, which continued in existence till 1852 – Craig having left in 1835 – differed from all the other agricultural schools of its day in that it blended two separate traditions: the working-class Owenism from which Craig had sprung, and the patrician ethic of Fellenberg, in which Lady Byron ardently believed. Craig viewed agricultural labour technically, assessing its value to the individual in educational terms, but Lady Byron saw it largely as a moral agency. In practice this fusion of purpose produced something far more original and stable than other simpler and more short-lived institutions.

Cheam School is a good example of the influence of Pestalozzi; Ealing Grove is a good example of the influence of Fellenberg.

9 KAY-SHUTTLEWORTH AND THE CONTINENTAL REFORMERS

SIR JAMES KAY-SHUTTLEWORTH's reputation began in his own lifetime when W. E. Forster, introducing the 1870 Education Bill, referred to him as 'a man to whom probably more than any other we owe national education in England',[1] and Kay-Shuttleworth's position as a founding father is still virtually unshaken today. This has tended to obscure his great interest in the theories and methods of Continental reformers, particularly those of Fellenberg and Pestalozzi, and his attempts to introduce Pestalozzian teaching methods into the inspected elementary schools of England have only recently begun to be appreciated.[2] The appointment of inspectors in 1839 was inspired by European practice, and his belief in the feasibility

[1] *Parl. Deb.*, 3rd ser., cxcix (17 Feb. 1870), 447.
[2] Cf. H. M. Pollard, *Pioneers of Popular Education, 1760–1850* (London, 1956), pp. 214 ff.

of a widespread system of pupil-teachers owed much to what he had seen in Holland and elsewhere.[3] Both the educational ventures in which he had controlling interest, the Norwood School of Industry and Battersea Normal College, breathed the spirit of Pestalozzi and Fellenberg. 'The principles on which it was founded,' wrote his friend Carleton Tufnell, 'were those we had learned from inspecting the institutions set on foot by Pestalozzi and Fellenberg, and by a careful study of their doctrines....'[4]

Kay-Shuttleworth came to education relatively late in life, and his experiences were rooted in the narrow world of the Poor Law and the provision for pauper children. Charged with carrying out the provisions of the Poor Law Amendment Act of 1834, as assistant commissioner of the Central Poor Law Board in the counties of Norfolk and Suffolk, he found in 1835 several thousand children 'herded with the adult paupers' in the workhouses of the Board. The pauper child 'might be an orphan, a bastard, the child of a convict, or deserted by his parents, or dependent because the surviving parent could not provide for him.'[5] In the ill-equipped and inadequate workhouse schools these children were taught 'by the least objectionable pauper inmates'.[6]

The necessity of providing a reasonable standard of education for these children began to concern Kay-Shuttleworth, and the lines on which his ideas developed came from his estimate of the effects of pauperism in society. His experiences as a young physician in Manchester during the late 1820s and early 1830s had given him a wide knowledge of first- and second-generation urban workers in the industrial north, whose characteristics he tended to take as a scale for the measure of the contemporary working man. The Lancashire cotton operatives, he felt, were 'a race full of rare qualities – hardy, broken to toil, full of loyalty to the traditions of family

[3] Cf. W. H. G. Armytage, *Four Hundred Years of English Education* (Cambridge, 1964), p. 115.
[4] E. C. Tufnell, 'Sir James Kay-Shuttleworth', *Journal of Education*, n.s., ii (1877), p. 308.
[5] B. C. Bloomfield (ed.), 'The Autobiography of Sir James Kay-Shuttleworth', *University of London Institute of Education, Education Libraries Bulletin, Supplement* 7 (London, 1964), p. 27 (hereafter 'Autobiography').
[6] Ibid.

and place',[7] and he compared them favourably with the East Anglian agricultural labourer, who had 'a shambling gait, a depressed expression, little activity or energy' and whose strength and vitality 'were far less than what I had been accustomed to observe in the operatives of the north'.[8]

He had early decided that education was one of the best antidotes to pauperism,[9] and he determined to raise the quality and quantity of instruction for pauper children. The great problem that faced Kay-Shuttleworth was to find teachers of quality who could understand and practise the Continental innovations in schools of the Norwood type. They could only be produced in numbers by training and the next logical step was to set up a normal college for the purpose. His appointment as secretary of the Committee of Council on Education in 1839 seemed to Kay-Shuttleworth a heaven-sent opportunity to inaugurate a college under government auspices, but when he found that religious rivalries made this impossible he set about finding his own. Characteristically, before doing so, he paid a further visit to the Continent, going to Holland, Prussia, Saxony, France, and Switzerland. He was particularly interested in the normal schools at Versailles and Dijon, and the School of the Christian Brothers in Paris. He visited Père Girard and Fellenberg, but was most impressed by Wehrli's normal school at Kreutzlingen in the canton of Thurgovia, which he believed could form a model for restoring the virtues of the English plebeian, and he devoted over four pages of his first report on the training school at Battersea to a description of Wehrli's school. What struck him most was the fact that the school made a point of educating the heart and feelings as well as cultivating the intellect.[10]

In February 1840 Battersea College was opened in a large manor-house on the banks of the Thames. The students were made up of apprentice teachers, who had come from the school of industry at Norwood, assistant teachers from the schools of

[7] J. Kay-Shuttleworth, *Four Periods of Public Education* (London, 1862), pp. 100–1.
[8] 'Autobiography', p. 22.
[9] J. P. Kay, 'Report on the Training of Pauper Children', *Fourth Annual Report of the Poor Law Commissioners for England and Wales*, P.P. (1838), xxviii, p. 140; 'Autobiography', p. 57.
[10] Kay-Shuttleworth, *Four Periods*, pp. 300 ff.

industry for pauper children, and a number of trainee teachers between twenty and thirty years of age.[11] The college was run as a household on simple, frugal lines. The school day lasted from 5.30 a.m. to 9 p.m., with work in the garden, in a manner professedly copied from Ealing Grove School, as an essential part of the regime. Most of the subjects in the curriculum were taught on the inductive method based on Pestalozzi's principles, with the simple preceding the complex, familiarity with examples preceding the rule, and the use of natural objects and illustrations coming before the use of books.

The object of Battersea was to turn out teachers who would devote themselves to the task of improving the mental, moral, and physical condition of the poorest and most demoralized section of the population. To achieve this the college wished to develop in the students a sense of dedication and service, and the regime was deliberately made rigorous and austere so that they might be in tune with the actual teaching condition that they would find in the schools after graduation. Battersea went too far in this direction, and the segregated, semi-monastic life, inspired by the seminaries of the Christian Brothers that had so impressed Kay-Shuttleworth, isolated the college from the world into a narrow puritanism.

Kay-Shuttleworth lost control of Battersea over the religious issue. Despite his attempts to meet their objections, influential members of the church and the Conservative Party regarded the college with suspicion, partly because it did not explicitly refuse admission to Dissenters. With this opposition in the background, Kay-Shuttleworth was unable to persuade the government to cover the deficit in the costs of running the college, and failed to raise the necessary subscriptions from any other source. In the end Battersea was handed over to the Anglican educational organization, the National Society, which preserved the curriculum more or less intact, except for additional religious instruction and church history.[12] Other

---

[11] This account is based on ibid., pp. 310 ff.; R. W. Rich, *The Training of Teachers in England and Wales during the Nineteenth Century* (London, 1933), pp. 55 ff.; Rev. J. Allen, 'Report on the Battersea Training School and the Battersea Village School for Boys', *Minutes of the Committee of Council on Education, 1842-3*, P.P. (1843), xl, pp. 12-21.

[12] Rev. H. Moseley, 'Report on the Battersea Training School and the

colleges, inspired by Battersea, were set up and the work of Kay-Shuttleworth was not entirely lost. The training of teachers in England was thus begun on lines that owed something, at least, to the genius of Pestalozzi.

Kay-Shuttleworth's idea of what constituted Pestalozzianism was extremely vague. His tours of Europe were made ten years or more after Pestalozzi's death and the schemes that attracted his attention were second- or third-hand, and the adoption in England of the schemes of Prinse, Labarre, Wilhem, Dupuis, Mulhäuser, and others did little to counteract the impression. Nevertheless, the educational ideas of these men were unorthodox and innovations in themselves.

At this distance of time we may be able to see Kay-Shuttleworth and his work in a more balanced perspective. The other innovators we have considered were either actively interested theorists or philanthropists like Rousseau or Edgeworth or Lady Byron, or else they were practitioners who valued the unorthodox, like Williams, the Hill brothers, Fellenberg, Wehrli, Mayo, or Buchanan. Only one was an administrator, Kay-Shuttleworth, the secretary of the Committee of Council on Education. Trained as a physician, knowing at first hand the lives of the poor in the city and the country, he was not a professional politician, nor was he a professional educator, but he held the chief administrative responsibility from 1839 to 1848 when the debate between church and state in education was tense and the extension of secular education backed by national funds was in a critical position. Hickson[13] and others say that Kay-Shuttleworth was timid in his reforms, tending to compromise before the consequences of a firm stand were fully tested, but they were not trying to affect a whole national policy as he was.

In the late 1830s and early 1840s, the time of the Corn Law, prices were high in a period of industrial depression, upheaval, and unemployment; rioting was reported as freely as the appalling conditions of the poor in the textile mills and the coal and iron mines; the pitiable lot of children in all branches of

---

Battersea Village School for Boys', *Minutes of the Committee of Council on Education, 1845*, P.P. (1846), xxxii, pp. 244–57, *passim*.

[13] [W. E. Hickson], 'Educational Movements', *Westminster and Foreign Quarterly Review*, liv (Jan. 1851), pp. 402 ff.

industry and manufacture was made public in report after report. Chartism was militant early in the period and the beginning of urban trades unions appears later. During the nine years when Kay-Shuttleworth was secretary of the Committee of Council on Education the economy climbed painfully to some stability and the government marked time on educational legislation.[14] Many believed, as did Graham, the home secretary, that to provide more education was to unsettle the masses still further and that what they needed was something much stronger.[15]

Kay-Shuttleworth was a tactician and an innovator. He transformed the monitors into pupil-teachers and introduced the Queen's Scholarships for the training of promising young students. He started a training college, he developed the inspectorate 'as a means not of exercising control, but of affording assistance'. He introduced as directly as he could experimental methods of teaching. In all of these things he was influenced by the innovations he saw in Scotland, Holland, France, and parts of Germany. He negotiated with the church, and he tried to accelerate and increase national financial support, but 1838–48 were lean years for the economy and for education within the economy. When his health broke down in 1848 he retired from his post, and when the Revised Code was approved in 1862 Kay-Shuttleworth denounced it as the negation of the humane and mildly experimental regime for which he strove in all his educational ventures. He did not welcome universal free education, and his views on education for the masses were patriarchal; he believed that administration, like politics, was the art of the possible. For him what was liberal was feasible as a national policy: what was radical was tactically unwise; but he certainly was a founding father of the modern English educational system.

[14] C. C. Greville, *A Journal of the Reign of Queen Victoria from 1837 to 1852* (London, 3 vols., 1885), ii, p. 212.
[15] Smith, *Kay-Shuttleworth*, p. 140.

4 Some General Themes

10 LABOUR AND EDUCATION: 1780–1850

IN THE later eighteenth century Continental educationalists had stressed the value of manual arts in education. Rousseau, in *Émile*, considered that manual labour was the pursuit that came nearest to a state of nature.[1] He would have children learn a trade and gave it the same importance as the more traditional subjects. 'He must work like a peasant and think like a philosopher,' he wrote of Émile, 'if he is not to be as idle as a savage. The great secret of education is to use exercise of mind and body as relaxation one to the other.'[2] This recognition that work with the hands could be an important aid to mental education was developed by Pestalozzi, Fellenberg, Basedow, and other Continental educationalists,[3] and Fellenberg's agricultural estate at Hofwyl took the principle to a high level. Thousands of visitors to Hofwyl carried the ideas away into almost every country in Europe, where they became the subject of discussion and experiment within various national cultures.

In Britain in the later eighteenth century there were two types of school in which manual labour formed an important part of the curriculum – schools of industry and certain Quaker schools. Neither, however, owed anything to Continental models. Nor was there any connection between them, each springing from quite different circumstances and educational assumptions. In neither case, however, were the implications of the significance of manual work fully faced. At the Quaker schools of Ackworth, Sidcot, and Wigton, at the turn of the century, the boys carried out a variety of domestic tasks and worked on the land attached to the school and in the school gardens. In no case, however, did the schools of the

---

[1] Rousseau, *Émile*, pp. 151, 158.
[2] Ibid., p. 165.
[3] C. A. Bennett, *History of Manual and Industrial Education up to 1870* (Peoria, Ill., 1926), pp. 82–6.

Society of Friends succeed in effecting an educational synthesis of manual and intellectual work. The reasons for the introduction of labour were in all cases social or economic, never educational.[4]

Schools of industry date back to the seventeenth century, but found a new lease of life in the early period of the Industrial Revolution, taking in the unemployed children of the non-manufacturing districts. Information on these schools can be found in Sir Thomas Bernard's *Of the Education of the Poor*. In these schools a variety of tasks was carried out: spinning, knitting, weaving, gardening, farming, cooking, and the making of clothes, gloves, stockings, hats, infants' shoes and socks, and similar articles.[5] In all cases the manual work was the chief feature of the school and occupied most of the day; reading and religious instruction, and occasionally a little writing and arithmetic, occupied the rest of the time.

Industrial schools were first and foremost working schools, and the labour of the children contributed to the upkeep of the establishment. The children themselves earned a few shillings a week each. The work itself was supposed to give the children 'habits of industry', the great social panacea of the Evangelicals and reformers of the period. To this extent the introduction of labour was an attempt to influence the character of the children, because Satan had work for idle hands. Industrial schools were intended for the poor, and the lower strata of the poor at that, and few were willing to believe that this section of the population deserved anything but the barest literacy. The education they received in industrial schools was designed to fit the children for their place in society, by the inculcation of the habits of 'order, cleanliness and application'.[6] If we wish to discover the conscious application of labour to education with a view to something more than the teaching of social humility, we must turn to experiments in a different type of school.

Schools in which the manual labour of young children formed an important part of the curriculum fell into two main

[4] W. A. C. Stewart, *Quakers and Education* (London, 1953), pp. 167–70.
[5] [Sir Thomas Bernard], *Of the Education of the Poor: Being the First Part of a Digest of the Reports of the Society for Bettering the Condition of the Poor* (London, 1809), *passim*.
[6] Ibid., p. 205.

classes: those, other than pure industrial schools, in which technical skills such as printing were practised, and those that incorporated the agricultural arts into their curriculum. During the early part of the nineteenth century, few of the former were in evidence. Three such were the Printing School started by William Davis in 1808 in Whitechapel; Mrs. Tuckfield's Experimental School of Industry in Westminster in the 1830s; and Captain Brenton's reformatory school at Brenton Asylum, Hackney, also in the 1830s. All of these schools were concerned with a wide education as well as vocational training.

The agricultural schools were more numerous, and belonged almost entirely to the early 1830s, in most cases being a response to the agricultural distress and rioting of that period. Besides Lady Byron's school at Ealing Grove there were other well-known establishments – the Reverend W. L. Rham's school at Winkfield near Windsor, Lord Lovelace's school at Ockham in Surrey, James Cropper's school at Fernhead near Liverpool, and William Allen's school at Lindfield in Sussex. In these industrial and agricultural types of school there was a recognition of the value of manual labour not only in the development of a more balanced individual and the formation of a more favourable response to the rest of the curriculum but also as an aid to the learning of the academic subjects.

Perhaps the most that can be said on the theme of labour in schools in the nineteenth century is that in the first half a few pioneers tried to work out a relevant vocational training, whether in the town or in the country. It arose out of and was designed to meet the needs of those who worked with their hands, whether in trades, crafts, or agriculture, and stayed within the bounds of the social structure. The implications of practical work, its relationship with traditional crafts, with developing technology, with the whole school curriculum, and with a nation's culture, were not seen then, except in flashes by such men as Owen and much later by Ruskin and Morris. In schools they were explored again by Cecil Reddie at Abbotsholme in the 1890s and by many others since then. These implications are still being discovered and considered today.

11 REWARDS AND PUNISHMENTS: 1780–1850

In the period we are considering two of the suggested preconditions for the acceptance of corporal punishment as normal were in operation: a theological conception of the fallen nature of man and the depressed condition of the masses. There is abundant evidence that flogging and brutality were rife in nearly all types of school from the public school to the common day school. The attitude of the zealously religious parent of the early nineteenth century may be gauged from Mrs. Sherwood's story *The History of the Fairchild Family*, which went through five editions between 1818 and 1822. The youngest child, a boy of six, was flogged with a horsewhip, put on bread and water, and sent to Coventry for refusing to learn Latin. In 1838 Kay-Shuttleworth declared that education in day schools was generally felt to be best promoted by coercion and that the feeling among all classes in England was that 'the best way to make boys learn was to whip them well'.[1] It is in and around this 'classical period' of corporal punishment in education, however, that we find the first attempts to provide a substitute. The reaction against flogging gave rise to several experiments in school organization based upon humane and rational forms of discipline. Opposition to corporal punishment among educationalists might spring from a variety of reasons: a view of child nature that saw the child as essentially good and in no need of coercion, a generalized opposition to force and violence on social or religious grounds, a belief that teaching with the aid of punishment was educationally inefficient and harmful, or a mixture of all three.

The question was, what to put in its place? The common alternative was to replace corporal punishment and coercion by schemes that made the occupation of a high position in the eyes of the school dependent on good behaviour. Direct punishment of all kinds was reduced to a minimum and often consisted of solitary confinement or similar deprivation of liberty. Complicated systems of merit and rank, the award of medals,

---

[1] *Report from the Select Committee on the Education of the Poorer Classes*, P.P. (1838), vii, pp. 3, 4.

tokens, and tickets, the inscription of names in books of honour were worked out. Sometimes the children were made directly responsible for judging each other by means of school juries. Some of these experiments, in particular that in use at Hazelwood School, were of a complexity that almost defies description.

Robert Raikes used rewards as an encouragement to good behaviour both in prison reform and in Sunday schools about 1780. A similar line of reasoning was used by the Philanthropic Society, a body formed in 1788 to rescue the children of the vagrant and criminal poor. The Society provided schools of industry for the rehabilitation of its delinquent charges and, in its own frank words, attempted 'to unite the spirit of charity with the principles of trade, and to erect a temple to philanthropy on the foundation of virtuous industry'.[2] The children lived in several houses, and in each case a skilled tradesman such as a carpenter, a bricklayer, a shoemaker, or a tailor lived on the premises and taught the children his trade.[3] Three principles were established: virtuous action should be rewarded; the reward should be tangible; the reward should be lasting. These became the standard justifications for systems of material reward. A fourth was often added: reward and penalties should be cumulative, to enable a profit-and-loss account of vice and virtue to be built up.

The widely popular Sunday school movement and the well-reported activities of the Philanthropic Society did more than establish the norms of the ticket and rank system of discipline. They also popularized it and demonstrated its feasibility, and during the early part of the nineteenth century, with variations of detail and emphasis, the system was taken up by two educationalists who were in all other respects anything but progressive in the terms of reference of this study – Andrew Bell and Joseph Lancaster.

Bell and Lancaster are known to history as the popularizers of the monitorial system, the scheme whereby children were instructed by other children called monitors. Though Bell and Lancaster's methods differed in detail, both had the basic

---

[2] *First Report of the Philanthropic Society* (London, n.d. but 1789), p. 23.
[3] *An Address to the Public from the Philanthropic Society* (London, 1790), pp. 7, 15.

idea of making children teach other children the three R's. This was indisputably an innovation and certainly an ingenious method of making up for the lack of teachers. Dr. Andrew Bell aimed at giving a minimum amount of education to the greatest possible number of poor children in the most effective manner in the shortest possible time. He was not interested in a varied curriculum, the wide diffusion of general knowledge, or any improvement in method beyond his own. He condemned 'Utopian schemes, for the universal diffusion of general knowledge', which would 'confound that distinction of ranks and classes of society, on which the general welfare hinges ...'.[4] On the other hand, he was equally against the prevailing methods of corporal punishment used in the schools, which, in the context of the period, showed an enlightenment rare among his contemporaries. The key to Bell's disciplinary scheme was not that it was aimed at the detection, conviction, and correction of the offender (although the machinery for this existed), but that the unified nature of his plan and close interconnection of teachers, monitors, and pupils established 'habits of industry, morality and religion, tending to form good scholars, good men and good Christians'.[5] His maxim was that praise, encouragement, and favour should be tried before disapproval, shame, and disgrace. The authority of the master, however, was not abrogated and was to be maintained in one form or another.

The machinery for maintaining authority was very similar to that of the Philanthropic Society. It consisted of a register of the daily tasks performed and of the award of tickets for good work, with a weekly distribution of prizes for those with the greatest number of tickets. A register of daily offences, or Black Book, was also kept and the misdemeanours recorded here were tried at weekly sittings of a jury of twelve or more boys especially selected for the purpose.[6] This could decide on the form of punishment that the offence merited – either confinement in school or, in very extreme cases, solitary confinement in the 'black hole'. Bell had introduced this register of offences and a rudimentary form of the jury system in the

[4] A. Bell, *An Analysis of the Experiment in Education, Made at Egmore, near Madras* (London, 1807), p. 90.
[5] Ibid., pp. 13–14.   [6] Ibid., p. 2.

Madras Asylum in 1790.[7] The asylum was a charity school for the orphan children of British soldiers, many of them coloured. When Bell in 1789 took charge of this as chaplain to the forces, he was faced with a problem similar to that of Raikes and the Philanthropic Society, for the boys had developed corrupt practices encouraged by their mothers, and in school were 'stubborn, perverse and obstinate; much given to lying, and addicted to trick and duplicity'.[8] His introduction of new methods of correction was a recognition of the futility of corporal punishment in these circumstances. Bell was careful to leave the decision as far as possible in the boys' hands, and he only intervened when he thought that the formality of the trial and the sentence were insufficient as a deterrent.[9] Bell believed that by involving pupils in tasks and decisions that gave them practical experience of order and government, he fostered in them the qualities of punctuality, diligence, impartiality, justice, and concern for the welfare of others.[10] A similar line of reasoning was to be used by the Hill brothers at Hazelwood School.

Lancaster's system, though in principle similar to that of Bell, involved the use of one monitor in charge of a group of ten or more pupils, whereas Bell had each boy in the top half of a class teach his opposite number in the lower half. Lancaster's theory of reward and punishment rested on a very different basis from that of Bell. Whereas Bell saw his disciplinary and reward schemes as the means of stimulating positive values in the school community, Lancaster believed that rewards were a measure of a pupil's elevation to the ranks of the elect, or nobility as he termed it. He believed that even one or two boys of 'superior merit' could influence the whole school by their example and therefore deserved to be rewarded by prizes of silver medals, pens, or valuable books. He established an Order of Merit, whose members were distinguished by a silver medal suspended from their necks by a plated chain, and the condition of admittance to this order was a proficiency in

[7] A. Bell, *An Experiment in Education, Made at the Male Asylum of Madras* (London, 1797), p. 27.

[8] A. Bell, *An Experiment in Education, Made at the Male Asylum at Egmore, near Madras* (London, 1805), p. 24.

[9] Bell, *An Experiment* (1797), p. 27.

[10] Bell, *An Analysis*, pp. 14–15.

studies, consistent help to others, or endeavours to check vice. Lancaster looked upon membership of this order as evidence of a 'natural' nobility, a beneficial distinction that existed in all groups and societies. At the same time he saw the hope of reward as the motive force of society, and one that animated all members of it. Thus emulation, which produced a top layer of nobility, was also a stimulus for those of average ability.[11]

Unlike Bell, Lancaster believed in the salutary effect of public disgrace or shaming as an alternative to corporal punishment, an idea he doubtless derived from his association with the Quakers, who practised it widely in their schools although without the severity that Lancaster used.[12] If a monitor saw a boy misbehaving, the latter was handed a card on which was printed 'I have seen this boy talking', or 'I have seen this boy idle'. The card then had to be presented to the head of the school, from whom he received an admonishment. But if admonition failed and the boy repeated the offence, then he was liable for a series of much harsher penalties. These included tying a log of wood weighing up to 6 lb. round the defaulter's neck or fixing wooden shackles up to a foot long round a boy's legs, and forcing him to walk around the room till tired out. Sometimes up to six boys would be yoked together and paraded round the school, walking backwards. A bad offender would be put in a sack or a basket and suspended from the roof of the school. 'This punishment,' Lancaster remarked, 'is one of the most terrible that can be inflicted on boys of sense and abilities.'[13]

Lancaster considered that the most effective punishment of all was confinement after school hours. As he pointed out, it was attended by one unpleasant circumstance – it needed the presence of the master also. 'This inconvenience may be avoided,' he advised, 'by tying them to the desks in such a manner that they cannot untie themselves.' Alternatively, offenders could be tied up in a blanket and left to sleep at night on the schoolroom floor.[14]

[11] J. Lancaster, *Improvements in Education, as it Respects the Industrious Classes of the Community* (London, 3rd ed., 1805), pp. 93–6 *passim*.
[12] Stewart, *Quakers and Education*, p. 208.
[13] Lancaster, *Improvements in Education*, pp. 100–3.
[14] Ibid., pp. 103–14.

In the end Lancaster himself abandoned these punishments, and in his best-known school at Borough Road a simple system of merit tickets, which could be lost for bad behaviour, was put into force.[15] By the end of the 1830s, however, the award schemes in both British and National schools were breaking down, and corporal punishment taking their place. Nevertheless, the multifarious schemes of tickets, marks, coinage, medals, rank, and so on rose and flourished in the period when corporal punishment in schools was believed by many observers to be at its height. The systems substituted for the cane and the whip, based as they were on the principles of emulation, competition, and the acquisition of rank and prizes, obviously took their inspiration from the competitive capitalist ethic to which the growth of the Industrial Revolution was giving rise. The spirit of individual enterprise and the capital–wage–labour relationship were beginning to dominate society.

During the 1850s there was a large-scale operation of prize schemes for attendance in elementary schools, largely sponsored by the church or by private philanthropy, with the main object of keeping working-class children longer at school.[16] The Revised Code of 1862, however, with its prescriptions and payment of grants to schools on a basis of the numbers in attendance from six to twelve years of age, became a formidable obstacle to projects of this kind because it narrowed down the educational aims of these schools to results. At its most developed, the system of rewards up to 1850 was applied to many aspects of school life, and, as in Hazelwood and the Bell schools in Weardale, Durham, encouraged a good quality of response in the children. Payment by results after 1862 concentrated on a standard product, and thereafter rewards and punishments were directed to that end.

[15] *Report from the Select Committee on the Education of the Lower Orders in the Metropolis*, P.P. (1816), iv, pp. 182–3.
[16] A Hill (ed.), *Essays Upon Educational Subjects Read at the Educational Conference of June 1857* (London, 1857), pp. 125–215.

5 Epilogue: 1750–1850

IN SUMMARIZING the period 1750–1850 let me state again the four trends in educational innovation that have appeared. First, there is the stream of thought from the European Enlightenment and the romanticism of Rousseau, which flowed more or less directly into English schools through Williams, Day, and the Edgeworths, although there were idiosyncratics like Gilpin and Manson before them. Second, there is the period of assimilation by a man like Owen, whose educational work bears traces of the Enlightenment and Pestalozzi and Fellenberg, but whose modulation of middle-class thinking to working-class problems is one of the remarkable contributions to change in this period. Yet it would be to oversimplify if it were not admitted that utopian experiments were not always working-class ventures. The point is, however, that Owen represents a second-generation version, a British adaptation of the Continental influences. Third, there is the straight line of thought from Bentham and Mill to the utilitarian theory and practice of the Hills at Hazelwood for the children of the urban intelligentsia. Fourth, there is the stream of thinking that flows from Pestalozzi and Fellenberg to the philanthropically-minded innovators like Lady Byron and Kay-Shuttleworth, whose work for poor children in the country and in the town made their schools far more liberal and enlightened than was the common practice.

These have been the main lines of educational innovation in the historical context of the hundred years 1750–1850. The story changes as we move into the middle and later years of Victoria's reign, to the era of the great educational Commissions and towards the emerging outlines of general compulsory schooling, the decay of voluntaryism, and the beginnings of a state-provided system of elementary and secondary education.

Part Two

1850–1880

6 The Royal Commissions and After

12 NEW INFLUENCES AND THE INTELLIGENTSIA

THE INNOVATORS of this period were of the middle class, whose unorthodoxies, for the main part, affected children of the middle class. Writing in 1864, Matthew Arnold included in this range the middling manufacturers, retail tradesmen, and professional classes in addition to the traditional groupings of clergy, gentry, and army and navy officers; in economic terms they were those able to afford £25 to £50 a year for their sons' education.[1]

The education for which the middle class was willing to pay was widespread but variable. In 1851 some 500,000 children of the middle and upper classes were being educated in 12,000 'superior' and 'middling' schools.[2] Proprietary schools, untrammelled by ancient statute, among the best of which were King's College School (founded 1829), University College School (1830), and Blackheath (also 1830), were created specifically for middle-class needs. The Grammar Schools Act of 1840 opened the way for the development of a wider curriculum in endowed grammar schools by reversing the Eldon Judgement of 1805 which had prohibited Leeds Grammar School from using its endowments to further the study of arithmetic, writing, literature, and modern languages.

Despite these developments, and despite the fact that the first half of the nineteenth century was the golden age of the private-venture school, the more articulate members of the middle classes were becoming increasingly aware that the education available to them was unco-ordinated, inadequate

---

[1] M. Arnold, *A French Eton; or, Middle Class Education and the State* (London, 1864), pp. 47 ff.
[2] Census of Great Britain, 1851: *Education* (London, 1854), pp. xxxiii, xliv.

in content, and variable in quality. The growth of a more or less co-ordinated body of opinion with well-defined objectives on the kind of schools and curriculum acceptable to the increasing number of professional, commercial, and industrial groups did not really begin until the late 1850s. The founding of the National Association for the Promotion of Social Science in 1857 gave the initial impetus to, and provided a forum for, the advocates of organized middle-class education. The Social Science Association also had links with the contemporary and parallel agitation for raising the status of, and improving the educational provision for, women. George Hastings, the secretary of the Association, worked with Emily Davies, Barbara Bodichon, and others to open up opportunities in higher education for middle-class girls.[3]

In the following decade various aspects of the subject such as examinations, the training of teachers, and the curriculum were discussed. A number of books and pamphlets appeared in the same period, including T. D. Acland's *The Education of the Farmer, Viewed in Connection with that of the Middle Classes in General* (1857), Earl Fortescue's *Public Schools for the Middle Classes* (1864), Matthew Arnold's *A French Eton*, published in the same year, and J. N. Molesworth's Prize Essay on *The Great Importance of an Improved System of Education* (1867). These authors, with other writers and speakers on middle-class education, put forward a fourfold argument: that the upper classes had their own system of education provided by the universities and great public schools; that in recent years provision had been made for the education of the working class; that private schools catering for middle-class children were often of low quality and on the whole tied to a traditional syllabus; and that these facts pointed to the necessity for an organized provision of middle-class schools. A wider and more up-to-date curriculum was the chief feature of the movement for independent middle-class education, and it was to include science and modern languages, as might be expected in an age that welcomed Spencer's *Education: Intellectual, Moral, and Physical*. Apart from Spencer's considerable powers of argument, his readability, and the passion and logic with

---

[3] Josephine Kamm, *Hope Deferred: Girls' Education in English History* (London, 1965), pp. 184–6.

which he put his case, the success of the book can only properly be explained in terms of its fulfilment of the aspirations of a large section of educated public opinion. Spencer's text, that the teaching of classics should give way to the teaching of science, and his constant linking of the former with old-fashioned despotic traditions of life and thought and the latter with progress, enterprise, and individuality, could not fail to appeal to his readers. These were largely the Liberal-orientated industrial and commercial middle classes, who were in favour of *laissez-faire* and free trade and who welcomed an emphasis on science in education, which distinguished them from the supporters of the classics – mainly the religious and political establishment, Conservative and protectionist in general outlook.[4]

The Scottish educational renaissance of the 1830s and 1840s influenced the mid-century progressive movement in England considerably. The names of Stow and Wood are well known, but George Combe is less familiar. An Edinburgh lawyer, born in 1788, he became passionately concerned with psychology and education and with phrenology in particular.

Phrenology was based upon the researches into the localization of brain function of F. J. Gall, the German anatomist, and systematized by his follower Spurzheim.[5] At the lowest level it was represented by the fairground quack and his phrenological chart of the thirty-seven faculties of the mind, his plaster cast of the human head, and his offer to read a person's 'bumps', characterized in W. S. Gilbert's words:

> Observe his various bumps,
> His head as I uncover it,
> His morals lie in lumps,
> All round about and over it.

That the mind can be analysed into a number of faculties or functions; that these are localized in different parts of the brain; that the excess of one faculty is correlated with an en-

---

[4] A. Price, 'Herbert Spencer and the Apotheosis of Science: I', *Educational Review*, vol. 14, no. 2 (Feb. 1962), pp. 87–97.

[5] J. D. Davies, *Phrenology: Fad and Science* (New Haven, Conn., 1955), *passim*, for a recent account.

largement of that particular part of the brain; and that these variations have a corresponding effect on the exterior formation of the skull may have little scientific validity today.[6] In the scientific climate of the early nineteenth century, however, these propositions brought the mind within the operation of natural laws and up to a point enabled it to be studied objectively. Disorders of the mind, which hitherto had been ascribed to demoniacal possession, witchcraft, or miraculous agency, were now studied in relation to the whole human organism. Psychology was no longer seen only from the viewpoint of introspection and metaphysical speculation, and the ground was cleared for a rational observation of human beings. As a modern historian of psychology has said, phrenology was 'an instance of a theory which, while essentially wrong, was just enough right to further scientific thought'.[7]

The possibilities opened up for education by phrenology were far-reaching. At the lowest level it provided a sort of ready-made selection test: one had only to find out the faculties in which one was deficient and then set out to exercise and develop them. In this sense it was well suited to the age of Smilesian self-help, in which the application of science to industry had progressed sufficiently to interest the thinking man, but in which education was insufficiently developed to have established a widespread scientific response. To the practising teacher phrenology was of service, in the words of W. B. Hodgson,

> not merely in enabling him to form rapid and correct judgement of individual characters, but from its clear and simple philosophy of mind, the light it throws on the nature of the being to be instructed, and consequently on the true aim and widest methods of education.[8]

On the highest level also phrenology, with its humanism, its scientific basis, and spirit of rational inquiry, opened up new

---

[6] Cf. G. Combe, *Essays on Phrenology* (Edinburgh, 1819), pp. 1–28; *Elements of Phrenology* (Edinburgh, 1824), pp. 18–20; *A System of Phrenology* (Edinburgh, 1825), pp. 25–35.
[7] E. G. Boring, *A History of Experimental Psychology* (New York, 2nd ed., 1950), p. 57.
[8] *Phrenological Journal*, n.s., vol. ix, no. lxxxvii (1846).

New Influences and the Intelligentsia

opportunities for the investigation of the mind of the child, for criticism of educational orthodoxies, and a revaluation of traditional disciplines. J. D. Davies has pointed out that the educational aims and objects of the early nineteenth-century phrenologists sound today remarkably like those of twentieth-century progressive education:[9] the main impression one gets from reading Spurzheim's *A view of the Elementary Principles of Education*, published in 1821, and Combe's *The Constitution of Man*, which came out seven years later, is of a wide-ranging and comprehensive belief in rational progress, the perfectibility and educability of man, and the necessity of scientific and universal education.[10]

Combe divided the educational process into two parts: training (the exercise of the faculties) and instruction (the acquisition of knowledge for the tasks of life). Knowledge was of two kinds, instrumental and positive. Instrumental knowledge consisted of the three R's and useful languages, which were in themselves merely a means of acquiring positive knowledge, which consisted of a study of the world and man's place in it.[11] The emphasis on the usefulness of language necessarily meant that Latin and Greek were given a subordinate place in Combe's educational scheme. The prevailing faculty theory which was often quoted in support of the classics was rejected on phrenological grounds: the mind was not a unitary organism that could be trained by study in one discipline only, but consisted of numerous faculties only a few of which were suitable for language training.[12]

In religion, Combe took the deistical position that the Divine Ruler governed through the constitution and laws with which he had endowed the material world, and that man could best apprehend Providence through a study of that world.[13] He rejected the supernatural elements of religion, and in true phrenological fashion maintained that religion and

[9] Davies, *Phrenology*, p. 81.
[10] J. G. Spurzheim, *A View of the Elementary Principles of Education* (Edinburgh, 1821), *passim*; G. Combe, *The Constitution of Man* (Edinburgh, 1828), *passim*.
[11] W. Jolly, *Education, Its Principles and Practice as Developed by George Combe* (London, 1879), pp. xxxi–xxxvi.
[12] Ibid., pp. 69–86; G. Combe, *Discussions on Education*, in *Select Works of George Combe* (London, 5 vols., 1893), iv, p. 34.
[13] Jolly, *Education*, pp. 123–67, *passim*.

morality sprang 'from distinct and independent sources in the human mind'.[14] The teaching of orthodox Christianity was not included in his proposed curriculum.

Combe's detailed proposals for a curriculum followed logically from his pedagogical principles. The study of anatomy, physiology, and phrenology would give the child a knowledge of man's physical and mental constitution. The physical and moral sciences, including chemistry, natural history, social science, human geography, and political economy, would enable the pupil to place man in his relation to nature and society. The three R's were to be acquired for utilitarian purposes, but neither the classics nor religion was completely excluded.[15] Though this programme was seriously thought out on philosophical lines, Combe was aware that it lacked a humanist element, and in adding the study of literature, poetry, painting, and sculpture he was pioneering liberal studies, possibly to fill the gap formerly supplied by the study of classical cultures.[16] However, like all who proposed encyclopaedic, scientific curricula at this period, Combe's schemes were heavily weighted with inert knowledge. The pupils were expected to familiarize themselves with masses of fact and information, and Combe assumed that this knowledge would be of direct practical use to everyone.[17] Although his intention was to supersede the narrowness, obscurantism, and reverence of the past for its own sake which he felt was strangling education, he was limited by lack of knowledge and understanding of the value of experimental science.

Combe's writings on phrenology, education, and moral philosophy influenced many progressive thinkers in England, a number of whom became contributors to *Household Words* and its successor *All the Year Round*, periodicals edited by Charles Dickens, who was always open to publish accounts of anything new and unorthodox in education. These journals were one focus which provided a certain cohesion to the intellectual life out of which these educational experiments grew. Another focus was the group that gathered in the 1850s at the

[14] C. Gibbon, *The Life of George Combe* (London, 2 vols., 1878), i, p. 198.
[15] Jolly, *Education*, pp. 23-200, *passim*.
[16] A. Price, 'A Pioneer of Scientific Education: George Combe (1788-1858', *Educational Review*, vol. 12. no. 3 (1960), p. 225.
[17] Cf. ibid., pp. 224-5.

London house of the publisher George Chapman, a friend and associate of Dickens. Chapman was a man of great charm and energy, eager to embrace new and radical ideas. He published chiefly advanced religious and philosophical works, and from January 1852 was, with George Eliot, editor of the *avant-garde Westminster Review*. Among those who met at 142 Strand were Thackeray, Dickens, Mrs. Gaskell, Carlyle, Herbert Spencer, William Ellis, Barbara Bodichon, W. B. Hodgson, the Biblical critic R. W. Mackay, J. A. Froude, Harriet Martineau, George Combe himself, George Henry Lewes, and Thornton Hunt (son of Leigh Hunt), who in the 1850s conducted *The Leader*, a journal devoted to rational religion, economic reform, and a secular educational system.

Most of Chapman's circle were reformers concerned with the improved status and higher education of women, greater freedom in personal relationships within and between the sexes, and a generalized political radicalism. They all held a fervent belief in the importance of science in education and the national life, and the scientific aspects of phrenology provided an intellectual leaven for many in the group even before they had met George Combe. Herbert Spencer had been influenced by Spurzheim's lectures at an early age;[18] Combe's *Moral Philosophy*, read in her teens, had permanently influenced the thinking of Barbara Bodichon.[19] Ellis's determination to open schools that would teach social science was inspired by a re-reading of Combe,[20] and Hodgson had been lecturing on phrenology in Scotland in his early twenties;[21] while George Eliot had been sufficiently impressed by the arguments of the Coventry Owenite and phrenologist Charles Bray to have a cast made of her head.[22]

In the sphere of education, the sympathies of several members of the Chapman circle were with the general aims of the movement for middle-class education, particularly those concerned with the incorporation of science and modern languages in the curriculum. In addition, they evinced a general distrust

[18] H. Spencer, *An Autobiography* (London, 2 vols., 1904), i, p. 200.
[19] Hester Burton, *Barbara Bodichon* (London, 1949), pp. 14–15.
[20] Cf. below, pp. 125–31.
[21] *Dictionary of National Biography*.
[22] G. S. Haight, *George Eliot and John Chapman* (New Haven, Conn., 1940), pp. vii, 168 n.

of Christianity and of classical culture in the traditional system. The details of the foundation and organization of the various schools with which the members of this group were later connected differed widely, though each was a product of the age and could not have existed in that form at an earlier time. Besides emphasizing the place of science as against religion and classics in the curriculum, and developing new teaching methods and substitutes for corporal punishment, these schools demonstrated innovations such as co-education, the mingling of different social classes in the schoolroom, the teaching of social science, education in the ideals of international co-operation, and a new approach to infant development. All of these were of immense importance for the future.

13 HENRY MORLEY AND JOHANNES AND BERTHA RONGE

HENRY MORLEY trained as a doctor in the early days of King's College in the University of London. He practised in Somerset and Shropshire in the middle 1840s, but determined in 1848, 'the year of revolutions', to start his own school. Natural science, history, modern languages (Morley had been schooled by Moravian Brothers in Germany, and had travelled elsewhere in Europe), mathematics, geography, social and political science, and religious studies of a modernistic style were to be included in his school. Corporal punishment was to be abolished and a signed undertaking to act openly and speak the truth was required of each student. By this means the school could be conducted without coercion, prizes and rewards could reinforce the standards expected, and if necessary, as his punishment, a badly behaved pupil was to be forbidden to come to lessons.

Morley found no takers when he advertised in Manchester but in 1849 he started a school across the Mersey in Wallasey, where he ran a co-educational establishment for the sons and daughters, aged eight to fifteen, of Liverpool merchants. Morley was not a good administrator, although he must have been a very good teacher. His school closed in 1851 and he went to

London to join Dickens on the staff of *Household Words*, where he stayed for nearly fifteen years. He wrote about his educational ideas in the periodical and in its successor *All the Year Round*, he edited *The Examiner* from 1861 to 1867, and in 1865 he became professor of English language and literature at University College, University of London. Kay-Shuttleworth was a doctor by training who influenced English education by creative administration. Morley was also a doctor, an innovator who as a cultivated man of wide knowledge influenced old and young as a teacher, as a popularizer in the best sense, and as a writer.

Morley wrote an article in *Household Words* in 1855 on a remarkable kindergarten run by Johannes and Bertha Ronge, and this led to an innovation of even more importance than Morley's own. The Ronges were refugees from Germany after 'the year of revolutions' in 1848. Johannes had been a Roman Catholic priest in Breslau until he was outraged by certain attitudes and practices of his church, from which he resigned after a public declaration of his differences. Some called him 'the Luther of the nineteenth century' and in fact a German Catholic church was set up which renounced the authority of Rome, declared the authority of the Bible as the source of its faith, and extended toleration to all other faiths. But Ronge was no Luther, and by 1850 he had to flee the country. In the meantime, however, he had married Bertha, a daughter of the wealthy Meyer family and a disciple of Friedrich Froebel, the progenitor of the kindergarten movement in Germany, whose emphasis on the development of individual character and the removal of restraints upon growth harmonized well with the religion of humanity preached by Ronge and the German reform committees. When Ronges came to London in 1850 they had experience of Froebelian kindergartens even if they had little English.

Froebel adapted the child-centred principles of Rousseau and Pestalozzi to infants and furnished an elaborate theoretical and practical basis for his schools with children's play at its heart. The Ronges allied Froebel's theory and practice to their religion of humanity, providing not only a kindergarten for children from three to seven years of age, but the prospect of a training school for teachers and an establishment based on

Froebel's principles to follow for older children. The teachers were to be 'well-educated and accomplished ladies of modern society', and certainly the refinement was quite different from the best that Buchanan and Wilderspin, the originators of schools for infants in the first half of the century, could offer. The Ronges, with a committee of parents and co-religionists, founded an Association School for older children based on the same child-centred and academically fluid principles as the kindergartens and the children were taught geography, natural science, social economy, languages, and 'human culture'. The two schools together were called the Humanistic Schools.

The kindergarten movement was one of the few nineteenth-century experiments in education that established themselves on a permanent basis. In 1857 the Ronges had visited Manchester, here they helped to form the Manchester Committee for the Extension of the Kindergarten System. Several German teachers resident in Manchester helped to found kindergartens there. In 1873 the Manchester Froebel Society was founded, followed in 1874 by a similar organization in London, and in 1893 the Home and Colonial School Society, which in the middle of the century had accepted Froebel's principles, was incorporated in the National Froebel Union, which still flourishes today.[1] The Ronges' schools lasted for only ten years from 1851, but they undoubtedly started the movement in England.

The Humanistic Schools did not last beyond 1861, when Johannes Ronge returned to Germany under the amnesty of that year to join his wife, who had gone there shortly before because of ill-health. She died in 1863 and after her death Johannes went to Austria, where little more is heard of him before his death in 1887. Their schools in England were taken over by the Misses Rosalie and Mina Praetorius, who came from Nassau,[2] but the reforming impetus had gone out of them.

[1] P. Woodham Smith, 'History of the Froebel Movement in England', in E. Lawrence (ed.),, *Friedrich Froebel and English Education* (London, 1952), *passim*.
[2] Ibid., p. 43.

14 BARBARA BODICHON AND PORTMAN HALL

On 6 November 1854 a day school for boys and girls was opened in Portman Hall in Carlisle Street, off Edgware Road. The hall was used in the evenings for temperance meetings, and the benches and temperance texts had to be put back at the end of every day. The school was run by Barbara Leigh Smith, a woman of twenty-seven, better known under her later married name of Bodichon. Her friend Elizabeth Whitehead (later Malleson) was in charge of the teaching, assisted by Barbara's sisters Isabella and Anne, and Octavia Hill, the housing reformer.

The experimental nature of the school caused initial difficulties. In the words of her biographer, 'Barbara's school was like nothing any of her contemporaries had ever seen before ... grave doubts about the propriety of the school and the religious convictions of its founder were held by people otherwise open to reason and reform.' Octavia's sister, Miranda Hill, for instance, was warned not to teach there by the Reverend F. D. Maurice, the Christian socialist, because of his dissatisfaction with the religious *bona fides* of the establishment.[1]

The school broke with tradition in many ways. In the first place it educated young boys and girls together. Co-education, in the eyes of the mid-Victorian middle class, was permissible for working-class or very young children, but was supposed to present peculiar problems in the case of children of a higher class. Barbara Bodichon's belief that girls should be treated in schools on equality with boys was bound up with her advanced views on the social position of women. She told the Newcastle Commission in 1861 that the education of girls would always be neglected until women had received better legal and social rights; if the education of women was to improve, then women in the educational world must have equality with men.[2] In Barbara's school the alleged difficulties and dangers of co-education were either ignored or overcome.

---

[1] Burton, *Barbara Bodichon*, p. 50.
[2] *Report of the Commissioners Appointed to Inquire into the State of Popular Education in England*, P.P. (1861), xxxi (5), pp. 103-4.

Portman Hall School further outraged Victorian propriety by mixing together different social classes. Children of middle-class parents sat side by side with the sons and daughters of the neighbouring tradesmen and artisans. The school was also a demonstration of racial tolerance: children of various nationalities were welcomed as pupils there. For a short while Ricciotti, the younger son of Garibaldi, attended the school. He was a crippled child, but he was more active on his crutches than most of the normal children were on their legs, and he used to terrify the younger ones by leaping wildly across the benches.[3]

As far as possible punishment was not administered, and few prizes were given for school work. The aim was to make lessons short and pleasurable and to use attainment and a sense of acceptance as the stimulus to improvement. Several innovations were made in teaching method. The teachers made great efforts to work out for themselves the most rational way of presenting arithmetic and English, and in arithmetic many of the reforms of William de Morgan were anticipated, mainly, as Miss Whitehead recalled, by 'infinitely hard work'. Much attention was paid to what were considered by some to be educational extras – visits to museums or picture galleries, and the use of a school lending library. Physiology and the laws of health were an important part of the curriculum,[4] an innovation deriving from the work of Combe and Ellis.

The progressive schools of the previous generation had either disappeared or, as in the case of Bruce Castle, were lapsing into orthodoxy. Behind the challenging practices of her school stood Barbara Bodichon's own strong predilections for radicalism, rationalism, internationalism, feminism, and freedom in personal relationships. She clashed head-on, both personally and through her school, with the strongest of the Victorian prejudices, and to do this required independence and courage of a high order.

She was born Barbara Leigh Smith in 1827. Her father was Benjamin Leigh Smith, a Unitarian and a Radical, and M.P. for Norwich at the time of the repeal of the Corn Laws. Her

---

[3] Elizabeth Malleson, *Autobiographical Notes and Letters* (London, 1926), p. 49 n.
[4] Burton, *Barbara Bodichon*, p. 51.

grandfather had been William Smith, a noted Abolitionist and ally of Wilberforce, and a sympathizer with the ideals of the French Revolution.[5] The family had a reputation for supporting advanced and unpopular ideas. Her father objected to sending his children to a traditional school, but since they might meet Richard Cobden, Harriet Martineau, or Henry Brougham discussing free trade, philosophy, or economics at the dinner table, this hardly seemed a disadvantage. The education of the Smith children largely consisted of private tutoring and private reading, interspersed with journeys in Britain and abroad in a large family coach, well supplied with books and sketching materials. For holidays they might go hop-picking, fishing, or walking in Scotland. When in London Benjamin Leigh Smith made his daughters attend Westminster Infant School and assist James Buchanan, the master. The Leigh Smith family gave money to build schools, endow hospitals, finance students, and help refugees; their house in Blandford Square was often full of exiles from Poland, Hungary, Italy, and France.[6]

On her twenty-first birthday, in April 1848, Barbara's father settled on her £300 a year. She celebrated her independence by enrolling, in 1849, at the newly founded Ladies' College in Bedford Square, where she became particularly interested in drawing and painting. The following year she made a tour of Europe with Bessie Parks, great-granddaughter of Joseph Priestley and later the mother of Hilaire Belloc. She became friendly with many of the leading women intellectuals of the day, including Mrs. Somerville, Mrs. Opie, and Lady Byron. In 1852 she was introduced to George Eliot at one of Chapman's evening parties, and the novelist later made her the model for Romola:

> The hair was of a reddish gold colour, enriched by an unbroken small ripple, such as may be seen in the sunset clouds on grandest autumnal evenings ... there was the same refinement of brow and nostril ... counterbalanced by a full though firm mouth and powerful chin, which gave an expression of proud tenacity and latent impetuousness; an

[5] Ibid., pp. 1–2.
[6] Ibid., pp. 3 ff.

expression carried out in the backward poise of the girl's head, and the grand line of her neck and shoulders.[7]

In 1854 Barbara published *A Brief Summary in Plain Language of the Most Important Laws Concerning Women.* This was written with the help of Matthew Davenport Hill, the recorder of Birmingham, an old family friend of the Smiths, who thus had connections with Hazelwood, and stressed the complete absence of rights of the married woman. It created a sensation at the time and was one of the first shots in the campaign that resulted in the Married Women's Property Acts of the 1880s and 1890s.[8]

In 1857 she published *Women and Work,* a plea for women to be accepted into the trades and professions, and the following year she helped to found *The English Woman's Journal,* which campaigned for the rights of women.[9] She felt, however, that this activity neither absorbed her whole energies nor was of sufficient practical benefit. She believed that all women should have the advantages in life that she herself had enjoyed, and her dissatisfactions with the Victorian conventions led her into an affair with John Chapman. She assessed herself thus:

> I am one of the cracked people of the world, and I like to herd with the cracked ... queer Americans, democrats, socialists, artists, poor devils or angels; and am never happy in an English genteel family life. I try to do it like other people, but I long always to be off on some wild adventure, or long to lecture on a tub in St. Giles, or go to see the Mormons, or ride off into the interior on horseback alone and leave the world for a month.[10]

It was this dissatisfaction with what seemed to her the stifling morality and artificiality of Victorian middle-class social life that attracted her to Eugène Bodichon, a French doctor domiciled in Algiers, a socialist, republican, and self-styled eccentric, who was not above scandalizing London society.

[7] G. Eliot, *Romola* (London, 3 vols., 1863), i, p. 79.
[8] Burton, *Barbara Bodichon*, p. 61.
[9] Ibid., pp. 99–100.   [10] Ibid., p. 92.

Barbara Bodichon's school embodied many of the ideas that she had acquired during her lifetime, and was in consequence a protest against educational convention. The three main influences on her educational thinking were James Buchanan, George Combe, and William Ellis, although she was also well acquainted with all the current literature on education and, before opening her school, had visited various National, British, Secular, Catholic, Ragged, and other schools and taught in some of them.[11] Combe she had come across in her late teens, and from his *Moral Philosophy* she had derived much of her faith in rationalism and social progress.[12] The assistant teacher at Portman Hall came from Edinburgh and had been trained at George Combe's school there.[13] In addition to these influences, the moral atmosphere of Portman Hall School owed much to the example of Owen and Buchanan. 'My school ... was the child of Robert Owen's, child of James Buchanan,' she confessed.[14] She was also impressed by her friend William Ellis's Birkbeck school at Peckham, which she considered to be the most advanced school in London, and she suggested that Elizabeth Whitehead should spend some weeks there before taking charge of Portman Hall.

Elizabeth Whitehead, whom Barbara had met through a friend of her father's, William Johnson Fox, M.P. for Oldham, was born in 1828, and came like Barbara from a Unitarian and Radical family. She later played a leading part in the founding of the College for Working Women in 1864, and campaigned against the Contagious Diseases Acts and for women's suffrage and other causes.[15]

Elizabeth Whitehead was forced to give up full-time teaching at Portman Hall after one year because of overwork. It was due to her vitality and ability as a teacher that the school had been placed on the road to success, and after her marriage to Frank Malleson she retained inspectorship of the school and her husband gave generous subscriptions to it. Barbara Bodichon herself finally gave up the school after her marriage

---

[11] *Report of the Commissioners Appointed to Inquire into the State of Popular Education in England*, P.P. (1861), xxi (5), p. 103.
[12] Burton, *Barbara Bodichon*, pp. 14–15.
[13] [Buchanan], *Buchanan Family Records*, p. 18.
[14] Ibid., p. 25.
[15] Malleson, *Autobiographical Notes*, pp. 39, 55 ff.

to Eugène Bodichon in 1857. She spent half the year in Algiers and found she could not give the close superintendence that she felt the school needed. She later donated the school equipment to Mrs. Malleson for the Working Women's College.[16] Her school lasted just over three years, preceding the great Commissions of the 1860s and the Revised Code, and was in the genuine progressive, radical succession.

15 THE INTERNATIONAL SCHOOL

IT was a widely held belief, associated particularly with the name of Richard Cobden, that the unrestricted flow of commodities between nations must eventually lead to the disappearance of international rivalries.[1] Cobden's views on trade, in the words of his biographer Morley, 'were only another side of views on education and morality'.[2] Many leading advocates of free trade hoped to realize their vision of international harmony by the creation of a new type of education which would enable the citizens of different countries to become international ambassadors. Free trade was breaking down barriers between nation and nation, but they were, it was felt, still divided and kept apart by ignorance of each other's culture and language.[3] The provision of boarding-schools in the major industrial countries which pupils could visit in turn to study the language of the country was put forward as a means of bringing nations together. The one genuine and successful attempt at international education in the nineteenth century was made at the height of the free-trade era.

Specific proposals were made independently on three oc-

[16] Burton, *Barbara Bodichon*, p. 52.
[1] 'I believe that the desire and motive for large and mighty empires, for gigantic armies and great navies – for those materials which are used for the destruction of life and desolation of the reward of labour – will die away; I believe that such things will cease to be necessary, or to be used when man becomes one family, and freely exchanges the fruits of his labour with his brother man'; J. Bright and J. E. T. Rogers (eds.), *Speeches on Questions of Public Policy by Richard Cobden, M. P.* (London, 2 vols., 1870), p. 363.
[2] J. Morley, *The Life of Richard Cobden* (London, 2 vols., 1881), i, p. 93.
[3] 'International Education', *Reader*, vol. v, no. 129 (17 June 1865), pp. 678–9.

casions between 1855 and 1862 in favour of international education, two by Frenchmen and one by a Scot. The first proposal was made by Eugène Rendu, inspector-general of public instruction, in France in 1855, but for political reasons it was not published until 1862. The next person to put forward a similar proposal was James Lorimer, a Scottish lawyer. In two remarkable articles in the Edinburgh *Museum* in the summer of 1861 he outlined a scheme very similar to that of Rendu.[4] There was no doubt, however, that the latter's proposals were completely unknown to Lorimer. Like many thinking men of his generation he deplored international antagonisms, and his articles were a plea for the rational study of languages and the use of travel in the service of international understanding. The third proposal for international schools was made in 1862 by a French manufacturer, Aristide Barbier of Clermont-Ferrand, on the occasion of the International Exhibition held in London that year. Barbier donated five thousand francs to the French Committee of the Exhibition as prizes for the best essays on the means of establishing international education in Europe. Though he had mooted his plan the previous year, he felt that the exhibition provided a good opportunity for public men of different nations to meet and discuss plans for a form of education that would be the intellectual counterpart of the exhibition's objects.[5]

Barbier suggested the creation of four colleges, one in each of four countries, for children of ten to eighteen years of age, and invited specific and detailed proposals on these lines.[6] To judge the essays an international jury was set up, which included Sir James Kay-Shuttleworth, Richard Cobden, and Michel Chevalier. The first prize was won by Edmond Barbier, a French tutor resident in England (not related to his namesake Aristide) and translator of the definitive French edition of Charles Darwin's *Origin of Species*. His prize-winning essay was in all essentials a detailed working-out of

[4] J. Lorimer, 'Reciprocal Naturalisation. I: International Education', *Museum* (Edinburgh), no. 1 (Apr. 1861), pp. 77–87; 'II: The International School the Complement of the International Exhibition', ibid., no. 2 (July 1861), pp. 174–81.

[5] 'Proposed International Schools', *Journal of the Society of Arts,* vol. xi, no. 540 (27 Mar. 1863).

[6] A. Barbier, *Éducation Internationale* (Paris, 1862), *passim.*

the main ideas put forward by Rendu, Lorimer, and Aristide Barbier. Briefly, he suggested that four colleges, of about 120 pupils each, should be set up in Paris, London, Berlin, and Florence. The children were expected to start at eight or nine years of age and study the languages of the four countries concerned. They then had to spend one year in each country in turn, thus visiting each country twice in the course of their eight years of school life.[7]

The first response to Aristide Barbier's initiative was the organization of a European Association for International Education, with Eugène Rendu as secretary and with sub-committees to be set up in the four countries concerned. The first sub-committee was set up in France, consisting of leading educationalists and public men, and the prototype school was founded in France in 1862, in Saint-Germain-en-Laye, a few miles from Paris, with Jules Brandt as director.[8] It combined modern languages with advanced classical studies, with the object of preparing pupils for professional work in the major European countries. Two hours a day were devoted to courses in English, French, German, and Italian, and religious instruction was barred from the curriculum. The pupil–teacher ratio was low and classes did not exceed twenty pupils. The individual responsibility of the pupils was fostered as far as possible, and sport played an important part in the curriculum. A doctor visited the school daily to look after the health of the pupils,[9] who were drawn from the upper classes of society.

In England the scheme did not get under way until 1863. A provisional committee was set up that included Richard Cobden (who died before the school was opened), Dr. W. B. Hodgson, and Thomas Twining, later an advocate of technical education. The scientists John Tyndall and Thomas Henry Huxley also became members, and Edmond Barbier acted as secretary to the committee.

The committee sent out a circular letter in 1863 outlining the aims of the college as described in Barbier's prize-winning

[7] Ibid., pp. 49–78.
[8] 'International Education', *All the Year Round,* no. 281 (10 Sept. 1864), pp. 106–8.
[9] Prospectus entitled 'École Internationale de Saint-Germain-en-Laye', dated Feb. 1867.

essay. The circular also attempted to answer various criticisms of the project, particularly the charge that the pupils would, during their time at an international school, lose all sense of national feeling. The circular also pointed out that, although the curriculum was very wide – in addition to six languages the pupils would have to study a range of scientific subjects, modern politics, and political economy – 'complete' instruction would be given in the three R's and languages and only 'the elements' of the rest would be taught.[10]

Sufficient support was forthcoming for the school to be opened three years later. The main benefactor was William Ellis, who advanced a very large part of the money required for the purchase of the site at Isleworth in Middlesex and the erection of the buildings, which were opened on 1 May 1866.[11] It was not until 10 July of the following year that the college was completed and the formal opening was performed by Ellis's old pupil, the Prince of Wales, with great ceremony amidst the fluttering flags of different nations.[12] The first headmaster was Dr. Leonard Schmitz, who had been rector of the High School in Edinburgh and a former associate of George Combe.[13] The official name of the school was the London College of the International Education Society.

In 1867 there were twelve day scholars between the ages of ten and fourteen, and fifty-eight boarders. The fees were extremely high even for this class of school: boarders paid eighty guineas a year and day scholars twenty-four guineas. The amenities of the school, however, were very good. There was one master to every ten pupils, each boy had his own bedroom with, it was claimed, 970 cubic feet of breathing-space, and the catering arrangements were similarly generous. The school stood in eight acres of ground, and the boys had fifteen hours of playtime a week in the winter and eighteen hours in summer. There was no corporal punishment and discipline was maintained by confinement during play hours, the imposition

[10] *Brief Statement of the Proposed Plan for International Schools* (London, 1863), *passim*.
[11] E. K. Blyth, *Life of William Ellis* (London, 1889), p. 266.
[12] C. Bibby, 'A Victorian Experiment in International Education: The College at Spring Grove', *British Journal of Educational Studies*, vol. v, no. 1 (Nov. 1956), p. 27.
[13] Gibbon, *George Combe*, ii, p. 243.

of extra lessons, or the deprivation of privileges.[14] In 1871 the college buildings were extended to include a new wing and a gymnasium at the additional cost of £10,000.[15]

Apart from the pupils from France, Germany, and Italy, the college attracted a number of scholars from all over the world, including Spain, Portugal, the United States, India, Brazil, Chile, and Nicaragua. Among its most distinguished English pupils were the composer Frederick Delius and the novelist Maurice Hewlett. Hewlett never settled down at Spring Grove, where he saw only conflict and hostility in the clash of different nationalities:

> There were no traces in my time of the Brotherhood of Man about it.... The raw Brazilians, Chilians, Nicaraguans and what not who were drawn from their native forests and plunged into the company of blockish Yorkshire lads, or sharp-faced London boys, were only scared into rebellion, and to demonstration after their manner. They used the knife sometimes – they hardly ever assimilated; and they taught us nothing that we were the better of knowing.[16]

The initial prospectus of the school defined the curriculum as follows:

> English language and literature; modern languages; Latin, Greek; mathematics (arithmetic, algebra, geometry, etc.); natural sciences; history; geography; moral science; religious instruction; military drill; gymnastic exercises; vocal music; and drawing in its several branches.[17]

The Schools Inquiry Commission described the general character of the school at the beginning of 1867 as 'classical',[18] though the *Illustrated London News* had in the same year drawn attention to the prominent place given to the physical

---

[14] *Report of the Endowed Schools Inquiry Commission*, vol. xii: *South Midland Division, Special Reports of Assistant Commissioners*, P.P. (1867–8), xxviii (10), p. 526.
[15] Bibby, in *British Journal of Educational Studies*, vol. v, no. 1, p. 33.
[16] Ibid., p. 35.
[17] *Schools Inquiry Commission*, p. 525.
[18] Ibid., p. 526.

sciences in the curriculum.[19] The original aim of making modern languages the core of the curriculum was obviously not being carried out: Italian, for instance, was not taught at all in the early years. The leaning towards the classics was due to Schmitz: unless a large proportion of time was given to their study, he felt, they were not worth studying at all.

Thomas Henry Huxley, on the other hand, despite the general aim of making the college an international language institution, wanted to make science the backbone of the curriculum and proposed an ambitious scheme that would include physics, chemistry, biology, advanced social science, and the natural history of man;[20] but this was not accepted by Schmitz. In addition to its relatively low place in the curriculum, science was apparently not very well taught. In 1872 Charles Hooker, one of the pupils there, described the science teaching at Spring Grove as 'an utter sham, worse by far than nothing and calculated to bring the thing into contempt'.[21] By 1880, however, the science teaching had been improved by the provision of two laboratories for practical scientific work. The teaching of modern languages had also been improved and extended, and five years after the opening it was reported that the pupils could converse equally well in English, French, German, and Italian.

According to the Memorandum of Association of the college, the fundamental principle of all educational institutions under the direction of the International Society was that no theological studies should form part of the general course of education, but arrangements were made for giving all pupils such special religious instruction as their parents or guardians desired. There were two lessons of religious knowledge a week at which the Bible was read and explained, but no boy whose parents objected was compelled to attend. The school day began and ended with prayers (presumably undenominational) composed by the headmaster.[22]

By the early 1870s the Isleworth College had established itself very much on the lines of the original aims of the

[19] *Illustrated London News*, 20 July 1867, cited in Bibby, in *British Journal of Educational Studies*, vol. v, no. 1, p. 28.
[20] Bibby, in *British Journal of Educational Studies*, vol. v, no. 1, pp. 28–31.
[21] Ibid., p. 33.
[22] *Schools Inquiry Commission*, pp. 525–6.

founders. It had become truly international in scope, teaching the languages of four of the most important countries of Europe – England, France, Germany, and Italy – to a wide variety of nationalities. It continued its work throughout the 1870s and 1880s, and in 1874 H. R. Ladell replaced Schmitz as headmaster. In its last years it had a hundred pupils and fourteen masters and had several scholarships tenable at English universities. In 1889, however, the college came to an end and in 1890 the buildings were occupied by Borough Road Training College.[23] No reliable information has been obtained as to the reasons for its closure.

During the twenty-three years of its life the college had given in some degree a practical experience of internationalism to many hundreds of pupils. In addition, by giving science and modern languages a prominent place in the curriculum, it had, despite Schmitz's preference for classical studies, carried forward the movement for curricular reform. The Isleworth International School was in many ways far ahead of its time. If its original impetus in the 1860s had lain in visions of universal peace and prosperity arising from free trade and the spread of culture, in practice it had to adapt to the era ushered in by the Franco-Prussian War of 1870. Dickens's journal *All the Year Round* had welcomed the project in its earliest days as 'the truest expression of the law of education in the nineteenth century', and saw in it a revival of the republic of letters of the medieval universities.[24] Perhaps the most remarkable feature of the English college was that it lasted so long in an atmosphere of war and international rivalry.

The idea of a linked group of schools has been revived from time to time, notably by Cecil Reddie of Abbotsholme and more recently by Kurt Hahn. It has usually foundered on the difficulties of practical arrangements, and the chief form that the principle has taken is of a parent school with direct links with similar schools in other countries. By any standards the International School of 1866–89 was a remarkable achievement, a product of the liberal intelligentsia for their children.

[23] Bibby, in *British Journal of Educational Studies*, vol. v, no. 1, pp. 35–6.
[24] *All the Year Round*, no. 281, p. 107.

16 WILLIAM ELLIS AND THE BIRKBECK SCHOOLS

WILLIAM ELLIS, businessman and educationalist, tutor to Queen Victoria's children, praised as a teacher by Florence Nightingale ('the best and most effective teaching I have ever heard'),[1] the friend and patron of William Lovett, the veteran Chartist, was the founder of a series of remarkable schools during the mid-Victorian period which attempted, as no other schools had done, to make the education provided correspond closely to the economic and social life of the times. This involved changes in curriculum and teaching method that were of interest and value for education as a whole.

Ellis had little time for the conventional curriculum and did not believe in the neutrality of the teacher or in keeping politics out of the classroom. He thought it 'quite within the scope of school instruction' to persuade children of the follies of joining unions or of taking part in strikes, and to teach them a morality based upon the doctrines of classical political economy, to which he gave the general name of social science.[2]

Ellis, born in 1800, the son of an underwriter at Lloyd's who was ruined by the blockades of the Napoleonic Wars, was forced to leave school at thirteen and live a frugal life as a clerk. ('... we were allowed a penny a day each for lunch,' he recalled. 'We used to buy a small biscuit with seeds in it for the penny; but corn was dear and it was not much for a hungry boy....')[3] By self-denial and hard work, however, he progressed in the true Smilesian manner, becoming manager of the Indemnity Marine Insurance Company at the age of twenty-six. Under his guidance the company rapidly became one of the largest of its kind in the country.

'I met Mr. James Mill,' he said, 'when I was about twenty, and he worked a complete change in me. He taught me how to think and what to live for.'[4] He became a member of John

---

[1] Blyth, *William Ellis*, p. 98.
[2] W. Ellis, 'Combinations and Strikes from the Teacher's Point of View', *Museum and English Journal of Education*, vol. ii, no. 8 (June 1865), p. 81.
[3] Florence Fenwick Miller, 'William Ellis and his Work as an Educationist', *Fraser's Magazine*, n.s., xxv (Feb. 1852), p. 234.
[4] Ibid., p. 236.

Stuart Mill's Utilitarian Society and later of George Grote's discussion group, where he read and discussed the works of James Mill, Ricardo, and Hartley. The views he formed strongly affected his attitude to education, which he believed should be brought into a closer relationship with life:

> I consider it a disgrace to our civilization that a boy should leave school at the age of 13 and not have something like a clear perception of the world he is going into, and the duties that he will have to perform, and I consider that he cannot have that unless what I understand by the name of elementary social science is taught.[5]

Ellis was disturbed by the gap between the traditional subjects of the school curriculum and the nature of the expanding industrial and commercial society that formed the environment of the school. The target, Ellis had no doubt, should be a thorough acquaintance with industrial capitalist society and an appreciation of the place of the individual, particularly the working-class and lower-middle-class individual, in it.

Society, however, was plagued by social discontents, which Ellis divided into two groups: permanent evils, among which he included destitution, bad housing, crime, and improvidence, and intermittent upheavals, such as commercial panics, combinations, and strikes.[6] He did not condemn strikes with the horror common to many of his middle-class contemporaries, for he took the view that the real causes of industrial and social unrest lay in error and maladjustment on the part of the workers themselves. The causes of human misery, he maintained, could be shortly summed up: 'Four names will suffice to embrace them all: ignorance, unskilfulness, depravity of disposition and bad habits....'[7]

Ignorance and ill-conduct were, of course, removable by

---

[5] *Report of the Endowed Schools Inquiry Commission*, P.P. (1867–8), xxviii (4), p. 507.

[6] *Report of the Commissioners Appointed to Inquire into the State of Popular Education in England*, P.P. (1861), xxi (5), p. 181; W. Ellis, 'On Economic Science', *Journal of the Society of Arts*, vol. ii, no. 91 (18 Aug. 1854), pp. 667–9.

[7] W. Ellis, *Thoughts on the Future of the Human Race* (London, 1866), p. 133.

the general spread of education, but the special kinds of ignorance that Ellis saw manifesting themselves in society needed special kinds of instruction and disciplines to overcome them, and it was in this connection that social science, particularly the economic part of it, was relevant. It could teach the working class about the sources of wealth, the connection between capital and labour, the importance of respect for property, and 'the suicidal folly' of organizing combinations, strikes, and turnouts, of impeding the introduction of new machinery, and of opposing the free movement of capital and labour.[8]

After twenty years of attending to his business interests Ellis turned to education, and the occasion for this, as with other reformers of the time, was a reading of George Combe's *The Constitution of Man*, which revived his interest in population restraint (a favourite theme of Combe's) and related aspects of political economy. He wrote to his friend W. B. Hodgson in 1847:

> Combe dwells more than once on the importance of a rational restraint upon population, and my conviction of this, more than anything else, led me last year to resume actively what I had laid aside for twenty years – the teaching of political economy.[9]

Ellis's strategy was to found and equip a number of schools, later called Birkbeck schools, after the founder of the Mechanics' Institutes, in which social science would be not merely another subject in the curriculum but the very staple of the education given. Ellis was not the first to advocate the inclusion of political and economic doctrines in the curriculum of elementary schools. The economist John Wade and Sir Thomas Wyse had, in the 1830s, suggested political economy as a suitable ingredient in working-class education.[10] Ellis, however, was the first to found and equip schools for this purpose.

[8] *Commission on Popular Education*, xxi (5), p. 181.
[9] Blyth, *William Ellis*, p. 58.
[10] Cf. J. Wade, *A History of the Middle and Working Classes* (London, 1833), pp. 494 ff.; T. Wyse, *Education Reform; or, the Necessity of a National System of Education* (London, 1836), pp. 313–23.

Two further things were necessary, suitable textbooks and well-trained teachers, and with typical thoroughness Ellis wrote his own books and set about training his own teachers, who had to have not only an enthusiasm for the doctrines of social science but also the skill to impart the knowledge in a manner favoured by Ellis. For many years during the 1850s he carried out the job himself, giving weekly instruction to a class of about fifty teachers,[11] using the first Birkbeck school in Southampton Buildings as a sort of training college for teachers in other similar schools.[12] Ellis did, however, discover some teachers who fully shared his views and who could, without much further instruction, conduct his schools as he wished.

The importance given to social science (despite the criticisms that could be made of its content) brought the curriculum closer to the affairs of the outside world and the future lives of the pupils than was the case in almost any other school in the nineteenth century. However, the curriculum also included study of the natural sciences, and few schools of this type taught science on such a scale at such an early date. Traditional subjects that did not further Ellis's aims were excluded from the curriculum and so the classics were not taught, Ellis dismissing classical scholarship as 'groping among the rubbish, the filth and superstition of by-gone times ...'.[13] Literature, poetry, and history were also excluded, poetry because Ellis considered that it led to undue exaggeration and history because of the unsatisfactory work of historians.[14]

He claimed that the main teaching method was a Socratic dialogue between pupil and teacher, because this was considered by Ellis to be the best way of presenting the principles of social science. In addition, the general mode of presentation of lessons was as far as possible practical, and it should be remembered that from 1862 onwards the National and British schools had to work to the Revised Code, which necessitated fairly rigid rote-learning. The Birkbeck schools were completely secular, there being no religious teaching of any kind,

---

[11] *Commission on Popular Education*, xxi (5), p. 407.
[12] Blyth, *William Ellis*, p. 96.
[13] W. E[llis], 'Classical Education', *Westminster and Foreign Quarterly Review*, liii (July 1850), p. 409.
[14] Blyth, *William Ellis*, pp. 45–6.

and the Bible was not even used as a reading-book. No corporal punishment was given, and in this Ellis demonstrated as other progressive educationalists had done that it was possible to run large schools without the use of the cane.

All these features clashed with the dominant educational spirit of the age in a way difficult to comprehend today. A contemporary of Ellis wrote that 'they formed astounding innovations, opposed by all the old wives of the political, social and theological worlds, as tending to subvert the order established by Providence for keeping us, in every sense, in our proper stations'.[15]

Nevertheless, there were obvious disadvantages in the schools, the main ones being a bleakness of atmosphere and semi-vocational bias, which the doctrines of social science did nothing to alleviate. Many critics of the Utilitarians opposed Utilitarian doctrines on the grounds of their inhumanity, as John Stuart Mill had pointed out: 'Utility was denounced as cold calculation; political economy was hard-hearted; anti-population doctrines were repulsive to the natural feelings of mankind.'[16]

This was fair comment on the Birkbeck schools, made all the more apparently convincing because the schools and the curriculum lacked any aesthetic sense and feeling. The buildings were ugly, scarcely any humane subjects were taught, the monitorial system was used in the schools, mainly to save the expense of teachers' salaries, and this diminished the benefits that the personality of good teachers and the best of the Socratic teaching gave.

Ellis's approach was fundamentally different from the educationalists of the Enlightenment and their followers. His point of departure was not the child, his interests, capacities, and potentialities, but society and its presumed necessities. Where Morley or Barbara Bodichon tried to shape a curriculum and teaching methods at least in part to the interests of their pupils, Ellis assumed that if the curriculum and methods were in his view important and necessary for children to learn, then the children automatically appreciated them, an assump-

[15] W. Jolly, 'William Ellis, Educationalist and Philanthropist', *Good Words*, 22 (1881), pp. 543–4.
[16] J. S. Mill, *Autobiography* (London, 1873), p. 111.

tion he never fully demonstrated. To him the facts of social science were given and the correct values stressed, and thus the children would, later in life, possess a chart for self-guidance and adjustment in society.

Notwithstanding the forbidding bleakness of the Birkbeck schools, Ellis was probably the most influential educator of the mid-nineteenth century. He helped to finance the International School at Isleworth, Middlesex, and he found money for the Edinburgh Secular School, started by George Combe and James Simpson. Between 1850 and 1853 he helped financially two schools founded by the Glasgow Secular Society, and in the same period provided much of the finance for two schools in Manchester together with other schools in London, Dorset, and Norfolk: in 1858, for instance, he was helping and teaching in St. Thomas's Charterhouse, founded by the Reverend William Rogers.[17] Ellis gave practical training to Barbara Bodichon's schoolmistress, Elizabeth Whitehead, and he was the moving spirit behind William Lovett's National Hall School, opened in 1848, in which, Lovett claimed, he pioneered the teaching of physiology in English elementary schools.[18] Ellis not only underwrote the school financially but also taught social science there. He founded at least eight other day schools in and near London, and his influence extended abroad, for in 1864 Mme. Salis Schwabe founded schools on the Ellis pattern in Naples.

Most of the schools founded by Ellis, however, did not survive the competition of the Board schools, and were either closed or absorbed into the state system. The process of time had also changed Ellis's views on the new educational climate after 1870. The writings of Ruskin (which Ellis, who was no utopist, typically called 'noxious rubbish')[19] had helped to humanize political economy, and Ellis's pamphlet *A Few Words on Board Schools*, published in 1875, showed that he had modified his conception of social science. It advocated that lessons on social life should be drawn from the surroundings of the children and include instruction on food, plants,

[17] Blyth, *William Ellis*, pp. 111–19.
[18] *The Life and Struggles of William Lovett* (London, 1876), pp. 360 ff.; W. Lovett, *Elementary Anatomy and Physiology* (London, 1851), *passim*; Jolly, *Education*, pp. 224–30.
[19] E. E. Ellis, *Memoir of William Ellis* (London, 1888), p. 165.

streets, vehicles, natural phenomena, communications, and so on, illustrated where possible by objects, drawings, models, diagrams, and maps.[20] Thus even in Ellis's lifetime the content of social science had begun to change from classical political economy to something resembling modern civics, a change that is symbolized in the decline of the Birkbeck schools. This transition is notable in the work of the new wave of progressive schools that began in the 1890s, partly as a result of the rise of the Labour movement and partly from the concern of the liberal intelligentsia. However, Ellis had made a lasting mark in the period from roughly 1850 to 1880 as teacher, educational thinker, and philanthropist of a characteristically radical-capitalist stamp.

[20] Blyth, *William Ellis*, pp. 298–9.

7 Epilogue: 1850–1880

I

IN 1856 a Royal Commission under the Duke of Newcastle was instructed to survey the elementary educational system that had grown up since the first national grant of £20,000 in 1833 was shared between the National Society and the British and Foreign Schools Society. The Newcastle Commission recommended in 1861 that in future government grants should be paid only to those schools that were reported by Her Majesty's Inspectors as efficient in the teaching of the basic subjects. A detailed schedule of work was laid down for each 'standard' or age-group by the Revised Code of the Education Department and on this children were examined by Her Majesty's Inspectors on a given date each year and grants paid on the standards achieved. This, while seeking to ensure some evenness of standard in the battle against illiteracy, began the long history of oppression, hostility, and organized deception in elementary schools that continued till 1902 and after, although the Revised Code began to break up in 1895. The reverberations in the attitudes of teachers in elementary schools lasted until well into the twentieth century and the thought of an experimentation in state-supported schools during the period from 1862 was quite killed.[1]

In 1861 the Clarendon Commission began its inquiries into the affairs of nine public schools: Eton, Harrow, Rugby, Winchester, Westminster, Shrewsbury, Charterhouse, St. Paul's, and Merchant Taylors'. By 1864 the report was available, and the Public Schools Act of 1868 ensured that reforms in the government and financial conduct of these schools as well as recommendations on organization and practice were carried out. Many schools regrouped themselves, others were founded as new public schools, and for fifty years this kind of institution gained a firm hold on the public imagination.

[1] See C. Duke, 'Robert Lowe – A Reappraisal', *British Journal of Educational Studies*, vol. xiv, no. 1 (Nov. 1965), pp. 19–35.

The Endowed Schools Inquiry Commission reviewed the grammar, proprietary, and private foundations between 1864 and 1868, and in the twenty volumes of their report included consideration of art schools, museums, natural science laboratories, girls' schools, and the extent of parents' co-operation. The report revealed an alarmingly low standard in a large number of the nearly eight hundred establishments that were investigated, and Matthew Arnold's reports, in one of the volumes, on the educational systems of Continental countries showed England to have little understanding of the need for civic organization as compared with the educational forethought and design of France, Prussia, Holland, and Switzerland. All these countries had accepted the need for, and principle of, state participation in secondary and higher education, and the education offered in their schools was vastly superior in quality and range, especially in science, to anything offered in secondary schools in England. Arnold prophetically outlined the reforms called for in national and local government in order to end the chaos of *laissez-faire* in education and to provide reorganization of secondary and higher education. The Endowed Schools Act of 1869 recommended that countless bequests and educational benefactions should be brought under endowed schools commissioners, who later became the charity commissioners. The first firm steps towards involving local and national government in education had been taken and the end of voluntary initiative as the basis of school provision was in sight.

In 1870 W. E. Forster introduced the Act that set up elected school boards and began to cover the country systematically with elementary schools supplementing the existing foundations. By 1880 it was possible to insist on compulsory attendance, at least for part of the day. By the end of the century local education authorities and a national Board of Education had been set up with political accountability on one side and the structure of a permanent secretariat of officials on the other.

During the second half of the nineteenth century in England the population increased by more than 75 per cent, and the concentrations in cities became increasingly oppressive. The franchise, which had been narrowly extended in 1832, had by the end of the century become available to nearly all men in the town and in the country, and local government was sustained by the County Councils Act of 1888 and the Local Government Act of 1894. The industrial developments of the first half of the century in England were matched by the later, faster growth of industry and transport in Europe and the United States. Where in the eighteenth century foreign export was a minor feature for a self-supporting nation, by the nineteenth century overseas trade became a survival factor for England, and in the 1870s agriculture was starting upon its sharp decline and England began to depend on imports for its food, for which it paid in industrial or service exports.

II

Alongside the Royal Commissions, the Education Acts, the emerging state support, the accountability of payment by results, and the economic, political, and social changes in England, the work of the educational innovators so far considered from 1850 to 1880 was done. What can now be said of it?

These schools were institutions in protest and their distinctive features can show what was commonly thought to be wrong in practice. The area of knowledge and curriculum is an obvious territory for innovation. Without exception Morley, Ronge, Barbara Bodichon, and William Ellis were interested in presenting a wide range of subjects. They rejected the three R's for poor children and they considered the classics, as they were commonly taught, an impoverished curriculum for well-to-do children, and in this they reiterated what some of the reformers like Williams, Owen, Craig, and the Hills had pioneered, as we have seen, and they anticipated what the Newcastle Commission recommended for the elementary schools in 1861, the Clarendon Commission for the public schools in 1864, and the Taunton Commission for the grammar schools in 1868. Science, history, and very often the elements of economics and social science were thought to be necessary for children of what we should now call secondary age. All of the innovators after 1850 mentioned above were concerned to see that children were taught to think about international matters, and Morley, Ronge, Ellis, and Schmitz of the Isleworth International School tried to approach this through world history in one form or another. These were the years when economic and political power both at home and overseas made the relevance of social science and international affairs obvious in schools. Yet very few followed the lead of Morley, Bodichon, Ellis, Lorimer, or Schmitz.

Foreign languages were another aspect of the same awareness of a world in which communications were becoming steadily more effective. In this whole area of knowledge the innovators showed in the second half of the century that the curriculum of a school was relevant, flexible, and changing, and that science, social science, history, languages, and the arts were more appropriate in educating children than the three R's or the classics.

The leaders in this were middle-class men and women, as they usually were in the first half of the century, but where between 1820 and 1850 there had been an Owenite working-class movement striving for educational innovation, there was nothing to correspond to this between 1850 and 1870. Simon says that 1850–70 were years of prosperity, rapid industrial development, and colonial expansion. He also says that in these years, by the Royal Commissions and Acts of Parliament, the Victorian upper middle class transformed the school system into an effective hierarchical structure in which the Forster Act established elementary schools for the working class in 1870, three years after the Franchise Act of 1867 had added a million artisans to the voters' roll. The connection between the extension of the franchise and mass popular education can easily be seen, and Simon's point is that from 1870 onwards the working class became more explicitly coherent and socialist as the crude tools of mass education and voting powers enabled them to organize political participation and exert pressure.[2]

A teacher's concern for the interests and motivations of children is an index of the importance he attaches to the pupil in the learning process, and in this there is very little to choose between David Williams in 1776, Charles Mayo in 1836, or Johannes Ronge in 1856. The social context is differ-

[2] B. Simon, *Education and the Labour Movement, 1870–1918* (London, 1965), pp. 11–18.

ent, the data are different, and Ronge taught younger children, but the willingness to encourage boys to be initiators is the same.

It is not often realized that co-education for older children was in existence in England before Bedales took it up in 1898, but Henry Morley and Barbara Bodichon accepted it fifty years earlier, although William Ellis did not. Mme. Bodichon was clearly an early champion of women's rights and a resilient opponent of convention whether in education, politics, literature, or sex. Where she would appear, as a member of the affluent liberal intelligentsia, to be politically and socially to the left, Morley would appear to be a self-made man, a *laissez-faire* humanist whose public conscience combined his considerable income with educational concern to produce practical and original results in his schools.

This interest in children as initiators is allied to a deeper concern for the quality of the relationship between the teacher and his pupils, and one revealing aspect of this is the kind of punishment thought appropriate. All of these schools rejected corporal punishment, but each of them retained a sanction of some kind, whether it was a school jury sitting in judgement and passing sentence, or fatigues, correction exercises, or the like. Equally, the competitive motivations stimulated by rewards, marks, ranking, and the snakes-and-ladders of a highly worked-out system, represent the encouraging obverse of punishment. But in all these unorthodox schools of 1850–70 nothing has appeared in relation to methods of correction that has not already been seen in the first half of the century.

One other feature that is common to the innovators of 1850–70 is their radical views on religion. Henry Morley had been trained in a Moravian community and became what may be termed an ethically-minded theist who was not aligned to any doctrinal or ecclesiastical position. Something similar could be said of Johannes Ronge, whose Catholic allegiance was broken so dramatically in the late 1840s before he came to England with his wife and founded what he called the Humanistic Schools. Ronge not only preached his religion of humanity and denounced creeds and churches but he also treated the children in his kindergarten, aged between three and seven, in the spirit of these numinal beliefs, which had many affinities with the spirituality of Froebel's understanding of childhood that Ronge did so much to proclaim. Barbara Bodichon was from a Unitarian family and had no Christian doctrine taught in her school. At the London College of the International Education Society theological studies were excluded from the compulsory course, but optional instruction was offered. William Ellis was more severe still, excluding religious instruction and the reading of the Bible even as an ordinary school book. John Stuart Mill and Bentham were the rationalist saints in Ellis's gallery, although he, together with Mme. Bodichon, knew of the esoteric Swedenborgian position of Buchanan and Wilderspin. Again, Morley, Ellis, and Mme. Bodichon knew of the theories of phrenology, an attempt at a rational theory of psychology that nevertheless had many irrational consequences of an almost religious kind.

This religious unorthodoxy was the cause of deep-seated hostility between the churches, especially the Anglican church and certain free churches, and the innovating schools. Whereas in the period before 1850 Dawes at King's Somborne was an Anglican cleric, as was Mayo at Cheam, and Kay-Shuttleworth was an influential layman, there is no instance of an Anglican among those we have considered from 1850 to 1870 as educational innovators. It is understandable that as one of the two main providers of schools Anglicans should attach great moral significance to the influence that radical institutions exerted on young people, and bearing in mind the intensity of the struggle during the two middle quarters of the century between the ecclesiastical and secular interests for the control of the nation's schools, the generally hostile response of the churches to the educational radicals is to be expected and is an index of the changes in theological orthodoxy in the country in the second half of the century.

The powerful theoretical influences in education in the first half of the century were Rousseau, Pestalozzi, and Fellenberg, together with a generalized liberalism from the French Enlightenment and a combination of English eighteenth-century empiricism and nineteenth-century romanticism. I have tried throughout this study to avoid giving names to large-scale influences without pinning them down by example and illustration; indeed, I have aimed at precise examples without a great deal of generalization in order to let the evidence speak for itself. The point to make here, however, is that the Continental theorists who affected English education directly between 1770 and 1850 had, as might be expected, receded in importance by the third quarter of the century. Their theory and practice had been assimilated by the innovators and England had produced out of its own history and resources an indigenous progressive mode in education of which Henry Morley, Charles Dickens, and William Ellis, together with Combe and Simpson from Scotland, are illustrations in ways that we have seen. The Utilitarians like Mill and Bentham and later Herbert Spencer have more significance than the Continentals, and the theological and scientific arguments, at the centre of which were Huxley and Darwin, needed no imported fuel for their conflagration, although higher and lower criticism of the Bible brought material from Germany and elsewhere. If any one Continental theorist in education had to be named whose influence grew in the second half of the nineteenth century it would be Froebel, and I have already shown how important a part in this was played by Johannes and Bertha Ronge. Buchanan and Wilderspin between 1820 and 1840 made the first real contributions in England to the enlightened education of young children at the kindergarten and infant-school levels, and these two were more influenced by Owen and their own teaching gifts and Swedenborgian beliefs than by Rousseau or Pestalozzi. The Ronges, on the other hand, made a formidable combination of theory and practice and were convinced of the truth of Froebel's educational principles. The organizations that were begun in Manchester which led to the Manchester Froebel Foundation in 1873 and later to a London and national Froebel movement, represent an institutional continuity that Rousseau and Pestalozzi never properly achieved in England.

I have stressed the interest of the innovators in original teaching methods, and the details are scattered through these pages. I have also emphasized and illustrated their interest in moral education in the sense that Castle so excellently sums up at the end of his book:

What matters is that those responsible for the moral education of the young should think more in terms of weaning and development and less in terms of shaping and inoculating.[3]

III

When all is said, however, the evidence shows that the variety and range of educational innovation in the first half of the nineteenth century are far greater than in the period 1850–80. Some of the reasons for this are obvious. Transition from an agrarian to an industrial society, from a powerful landed class to thrusting individualist capitalists, from a traditional to a *laissez-faire* order, made the first half of the century more inchoate. The values of the Enlightenment, of the Romantic movement, and of public-minded Christianity called for education in many forms and schools were founded in great numbers.

By 1850 the needs of the urban masses were relatively clear and the embryonic organization of political and economic power in a working class was beginning to take shape. General compulsory education could not be evaded, must be paid for, and could be seen to be an instrument for cohesion, disruption, and power, and at the same time a matter of conscience for Christians and humanists alike. But the main needs of the new era of mass education were for economic and social continuity without revolution, and the unique role of the middle classes in England is to be seen here. In education, organization of a kind was arrived at in the second half of the century and the elementary school, with a basic curriculum for all children whose parents did not want or were not able to pay for their schooling, was provided. The government of grammar schools and public schools was reformed, and all of this was done in the period 1850–80.

The consolidation of Empire and industry caused schools to spread across the land and produced only the kinds of unorthodoxy in education that we have seen in Morley, Ronge, Bodichon, and Ellis. These do not match the daring of Owen and the Hills and Kay-Shuttleworth or of David Williams, Lady Byron, and the Mayos. Rousseau, Pestalozzi, and Fellen-

[3] E. B. Castle, *Moral Education in Christian Times* (London, 1958), p. 337.

berg are more massive in their educational influence and principle than Bentham or Mill or Spencer. In any case, the Commissions of the 1860s had indicated the innovations needed: the national house was swept and remained only to be garnished. It is more difficult for progressives to be seen to be so when the government is practising some of their best theories.

Here then is a point of rest in this study of innovation in English education. The next point of departure in the progressive movement appears in 1889, when a new school was founded at Abbotsholme in Derbyshire, and significantly this new school looked first, but very briefly, at the Labour movement, and secondly, with intense, critical attention, at the public school.

Part Three

1889–1970

8 The Growth of Schools: 1889–1898

FOR ALL the innovations in the last quarter of the century at Winchester, Rugby, Harrow, and Uppingham that followed the Public Schools Act of 1868, the evidence is still overwhelmingly that in the 1870s, 80s, and 90s classics, 'the grand old fortifying curriculum', took up most of the timetable for everyone. When the Endowed Schools Act of 1869 sought to give legislative strength to the recommendations of the Taunton Commission for the grammar schools, one of its main consequences was to make the grammar schools feel that they were the poor relations of the public schools, and most of the grammar schools of England modelled themselves as far as possible on what the public schools did between 1870 and 1920. The achievement of universal elementary schooling by state provision after 1880 and especially after 1902 was itself the major objective for the education of the poor, and the aftermath of payment by results left its own distinctive mark probably until the 1930s.

By definition the progressive schools in the last decade of the nineteenth century were in protest, with theory and practice to support their claims. By definition they were enthusiasts who not only protested against something but also urged a positive alternative with conviction. But these schools urged different alternatives: some were for boys or girls only, others were co-educational; some were boarding-schools, some day; some were based on religious convictions, some were firmly rationalist, some were neutral; some accepted a hierarchy of authority in the school, others rendered it minimal. One thing is clear: from 1889 to the beginning of the First World War the progressive movement in education was a middle-class movement for middle-class children, substantially as we have seen to be the case for the period 1850–80.

17 ABBOTSHOLME

CECIL REDDIE was the first headmaster of Abbotsholme in Derbyshire, founded in 1889, and he was the first of the educational radicals of the new wave in the nineteenth and twentieth centuries.[1]

Reddie was born in London in 1858, but was orphaned by the age of twelve and had the rest of his education in Scotland and Germany. He went to Fettes College in Edinburgh, a public school based on the English pattern, for more than seven years and then to the University of Edinburgh, where, although he had taken the classical training at school, he ultimately read natural sciences, having started on medicine but withdrawn from it. On graduating he won a scholarship which enabled him to study in Germany for over two years, and there he took a distinguished doctorate in chemistry. On his return to Scotland in 1884 he worked as a university demonstrator and then for a year or so returned to Fettes to teach chemistry, from which he transferred to Clifton, a public school near Bristol, to teach science for nearly two years. Clifton, founded in 1862, while giving pride of place to the classics, specialized in systematic scientific teaching. However, despite this novelty, which no doubt had attracted Reddie in the first place, he came to feel 'that reform within the old type of school would be difficult if not impossible' and at the age of twenty-nine he applied for the headship of a new day school in London with the support of Dr. Wilson, his Clifton headmaster. Reddie did not get the post but he says that Wilson's cordial recommendation put the idea into his head that he might 'open a school in which our dreams and aspirations might, perchance, find fulfilment'.[2]

During the 1880s Reddie was an active socialist, influenced by the writings of Carlyle and Ruskin, of Hyndman and William Morris, of Edward Carpenter and Walt Whitman. In 1883–4 in Göttingen as a doctoral student he heard a number of lectures on Marxism, and when he returned to Edinburgh he joined the Fellowship of the New Life, a movement devoted

[1] For a fuller consideration of Reddie and his work, see Chapter 10 below.
[2] Dr. Wilson on retirement became a canon of Worcester and later lived close to Bedales School and had some influence on Badley.

to purifying cupidity in society by the labours of reformed and redeemed individuals who, through a self-supporting life based on manual work in communities, through education and religious communion and steadfast attention to social change, could reconstruct society. The Fellowship was started in 1883 and one of its leaders, J. C. Kenworthy, wrote later in the Fellowship's journal: 'In economics we are Socialists; in our ideal we are Communists, in politics we are, some of us, Anarchists of Peace.'[3]

The Fellowship was seeking the ideal society and church combined, and although its communitarian methods were supposed to apply to the town as well as the country, the communities which actually came into existence were mainly in the country or on the outskirts of towns like Nottingham and Sheffield. The Garden City movement was a later application of the Fellowship principle.[4] It is interesting to note that Cecil Reddie, a member of the Fellowship of the New Life in the 1880s, moved to Welwyn Garden City on his retirement from Abbotsholme in 1927 and lived there till his death in 1932.

Abbotsholme, the school in which Reddie's dreams and aspirations 'might, perchance, find fulfilment', was called in the preliminary announcements 'The New School' and named 'A Fellowship School' in the journal of the Fellowship of the New Life, *The Sower*, of July 1889 – this later became *Seed Time*:

> Some time ago [actually 1886] the New Fellowship issued a proposal for the establishment of a school on lines consistent with the principles which it advocates. Up to the present, circumstances have not admitted of the practical realization of this scheme under the direct auspices of the Fellowship, but the members hail with great satisfaction a separate effort which some friends and associates are about to make to establish just such a school as was contemplated in the circular which the Fellowship issued. An attempt will be made to develop harmoniously all the faculties of the boy – to train him how to *live*, in fact, and become a rational member of society.... Negotiations are almost completed for the lease of a commodious house called Abbotsholme, with

---

[3] *Seed Time*, Apr. 1895.
[4] See Armytage, *Heavens Below*, pp. 370–84.

adjoining land, on the banks of the Dove, near Rocester, Derbyshire, a picturesque yet accessible region. The school will be opened in October next [1889].

A preliminary announcement appeared in the summer of 1889 informing the public that the school was going to open and naming Edward Carpenter, R. F. Muirhead, and William Cassels as partners with Cecil Reddie in the venture. The document admitted the importance of the public schools because they aimed to cultivate not only intellectual powers but also the physical, social, and moral nature of boys as well, and said that these features were appreciated abroad as well as in England: 'Any improvements therefore in education should be based on the ground-idea of the "Public School" system.'[5] Having made these polite preliminaries and shown the company in which Abbotsholme should be considered, the attack was then developed. The public schools were out of touch with contemporary needs, boys spent far too much time on the classics, for which in any case the majority of them were quite unsuited. A modern curriculum in history, languages, and science was neglected and no time was given to mental and physical hygiene or to the study of society outside the school. The games fetish was denounced, together with the desperate waste of time spent in compulsory spectating by the mass of boys so that few interests could be developed other than athletic 'shop': 'The want simply of more ideas is one of the chief sources of the corrupt imagination and conversation found in schools.'[6] Reddie considered the university hold on the public schools was damaging and proposed to start a school on the lines suggested by 'the modern Science and Art of Education'. There was to be a carefully worked out programme of general education caring for physical and manual skills, for artistic and imaginative development, for literary and intellectual growth, and for moral and religious training. Manual labour in the house, the garden, and the field was to be as important in physical training as games, and would familiarize the boys of affluent parents with work which was commonly done for them by servants. The boys were to be taught tailoring, boot

[5] *A New School*, pamphlet published Apr. 1889.
[6] Ibid.

making, and cookery – we can here detect the influence of Ruskin and Edward Carpenter, but as a matter of fact Reddie did not get the tailoring, boot making, and cookery going.

Boys were to learn the rudiments of agriculture and gardening and the care of animals, which besides anything else would be 'a sound preparation for colonial life'. Their school was to be made to look beautiful, and as far as possible by the boys themselves: 'In this we shall follow Ruskin and Thring.' Carpentry, carving, metalwork, and other crafts would be taught to make it possible to achieve such aims.

English, not classics, was to be the foundation of the curriculum, and French or German was to be the first foreign language. Latin was also to be taught to everyone without being given any special prominence. The country and industry in towns near at hand were to be explored in excursions, expeditions, and visits, the sciences were to be attended to and music was to be given a high place. Religion would be undogmatic and non-sectarian and services beautiful, simple, and not according to any particular communion.

While boys were to be prepared for entry to 'the Universities of Britain and Germany' and for other careers of all kinds, Abbotsholme did not intend to cram boys for prizes and scholarships and would use only the mornings for classroom subjects. This was to be a school which would be aware of the British Empire and was aimed at national regeneration, and Reddie, for whom the faintest symbol had the lure of Circe, chose for a few years red, white, and blue as the school colours.

Abbotsholme was a school for English boys aged from eleven to eighteen 'belonging to the directing classes', and it was laid down as a principle that cordial trust was to be developed between boys and masters and all members of the school. The teaching of hygiene involved systematic courses in sex instruction, and necessitated carefully designed buildings and specially made clothes for the boys, introducing patterns which later became common in other schools – a knickerbocker suit, either no hat or a beret.[7] This was all very different from Eton suits,

---

[7] Hely Hutchinson Almond, headmaster 1862–1903 of Loretto, a boys' public school for 150 near Edinburgh, encouraged fitness and toughness in his boys by introducing in the 1860s open windows, flannel shirts, tweed shorts, morning cold baths, no caps, no 'tuck' between meals. Fettes and Loretto have always been great rivals.

F

stiff collars, and top hats or bowlers, the usual uniform at other schools, and was part of the dress reform movement of the time.

Reddie produced the most minutely detailed plans for every part of Abbotsholme life. He was building the prototype school from which he hoped others would follow as Abbotsholme 'colonies'. He was strongly opposed to co-education, and his ideal was a boarding-school for about one hundred boys aged eleven to eighteen. He quickly quarrelled with his partners and one term after Abbotsholme opened Reddie was the sole owner and remained so until he retired in 1927. In the first decade the school prospered, but from 1900 onwards its progress was erratic; after a temporary revival in the post-war boom, things went from bad to worse until in 1927 there were only two boys in the school. The main reason for this failure was Reddie himself. He wished to direct everything and quarrelled with almost everybody – colleagues, parents, boys, Old Abbotsholmians, other educationalists, tradesmen, women, the plutocracy, the aristocracy, the working classes. Few things in England were done well, most things in Germany were, with the exception of the period of the First World War, which deeply disturbed Reddie's convictions though it did not prevent him explaining why Britain did not deserve to rule its Empire.

The Fellowship of the New Life came to an end in 1898 and by that time Reddie was no longer a socialist, but he remained a radical, this time of the right, with political views as extreme and idiosyncratic in the other direction. Even though he nearly ruined Abbotsholme, others more stable than he were excited by what he started in Derbyshire and carried forward and developed his ideas both in England and also, more widely, in Germany, Switzerland, France, and elsewhere. In 1927, when a council of Old Abbotsholmians was re-establishing the school after Reddie's retirement, a pamphlet was published in which it was stated that nearly one hundred schools in various parts of the world had sprung directly or indirectly from the 'New School'. Abbotsholme must be undoubtedly the first school, as Reddie must be the first man, to come into our reckoning during the last decade of the last century.

Colin Sharp took over from Reddie in 1927 and the school was saved and built up its numbers beyond anything Reddie achieved. Where Reddie centralized Sharp delegated, where Reddie dominated Sharp suggested. We can examine the changes in detail later as they took place under Sharp and his successors.

18 BEDALES

ONE of Reddie's first appointments in 1889 was John Haden Badley, a man of twenty-four whose affiliations and thinking appeared very similar to Reddie's but whose background was very different. Badley and his three elder sisters were born into the family of a quietly affluent Midlands doctor at Dudley, near Birmingham. His childhood was secure and affectionate in a restrained and disciplined style. His parents were enlightened in many things although not demonstrative, and close affection and regard bound Badley and his sisters throughout their long lives. He went to Rugby, from which he got the top classics exhibition to Trinity College, Cambridge, where he took a First in the Classics Tripos. He did not want to enter academic life, was dissatisfied with the thought of teaching classics at Rugby or any other public school, and at this moment of uncertainty in 1889 was told of Abbotsholme, about to open.[1]

Badley had read and admired Edward Carpenter's writings, and was and remained generally sympathetic to the left in politics. Abbotsholme seemed to embody his own social thinking and at last gave an unequivocal lead on his future career. Almost all the distinguishing features of Abbotsholme outlined above chimed exactly with Badley's thinking, and he threw himself with immense satisfaction into the life of the school. There were three main problems for him: the first was Reddie himself, with his dominating energy, the second was Reddie's antipathy to girls and women (with one or two exceptions, including the accomplished and beautiful Duchess of Sutherland), and the third was Badley's wish to marry.

It is clear from the accounts of life at Abbotsholme in those first three years that Badley was a mainstay of the school and

[1] For further treatment of Badley and Bedales, see Chapter 21 below.

that he learned a vast amount from Reddie, Badley thought that Reddie would not accept his wife at Abbotsholme, and in any case Badley knew his wife, herself a teacher of music, would want to interest herself in the school and that Reddie was 'averse from giving to women's influence the scope and weight in the school that we felt it should have'.[2] So Badley decided to start a school of his own with his wife's help, although as he says, after more than two years at Abbotsholme, 'I could not contemplate continuing school-work except under similar conditions.'

When he told Reddie of his intention he had hoped that proposed imitation would flatter, but Reddie saw it all in terms of disloyalty, intellectual theft, and institutional rivalry. According to Badley, Reddie proposed that the young couple should open what amounted to a preparatory school to Abbotsholme on lines laid down by Reddie. This Badley refused as he wanted freedom to work with older children too, so he resigned in the hope that Reddie would come to think that his influence was really being extended by new and clearly indebted foundations.

On the other hand a revolutionary new school owing the originality of its ideas entirely to one man was in the third year of its life, and one of its most promising masters, not yet twenty-seven and with only two and a half years of experience, wanted to take the public notice given to Abbotsholme as a support to his own new venture. Although Reddie may have been domineering and in any case was powerless to prevent Badley from carrying out his intention, his exasperation was not altogether surprising. Certainly, Reddie for many years was publicly hostile to Bedales; Badley appears to have made no reply, although many members of his staff, some of them refugees from Abbotsholme and Reddie, said some very uninhibited things about the monarch of Abbotsholme.[3]

Badley set out his aims and intentions in a pamphlet published in 1892 before his school was opened.[4] He had found a suitable house and grounds called Bedales near Haywards

[2] J. H. Badley, *Memories and Reflections* (London, 1955), p. 119.
[3] See C. Reddie, 'The Relation of Abbotsholme to Bedales', in *The Abbotsholmian*, vol. ii, no. 3 (July 1908), pp. 13–16.
[4] *Bedales (Hayward's Heath, Sussex), A School for Boys: Outline of its Aims and System*, 16 pages.

Heath in Sussex, and here he and his wife began in January 1893 his school for boys aged nine to fifteen with due acknowledgement and deep obligation to the New School, Abbotsholme. Like Reddie, Badley began with polite deference to the public school as one who loved in boyhood 'the place of *Tom Brown's School-Days* ... and later trod the proudest court in Cambridge ... and who respected and admired the many admirable points in these and the like grand ancient institutions'. Then he showed how faulty they were by the narrowness and intensity of the competition, their early specialization, and the limits of their concept of character training. One new idea appears in the Bedales prospectus, befitting a man married a few months before the school opened – the presence and direct influence of women. For the rest, the ideas are almost identical with those of Cecil Reddie, sometimes differently ordered, co-operation is stressed instead of competition, and the older boy is to be trusted with a measure of direction. There must be nothing of luxury about the school, but something of comfort and beauty. However, not a word about 'the sons of the directing classes'. And no mention of the German example.

Three boys came in January 1893 and by 1894 there were thirty, with seven academic and domestic staff, and the school grew slowly. In 1898 the best-known feature of Bedales appeared. By now the children were aged nine to eighteen and four girls joined the school for lessons and other activities, living in a house near at hand. This is not foreshadowed in the early prospectuses and Badley maintained that co-education grew as the principle of natural development in the school suggested this change – the mother of a Bedalian boy, widow of an Oxford don, suggested that her daughter and three other girls should join the school and that she would look after the house in which they at first lived. Badley said that he and his wife had had the education of girls in mind from the first, but it was impracticable, and in this somewhat haphazard way the education of the four girls became co-education.[5]

The Bedales curriculum and organization were very like

---

[5] One account of this development appears in J. H. Badley, *Bedales: A Pioneer School* (London, 1923), p. 69. Another account is in his *Memories and Reflections*, p. 136.

Abbotsholme's, even including the earth-closet sanitation in which both Reddie and Badley believed, giving back to the earth what it needed and preserving the natural cycle. Physical and manual skills, artistic and imaginative development, literary and intellectual growth, and moral and religious training had the same kind of nurture as at Abbotsholme, and Bedales was at first known as an offshoot of Abbotsholme.[6]

Reddie and Badley were unorthodox in their religious belief, though not in the same way. Reddie had developed a liturgy at Abbotsholme, where there was and is a special chapel. Bedales, although possessing in 1901 a school psalm and hymn book, used its assembly hall for services: Badley's position was somewhat that of a Unitarian moralist not much interested in religious symbolism.

There was probably more freedom in school government at Bedales than at Abbotsholme in the sense that Badley directed less from the centre than Reddie. Each school was opposed to cramming, and it was not until 1913 that Bedales took the General Schools Certificate, thinking the London Matriculation too cramping for the school's general education programmes.

Bedales grew up in its own way and developed an identity very different from Abbotsholme's. When it became co-educational in 1898 and moved to its present site near Petersfield in 1900 it became better known than Abbotsholme. Badley was far more successful in building up his school than Reddie, and a measure of his success is that a scholar like E. C. Mack can nominate Bedales as the parent of the progressive movement in England and make no mention of Abbotsholme.[7] Bedales may have owed its origins to Abbotsholme but within ten years of its beginning it was a very different place, more unorthodox

---

[6] See *Pall Mall* Gazette, 22 Aug. 1892 and 5 Oct. 1892; *Review of Reviews*, 15 Nov. 1893.

[7] Mack, *The Public Schools and British Opinion since 1860* (New York, 1941), p. 255. There are various other small errors in the sections of this important book concerned with progressive education. J. H. Simpson was headmaster of Rendcomb College not of Churnside, the pseudonym he gave to the school in his account of it in *Sane Schooling* (Mack, p. 382). A printing error calls Bembridge School Bunbridge (p. 376). Mack speaks of the foundation of a number of schools in the inter-war period quite correctly but includes Friends' School, Saffron Walden (founded 1702), Sidcot (founded 1808), and Sibford (1842) (p. 376).

than Abbotsholme in many ways, less doctrinaire, more democratic. Reddie and Abbotsholme represent one shade in the spectrum of educational radicalism and Badley and Bedales another.

19 CLAYESMORE

ALEXANDER DEVINE was born in 1865, the same year as John Haden Badley. Devine was the son of a flamboyant Manchester merchant, whose ancestors were Irish, and a mother whose ancestors were Greek. Devine *père* had begun life as a Roman Catholic but moved to Congregationalism as time passed and Alexander (who was nearly always known as 'Lex' later on, and 'Mr. Lex' to his pupils) thus grew up in a religious background of unusual fluidity. Devine senior was a remarkably temperamental businessman whose inspirations led almost as often to bankruptcy as success and his son as a result had a limited schooling in Manchester day schools, leaving early to serve an apprenticeship to a printer and later becoming a journalist on Manchester papers. Like many young reporters he had to work in the police courts of the city, and his warm and energetic temperament responded to the needs of young offenders often only a year or two junior to himself. He became familiar with the appalling living conditions of many of these lads and their friends and the complete lack of leisure amenities. When he was twenty years of age he was the prime mover in starting the Working Lads Association in Chorlton-cum-Medlock and became secretary to three clubs. Like his father, Lex proved quite unable to balance his budget and his committee asked him to leave. In 1888 he began the Gordon Boys' Home in Manchester, having engaged local support which became much greater when, to the chagrin of many, Lex engineered a visit to the home by Prince Albert Victor of Wales in October 1888 during the latter's short scheduled stay in Manchester. This home was part of what amounted to a personal probation service which Lex had started for boy first offenders in the Manchester area. He lived with them and he worked for them, trying to place them in jobs, to guide and befriend them, and to steer them clear of criminal careers. But again Lex could not work with his supporters, in that as he saw it he could not get the expansion he wanted and as they saw it he was reckless about financial practicalities.

Devine migrated to London in the early 1890s and for a few years tried a number of different jobs, including what he called 'a reformatory for bad boys of the Public Schools', his Gordon House venture transposed to a different social key. Creditors still wanted to be paid and Devine had to move more than once either to meet or to evade them. All through his life he displayed his father's irresponsibility about money, professing in a euphoric way that the importance of his projects mattered more than balancing accounts. On this his friends would say he had a blind spot and his enemies would say he was dishonest. Each would admit that he appears to have had unquenchable confidence. J. H. Badley said of him:

> [He never could control money and was] quite unable to keep check on his expenditure, or to think of loans as anything but gifts. In each fresh crisis he would turn to anyone, friend or stranger, for help with which to extricate himself....[1]

By 1896 he had decided not to continue dealing with delinquents and problem children from the public schools because he had come to realize that there was much at fault with the schools themselves. So he founded a school to be 'a liberal, democratic state, not a reactionary dictatorship' and it opened at Enfield in Essex in February 1896. The estate which Devine took on a lease was called Clayesmore, and the school kept this name when it moved to Pangbourne in Berkshire in 1902, to Northwood Park near Winchester in 1914, and finally to its present location at Iwerne Minster in Dorset in 1933.

Devine had acquired a number of connections with public-school headmasters by 1896 and they continued to recommend boys to him who had a difficult background; therefore his plan to promote 'a reformed school rather than a reformatory' took time to realize – indeed some of the first boys at Clayesmore transferred there from the earlier 'reformatory' Glebelands.

[1] *Memories and Reflections*, p. 202.

After very few years Devine refused to accept any boy who had been expelled from another school and decided to act on recommendations only, although his self-generated idea of himself as Puck (his biographer suggests that it co-existed dangerously with a picture of himself as Napoleon) sometimes permitted him to stretch a point for a particularly stimulating malefactor.[2]

Devine visited Badley and Bedales quite frequently during term time and vacation, and they speak of one another with considerable regard. Badley had a number of reservations about Devine, as will be seen, but still he says: 'he remains in my memory as a man of powers as remarkable and of charm as great, as I have known in anyone.'[3] Devine also knew Reddie, but with him he had little in common as a man, with which Reddie pungently agreed. But Devine knew Abbotsholme's educational principles and the connection with Bedales, and writing in 1903 to Edward Lyttleton, then headmaster of Haileybury, he said with characteristic aplomb:

> Clayesmore is the third and latest of the 'new' schools; and though I have not had the advantage or disadvantage of discipleship to either Reddie or Badley, I am quite prepared to admit that there is something in the aim of the three schools which is identical.

By 1900 Devine had a school of fifty boys at Enfield, and he began a typical and unusual venture early in the school's history. Bearing in mind his Manchester work for underprivileged and poor people and his concern to share his advantages, Devine decided to invite 'ordinary working men' to visit the 'New School' at Clayesmore. He advertised in a generalized form by letters in the papers and soon had a stream of visitors at the weekends, some coming regularly. There was seldom any formal business but always the opportunity for talk and tea and the chance for boys, masters, and headmaster to make this kind of contact with men whose daily life was very different from their own. In inviting the visitors Devine had

---

[2] F. Whitbourn, *Lex: Alexander Devine Founder of Clayesmore School* (London, 1937), p. 221.
[3] *Memories and Reflections*, p. 202.

asked them to come 'to relieve him from the small world of miniature folk over which he reigned supreme', and over the period of five years at Enfield for which the arrangment lasted it is estimated that three thousand visits were paid by these guests. It was not possible to continue similar contacts at Pangbourne or Northwood Park by reason of distance, and in any case perhaps Devine's outlook was somewhat changed by then.

Like Reddie, Devine remained a lifelong bachelor and like him he did not approve of co-education. He had declared in his early prospectus:

> The School makes no pretence to the possession of any elaborate new system; we are in need of no educational fads.... The school makes a practical protest against the neglect of the average boy.[4]

He did not attack the public schools with the sustained criticism that Reddie and Badley brought to bear, and in the letter to Lyttleton already mentioned he criticized Reddie because:

> he has apparently shut his eyes deliberately to the virtues and values of our good old schools, has resolutely ignored the useful and splendid work of individual headmasters and takes his stand on the platform of 'There is but one Education, the new Education and Reddie is its prophet!'

Devine had had no direct experience of public schools either as a boy or as a master, and as a teacher of misfits he really wanted to reform what he knew of them. But he was fond of men of title, fame, and money, was a great name-dropper, and knew on which side his bread was buttered. Nevertheless, he admitted to Lyttleton that he found Reddie's ideas 'sound at the root, and ... great because they are scientific ideas'. But his characteristic complaint was that Reddie was carrying them out in a small way. Devine was an impresario who wore a cap and gown, lived at Claridge's, became in 1919 the minister plenipotentiary for Montenegro in London, enjoying his status and decorations, and inviting as many men of distinction to

[4] Pp. 10–11.

lend their names to Clayesmore as possible. He offered the suggestion to Reddie and Badley that the three schools should form the ABC of educational reform, which amused Badley and infuriated Reddie. At the same time Devine kept some of the practices of the public schools: classical and modern sides in the sixth with the tutor system; Eton jackets and top hats on Sundays in winter and spring terms, straw hats with bands in the summer; fagging on a hierarchical basis; ritual caning for certain types of offenders in the library by the headmaster – often at 10 p.m.

There were, nevertheless, many ideas from Abbotsholme and Bedales at Clayesmore: the morning run and shower, manual labour and digging and building, the shorts and Norfolk suit for everyday wear. General education was maintained at least until the boy was fifteen with much the same range of options for everyone. Specialization came after that and so the classical grind was avoided. Devine disapproved of the games fetish and the dominance of 'colours', and first of all provided a variety of games and secondly offered estate work as a required alternative on one or two afternoons in the week. He insisted on time being allowed in each boy's programme for art, craft, and music. No public examinations were taken below the age of fifteen and at a later age only when necessary. In any case Devine, like so many other teachers considered earlier in this book, wanted to reform the usual type of informational check and to produce tests of understanding and real comprehension. Although not well-equipped technically in psychology, he wanted teaching at Clayesmore to be based on a proper understanding of the importance of interest as a basis for mental discipline rather than compulsion. Equally he wanted his pupils to be challenged by the genuine reasoning required in experimental inquiry and the initiative expected for research or project work. Like Reddie he was critical of the lack of preparation in the craft of teaching for public-school masters. Devine wanted schools to accept responsibility for the apprenticeship of beginners, although he had no formal training himself.

He was a difficult man to work with and few masters stayed with him for long. Payment of salaries was several times delayed over the years, and in his open letter to new staff he said blandly: 'the married or about-to-be married Master is a difficulty, I admit. During term-time you have the boys and your wife. Which are you going to neglect?' He commanded and expected loyalty from masters and boys but seemed to be jealous of marked popularity in a colleague, and more than once his biographer tells of Devine's tendency to side with boys in scoring off colleagues, as when he took boys off on swims late at night unknown to and against the orders of the housemaster. One of his beliefs was that the boy is always more or less of a statesman, balancing masters' and parental interference to a nicety and creating a policy to meet each situation.

In the early prospectuses there are references to 'self-regulated independence', to 'a system of self-government', and to 'greater liberty than is common', but details are lacking on the working out of these things. There is one gnomic and unwittingly ambiguous sentence in connection with discipline: 'The School does not legislate either for the mature man or for the incorrigible offender.' Devine himself was too much of a virtuoso to develop the settled regime with colleagues necessary for the school to grow steadily as a democracy.

In 1904, two years after moving to Pangbourne, the bailiffs came in at the end of a term and took off the furniture while Devine photographed the scene for his album as 'An incident in the history of the school' and took a bet with the removers that the furniture would have to be brought back. His friends founded a limited company and Devine was able to win his bet at the cost of becoming a salaried headmaster with a bursar appointed to care for the school's finances, and for ten years (which Devine called 'his years of slavery') the school prospered. In 1914 the ownership of the school reverted to Devine and he moved it with about one hundred boys from Pangbourne to Northwood Park. During the ten years when the general control of business matters was in the hands of a governing body there was an improved chance of stability for young staff, and the historians of the school record that despite the difficult and possessive attitudes of Devine some wise masters gave a steadiness to the school which enabled it to grow at that time.

The war provided as many hardships for Claysmore as for other schools of its kind, and this put burdens on Devine. The school had further difficulties when Devine himself went to Montenegro in 1915 and again in 1917 at the invitation of the Red Cross to inquire into the fate of Montenegrin refugees – he had been a war correspondent there as a young reporter in the Balkan Wars of the 1880s. Despite his absences for some months on each occasion the school continued, and after the war began a boom which subsided somewhat in the years of depression which followed. Devine fell ill in 1927 and was never really fit again before his death at Clayesmore in 1930.

The vice-master, who had been Devine's deputy for nine years, succeeded him and the school moved to its present location in Dorset three years after Devine's death. In 1935 numbers had fallen to about fifty and bankruptcy threatened the school again; a limited company of friends and old boys was formed to rescue Clayesmore once more. Within a year under a new head the numbers had risen to one hundred and twenty and have continued to rise – this recovery being financially strengthened by the Desmond Coke bequest in the mid-1930s. In the 1960s we read:

> Clayesmore is a Public School which is deliberately kept to a moderate size with the object of enabling the Master and every member of the staff to know each boy as an individual. The strength of 210–218 is nevertheless large enough for a full corporate life with a complete range of activities.[5]

The *Book of Clayesmore School* claims that from its earliest days Clayesmore has been a pioneer school in education and that many of its ideas which were regarded as revolutionary when first adopted are now accepted as sound educational practice. It quotes Devine's words incorporating the importance of the interest of the learner and the psychological understanding of the teacher and reaffirms them as the educational aim and faith of Clayesmore today, claiming that they blend with the great character-founding traditions of the English public school. Manual work in the open air (which the *Book of Clayesmore School* claims, perhaps misleadingly, that

---

[5] *The Book of Clayesmore School*, p. 1. There is in addition a preparatory school for about one hundred boys aged eight to thirteen years, eight miles from the main school.

Clayesmore pioneered) continues and so do creativeness in the arts and crafts together with the enjoyment of the country, and all of these 'without any sacrifice of learning'. Another account of the school's work puts it like this:

> ... while adapting itself to the growing need for success in examinations, the School still holds by its first vision. Every boy is encouraged to make something or do something for the common service ... and far from over-working the boy who is preparing for examinations, it refreshes him.... Verses are produced, printed and bound into books, trees are felled, land is tilled and music made, pictures are painted, loud speakers installed for out-of-door occasions, walls built, concrete laid, trenches dug, the School cinema operated, costumes and scenery devised for plays, lighting effects produced, animals cared for.... Through many of these avenues boys are led to careers at least as happily as through the examination room.[6]

The Memorial Chapel opened in 1956 offers a very different setting for the Anglican order of service from the evening services in the school of Devine's day (though he enjoyed Northwood Park partly because it had its own chapel). He preached often to the school and later in the evening held in his own study an informal gathering of boys which was characteristically called a levee, where reading, story telling, singing, and piano music were mingled with conversation and yarn-spinning.

Clayesmore had and has many of the features of the 'New School' movement while being nearer to the traditional public school than either Abbotsholme or Bedales (the school has been for some years a member of the Headmasters' Conference). Like the two earlier schools it had a remarkable person as its founder-headmaster with whom it is easy to be exasperated. To be sure he became a poseur, a snob, an adventurer, but he inspired shrewd men to enable him despite many crises to run a fairly radical school for thirty-four years and clearly his personal magnetism attracted boys. His biographer may have laid the colour on rather thickly, but the likeness is there:

[6] *The Public and Preparatory Schools Yearbook* (London, 1964), p. 115.

Lex's boys worshipped him, but they were not blind to his weaknesses. They were ready to laugh at him among themselves; but never would they betray him to any outsider.... He may not have paid his bills ... he may have broken his promises ... but his boys loved him.[7]

He did not attract Reddie at all, who wrote, when two masters dismissed from Abbotsholme after the 'great row' of 1900 went to Clayesmore and two others to Bedales:

If you please, a great effort has been made to get me to enter into a sort of federation ... with these two schools for the sake of pressing the claims of the New School Movement upon the public attention. Carefully worded articles ... talk of the three schools as if like lovebirds on one perch they were all billing and cooing together in the most fraternal manner.... By what we know of these two places we can only say the heroes [the four masters] have gone to their own Valhalla.[8]

We have already quoted some of Badley's comments on Devine and Clayesmore, and we finish this section on the school with his shrewd and sympathetic assessment of its founder:

It was in the early years [of Bedales] that I first met one of the most remarkable men I have known.... As Head Master [Devine] was a curious combination of sound educational ideals, great ambitions, boundless self-confidence and an artless egoism. He had – so I thought – little judgment in choosing his staff, and it was only by a process of trial and error that he found some devoted helpers. Of boys, on the other hand, he had a profound understanding ... and won from them a corresponding loyalty and affection.... Puckish humour and an endless fund of amusing stories and his charming manner could carry off the constant self-dramatisation which gave him at times more than a touch of the charlatan.[9]

[7] Whitbourn, *Alexander Devine*, p. 138.
[8] From typed record dictated by Cecil Reddie in Abbotsholme archives.
[9] *Memories and Reflections*, p. 202.

20 KING ALFRED'S

THE last school founded before 1900 to be considered is very different in its origins from any of the three schools already mentioned. In July 1897 a preliminary circular was distributed to householders in the north-west London residential suburbs of Hampstead and Golders Green outlining 'A Proposed Rational School' and issued in the name of 'a few parents residing in this neighbourhood'. The circular in its preamble stated that nearly all the high schools and private schools of that decade 'were out of touch with the broader and healthier views of the training of children that science and the scientific study of child nature have roused'. This rational spirit ought to find expression in books and in periodicals but also in institutional form in a school. It was proposed, therefore, 'if sufficient support is accorded to the scheme', to start a school in Hampstead where boys could be educated up to the age of twelve in preparation for entry to the public schools, or to sixteen after which they could prepare for their careers. Girls were to be educated so that at sixteen they could prepare themselves to enter one or other of the women's colleges, or at age eighteen they could take up a career which needed no specialist training.

The school was to have a number of distinctive features. As the beginnings might have to be gradual the expected age-range was eight to twelve years and classes would be limited to twelve or fifteen children in each. The aim of the school was to provide an individual training in mental, physical, and moral development, calling upon the help of a medical officer with a special knowledge of children and keeping thorough and cumulative records of each child as he or she moved through the school. As far as the arrangement of studies went, the school was to make every effort to co-ordinate the curricula in order to avoid subject-separation and to enrich the children's understanding. Learning was to be for its own sake and the increasing maturity which came from it, and as a consequence all prizes or awards were to be eschewed and the pressures of a competitive system avoided. There was to be no homework, at least for the juniors, and while it was hoped that the school would exemplify a religious spirit, no direct teaching of a religious creed would be permitted. Co-education would be a principle of organization on the grounds that this was in line with family living, and as a supporting argument the pamphlet says that educating boys and girls together 'is the custom in Scotch schools' and that it was well tried in England – not a valid statement in respect of secondary school children, for whom co-education was (and still is) in England a minority practice. The promoters thought that a school based on these rational principles would produce far less strain, and 'the need for the present extravagantly long holidays will cease'. They accordingly proposed ten weeks' holiday each year: two weeks at Easter, one at Christmas, and seven in the summer. Finally, they proposed that the school should be controlled by an elected governing body which should, in turn, elect a small executive committee.

As a result of this circular the King Alfred School Society came into being, with formal registration of the Society under the Companies Act in June 1898. A number of the matters outlined in the preliminary circular of July 1897 were modified or extended in the Memorandum of Association. Among the objects for which the Society was established was 'to carry on Schools to give practical expression to the best theories of Education extant, and particularly to the theories enunciated by Educational reformers, such as Pestalozzi, Froebel, Herbart, Herbert Spencer, Louis Compton Miall, and others working on similar lines'. In addition the Society was committed 'to promote the advancement of Educational Science ... by the diffusion of knowledge relating thereto', and to establish colleges or departments for students of education in order to equip them professionally to teach in the Society's schools or similar foundations. In fact the Society founded only King Alfred School, no training college or department, and its membership has tended to be the parents, staff, and old pupils of the school together with a few well-known educational radicals like Mrs. Beatrice Ensor and J. H. Badley, who became vice-presidents of the Society. Conferences have been held, but it is true to say that the expansionist plans of the King Alfred School Society of 1898 have not been realized.

The signatories of the Memorandum of Association and the

first members of the Society's Council were F. W. Miall, a journalist, Cecil J. Sharp, the well-known collector of folk-music, described as a musician, Alice Mullins, designated the wife of E. Roscoe Mullins, Hans Thornycroft, sculptor, Gerald C. Maberly, barrister-at-law, Isabel White Wallis, wife of E. White Wallis, and J. Godfrey Hickson, solicitor. These were the guarantors, none of them practising educators (although Sharp taught music at King Alfred's in the early days), none of them aiming to be the head of the school or school to be founded which 'shall be conducted upon curricula based upon the theories hereinbefore mentioned, and not upon the requirements of examining bodies, and the preparation of pupils for examinations, prizes, scholarships, and honours shall be avoided'. However, in addition, pupils over twelve could be prepared for entrance examinations to other institutions, or if over fifteen for scholarships or prizes at some place of further education. Thus competition was avoided in internal organization but pupils able to contend for scholarships or transfer examinations were not to be penalized. Parents of pupils were to have representation on the governing body if they were members of the Society, and the school was to be inspected from time to time by a person sympathetic to the Society's aims and chosen by 'some public educational authority wholly independent of the Society'.

The school was opened in Ellerdale Road, Hampstead, in 1898 under its first headmaster, Charles E. Rice, who had been one of the first two masters at Bedales with Badley in 1893. For four years, from 1893 to 1897, he taught mainly science there, but he was a man of considerable range of intellectual interest and practical skill. He introduced exploratory and experimental methods in nature study, he taught wood- and metalwork together with some English and mathematics. He had intended to train as a doctor and retained an interest in research, leaving Bedales in 1897 to go to the Royal College of Science to pursue further studies. It was with this background that he was invited to become the first headmaster of King Alfred School in 1898. Badley remarks: 'He was the first of a dozen members of our staff who have gone from their experience at Bedales to become Heads of schools of their own and thus helped to diffuse more widely the new educational ideal.'[1]

Rice found conducting a school in a number of semi-detached houses in a London suburb very different from Haywards Heath, where Bedales then was. The children lived at home and were not available all the time, and although Bedales started to become co-educational in 1898 it had not been so in 1897 when Rice left. Bedales was concerned with country activities, like estate work and farming, impossible to pursue at King Alfred's. Bedales had a liberal Christian basis and King Alfred's was firmly rationalist. Badely was the owner-legislator of Bedales, democratic though he was; the headmaster at King Alfred's had the Council of the King Alfred Society, usually meeting monthly, as his potential advisers, and while the evidence over the years is that the Council on the whole gave the headmaster and his staff a wise freedom, there are instances of friction, some of which occurred in Rice's period of office. In 1901 there was a split on the School Council and it would appear that this was largely due to the desire of some Council members to have considerable control of the day-to-day affairs in the school. Rice was forced to resign, and he decided to start another school in Hampstead on King Alfred principles with himself as sole headmaster and independent of the Society's management, but perhaps with a common bond as the Memorandum of Association had suggested in 1897. He was prepared to have routine inspections by an expert nominated by the Society and to continue to support 'the course of rational education'. The Council rejected the proposal and Rice had to sever his connection with the school. A minority on the Council, including Cecil Sharp and the chairman, F. W. Miall, resigned in support of Rice, who started a school not far away in Ferncroft Avenue, Hampstead, which came to an end just before Rice (who was married to one of Badley's sisters) returned to Bedales in 1908.[2]

The age range at King Alfred's was, at first, eight to fourteen years with a considerable group of both boys and girls leaving at thirteen to go to public and secondary schools. During the 1920s J. H. Wicksteed, then headmaster, added a nursery and

[1] *Memories and Reflections*, p. 128.
[2] *The Bedales School Roll 1952*, ed. B. Gimson, p. 358, is in error in stating that Rice was head of King Alfred's 1898–1908.

infant-school group aged from three to eight years taught on Montessori lines, for he, like many others in the 1920s and earlier, was a great admirer of the *dottoressa*. This nursery and infant school still exists at King Alfred's.

But to return to Rice. In 1908 he returned to Bedales to teach and remained there until 1911, but then, after nearly twenty years of schoolmastering, he decided that it did not offer him the scope that he wanted and so he reverted to his original intention to train as a doctor and followed that career for the rest of his life.

His successor at King Alfred's in 1901, John Russell, was a very different person. He remained headmaster until 1920 and became the father-figure of the school. He was a foundation scholar of St. John's College, Cambridge, and a certificated teacher who came to King Alfred's with seventeen years of teaching experience, mostly in conventional day schools. He was interested in the work of educational reformers and had edited a work on Pestalozzi and his successors, and had travelled and taught on the Continent. Russell was a strong supporter of the suffragette movement and the campaign for women's rights, and co-education had for him a significance far greater than mere educational wisdom: it was a symbol of achievement by and for women. He was a person with a considerable presence and a fine sense of drama: A. S. Neill, who worked under Russell at King Alfred's from 1918 till 1920, told the present writer that Russell had a voice like Henry Irving and was a born actor. He made the school conventions more formal, introducing blazers and ties and gymtunics, having the classes stand up on his entry, and enjoying the position the children accorded to him. He was a remarkable correspondent and kept in touch with many of his old pupils over the fifteen years or so of his tenure of office, which, of course, included the period of the First World War. When he retired in 1920 there were about seventy pupils at the school and he had been able to persuade the Council to consider moving the school to a larger site where both buildings and playing fields were available.

It was Russell who introduced the Children's Council with pupil representation on which the later organization was based. Under him the school was organized, controlled, and led in a way quite different from Rice's regime. Neill, back from the war and fired by his admiration for Homer Lane, writes of the last two years of Russell's headship:

> Old John Russell was Head, dear old J.R., a kindly, humane soul one could not help loving. Alas, under Lane's influence, I began to be a heretical assistant. I kept asking for self-government, stupidly of course, for what self-government can one practise in a day school? In the end [in 1920] I had to resign.[3]

Russell was highly regarded by the Council of the King Alfred Society and given good support by them in his enterprises, although not always without resistance. He was the stabilizer in the first twenty years of the school's existence. He followed the precepts of co-education, rationalism, co-operation rather than competition, liberal education rather than examination pressure, and participation of parents in the affairs of the school community, as laid down in the first memorandum of the King Alfred School Society.

When Russell retired in 1920 Joseph Wicksteed was appointed as his successor. He came, like Charles Rice, from a few years of service on the staff of Bedales. He was a son of Philip Wicksteed who had in the last two decades of the nineteenth century taken part in many utopian schemes, including the Labour church movement.[4] Joseph Wicksteed had been influenced by the Unitarian wing of the free churches and later by the Theosophical Society, which through the Theosophical Fraternity in Education, founded in 1915, had provided the effective beginnings of the New Education Fellowship. Wicksteed was a considerable Blake scholar, and so exemplified the combination of leftist politics, mystical and non-dogmatic religion, and a belief in internationalism which marked a number of educational innovators of the period.

Most of the principles of work at King Alfred's were very similar to those of the Theosophical Educational Trust, which had been founded in 1916. Wicksteed followed the Trust in

---
[3] A. S. Neill, 'My Scholastic Life: 2' in *Id*, journal of the Summerhill Society, no. 3 (Oct. 1960), p. 4.
[4] See Armytage, *Heavens Below*, pp. 321–3.

his stress on outdoor life and continued the argument which Russell had begun on moving the school. Eventually he succeeded. The new site (still the site of the school) was spacious enough to allow the children to camp, to build tree-houses, to garden. Wicksteed, who had been connected with the Garden City movement twenty-five years before, had Barry Parker, one of the Hampstead Garden Suburb architects, to design the main buildings of the new school.

During Wicksteed's period of office the old rationalism was slightly modified. In the original memorandum it was stated that the education given by the school would be free from any connection with religious organizations or denominations and from political associations, and that no inquiry was to be made about the religious beliefs of anyone connected with the school. During the 1920s King Alfred's began to teach comparative religion, and the study of the Bible was permitted in the context of literature and history.

The school was recognized as efficient by the Board of Education in 1928, having been refused recognition after an inspection in 1921, and had grown from approximately seventy children of all ages at the beginning of Wicksteed's period of office to about one hundred and thirty at the end in 1933. From the beginning he had Miss V. A. Hyett as his senior mistress, and her mark upon the school up to her retirement in 1948 was unmistakable. She came from Wallasey Grammar School with a very different experience from Wicksteed's, and she combined practicality in administration with considerable achievement as a historian and teacher of history. She was an ardent feminist, leftist in her politics, and active in the affairs of the Society for Cultural Relations with the U.S.S.R. and of the Left Book Club. When Wicksteed retired in 1933 Miss Hyett became joint-head with a former senior master. H. de P. Birkett, and it was she who took charge of the school when the children were evacuated during the Second World War.

From 1930 the refusal to admit examinations into the educational practice at King Alfred's was changed and the General Schools Certificate began to be a feasible goal for pupils. Miss Hyett had a great deal to do with this stiffening and rationalizing of procedure, and from 1933 children in the fifth form were normally expected to take the Schools Certificate examination with its required grouping of subjects. However, as there was no entry examination of the eleven plus selection type or the thirteen plus Common Entrance type at King Alfred's, there were children representing a wider spectrum of ability than would usually be found in a grammar school. The school was too small to stream the classes so the compromise has been applied, for more than thirty years, of a modified Dalton Plan – a varying minimum of oral class teaching according to age, together with work in what are called supervised open rooms where the teacher is available for individual instruction as required. B. H. Montgomery, who was a master at King Alfred's, 1932–40, and returned as headmaster and later as joint-head, 1944–62, wrote in a recent account of the school:

> During the past ten years we have found it necessary to modify considerably our attitude to examinations. Competition for university places has become increasingly keen, and many employers now require a good G.C.E. certificate as evidence of a good education.... We aim to produce people who are emotionally stable and who are independent and enterprising.... At the same time we fully recognize the need for them to gain academic qualifications.[5]

The Children's Council has been in existence in one form or another for over fifty years. The school is compact enough for all children over ten (about two hundred) to attend meetings of the Children's Council where their elected representatives discuss school problems each week. The Council is advisory only, with certain defined responsibilities: the heads have a right of veto on decisions if need be, though this is apparently scarcely ever necessary. There are also regular staff meetings, often weekly, and from this democratic structure much of the general concern and informality of the school derive. Mr. Montgomery sums up the principles of King Alfred's as follows:

1. We believe in co-education for boys and girls throughout their lives.... We have no reservations.

[5] *The Independent Progressive School*, ed. H. A. T. Child (London, 1962), pp. 90–1.

2. We believe in the educational value of personal liberty....
3. There is no formal religious observance or instruction.
4. There is no formal selection of pupils at entry.[6]

Mrs. Paul-Jones, the joint-head of King Alfred's, writes in the same article:

> There is still, in my opinion, a great differenec between schools like King Alfred's and the majority of grammar and secondary schools. Fundamentally ... it rests on the attitude we hold to education and the principles on which we base our work.... We feel certain that where there are more children in a community than the Head can know as individuals, something vital is lost.... We believe that children of varying abilities and widely differing interests and capacities (including those who have little or no academic skill) have something to contribute to one another's work and social life.[7]

The King Alfred Society, to which one or both parents of each pupil are expected to belong, has a Council which constitutes the School Council, and as the heads are *ex officio* members of the Council the parents have a significant liaison with school policy and practice through their representatives. There is no school uniform and a number of the staff are known by their Christian names, features of a modern idiom which has not always been there. A town day school, different thereby from Abbotsholme, Bedales, and Claysmore, King Alfred's was rationalist and co-educational from the start and thus different from them again. In most of the rest they are all four recognizably similar. In the hoped-for understanding and friendship between teacher and pupil, they all aim for the same things, however different the human context may be. I end these comments on King Alfred's with the obituary of a six-and-a-half-year-old girl writing of Miss Hyett, who died in 1949 (the school was evacuated to Royston during the war):

She is very kind Because she loves flowers She used to take

[6] Ibid., p. 87.   [7] Ibid., p. 92.

me to her shelter where she slept at Royston we had tea there on the grass.

She used to teach Anthony and me to throw sticks into the river and watch them come out of the other side of the bridge. I love her and miss her terribly terribly.

These four schools were founded before the Board of Education came into existence in 1899 and the local education authorities in 1902. However, these four progressive schools had nothing to say about elementary schools and make no attempt to locate themselves in relation to the maintained sector. Each school aimed to be an educational environment of the highest quality both in theory and in practice for all its members. In addition each school community claimed, either explicitly or implicitly, that it was a model which other schools, and society as a whole, ought to attend to and where possible learn from.

The point must be made early in this study that the educational radicals of the 1890s were, not surprisingly, middle-class intellectuals, many of whom had sympathy with the political left, at least at first, but who ran schools which charged considerable fees and so made any real penetration of working-class life impossible. Yet even this stock economic argument is too simple. The kind of educational reform which Reddie, Badley, and the others had in mind could be based only on an educational sophistication of some refinement, which the teachers in the elementary school seldom had. Reddie and Badley were really attacking a culture which was impoverished for the public school boy and for the elementary school boy in quite different ways, and even if they had wanted to, Reddie and Badley could not have provided a school which would have been sufficiently satisfying for each kind of boy.

Their triangulation point was the public school, the most independent yet the best organized branch, the most individualistic yet the most collectively powerful, free from inspection or control but intellectually almost as constricted by the classical curriculum as the elementary schools were by the Revised Code. Reddie staged a characteristic assault on the public schools: Abbotsholme was for boys of eleven to eighteen years belonging to the directing classes, and the New

School, by the simple appeal of its superior commodity, would win away such boys as at that time were going to the public schools. The New School, like Eton or Winchester, would begin at the top.

Reddie knew very little of the English public schools at first hand, although it would not have made much difference to his direct challenge if he had; Badley, on the other hand, knew a great deal about them and was even more fundamental, though less belligerent, in his radical opposition, because he added co-education to his challenges. Devine temporized more and seems a well-intentioned opportunist rather than a proper innovator, something of an outsider in both camps. King Alfred's has to be compared with the day public schools like St. Paul's or Merchant Taylors', and the day grammar schools. It was not one man's protest, but an affirmation by members of the intellectual middle class of a London suburb with a liberal reputation.

From 1902 onwards the public schools were also the triangulation point for many of the grammar schools of the new local education authorities, but more for emulation than rejection. The four radical schools of the 1890s found the public schools an extremely powerful educational and social influence, to be strengthened after 1902 by the grammar schools. The elementary school and the higher grade school were nothing like so powerful because they were only really beginning, and that from a very inferior position.

In 1900 there were not two, but really three separate systems, public, grammar, and elementary. In a very real sense the four radical schools represented a tiny fourth system because of their opposition to one kind of poverty in the education offered in the public and grammar school and to another kind of poverty in the Revised Code of the elementary school.

9 Merging into Educational Radicalism: 1898–1918

THE FOUR schools already described represent the beginning of a new movement. Besides these four, however, there were schools already in existence which had many similar features or which began to adopt quite explicitly many of the principles of the innovators. Of these we propose to mention the schools of the Society of Friends scattered throughout England, and Badminton, the girls' school near Bristol. These schools merged into the progressive school movement by the time of the outbreak of the First World War. One other group of schools is also to be considered in this period, and these are schools started by, or associated with, the Theosophical Educational Trust which came into existence in 1916. They were not individual ventures like those of Reddie, Badley, Devine, or the group of Hampstead parents, but separate expressions of the insights of Theosophy in education.

The educational radicals did not sweep the country before the First World War and there were many reasons for this. First of all, they did not try to do so – it is true that Reddie spoke of helping to create a higher type of human being and of regenerating England, but he also spoke of Abbotsholme as a state, a *kosmos*, and in fact each of the headmasters gave his energy to getting his own school started. The ABC of educational reform as Devine suggested it came to nothing. The King Alfred Society had visions of a number of schools, a training college, and other ventures, but the single school was all that was actually achieved. A second reason for the modest expansion of the progressive school movement was that the national educational system was being planned and enacted in the two decades on either side of the turn of the century and this took up the energies of many men of educational good will. Thirdly, although the New School movement was associated with the beginnings of the Labour movement in the confused days around 1890, by 1900 the outlines of a proletariat with a parliamentary future were becoming clearer and this was going to be a movement of the working class and its sympathizers in society as a whole. The New Schools were by then financially out of reach and intellectually out of touch with the working class. They were for the children of the liberal intelligentsia, who are by definition a very small percentage of the population. In any case, after the Balfour Act in 1902 the elementary schools had not the experience or confidence or desire to adopt the principles and practice of what they thought to be the lunatic fringe.

While, therefore, there are mergings into the radical movement in education, there are scarcely any new foundations before 1914. These came after the war for reasons which will appear.

21 QUAKER SCHOOLS

THE Society of Friends, commonly called the Quakers, is a minority group of about 20,000 which deservedly enjoys a wide respect for its religious integrity and its lively concern in social affairs. Since the foundation of Ackworth in Yorkshire in 1779 there have been schools in England officially associated with the Society and at the present date there are nine English Quaker schools.

In the middle of the seventeenth century, when the Society of Friends first took form, the three main traditions and emphases in the Christian approach to God can be seen. First there was the emphasis on the authority of the church as Roman Catholics accepted it, 'a visible, hierarchical institution, which is the divinely commissioned vehicle and guarantee of the truth and grace of the Gospel'.[1] Second there were those who emphasized the main authority of the Bible, and historic Protestantism might serve as the type for this; the Anglican, the Calvinist, and the Lutheran had this belief in common. The third main stream of tradition and emphasis may be called rather loosely the mystical and has its sanction for, and its source of faith in, the spirit of the worshipper, the individual Christian; of this the Quaker, with his belief in the Inner

[1] J. S. Whale, *Christian Doctrine* (London, 1942), p. 14.

Light, may be taken as the example. Early Friends considered that they were the restored church of Christ drawing on a unique experience of God speaking to their own hearts. There is a body of belief which is characteristic of Quakerism from a very early period and which we must consider briefly in so far as it influences educational theory and practice.

Friends say that all men have a capacity to listen to, understand, and share spiritual experience. This capacity is often called the Seed or the Inner Light and is, so to say, God's immanence in each human spirit. The belief presents a potential separation of 'natural' and 'spiritual' man which can be seen in Calvinism in different forms at this period. The potential separatism appears sharply for Friends in the relationship between the Inner Light and intellectual learning, and much has been written on this in Quaker literature in philosophical, psychological, theological, and metaphysical terms. We will not explore these aspects here, but sketch instead some of the practical outcomes in the Quaker schools.[2]

The response of early Friends to the classical languages was favourable for they, with Hebrew, were biblical languages and had thereby a sanctified utilitarian value. However, the children did not study the language by means of the usually accepted texts, but from books written by Friends like Christopher Taylor and John Matern, whose book *Institutiones Pietatis*, written in 1676, was full of Quaker precepts and what they called 'savoury and wholesome good matter that may not corrupt children's minds' as the classics would in their estimation if taught as they usually were straight from the heathen authors. So in their schools from an early date Friends tried to make the classics relevant to children's needs as they saw them, and in choosing this method they largely discarded the sense of an ancient literature and a linguistic tradition. Besides this break with the classical tradition, Friends emphasized that classics was only one subject among many others and English rather than classics was the basis of the curriculum from the start. Some of the schools in the eighteenth century were 'for the poorer sort and quite excluded Latin'.

Perhaps the most noticeable feature of the educational

[2] For fuller treatment, see Stewart, *Quakers and Education*, especially chs. i and ii.

implications of the relationship between the Inner Light and intellectual learning was the interest shown in science. The natural creation was part of God's plan and in it He could be perceived, but the expression of this point of view in science teaching did not really take shape until early in the nineteenth century.

Friends held clear views on the dignity of labour, believing that no task was degrading since the Inner Light was available to any man who wished for peace and power. Practical work, therefore, whether it be household duties, the fetching of supplies, the mending of linen and clothes, the care of the land, has always been recommended in one way or another in Quaker schools.

A consequence of the belief in the Inner Light was the particular position Friends take on what may be called the priesthood of believers. If God spoke to each spirit, it was without the need of a teacher or intercessor. No one was to have the special calling of priest because all were called to be priests, so there was no hierarchy in the Quaker church but an assumption of spiritual equality, with women as equal in the priesthood with men.

Friends are well known for their insistence on directness and 'plainness', which has consequences in the meeting for worship based on silence and liturgy. Another consequence is the emphasis on ideas of service and probity and a non-violent spirit. One Friend, writing of the Quaker view of children says:

> The historic Quaker tradition is between the extremes of Calvinism and Progressivism. The child is not naturally good nor is he naturally evil: he is simply innocent.... In view of these considerations we find that the Quaker school should be neither authoritarian after the Puritan model nor anarchistic after the ultra-progressive model.[3]

Even from these very brief indications of the point of view of the Society of Friends it is clear that many important educational practices ought to follow, some of them directly in line

---

[3] H. H. Brinton, 'Quaker Education in Theory and Practice', *Pendle Hill Pamphlet*, no. 9 (1940), pp. 79–83. See also H. Loukes, *Friends and their Children* (London, 1958).

with the distinctive position of the radical schools. Before looking more closely at this we should learn something of the Quaker schools which are in existence and a little of their history.

Monthly meetings of the Society of Friends are regular gatherings of representatives of neighbouring local meetings, often for the purposes of conducting business or making decisions and communicating these either to the central organizations of the Society or to the Quarterly Meeting, which is the regional organization. Yearly Meeting in England is the annual gathering of all the Quarterly Meetings and in 1779 Yearly Meeting undertook to be responsible for Ackworth School, founded near Pontefract in Yorkshire, to which the children of Friends 'not in affluence' were entitled to go. The school taught both boys and girls organized as separate 'sides', and this dual formation continued with cumulative modifications until in 1947 Ackworth became fully co-educational, the last of the co-educational Friends' schools now in existence to make the change.

The concern of Yearly Meeting to support the foundation of Ackworth in 1779 followed upon a report presented in 1760 by a special committee which had examined the state of education in Friends' schools. If the period 1695–1725 might be regarded as the high-water mark of the Society's interest in its schools, the state of affairs in the middle of the eighteenth century was serious.[4] For years after the publication of the report in 1760 nothing appeared to be happening until John Fothergill, an eminent Quaker physician, David Barclay, a respected financier and banker, and William Tuke, a well-known York merchant, took the matter in hand. Following on the foundation of Ackworth in 1779 the West Country Quarterly Meeting founded Sidcot School near Bristol in 1808 on a plan somewhat similar to that of Ackworth.

There was already in existence in Clerkenwell in London, founded in 1702, a Quaker workhouse for old and infirm people together with a boarding-school for some young children. The school was separated in 1786 and moved to Islington, where it was reformed in 1811 to approximate to Ackworth.

---

[4] See D. G. B. Hubbard, 'Early Quaker Education 1650–1780' (unpublished M.A. thesis, University of London, 1939), pp. 160–1.

The school moved to Croydon in 1825, and to Saffron Walden in Essex, its present location, in 1879, and Her Majesty's Inspectors say that Saffron Walden in 1876 was for east London, Essex, and the Fen district what Ackworth was for south Yorkshire.

The Quarterly Meeting of Cumberland and Northumberland founded Wigton near Carlisle in 1815, and its general rules are almost verbatim the Ackworth rules drawn up in 1789. All four of these schools were for boys and girls taught separately and from relatively poor Quaker homes. In 1829, however, York Quarterly Meeting gave its official support to a boys' school which had been running for five years as a private venture in the city. This was Bootham School, which was to give 'a liberal, guarded and religious education, on moderate terms, to the sons of Friends who are not considered the object of Ackworth School'.[5]

In 1831 York Quarterly Meeting founded a girls' school 'similar in its character and general management to the boys' school'.[6] This was The Mount School, which was and is the only girls' school in England under the auspices of an official Quaker committee. These two establishments were for the children of Friends who could afford to pay more, and offered a more advanced education. One of the Taunton Commissioners in 1867 said of The Mount: 'The curriculum of instruction is remarkable for the small proportion of effort devoted to accomplishments, and the large share to intellectual culture.'

In the 1830s and 1840s four schools were founded by Quarterly Meetings, two of which have survived, for the children of those 'disowned'. These were the children of men or women who had been members of the Society but who for one reason or another had turned away from, or had been turned out of, the Society, mostly for marrying a non-Friend. This strict rule of exclusion affected not only those who 'married out' but also members of their family who sympathized with them, and it depleted the Society seriously in the first half of the nineteenth century. By 1860 the rule of exclusion had

[5] *History of Bootham School 1823–1923* (London, 1926), p. 22.
[6] H. W. Sturge and T. Clark, *The Mount School, York, 1785–1814, 1831–1931* (London, 1931), p. 36.

been rescinded by many meetings – incidentally W. E. Forster, the architect of the 1870 Act, was a birthright Friend who was disowned for marrying Jane, a daughter of Thomas Arnold. Forster had been educated at two Quaker private schools, Fishponds and Tottenham.

With the rescinding of the practice of disownment the schools set up for those disowned became ordinary Quaker schools, again for those not in affluence. The two existing schools which have this origin are Great Ayton in north-east Yorkshire, which was founded in 1841 as the North of England Agricultural School, and Sibford, founded near Banbury in 1842 by the Berkshire and Oxfordshire Quarterly Meeting.

The only other Friends' school to name is Leighton Park. This was founded in 1890 at Reading by the Friends Public School Company, a group of concerned Friends who formed a governing body to which Yearly Meeting added representatives. The school was to provide about one hundred boys with preparation for a university or other advanced training. It corresponded in the south to Bootham in the north and it has continued as a Quaker public school, a member, like Bootham, of the Headmasters' Conference. So the Quaker schools are Ackworth (1779), Sidcot (1808), Saffron Walden (1811), Wigton (1815), Bootham (1823), The Mount (1831), Great Ayton (1841), Sibford (1842), and Leighton Park (1890).

During the nineteenth century the integrity and hard work of Quakers had given them an influential position in industrial England, and so too had their active concern for human welfare in prison reform, the abolition of slavery, factory legislation, the care of the sick and the insane, the alleviation of poverty. Their pacifism and plainness tended to isolate them from everyday life as a special group, and while they were committed to the relief of human suffering and to the honest conduct of ordinary affairs they were also aware of their separateness and need for solidarity. Throughout the century one is aware of the conflict between cautious 'guarding' advices and a more expansive, questing outlook. For instance the distinctive Quaker dress had disappeared from Friends' schools in the 1870s, and by the end of the century the pupils were dressed like other children. The special forms of Quaker speech, employing 'thee' and 'thou' and other particular idioms, had almost disappeared from the schools by 1879. Non-Friends were admitted to Friends' schools both as pupils and as teachers from about 1870, and the present fluctuating average proportion of Quaker children and teachers in Friends' schools is rather less than half. The crucial decade for these changes was the 1870s, though the roots of change stretch back long before that. In the twentieth century the Society of Friends has ceased to be a separatist group in English society, which in some senses it never really was. As in society, so in education the older 'guarded' concepts have had to be replaced by new modes of perpetuating the Quaker message and beliefs.

In 1864 the Taunton Commission had examined the York schools and given them a favourable report. In the 1860s and 1870s most of the Friends' schools began to accept regular inspections by officers of the Cambridge Syndicate or the British and Foreign Schools Society, and in 1879 there was an important conference of Friends on education. From this report we can see how the wind of change was blowing:

> If we want to train good teachers ... we must send them out into the world, to learn from intercourse with the highest minds outside what are the new systems of teaching.[7]

A realistic appraisal of the Friends' schools at that time showed that changes were needed:

> There is not an education offered for all classes in [the Society].... We should have a thoroughly well-educated class of men who will be able to take any position in regard to the education of the sons and daughters of any class in our Society.[8]

The Society's schools are clearly seen to be in intellectual competition with other schools, and they reflect the social standards of the Society as a whole in late nineteenth-century class structure. Ackworth, founded a century before for the children of those 'not in affluence', was said to have had the effect of raising the families from which the boys and girls came 'rather above the middle class in life' and making rich men of many who would otherwise have been in humble cir-

---

[7] *Report of the Education Conference of the Society of Friends, 1879*, p. 116.
[8] Ibid., p. 135.

cumstances. Two out of three leavers entered commercial careers and about one in ten went into the professions.

The status of Friends by the 1880s and 1890s was such that they became important figures in local government when the Act of 1888 opened the way for local authorities. An American Friend reported in New York in 1881:

> Every person at all familiar with English affairs, knows that a large number of Friends occupy positions of great responsibility and influence. Two are members of the Government, nearly a score are members of Parliament, several are mayors of cities, a considerable number occupy highly important places on school boards.... The numbers ... are out of all proportion to the Society's membership in the nation ... I can see no significant cause but education, combined with public confidence, and those things difficult to define which are included in the term of 'respectability'. Wealth has a degree of influence, but it does not fit men for such positions, except as it gives them useful information, discipline and culture.[9]

Quaker schools had played their part in helping to bring about this shift in social standing. Many Friends were no longer reluctant to seek political power, and the Board of Education reported on Friends' schools in 1905:

> The Schools have been affected by a tendency which is almost universal in England. Schools which have been founded with special regard to the children of the poor have gradually increased their fees and the standard of education, so that they now do a work quite different from that which was originally contemplated.... The ambition of a successful school is not to do better the work which it began with, but to pass on to work of a more ambitious character.[10]

By 1900 the nine schools were offering 'a sound education of the secondary school type', the York schools and Leighton Park clearly to a more advanced standard. Much of what they did was parallel to what was being done in the radical schools

[9] J. Wood, 'Education among Friends in England', in *Proceedings of a Conference called by the Committee on Education of New York Yearly Meeting* (1881), pp. 44–5.

[10] *Inspection of Friends' Boarding Schools by the Board of Education* (1905), p. 9.

already mentioned. The classics took a position in the curriculum subordinate to English. The modern languages had their place and the sciences had been taught in the schools since their foundation – Bootham was said to have one of the earliest laboratories in an English secondary school, opened in 1879, and its Natural History Society, founded in 1834, was an early example of this kind of organization. The arts, including music, had received a general, if cautious, approval by the 90s of the last century: choral singing *in unison* was permitted in the 1870s and by the 80s harmonies were allowed. By 1880 class teaching of instruments was widely approved and by the beginning of this century pupils were going to concerts.

By the 1870s and 80s there were craftrooms and workshops in most of the schools, in which turning, fretwork, boatbuilding, bookbinding, and metalwork reached a good and sometimes excellent standard, according to the Board's inspectors in the early years of this century. The girls had for many years been engaged in all branches of housecraft, and in some of the schools (Ayton, Sibford, and Saffron Walden, for instance) estate work was done in the two middle quarters of the century but had been dropped in the last quarter, although ordinary household work was done by the children in all the schools.

Many Friends' schools had been groping towards co-education in the last two decades of the century. The priesthood of believers was a principle which Friends did not apply to the position of men and women as equal in the Society's councils until 1907; by that time Sidcot had become fully co-educational and so too had Ayton, Sibford, and Wigton. Saffron Walden followed in 1910 but Ackworth did not do so finally until 1947. The Mount remains a girls' school and Leighton Park and Bootham are still for boys only although there have been, and are, moves to consider co-education. Sidcot made the change in 1902 under Dr. Bevan Lean and the other three schools had done so by 1904–5, when the Board of Education produced a report on Friends' schools. The inspectors in their report said that if co-education in boarding-schools could be adopted anywhere with safety and success it would be in schools such as these with their traditional bond of a quiet family life and the restraint of strong religious influence.[11] It is probably this feature of co-education more than any other which brought Friends' schools into the same bracket as progressive schools.

Another feature of Quaker educational practice which linked their schools to the innovating group was the growth of Children's Councils in the 1920s and the readiness to give to children a limited sense of responsibility. This is a reasonable application of Friends' belief in the Inner Light, but in the schools no great freedom or power has been given to these Councils: they have been more of a patch on the fabric of the existing hierarchy. Again the non-violent spirit of Friends has made their discipline within the last hundred years relatively humane, though it was often surprisingly cruel before that. They discarded corporal punishment about the middle of the last century, but some harsh and damaging alternatives like solitary confinement and a generalized ridiculing have not been uncommon.[12]

By 1914 Friends' schools had merged into the progressive movement quietly but inevitably as they began to apply their own principles to the twentieth-century educational situation. Quakers were, and are, as a body on the right wing of progressive education. They value order and the sense of continuity and tradition, the need to focus on something beyond the school, the consciousness of religious foundations. They also value, however, the individual spirit and the vision each man or child may have, they respect telling the truth in love, and the right to have conscientious objection. Professor Castle, writing in 1936 when he was the headmaster of Leighton Park School, put it like this: '[Progressive schools] are schools of protest, self-conscious in their efforts, uncertain in their aims, usually non-religious in their foundation ... I do not believe they are the schools our Society can accept as substitutes for our own.'[13] This might be true of some of the foundations of the 1920s, but Friends' schools grew nearer to the first four pre-1914 progressive schools than to any other group.

[11] Ibid., p. 36.
[12] For fuller treatment, see Stewart, *Quakers and Education*, pp. 259–67.
[13] E. B. Castle, 'The Position of Friends' Schools', in *Friends' Quarterly Examiner*, 70 (1936), pp. 28–9.

22 BADMINTON

In August 1858 a school for girls began in a small way in Bristol which took the name by which it is now known when it moved to Badminton House, Clifton Park. Mrs. Badock, the founder, said in her first prospectus that 'her aim invariably is first to secure [the girls'] affection and confidence and then, by a careful study of the character and mental capacities of each to develop moral and religious principles and impart instruction in the manner best adapted to their individual tastes and dispositions'. Mrs. Badock encouraged her pupils to take the Cambridge Local Examinations from the 1860s onwards, and invited teachers from the University College as it then was to lecture to her girls on a range of subjects including botany, natural history, and elementary physics. The girls supported quite a range of school societies.

Mrs. Badock retired after thirty-five years of enlightened work which was not quite sufficiently unorthodox to merit including Badminton in the group of radical schools. There were fifty-five girls in the school when Miss Bartlett, aided by two sisters, became headmistress in 1893. Miss Bartlett had been a pupil and a member of staff, and by 1904, when a junior section was started, the school had seventy girls aged between thirteen and eighteen, forty of them being boarders. There is an illuminating account of the school at this time in which the writer says that the girls did not work very hard and that not many took public examinations. There was no prefect system and the school centred round Miss Bartlett: 'though we loved her, we all – girls, staff, and parents – held her in a very wholesome awe. She was petite, very clever and very charming to look at.'[1] The days were strenuous and long walks in all weathers were a regular feature. Another writer says of the period 1907–11:

It was a good, quiet, old-fashioned school – I mean old-fashioned in its own day – not coveting academic honours but giving a very fair grounding in at least English language

[1] *Badminton School 1858–1958* (published by the school), p. 6.

and literature. The girls were average, too, in attainment and conduct ... our goodness was rather negative. Looking back fifty years I feel that on the whole I enjoyed it.[2]

In 1911 Miss B. M. Baker became headmistress with Miss Randall as second mistress. This was their first experience of a boarding-school, to which they had been attracted by the greater opportunities it offered of developing girls' education than a day school, and 'they absolutely shook the school'. The old-fashioned school clothes were replaced by lighter, more hygienic, and more attractive dress, the academic standard was stiffened all round and weakness in particular subjects was taken care of by flexible 'setting' arrangements. Newspapers had to be read and matters discussed; meetings and lectures were attended in Bristol; the school took part in social work and in something like what we would now call youth club activities with children in poor and difficult circumstances in the city; the seniors went to the theatre not infrequently and saw the *avant garde* works of Shaw, Galsworthy, and Wilde. The political and social problems of the world were proper matters for Badminton girls. But before going further we should take a glance at girls' secondary education in England in the second half of last century.

The Girls' Public Day School Trust was founded in 1872 and high level day secondary schools for girls multiplied over the country, giving a chance of work of good academic standard intended as a preparation for professional and university careers which had not been easy for women to come by. There had been a few such boarding and day schools in the first half of the nineteenth century – Godolphin School, Christ's Hospital, and for the daughters of clergy St. Brandon's and St. Elphin's, and The Mount School for Quaker girls. Very active and sustained effort, some of it by university teachers of the new University of London, led to the foundation of Queen's College in Harley Street in 1848 and of Bedford College, which had its beginnings in 1849 and developed to its present status as a constituent college of the University of London in 1909. Frances Mary Buss, a former pupil of Queen's College, transformed a school run by her mother into the North London

[2] Ibid., p. 11.

Collegiate School in 1850, which was the prototype for the Girls' Public Day School Trust. Dorothea Beale, also formerly of Queen's College, took over in 1858 the Ladies' College at Cheltenham, which had been founded as a day school in 1853 with eighty-eight pupils. Twenty years later it was the leading girls' boarding-school in the country with over five hundred girls.

The Taunton Commission in 1869 supported the obvious growth of the education of girls and women and said that the education of girls was as much a matter of public concern as that of boys and even ruled that where charitable trusts did not mention girls in their instruments of foundation, funds could be used for their education unless they were explicitly excluded. In 1869 a report was issued by a Commission on the Education of Girls under the chairmanship of Miss Beale. In the 1870s Girton and Newnham made their beginnings in Cambridge; the Oxford women's colleges were founded in the late 1870s and after. The University of London opened its degrees and prizes to women in 1878, the University of Manchester did the same in 1880. Oxford and Cambridge at the same time made their grudging admission of women to courses and by courtesy to examinations, but not to official degrees for fifty years and more. After 1902, of course, maintained girls' and co-educational schools were founded to extend the provision at all levels made after the 1870 Act.

These comments are offered as background to the changes at Badminton after 1911. In a sense it was more difficult to transform a conventional girls' school than to give girls a progressive education in an obviously odd organization like Bedales or King Alfred's. For the new girls' boarding-schools, and many of the day schools, the boys' public school was the principal pattern. At Badminton the new idea in 1911 was to maintain a high academic standard while widening the range of interests to include social responsibility at home and interests in international affairs abroad. Miss Baker was headmistress through two world wars and retired in 1946, by which time work in the arts, in citizenship, the course in the history of civilization, and a considerable range of responsibility for girls' committees had long been established.

Badminton is and has been an undenominational school.

Girls go to their own churches on Sundays and there is a non-sectarian school service in the evening. In the post-war years Badminton took an active interest in the League of Nations, and parties of girls visited Geneva to learn of the League's work and attend sessions of its committees and assemblies; in 1922 a visit was made to Germany and Austria 'to make the acquaintance of our recent enemies'; during and after the war more than one member of the staff took part in the relief work on the Continent organized by the Society of Friends; the school made a point of encouraging girls from overseas to become pupils and they came from many nations in Europe, the Commonwealth, and elsewhere. After the First World War there were refugees from Poland and Russia, and in the middle and late 1930s there were Spanish and Basque children, Germans, Austrians, Czechs. The influx of foreign children in the decade before the Second World War was not just the consequence of a sudden general wave of sympathy for suffering Europe. Miss Baker and her colleagues had been explicit since 1911 on international sympathy and responsibility. When Miss Sanderson, her successor, wrote of the Conference of Internationally-Minded Schools founded under the auspices of UNESCO in 1949 it was natural that Badminton should be a leading member in England.[3]

The curriculum of the four innovating schools at the beginning of this century became the curriculum of Badminton after 1911 – no dominance of the classics, but a broad academic course with an emphasis on English studies. The arts and crafts and music were given a high place in the general education provided. Modern languages, science, and mathematics were important, as were informal and friendly relations with the staff. Cramming and specialization, prizes and competitiveness were avoided. Cold baths were the morning rule at Badminton for many years but estate work was not encouraged – partly it was thought to be unsuitable for girls and partly the grounds did not appear to permit it. The traffic of affairs with the city of Bristol could not be emulated at any of the four progressive schools except King Alfred's, and that was a day

---

[3] B. M. Sanderson, 'Badminton', in *The Independent Progressive School*, ed. Child, p. 29. Miss Sanderson has been chairman of the Executive Committee of C.I.S.

school. Badminton's insistence on an intelligent interest in history, politics, and current affairs was better organized than in any of the other four, as was its social work in the school's own rehabilitation house or at the University Centre. The School Council goes back nearly fifty years and has had a predominantly useful role in an advisory capacity all that time. Badminton is a girls' school but its senior pupils have had contacts for many years with neighbouring boys' schools and taken a full part in co-educational summer meetings of the old League of Nations Union and the modern Conference of Internationally-Minded Schools. Even until 1939 many of these things, now commonplace, were quite unorthodox.

This was a girls' school which aligned itself with the progressive movement in 1911 and had merged with the progressive schools by the end of the First World War, as the practices already summarized have indicated. The temper of Badminton has always been liberal, and the school may be taken with the Friends' schools as moderately progressive without being radical. In 1931 Badminton became a public school with a Board of Governors, of which Professor Gilbert Murray was for a long time the president. Yet it is with the innovators that Badminton is not willing to be associated, as Miss Baker's contribution to Blewitt's symposium in 1934 and Miss Sanderson's to Child's in 1962 both indicate.[4]

23 THEOSOPHICAL SCHOOLS

THEOSOPHISTS have made important contributions to educational innovation in England, but it is necessary to set the stage rather carefully so that their work may be seen and understood. Friedrich Max Müller was born at Dessau in the Duchy of Anhalt in 1823, where his father was ducal librarian. The boy proved to be a linguistic scholar of outstanding talent, and after studying oriental languages in circumstances of great poverty in Leipzig, Berlin, and Paris, he came to London to work on the rich store of Sanskrit documents in the library of the India Office. He became a fellow of All Souls and pro-

[4] *The Modern Schools Handbook; The Independent Progressive School.*

fessor of comparative philology at Oxford, and for nearly fifty years until his death in 1900 he edited first the *Rig Veda*, the Hindu hymns which were hitherto unpublished even in India, and then a massive series of translations of the sacred books of the great religions of the world in fifty volumes entitled *The Sacred Books of the East*. This monumental scholarly achievement enabled many Englishmen in the second half of the nineteenth century to have some knowledge of Eastern religions and provides an important part of the literary background to Mme. Blavatsky, Annie Besant, and the Theosophical movement in this country.

Mme. Helena Petrovna Blavatsky was born near Odessa in 1831 and died in her sixtieth year in London. She is supposed to have spent about a third of her life in wanderings during which she discovered in Tibet and the borderlands of the Far East the mysteries of spiritualism and oriental gnostic religions. She wrote many books, and with Colonel H. S. Olcott founded the Theosophical Society in New York in 1875. In 1890 Mrs. Annie Besant became a convert to Theosophy, largely through reading for review books by A. P. Sinnett and Helena Blavatsky herself, in particular the latter's major work *The Secret Doctrine*. The vision opened up by these writings astounded Mrs. Besant, who had already had a notorious career.

In 1867 Annie Wood married Frank Besant, vicar of Sibsey in Lincolnshire, when she was twenty. Six years later, after bearing him two children, she left him because she had ceased to be a Christian, and later she was legally separated from him. In 1874 she joined the National Secular Society and began to work actively with Charles Bradlaugh, with whom she was prosecuted and acquitted in 1877 for the publication of Knowlton's *Fruits of Philosophy*, which advocated and defended birth control. In the same year she published her *Gospel of Atheism* and was deprived of the custody of her children. Her sympathy was with the left in politics and she joined the Fabian Society in 1885; it was over this that she broke her association with Bradlaugh, who rejected socialism.

Mrs. Besant was militant in her choice of constitutional weapons. In 1888 she helped to organize the match-girls of Bryant & May (a firm with Quaker connections) in their strike for better conditions, and she remained a firebrand of splendid oratorical power in Fabian causes until she began to adopt a Theosophical outlook in 1889. The oratory remained but the loyalties changed. Mme. Blavatsky and H. S. Olcott realized what a remarkable acquisition Mrs. Besant was, and she came into the movement at the top. When Mme. Blavatsky died in 1891 Mrs. Besant was clearly one of the leaders in England, and in 1907 she became president of the world movement. In 1893 she visited India and thereafter spent the major part of her life there and in the United States until her death in 1933. India was the sacred land in which Mrs. Besant felt that the full meaning of Theosophy could be understood, and it was at Adyar in Madras that the headquarters of the movement was established and still is.

In 1895 William Quan Judge, an American leader in the Theosophical Society, led a secession movement with which many of the American and some European members allied themselves, forming a new organization, the Universal Brotherhood and Theosophical Society. There were further fragmentations later in the world movement and a major split in 1913 between Mrs. Besant and Rudolf Steiner, who had led the German section of the Theosophical Society since 1902. Steiner and his followers at once set up the Anthroposophical Society, which I shall consider separately later, for Anthroposophists have founded a number of progressive schools in England.

The eclectic spirituality of the Theosophical movement brought to it many men and women for whom orthodox Christianity, whether Roman Catholic, Anglican, or Dissenting, was too constricting. A generation nurtured on the cosmology and cosmogony of Swedenborg, Blake, Carlyle, and Ruskin, and with Müller's translations available, could quickly savour and taste Theosophy even when it did not swallow it.

Theosophy is based on belief in an immutable, all-pervading principle which pre-exists creation and from which the universe, spirit and matter, growth and decay, all flow. Life, and the human mind which is aware of life are ensouled by this principle, this God. What man calls evolution in the world of matter is part of the divine potential which is unfolding itself through the elements, through mineral, vegetable, and animal existence up to the self-conscious phase of humanity. The physical world as men know it is the most dense and obvious, but each man possesses also an astral body which through clairvoyance and telepathy can effect a line of communication forming a second plane of the universe. The third plane of the universe is explored by man's mental body, which develops what one may, by metaphor, call the 'senses' appropriate to comprehending the entirely different scope of the spiritual plane. There are four higher planes, known only to adepts, which we will not here attempt to describe. The physical, astral, and mental bodies represent man's usual working instruments even for an average Theosophist, whose task is, of course, to deepen and extend his spiritual life.

At death man is evolving according to his deeds and understanding of the life just ended, and the unfolding of powers, the evolution of human experience, demands reincarnation as a consequence by means of which experience can be assimilated and physical, astral, and mental bodies which have been outgrown may be superseded. For this progression to be maintained the principle of *karma* must also operate, which is only the immutable principle, the God, maintaining the growth of the spirit through successive lives. 'As ye sew, so shall ye reap' is a gospel which makes perfection possible seen in the perspective of reincarnation and *karma*. On the other hand these two principles can also help to explain apparent injustices in the world and the mental, moral, and social inequalities which exist. Mme. Blavatsky claimed that her special insight into all these matters was based on the esoteric tradition of a Tibetan brotherhood into which she was initiated, whose spiritual discipline and study had produced the evolutionary structure on seven planes described above.

There are many other instances of the Theosophical tradition in the Christian world: Plotinus, the Gnostics, Meister Eckhart, St. John of the Cross, Jakob Böhme, C. G. Jung. This eclectic spirituality enabled the Theosophical Society to state that it had no dogmas, no creeds, that it included adherents of all faiths and none, that it represented those schools of religious thought which were seeking insight into the nature of God by mystical or occult experience or from sacred books or esoteric traditions. Doctrines, dogmas, theologies, they said, trapped only part of the meaning and the mystery. However, generalized and vague common agreement developed later into a discovery of difference, a definition which led to schism, as we have seen in the case of W. Q. Judge and Rudolf Steiner and as was also true of Cecil Reddie's friends Edward Maitland and Anna Kingsford, who broke from Theosophy and formed the Hermetic Society. Nevertheless it was Theosophists who made possible an important development in progressive education.

By 1907 there were 655 branches of the Theosophical Society all over the world, and the British section, although it had done nothing collectively in education, had a good number of members engaged in teaching at various levels. Armytage has shown that a number of Theosophists were connected with the Fellowship of the New Life and later with the Garden City movement at the turn of the century.[1] Mrs. Besant, George Arundale, A. P. Sinnett, and others made Theosophy 'almost fashionable' from 1910 to 1915, according to one of the surviving leaders of the movement at that time.[2] Almost annual visits to England for congresses and other matters enabled Mrs. Besant to publicize her message. The appeal to professional people was considerable, and by 1914 the obvious question of education as a piece of public service for Theosophists through schools of their own and through participation in national and local administration was becoming urgent.

The Theosophical Society in 1875 in New York had had one general statement of aim: to form a nucleus of the universal brotherhood of humanity without distinction of race, creed, sex, colour, or caste. There were two other aims which were more tentative: the first was to encourage the study of comparative religion, philosophy, and science and the second to investigate the unexplained laws of nature and the powers of man. In 1915 the same kind of spirit appeared in the formation of the Theosophical Fraternity in Education.

In England for a few years before the outbreak of war an informal group sharing similar liberal views on education had met to discuss a variety of subjects. In the group was Edmund Holmes, whose books *What is and What Might Be* and *In*

[1] Armytage, *Heavens Below*, especially phase iv, pp. 289-384.
[2] In recorded conversation with the author.

Quest of an Ideal, written after his enforced retirement from the post of chief inspector for elementary education at the Board of Education, made such an impact. Miss Belle Rennie, Wyatt Rawson, Beatrice de Normann (later Mrs. Ensor), J. H. Simpson, Miss Alice Woods, and later T. F. Coade, headmaster of Bryanston, were also strong supporters of this group, which took the title 'New Ideals in Education' and held its first conference at East Runton in Norfolk in 1914, its main theme on that occasion being the theory and practice of Mme. Montessori. There followed a sequence of annual conferences which lasted till just before the beginning of the Second World War. Reports of these conferences were published separately and the papers appeared in the journal of the group, *New Ideals Quarterly.* The members of the group came from all points of the religious and educational compass but had a certain shared attitude, summed up in the introduction to the report of the 1923 Oxford conference:

> Having begun as an informal association of friends of education sharing the same views and sympathies, the Conference Committee has now assumed the character of a permanent Council. It does not exist to voice the opinions of any particular pedagogical school or to give exclusive assistance to any sectional propaganda. Its members work together upon the basis of a common conviction that a new spirit, full of hope for the world is stirring in education.... The essentials of the new spirit ... are reverence for the pupil's individuality and the belief that true individuality ... grows best in an atmosphere of freedom.[3]

The Theosophical Fraternity in Education was started within the larger organization of the Conference of New Ideals in Education. The moving spirit was Beatrice de Normann, who married in 1919 and whom we shall call by her married name, Mrs. Beatrice Ensor. Mrs. Ensor was a qualified teacher without a degree who in 1910 became the first woman inspector appointed by the Glamorgan County Council. Her duties were to supervise day and evening work for women and girls in the

[3] 'The Discipline of Freedom', *Conference of New Ideals in Education* (1923), introduction.

county, and after a few years she was appointed His Majesty's Inspector of schools mainly concerned with domestic science. This appointment she took up in the early days of the war and Mrs. Ensor, beyond her normal duties, found herself reporting on schools for girl delinquents in the south of England and inspecting the working conditions of women in factories. During the years 1910–15 she became sharply critical, by reason of her varied first-hand experience, of the practices in very many schools. The buildings were tasteless and gloomy, the classes dispiritingly large, the discipline was stark regimentation and when she went to see a Montessori school she found the opportunities for self-development and self-discipline admirable and enviable. As a fellow H.M. Inspector she read Edmond Holmes's writings with eager appreciation, knowing that his model school of 'what might be', presided over by 'Egeria', was at Sompting in Sussex. Homer Lane's Little Commonwealth, begun in Dorset just before the beginning of the war, gave her the idea of forming a group of teachers within the Theosophical Society, of which she was a member, to study the changes needed in education, and this became the Theosophical Fraternity in Education, of which the keynote was faith in human nature and the spiritual powers latent in every child. The international contacts of the Theosophical Society gave Mrs. Ensor the chance to link together with like-minded persons in many lands. The Fraternity had sections in France, the U.S.A., India, Australia, and New Zealand.

For five or six years the English Fraternity Group attended the annual conferences of the New Ideals in Education organization, holding sectional meetings of their own during the larger gatherings, until in 1920 with a membership of over five hundred the Theosophical Fraternity was big enough to need to hold its own conference, which it did at Letchworth. From this meeting grew the idea and the organization of what we now know as the New Education Fellowship, and this we shall examine in detail later. For the moment it is sufficient to say that as the New Education Fellowship grew the Theosophical Fraternity in Education in England withered away. The inclusive and generalized tenets of Theosophy made it possible for many who would not call themselves theists to co-operate with the Fellowship. However, as Mrs. Ensor says,

'It is only fair to record that the first members [of the New Education Fellowship] being mainly Theosophists did give the Fellowship a spiritual impulse which made it a creative and powerful force.'[4]

The Fraternity and the New Education Fellowship represented Theosophy's contribution to theory and practice in education at large.[5] Theosophists also wanted the Society to set up schools of its own to make its point of view more explicit. Mrs. Besant had said at more than one international conference that the Theosophical Society ought to engage through its members in practical affairs, and for three or four years before the outbreak of the war Mr. H. Baillie-Weaver, the general secretary of the British branch, discussed with Mrs. Ensor and others a proposal for setting up an educational trust. Baillie-Weaver was a Scottish barrister of Labour-humanist sympathies, who had lived in the Paris Latin Quarter for a while earlier in his life and who was a firm supporter of feminist causes:

> Le mouvement féminin est un mouvement pour lequel j'ai beaucoup travaillé, étant convaincu que la responsabilité de la bonne administration de la nation incombe non seulement aux hommes mais également aux femmes qui la composent.[6]

He had great faith in the ability and competence of Mrs. Ensor and, in his turn, was trusted by a group of influential and wealthy Theosophists, among them Miss Dodge, an American heiress, and Mrs. Douglas-Hamilton, whose considerable income came from Wills, the tobacco company. From this group the money for the Theosophical Educational Trust (in Great Britain and Ireland) Ltd. came and Mrs. Ensor

[4] From an unpublished manuscript sent to the late Dr. William Boyd by Mrs. Ensor and made available for the present author's use. This material has been quoted in W. Boyd and W. Rawson, *The Story of the New Education* (London, 1965), pp. 67–8.

[5] The two aims of the Fraternity were: 1. To further the ideal in all branches of education; 2. To secure conditions which would give freedom for its expression.

[6] H. Baillie-Weaver, 'La Co-éducation', in *The Creative Self Expression of the Child*, Report of the First Summer Conference of the New Education Fellowship in Calais (1921), p. 44.

was appointed director when the Trust was formed in the early months of 1916, resigning from the Board of Education in order to give her time to the Theosophical Fraternity of Education, the Conference for New Ideals in Education, the Theosophical Educational Trust, and the tender growth of the New Education Fellowship.

In 1915 the Garden City Theosophical School was started in Letchworth, the model community near London with which Theosophists, Quakers, members of the Alpha Union and of the Fellowship of the New Life had had so much to do since the turn of the century. This became the Arundale School, named after G. S. Arundale, one of Mrs. Besant's best-known English disciples, when it passed into the hands of the Theosophical Educational Trust as a co-educational boarding-school for about eighty pupils. There was a private Theosophical venture in which Mrs. Douglas-Hamilton was specially interested on the outskirts of London at Bromley in Kent, where handicapped children or those from broken homes were cared for, at first dealing with babies, normal children, and crippled or invalid children, but quickly finding this impossible in the limited accommodation and reorganizing to take normal children of three years old and upward from undesirable homes or from none at all, many of the thirty-five pupils being illegitimate. This school, together with several others in different parts of the country, passed into the hands of the Theosophical Educational Trust.

Mrs. Ensor came to think that it would be a notable contribution if the Trust could centre much of its effort on Letchworth, which had no secondary school other than Arundale School and a girls' school for forty-six pupils. The trust took over this establishment, the Modern School, in 1918 and expanded it to accommodate one hundred boys and girls, converting Arundale School into a boarding-house for the Modern School, which quickly changed its name to St. Christopher. In the first prospectus we read that this was 'a Day School for the co-education of Boys and Girls up to the age of 19 and the standard of University scholarship'. A report of the Trust's activities in 1920 noted that 'this brings the secondary education of Letchworth largely into the hands of the Trust'. St. Christopher also added a Montessori junior section.

The Theosophical Educational Trust laid out its aims in its second annual report:

> to form miniature communities – co-educational and run on democratic lines. The boys and girls are co-citizens, learning self-discipline, first by the Montessori method and then by gradually assuming partial government of the school, with the teachers as elders and guides. The children help so far as is practical in the service needed for the upkeep of the community. On the domestic staff are gentlefolk who have been properly trained in their own particular line, by whom the children are instructed in cookery, housecraft, gardening and woodwork.... A factor in the educational life of all, the practical side is yet not allowed to interfere with the culture side. We are most anxious that the standards of work in all directions shall reach a high level of efficiency, and with a view to obtaining this we have appointed well-known experts in the chief subjects to act as advisers.[7]

Freedom to develop special talents and to grow according to the laws of his being was accorded to each child by means of a well-understood discipline based on physical, emotional, and mental self-control. Punishment in this context was really a last resort, and corporal punishment was totally rejected. Theosophists had a deep awareness of 'nature', and their schools were often called garden schools because they conducted their work and life as much as possible in the open air. They were aware of the importance of diet in matters of health but also in the understanding of nature and belief in the divinity and unity of all life:

> If this means anything at all, it will not stop at mankind, but embrace the animal creation.... Thus, the diet of the whole boarding community is meatless; and the same belief in the oneness of life finds expression in our attitude towards man's treatment of animals and towards the diseases of his own bodily frame.[8]

[7] Nov. 1918, p. 3.
[8] L. B. Pekin, 'The Way of Life at St. Christopher School, Letchworth', in *Progress Today*, vol. xvii, no. 1. 'L. B. Pekin', a well-known writer on progressive education, is the pseudonym of a member of the staff of St. Christopher of many years' standing.

These last two references relate to the antivivisection principle and to homoeopathic practices in medicine accepted by Theosophists. The Trust, in the report already referred to, said that science was taught so that materialistic tendencies were avoided, no dissection of the living animal body was practised and synthetic as well as analytic habits of mind were encouraged. Eurhythmics, relating in one direction to games and in another to the aesthetic harmony of music, art, and drama, led to an acceptance of effort and an absence of tension. Voluntary tests instead of set examinations, a great deal of individual rather than class teaching, the encouragement of co-operation rather than competitiveness – these led to a proper understanding of learning in which 'the highest reward of attainment is to be appointed a coach to backward or younger children'. Children so educated, the report commented in passing, should pass Matriculation at seventeen without extra preparation. Civics and sociology were considered in 1918 proper studies for St. Christopher, provided they were taught practically, and the religious teaching was to be based on Christianity presented in a non-sectarian way. While it was not compulsory for any child to attend any religious observances, it was hoped that they all would. Most of these principles still apply to St. Christopher fifty years later. But to return to its beginnings.

In 1919 Mr. and Mrs. Lyn Harris were appointed as joint-heads of the co-educational junior school at Badminton. He was a Friend, educated at Leighton Park and then at a Hampstead co-educational school and Cambridge, and during the war he had been imprisoned as a conscientious objector; in 1923 he and his wife moved to St. Christopher as vice-principals to Miss King.

The Theosophical Educational Trust applied the communitarian principle proper to Letchworth by setting up in the town a number of guilds, which were supposed to be self-supporting examples of co-operative life which at the same time offered to the boys and girls the opportunities they needed for first-hand, meaningful experience of economics, commerce, sociology, and the basic crafts of life. There was a printing guild, a tailoring guild, and guilds for weaving, poultry rearing, and fruit farming with, in addition, a grocer's shop and a pure food factory. Ruskin, William Morris, Tolstoy, the Fellowship of the New Life are in the ancestry of such undertakings; so, too, for Theosophists, was Santiniketan, fifty miles north-east of Calcutta, where in 1901 Rabindranath Tagore established his sanctuary school as an *ashram* where children and adults learned from one another and lived together.

The printing guild was the only one to develop and it tried to take some part in the education of the children, but found its role and organization as a commercial undertaking made this increasingly difficult. When the Theosophical Educational Trust came to an end the press went into the town of Letchworth as a full commercial concern, continuing to have interest in and association with the school but more for old time's sake than in any organic way.

In 1925 there was a severe premonitory shock to Theosophical education which coincided with disturbances within the Society as a whole. Mrs. Ensor resigned from her directorship of the Theosophical Educational Trust after some major differences on policy and on personal matters, and Miss King, the principal of St. Christopher, who was a close friend of Mrs. Ensor's, resigned also. From that date the Trust as a living and active concern began to fade away, disappearing finally in 1930. Mrs. Ensor and Miss King were appealed to by parents to start a school elsewhere on similar lines to St. Christopher, and Mrs. Douglas-Hamilton, whose generous support of good causes had brought many needy children to Letchworth, agreed to help a new foundation. In this way Frensham Heights was started in 1925, with Miss King as the teaching head and Mrs. Ensor as the administrative head. The school was (and is) located in a mansion near Farnham in Surrey and was to be almost entirely a boarding-school as compared with the combination of day and boarding pupils at Letchworth. The Charrington mansion at Frensham was very different from Arundale House and Farnham was no Garden City. Theosophical principle had to be reinterpreted in a very different setting, for Letchworth had been the community symbol of the new century on which Mrs. Ensor saw that the effort and the physical plant of the Theosophical Educational Trust could best be concentrated.

Mrs. Douglas-Hamilton died suddenly in 1927 and left the

major portion of the Douglas-Hamilton Trust to her husband, who did not share her concerns for Theosophical causes. In the circumstances Miss King and Mrs. Ensor resigned from Frensham, and effectively all connection with Theosophy ends two years after the school started. Mr. Paul Roberts, who had been teaching for some years at St. George's, a co-educational school for boarders and day-pupils started by the Reverend Cecil Grant in 1907 at Harpenden, north of London, was appointed headmaster. Frensham continues to work under the Douglas-Hamilton Educational Trust, with many of the Theosophical principles and practices unaltered in so far as they are general progressive principles too. Farnham is close to Petersfield and Bedales and a long way from Letchworth, and in the last thirty-five years the connection and the rivalry between Frensham and Bedales have replaced any historical association with St. Christopher, the more particularly since the two headmasters who succeeded Mr. Roberts, who retired after the end of the Second World War, came from the Bedales staff.

To return to St. Christopher in 1925. With Mrs. Ensor and Miss King gone, taking a number of the children and one of the main financial supporters of the school with them, St. Christopher and the Theosophical Educational Trust were in severe difficulties. Still further hardships came when Miss Dodge, the American heiress, moved her allegiances from the Theosophical Society to a new group.

St. Christopher and the Theosophical Educational Trust found themselves by 1927 without the secure financial support and the executive leadership which they had had for ten years. Mr. Lyn Harris was appointed principal in 1926 and saw the whole project being gradually dismantled by the Trust under his eyes. In the autumn of 1929 he and his wife, who always worked with him, resigned in protest and this produced an objection from the parents, who in many cases were prepared to withdraw their children. An arrangement was reached enabling Mr. and Mrs. Harris to float a company, the St. Christopher School Estate Ltd., which bought the school through a mortgage to the First Garden City Company and to a group of parents and friends, and through a second mortgage to the Theosophical Educational Trust, which the Trust later renounced in favour of the school. The St. Christopher School Estate Ltd. leased the property to the Harrises for use as a school, which enabled them to acquire large and suitable buildings at a small rental, and from 1930 until 1956 the financial responsibility and all capital undertakings were borne by Mr. and Mrs. Harris themselves. The school grew from seven pupils in 1915 to three hundred and sixty in 1955. In 1956 Mr. and Mrs. Harris retired and handed over the responsibility of running the school to their son, Mr. N. K. Harris, and a public non-profit-making company, St. Christopher School (Letchworth) Ltd., was registered with a Board of Governors, still essentially a family group.

By 1918 there were at least the fifteen progressive schools we have mentioned. Fourteen of these were religious foundations, and at King Alfred's although the rationalist pulse was strong, a Theosophist headmaster in 1920 brought comparative religion over the threshold.

The New Education Fellowship was beginning to take shape by 1920 and although its development and influence came later, we must take note that there was already in other countries a progressive school movement which arose out of the work of Reddie, Badley, and the rest. It was in existence by 1914 and provided a foundation on which the New Education Fellowship could build after the war. We are accustomed to think that progressive education has its origins in the work of Rousseau, Pestalozzi, Fellenberg, Froebel, and Dewey, and in a sense this is true, as the theory of one or another of these outstanding men has been applied in different countries. But the international organization which provided a forum and a fellow-feeling originated in Great Britain and in Geneva in a non-political, idealistic movement with a tiny administrative staff, and we must see how this came about.

10 New Schools and Europe: 1890–1918

I

CECIL REDDIE said that three or four years after opening Abbotsholme in 1889 he needed some advice on developing classroom teaching and J. J. Findlay told him to visit Professor Wilhelm Rein at the University of Jena. This Reddie did at Easter 1893. He visited the Training School intending to stay in Jena for two nights: 'We saw for the first time what teaching was and for a full fortnight we sat five mortal hours, one after the other, and drank in that which is creating modern Germany.'[1]

He read Rein's *Pädagogik im Grundriss* and saw in Herbartian theory 'a new instructional heaven and earth'. He met Rein and one of his tutors, Dr. Hermann Lietz, a man of peasant stock who had studied both theology and pedagogy. Rein paid a short visit to Abbotsholme in 1896 and Reddie was able to arrange for Lietz to spend a year teaching at Abbotsholme, as a result of which he published *Emlohstobba* in Berlin in 1897, a detailed account of a flawlessly harmonious Abbotsholme. The book had a considerable vogue in Germany and Switzerland and Reddie translated it into English.[2] The experience of the school had an immense effect on Lietz. One of his German colleagues wrote: 'To think of Lietz without C.R. is impossible. His experiences at Abbotsholme altered both himself and his aims.'[3]

In 1898 Lietz established the first of his *Landerziehungsheime* at Ilsenburg in the Harz mountains of central Germany, for boys and girls aged six to twelve years in the proportion of one girl to three boys. In 1901 in Thuringia,

---

[1] C. Reddie, *Abbotsholme* (London, 1900), p. 115.
[2] Ibid., pp. 263–380.
[3] *Fifty Years of Abbotsholme*: article by Alfred Andressen, who was one of Lietz's successors as director of the Lietz Country Boarding Schools.

nearly one hundred miles south-west of Ilsenburg, he started Haubinda for boys aged thirteen to fifteen years, and in 1904 he completed the range by opening Bieberstein for boys aged sixteen to nineteen in the neighbourhood of Fulda in the Rhön mountains north-east of Frankfurt. Lietz was the principal of all three schools while being headmaster at Bieberstein, and according to Andressen he copied Reddie's work to its smallest detail although in German contexts something different emerged. At Ilsenburg, with the junior boys and girls, the routine of rules and orders was kept to a minimum and the custom of a family community in houses of twelve or fifteen was to be the guide. In the curriculum there was as little formal teaching as possible and what we might now call projects or individual work was the method, a kind of guided experience. Religion and morals were presented through the family life, through stories from literature, and through Christian teaching free from dogma. With the boys in the middle school at Haubinda, Lietz followed Reddie's lead in the agricultural and craftwork and extended it to bring in local workmen and craftsmen or to send the boys to work with them. To Lietz, a farmer and the son of a farmer, this was near to the heart of education, and the same actual and symbolic labour was continued at Bieberstein with the older boys, whose curriculum also included more work in science and mathematics than was usual. Wilhelm Rein wrote a foreword to *Emlohstobba* in which he spoke of an English school 'which is carrying into practice the high aims so long familiar to us Germans in the works of our great teachers, Pestalozzi, Herbart, Froebel'. Lietz's own admissions and his imitation of Abbotsholme show that, whatever Rein might write of the great German teachers, Lietz thought that no German Abbotsholme existed in fact.

Dr. Erich Meissner had a unique experience of the Lietz schools and their history. He was a pupil at Ilsenburg under Kramer, the first headmaster after Lietz moved on to Haubinda in 1901. He then moved on in the normal sequence to the middle school, where Marseille was headmaster, and later completed his schooling at Bieberstein. He studied at the Universities of Berlin and Göttingen and was contemplating an academic career for himself as a historian when he was invited to return to Haubinda as headmaster in 1924, straight from the university and the youngest man on the staff. Lietz had died in 1919 and the post-war confusion and depression had damaged the schools badly. Dr. Meissner remained at Haubinda until 1931, when he left to join Kurt Hahn at the Salem group of schools, and with him Dr. Meissner worked for the rest of his career, as we shall later see.[4] Salaries in the Lietz schools were low but the devotion, versatility, and energy which Lietz and his wife displayed were often able to win a corresponding dedication from their colleagues. As Dr. Meissner recalled, it was like being in an order, for life was simple and spartan.

Alfred Andressen was the director of the three Lietz schools in 1923, when a further group was founded, all but one relatively close to the existing schools, though in these days the border between East and West Germany separates those that remain. Gebesee near Jena, and Ettersburg near Weimar were founded in 1923, Buchenau near Bieberstein in 1924. Later a girls' school at Hohenwerda was started, also close to Bieberstein. In 1928, after Ilsenburg had closed, a new venture was begun on the Frisian island of Spiekeroog not far from Bremerhaven, where the rough climate and coastal storms made seamanship a main necessity in the school life of those boys of sixteen and over. An orphanage for boys and girls at Grovesmühle was begun in the Lietz group in the 1920s when after the war so many children without families had to be cared for in Germany.

These eight schools (Ilsenburg, Haubinda, Bieberstein, Ettersburg, Gebesee, Buchenau, Spiekeroog, and Hohenwerda), together with the orphanage at Grovesmühle, are the schools which were founded on Lietz's, and so Abbotsholme's, principles and they represent in themselves an export from Great Britain which has been too often invisible in discussing progressive education. Of the eight schools, Ilsenburg closed after the First World War. Haubinda, Gebesee, and Ettersburg have been, since the Second World War, in East Germany, the first two continuing as schools and the third not. Bieberstein, Buchenau, Spiekeroog, and Hohenwerda con-

[4] Dr. Meissner, who died in 1964, lived in retirement at Hohenfels School near Salem, where he talked with the author.

New Schools and Europe: 1890–1918

tinue, the headquarters of the administration of the Lietz group being at Bieberstein.

Gustav Wyneken and Paul Geheeb worked with Lietz in the earliest days of Ilsenburg and Haubinda but came to disagree with his opposition to co-education for adolescents. They also thought that the adults' responsibility in setting an example to and controlling the children gave the boys too little chance to take a full part in the running of the school. In 1906 Wyneken and Geheeb set up the Free School Community (*Freie Schulgemeinde*) at Wickersdorf, a co-educational school for children aged nine to nineteen with a good deal of freedom and weekly school meetings of teachers and pupils to deal with many matters of school government. In 1910 Paul and Edith Geheeb broke away from Wyneken and founded the New School at Odenwald, where they worked for twenty-five years before they left Germany under Hitler for Switzerland. There they set up the *École de l'Humanité* in which Geheeb worked till shortly before his death in 1961.

Other schools were started early in the century by Lietz's men, and a leading member of these schools says of the present-day situation: 'There are today about twenty *Landerziehungsheime* and *Landschulheime*. Only six or seven are of more than local importance.'

There were foundations in German Switzerland as well. In 1902 Clarisegg was founded by Werner Zuberbuhler, who had worked at Abbotsholme for a while and in Lietz schools. Herman Tobler founded Hof Oberkirch in 1906, and a French-Swiss Country Boarding-School, the *École Nouvelle de la Suisse Romande* was opened in the same year near Lausanne.

Sufficient has been said to show that Reddie, through Lietz, had helped to start a movement in Germany. When Reddie visited several of the *Lietz-Stiftung* – in 1924 at the age of sixty-six – he found himself greeted as the Grossvater of the New School movement, and this is no more than the truth, although some of his grandchildren were far from the old man's views on religion or discipline or co-education.

One other name might be mentioned here for later reference. Kurt Hahn, as a schoolboy about to go to Berlin University in 1902, met three senior Abbotsholme boys and went for a walking tour of the Tyrol with them, led by his uncle.

Here they told him of Reddie and Abbotsholme with such pride and enthusiasm that Hahn, having read *Emlohstobba*, thought how different such a school was from his own *Gymnasium*, and how preferable. As he said, recalling this incident in 1962 to the present author, 'My fate cried out to me.'[5] Salem and Gordonstoun come later in this story, but Hahn admits that, although he never met Reddie and differed from him in many things, Reddie was nevertheless important to him through those boys long ago and through Lietz, whose schools have much in common with Salem, although Hahn never met Lietz either – he died in 1919 before Hahn had taken up his work at Salem.

The Country Boarding-Schools turned from the towns and from the day schools, and sought to regain by labour and living the country ways and natural virtues. This feeling for nature, history, and the good earth was, of course, a romanticized sentiment, and in Germany the intensity of passionate folklore modulates too easily into mystique. In 1904 Berlin students and intellectuals formed companies of 'wandering birds' (*Wandervögel*) whose purpose was to rediscover the country, the peasantry, the customs, and the lore of the immemorial German land. The young people walked the forests and hills at weekends and in the holidays, they camped in the woods, read poems and legends, sang folk-songs, met the countrymen, joined in country dancing. The older people often felt this was leading to general unsettlement and moral breakdown, and undoubtedly there was a hectic and erotic quality in the movement. There was also an ascetic and high-minded strain; the puritan improvers who shunned alcohol and tobacco and were concerned with hardihood and fitness and the regeneration of the Fatherland. It is easy to see that the *Wandervögel* of 1910 had much in common with the outlook of the Country Boarding-Schools. Gustav Wyneken even proposed a merger of the two movements so that young people of all kinds and in all circumstances could learn from one another, pamphleteering against the domination of adults and the consequent subjection of children in school and in the home. He advocated the extension of his Wickersdorf Free

---

[5] This incident is also reported in Abbotsholme sources and in Stanley Unwin, *The Truth about a Publisher* (London, 1961).

School Community to enable other schools to lead a life of freedom, with liberally-minded teachers often taking their pupils away from the circumscribed and authoritarian life of the classroom to live and learn like the outdoor *Wandervögel*. In 1913 the short-lived *Freideutsche Jugend-Bewegung* was founded at Hoher Meissner, taking as its oath: 'We seek to order our lives with full personal responsibility and in concord with the truth that is within us.'

Distant as the comparison is, the nearest British equivalent would probably be the Boy Scout movement, which started in this country in 1908 and to which Reddie in particular was quick to respond, for the movement sought to promote good citizenship through woodcraft, camping, nature study, and the outdoor life, a combination of scouting crafts with a code of honour like a medieval knight's. Even the sectional organization by age into Wolf Cubs, Scouts, and Rover Scouts was pleasing to Abbotsholme, for in this and most of the earlier features the Scout movement gave a particular form to principles which the school had proclaimed from its beginnings.

II

When Patrick Geddes was studying in Paris in the early 1870s, at T. H. Huxley's suggestion he met Edmond Demolins, the French sociologist and disciple of Frédéric Le Play. Ten years later Geddes was back in Edinburgh, and at one of the university summer courses in August 1894 Demolins was present. Also present was Reddie, and the two men were introduced by Geddes. Demolins subjected Reddie to a close interrogation, and each has a record of the meeting:

> We [Reddie] met, for the first time, M. Demolins, little dreaming, as he pertinaciously catechized us about our school, that he meditated incorporating our chance conversation in a book.[6]

Demolins wrote up the conversation in *La Science Sociale*,[7] and from this it is clear that Reddie and Demolins must to-

[6] *Abbotsholme*, p. 118.   [7] Oct. 1894.

gether have had a verbal marathon. In 1897 Demolins incorporated the account in his book (published in Paris) *A Quoi Tient la Supériorité des Anglo-Saxons?*, which was translated into English in 1898[8] and in which he tried to demonstrate that the Anglo-Saxons had been far more successful than Frenchmen as colonizers in Canada, America, and India; more prosperous as traders; more stable in their governments; more venturesome as explorers. Demolins saw socialism as limiting both the risks and the opportunities open to a man, and considered this kind of 'collectivism' to be the natural enemy of enterprise. Despite the Revolution, Frenchmen are not Socialists, said Demolins, and they rely on their family, their connections, a safe post in the government, for their security: for this attitude of mind he coined the word 'communitarian'. The third, and for Demolins the desired classification he called 'particularist', characterized by qualities of independence, resource, and energy. It was in these that the reasons for Anglo-Saxon leadership were to be found, and to support the thesis he analysed deficiencies in French attitudes and competence, showing in each case how the Anglo-Saxons had developed the compensating efficiencies. The Germans came in for even less flattering treatment than the French, and as one reviewer remarked: 'His chapter on education in Germany and the Emperor's views thereon, will more than suffice to cause [the book's] confiscation beyond the frontier.'[9]

Demolins attributed the superiority in part to the habits of family training and the education provided in England. He chose three schools to illustrate his point: Abbotsholme, Bedales, and Colonial College, Hollesley Bay, an agricultural college near Felixstowe which a few years later (1904) was converted into a community for the unemployed under the Central Unemployment Committee. Many English reviewers took up his selection, and the *Journal of Education* said:

What does astound us is that it never seems to have dawned on M. Demolins that these schools, so far from being typical of English schools, are almost unique of their kind and that three schools (it would be difficult to name a fourth) are a

[8] *Anglo-Saxon Superiority: To What Is It Due?* (London, 1898).
[9] *The Westminster Gazette*, 15 Nov. 1897.

narrow and unstable basis on which to rest a glorification of Anglo-Saxondom.[10]

Demolins had visited Bedales after his Edinburgh conversations with Reddie and had been so impressed by what he saw there that in 1896 he sent his son, Joseph Jules, to the school as a pupil. He followed this by establishing near Verneuil in Normandy the *École des Roches* in 1899. Badley remembers him as a stocky man who was a better talker than a listener, sure of himself and his ideas and 'impatient not only of contradiction but of any slowness in acceptance of the principles he laid down'.[11] In France, Demolins and his associates at the school were considered *des bêtes curieuses*.

In 1901 Demolins wrote a second book to explain the provenance of the *École des Roches* and to outline its programme. This was *L'Éducation Nouvelle*,[12] and the book is freely illustrated with pictures principally of Abbotsholme and Bedales. Joseph Jules returned from Bedales in 1899 to finish his schooling at the *École des Roches*, and Demolins recommended to French parents that they continue to send their boys to Abbotsholme and Bedales while also drawing their attention to the French equivalent at Verneuil-sur-Arve, complete with *Champ de Foot-Ball et Champ de Cricquet*. His acount of the new-style schoolmaster could well have been taken from his son's experience at Bedales,[13] and 'La Vie de l'École Nouvelle décrite par les élèves'[14] is taken almost entirely from the *Bedales Record*.

It is to be noted that the *École des Roches* was a boys' school, which fitted the French situation more conveniently, but thereby in 1898 they were following the Bedales plan, for the English school did not change to co-education until after Joseph Jules left. A few girls were admitted later when Demolins had left the running of the school to the new headmaster, but this was not co-education as it developed at

---

[10] Nov. 1897. The reviewer would have been even more astounded had he known that Demolins never visited Abbotsholme, but rested his account on his talk with Reddie. For similar strictures, see *Manchester Guardian*, 11 May 1897; *The Spectator*, 18 Sept. 1897; *Academy*, 24 Sept. 1898; and *The Westminster Gazette*, 30 Sept. 1898.
[11] *Memories and Reflections*, p. 203.   [12] Paris, 1901.
[13] *L'Éducation Nouvelle*, pp. 52–98.   [14] Ibid., pp. 196–258.

Bedales. The school continues and thrives today.[15]

There were two or three other schools in France, but the *École des Roches* is the important foundation because it followed upon Demolins's controversial thesis of Anglo-Saxon superiority, and because of the place of Abbotsholme and Bedales in bringing this about. The book had immense publicity[16] and as a result the two English schools had many visitors from a great range of countries. There were countless foreign press notices and an avalanche of letters from all parts of the world asking for information and applying for admission. Both schools responded as far as they could, but Reddie had no intention of letting Abbotsholme become a 'Cosmopolitan School', and Badley said that if every pupil who came from overseas was counted, whether from the Commonwealth or not, of the first 1,400 former pupils of Bedales just under 20 per cent were 'foreigners', which is significantly high.

At this point we can say that the New Schools, Abbotsholme and Bedales, had international reputations by 1900, especially on the continent of Europe, and served as a pattern for a number of schools in Germany, Switzerland, France, Belgium, and Holland. The Quaker schools and the Theosophical schools had international sympathies by reason of the faith and works of their parent bodies. Badminton from 1911 was an internationally-minded school. The time was ripe to try to bring them all together in some way.

III

A young Swiss, Adolf Ferrière, read *A Quoi Tient la Supériorité des Anglo-Saxons?* in 1898 when he was nineteen years of age. He had a comprehensive university training in philosophy, sociology, and zoology, and his doctorate was in sociology. Ferrière first heard of Reddie and Abbotsholme through Demolins, and he resolved that teaching was his vocation, with the New School movement as his chosen environment. He went to Germany and started teaching under Hermann Lietz at Ilsenburg in 1900, where he read *Emlohstobba*, and he had the opportunity to meet Reddie at Haubinda in 1901, sensing

[15] There are accounts of the work of the school in conference reports, in *The New Era* during the 1920s and in *Pour L'Ère Nouvelle* at the same period.
[16] It ran to ten impressions in the first year.

his intellectual daring and magnetism at once.

In 1899 Ferrière started the International Bureau of New Schools in Switzerland at Les Pléiades-sur-Blonay in the canton of Vaud. He had no staff and had to rely mainly on his own money for expenses, but by conducting a massive correspondence and making visits when his teaching duties permitted he built up an unrivalled range of contacts. Over the years he tried to clarify the definition of a New School, for there were many variations on the Reddie–Lietz theme. At one point Ferrière defined such a school as 'a self-governing country boarding-school in which all education is based on personal interest and experience, and intellectual work is combined with manual activities in workshop and fields'.

Throughout the 1914–18 war Ferrière was able to keep his records going only to lose them all in a disastrous fire in 1918. The Bureau, however, continued to work alongside the developing New Education Fellowship from its inception in 1921, and Ferrière became in 1922 the editor of *Pour L'Ère Nouvelle*, the French version of *The New Era*, the Fellowship's periodical. In 1926 the International Bureau of New Schools merged with the International Bureau of Education which had been founded in Geneva a year before by a grant from the Rockefeller Foundation and placed under the auspices of the *Institut Jean-Jacques Rousseau*. In 1929–30 the *Institut* was officially supported by the authorities of Geneva and the other cantons while retaining its position as an independent organization and thus ceased to have to rely upon voluntary money.

The publications of the International Bureau of Education no longer have a particular interest in the New Schools and Ferrière's work has been carried forward since 1922 largely through the New Education Fellowship, *Pour L'Ère Nouvelle*, *The New Era*, and the German equivalent, *Das Werdende Zeitalter*. His expansive aims for the Bureau in 1912 have been realized up to a point in the Fellowship's programme. Ferrière died in 1960, having started and participated in many New School ventures and still maintaining a phenomenal literary output including forty books, countless articles, and a correspondence often averaging four thousand letters a year.[17]

[17] See an obituary notice in *The New Era*, Aug. 1960.

IV

There were New Schools in Canada and the U.S.A., many of which Reddie saw when he crossed the Atlantic in 1906. In 1919 one of the first bulletins of the newly formed American Progressive Education Association described the work of the International Bureau of New Schools, calling particular attention to Reddie and Abbotsholme, to Demolins and the *École des Roches*, to Lietz and the *Landerziehungsheime*.[18] The tentative association of the American Association with the New Education Fellowship developed quickly in the 1920s, but for the moment the point to make is that the impulses from England's New Schools spread principally to Europe from 1890 to 1920. To put it over-simply but not unfairly, Abbotsholme and Reddie and to a lesser extent Bedales and Badley were originators of the Country Boarding-School movement in Germany, Switzerland, France, Holland, and Belgium. The schools were often started by sparks of conflict struck between enthusiasts, and in any case no new experiment wants for long to dwell in the shadow of the orthodoxy from which it sprang. So Bieberstein was not for long another Abbotsholme, Wickersdorf was not another Haubinda, Odenwald another Ilsenburg. But individualists though they might be, there was a family likeness and the fellow-feeling that pioneers have for one another over against the cohorts of the conventional.

Reddie admitted a deep debt to Rein and to Herbart and to German initiative, solidarity, and organization. But through Lietz, Ferrière, and later Hahn he repaid it. Badley's influence was mainly in the first place with Demolins, but as Reddie's temperamental waywardness diminished his and Abbotsholme's influence, Badley's stability and co-educational daring caused his and Bedales' influence to increase.

The post-war international organization for progressive education becomes more diffuse, but there can be no mistake as to the examples by which the pre-war European impulses were activated.

[18] L. A. Cremin, *Transformation of the School* (New York, 1961), p. 248.

11 Preface to the Post-War Surgence

THE WORK of Maria Montessori and of Homer Lane made a deep impression on progressive education in this country after the First World War. Each of them claimed to have rediscovered the significance of freedom for children, but their practical conclusions were vastly different, so variant that without misprision they may be called the two magnetic poles round which for a time the lines of force in English innovatory education formed themselves.

24 MARIA MONTESSORI

MARIA MONTESSORI was born in Rome in 1870 and spent her early years in the uncertain world of hard-won Italian unity. She was in the mould of European feminists, and in 1894 she qualified in the University of Rome as the first woman doctor of medicine in Italy. She worked in asylums and psychiatric clinics and became especially interested in feeble-minded children, for whom she tried to devise a training which would give them the best opportunity to use the limited capacities they had. She read, and later translated into Italian, the works of Séguin on the treatment of idiots[1] and the earlier classical account by Itard of his attempt to educate the Savage Boy of Aveyron.[2] There were others, like J. R. Pereire and Giuseppe Sergi, in whose work Dr. Montessori was interested, but it was Séguin whose writing and design of inquiry meant most. Another pioneer in the education of young children, Margaret McMillan, also read Séguin but, of course, without Montessori's professional insight. For Séguin, instinct, emotion, and the senses provide the materials with which comprehen-

---

[1] E. Séguin, *Idiocy and its Treatment by the Physiological Method* (1866); *Traitement Moral, Hygiène Éducation des Idiots* (1846); *New Facts and Remarks on Idiocy* (1870); *Report on Education* (1876).

[2] J. E. M. G. Itard, *An Historical Account of the Discovery and Education of a Savage Man* (trans. 1802).

sion may be built. But, and this is important, the comprehension is the child's and it is most secure and resilient when he is able to initiate his own experience. With idiots, says Séguin, a teacher will enforce obedience by coercion more often than with normal children:

> *Liberty* and *will* are two words which are permissible only when two preceding words are understood: *obedience* and *authority*, words which are too often divorced and which, when divorced, have no meaning.[3]

Séguin has a grasp of the growth and cumulative mastery of a child's mental, moral, and social development, and he says that the aim of education should be not passivity, but liberty, the first condition of which is the desire to be free. When this desire is combined with confidence in one's own competence within a certain range, then the normal pressure of meaningful activity will indefinitely extend the competence and, in normal people, the range. So, to restate the two key principles in Séguin's work, the first has to do with training and directing or redirecting basic impulses, using the detailed knowledge of each child's neural, muscular, and motor mechanisms to the full and observing these working in his actions while bringing the same precision to bear on his sensory and intellectual training. The second principle gives scope to the child's initiative and curiosity operating within a contrived 'educational' framework, but also accepting the chance, intricate, dense experience gained from the influence of child upon child as well as of child and adult upon one another.

When Montessori was working with feeble-minded children in the Orthophrenic School, which she conducted in Rome from 1898 to 1900, education for her was at first concerned with preventing the ultimate consequences of degeneration and disease and with the removal of obstacles. Her apparatus aimed at improving discrimination of length, size, weight, shape, colour, texture, and, like Séguin, she had to perfect both the apparatus and a precise method of observation, at first leaving little individual scope to the backward child until necessary skills had been mastered as tools. She began with

[3] *Traitement des Idiots*, p. 651.

normal children by providing a physical and educational environment in which things were constructed to make use of each child's physical and sense mechanisms and the regime was ordered so that the children were confronted by but not forced into dealing with these challenges. She found, of course, that normal children could much more quickly see the purpose of the tasks they were set and connect up the knowledge they obtained from the different pieces of apparatus. McCallister goes so far as to say that only then for the first time did Montessori envisage freedom as a means of enabling the pupil to educate himself. She was very successful in improving the standard of reading and writing of her backward children and began to wonder why normal children did not do much better than they did.

In 1907 a philanthropic organization in Rome conceived the idea of having schools attached to tenement buildings in which young children between the ages of three and seven could play and work under the care of a teacher who also lived in the tenement, and Dr. Montessori undertook the educational direction of the enterprise. For four years her Children's Houses enabled her to test her methods upon normal children and to perfect her theory of the teacher as background directress rather than pedagogue. She presented the fruits of this experience in the bok translated into English as *The Montessori Method*.[4]

Her methods and her apparatus aroused world-wide interest, support, and criticism. She was uncompromising in defence of her ideas, taking the line that hers was a scientific approach to child development built without any predisposing theory except loyalty to the truth and a readiness to test the results of experiment, and that the same could not be said of the works of most other theorists on child development. But her fiercest denunciation was reserved for conventional class teachers and believers in 'discipline'. In her later writings this became apocalyptic:

> In fact in every educational ideal, in all pedagogy up to our

---

[4] The third edition has been newly translated and entitled *The Discovery of the Child*. It was published in Adyar, Madras, the Indian headquarters of the Theosophical Society.

own time, the word education has been almost synonymous with the word punishment. The end was always to subject the child to the adult.... Thus the child repeats the Passion of Christ.... The mistress [in the classroom] commands that group of souls, with no witness or control. She will shut the door....

Henceforth those delicate, trembling limbs are held to the wood for more than three hours of anguish, three and three for many days and months and years.

The child's hands and feet are fastened to the desk by stern looks which hold them motionless as the nails of the cross in the feet of Christ.... And when into the mind athirst for truth and knowledge the ideas of the teacher are forcibly driven, as he wills, the little head humbled in submission will seem to bleed as by a crown of thorns.[5]

Written when she was sixty-five, this is not scientific refutation and it reveals the intensity with which the *dottoressa* felt about children, her own work, and conventional parents and teachers. As we shall see, there was also a battle between two armies of freedom: we may loosely call these the Montessorians and the other educational radicals. Mme. Montessori developed the didactic apparatus, which had to be used complete and not as an incidental aid. She trained her followers personally, and as her two staunchest present-day supporters say:

Though her attitude was bitterly resented at the time, Dr. Montessori was probably far-sighted in creating first of all, a body of disciples all trained personally by herself, and in resisting the many facile temptations to go too quickly, for fear of going more slowly in the end.[6]

She designed the furniture, she put the child in the way of teaching himself in his own good time under the discreet con-

[5] Maria Montessori, *The Secret of Childhood* (Calcutta, 1936), pp. 274, 279, 281-2.
[6] Mario M. Montessori and C. A. Claremont, 'Montessori and the Deeper Freedom', in *Year Book of Education* (1957), p. 426.

trol of the directress. The shift of focus was astounding, and there were many in England who testified to it. Miss Finlay Johnson, Edmond Holmes's Egeria of the Sussex village, had completed her experiment 'before the name of Montessori had been whispered in this country',[7] but MacMunn himself says: 'As the doctrines of Rousseau were to the social revolution of yesterday, so, it seems to many of us, the doctrines of Montessori will be to the revolution of tomorrow.'[8]

Edmond Holmes wrote a warmly favourable report on Montessori's work for the Board of Education, and in 1912 told the Reverend Cecil Grant, head of the relatively conservative co-educational school St. George's at Harpenden, of the *dottoressa*'s Roman school, which Grant visited in 1913: 'I knew that I was in the presence of a greater than Pestalozzi and Froebel.'[9] On his return he roused Harpenden to start a Montessori class adjacent to the senior school, and persuaded the originator of the movement to visit Harpenden and speak at a special meeting in 1919.

In the first issue of the journal which a year later became *The New Era* there appears a statement by Mrs. Beatrice Ensor, the editor: 'In our opinion the Montessori System is a most valuable element in the forward movement in Education, and we propose to devote a few pages to this subject every quarter.'[10] Professor Culverwell of the University of Dublin had published in 1913 as 'a keen enthusiast and careful critic' a book on the new movement.[11] In 1920 Dr. Percy Nunn wrote of the contrast between the bondage of old methods and the calm, happy, absorbed industry of the Montessori class, before which he thought 'the most cautious observer ... would find it hard to remain a sceptic'.[12] In 1919 Dr. Montessori conducted a training course in London: about one thousand inquiries were made but only three hundred could be admitted. A Montessori Committee led to organized support in this country in pre-war

---

[7] N. MacMunn, *A Path to Freedom in the School* (London, 1914), p. 45.
[8] Ibid., p. 7.
[9] C. Grant, 'St. George's School: A Retrospect': address to St. George's Parents' Association, 5 July 1941, p. 20.
[10] *Education for the New Era*, vol. i, no. 1 (Jan. 1920), p. 11.
[11] E. P. Culverwell, *Montessori Principles and Practice* (London, 1913).
[12] T. P. Nunn, *Education: Its Data and First Principles* (London, 1920), p. 101.

days, and schools were started in many places for children of nursery-school and infant-school age. While the Montessori methods were being worked out with older children and for adolescents, it was mainly with three- to seven-year-olds that they gained their position in England. Mrs. Ensor and the Theosophical Fraternity in Education, and later the Trust, found Mme. Montessori's emphasis on the child's freedom to grow, to learn, and to teach himself, in harmony with their views, and it is no wonder to find a Montessori nursery school and children's house at St. Christopher, Letchworth. Mr. and Mrs. Lyn Harris had had a similar school at Badminton before they moved to Letchworth. From 1917 Bedales had one of the best-known junior houses in England at Dunhurst, run by Mrs. Fish and later Miss Clarke on Montessori lines. King Alfred's has had a Montessori department for fifty years and so has St. George's, Harpenden, although here the junior school is a separate organization. Some of the Friends' schools have had preparatory departments run mainly on Montessori lines at least for a while.

The progressive schools were active in developing Montessori interests in England, but the militant Montessori movement cannot really be said to have swept the country. Old battles have led to treaties, truces, modifications, and near-alliances, but for the moment we must look back to the 1920s to understand how severe the conflicts were.

There were four main kinds of objector to Montessorianism. First, the out-and-out opponent of a system which, as was so often said, represented a 'go-as-you-please' regime for the children: teachers and adults generally were resigning the authority they ought to exert. Second, there were those who criticized parts of the system: the apparent discouragement of individual imagination in the child in the interest of precision, the apparent discrediting of class teaching in the interest of auto-didactic apparatus. Third there were those who were already committed to another system, like Charlotte Mason, who says in a summary of her method as seen in the work of the Parents' National Educational Union:

When we say that 'education is an atmosphere' we do not mean that a child should be isolated in what may be called a 'child-environment' especially adapted and prepared, but that we should take into account the educational value of the natural home atmosphere both as regards persons and things, and should let him live freely among his proper conditions. It stultifies a child to bring down his world to the 'child's level'.[13]

Cecil Grant, after returning in 1913 from his visit to the Montessori Centre in Rome, intended to go and see Miss Mason of Ambleside, 'whose experimental method was our nearest approach to Dr. Montessori's scientific discovery.... Before I could do so, an enemy had sown tares in her mind and she became the Dottoressa's most formidable opponent.'[14]

Margaret MacMillan, who with her sister Rachel founded an open-air nursery school for poor children in Deptford in 1914, and who was founder and first president of the Nursery Schools Association in 1923, wrote in 1926 that many people were suggesting that these schools were the product of the Montessori movement. While admitting that Mme. Montessori was 'the most successful and popular educational leader of our time', she thought that the nursery school was nearer to the ideas of Froebel than of Montessori but that, in any case, it was really a new entity: 'The Nursery School is itself – no part or element of any other things. For lack of plain speaking we have seen the new birth strangled entirely between the older societies who do not represent it. This must end.'[15]

A former student said of Margaret McMillan that she was convinced that a child's imagination was of primary importance in the growth of his own understanding and education, and that she was equally convinced that Dr. Montessori had left this out of her reckoning. This conviction was apparently so emotionally charged that she would brook no discussion of the matter. The same writer quotes Margaret McMillan as follows: 'We [Dr. Montessori and Miss McMillan] have nothing in common. My educational system and hers are entirely

---

[13] *A Short Synopsis of the Educational Philosophy Advanced by the Founder of the Parents' National Educational Union* (n.d.).

[14] Grant, 'St. George's School', p. 21.

[15] Margaret McMillan, 'The Nursery School', Child Study Society, London, *Journal of Proceedings*, vi (1926), p. 47.

different. I do not want her name to be used in connection with my work.'[16]

The fourth group of objectors was small but the most radical of all, and A. S. Neill is the most obvious example. Where the first group objected because there was too much freedom in Montessori schools, the fourth objected because there was too little. Writing in *The New Era* as Mrs. Ensor's assistant editor from the Dalcroze School in Dresden, Neill said in 1921:

> One thing pleases me: among Dalcrozians there does not appear to be that unfortunate Montessorian habit of waiting for guidance from the Fountain-head. I see Montessorianism becoming a dead, apparatus-ridden system.... Thank heaven there is no apparatus required for Eurhythmics![17]

Neill thought Montessori did not really leave the children free at all but simply disguised her moulding control. McCallister takes a similar position in a more theoretical examination of the Montessorian theory and practice:

> ... one looks in vain for any definite recognition of those differentiations of the environment which are necessary for the growth of strongly individual tastes and qualities. There seems no room for any real self-determination of the forms which growth shall take. The pupil of eleven or twelve years usually shows a decided tendency to enter upon a higher form of spiritual integration than the Montessori exercises permit.[18]

Montessori shifted the focus from the teacher to the child more completely than any other educationalist. The teacher as expositor, as inspirer, as initiator, as example, is at a minimum and the child teaches himself to conquer an ingenious and exciting set of problems with built-in answers. Make-

---

[16] 'A Former Student' writing in G. A. N. Lowndes (ed.), *Margaret McMillan* (London, 1960), p. 33. This is a centenary volume produced a century after Margaret McMillan's birth by the Nursery Schools Association.

[17] *The New Era*, vol. 2, no. 8 (Oct. 1921), p. 221.

[18] W. J. McCallister, *The Growth of Freedom in Education* (London, 1931), p. 430.

believe and fantasy and anti-social aggressiveness are beyond the customary standard deviation which may be permitted in the group.

Montessori represents a biological individualism in the midst of the group and has produced an excitingly conceived rationalist training for small children. The ferment of ideas and practice which she helped to stir up resulted in some passionate conflicts of dogma; nevertheless the concern for knowledge of child development and enlightened educational procedure has gone furthest and spread most widely in work with pre-adolescents. Pestalozzi, Freud, and Froebel have their place of honour in this outcome and so too has Montessori, though in the 1920s it was mainly the innovating schools that gave her recognition in England.

25 HOMER LANE

In 1912 Mr. George Montague, later the Earl of Sandwich, visited some of the Junior Republics which had grown up in the United States with a view to seeing if the same kind of community might be set up in England. He was greatly impressed by what he saw, and his uncle, then Earl of Sandwich, offered Flowers Farm, an unoccupied holding in Dorsetshire near Dorchester, as a home for the new venture, the English version of the George Junior Republic. A committee was formed of people interested both in penal reform and in progressive educational ideas, and they asked Mr. Homer Lane, an American who had worked in the Ford Junior Republic with success, to come to England and advise them and the first superintendent, Harold Large, on setting up the Little Commonwealth. He came in 1913 and stayed to replace Large as the leader of the whole enterprise, his wife and family joining him before the end of the year.

W. R. George had been a holiday-time worker with tough and often delinquent youths, and later he and his wife set up a permanent residential community at Freeville in New York State for boys over the age of twelve, which he subsequently raised to sixteen, a Junior Republic which was copied in a number of other parts of America.[1] He was no permissive psychologist and for a considerable time, as he says, he had not sufficient faith in the boys he worked with to delegate to them any real powers of self-government. His early acts of generosity to individual boys did not produce a good spirit in the Republic or a general respect for other people's property. George concluded that an economic basis for the life of the community was essential, and work ought to be done for wages both to keep the community going and clean, but even more importantly to enable the boys to acquire and value possessions. There were, of course, lazy and thieving members of the community, but George found that the boys were far more zealous in seeing that their own laws were applied than they were with any of his devising. In the end George gave up thrashing and disciplining and passed over the administration of punishment to the community, who, through a judge and jury of citizens, maintained order with some rigour. People who lazed and so were paupers in the Republic on the charge of the taxpayers were shocked by a law passed through the legislature saying that if boys who could work did not do so they could be left to starve to death.

The community was organized like a state with a constitution based on the American Constitution, and incorporated a judicature, a legislature, a police force, a civil service (with appropriate examinations for membership), a miniature army with wooden rifles, and a gaol. George was the first resident and adults at first took the main senior offices. The gradual relinquishing of these positions in favour of the boys was part of the educational technique of the community and, as George frankly confesses, he proceeded in this and in other ways as his own understanding and insight grew. The boys worked from 8.30 to 12 noon and were paid according to their output in the Republic's own currency, and instruction was offered in school for part of the day. McCallister has this comment to offer:

> The Junior Republic, then, is the history of a successful attempt to take boys at their own level and to lead them gradually to perceive the justice and relevancy of communal

[1] See W. R. George, *Citizens Made and Remade* (New York, 1913); *The Junior Republic: Its History and Ideals* (New York, 1910).

demands. Its evolution shows that community control is a much more influential and efficacious force in the adolescent life than the old method of adult domination. Control of this kind frees many of the life forces and gives them glimpses of reasonable and relevant lines of self-assertion.[2]

George's methods spread elsewhere in the United States and were tried in schools, clubs, and prisons in other countries as well. Homer Lane claimed that he came to his similar solutions in Detroit about the same time without any knowledge of George's work.

The story of the Little Commonwealth has been well told by Miss Bazeley and Mr. Willis.[3] The community beginning in the autumn of 1913 was for boys and girls, as distinct from the Ford Republic which Lane had run in Detroit for boys only, and they were all difficult and usually delinquent children. From the chaos of noise and aggression the children were supposed to discover the need for some kind of law, and from the readiness of some children to break the law the community was expected to see the need for order and so set up the parliament and the court. But the turmoil and disorder that occurred before these decisions were even remotely accepted are painfully clear in Bazeley's and Lane's accounts.[4] Through it all Lane says he preserved outward calm and watched, and by 1916 the citizens had assumed entire responsibility for their government, the reason for this being that in the Commonwealth the children were encouraged both in good actions and bad ones. Lane claims that he took no authoritative role but really left the children to learn how to be citizens and how, as officials, to deal with brazen defiance. James the destroyer, whose ferocious resentment, encouraged by Lane, was vented on breaking cups, plates, and saucers, was finally tested to a shattering climax by the offer of Lane's gold watch to smash, which he furiously refused to do. In the traumatic catharsis (which loses nothing in the telling on the printed page and must in the original lecture have had the audience by the

[2] McCallister, *Growth of Freedom*, pp. 518–19.
[3] E. T. Bazeley, *Homer Lane and the Little Commonwealth* (London, 1928 and 1948); W. David Wills, *Homer Lane* (London, 1964).
[4] Homer Lane, *Four Lectures on Childhood: The Age of Loyalty*, ed. Rev. H. H. Symonds.

throat), according to Lane, James worked off his delayed self-assertive tendencies and caught up with his new social responsibilities.[5] This is the justification for encouraging children both in their good and their bad actions, because only so will they discover how to discard futile and false ideals.

Lord Lytton, of the Executive Committee of the Little Commonwealth, writes that there were three principles in the experiment which could be of universal application. The first was the law of love in the sense that Lane was on the side of each child, prepared to approve and champion him in whatever he did, believing that 'badness' was simply misdirected goodness. The second principle was to teach the citizens that there is no such thing as absolute freedom because we can never escape the consequence of our own actions. The main compulsion by which this lesson was learned was economic. The citizens kept the community solvent and viable and were paid for their labour. They all started in debt to the community for their clothes and their food and until and unless they earned they were a charge on the household in which they lived. The freedom of Homer Lane's Commonwealth was the liberty to discover that a community disintegrates if it does not discover how to maintain itself. The 'go-as-you-please' version of the regime arose from the agonizing conflicts and crises which disturbed children produced in one another and which Lane, with a kind of terrible meekness, often persisted in precipitating for obviously generally exhausting psychological reasons.

The third principle was concerned with self-government. The members of the community elected the authority they were prepared to accept and made their own laws. Eighteen boys and girls living in one house normally formed a family, together with the house-mother and one or two adult helpers. The boys had rooms at one end and the girls at the other, with living rooms used in common. The family was the economic and emotional anchorage of the system, and the community meeting was the gathering of the families (for most of the Commonwealth's existence there were two main families) for community discussion and decision-making twice a week. The

[5] See the three versions of the same story reported in Wills, *Homer Lane*, pp. 140–4.

family made the rules which governed the life within the cottage and enforced its own discipline:

> The Little Commonwealth was not an inimitable institution, the product of a single genius, but a model reformatory the principles of which could be applied with equal success to other institutions for the reformation of adult criminals as well as in the treatment of delinquent children.[6]

Lane always strenuously denied that as a person he was responsible for any success the Commonwealth may have had, but all commentators make clear the dominant part he played in his role as non-directive counsellor. He claimed that any children's community given real freedom within the demands of economic self-sufficiency could succeed as the Little Commonwealth succeeded, but when all the necessary reservations are applied it can be seen, as Lane affirmed, that good qualities do not unfold spontaneously in the free atmosphere, but that results have to be worked for with every resource. Despite five years of careful preparation Lane did not really get the teaching side of the work started. The children were, of course, over fourteen, the age of compulsory schooling, but were often backward and in need of remedial teaching. Nevertheless, while the needs of the war effort made it difficult to extend the basic farm work, the citizens were not really ready to receive instruction, nor were they prepared to think with any constancy about religious issues, no matter how sensitively Lane and his helpers tried to bring these questions forward. Miss Bazeley sums up with characteristic candour:

> During the last two years of the Little Commonwealth Mr. Lane was working for and expecting the development of a final phase in the life of the community and this final phase did not arrive. He had all along expected that the very strong Commonwealth spirit of loyalty to the community would, at any rate at points, be touched into loyalty towards higher ideals and towards the spirit behind ideals. He did

---

[6] Lord Lytton, introduction to Bazeley, *Homer Lane and the Little Commonwealth*, p. 19.

expect that we should develop from communal loyalties towards spiritual ones – and this did not happen.[7]

The story of the end of the Commonwealth is well known and pathetic. On 30 December 1917 Florence and Annie, two citizens of the Commonwealth, having robbed the office safe ran away and charged Lane with sexual improprieties towards them. The home secretary, Sir George Cave, proposed to withdraw the certificate of recognition which had been given to the Little Commonwealth in March 1917, but the Committee of the Commonwealth persuaded him not to do so at least until they, together with the chief inspector of reformatory and industrial schools, had investigated the matter fully. The Committee had already made a preliminary inquiry, and despite the discovery of a history of severe unrest and serious premonitory warnings in Florence's case, had given Lane a unanimous vote of confidence. However, before the proposed full investigation was begun the home secretary decided to hold a private inquiry into the affairs and government of the Little Commonwealth and appointed Mr. J. F. P. Rawlinson, K.C., M.P., to carry it out. He began on 30 January 1918 and completed his interviews early in April. On 6 June the Home Office wrote to Lord Sandwich, representing the Little Commonwealth Committee, to say that the certificate of recognition would be withdrawn if Lane continued as superintendent but would be continued if another superintendent were appointed and certain modifications of practice were made. In these circumstances, and still offering their belief in Lane's innocence, the Committee closed the Commonwealth 'with the greatest reluctance ... for the duration of the war. They have every intention of reopening it when the war is over and when conditions are more favourable for securing an adequate income and a sufficient staff to deal with all the phases of this educational experiment.'[8]

Lane turned to the practice of psychotherapy with adults in London, hoping to return to work with children. In 1925 he failed to notify a change of address and this offered a technical

[7] Ibid., p. 146.
[8] From the *Report of the Committee on the Closing of the Little Commonwealth*, July 1918. Wills, *Homer Lane*, has given the fullest account available of these transactions.

reason under the Aliens Act for the police to demand his exclusion from Great Britain. A few weeks later in September 1925 he died of heart failure at the American Hospital in Paris.[9]

> [The Little Commonwealth] failed only in establishing the general applicability of the principles on which it was conducted.... It was the tragedy of [Homer Lane's] life that to the end men never said of him, 'What admirable principles, let us adopt them,' but always 'What a marvellous man, he is inimitable.'[10]

While this is substantially true in the case of work with delinquents in the 1920s it is not true of radical educationalists in general, and we choose three examples of men who saw in Lane's work a lead for their own practice with children who had not fallen foul of the law.

Norman MacMunn was a teacher of modern languages who worked for a while in grammar schools before and during the First World War, developing at first a partnership system between pairs of pupils learning French, as a beginning of his practical experiments in freer methods.[11] MacMunn saw in Homer Lane's work what he called a wonderful and inspiring example, of which he wrote:

> Surely every logical and progressive teacher should be tempted by such victories of the principle of liberty to remark: 'Either these young criminals are better than my boys, or my boys are not quite so incapable of self-direction as I have been taught to believe.'[12]

MacMunn went on to try to practise at Tiptree Hall in Essex many of Lane's principles with a small number of boys (usually about nine or ten), and although the school did not have a long life, his book *The Child's Path to Freedom* (1926) was written

[9] Again Wills, *Homer Lane*, has the fullest available account of this period of Lane's life up to the time of his death.
[10] Lord Lytton, introduction to Bazeley, *Homer Lane and the Little Commonwealth*, p. 13.
[11] N. MacMunn, *Differential Partnership Method of French Conversation* (London, n.d.); *The MacMunn Differentialism: A New Method of Class Self-Teaching* (London, n.d.).
[12] MacMunn, *A Path to Freedom in the School*, pp. 7–8.

to prove that self-government of the Homer Lane pattern was going to be the basis of the education of the future: 'From the commonwealth colony for young delinquents to the commonwealth school for normal boys is scarcely a step at all.'[13] The only restraints would be imposed on boys (MacMunn was not convinced about co-education) by the collective will of their fellows through courts and school meetings. As an admirer of both Montessori and Lane, MacMunn wanted his pupils to create a new spirit in which their willing partnership blurred and later abolished the border between work and play, where living-rooms and classrooms would not be distinguishable. He rejected the desire of teachers to 'appropriate the souls of those whom they teach' on the excuse that Arnold and Thring had set the example, for according to MacMunn few teachers had the equipment and gifts to make this transaction anything other than a violation of freedom and an unwarranted presumption.[14] MacMunn thought that in theory and practice Montessori and Lane had most nearly reached the stage to which he aspired: 'The will to guard and to develop the freedom of another can only come when man is entering upon a supremely great stage of racial development.'[15]

The second man who acknowledged a deep debt to Homer Lane was J. H. Simpson, and probably more than anyone else in England Simpson carried out Lane's principles for a number of years in different contexts. James Simpson had been a boy at Rugby in the 1890s, of which he wrote a sympathetically critical account in 1954[16] from which we find that most of Badley's comments on the school where he was a pupil twenty years before Simpson were still applicable. After graduating at Cambridge and teaching at several schools, including Gresham's at Holt,[17] Simpson returned to Rugby as a master in January 1913 and it was during the autumn of this year, when Simpson was visiting Holt, that he met Homer Lane, an American 'working at some kind of reformatory'. His talk on that occasion began to effect a radical change in Simpson's whole outlook on education. He visited the Little Common-

[13] Ibid., p. 149.
[14] *The Child's Path to Freedom* (London, 1926), p. 30.
[15] *A Path to Freedom in the School*, p. 7.
[16] *Schoolmaster's Harvest* (London, 1954), ch. 2.
[17] J. H. Simpson, *Howson of Holt* (London, 1925).

wealth at Christmas 1913 and on many occasions during the succeeding three years: 'In those years I came to know the Commonwealth pretty well, possibly as well as anyone who had no definite connection with it.'[18]

Simpson regarded Lane well this side idolatry – he thought Lane's denial of personal influence absurd and said his tendency to dramatize incidents went over the brink of self-deception, while his non-directive role in general meetings of adult helpers and disturbed children led in Simpson's opinion as often to public agonizing as to understanding. But Simpson had seen enough of Lane's intentions to want to try out some kind of self-government, and MacMunn's experiments in teaching (themselves inspired by Lane's work) suggested to him that a single form in a school might serve as a beginning. It says much for Simpson and Dr. David, his headmaster, that he was able to do this original work at Rugby.[19] It should be added that Dr. David was a member of the Managing Committee of the Little Commonwealth.

In 1919 Simpson was invited to become the first headmaster of Rendcomb College and here from 1920 till 1931 he was able to work out his ideas in much greater detail, as we shall see later. For the present I want to acknowledge the continuity of Homer Lane's educational principles.

> I wish to express my gratitude to Mr. Homer Lane, whose work is a continual source of inspiration.... [The Little Commonwealth] is the most inspiring educational establishment in England. [I dare not] attempt to express the measure of my personal debt to Mr. Lane, which is indeed incalculable.[20]

This young schoolmaster, already impatient with public school conventions and restrictions, responded to the liberty and responsibility which when given to Lane's young delinquents seemed to call forth unsuspected qualities and capacities. Yet his was not always an eager, spontaneous response: 'Occasionally the challenge to my beliefs and prejudices at a previous visit had been almost unbearable, so that in

[18] *Schoolmaster's Harvest*, p. 138.
[19] See J. H. Simpson, *An Adventure in Education* (London, 1917).
[20] Ibid., pp. ix, 3.

my thoughts of the next there was some faint mixture of reluctance.'[21]

The third man to respond to Lane and his work is the best known. A. S. Neill says that it was a fan letter from a lady in Hampstead who had read and enjoyed *A Dominie's Log* and *A Dominie Dismissed* (Neill never has been dismissed and considers this book a kind of fictional autobiography) which first brought Homer Lane to his attention. The lady said that Neill might be interested in Lane's work and enclosed a copy of one of his lectures. As an officer-cadet in the artillery in 1916–17 Neill was stationed in Trowbridge in Wiltshire and wrote to Lane, who agreed to his visiting the Little Commonwealth. The consequence is best told in Neill's own words:

> That weekend was perhaps the most important milestone in my life. Lane sat up till the early morning telling me about his cases. I had been groping for some philosophy of education but had no knowledge of psychology. Lane introduced me to Freud. I asked Lane if I could come to work in the Commonwealth after the war and he said he had just been going to ask me to come, but when I was free the Little Commonwealth had been closed by the Home Office.
>
> I owe a great debt to Lane. It was from him that I learned that unless a teacher could see a child's motives he could not help him to be happy or social. He was a genius although his 'education' was limited. He spoke from his unconscious mostly. He found writing, even writing a letter, difficult. But with delinquent children he was simply wonderful. I consider it appalling that, since he died in 1925, so far as I can see his great experiment has had no visible influence on the State treatment of delinquent children.[22]

Neill had a long psychological analysis from Homer Lane in London in 1919 which he recalls as being 'far from perfect' because he considered Lane's interpretation as clever, satisfying the mind but not the emotions. This reservation notwithstanding, Neill reaffirms in his eighties his primary debt to Lane, and Summerhill has many practices which are recognizably similar to those of the Little Commonwealth.

[21] *Schoolmaster's Harvest*, p. 138.
[22] Neill, 'My Scholastic Life: 2', in *Id*, no. 3, p. 3.

Both Montessori and Lane considered that their methods were based on the freedom and self-determination open to the child. However, in the practice of each of them the teacher's control of environment and the structure of authority in the group are very different. Montessori's directress has furniture, play equipment, teaching material, and a school and classroom organization which are devised to stimulate learning. She knows within limits what she wants the child to discover he wants to learn, and her teaching skill and tact consist in presenting the problems and data when the child most wants to confront them. Although the order that exists in a Montessori class seems to reside in and be maintained by the children's group, the background directress is a *dea ex machina* who separates the anti-social child from the rest, permitting him to have the things he wants and relying on the magnetism of the group to make him want to join in again on the generally approved terms. Hers is the ultimate but unobtrusive authority.

Homer Lane's self-government was with older children, and its framework was the need of a self-supporting community to live together and pay its way. The children never got as far as academic learning in a school context. 'Daddy', as they called Lane, had no more say in the self-governing councils than the boy or girl chairman allowed him. He did not want his word to be law, he wanted the children to discover the need of law and to legislate as their collective wisdom guided them.

Montessori's teaching arranged the group and the scale of problems to stimulate motivation to learn while keeping the disruptive factors within adult control. Lane's teaching prescribed very little: money had to be earned by work, and the will of the school community as expressed by a majority vote had to be the controlling authority – and even this piece of raw politics was hammered out after newcomers had ruined the sleep and peace of mind of their fellows by a tireless racketing.

To what extent do children know what is best for them? This is the key question which sorts the Montessorians from the Laneites, to which Summerhill gives one answer, Abbotsholme another, and Winchester another.

12 The Post-War Surgence: the Twenties

26 BEGINNINGS OF THE NEW PSYCHOLOGY. BEMBRIDGE, RENDCOMB

DESPERATE ELATION and exhaustion were part of the post-war reckoning, an emancipated disenchantment discerning an ideal in the League of Nations on the one hand and revealing bitter hostility in the General Strike on the other. The second wave of radical schools in England appeared in this decade and in their beginnings made manifest the latent social, economic, psychological, and religious currents of the time.

I

John Howard Whitehouse was born in Birmingham in June 1873, the son of George Whitehouse, a brass founder and plate-worker and a staunch Gladstonian Liberal. George Whitehouse became, after 1870, a local inspector of schools and his son attended board schools in Birmingham until the age of fourteen, when he left to earn his living, first in an accountant's office and then with a saddler. The young lad educated himself in the evenings at the Birmingham Institute and Mason's College, which has since become part of the University of Birmingham.

In 1894 at the age of twenty-one Howard Whitehouse went to work at Cadbury's, and this experience of enlightened industrial practice and the place of welfare and educational programmes in the life of the work people greatly influenced his whole way of thinking and his career. He moved from office work to take part in the social and educational enterprises of the Quaker policy-makers. He worked mainly with young employees, establishing a library and a youth club, whose members often travelled and camped away from Birmingham.

Liberalism and Quakerism were two of the formative principles of Whitehouse's life. A third was his deep respect for

Ruskin's politics, social and artistic ideals, and writings. We have already seen how Reddie, Badley, and the communitarian left had the same deep admiration for the great man's work and how his palpable decline before his death in 1900 had saddened his followers. Whitehouse had from an early age organizational flair of a high order to go with his Liberal, nonconformist convictions. He founded the Ruskin Society of Birmingham and made a great success of its programmes before, at the age of thirty-one, he left Birmingham to spend a short time as first secretary of the Carnegie Trust in Scotland. It was here that he met Patrick Geddes, whose work for sociology we have already noted, and whose friendship with Reddie brought him into the New School movement. Geddes acted as an inspector at Abbotsholme in 1904, round about the time when he met Whitehouse. Both Geddes and Whitehouse were active in the affairs of the Guild of St. George, as it came to be called, the society formed to perpetuate the principles and the memory of Ruskin, and Geddes remained for Whitehouse an admired and influential friend.

Whitehouse left the Carnegie Trust and Scotland after only a few months and moved to the Toynbee Hall Settlement in London's East End, founded as a memorial to Arnold Toynbee, the economic historian, who was one of the pioneers of the Balliol tradition in adult education and social work among poor people. The settlement was opened in Whitechapel in 1884, a year after Toynbee's death, as a centre of reconciliation between young men from university and privileged backgrounds and the working classes. When Ruskin had been a professor at Oxford, Toynbee had been one of his disciples and derived much inspiration from the ideas of the master. It is no wonder, then, that the movement to Toynbee Hall attracted Whitehouse and that he found kindred spirits there. W. H. Beveridge was a sub-warden and a joint-editor, with Whitehouse, of *St. George*, the magazine of the Ruskinian Guild. The warden was a Friend, T. E. Harvey, and another member was E. T. Cook, one of the editors of the massive edition of Ruskin's works.[1] Whitehouse was the secretary of the settlement and became a school manager and the founder

[1] E. T. Cook and Alexander Wedderburn, *The Works of John Ruskin* (London, 1905).

of the National League of Workers with Boys, through which he came into contact with Baden-Powell, who began the Boy Scout movement in 1908, the year when Whitehouse moved from Whitechapel to St. George's School, the co-educational school founded in 1907 at Harpenden by the Reverend Cecil Grant, who transferred his school from Keswick in Cumberland. Despite its name, St. George's had no connection with Ruskin, and after a year as sub-warden Whitehouse moved, at the age of thirty-six, to be warden of Manchester University Settlement at Ancoats, the Toynbee Hall of the north.

It appeared as though this might be the ideal post for a man of Whitehouse's experience and social conscience. Reared in industrial Birmingham, nurtured by Quakerism, Gladstone's Liberalism, and the beliefs of Ruskin, versed in social work in a Whitechapel settlement, eager to encourage youth movements, he had all the opportunity in Ancoats a man could want to promote social improvement. But in 1910, a year after he became warden of Manchester University Settlement, Whitehouse became a Member of Parliament, elected for the mining constituency of Mid-Lanark, which he held until the end of the war. He was parliamentary private secretary at the Home Office for a while, where his concern for the social welfare, especially of children and refugees, had scope. Later he served at the Treasury when Lloyd George was chancellor of the exchequer, but Whitehouse broke with him in 1916 when Lloyd George introduced conscription. Ruskin and Gladstone were still important influences in Whitehouse's thinking, and between 1916 and 1918 he made a journey to the United States as a member of a minority opposition in the coalition government seeking to bring about a negotiated peace. Whitehouse lost his seat in the House of Commons in 1918; he contested every election between 1922 and 1935 in his efforts to re-enter the House, but his parliamentary days were ended.

In 1919, at the age of forty-five Whitehouse founded Bembridge School in the Isle of Wight, of which he remained warden until 1954, dying on 29 September 1955, aged eighty-two. Once again I use the public schools of the time as a point of reference by which to trace the differences of belief and practice in this new school. Whitehouse was a prolific writer and a public lecturer who often gathered his addresses into printed symposia or brochure form, and from these and the school records it is possible to piece together what he hoped to do at Bembridge, 'a school where, without, we hope any weakening of the literary and academic side of education, arts and crafts ... are regarded as instruments of spiritual and intellectual education'.[2]

This is what one might expect from a devoted Ruskinian. He considered creative education to be that which leads to a child finding out what he can do, what interests him, and for this manual activities, especially in art and craft, were potentially of the greatest importance and should have a place of honour in every school. To this end Bembridge had, almost from the start, a museum and art gallery in which every term there was a special exhibition of paintings or furniture or drawings or scientific exhibits or the like. One term each year was devoted to exhibitions of work by the boys in the school, which, for example, on one occasion illustrated the history of the Isle of Wight and where on others boys exhibited their paintings, poetry, models, craftwork, and printing. A printing press was an important part of the school's apparatus and such equipment was found at Abbotsholme, St. Christopher, Bedales, and a number of other schools. It was in line with Ruskin's pride in craft and workmanship and with William Morris's Kelmscott Press. Whitehouse maintained that work at the press helped to acquaint boys with good writing while incidentally improving their spelling, it encouraged taste and discrimination in type-face and layout, it opened a small window into the work of an ancient craft and a modern industry, it gave to some boys a real interest and a skill.

The painting, drawing, woodwork, pottery, script writing, and play production characteristic of Bembridge ring familiarly in these days, but in 1919 few of these were encouraged in public schools (Whitehouse called Bembridge a public school, not a progressive school) and they were certainly not given a firm place in the school timetable. Natural history and biology were more favoured at Bembridge than chemistry and physics, and history was merged with a real concern for the recent past, the present, and current affairs. Whitehouse

[2] J. H. Whitehouse, *Creative Education at an English School* (Cambridge, 1928), p. 2.

was a great admirer of America and introduced a study of American history to Bembridge.[3]

He gave his boys practical responsibility for organizing societies and meetings and, like Badley, Reddie, and Devine, he thought that games ought to take a part only of a boy's free time: 'We want a richer and nobler range of activities than would be afforded merely by games.'[4] Yet with all this concern for personal development and despite his position as chairman of the Society for Research in Education (there is no evidence that he took part in what would today be called research), he had no place for the Dalton Plan: 'I am filled with something approaching horror when people tell me that if I dole out a programme to a boy or girl a month or a year ahead that is going to lead to anything satisfactory.'[5]

Whitehouse was sympathetic to and influenced by the Society of Friends and he spoke of religion as the practice of goodness in the spirit of Jesus Christ without the teaching of dogma. Equally, Whitehouse spoke with asperity and vigour against all military training in schools and sought to promote the ideals of kindness and gentleness. He wanted all schools 'dissociated from the War Office', and to his implacable opposition to Officers' Training Corps he added his perpetual hostility to fagging at public schools, which he considered to be a degradation and waste for the younger boy and a lure to cruelty and exploitation for the older.

Reddie, Devine, and Whitehouse were all bachelors who devoted themselves to work with boys. Reddie and Devine were both thirty-one years old when they started Abbotsholme and Clayesmore, and Whitehouse was forty-five at the foundation of Bembridge. Reddie had a very good academic record, Devine had none. Whitehouse used the evening facilities offered by Birmingham, and later in his life was made an honorary M.A. of Oxford. His political and social work had given him the acquaintance and friendship of a large circle of liberals. Indeed, his obituary suggests that he had 'too many irons in too many fires',[6] which was also true of Devine, but

[3] See J. H. Whitehouse, *America and Our Schools* (Oxford, 1938).
[4] J. H. Whitehouse, 'Ideals and Methods in Education', in *A Boy's Symposium* (London, 1932), p. 26.
[5] Ibid., p. 27.
[6] *The Times*, 30 Sept. 1955.

certainly not of the single-minded monarch of Abbotsholme. Whitehouse's school, while the first of the post-war wave, was one of the least radical of the new schools, and by 1919 Ruskin was regarded as being on the right of socialism, which now had a militant working class and a Russian revolution as its spearhead.

Bembridge can be thought of as in continuity with Abbotsholme, Bedales, and Claysmore, but the new schools of the 1920s were to go much further than Whitehouse was prepared to go.

In his days in Whitechapel and Ancoats the young Whitehouse came across at first hand the elementary schools of the mass of the people, and in 1908 in the magazine of Toynbee Hall he wrote an article on reform in the elementary schools.[7] In it he pleaded for an end to the building of schools isolated from each other in crowded districts of cities where sites are desperately difficult to come by and play space is always too little. He proposed that schools should be built in groups at certain bases which could afford amenities for the children in that section of the city. The parks would be near and a swimming bath, a gymnasium, kitchens and dining-rooms, library, concert rooms, and art rooms could be shared by a group of schools and so more adequate recreation and culture space be found. In 1908 these were revolutionary ideas and they came to nothing, though the Cambridgeshire Village Colleges of Henry Morris in the 1930s belong to the same family of ideas.

In 1943, just before the 1944 Act, Whitehouse wrote again on the school base:

Under this scheme every town would be divided into areas, and each area would have its own School Base in the country. In many cases it would be within two or three miles of the area.... It would be possible to provide all the educational needs of a big town at one base.... Except in the case of small towns, more than one School Base will be required.[8]

Here, for the whole country, Whitehouse sketched the resources of Bembridge and the Cambridgeshire Colleges writ

[7] *The Toynbee Record* (1908).
[8] J. H. Whitehouse, *The School Base* (Oxford, 1943), p. 11.

large. Some later writers have tangled these ideas up with proposals for the comprehensive school, but the sketch in this booklet of forty-seven pages is far too general for that. Whitehouse believed that for older children the school base should be in the country, but he travelled no real distance in facing up to the practical implications of this. Bembridge was his most complete contribution to progressive education, not a very radical school, and nowadays unwilling to be in the progressive group. As the *Times* obituary of Whitehouse put it: 'No one could consider Bembridge a "freak school".' But no one could confuse it with Harrow, either.

II

Bembridge was not the only unorthodox foundation in 1919. Rendcomb, near Cirencester in Gloucestershire, was started by J. H. Simpson, who was appointed in 1919. Simpson was like Badley a Rugbeian who went on to Cambridge. He taught for a little at Charterhouse and Clifton and for two and a half years at Gresham's School, Holt, in Norfolk, where he developed a strong admiration for G. W. S. Howson, the headmaster, a man of conservative educational ideas and very strong moral principles which he expected the boys to share. Later in life Simpson became more critical of Howson's personal dominance, but he admired the honesty and vitality in the school. After Gresham's Simpson returned to Rugby as a master, but not before he had two years as a junior inspector of the Board of Education. He found the prevailing attitudes in elementary education coarse and depressing, but the conditions in which the teachers worked and the needs of the children he never forgot. He was, like Whitehouse, a manager of elementary schools, but he differed from the Bembridge warden in that he had been academically and professionally trained to teach. He was one of the few heads of progressive schools who up to that time had taken an education qualification as well as a degree.

Simpson was critical of the educational class structure. His year in Bolton as a junior inspector, contact with the deprived and impoverished delinquents of the Little Commonwealth, work on the boards of management of elementary schools –

all these things are straws indicating his growing hostility to the public schools which reared him. This is summed up in a pamphlet he produced as late as 1943, in which he wrote:

> I do not feel guilty of the least inconsistency in admiring their past achievements and certain educational virtues which the best of them still retain and believing at the same time that they are not the schools which this country will require in the coming years.... It is the specially favourable jumping-off place afforded by the public schools to boys of quite ordinary ability and character which excites the strongest hostility.[9]

Simpson was an assistant master at Rugby from 1913 till 1919 and during that time he had special responsibility for boys of only average ability, who, he thought, were given a far less apt and rewarding education at Rugby than the intellectually gifted. He put all the routine of orderliness, punctuality, timing, and delivery of work in the hands of a committee of boys of his form, and later he gave the form a much larger say in the arranging and assessing of work programmes. When Simpson went into the army in September 1917 he had discovered how demanding, exciting, and limited his Rugby experiment in self-government was.

F. Noel Hamilton Wills of Misarden Park, Oxford, wrote to Simpson shortly after his demobilization in January 1919 saying that he had read Simpson's book *An Adventure in Education* with great interest and asking for the opportunity to discuss:

> an educational experiment which has been in my mind for some eighteen months. Briefly, the idea is as follows: A school for 50 boys, selected by scholarship examination from the Primary Schools [of Gloucestershire]. It is hoped that by giving the best possible education at this establishment a proportion of the boys (who would be a very select community, picked out of some 40,000 children) might prove able to take scholarships at Public Schools and some of them

[9] J. H. Simpson, *The Future of the Public Schools* (Rugby, 1943), p. 6.

later at the Universities. These scholarships would be subsidized under the scheme.[10]

Wills, 'with a good bit of help from my brother', was going to provide the money to found this school, which had at first no unusual educational ideas about it. Simpson agreed to become the first headmaster, and after the school opened in June 1920 quickly persuaded his Governing Body to drop the principle of sending scholars on to the public schools, which would at once have made Rendcomb into a preparatory school. In 1922 the government agreed to a suggestion made by Simpson that fee-payers should be admitted. This was a change occasioned in part by Simpson's discovery that the endowment was not sufficient to enable the school to expand beyond forty boys, and he wanted it larger for educational and economic reasons. Part of the educational reason was to achieve what Simpson called 'a social mixture'. The fee-payers could come from any part of the country and from many home backgrounds and so the purpose and range of the school were widened. Again, one of the attractions of Rendcomb for Simpson was that it gave him the chance to bring into being what he called a 'self-governing' school. It was based on the Little Commonwealth, but with several differences.[11]

There was a General Meeting to which boys aged thirteen and older belonged. Offices were held for a term and holders were elected by the boys, as were appointments to the many sub-committees, the Games Committee, the Finance Committee, the House Committee, and so on. There were games wardens, three shopkeepers, a banker, an auditor, and a Council of seven boys who were elected for the duration of their school life and who acted as a boys' judiciary. There was formality and order in the General Meeting and after various experiments the staff were not included as members and

[10] From a letter to J. H. Simpson dated 7 Jan. 1919. Copies of correspondence relating to Rendcomb, biographical information, and many other valuable records were made available by Mr. C. H. C. Osborne, a former colleague and close friend of Simpson, and Mr. A. O. H. Quick, headmaster of Rendcomb College. To these gentlemen I am greatly indebted for their help and kindness.
[11] Full accounts are given in Simpson's books, *Sane Schooling* (London, 1936) and *Schoolmaster's Harvest*, ch. v. In *Sane Schooling* Rendcomb is called Churnside.

Simpson sat in as a non-voting attender. Minutes of the first General Meeting are dated 30 June 1920, a month after the school opened.

Responsibility was real and money was spent by the officers on behalf of the boys. In 1921 Simpson persuaded the Governing Body not to provide money for equipment directly to the school, but to make the grants as an allowance to each boy with the instruction that they were to provide all necessary games equipment and arrange to keep the grounds in order. Thus the boys were given a task to do involving committee decision, estimating, and some quite considerable budgeting.

> Economics ... give a solid basis of reality to the 'self-government' and, above all, make it easier to let the boys learn by making mistakes.... They should learn to spend judiciously, and sometimes boldly, and at the same time the results of their efficient, or inefficient, management should be seen immediately in their everyday life.[12]

This is a feature which continued although Simpson left Rendcomb in 1932. With such scope for the participation of boys in the disciplinary and economic life of the school, he coupled active learning in group situations, and he took the unusual course of adopting Greek as the main ancient language for study. He thought it a language with a richer literature and mythology than Latin. The teaching was enlightened and experimental, and in a school of forty to fifty pupils it could be personal. But this was not the distinctive pulse of Rendcomb among the innovatory schools of the 1920s, and in trying to discern it we discover again the change of thought patterns in the last fifty years.

Noel Wills, as Simpson recalls him, was sensitive, versatile, generous alike in thought and action, courageous to think of supporting elementary school boys at a boarding-school against the encrusted prejudice of county families, convinced of the need to make a new world of understanding after 1918. The proposal was to pay the fees of about fifty of Gloucestershire's most capable eleven-year-olds, to give them 'the advantages of opportunities which have hitherto ... been restricted to boys

[12] *Schoolmaster's Harvest*, p. 162.

of gentle birth'. This was said by Wills in another way in an article he wrote for *The English Review* in June 1924: 'Rendcomb College was founded in the belief that the true aristocracy among men is in reality simply an aristocracy of brains and character.'[13] The Gloucestershire authority gave the responsibility of selecting pupils to the governors.

Noel Wills had seemingly not greatly enjoyed his own public school days but perceived how they could have been enriched. He was a man of wealth, belonging to the family for which the tobacco concern of W. D. and H. O. Wills and later the Imperial Tobacco Company had built prosperity. The Wills family had a tradition of generous giving and of public service – Noel's brother, Gilbert Alan Hamilton Wills, who became the first Baron Dulverton in 1929, was a Member of Parliament 1912–22, president of the Imperial Tobacco Company, and a founder of the Dulverton Trust. An earlier generation had given handsome support to Bristol University, and it was from the same family that Mrs. Douglas-Hamilton came, whose generous support of the Theosophical Educational Trust during the period 1916–27 we have already seen.

> ... While recognising that I must not tie the hands of a Head and specialist, I repeat that I want to enjoy a position of mutual confidence and co-operation and to be sure in advance that there exists a fundamental conformity in our aims.
>
> The aim is decidedly social, moral and intellectual education, rather than mere scholarship; the latter being only a desirable evidence of the better things.[14]

By the beginning of 1922 local resentments and suspicions had produced the scandals and rumours which we have seen at other progressive schools, and Sir Thomas Davies, a Member of Parliament, was invited to visit the school and report to the governors. He said that charges had been made that the school was irreligious, but he found Scripture on the timetable although church attendance was not enforced. Again it was alleged that the boys were luxuriously fed, lodged, and clothed and Davies reported that the governors provided every-

[13] p. 797.   [14] Letter dated 15 Apr. 1919.

day wearing apparel as part of the boys' equipment while parents provided underclothing. As for the accommodation and food, it was such 'as would be found in, say, Cirencester Grammar School'. Rumour suggested that the boys could do what they liked in their free time, but Davies stated that games were played and that committees saw to many day-to-day arrangements and routines. Davies made one or two tentative criticisms, but concluded 'the various rumours and reports about the conduct of the school and its pupils have no foundation'.[15]

Wills did not have a social and educational manifesto. He wanted as many boys as he could afford to maintain given the 'advantages' of an enlightened boarding-school. Simpson wanted an experimental boarding-school, an educational corrective to the complacent public school. He had a general sympathy for the underdog, but he was neither an uncrital admirer of the underprivileged nor a devoted servant of freedom in the Rousseau style. He spoke of the majority of elementary teachers in his junior inspector days as timid, unimaginative, hurried, harried, and either cowed or falsely aggressive and none too careful of elementary personal hygiene. After he left Rendcomb in 1932 he became the principal of a Church of England Training College for men, St. Mark and St. John in Chelsea. He said that here he struck something new in collective bad manners, a coarse juvenility that compared ill with all that he had aimed for at Rendcomb.[16]

As to freedom in school, even in a progressive school, Simpson, writing in 1954 of his work at Rendcomb thirty years before, said that he believed in the limited value of self-government to teach the use of a committee structure. He believed too in the economic scheme and in the general feeling that the rules were 'ours' not 'theirs', which helped boys to shed inferiority, to become tolerant and sanely critical, and far less likely to be the slave of obsessional schoolboy customs. Yet Simpson admitted on reflection to being guilty of confused thinking, because he attributed to self-government what was equally due to the ethical tone and spirit of the school as a

---

[15] From a letter to Sir Francis Hyett, one of the governors, dated 7 June 1922.
[16] See *Schoolmaster's Harvest*, ch. 6.

whole. In his zeal for his *idée fixe* he thought he underplayed direct ethical teaching, and even more, religious education. He considered that like many another post-war left-wing schoolmaster (his own terms) he groped for the meaning of freedom in education at the expense of the virtues of religious education: 'It seemed easier and safer somehow to think of social education solely in terms of human relationships, without asking whether human relationships can be perfect except in the knowledge of a personal God.'[17]

Again, under the influence of 'the new psychology', he assumed that strong personality in a headmaster meant a repressive and dominating leader, and so used self-government as a protection for himself and his pupils against his own potential despotism. However, he considered that the extreme cult of self-effacement could be rationalization for a kind of cunning directed at a more pervasive, a subtler kind of manipulation. Equally, he considered the *laissez-faire* principles by which some headmasters tried not to inhibit their pupils represented a failure to face responsibility. Steering, therefore, amid these reefs and shoals of self-deception and lazy thinking, he remarked that his own attitude to self-government entailed patience to permit things to go wrong, and faith in adolescents to detect error and discern how to correct it. Yet Simpson did not abrogate authority and give it finally to his boys. His criticism of Homer Lane was that he said he tried to do just this, and sometimes the anguish for children was too costly; Simpson, however, used his judgement to give a lead, to quell a riot, to drop a hint. After all, he was a schoolmaster and not a psychotherapist.

Noel Wills died in 1927 at the age of forty. His family still plays a leading part in the Governing Body of Rendcomb, but this particular philanthropic impulse did not extend to other families in other parts of this country. That Wills found Simpson was the happy accident that made a social venture into a progressive school. Yet, although its ideas were original its impact has not been great, and this is partly a consequence of its small size. Fifty boys in 1926 became one hundred and nine in 1963, with the promise of further expansion to come. More significantly, the egalitarian experiment which suggests

[17] Ibid., p. 178.

a precedent for proposals like those of the Fleming Report, has not produced consequences in other areas, or even elsewhere in Gloucestershire. The desirable feature is the boarding-school, and a few authorities like the Greater London Council, Suffolk and Lancashire have lately begun to provide their own.[18]

[18] Also see R. Lambert, *The State and Boarding Education* (London, 1966).

13 The Post-War Surgence: the Twenties

27 THE WAVE OF THE NEW PSYCHOLOGY: SUMMERHILL, THE MALTING HOUSE

IN HIS biography of Sigmund Freud,[1] Ernest Jones places the beginnings of international recognition for the psychoanalytic movement between 1906 and 1909. There were tiny signs before 1914 of some interest in psycho-analysis in England at the meetings of the British Medical Association. But it was not until after the war that translations of all Freud's works, from a number of hands, appeared in England and the United States. There was a great deal of talk about Freud and his theories in intellectual circles in this country. The British Psycho-Analytical Society was reorganized in February 1919 and psycho-analysis extended into the discussions of at least the new Medical Section of the British Psychological Society.

In 1920 Percy Nunn, professor of education in the University of London, brought out a remarkable and influential book, *Education: Its Data and First Principles,* in which he tried to chart his way between theories of natural selection and physical inheritance and McDougall's postulation of a varying number of innate tendencies, instincts and capacities; between the 'adjustment' model of Dewey, the *élan vital* of Bergson, and the genetic forces of Freud, Jung, and Adler. Nunn wrote as a liberal thinker who wished to enable each child to realize his potential more completely, and he called upon knowledge of human psychology and educational practice for this purpose. While his examples from schools are chosen both from within the maintained system and from the independent sector including public and progressive schools, there can be no mistake that his prescriptions advise emancipation, the chance to

[1] E. Jones, *The Life and Work of Sigmund Freud* (London, 3 vols., 1953, 1955, 1957).

experiment, to play, to create. He acknowledges the place and necessity of routine and ritual, but as a ground and soil for the security from which independence grows. These are principles dear to the heart of the educational innovators.

Far more than Herbert Spencer before him, Nunn represents an educational theory based on science (especially the emerging science of psychology) and philosophy, and he focused for a decade the thinking of many people concerned with education and teaching. Educational innovators saw in him an ally who gave theoretical depth to their practice, a sympathizer who instanced what was being done by Homer Lane, by J. H. Simpson, by Badley, by Caldwell Cook in Cambridge and put it all into a much larger intellectual framework. But although he gave space to the work of the dynamic psychologists, Nunn's impact was nothing like as profound on the progressive schools as Freud's, whose concentration of attention on the significance of infantile experience was of the greatest importance to radical thought in English education. I can illustrate this best from individuals and the schools which they started.

I

We shall return to A. S. Neill and his school in fuller detail later and here we need say only enough to put him in his position as the first of the Freudian radicals in education.[2] Neill is an east coast Scot who was born in 1883 as the son of a Scottish dominie and one of a large family. His school record was bad and he seems to have stumbled into pupil-teaching when his father could not think what his youngest son might do. He reached Edinburgh University as a mature student, read English for his degree, and when he graduated in 1912 went into publishing and contributed many pages to an encyclopaedia of the time. As we have already seen, he met Homer Lane in 1916 and would have returned to work at the Little Commonwealth had it still been open when he was demobilized. Instead Neill went to teach at King Alfred School in Hampstead, where he stayed for two years, becoming increasingly galled by the limits placed on the children's free-

[2] See ch. 22.

dom, as he saw it. In 1920 he resigned and began four years of work in Germany, Austria, and Holland, dealing with refugee children and ultimately conducting schools on the outskirts of Dresden and then in Austria.

During these years Neill met Wilhelm Stekel, who had been one of the original group of psycho-analysts in Vienna. In 1911 Stekel had broken away from Freud but, much of his analytical technique was like Freud's. Neill had an extensive period of analysis with Stekel which he later said was of little help. Nevertheless Neill saw psycho-analysis as the chart by which he wished to steer and Freud as his pilot. When he returned to England in 1924 he started Summerhill near Lyme Regis, and the ideas he had expressed in *The New Era* when he was joint-editor for two years with Beatrice Ensor now had the chance of coming to reality. While there have been some changes in his outlook and practice over the last forty years, probably Neill's Summerhill has remained the most consistent and the most extreme of the radical schools:

> Freud showed that every neurosis is founded on sex repression. I said, 'I'll have a school in which there will be no sex repression.' Freud said that the unconscious was infinitely more important and more powerful than the conscious. I said, 'In my school we won't censure, punish, moralize. We will allow every child to live according to his deep impulses.'[3]

This school, first in Dorset and later in Suffolk, was the first of the new wave of the radical schools of the twenties whose main differences from the other groups that we have mentioned so far are directly related to the emphasis on the nature, interpretation, and importance of infantile experience to be found in psycho-analytic theory and practice.

II

No one English educationalist, by reason of her teaching, writing, and practice, has had more influence on the treatment and understanding of young children than Susan Isaacs. She was

[3] A. S. Neill, *Summerhill: A Radical Approach to Education* (London, 1962), p. 294.

The Wave of the New Psychology

a student at the Universities of London, Manchester, and Cambridge in the first decade of this century, being trained in philosophy and psychology to which later she added a deep understanding of psycho-analysis both as a student of its theory and as a practising analyst concerned particularly with children's problems. In addition to this impressive academic preparation she had trained as a teacher and had taught in schools, a training college, and just before the outbreak of the war in the University of Manchester as a tutor in logic. In 1924, at the age of thirty-nine, she became the first and only principal of the Malting House School in Cambridge for children mainly aged from three to seven years, attracted to this unusual enterprise by the prospect of pioneering teaching and research. However, before we consider the school further, we should turn back to the work for young children of another remarkable woman, whose name we have already mentioned – Margaret McMillan – and who may be regarded as a forerunner of Susan Isaacs in some ways.

Rachel and Margaret McMillan were born in New York State in 1859 and 1860 to Scottish parents who had emigrated to America after the clearances of the Scottish Highlands. Their father and a beloved younger sister died when the girls were five and six years old and Mrs. McMillan took her two young daughters back to her parents in Inverness. Life became austere and subdued for all three of them: 'Hitherto we had been the objects of quiet but intense interest and solicitude. Now we have no claims.... Our mother had passed into shadow. It was as if she had done something wrong in becoming a widow.'[4] The girls were given a 'good Scottish education' at Inverness Academy, where, as Margaret wrote, there was little child study but there was scholarship. In a letter written to a friend sixty years later Margaret said that her school life had made her a rebel and reformer.

Rachel stayed in Inverness and nursed her grandmother for eleven years until her death in 1888, and then at the age of twenty-nine Rachel became junior superintendent of a work-

---

[4] M. McMillan, *The Life of Rachel McMillan* (London, 1927), pp. 15, 16. Yet Margaret McMillan dedicated *Labour and Childhood* (London, 1907) 'To the memory of my grandfather who was as a father to me and whose gentle and chivalrous character first taught me to have faith in humanity'.

ing girls' hostel in London, where Margaret, who had trained in Switzerland and worked as a governess, joined her. The sisters became devoted servants of the socialist cause, hearing the leading speakers, meeting Keir Hardie, Hyndman, William Morris, Shaw, Annie Besant, and many others, reading and distributing literature.

In 1887-8 the two sisters tried to befriend Whitechapel working women, to introduce them to poetry and singing and to show them some simple political facts: '[The Whitechapel girls] I am bound to say led me a dreadful life ... and my school was a Babel where everyone amused herself as she chose.... The East End did not want me. It had no use for my feeble powers and vain offerings.'[5]

Depressed by this experience, but as staunch a socialist as ever, Margaret took employment with Lady Meux in 1888 as governess to a child she had adopted. Lady Meux was a quixotic and modish society hostess who regarded this striking and idealistic woman as a rare acquisition. Margaret was given beautiful clothes and trained over many months as an actress by leading producers, experts in voice production, and a doctor who taught her to understand the importance of developed breathing to health itself as well as to elocution. By 1892 Margaret had finished two trainings and no longer wished to be either a governess or an actress. She had also come to sense that she had been exploited as a novelty in what she called Lady Meux's 'cynical kind of Bohemia backed by Mammon'.

The stresses in this explosive patronage became dangerous. Margaret wrote an article in 1889 in *The Christian Socialist* which attacked the church for its failure to examine political and economic conditions. One of Lady Meux's friends heard Margaret speaking in Hyde Park on May Day 1892, supporting action by the workers against exploitation. The governess had not been tamed, and this realization intensified 'the intermittent fever' of Lady Meux's whims and produced the final break in 1892 when, according to Margaret, Lady Meux spoke as her final, histrionic word: 'Go! You may blot me out of your memory!' However, they saw one another and wrote from time to time.

[5] Ibid., pp. 38, 39, 42.

In 1892 we come to the beginning of the known achievements of the McMillan sisters, but even these few brush strokes covering the first thirty years of their lives give some hint of how different their story is from that of Reddie, Badley, and Devine. When Rachel and Margaret went to Bradford to start upon their life's work for child health and nursery schools Susan Isaacs, whose life was also so very different, was eight years old.

The two sisters found themselves members of a Labour church and of the newly formed Independent Labour Party. Margaret was to be a propagandist and in time was to run as a Labour candidate for election to the School Board. She lectured pretty well all over the country, especially around Bradford, and now 'our Margaret' found she was not at odds with Whitechapel working women but was at one with the positive Yorkshire working-class movement. The Independent Labour Party was committed to war on capitalism and competition, to promoting the creation and distribution of wealth in a new way and to caring for the unemployed and the needy. In 1894 Margaret McMillan was elected to the Bradford School Board, scraping in at the bottom of the poll: 'I was elected to fight ... the battle of the slum child.'[6]

There were four services that Margaret McMillan fought to have provided: school baths, the provision of school meals, medical inspection and treatment, and finally nursery schools. In Bradford she and her colleagues were able to obtain the first school baths and even the first recorded medical inspection of schoolchildren.

Margaret resigned from the Bradford School Board and left Bradford in 1902, the year of the Balfour Education Act, to return to London to be with Rachel, who had meanwhile completed a training as a sanitary inspector and was working for the Kent Education Committee, mainly teaching mothers and children some elementary hygiene. Margaret lectured for the Ethical Society, for the Workers Educational Association, founded in 1903, for the Independent Labour Party on whose National Administration Council she sat in 1907, and she was on the Council of the Froebel Society. In 1900 she produced *Early Childhood*, a book which called on her practical experi-

[6] *Rachel McMillan*, p. 86.

ence as a teacher of young children. She wrote of their moral and manual training, of the needs of feeble-minded children and the fatigue of half-timers, youngsters who worked half-time in mills and factories and spent the rest of their time in school. In 1904 she wrote *Education through the Imagination*, from which many of her later disagreements with Dr. Montessori may be deduced. She wrote a number of pamphleteering articles about this time, like *The Child and the State* in 1907, attacking the evils of dirt, drink, disease, and hunger, and *Citizens of Tomorrow* (1906), in which she placed educational development 'in the radiant light of the forward-swinging torch of medical science'. Other titles which speak for themselves are *Schools of Tomorrow* (1908) and *London Children: how to feed them and how not to feed them* (1907). She crowned this with her book *Labour and Childhood* in 1907. Ten years earlier she had been a frequent contributor to Blatchford's *Clarion*, Campbell's *Christian Socialist*, and the *London Echo*. Besides this output in writing and speaking she and Rachel were able to see a seal set on this part of their life's work when in 1906 the Education (Provision of Meals) Act was passed and in 1907 the Education (Administrative Provisions) Act, which included as Clause 13 the provision for medical inspection of schoolchildren by a local authority.

In 1908 Margaret and Rachel followed on their Bradford venture by opening up a school clinic at Bow in East London. For two years it was not a great success, despite heroic work. In June 1910 they moved over the Thames and a few miles upriver towards the City, to Deptford. This time they had about £500 a year from that tireless and wayward philanthropist Joseph Fels, and the use of a house and a hall without rent. The clinic was opened by Sir John Gorst, president of the Board of Education, and Sir Cyril Jackson, Chairman of the London County Council. About six thousand children a year attended. In 1911 an open-air camp school in the garden of their Deptford house was opened. Seventeen girls aged from six to fourteen slept under canvas each night, taking shower baths beforehand, and soon on nearby wasteground a similar camp for boys was started. There was suspicion and hostility locally and dire results were prophesied, but Margaret, calling upon her earlier training, had great faith in correct posture, carriage, and breathing and found that the open air and cleanliness, even in the slums of Deptford, made the children healthier. A day nursery school was started for children under five and the medical care and educational provision developed all the while, both the sisters working ceaselessly and gaining the respect and grudging admiration of their neighbours. After the outbreak of war in 1914 they ran a night-and-day nursery school in what was a dangerous area, and they found their task a killing one as the call for women munition workers became more insistent. Their premises were badly damaged by a bomb, and Rachel died in 1917 after herculean labours for which, as Margaret wrote, the training of finely nurtured English girls did not equip them. Both the sisters, with all their love of children, knew in their heart's core 'the brutishness, the vermin and all the plagues of the pit'.

In 1918 the president of the Board of Education, H. A. L. Fisher, opened the new nursery school building, and Margaret of the I.L.P., the Ethical Society, and the suffragette movement was made a C.B.E. In 1921 Queen Mary opened the extension to the nursery school and in 1930 she opened the Rachel McMillan Training College, Margaret's memorial to her sister. Margaret, having been awarded a Civil List pension in 1927, was made a Companion of Honour a few months before her death in 1931.

In 1923 Margaret McMillan became founder-president of the Nursery Schools Association and in an article she wrote in 1926 she summed up its aims. Nursery schools were to be for children from two to five years of age, although this could stretch to seven or nine, and the children should spend much time in the open air. Close contact was to be established with parents and the training of the children was to be related to their own sense experience, learning developing imaginatively from common objects, animals, and happenings and not from the didactic apparatus of Montessori. The Fabian socialist, the member of the I.L.P., the political evangelist, appeared in the assertion that such a school would help to break down class and professional prejudice:

> The open-air nursery-school as envisaged by Margaret McMillan is the starting point of new 'preventative medicine'

where the doctor will no longer be needed. She prophesied that the extension of its principles into education, and still further projected into the people's health centres of the future, could effect a revolution as yet undreamt of. Research and experiment on these lines, she said, would lead to startling discoveries.[7]

Which brings us back to Susan Isaacs and the Malting House School.

On 22 March 1924 a full-page advertisement appeared in the *New Statesman* seeking

> An Educated Young Woman, with Honours degree – preferably first class – or the equivalent, to conduct the education of a small group of children aged 2½–7, as a piece of scientific work and research ... someone who has considered themselves too good for teaching and who has already engaged in another occupation.... Large salary.... Preference will be given to those who do not hold any form of religious belief, but this is not by itself ... a substitute for other qualifications.

The advertiser was Geoffrey Pyke, a man of erratic and eclectic brilliance. In 1921 his son had been born and Pyke, having read some psycho-analytic writings, decided characteristically that the infant must be educated free from neurosis. From the time of the child's birth the father began to read widely in educational literature and he decided on four things. First, that he would have to undergo psycho-analysis in order to equip himself to discharge his duties and responsibilities as a wise father. Second, that his son must go to school early to grow up and learn with other children. Third, no school that he knew in Cambridge could provide the emancipation and challenge that he wanted, so he would have to get one started himself. Fourth, that this school would discover things that would benefit other schools and in time it could affect the education given to young children throughout the country provided that a research function were realized from the beginning.[8]

[7] Lowndes (ed.), *Margaret McMillan*, p. 103.
[8] For a fuller account, see D. Lampe, *Pyke the Unknown Genius* (London, 1959).

Pyke rented the Malting House in Cambridge with its spacious garden and Susan Isaacs agreed to become the principal provided that she was in full charge and was responsible for all the educational decisions. The school opened in October 1924.

Susan Isaacs saw the importance of sequence, of challenge, of sensory material, and of individual learning in the Montessori system. However, she was also interested in the work of John Dewey, who had started with his wife the Laboratory School at the University of Chicago in 1896, 'to discover in administration, selection of subject-matter, methods of learning, teaching and discipline, how a school could become a co-operative community while developing in individuals their own capacities and satisfying their own needs'.[9] In 1899 Dewey published *The School and Society*, three lectures he gave to parents and patrons of the school, in which he said:

> [We must] make each one of our schools an embryonic community life, active with types of occupations that reflect the life of the larger society, and permeated throughout with the spirit of art, history and science.[10]

Mrs. Isaacs knew Dewey's work as an educationalist and a philosopher and accepted the stress placed on the social role of the school both in its internal organization and activity method, and in its adaptation outwards of curriculum, method, and aims to the requirements of a society undergoing rapid transformation.

There is a vast literature by and about Dewey, and in much of it the social emphasis is so heavily stressed that Dewey's insistence on the ultimate understanding and participation by individuals is often overlooked: '[Education] is that reconstruction or reorganization of experience which adds to the

[9] K. C. Mayhew and A. C. Edwards, *The Dewey School* (New York, 1936), pp. xv–xvi.

[10] pp. 43–4. These ideas are developed in range and complexity in *Marol Principles in Education* (New York, 1909), *How We Think* (New York, 1910), *Interest and Effort in Education* (New York, 1913), and above all in *Democracy and Education* (New York, 1916), and in a number of other books and articles, some of them devoted, like *My Pedagogic Creed* (New York, 1897) and *The Child and the Curriculum* (New York, 1902), to the business of how and what to teach.

meaning of experience, and which increases the ability to direct the course of subsequent experience.'[11] In other words education is for fullest individual growth. Mrs. Isaacs recognized the significance of this rather heavily self-evident maxim expressed in Dewey's radical and most original practice. She described the Malting House School in the first volume of what was intended to be a trilogy,[12] and acknowledged that what she did might well have been the first expression in England of Dewey's practice. She said in the later volume:

> I was a trained teacher of young children and a student of Dewey's educational theories.... [The school] was an application to the education of very young children of the educational philosophy of John Dewey. This was my active inspiration.[13]

Whereas the Deweys in their Laboratory School started with sixteen pupils in 1896 and reached one hundred and forty in 1902, the Malting House School opened with ten boys in 1924 and ended as far as Mrs. Isaacs was concerned with twenty boys and girls in 1927. This small school, where the age range varied from two years eight months to ten years five months at different times, provided all the data for the two important books. As the location was Cambridge the children were mostly from professional families, many of them university families, and the mental ratio ranged between 114 and 166, with a mean of 131. At first it was a day school only but boarders were taken in the second year, and in the end about one-third of the children lived in a house attached to the school and in another a little way away. In all cases the children had their own bed-sitting-room built to scale, brightly painted and with a lock on the door, the key being in the possession of the occupant.

There was a hall which gave on to a larger garden where trees, sand pits, and water pools, and the first 'jungle gym' in England, provided chances for adventure and discovery in

---

[11] *The School and Society*, pp. 89–90.
[12] *Intellectual Growth in Young Children* (London, 1930), ch. ii, pp. 14–18. The second volume, *Social Development in Young Children*, appeared in 1933. The third one was to be case studies of children and this did not appear.
[13] *Social Development in Young Children*, pp. 18–19.

plenty. At the back of the hall was a gallery where visitors, including parents, could observe this unusual school in action. However, after a while the number of visitors grew too great and a ban was enforced. Under the gallery climbing bars and swings offered undercover agility. The children were encouraged to cook, bake, and make drinks, using the gas cooker, utensils, and crockery provided. Shelves, tables, chairs, and simple beds were all made to scale, and paper, clay, plasticine, crayons, paints (both artist's colours and the housepainter's variety), blackboards, and easels were available. A complete kit of tools, including a double-handed saw for cutting up logs, was in constant use together with the miscellaneous materials needed in any informal work with young children – rope, paste, paper, building bricks, and fabrics of all kinds. These children also had a hand lens, Bunsen burners, flasks, tubing, tripods, and the impedimenta of simple science teaching. They had dissecting instruments, specimen jars, a human skeleton, anatomical diagrams, and a small menagerie of pets and animals ranging from rabbits, mice, dogs, and cats to snakes, salamanders, and silkworms. On the formal side of teaching the Malting House had the entire Montessori equipment and several of the specially constructed sets of books and materials for reading and number, not to mention a typewriter and a range of maps.

Mrs. Isaacs believed that many nursery and junior schools in the 1920s encouraged art and craft, literature and music, all the arts of self-expression, together with reading and writing. She wanted to make use of children's curiosity about everything, the electric light, drains, water supply, the gas cooker, the telephone, the policeman. And, of course, after a while, their own bodily development and habits. This factual curiosity was as important to Mrs. Isaacs's view of education as the ideals of self-expression and make-believe and the basics of reading, writing, and computing.

There was no fixed curriculum and no class teaching but an emphasis on discovery by the child, with a corresponding quick-wittedness in the teacher to take the chance offered by a question like 'Where does the stuff we use in sewing come from?' to begin simple weaving and to visit a shop to see how big the bales of cloth could be when machines were used. Or to start on a dissection when a dead mouse or rabbit had been found and curiosity led that way before the obsequies supervened.

Free discussion was characteristic of the method and little or no restraint was placed on the children – they were co-investigators with their teachers. They were also expected to be precise and responsible about certain things: they had to wash up their own crockery, to clear up apparatus at the end of a lesson, they had to order their meals from a menu with prices, often on a limited budget, and the order had to be lodged with the cook by a certain time or a meal from the menu was not provided. There was no retributive punishment but there was the discipline of a required routine. The older children could prepare itineraries from maps and go on a sight-seeing bus tour, having established the cost and the timing of the whole operation. Many of these features arise out of an approach to school that is strikingly like John Dewey's. The connection was strengthened for a short while in 1927, when in answer to another of Pyke's full-page advertisements (in *The Times* on this occasion), for 'a scientist of the first order ... for the beginnings of a research institute into the problems connected with education ...', Richard Slavson, a thirty-six-year-old Russian-born educator from New York, was engaged from over one hundred and fifty applicants, seven of them university teachers. However, difficulties in the relationship with Pyke were beginning to appear and Slavson was only in Cambridge for a few months.

We have already seen that Mrs. Isaacs was sympathetic to Dr. Montessori's methods, but not a committed disciple. She thought that:

> [Dr. Montessori] has given her genius for devising techniques to the narrow ends of the scholastic subjects.... To us the direct interests of the child in the concrete processes in the world around him seem far more significant in themselves, and as a medium of education, than knowledge of the traditional 'subjects' of the schoolroom. In other words we see no reason to let the school and its conventions stand between the child and real situations in the world.[14]

[14] *Forum of Education*, vol. v, p. 131.

The third influence upon Mrs. Isaacs's theory and practice was Freud. If Dewey gave an unusual and permissive informality to the Malting House routine and regimen, while Montessori and other teaching aids gave a certain experimentalism in pedagogic techniques, Freud brought the most shocking of the innovations. Susan Isaacs could say that she had been a student of Dewey's and Montessori's ideas long before she knew anything of Freud, but it was the cross-indexed detailed evidence supporting infantile sexuality in its oral, anal, and genital phases which was the most explosive material in *Social Development in Young Children*, and in the articles which preceded it: 'I was just as ready to *record* and *study* the less attractive aspects of [young children's] behaviour as the more pleasing, whatever my aims and preferences as their *educator* might be.'[15]

In her introduction to *Social Development* Mrs. Isaacs gives a clear account of her difficulties. She knew that the absence of reproof and the freedom of behaviour would lead to an obvious and aggressive interest, either verbal, actual, or symbolic, in sexual and excremental detail, and this shocked a number of parents and helped to spread the *canard* in Cambridge to which we have become accustomed in other progressive schools. The Malting House was a bedlam of foul-mouthed, unwashed, sexually precocious brats according to this report. Mrs. Isaacs's own account of the pupil's subdued beginning, followed by the discovery of the freedom to run about, to play, to quarrel without adult reprisal and the resultant aggression and hostility reminds one of the accounts of the behaviour of Homer Lane's adolescents: 'Then gradually, and with occasional resurgences of mere wild disorder, the group began to take a definite social shape ... until by the end of the year ... [there was] full give and take of friendly adaptation.'[16]

Miss Evelyn Lawrence, who started teaching at the Malting House in 1926, wrote of the expression of crudity and savagery and of sexual interest and curiosity. 'If Malting House children hate a person they tell him so,' if they wanted to smoke they did so with the adults present, if they felt like swearing

[15] *Social Development in Young Children*, p. 19.
[16] Ibid., p. 22.

they could, and talk on sexual subjects was not shameful and unmentionable. 'I was not without doubts about the possible effects on the children's future manners and habits of the degree of freedom which they were allowed.'[17] She wondered what would be the outcome in the growth of kindliness, unselfishness, and restraint in personal relationships, but came to the conclusion that she need not have worried, to judge from her later knowledge of the easy manners and social conscience of her former pupils.

The school received much public attention; journalists visited it and wrote many articles with varying degrees of sympathy and understanding. Pyke began to favour a large expansion, intending to take in a cross-section of all people. While Susan Isaacs was not averse from some growth and expansion, she was anxious not to upset the research function and the continuing precise recording of data. Difference on this and other issues led to some fraying of relationships between the two, and without declared hostility Susan Isaacs resigned in 1927. Slavson returned to the United States and for inescapable reasons Pyke closed the school in 1928. Before his death nearly twenty-five years later he had a number of further different careers, each of them characterized by a *dégagé* brilliance.

Margaret and Rachel McMillan were political reformers fighting poverty, squalor, dirt, and undernourishment. Public health, hygiene, and preventive medicine were their arenas at first, and they were campaigning for twenty years for these causes as part of the socialist strategy before they stumbled upon the need to care for children even before they came to school. Although they were well-read women with educational ideas, the Deptford open-air school had as much to do with hygiene and health as it had to do with teaching.

Susan Isaacs was not dealing with poor children or with ignorant parents. She could take physical health and cleanliness for granted from the home interest and solicitude. In the course of her two main works, not only does she refer to Dewey, Montessori, and Freud as important to her thinking but she

---

[17] E. Lawrence, *National Froebel Foundation Bulletin*, Feb. 1949. Miss Lawrence married Nathan Isaacs some years after Susan Isaacs's death in 1948.

subjects the hypotheses of Jean Piaget to a most searching scrutiny, providing evidence to suggest that his generalizations might be too dogmatic, especially in relation to particular chronological ages of children. Her synthesis has in it a Freudian element altogether absent from the thinking of Dewey, Montessori, Piaget – and Margaret McMillan.

The radical nursery school for Margaret McMillan was the by-product of poverty, want, ill-health, and need, and for Susan Isaacs it was the laboratory of the children of the intelligentsia and the occasion for a unique piece of research. These women revived something which Robert Owen, James Buchanan, and Samuel Wilderspin had explored each in his own way a century before. Although the Malting House School existed for only three years, its indirect influence has been out of all proportion to its life-span or size: 'The fact that the nation as a whole is advancing rather rapidly in its ways of handling young children both at home and at school is due to [Susan Isaacs] more than to any other single person.'[18]

[18] From an obituary by Evelyn Lawrence, *The New Era* (Dec. 1948), p. 223.

14 The Post-War Surgence: the Twenties

28 THE NEW COMMUNITIES: DARTINGTON AND BEACON HILL

I

OF ALL the schools considered in this book there is only one which was founded as part of a larger social experiment. Dartington Hall Trust began as a rural community enterprise in which the school was a necessary development which did not come right at the beginning. But we must go back before 1925 to see how all this came about.

Leonard Elmhirst is a Yorkshireman whose family have lived in that county for over six centuries. After graduating at Cambridge he went to India in the army from 1915 to 1918, where he became deeply concerned in the social, political, and agricultural problems of the sub-continent. When he left the army in 1919 he decided to undertake a training in agriculture, and finding no course in England to satisfy his needs he chose Cornell University, where the programme included a training in science and economics as each is related to practical farming, which was what Mr. Elmhirst saw as the kind of preparation needed. In 1921 he completed his degree at Cornell and in the same year he met Rabindranath Tagore in New York: 'I remember how you came fresh from your university and you were absurdly young, but you were not in the least academic or aridly intellectual.'[1]

Tagore had a sanctuary school at Santiniketan which preserved and in some sense transformed the Indian style of life in dance, music, drama, and poetry. He saw the need to extend this liberal education for the children of prosperous parents

[1] From a letter to Mr. Elmhirst from Rabindranath Tagore quoted in a book edited by the former, *Rabindranath Tagore, Pioneer in Education* (London, 1961), p. 28.

much farther and wanted to help in the reconstruction of the social and economic life of the villages, and he saw in Leonard Elmhirst the man to lead the venture. In February 1922 Mr. Elmhirst, with a tiny staff and ten Indian students, all of whom said they wanted to be farmers, went at Tagore's invitation to the village of Surul about a mile and a half from Santiniketan. The new school was called Sriniketan, 'the abode of grace', which they preferred to the English title, the Institute of Rural Reconstruction. At that time Mr. Elmhirst found, as he said, 'monkeys, malaria, and mutual mistrust', and it was his task to conquer hostility and apathy and to present a subsistence programme not at all unlike the later Basic Education programme of UNESCO and United Nations.

Mr. Elmhirst was able to rouse village boys and girls to grow vegetables, to put out fires, give first aid, sing songs, administer quinine and 'see the pill swallowed'. Craftsmen who were starving were subsidized and retrained and some of the elements of orderly marketing were presented. After a period of mistrust village scoutmasters began to come forward and by the time Siksha-Satra was ready to start, many of the features which appeared in its five-day boarding-school week had been tried out in the Sriniketan experiment. Duties in the dormitory, the kitchen, the garden, poultry-run, and dairy were coupled with weaving, preparing food, washing, ground cleaning, and clearing drains. The closeness to the needs of village life effected many changes in the community for the better, for lessons in rotation of crops were taught, public responsibility was accepted in guarding against fire and against theft and in the constant attack on mosquitoes and bacteria. Mr. Elmhirst thought that by a little practical training 75 per cent of the ill-health of rural India could be eliminated in a few months by the children and as an example he chose malaria, which affected 90 per cent of any village which it attacked. The children could map out the village, its dwellings, storage tanks, drains; cesspits and water channels could be dug, all of this being an aspect of social geography. Keeping health records, tracking and locating the breeding ground of anopheles and disinfecting brought knowledge of chemistry, bacteriology, zoology, and social welfare. To understand the linkages between cleanliness, water supply, pollution, sanitation, and the need for firm laws with police sanctions in the interests of health was to learn lessons in civics, local politics, morals, and hygiene which showed more than anything else how closeknit the village community is. At the other end of the scale the experiments carried out by the boys in growing vegetables and producing new crops contained lessons in nutrition and agricultural botany that adults might pick up from their children.

Behind the immediate local problems which faced him Mr. Elmhirst saw the huge issue of India poised between three cultures: the ancient traditional fatalism; the ancient and modern folk-education later seen in Gandhi's village *Nai Talim*; and the inevitable modernism of the machine.

The book on Tagore which has already been mentioned has as its dedication: 'To Dorothy Whitney Straight who made Sriniketan possible'. Dorothy Whitney was the daughter of William C. Whitney, a noted American financier who left her an independent fortune. She took her university education in New York at a time when Dewey, Thorndike, and James Earl Russell were building the international reputation of Teachers' College. In 1911 she married Willard Straight, whom she met in Peking while on a world tour. Straight was a graduate of Cornell University who after volunteering in 1917 died in France in 1918 leaving his wife with three young children, and in his will he asked that something should be done 'to make Cornell a more human place'.[2] In working out a plan for a Students' Union called the Willard Straight Hall, Mrs. Straight called on the help and advice of Leonard Elmhirst, who was at Cornell from 1919 to 1921. When he went to India, to Surul, Mrs. Straight gave financial backing to the enterprise and continued to support it until 1947. When Mr. Elmhirst returned to the United States he and Dorothy Whitney Straight were married in April 1925; they came to England, and in September 1925 they brought the estate at Dartington near Totnes in Devonshire to which the whole of the rest of their life together was devoted.

Dartington was an estate in pre-Norman times and maintained continuity through a thousand years. The Elmhirsts had two principal aims: to develop the natural resources of

[2] Quoted from information supplied by Mrs. Elmhirst, who died in 1969.

the estate and rehabilitate it both for itself and as a source of employment and livelihood; and to provide the housing social services, aesthetic activities, education, and personal enrichment necessary for country life to gain and regain a health of its own.

In 1931 the Elmhirsts established a Trust in which are invested all the land, buildings, and services, and the shares in commercial enterprises both inside and outside Dartington. The commercial enterprises owned or partly owned by the Trust provide the money which gives backing to other activities that may and usually do not run at a profit. Dartington Hall Ltd. controls farms, a textile mill, and a shop selling products from Dartington and elsewhere; Dartington Woodlands Ltd. manages 2,000 acres of forest as a commercial undertaking; Staverton Contractors Ltd. is a building and civil engineering firm with an extensive joinery and furniture shop attached; the Dartington Sawmills Ltd., partly owned by the Trust, deals in cut timber in all forms of the trade.

The non-commercial activities are called the Trustee departments and include the school, the Arts Centre as it was formerly called,[3] the Adult Education Centre, research projects, grounds and gardens, and the estate department responsible for the maintenance and upkeep of all land and buildings. The progress of the scheme owed nearly everything to the generosity of the Elmhirsts in the early years, but now the Trust has a balanced budget as a considerable enterprise.

In a world of rural conservatism the new Dartington community was cosmopolitan and politically far to the left; the interest of foreigners, socialists, and pacifists in the experiment introduced strange and controversial persons to Totnes. The work done in the arts brought painters, sculptors, composers, musicians, actors, and dancers to Dartington. The revitalization of the country crafts had some colour of local success in the first ten years, but the life of the arts centre was too violent a contrast for rural assimilation. Even the new enterprises in forestry, farming, and general agriculture ran into trouble

---

[3] This enterprise is now called the College of Arts and is mainly concerned with the training of teachers in the arts, in conjunction with the Institute of Education of the University of Exeter. Dartington has long been famed for its work in music.

because of their sheer enlightenment. Buildings were erected or remodelled with taste and style, new houses for estate workers were architect-designed. According to Bonham-Carter, in the first five years pay was more generous than was offered by many local farmers, and pensions, sickness benefits, holidays with pay were all disturbingly liberal in a traditional farming county.[4] Some neighbouring employers resented the unfair advantages offered by these inexperienced intruders and were aggrieved at the competition in a time of high unemployment. All kinds of obloquy were levelled at Dartington, and Bonham-Carter writes that while some of it was ignorant, prejudiced, even vicious, in other cases Dartington asked for it by its aggressive, *avant-garde* self-sufficiency, by the amateurs, the eccentrics, and the fanatics who took advantage of the generosity of the Elmhirsts and the Trustees. At the centre of the Dartington community was the school, and this too was conceived in the spirit of radical liberalism of the rest.

Mrs. Elmhirst had three children by her first marriage, who had been educated at Lincoln School, New York, founded by Abraham Flexner in September 1917 by arrangement with Teachers' College, to which the school was attached, and with the General Education Board of the Rockefeller Foundation, by which the school was generously financed. Flexner's curricula were organized around the themes of science, industry, civics, and aesthetics, together with a wide range of options. He employed an extended 'centre of interest' method, developing many of the lines of theory and practice started by Dewey and his wife over twenty years earlier in Chicago. Flexner regarded Lincoln School as a laboratory which would test and evaluate the bases of its own theory and the results it produced, and these are words almost identical with those used thirty years earlier by Reddie about Abbotsholme.

The Elmhirsts had in mind as part of the Dartington idea that a fully equipped and staffed co-educational boarding-school could provide the basis of a common life for pupils. The estate undertakings could be used as part of an education as utilitarian, pragmatic, and unstructured as American experience, amateur enthusiasm, and secure finance could make it. In the first five years the numbers grew to fifty and the

[4] See Victor Bonham-Carter, *Dartington Hall* (London, 1958), pp. 25 ff.

transience of staff (twenty-two in this period) produced a somewhat unsettled community. On the principle of equality, no one on the staff was given the authority and responsibility of being the head of the school. Each child had a 'second' or moral tutor whose task was to act as counsellor to the boy or girl and adviser to the parents, to whom personal reports were sent if requested, but not as a termly routine. One of the masters offered rudimentary psychotherapy to the children if needed, part of the technique being dream-interpretation.

After about eighteen months Dr. Williams, the school doctor, reported that the children were being fatigued and burdened by too much discussion and consultation, with consequent effect on their schoolwork, and that the belief in freedom at the cost of routine and secure order had gone too far. In June 1928 Dr. Bonser of the Teacher's College, Columbia University, was invited to report on the school (the Trustees have a willingness to invite outsiders frequently to scrutinize and assess what is going on), and this American critic from a stronghold of pragmatism and freedom in education said quite roundly that while Dartington relied on advanced psychological theories it had not a sufficiently experienced team of teachers to make the theories effective. The children were unpunctual and undisciplined, the psychotherapy given by a master was unsuccessful and undesirable. If the children's resistance to hard work was overcome by a disciplined approach to learning, their progress would bring its own reward. Bonser was equally severe with the practical work. He said that the estate departments were unsuitable agencies for educating the boys and girls. The children needed constructive and well-devised tasks for their own mental growth and the commercial enterprises were presenting them with problems connected with buying, selling, and profit-making. Besides this, the estate managers had neither the time nor the training for teaching and if a link was to be forged between the school and the estate it would have to be striven for by a better planned organization in pottery, gardening, woodwork, and estate work.

This report led to a new disposition of occupational interests between the school and the estate. The commercial enterprises were put under a Management Committee in 1927 and a limited company was founded in 1929. An Education Committee was constituted in a definite form in 1928, and the intimate structure of the early experiment began to disappear. The Bonser Report showed that expert knowledge and teaching skill were needed for a progressive school (perhaps especially for such a school) and that the existing staff were mostly amateurs.

The Committee took note of this advice and decided to appoint a head of the school who would also be director of education for the estate as a whole. The nursery and primary schools which it had been decided to add were to be the nucleus of a department of child study staffed by the director, the nursery school teachers, a psychologist with part-time help from a doctor, a nurse, and a dietician. The help of a secretary and a household manager with assistants was to provide the ancillary aid by which enlightened teaching and the research function could take place. The Elmhirsts looked for their staff in America, where they found Winifred Harley, an Englishwoman working at the Merrill-Palmer School in Detroit. The Merrill-Palmer tests were to be used to assess the progress of the Dartington children, and an English psychologist was sent to the University of London by the Elmhirsts to restandardize the American material for English use.[5] In 1931 the director was appointed, and his responsibility included the oversight of nursery, kindergarten, and later the middle and senior schools, together with the adult education programme and the School of Dance and Mime. The first head was William Burnlee Curry, who served the school from 1931 to 1957 and became, with Badley and Neill, one of the best-known names in progressive education.[6]

Curry was a Northumbrian born at the turn of the century. He did well at Alnwick Grammar School, ending as head boy and senior scholar of Trinity College, Cambridge, where he read mathematics in the first part of his Tripos in 1919 and natural sciences in the second part in 1921, gaining a Third in each, results not at all in keeping with his quality of mind. One of his former colleagues writes: 'Many of his staff had

---

[5] See a reference to this work done by Miss Hilda Bristol in H. R. Hamley, 'The Testing of Intelligence', *Year Book of Education* (London, 1935).

[6] Curry died after an accident in the summer of 1962.

Firsts in the early days, and he was unquestionably their intellectual superior. I suppose one can make various deductions, according to inclination!'[7]

Curry says of his own school days that he had been brought up conventionally and had been more than content with his success at an orthodox grammar school. He was not among those who turned to progressive education in bitter revolt – interestingly enough, neither has any other educational innovator whom we have mentioned. Critical of the public school or grammar school teaching they all were, but with the exception of Neill, none of those so far considered smouldered at his own schooling, at any rate while he was undergoing it. Curry, like Reddie, Badley, Simpson, and Susan Isaacs, said that while he was at school he saw no reason to question the system. In 1919, however, he read Bertrand Russell's *Principles of Social Reconstruction* and found his assurance deeply disturbed. The book was based on a series of lectures that Russell gave in London in 1916 on the conduct of the war (he advised the immediate conclusion of a peace on the best terms available); on a rational approach to marriage as the basis of the family and a form of social contract but not as an indissoluble relationship; on notions of authority, liberty, and intellectual freedom; and, of course, on education. Russell noted that at the beginning of 1914 men and women seemed to have a zest for the war, and he saw the positive growth of freedom in infancy as being of central importance for future peace and discerned in repressive systems of education a predisposing influence towards aggression and savagery.

In 1916 Russell had been tried before the lord mayor at Mansion House for issuing 'statements likely to prejudice the recruiting and discipline of His Majesty's Forces' – as a member of the No Conscription Federation he had written a leaflet objecting to and publicizing the sentence of two years' hard labour passed upon Ernest Everett, a conscientious objector who had been conscripted and then refused to obey orders. Russell was found guilty and fined £100. The Council of Trinity College, Cambridge, decided unanimously in July 1916 to dismiss him from his lectureship. Three years later Trinity was Curry's college and he found as an undergraduate

[7] In a letter to the author in December 1962.

at Cambridge with the veterans of the post-war generation, that Russell and the whole post-1918 world were detonating explosions in his schoolboy assumptions. If Russell was the passionate sceptic, Curry was beginning to become the passionate rationalist, and Curry quotes this passage from Russell more than once in his writings as an early inspiration:

> Where authority is unavoidable, what is needed is *reverence*. A man who is to educate really well and is to make the young grow and develop into their full stature must be filled through and through with reverence.... The man who has reverence will not think it his duty to 'mould' the young ... [he] can wield the authority of an educator without infringing the principles of liberty.[8]

Not only at Cambridge, but through nearly all his life thereafter Curry found in Russell's writing and conversation a stimulus and a clarification for his own thinking.

Curry's first teaching post was at Gresham's School, Holt, where Simpson had been ten to fifteen years earlier. Simpson had found Howson's 'honour' system at the time an astringent and bracing experience, but Curry unequivocally detested it as a form of moral and emotional blackmail.[9] In 1922 he went to Bedales, where he taught physics until 1926 and where his first experiences of experimental education began to take shape. Like Russell, Curry thought that the fundamental questions had to do with the kind and quality of life that was worth living and the conditions which could make it possible. Three special questions plagued him all through the years: peace was a necessity for the quality of life he sought; people were not emotionally and intellectually prepared for the rational alternatives to war and nationalism; the existing methods of education did not put the prerequisites first – the fundamental social attitudes of children growing up to a world needing understanding and international law. These preoccupations are best summed up in Curry's own words:

[8] Bonham-Carter, *Dartington Hall*, p. 196. The passage is from Russell's *Principles of Social Reconstruction*.
[9] For a personal account of the system about the time that Curry was at Gresham's, see W. H. Auden, 'Honour', in *The Old School*, ed. Graham Greene (London, 1934), pp. 9–20.

The New Communities

A modern school is one which recognizes that the social order must be radically changed if civilization is to survive at all and which also recognizes that education will have perhaps the most difficult and the most important part to play in the changes which must come about.[10]

Elsewhere in the same book he said that the primary aim of education was the creation of civilized communities: that the school should provide a model for such communities was possible only when art, intelligence, and knowledge were acknowledged as good in themselves and not only as servants to usefulness. In civilized communities citizens were sociable and responsible without necessarily being gregarious, they were tolerant and valued liberty while also permitting talent to thrive. Co-operation in such a society would mean more than competition, moral and intellectual autonomy would be prized and understood. More and more it would tend towards becoming a world society. These were the guide-lines for politics and education in his writing and his practice.

Curry had reason to be grateful to Badley and to Bedales for his first real glimpse of co-education and innovation in education, but he did not think it was radical enough. Badley, for his part, remembered Curry as a good teacher, lucid in discussion and argument and as much concerned with politics as with teaching – a headmaster recalling a polemical assistant thirty-five years his junior.[11]

Curry went from Bedales to Oak Lane County Day School in Philadelphia, which had been started in 1916 by a group of local businessmen wishing to finance and begin a school which would apply John Dewey's educational theories. The sponsors and participating parents then hired the teachers in the usual American pattern. When Curry arrived in 1926 Oak Lane was well established, and in 1927 he became head of the school and remained in Philadelphia until his appointment to Dartington in 1931. He brought three main impressions back to England with him: first, a concern for individual children and their way of learning; second, the need for and the predicaments of pupil participation in school government; third,

[10] W. B. Curry, *The School* (London, 1934), p. xii.
[11] In a recorded conversation with the author in 1962.

an exasperation with the assumption by uninformed parents in Philadelphia that their views on education and teaching could be pressed upon teachers. Curry felt that the head of a progressive school should work according to his own conscience, listening to criticism but not necessarily accepting it, especially if it came from the more conventional world 'outside'.

Curry became the first (indeed the only) director of education for the Dartington estate as a whole. He had general control of all kinds of educational work with children and young people aged from two to eighteen (including Miss Harley's nursery sector) and with adults both on and off the estate. Not long after his appointment the director told the Trustees that he could not manage oversight of all this work and his proposition that he should concentrate on the school, or schools, was accepted and responsibility for the adult education programme and the School of Dance and Mime was transferred to others. The concept of the grand strategist in education for Dartington faded away and did not revive.

Curry dedicated *The School* in 1934 to Mr. and Mrs. Elmhirst 'for the opportunity to practise what I preach' and said a year before his retirement that the views he set out in that book 'are still substantially my views in 1956'.[12] While the Trustees had the general planning responsibility for Dartington as a whole, there can be no doubt that Curry's was the guiding mind for twenty-six years. During that time the school became one of the best-known co-educational schools in England.

The school is co-educational and now houses over three hundred and fifty boys and girls aged from eleven to eighteen, having grown to this size from the thirty-two with which Curry started in 1932. In terms of physical organization Dartington is on principle and in practice the most consistently co-educational of all. While I shall concentrate for the sake of brevity on the secondary age group, the same ideas, with only slight modifications, apply to the other age ranges. Each child has a study-bedroom of his or her own, the school is split into three houses for social and not competitive purposes, and boys and girls have their rooms next to one another as they

[12] Bonham-Carter, *Dartington Hall*, p. 189.

might do in a family. The washing and sanitary arrangements are shared as in a household, and Curry and the Trustees planned the buildings in this way with a housemother for each group of about forty boys and girls. There never has been a school uniform and dress is as informal as children may wish to make it.

A large part of the discussion of progressive education is concerned with aspects of freedom, authority, and discipline: 'No good society is conceivable except in terms of good individuals, and good individuals cannot be produced by educators lacking in respect for personality.'[13] Curry accepted the need for authority and thought that educators should do all they could to encourage love of truth, vitality, initiative, and friendliness. He was fond of quoting Whitehead's dictum that an education which does not begin by evoking initiative, and end by encouraging it, must be wrong. For such an education one of the basic requirements was the security consequent upon a right relationship with adults, one in which the adult is seen to be on the child's side. To this end there was and is at Dartington a considerable degree of self-government. Curry was opposed to complete self-government for much the same reasons as Dr. Williams and Dr. Bonser, who, as we have seen, reported on this and other matters a few years before his arrival. According to Curry, putting nearly everything in the hands of the pupils would give too heavy a load of responsibility, reduce the sense of security which adult support and competence could afford, and probably lead to harsher rules and punishments than were necessary. However, to give children the chance to obey and often to make the law and to understand why they do so is to enable them to see the world in terms of the victory of persuasion over force. At various times Curry had a Headmaster's Advisory Council, which later became a Rule Making Body which discussed and amended rules, and later still developed into a School Council and to the Moot, which was served by an inner cabinet or Agenda Committee. Curry gives a full account of the changes which took place over the years in the organization of the widely permissive self-government by the pupils.[14]

[13] Curry, *The School*, p. 25.
[14] See W. B. Curry, *Education for Sanity* (London, 1947).

For a time there was a pupil chairman, changing at regular intervals. Later Curry became the chairman and had the right of veto, which he scarcely ever needed to consider using. Where Neill's School Meeting decides almost everything and is chaired by an elected pupil, Dartington for a time moved away from this, although for several years now pupils have acted as chairmen. The agenda is prepared and displayed after due notice from suggestions submitted, and only these items can be discussed at the meeting of the Moot, which the whole senior school and the staff can attend at will, although other matters can be raised under 'any other business'. In the summer term of 1961 the Moot gathered together, codified, and promulgated twenty-five rules with sub-sections, many of them rules that were already in existence, but not collected in this form. The twenty-five rules covered such things as time limits within which general noise, including the playing of radios and gramophones, was permitted; areas in which ball games might be played; a prohibition on electric heaters in private rooms, on riding pillion on motor-cycles at any time, and on airguns or other weapons, including catapults; and the inspection of bicycles. According to these rules permission from parents had to be obtained for a number of undertakings such as canoeing or spending a night away from Dartington; smoking was permitted in private rooms and common rooms only; except in cases of illness classes could only be missed with the permission of the tutor; teachers might make any rules of conduct they considered desirable for their own rooms (it may be noted that this does not give to teachers control of the pupils' behaviour in the rest of the school, or in the children's own rooms). Anyone who wanted to go swimming or to climb in a nearby quarry had to have responsible companions with him. Some pupils thought that one rule was the most important of all, maybe the only necessary one: 'Every person should at all times behave with due consideration for the happiness and convenience of others.'

These rules indicate that Dartington is not a school without discipline or without a structure of law. The pupils cannot 'do what they like' as the cliché of critics often puts it. But they have more freedom from convention and expected behaviour than is usual. Curry believed that the nature of the society taught more effectively than proclaimed rules; for him a school was an actively functioning society, not just a collection of children learning lessons and obeying orders. He accepted such moulding of young lives as took place on the assumption that children were able to manage their own affairs wisely when sympathetic adults gave them the freedom and security to do so. As his prospectus had it: 'Good feeling is more important than good behaviour and will ultimately lead to it.'[15] The authority of the adult was seldom displayed, and Curry wanted children to learn to understand and accept law rather than simply obeying superior persons.

Curry saw co-education as a necessary condition for the proper education of the emotions and for the harmonious development of sexuality: 'It is surely best that this problem should first be faced under conditions which are deliberately devised in the light of educational considerations.'[16] He believed that in the family context of the school the naturalness of affection, of heterosexual feeling and desire could easily find expression and the community could create the necessary controls. Nude bathing for boys and girls was permitted in Curry's day as part of the family ethos although there have been modifications of the arrangements in more recent years. When Curry was challenged about this as he often was, not least by His Majesty's Inspectors after an inspection in 1949, he said that children who found it in any way embarrassing or upsetting were free to wear a costume and the rest of the school family would accept this as an understandable preference.

Over the years each pupil at Dartington has had a tutor whom he or she can, within very wide limits, choose, and it is the tutor's responsibility to keep general oversight of his charges, usually seeing them once a week to offer general advice and help and to keep their class attendance and work record constantly under review. In general terms Curry recognized that not all children wanted to work when expected to do so, and in 1956 he spoke in the prospectus of some children 'to whom pure scholarship is largely meaningless, and we foresee the possibility therefore that we may have to refuse in special

---

[15] Prospectus for 1954.
[16] Article on 'Dartington Hall' by W. B. Curry, in *The Modern Schools Handbook*, ed. T. Blewitt (London, 1934), p. 63.

cases to prepare children for examinations'. However, in 1949 the school had been inspected by six of His Majesty's Inspectors following through from the right of the minister consequent upon the 1944 Education Act to inspect all schools. The Dartington Trustees invited the visit of the inspectors, but Curry had resisted inspection as long as possible. Nevertheless he found the inspectors thorough, experienced, and considerate, with a gift for candour and tact. Their candour compelled them to indicate serious inadequacies in some of the teaching, as well as high ability elsewhere. As we have seen in some other reports on progressive schools, the inspectors sometimes found too little zest in both pupils and teachers and in a few cases their criticisms were precise and mordant. Later visits by the inspectorate have indicated how this has changed, and in 1959 the school became 'provisionally recognized', a formal step from its full recognition by the ministry which took place finally in 1965 after another full inspection.

Curry retired in 1957 after twenty-five years at Dartington, and he was succeeded a year later by Hubert and Lois Child: 'When we took up our duties in 1958 it was at our own wish that, both having the appropriate qualifications, we should hold the headship jointly as man and wife.'[17] Mr. Child is a scientist, educated originally at Oundle and Cambridge, who saw service in education in northern Nigeria before returning to England to teach at Bedales, where Mrs. Child was at that time also teaching. Mr. Child was able later to follow up his interests in vocational guidance and psychology, and after leaving Bedales worked with the National Institute of Industrial Psychology and during the war as a psychologist with the Admiralty. For ten years after the war he was the senior educational psychologist to the London County Council, in whose service one of Mr. Child's distinguished predecessors had been the then Dr. Cyril Burt. From the L.C.C. Mr. Child with his wife, who had been working in a training college, moved to Dartington to share the headship so that a man's and a woman's point of view could be available in a co-educational school. In principle many of their views coincided with Curry's, but they also made their own mark.

Where Curry had spoken in 1956 of possibly refusing to

[17] *The Independent Progressive School*, ed. Child, pp. 42–3.

prepare some children for examinations, the Childs, who retired from Dartington in 1968, expected nearly all children to take Ordinary levels or similar tests and to start the school course with a full range of subjects which could be modified later on tutorial advice – 'the necessity of taking external examinations inevitably makes demands which cannot be ignored'.[18] In 1956 Curry had said that it was part of the tradition of the progressive school movement to give a new emphasis to art and craft right through to the sixth form, and this Dartington continues to accept. The school is rightly proud of an art and craft block built in the early 1960s which matches the excellent laboratory and library provision, and the proximity to the full facilities of the new College of Arts at Dartington has already been mentioned.

Curry could say that there was no religious instruction in the sense that the school presented no particular religious doctrines, although the children were encouraged to discuss religious questions and to attend church if they wished. The Childs maintained this position, claiming that the school society taught good social habits and that freedom of spirit in a child was more important than any dogma or ritual. For the oldest boys and girls a class in comparative religion was provided.

In 1960 two Bedalians visited Dartington for a short while and later wrote some highly critical impressions for the *Bedales Chronicle*.[19] In a later issue of the same journal some Dartington pupils made reply, correcting many factual errors and denying the charges of apathy and mediocrity made by the Bedalians.[20] Round about the same time, however, the Childs themselves said that some pupils were doing the minimum of intellectual work and that improved rapport in teaching technique as well as a change from 'the casual "get-by" attitude' of the pupils was needed. This is a standard criticism of progressive schools by more conventionally-minded educators, but these reservations by the Childs themselves at the time lend colour to the view. A number of visitors have written about Dartington more recently, and Edward Blishen refers in an

[18] Prospectus, p. 8.
[19] Vol. 44, no. 2 (spring 1960).
[20] Vol. 45, no. 1 (1960), pp. 4–5.

article to matters considered at greater length by Jusmani and others.[21] Blishen says that there are three rather large gnats at which conventional educationalists would strain. First, 'the uncompromisingly genuine co-educational quality of the school', which is faced and backed by the Childs' declared opinion that sexual restraint is the price of freedom and that if any individual is unable to exercise it Dartington cannot be the right place for him or her. Second is the problem of academic pace, and here Blishen asserts that until the sixth form is reached the rate of work is slower than in conventional schools: this is a comment we have often met in the other progressive schools. Dartington sees this as the virtue that enables children to grow at their own pace, but a critic would say the pace is being kept too slow, although the Childs sharpened it in their ten years of office. Blishen offers the opinion that Dartington has opted out of the academic rat-race with perhaps some loss in the intensity of learning, but to the general benefit of the children and at no apparent cost in opportunities for higher education: this is the traditional progressive school argument. The third gnat is the secular humanism that is the prevailing moral and ethical spirit of the place. However, Blishen and Jusmani agree with Curry and with the Childs in thinking Dartington 'a remarkably law-abiding yet dynamic society'.

In the matter of discipline Dartington stands well to the left of Abbotsholme and rather less to the left of Bedales, but well to the right of Summerhill, though Neill claims that he was nearer to Curry than almost all the other progressive heads. Heckstall-Smith went to Dartington after a period at Gordonstoun with Kurt Hahn and found the change 'like a dressing on a burn'. He says that Curry's 'tireless attempt to tell the truth as he saw it, was for me something wholly new in education'.[22]

Dartington is a progressive school in the setting of a thriving, liberal community which combines rural industries and agricultural craft with high excellence in the dramatic and visual arts and music. The school was conceived in 1926 by the

[21] E. Blishen, 'The Lessons are Now Compulsory', in the *Daily Telegraph*, 22 Apr. 1966; A. A. Jusmani, 'The Attitude to the Child in Progressive Educational Theory and Practice in England since 1890' (M.Ed. thesis, University of Leicester, 1961).

[22] H. Heckstall-Smith, *Doubtful Schoolmaster* (London, 1962), p. 141.

Elmhirsts as an educational experiment and an agency for social equality. While it remained the first under Curry and the Childs, it did not succeed in becoming the second: the style of life and the permissive methods were not really accepted by the estate workers. The financial support of the Trustees has given to the school buildings, equipment, and financial backing which must be the cause of envy in other radical schools.

Since the retirement of the Childs, Dr. Royston Lambert, the author of *The State and Boarding Education* (London, 1966), became head in January 1969 and his aims and programmes are different in a number of particulars. He wants to maintain the unorthodox quality of Dartington but to relate the school in an integral way with the state system, pairing it with one or more comprehensive schools in other parts of the country, letting pupils move in both directions at different stages of their school life. He also wants to make participation between Dartington and its immediate vicinity more active than it has ever been, and here he is following the lead the Elmhirsts gave in the twenties, but with a contemporary difference which is more aware of how the progressive style of Dartington needs to be translated into the idiom of the modern urban world. Dr. Lambert is much concerned with the importance of the boarding-school, its quality of life and what at its best it can do for many children who do not have the chance to attend one. A research unit worked with him on the subject of the state and boarding education and he has taken a research unit with him to Dartington, which again is in line with the Elmhirst principle. But at this stage it is too early to do more than note this next chapter in the development of the Dartington story.

II

Bertrand Russell married Alys Pearsall Smith, of American Quaker stock, in 1894 and this marriage was dissolved in 1921 after ten years of separation and before that a long period of estrangement.[23] There were no children. In 1921, aged nearly

[23] A full account of this period of Russell's life is to be found in his *Autobiography, 1872–1914* (London, 1967). In volume ii, *1914–1944* (London, 1968), he covers the period when he was at Beacon Hill, but says disappointingly little about his participation. He died in 1970.

fifty, he married Dora Black, and when Russell wrote *On Education* in 1926 they had two young children whom they were anxious to educate as well as possible. Pyke had started the Malting House School in 1924 for a similar reason, and the Elmhirsts had started their school at Dartington in 1926 for the enlightened education of their own and other children. It was this same impulse at about the same time that stirred the Russells.

Bertrand Russell had stood unsuccessfully for Parliament as a Labour candidate in 1922 and 1923 – he had been similarly unsuccessful as a Liberal candidate in 1907. Dora Russell, who had also stood as a candidate earlier, took over from him as the Labour candidate for Chelsea in 1924, but she too was not elected. Their parliamentary aspirations were not renewed and their concern for their children's education took on a new insistence. In the introduction to *On Education* Russell wrote: 'The cause of educational reform is forced upon conscientious parents, not only for the good of the community, but also for the good of their own children.'[24]

In September 1927 the Russells rented Telegraph House at Harting near Petersfield in Hampshire from Frank Russell, Bertrand's brother, who had succeeded to the earldom over forty years before. Here they tried to work out their educational theories as Pyke and Susan Isaacs, Neill, and the Elmhirsts were all trying to do. Where Pyke became a financial impresario to finance the Malting House and the Elmhirsts backed Dartington with a secure and substantial subsidy each year, Russell, as on many other occasions in his life, relied on his tongue and his pen to earn the necessary money. He admitted that he was writing entirely for cash and that he had no pride to prevent him earning from what he called 'pot-boilers'.

Dora Russell was the leading spirit in starting and running the school.[25] Bertrand Russell was there from 1927 to 1932 helping a little in teaching and much more in administering and in planning the programme and the regime. In 1932, at the age of sixty, he left Beacon Hill prior to a divorce from Dora Russell in 1935 and marriage in 1936 to Patricia Spence,

---

[24] B. Russell, *On Education* (London, 1926), p. 9.
[25] For a recent short account, see D. Russell, 'What Beacon Hill Stood For', in *Anarchy* (Jan. 1967), pp. 11–16.

who had been a helper at the school. Dora Russell continued to run Beacon Hill, taking it to various locations, and ending up at her house in Cornwall, where with very few children at the school in 1943 she decided to close it down. She had herself a distinguished academic record at a Girls Public Day School Trust establishment in Sutton and at Cambridge, where she was a scholar of Girton, taking a First in modern languages and later becoming a fellow for two years before her marriage to Bertrand Russell. In a letter to the present author she said that she had often been tempted to write about education after her sixteen years at Beacon Hill but she had not done so, her work having lain in other directions since the end of the war. If she had written, she considered that what she would have had to say would have been meaningless to present-day planners, and here is the key to the work which was carried out at Beacon Hill both during the five years of the joint-headship of Bertrand and Dora Russell and for the remaining eleven years of Mrs. Russell's control. It was concerned primarily and mainly with growing persons living in as much freedom as possible.

While admitting that they differed in many matters, it would be best from our point of view to consider the educational ideas of Bertrand and Dora Russell as though they were one. They were opposed to war, they were in an intellectual sense committed to the left in politics, they had both read Freud, Adler, and Jung, and had acquaintance with behavourist psychology, they both tried to find rational bases for the kind of influence they wished children to be exposed to. Russell was by this time what may be called a liberal-socialist whose original liberalism had been transformed by the war, which to him was a consequence of capitalism. He had maintained his rational rejection of war as a wildly stupid way to try to solve contentious problems and in 1918 had spent some time in Brixton jail. But he was not a doctrinaire pacifist. His biographer quotes a most significant passage:

> I have longed to feel that oneness with large bodies of human beings that is experienced by the members of enthusiastic crowds.... I have imagined myself in turn a Liberal, or a Socialist or a pacifist, but I never have been any of these

things in a profound sense. Always the sceptical intellect, when I have most wished it silent, has whispered doubts to me.... I would tell Quakers that I thought many wars in history had been justified, and Socialists that I dreaded the tyranny of the State.[26]

The intellectual, the fastidious rationalist, the critical individualist was stifled by the utilitarianism and indifference to beauty and humane values when he visited Russia in 1920, and *The Practice and Theory of Bolshevism* alienated many of his socialist and pacifist friends. He and Dora Russell did not take easily to the Labour Party in England in the 1920s, and after their conspicuous failure at the polls in 1922–4 they decided to start a school in order to make a statement about quality in living which they thought the Labour Party was not exemplifying. Russell's restless and formidable intelligence was too essentially aristocratic in its loneliness and distinction to be in willing submission to the proletariat. If politics is the art of the possible, it also rests on a man's skill in playing consensus against conflict. This Russell, the individualist champion of the human race, always found difficult.

The motto which Russell invented for education as for other human affairs was that it should be based on science wielded by love. A living example of this principle was Margaret McMillan, who was greatly admired by both Bertrand and Dora Russell, although in detail their programmes were different from hers. They believed that children should grow up in a group which tried to make explicit the main principles characteristic of a reformed society. Opposed as they were to war and militarist thinking, they considered that nationalism was a potent influence towards aggression. Their school would be international and it would welcome children from the age of two because, while the family was the matrix of growth, it could become a divisive and defensive agency, the cause of feud and faction. Children should learn to be members of groups wider than the family as soon as possible, so that cooperation and mutual helpfulness should be the counterweight to competition and limited sympathies. The school, like

---

[26] A. Wood, *Bertrand Russell: The Passionate Sceptic* (London, 1957), p. 115. This passage also appears in volume ii of Russell's *Autobiography*.

Bedales and Dartington, the Malting House, Summerhill, and Abbotsholme, was to provide a model community in which quality of life, content of curriculum, methods of teaching, and style of human relationships were to be in themselves a way of living and learning the good life. When they became adults the pupils would have had prior knowledge of the kind of community they wanted and how to set about getting it.

There was no direct religious or political teaching at Beacon Hill but the children became aware of religion and politics through their study of the history and economic structure of other societies, and their moral education grew out of the daily give and take of the community. The very small children had a regimen of their own in which the contributions of Montessori were given place with those of the McMillans and to some extent of Susan Isaacs, although Mrs. Russell had criticisms of her work, as we shall see. Children of three and four used hammers, saws, and scissors as they did at the Malting House School, and Dora Russell thought that by four years of age her boys and girls were more independent and developed than children brought up within the average family. Beacon Hill never had more than about thirty children on the roll, and the total staff for all purposes was, at its peak, nine or ten, which makes a very generous proportion of adults. The school was co-educational from the start although the Russells were prepared to admit that in adolescence the sexes might want to draw apart. This they did not have to decide because Beacon Hill did not have a sufficient number of children staying on through adolescence.

The Russells thought that children would signal their readiness to read soon enough and at that point the opportunities of good material would be offered to them. As their parents were often intellectuals, usually of the left, among them refugees and professional men, frequently the readiness developed quite rapidly. The Russells were believers in oral work, and the children produced and later wrote their own plays[27] and were introduced to French and German from the age of four or even earlier, Dora Russell herself being the main teacher of languages. She would have liked to teach Spanish,

[27] A number of these were collected and published under the title *Thinking in Front of Yourself* (London, 1934).

Russian, and Chinese because on social, economic, and political grounds she thought these were the languages of the future. In fact they did teach Russian for a time, one of their science masters being of Russian extraction, but French and German, the main Western European languages, proved more immediately relevant in 1927 than the long-term internationalism of the Russells.

As at the Malting House School, so at Beacon Hill science was taught by experimental methods to children of four or five, even before their reading capacity had enabled them to use books. This was not the nature study which was, and still is, found in many infant schools, for the Russells worked on the basis that many things were learned and left in the unconscious knowledge of young children, to emerge later as and when needed. They had a simple laboratory where children learned from elementary experiments about air pressure and the composition of the atmosphere, and about the behaviour of water. They grew crystals, they did simple experiments in physiology, they collected fossils and rocks and studied rudimentary geology. The Russells tried to be educationally original while retaining their regard for intellectual standards. History and geography were taught as aspects of 'the science of life', in which astronomy, chemistry, and biology were related to history, geography ,and archaeology in order to suggest some concept of the unity of mankind developing from primeval human beings to the diverse competence and organization of modern society.

Beacon Hill had its School Council on which every adult, from the principals to the gardener, and every child of five years old and over, had a place and a vote. On the Council ordinary community rules were discussed and agreed upon, the adults having the responsibility for seeing they were obeyed, and there is the usual history of changing decisions and methods. At one time attendance at lessons was compulsory but later this was revised, provided the absentees did not disturb the workers and kept away from the classrooms. At another the Council gave the matron the right to make the rules for community order, discipline, and cleanliness but later changed to as near to complete freedom in routine as possible, arriving in due time at a framework of necessary rules. Mrs.

Russell sums up the attitude as follows: 'The most important thing to our children seems to be the feeling that they are not being compelled, but are doing a thing from their own choice, either because they like to, or because they think the thing reasonable.'[28]

The Russells considered that adults force patterns of behaviour on children too early and that from this resentment builds up. Adult society and national aspirations showed clear signs of the impulse to dominate. The Russells accepted that in the school there was bound to be some assertive and domineering behaviour because children and adults were like that, but their main aim was to release children from adult controls and social directives so that they could win time in which to build a sense of personal values. The free community would be tolerant to stress and would respond with vigour and a dispassionate realism. Children who grew up in a school which had a humanist ideal, a scientific attitude to diet and hygiene, and a respect for developmental psychology, would grow to understand one another and the society they wanted to live in. The Russells had, at any rate for a time, the conviction that a model community of children would, as the years passed, have an impact on society and on other schools, but they were too sophisticated to prescribe a Beacon Hill type of education as the answer to aggression in all its forms.

Russell was a close friend of W. B. Curry, who, as we have seen, returned to England to work at Dartington Hall in 1931, and it was mainly through his interest in the education of his own children at Dartington and Curry's critical admiration of his ideas that Russell continued his association with radical schools after his departure from Beacon Hill.

The Russells were the most consistently intellectual of the heads of radical schools except for Pyke and Mrs. Isaacs at the Malting House, and the differences between them are important and interesting. It will be remembered that Geoffrey Pyke's first advertisement in 1924 was for an educated young woman 'to conduct the education of a small group of children aged $2\frac{1}{2}$–7, as a piece of scientific work and research'. Mrs. Russell's comment on the Malting House enterprise was that it was more of a study of children than a school and that Beacon

[28] *The Modern Schools Handbook*, ed. Blewitt, p. 38.

Hill was too often placed in the same bracket with the Cambridge school.[29] Pyke and Susan Issacs were working to a psychological model, making discoveries about learning theory, adjustment, motivation, and unconscious influences as the 'research' proceeded, and, of course, making certain internal assumptions about mental health as they went along. Bertrand and Dora Russell were working to a social and political model, in which democratic and anti-militaristic ends were to be reached along many of the same paths as those followed by Pyke and Susan Isaacs, and all of them often spoke of emotional maturity and stability.

The Russells began their school as a result of personal political conviction and experience and without previously having taught children, but with the conviction that other unorthodox intellectuals would want to send their children to Beacon Hill. Russell was never only an academic philosopher and in his attempts at full human engagement his concern for education both in exposition and practice was a sub-heading to the general title that life should be lived on a basis of science wielded by love. Dora Russell was the person who translated this into action, and where the Malting House lasted for three years and has left its mark in Mrs. Isaacs's books, Beacon Hill lasted for sixteen years and is reflected to some extent in the writings of Bertrand Russell on education and in the largely forgotten methods and regime of the school which in the 1930s was nearest to Summerhill and Dartington.

[29] In a letter to the author, April 1964.

15 The Post-War Surgence: the Twenties

29 RUDOLF STEINER AND ANTHROPOSOPHY

I

ALL THROUGH his writing Steiner proclaims that he could never accept the sense-world as an ultimate. Physical perceptions are real enough and so are sense-data, and everyone can agree that thinking and systematic logic represent an analysis of situations and experience which can be more or less verified:

> I wished to turn away from that road to knowledge which looked towards the sense-world, and which would then break through from the sense-world into true reality. I desired to make clear that true reality is to be sought not by such a breaking through *from without*, but by sinking down into the inner life of man.... When from within man sense-free thought comes forth to meet the sense-perception ... the human spirit, living its own life within, meets the spirit of the world which is now no longer concealed from man behind the sense-world, but weaves and breathes within the sense-world.[1]

This finding of the spirit within the sense-world is not a question of logical inferences or progression from sense-data. It is a further phase of man's evolution and so far much of the metaphysics of Steiner's analysis marches with the interpretations of Theosophy. For both an all-pervading principle pre-exists, or at any rate co-exists with and through, Creation. Life, and the human mind which is aware of life are transformed beyond matter by this manifestation of God. Man is able

[1] R. Steiner, *The Story of My Life* (London, 1928), p. 116.

uniquely to test and experience this, according to Steiner, because evolution is not simply a process of natural selection with men as the most developed and adaptable of the animals:

> It was a personal distress to me to hear men say that the material economic forces in human history carried forward man's real evolution and that the spiritual was only an ideal superstructure over this substructure of the 'truly real'. I knew the reality of the spiritual. The assertions of the theorizing socialists meant to me the closing of men's eyes to true reality.[2]

This discovery of the spiritual by Steiner took a long time to form itself. He was born in 1861, the eldest of three children, in Kraljevec on the border between Hungary and Croatia to the wife of a minor official on the Southern Austrian Railway. The parents were Austrian Catholics, though the father went through a period of 'free thinking' in middle life. There is no evidence of an intense religious atmosphere in the Steiner home. When the time came to choose Rudolf's secondary-school training, his father decided that he should attend the *Realschule* rather than the *Gymnasium* as he wanted the boy to follow him in a railway career. The *Realschule* emphasized the sciences and Rudolf was grounded in physics, chemistry, and mathematics, especially geometry. His own interest and ability enabled him later to undertake the classical work of the *Gymnasium*.

In 1879 Steiner entered the Vienna *Technische Hochschule*, ostensibly continuing at the university level the science emphasis of the *Realschule*. By this time he had read and been fascinated by Kant's *Critique of Pure Reason* and had begun on Fichte's *Wissenschaftslehre*. He officially enrolled for mathematics, natural history, and chemistry and in fact carried these studies through but his primary interest was in philosophy and literature and he attended classes both in the *Hochschule* and the university, for he felt in duty bound to seek through philosophy for the truth. When he was nineteen he read Goethe's *Faust* for the first time, about fifty years after Goethe's final version of the work. Steiner found the unity of

[2] Ibid., p. 104.

Goethe's sensibility such as to attract him to read widely in both his literary and his scientific writings, and in 1884 he contributed to a symposium on Goethe. At the age of twenty-seven he was invited to Weimar as a co-editor of the scientific papers for the standard edition of Goethe's works published by the Goethe Archives. For the first time he had some limited financial security, and his intellectual intensity brought him to the attention of many of the leading philosophers and social theorists of the time. He had been schooled in the thinking of Kant, Fichte, Herbart, and Haeckel, he had read Nietzsche, Marx, and Engels, and he later came to know the work of Breuer and Freud. Steiner had listened to leading German thinkers lecturing on the theories of Hume and Darwin, and his scientific training enabled him to assess Einstein's work on relativity. By the time he was forty he had arrived at the basic hypotheses of what later came to be called Anthroposophy, the wisdom of man the spiritual being. It is exceedingly difficult to describe this briefly, because Steiner's output in books, articles, and lectures was phenomenal and covers exposition of his difference from other *Weltanschauungen*, his notion of sensory reality, presentations on fancy and imagination, visual art, literature, drama, and architecture as expressions and symbols of the spirit. He developed a moral theory which he called ethical individualism, by which moral life was to proceed by the unfolding of the human spirit and not by way of precepts obeyed. If it is very difficult to describe Anthroposophy briefly, it is equally difficult to describe it clearly, because the starting-point is personal and unlikely to yield adequately to words: '[About 1900] the germ of Christianity was beginning to unfold within me ... as an inner phenomenon.... The evolution of my soul rested upon the fact that I stood before the mystery of Golgotha in most inward, most earnest joy of knowledge.'[3]

In his major work *The Philosophy of Spiritual Activity* and in other books like *Mysticism* and *Christianity as Mystical Fact* and in lectures, Steiner recounts examples of spiritual activity in classical times, before the Christian revelation, and in the Christian centuries in Gnostic and other mystical groups from the Rosicrucians to Jakob Böhme. He took the example

[3] Ibid., p. 264.

of Buddha as a precursor to Christ, but at all points he claimed that historical examples were not the evidence that he valued. His understanding was received by hard, sustained thinking to clarify the philosophic issues, and by inner discipline to perceive the existence and reality of the spirit world and to enter into it. From a Germanic training in philosophy and science, and a personal vision, Steiner had by 1900 accepted many of the Theosophical principles expounded by Mme. Blavatsky, which in her case were based on Eastern occult writings. Most obviously, the spirit-principle is common to both, and the belief in reincarnation and *karma*. The physical self, the astral self, and the etheric self are to be found in each, together with a multi-dimensional understanding of life and the universe. There were, however, chasms of difference, and perhaps the best way to make these clear is to look at Steiner's career in Theosophy up to 1913.

In 1902 the Theosophical Society decided to set up a German branch and invited Steiner to be its general secretary. He agreed, with a number of reservations. Steiner continued to proclaim Anthroposophy to German Theosophists, saying that he had made this position quite clear to Mrs. Besant and the Theosophical Society when first agreeing to the formation of the German section. He disapproved of the Society's impartial support of religions and its generally numinous attitudes. Yoga, Eastern techniques of spirit-composure, the practice of spiritualism, and above all the depreciation of the significance of Jesus Christ, made it increasingly difficult for Steiner to continue to give loyalty to the Theosophical Society. In his idiosyncratic way, he had become Christocentric. The life and death of Jesus were not, for Steiner, just unusually powerful manifestations of spirit-centred man which could take their place with the sacrifice of Socrates, the life and serenity of the Buddha, or the confidence and sacrificial courage of Mahomet. The Christ phenomena were the unique statement both of man's hostility to God, and of the permeation of God's spirit. The gathered self-knowledge of Jesus in his acceptance of the spirit-world was a sure guide to men. Again, Theosophists seemed to be too dependent on the past and had too little knowledge of the scientific revolution, whereas Steiner wanted to accept the society of today in so far as these were the conditions in which the self-knowledge necessary in Anthroposophists had to be won.

In 1910 the final rift between Steiner and the Theosophical Society began to appear when Krishnamurti was presented by Mrs. Besant as the boy in whom Christ would live in reincarnation. A group within Theosophy grew up to support 'the Star of the East'. Steiner and his followers refused to have a branch of this movement in the German section and began to found the Anthroposophical Society. In January 1913 Mrs. Besant wrote to Steiner to tell him that he was no longer to be regarded as the leader of the German section of the Theosophical Society, which included Austria, Germany, and German-speaking Switzerland. Steiner responded by holding the first General Assembly of the Anthroposophical Society a month later. He was over fifty years of age, an Austrian not very well known outside Germany and with a difficult and unpopular creed to proffer. Eighteen months after the foundation of the new Society, Germany was at war with the rest of the world and therefore the main impact of Anthroposophy on Europe as a whole and on Great Britain in particular was felt only after 1919. Steiner died on 30 March 1925.

II

Steiner had spent twenty years of his life from his university days onwards as a part-time tutor, usually to the children of well-to-do families. He also taught courses in an adult education centre, the Berlin Workers School, and among the countless lectures he gave in his journeys across Europe before 1914 was a series on education on which he later based a published essay, *The Education of the Child in the Light of Anthroposophy*, which contains the essence of his subsequent writings on the subject. The first practical test of his theories came in 1919 when Herr Emil Molt, the owner of the Waldorf Astoria cigarette factory in Stuttgart, decided to initiate improvements in the working conditions of his operatives and to try to transform the spirit of the working relationship. In the discussions which followed some of the reforms were effected, but many of the workers felt that educational programmes which Molt proposed were not likely to succeed with them. However, together with Herr Molt they proposed that Steiner should direct a school for their children, and so began the *Freie Waldorfschule*, the prototype of Steiner schools. While Steiner recognized that the division of labour was unavoidable for adults, he wanted the children who went through the school to have a depth and range of experience. For these spiritual resources unusual teaching was required, and he gathered his men and women from Germany, Austria, Switzerland, and even Russia. Few of them had trained to teach, and Steiner conducted three courses in the fortnight before the beginning of the first term. These were the skeleton on which later and more elaborate training courses have been constructed.

In 1919 there were three hundred boys and girls at the Stuttgart school, and within a few years there were a thousand. Numbers rose to thirteen hundred in 1938, when the Nazis closed the school as a potentially subversive institution. It was reopened six months after the end of the Second World War, and another school was started in Stuttgart. At present there are at least twenty-six Steiner schools in Germany, all receiving support from the state and eighteen of them rebuilt after the destruction of war. In Germany and Switzerland one child in every six thousand goes to a Steiner school, a small enough ratio, but about fourteen times larger than the proportion in Great Britain, which is one child in eighty thousand. There are now at least seventy-five Steiner schools spread throughout the world in Germany, Holland, Switzerland, France, Norway, Denmark, Sweden, Belgium, Great Britain, Finland, Austria, Italy, United States, South Africa, New Zealand, Australia, Mexico, Brazil, and the Argentine. These do not include the schools and homes for children in need of special care, for whom Anthroposophists feel particular concern – there are another one hundred and twenty of these. Nor do they include the training colleges for teaching which are run in conjunction with seven of the schools in Germany, Switzerland, Holland, England, and the United States.[4]

In the summer of 1922 Steiner gave a course of lectures in Oxford on education, which was published in 1947 under the title *The Spiritual Ground of Education*. In 1923 he gave a second course at Ilkley in Yorkshire. These lectures were pub-

[4] *Child and Man* (summer 1964), p. 5.

lished much later, in 1954, as *Education and Modern Spiritual Life*, and it was at this conference that Margaret McMillan presided. Each had a great respect and admiration for the other, and some of Margaret McMillan's beliefs in the last ten years of her life may well have had more than a tincture of Anthroposophy in them, although she was always unwilling to discuss them. After the Ilkley conference she wrote to a friend of hers, Mrs. Sutcliffe: 'Yes, Steiner is a wonderful, glorious man.... [He] came here [to Deptford] and everything seemed new and wonderful when he entered the room.... No one need tell him anything about themselves. He seems to see one.... He never condemns or criticizes or has bitter thoughts like me.'

Others felt this inspiration and magnetism, and a committee was formed and money promised to start a Steiner School in England. He was again invited to England in 1924, and at Torquay he gave the kind of training course to the pioneer teachers that he had given in Stuttgart five years before. It was one of his last public acts, for he died a few months later.

The New School was opened at Streatham in London in 1925, later transferring to Forest Row in Sussex, where it now is under its present name, Michael Hall. This school was recognized as efficient by the Ministry of Education in 1950, as was Wynstones School in Gloucestershire in 1952. The other four schools, one in Edinburgh and the others in Worcestershire, Derbyshire, and Hertfordshire, are either not yet ready for or are not seeking this approval at the moment.

The teaching body is a 'college', where the responsibility is shared and no one is, in the conventional sense, head. Ethical individualism and respect for spiritual harmonies in a like-minded community make hierarchy and the bearing of authority seem superfluous. It is not necessary to invoke promotion as reward for spiritual maturity or teaching skill. The teaching body in a Steiner school, of which a high proportion are Anthroposophists, is nearer to a lay order than to the staff of a conventional school.

The same attitudes and beliefs relate to the children:

Childhood assumes quite another importance for us if we learn to view it as an incarnating process which partly conforms to the laws of physical nature and partly transcends these laws. Indeed the true nature of man lives in his *non-nature*, in the world beyond nature which declares itself in him. Thus each human life is the revelation of an immortal spirit which *was* before birth and which *will* be after death.[5]

The consequence in Steiner education is that all formal instruction is avoided in the 'sleep' of infancy because the child needs all his powers for his bodily, moral, and spiritual growth, and to introduce intellectual forms during this period encourages a precocity which throws the balance of growth askew. Small children need kindness, encouragement, love, and trust and they will not only respond similarly, but these moral and emotional qualities will affect physical growth too, will relax and strengthen breathing, encourage muscle-use, bring general confidence and somatic harmony. The fullest scope in Steiner schools is given to spontaneity in play, in art and in movement, in drama, in folk- and fairy-tales and in seasonal festivals, the archetypes of experience. Singing in English, French, and German lays the basis for later and wider understanding. Undoubtedly practices in most nursery schools are similar to those in a Steiner nursery class, though the structure of the archetypal past, the forms of eurhythmy (not meant to be the same thing as Dalcroze eurhythmics, though obviously related), and the European languages and folk-tales are more theoretically consistent because they are based in Steiner theology and cosmology. The nursery class in a Steiner school continues without the introduction of reading or computing until the child is six or seven, a year or two after the child in a maintained school has started more formal work, however informally taught.

The second phase of growth for Steiner is the years of childhood from seven to fourteen, and he emphasizes that man has time to mature, he has the benison of restraint which no other animal has, and that this is true both physically and mentally. The ego is the aspect of self which co-ordinates thought, speech, action, and acts of will, and through the period of childhood Steiner sees the advantages of what Freud called the latency period. Anthroposophists would say that in these seven or eight years soul-awareness fuses with ego-consciousness and

[5] L. F. Edmunds, *Rudolf Steiner Education* (London, 1962), p. 15.

experience becomes far more personal and realized than in childhood. This is the period for education of the feelings, for deepening of response to others before the differentiation of intellect diversifies the self: 'If the heart forces are not educated rightly, the intellect, left to itself, isolates men one from another.... Then we have parties but not community.... The education we are describing sets out to try to overcome the primary evil, egotism.'[6]

In Steiner schools the chronological age determines entry to a class and there is no streaming. The class teacher remains with the class throughout the eight years of childhood, teaching many if not most of the lessons and making with his or her pupils a secure and sensitive family of learners – or, at least, this is what is postulated and often achieved. Brilliance in a child is deepened by experience of wisdom, patience, tolerance, and compassion and not whetted as an instrument in a competition with other children. Thus the transition from the fantasy of the small child to the abstract thinking of the adolescent should be a gentle process, and the intellectually able child should be protected from exploitation by society and by parents.

Anthroposophists believe that children not only recapitulate in their growth the biological history of the human race but its psychological and cultural history too, and they base their curriculum on these principles. This means that reading is not taken as a special enterprise but is built up by movement, gesture, painting, and ideograph, into writing and to an outcome in reading itself. The practical consequence of this recapitulation of man's story is that reading is usually delayed in Steiner schools longer than in the conventional school and it is at a late stage that letters are tied to sounds. Thus it is supposed that letters are not seen as conventional symbols only, but the alphabet and written communication are felt to be descended from more rudimentary needs and cruder representations. Hence, to use a common phrase in Steiner terminology, the growing self-identity of the child 'begins to turn earthward'.

The age of nine and ten is the heart of this childhood phase, the time of growing awareness for the child of the aloneness,

[6] Ibid., pp. 30–1.

of the individuality, of persons, others as well as himself. Again, Steiner says, the child needs the security of a past which is not only his shallow family childhood but his deep racial heritage, and in this the boy or girl can begin to bear and understand the polarity of continuity on the one hand and separation on the other. The Old Testament is the source for these personal and cosmic themes – Adam, the son of the Father and the rebellious man, Noah, Abraham, Moses, the Patriarchs, all of them with a sense of mission but with a sense of origin, too.

Other themes are also important at this time, like farming, the soil, the seasons, man the husbandman who knows, respects, and fears nature. Or housebuilding, the perennial statement of the need for shelter from which so many other activities flow, rooms for eating, for preparing food, for talking, for study, for washing, for excreting, for sleeping.

As children move closer to puberty so they become aware of growth, depth, and range, says Rudolf Steiner, and one of the consequences in the school is the study of geology, physics, and mathematics. The children bridge the discomforts of their own lack of co-ordination by the use of tools in carving, and in cultivating the soil. History is given the characteristic Steiner symbolism. The Romans are appropriate for study by the twelve-year-old because they were at once temporally competent and they made actual by law, by rational building, by respect for minorities what the Greeks had begun to do. These achievements form the prerequisite for the speculative thought of Byzantium and Islam and the prelude to the Arthurian legend. Steiner's use of history as a kind of textbook of cosmic themes has about it the daring, if not the range or precision, of Toynbee's vast historical undertaking.

The third phase of growth is adolescence, and here again Steiner has some unusual emphases to offer. At this time he sees the beginning of an independent life of thought, a questioning of the experience and opinion of others and of oneself, a search through ideas for some binding truth. This quest can take various forms of expression, nearly all of them restless: ambition, assertiveness, a factitious adulthood, romantic imaginings. Always, for Steiner, these represent a stirring of the spirit startled by the wakening mind and its self-sustained ideas, dismayed by the apparent loneliness and the personal inadequacy. For Anthroposophists there are two special antithetical difficulties in adolescence: egotism in material things and scepticism in spiritual things: 'the first makes too much of the earth, the other too little of heaven'.[7]

To maintain this balance Steiner schools lean heavily on art. From the start children have been encouraged to experience and to experiment with colour and through this to learn a language of moods and modulation. This is, of course, related to Goethe's theory of colour which Steiner studied and knew so well. In Steiner schools clear colours have qualities which can be modified and transformed in line and harmony: yellow is a confident, radiant colour which deepens and matures in gold and amber; blue has qualities of form and firmness and depth; red is the colour of energy, of passion. From the first day in the nursery class children in Steiner schools have a weekly lesson with simple watercolours, and from this, as they mingle the colours and shades, they learn a language of contrast, harmony, modulation, restraint, and conflict, with which they can paint their moods, their fears, and their understanding in colour compositions which Steiner considered far more expressive in the early years of limited control of the medium and restricted grasp, than the formless appearances of so much child art. The colours make a dialogue within a discipline that is appropriate in art for young children and is the basis of freedom within forms, which Steiner valued.

At puberty children in Steiner schools cease to work in colour for a while and use black and white. Steiner thought this was an appropriate change of medium to comport with a new awareness of contrast, a clarity of definition, a sustaining of the line of argument which develops in adolescence. The austerity required by the black and white medium is thought to aid children of fourteen or fifteen to a greater stability: when they return to colour around sixteen their compositions are expected to have more balance, often a more direct theme. Anyone familiar with the use of art in diagnosis and therapy as Jung and others have employed it will see resemblances to what Steiner proposed, although the Anthroposophical

[7] Ibid., p. 54.

doctrine may appear too cloudy in its psychological symbolism and too restrictive in its abstract colourwash form when one thinks of the sheer vitality of a great deal of child art.

Music, drama, eurhythmy, and the growing range of subjects like mathematics, geography, science, and English give to adolescents an intellectual challenge and the means of maintaining depth in the whole range of activity. Whereas in the years from six to fourteen the class teacher was the continuing parent-figure, in adolescence the teaching is by specialists as in most secondary schools. The child is expected to do more himself to bring together and to co-ordinate the subjects he is being taught; his interests are given every encouragement while the education is still kept wide. One distinctive feature in all Steiner schools is the main lesson, which is the first lesson of the day, and which usually lasts for two hours and is devoted to either mathematics, English history, geography, or science. This regime starts in the first class at the age of six or seven and goes through the school and into the upper school. Not only is there this daily concentration, but each subject may be taught each morning for several weeks before a change is made to the next. Anthroposophists maintain that this allows the children time both to receive and to give; they can listen to the teacher's words, they can translate them into movement, recitation, individual work, and discussion, and quite often this is undertaken in three-day cycles. Steiner postulates that what is taught on the first day merges into rhythmic functioning of the child during sleep on the first night and on the second night more deeply still into the child's metabolism. Again the spirit symbolism of Steiner unites ideas and mental activity with the working of the body.

Eurhythmy is an art of movement developed by Steiner which is related to gesture, to rhythm, to harmony of mood or idea, and movement. Ballet, mime, drama, dance are all part of this body-language, and in its medium it has a part to play in Steiner education as art does in a different mode. It is intended to have the expressiveness, freedom, discipline, and restraint which many modern schools of movement have built upon, and it was conceived to encourage creativeness and personal therapy while being another means of presenting archetypal themes in a stylized form.

In Steiner schools discipline is taken seriously, as might be expected when teachers speak of restraint as well as freedom:

> If children are left only to do as they will, what benefit can it be to them? Sooner or later it leads to a kind of exhaustion.... One gains the impression at times that with the self-expression enthusiasts anything 'odd' is accounted 'remarkable'. The only way to real freedom is through schooling.[8]

This might have been written by any *status quo* reactionary, but the particular meaning for an Anthroposophist is very different from a traditional 'us' and 'them' kind of view. Physical fear and corporal punishment have no place in a Steiner school, neither have prizes and obvious awards in competition, but correction for wrongdoing is regarded as both right and proper. The main initiative in maintaining discipline is with the teacher and there are no precise rules or methods of control or punishment available to him because it is assumed that both pupil and teacher, each from his own point of view, are prepared to accept co-operative enterprise as the real purpose of school and classroom – indeed of life as a whole. Bringing order out of disorder is not mainly a matter of organization but rather a therapeutic exercise both for teacher and child, and consequently any punishment, to be worth while, puts a burden on the teacher because the core of true discipline is willing discipleship. The heart of the matter is a deep sense of peace in heart and mind, in home and school, in these days especially in the school. There is no belief in child self-government: 'Contrary to the methods of self-government practised in other schools, in a Waldorf school authority rests only with adults.'[9]

The schools make no pretence of the fact that their purpose is to hold back a too rapid intellectual development in the interest of what they call 'greater force of imagination', and this means that they do not shape their courses in the upper school with national examinations in mind. 'The examinations required for entering college or the professional schools ... invade and compromise that curriculum of our upper classes.

[8] Ibid., p. 48.   [9] Ibid., p. 84.

... To safeguard the Waldorf curriculum the examinations are generally taken later.'[10] The phrase used in the prospectus of the Steiner schools on this matter is that pupils are prepared for the General Certificate of Education or its equivalent 'in as many subjects as are necessary for the career they have chosen'.

Anthroposophists have become widely known for the work they do with and for handicapped children, or as Steiner called them *Seelenpflegebedürftige*, children in need of special care. He wrote to one of his friends: 'Only the physical body sustains the injury, but the Spiritual Being which lies behind the physical body remains unharmed. This Spiritual Being is a reality for me, just as much a reality as the hydrogen in water is for the chemist.'[11] The problem for the teacher in a Steiner home for such children is to discover in what ways, if any, the etheric body and the astral body are damaged, as the physical body clearly is. The children are not regarded as simply unfortunate, but as human spirits with whom little successful contact through the intellect is going to be possible. The deeper self may be clouded because the physical body and the stunted ego offer little transparency. To Anthroposophists, however, the enigmas of the phases of reincarnation and *karma* exist, of which these abnormalities are clear and saddening expressions, and from this affliction the seeds of future growth and correction come. In this the work of the doctor, the nurse, and the teacher moves not only, or even mainly, in temporal cycles, It is not our main concern here to write of work with abnormal children, but it would be a serious omission not to mention, even thus briefly, the radical work done by Anthroposophists, based on their initial religious positions, for handicapped children and, come to that, maladjusted children.

We can sum up the purpose of the Steiner schools thus:

> To take the adolescent through the history and development of art as the revelation of evolving manhood; to educate him into the meaning and appreciation of poetry as the medium wherein the centre in man finds kinship with the heart of all creation; to unfold the nature of love, by way

---

[10] Ibid., p. 81.
[11] Quoted in Joan Ruder 'Curative Education', in *The Faithful Thinker*, ed. A. C. Harwood (London, 1961), p. 207.

of the great sagas and literatures of the human race, as the search of man for his own kingdom; to show that the ideals man carries are the earnest he has of his true estate, that there is conception in the spirit as well as in the body, that moral imagination is not a chimera of the mind but a power for renewing life; to discover that history follows a mighty plan of promise and fulfilment, that it leads from a state of moral and spiritual dependence towards the goal of self-mastery and self-determination, from community by descent in the past to community by assent; to demonstrate ... that as man grows in insight so will the ultimate goal of science be attained, the rediscovery of the divine; to come to an understanding of the spiritual heritage of the East and to an appreciation of the spiritual promise of the West ... to perceive mankind, with Paul, as many-membered but filled with One Spirit ... and to see the many deaths that man must die to gain immortality ... to pursue all this with enthusiasm and with faith.[12]

The Steiner epistemology, ontology, and teleology are not located fully in time, and the sense of the eternal moment is strong, at least in Anthroposophical writings on education. It is not surprising that one writer considering teaching machines in a recent issue of *Child and Man* found them to be the antithesis of what Steiner schools stand for, and that programmed learning was 'the stillborn offspring of desiccated calculating machines' intended to emasculate the human spirit. A spiritualized theology provides little nourishment for sociological thinking and so Steiner schools are, of all those so far mentioned, the most radical because they are the most comprehensively different. In their way they are as radical as Summerhill in its way, and the report drawn up by members of His Majesty's Inspectorate on Michael Hall when it was first inspected in the 1960s makes the same point:

We have visited many types of school in this country. The ethical colourings in those schools might be different according to whether they were state, public, private, denominational, progressive and the rest, but the actual education

[12] Edmunds, *Rudolf Steiner Education*, pp. 57–8.

offered was essentially the same in all of them. This is the first school we have met in which the philosophy of the school has totally altered the character of the education offered.

Anthroposophists consider their belief to be a way of living and they have no forms of worship. There is, for them, a distinction between approaching the spiritual world by means of individual initiative through thinking and approaching it through the common path of a religious liturgy, ritual, or form of worship. When individual understanding has been reached, Anthroposophists consider that there is no longer any need for a communal religious approach. Here is the heart of an apparent paradox: on the one hand the difficult, idiosyncratic life-view of Steiner forming a kind of imprecise orthodoxy, and on the other the truly anarchic principle of ethical individualism. So in education there is an agreed canon of Steiner theory and practice, different in many particulars from orthodox teaching in schools. It is different also from the ethos and practice in any of the radical schools we have so far considered. Whereas these grew out of English life and institutions and took up their stance in relation to the public schools, the liberalism of early political emancipating movements, religious unorthodoxy, and the anglicized transplanting of Freud, Steiner schools are and always have been based on a thought-system and a creed which bears clear marks of its Germanic origin.

The inspectors were right in saying that the character of the education in Steiner schools is deeply affected by the philosophy of life of Anthroposophy itself. As this is a product of German and Eastern thought it does not graft easily on to an English stem.

16 The Slackening Tide: Bryanston

IN THE first prospectus of Bryanston school, issued before the school opened in January 1928, appears the following statement:

> The Bryanston scheme has been launched to meet the difficulty felt both in this country and in the Dominions of gaining admission to our public schools.... Bryanston will therefore be a new English public school in which provision will be made for applicants from throughout the Empire.

The first headmaster was J. Graham Jeffreys, an Australian who graduated in Melbourne before going up to Christ Church, Oxford, and the school opened with twenty-three boys in what had been Lord Portman's fine house on a 400-acre estate near Blandford in Dorset. The building had been designed by Norman Shaw in 1897 and remains the main accommodation, although surrounded now by the additional buildings appropriate to a much larger school.

The explicit alignment to the public schools may be thought to rule Bryanston out of the radical group we are considering, and admittedly it is on the borderline, but in its later development it is more clearly like others on the right wing of the progressive group. The first issue of the school magazine in December 1929 contains a contribution from the head which shows the way he was thinking: 'Let [each boy] be a gentleman in the best and widest sense of the word – courteous, kindly, considerate, discreet'. A contribution to a later issue, thinking back to those early days, says that Mrs. Jeffreys helped with the cooking and the relationship in the school family was rather that of a club: 'Jeff seemed more like the breezy second officer of a ship.... [He had] tremendous promotional flair.'[1]

---

[1] *Anniversary Saga, 1928–1948*, article by M. P. Phillips from an early number of the magazine, p. 12.

Jeffreys claimed that Bryanston had been founded and directed by men who were old boys of great English public schools and who had imbibed their spirit. They started by admitting boys of thirteen to fourteen and a half on a test of general ability with a view to providing resilient systems of teaching, but in 1931 the more usual Common Entrance examination for thirteen- to fourteen-year-olds coming from preparatory schools was required. Jeffreys spoke more than once about this time of a public school which gave a realistic working method for average boys who wanted to enter the armed services or the learned professions or who had no pretensions to a professional career. They should all become honest, manly, and Christian citizens of the Empire. In the article in the *Anniversary Saga* already quoted, the author says of the first twenty-three pupils in January 1928 that all had this in common – 'we were either delicate or backward: I was both'.[2]

Corporal punishment was administered by masters only and not by prefects, and as an instance one stroke was given for every cigarette smoked in the term. Yet alongside these traditional public school patterns there were other features unusual for 1928. There was no classical side, although Latin and Greek were available for those who wanted them. Modern subjects included a variety of languages, as well as biology and the physical sciences. A seminar and discussion methods in teaching, classes of sixteen or less, and houses of not more than forty are reminiscent of the assumptions and methods of progressive schools in the 1920s. Boys at Bryanston were expected to dispense with personal domestic service to avoid 'undue luxury of living'. In the summer they wore shorts and open-necked shirts as weekday school uniform, and their winter outfit was informal by the public school standards of those days. On Sundays the differences were less obvious – for a few years bowler hats or straw hats were worn by all. Although they had to play school games for their first three years, they were free in the last two years in school to choose their own form of exercise. From the beginning there was a system of tutorials and what we would now call 'setting' for the teaching of certain subjects, and an organization closely

[2] Ibid.

akin to the Dalton plan, though in a number of public statements on the Bryanston scheme round about 1930 the absence of reference to Helen Parkhurst and the Dalton programme suggests that this was not a direct descendant. Here was another unusual feature in what might otherwise have been characterized as a new public school for not-so-bright boys from England and the Empire who were finding entry to the older schools too difficult.

In February 1932, with the numbers having increased in four years from twenty-three to nearly two hundred and fifty, Jeffreys resigned. He reported in the third prospectus, just before his departure, that the maximum number to be aimed at in Bryanston was three hundred. When His Majesty's Inspectors first made a full inspection of the school early in 1933 they reported that there were one hundred and ninety-two boys in the school, only fourteen of whom were doing sixth-form work: 'The first Head Master, who was the founder, has left very recently and the new Head Master has scarcely had time to make his influence felt.'[3] The new headmaster was Thorold F. Coade, who retired in 1959 and died in 1963, and although he was not the founder he represents for Bryanston what Badley does for Bedales: the sustained leadership for more than a quarter of a century of a remarkable man. In 1957 one of his old boys wrote: 'T.F.C.'s Headmastership may well come to be regarded by those qualified to judge as the most significant in educational development over the first half of this century; there is no doubt that T.F.C. will be looked upon as one of the outstanding headmasters of this age.'[4]

Making allowances for anniversary euphoria, we have here a notable tribute. Coade had been a young master at Harrow, and in correspondence[5] gives some indications of how his viewpoint on education developed. Between 1922 and 1932 he was a member of the informal group which took the title 'New Ideals in Education', and to which so many of those we have already mentioned also belonged. The group had its first

---

[3] *Report by H. M. Inspectors on Bryanston School, Blandford* (1933), p. 2.
[4] *Saga* (summer 1957), p. 4. This is the school magazine at Bryanston.
[5] Kindly lent to the author by R. A. Wake, H.M.I. Fuller treatment can be found in a collection of Coade's papers compiled by three Bryanston masters entitled *The Burning Bow* (London, 1966). I have called on this book *passim* in some of what is here written about Thorold Coade.

conference at East Runton in Norfolk in 1914 and later published a journal, *New Ideals Quarterly*. From 1922 Coade attended the group conferences and was familiar with the ideas of all the schools we have so far considered. It will be remembered from the account given earlier that the Theosophical Fraternity in Education and later the New Education Fellowship grew out of this group. Coade also speaks of the importance of the New Education Fellowship in helping to shape his educational thinking.

A number of able young men had returned from their war service to Harrow, and Coade, an old boy of the school, joined with a number of others in forming a Junior Masters Club to which speakers with interesting ideas were invited. It was from meetings arranged by this Club that the *Harrow Lectures on Education* appeared in 1930, which showed some of the unorthodox thinking going on at the time among the younger men. Coade had been a leading figure in arranging these meetings and edited the publication.

Miss Helen Parkhurst and her Dalton Plan of individual assignments had attracted his attention, mainly through his contacts with the New Education Fellowship. Another whom he said he met through this society was one of its leading French members, Professor Émile Marcault. 'Marcault illuminated my mind on this subject of individual education, "individual" in this sense being the exact opposite of "individualist". He defined leaders as "those who habitually live on a higher level of consciousness".'[6] This emphasis Coade sums up as essentially Christian, exemplifying the principle that the school community, like the Sabbath, is made for man and not *vice versa*. He laid great store by the quality of the life of the school community, which, especially in a boarding-school, gave scope and experience for the growth of Christian love, which he defined as the steady, determined activity of the mind directed towards fellowship. The writings of Evelyn Underhill gave Coade a clearer idea, as he said, of the nature of God as a Creator and as a lover of His creatures. Coade saw both these aspects merging into one in a good and lively school community, and for him the main factor in education was the impact of person on person, hence the paramount importance

[6] In private correspondence.

of the selection of staff and the attitude of responsibility which the older boys were expected to have to the younger. At the time of Coade's retirement in 1959 one of his former pupils wrote of Coade's arrival in 1932: 'A shy, diffident figure sidled down the main corridor.... Slowly the school grew round him, alive and sensitive.... He who loves God loves his brother also: such a man is Thorold Coade.'[7]

H.M. Inspectors said in 1951 that he delegated authority and avoided any appearance of being a figurehead, yet his personal influence was pervasive and the success of the school had to be attributed largely to him. He did not meet Reddie, nor did he see his ideas working out at Abbotsholme, though later he knew Sharp and the work of the school. Characteristically Coade gives Reddie all credit for being 'a great man and an innovator', but finds him from report and evidence of practice too much of an egotist. Coade did not meet Badley until his own views had become fairly clear and his Bryanston work was established. However, he came to know Kurt Hahn well from 1929 onwards, and in 1932 boys from Bryanston and from Salem exchanged schools for some weeks: 'I learned much from him about the need to get boys to focus on some worthwhile objective which might become for them a *grande passion* shepherding them through the difficult adolescent years; also his stress on physical achievement outside organized games struck me as highly important.'[8]

Coade had another concern, another emphasis. He wanted boys at Bryanston to use their hands, to feel, to know, and to create through the plastic arts, the crafts, and music. Every boy could have in some way his chance of a creative moment, and this really was an article of faith with Coade: again in 1951 the inspectors show how the school had matured in this since 1933, reporting a fine art and craft tradition, ambitious and successful sculpture, good pottery, woodcarving, typography, and a splendid development in music. Time was set aside for such activities for each boy in the normal run of work and on one or two evenings each week. This programme still exists and the 1961 inspectors also commend it.

The occasional caning in Jeffrey's time was not repeated

[7] G. S. Udall, *Saga* (winter 1959), p. 6.
[8] In correspondence.

under Coade, and the relaxed friendliness of relationships continued, punishment runs and gatings being found enough in the way of deterrents. But the most unusual feature was the consistent adherence to the Dalton Plan which began in some form under Jeffreys in 1930, as we have seen. In 1941 the first edition was produced of an account of this scheme as it was then working at Bryanston, and this was revised in 1947.[9] The principles of the system were that a boy should learn to work on his own initiative, discovering how to study and bridging the gap between classroom instruction and university work by making progress at his own pace on assignments which he completed by studying often by himself and sometimes with classes or groups. His teachers were available for advice, guidance, and teaching and the pupil kept a time-chart and a mark record.[10] All of this continues in substantially the same form and resembles fairly closely what Miss Parkhurst laid down.

At the age of sixteen Helen Parkhurst found herself in a log-cabin school in Wisconsin responsible for the teaching of forty children in eight grades. She started then to plan individual schemes of work, and enabled some children to work by themselves while she taught others. Over the next fifteen years she perfected this programme, visited other innovators and became a co-worker with Maria Montessori. In 1919 she was given charge of a school for crippled boys where she introduced her full 'laboratory plan', which quickly gained a great deal of public attention, made all the more intensive when Mrs. Murray Crane, a philanthropist much interested in education, urged the adoption in 1920 of the laboratory plan in the state high school of Dalton, Massachusetts, Miss Parkhurst's home town. The scheme came to England through Belle Rennie, the tireless secretary of the Conference of New Ideals in Education, who saw the Dalton school in operation right at the start and within three months had written to *The Times Educational Supplement*[11] offering full information to anyone interested. There were four hundred inquiries within a week. In November the paper stated that over six hundred schools were using the plan in Great Britain, and by 1926 it was claimed that over two thousand schools were working it. In

[9] D. R. Wigram, *The System of Work at Bryanston School* (1947).
[10] Ibid.   [11] 6 May 1920.

1921 a Dalton Association was formed with Miss Rennie as secretary, and Miss Parkhurst visited England to give lectures and see the schools. The method was practised in many countries in Europe and Asia and was even proposed as a national system for Poland and Japan. Yet within fifteen years it was dead in England as a radical novelty and in general had been either submerged by a return of class teaching or assimilated into an individualized assignment system. The teaching rooms tended to go, the individual assignments were accompanied by an encroaching amount of formal instruction, and the working group replaced the private study of an individual.[12] But Bryanston has kept to the Dalton Plan in all main essentials.

As reported by Wigram, the Bryanston scheme worked (and in all essentials still works) as follows. Usually the thirteen-year-old entry is placed in a year-block D, moving a year later to C, then to B, where General School Certificate Ordinary Level examinations are normally taken. For those who want it, two years between the ages of sixteen and eighteen are spent in block A, the sixth form in other schools, but boys of high ability go into block C on entry and spend three years in block A. Each boy has a monthly chart which has to be carefully kept; it records the number of forty-minute periods spent on each subject. The work of all these subjects is split up into topics and references, called assignments, and a space is left on the chart for recording marks given by the teacher on the work done in the assignments. These marks convey not only the quality of the knowledge displayed but, by use of colours, the degree of effort. Thus alpha in red indicates very good work and diligent effort. Blue markings indicate medium effort and black represents a lack of diligence and concentration. It is possible for a boy to get a blue beta for one subject and a black beta for another, showing that the quality of work is similar in each, but in one he scores low on diligence.

Each boy has a tutor who acts as his guide and adviser. The tutor decides with the boy at the beginning of each session

---

[12] See 'The Dalton Plan', in *The Times Educational Supplement*, 2 Aug. 1963, p. 149; H. Parkhurst, *Education on the Dalton Plan* (London, 1923); E. Dewey, *The Dalton Laboratory Plan* (London, 1924); A. J. Lynch, *Individual Work and the Dalton Plan* (London, 1924); *Adolescent at School*, ed. V. Mallinson (London, 1949), ch. vii.

what subjects he will take and will have previously consulted the parents. The curriculum offered is the usual grammar-school range with divinity, music, and current affairs taking a compulsory share of the total programme throughout the whole five years; physical education is also required in varying forms. The blocks are 'setted', an arrangement by which boys are grouped together and may work with others of their own standard. For instance a boy in block C may be good in mathematics and so in set C_1 for that subject, weak in Latin and in C_4 for that, and moderate in French and in C_2 for that.

Within this Dalton system there is scope for class or 'set' teaching, and there is a good deal more of this in block D than elsewhere so that new boys may learn gradually to acquire the necessary self-discipline. Some subjects need more of it than others: a modern language needs more than history, similarly mathematics more than English. There are no form rankings, no class prizes, and the story of a boy's performance and progress is to be found in his work-chart, which is filled in every day, gradings entered and initialled by the subject-master, and the whole record examined regularly by the tutor. This system permits of tests and examinations as required.

The basis of the whole plan is the assignment, a scheme of work set weekly or fortnightly, or over a longer period in blocks A and B, and provided on a typed sheet for each boy. The assignment has to be completed in a fixed period of time, and here the Bryanston scheme differs from the Dalton Plan, for in the latter children worked through the assignment at their own pace and no group could be expected to be at the same point in the programme at the same time. At Bryanston each set is kept working on basically the same assignment for the same length of time, the faster and abler pupils being expected to produce a deeper and more extensive coverage. The assignment is not only a statement of the work to be done but covers reading references, requirements of notes, questions for written answer, and correlations with cognate assignments in other subjects. By this means it is thought that pupils can see the strategy of the course, teachers have been compelled to chart their programme with long-term foresight and short-term care, and the record of a boy's achievement in all his subjects is kept by him on his chart.

The Slackening Tide: Bryanston

The whole system demands discipline and organization, as much from the teaching staff as from the boys, for work has to be marked and returned quickly, a variety of class periods taught, and availability for consultation arranged and known to both boys and masters. On the boy's side it is assumed that if he finishes a week's assignment in one subject in less than the total of, say, seven periods allotted for it, he has that time available to spend on a weak subject where he needs more time.

None of the other schools mentioned in this volume has organized its teaching on the Dalton Plan for so long or in such detail. Many of them had a programme of the kind for a while: Bedales, Abbotsholme, more than one of the Friends' schools, St. Christopher are examples, and vestiges of the organization remain in some cases. H.M. Inspectors in 1951 and again in 1961 speak well of the system at Bryanston and consider that ordinary boys show a cheerful attack on their work. One commentator, with impregnable condescension, considers that at worst the boys are not being bored and at best are developing maturely. As a gauge of the effectiveness of the Bryanston–Dalton Plan for boys going on to higher education, 44 per cent of those leaving the school between 1948 and 1951 went on to university, 'a proportion surpassed by few schools'. Of those leaving between 1958 and 1961, 41 per cent went to universities, and if one adds the boys who went to colleges of art, music, drama, or other forms of full-time higher education, the percentage is 59 per cent, which is conspicuously high by any standards. When we recall that in 1933, at the beginning of Coade's headship, only fourteen of the one hundred and ninety-two boys were doing sixth-form work we can see how the school has changed, and it was during this period that the Dalton Plan innovation was systematically organized and applied.

To work the Dalton Plan with any success it is necessary to have a good collection of books, whether in the central library or in the subject-rooms, and the 1951 inspectors thought that the total number of books was not large and that growth had not been rapid enough. In 1961, when there were about eleven thousand books in all for the school's use, the holding was thought to be commendable – the number now, in a school of over four hundred and fifty, is considerably larger.

All boys are expected to belong to the Sea Cadet Corps or to the Pioneers, a school organization which came into existence in 1933. In the early 1930s the mounting crisis of the ineffectiveness of the League of Nations and the rise to power of Hitler were accompanied by a desperate desire for peace and economic recovery after the Great Depression. It was no accident that the year after he became head, Coade brought the Pioneers into existence to provide in a school 'where much attention was given to individuality an organization aiming at a sense of corporate unity directed to positive ends through constructive work'. For Coade, who had served in the First World War, the Pioneers were an educational liberal's answer to the O.T.C. The aim was training for citizenship, the membership voluntary, and boys worked (as they still do) usually in groups of about six to ten on community service projects in building, maintenance, conservation, and improvement. Among many projects the Pioneers have built a new boathouse, and a causeway to the river, very necessary for a rowing school; they have put up a new rifle range and an observatory, and over a period of seven years have constructed a fine music school; the Greek theatre took two years to complete.

Many of these undertakings are now common practice in a number of maintained or independent schools not in the progressive categories, but Bryanston has been run on these lines since 1933 when this whole outlook was very new and compulsory games was the orthodox physical enterprise. Bryanston's schemes were, of course, related to Abbotsholme's and Bedale's estate work, to Leighton Park's venture scholarships and to Kurt Hahn's similar schemes first at Salem and from 1934 in Scotland at Gordonstoun, and in Outward Bound enterprises.

The Sea Cadets were started at Bryanston in 1946 to provide opportunities for pre-service training. In the 1930s the Pioneers had been a specifically non-military organization, but during the war many of the older boys had been active in pre-service and civil defence units and there was still, in the post-war situation of conscription, a body of opinion among boys and parents supporting some form of preparatory organization. Some parents were glad of this more formal and disciplined training and saw it as a valuable contrast to the informality of the school, even where no future career in the service was intended. Others saw this development as an extension of the range of careers for which a Bryanston education might be directly relevant. Still other parents thought it a surrender to orthodox practices, and the choice of Sea Cadets as the favoured organization shows a nice discrimination in trying to meet all shades of opinion.

In the liberal–conservative spectrum of the progressive schools Bryanston was and is at the conservative end. The traditional games, with rowing, swimming, athletics, and tennis, are played regularly and to a good standard. The more individual sports like climbing and canoeing are encouraged and it is the school's policy to leave boys free to choose what form of exercise they will take, with the proviso that it has to be strenuous, and they can choose their games each term only if they undertake to turn out regularly. Summerhill or Dartington or Bedales or the Steiner schools or St. Christopher are more permissive in these and other matters than Bryanston. In the matter of pre-service training among the progressive group Bryanston and Gordonstoun are almost alone.

There are about fifty clubs and societies in the school to which boys belong and time is given in the evenings and at other parts of the day for boys to engage in work in the societies of their choice. Without doubt this is a remarkable feature in the school. Art, pottery, photography, natural history, archaeology, printing, politics, sailing, gliding, science, sculpture are among the interests of the societies. Two of particular importance are music and drama, both abiding interests of Coade. The concerts, operas, and oratorios are notable occasions and there have been more than ten each year since the school was founded, many of them including original compositions by boys. The plays have been strikingly ambitious and consistently successful.

Since 1946 Bryanston has had a sister school, Cranborne Chase, founded on the same principles and intended to be a partner in many kinds of educational and social activities. None of the other single-sex progressive schools has done this except Bootham and its sister school, The Mount: Clayesmore, Bembridge, Rendcomb, Gordonstoun have no sister schools and Badminton has no brother school. Abbotsholme was a boys' school for eighty years before becoming co-educational in 1969. Bryanston and Cranborne Chase have shared teaching resources as well as offering one another the complementary advantages obvious in drama, music, and social life. The schools were originally rather more than twelve miles apart when Cranborne Chase was at Crichel but now are eighteen miles from one another as the girls' school has moved to Wardour Castle, and effective contact is difficult to maintain.

At Bryanston there are prefects and monitors who are responsible to the head for the discipline of the school, and a School Council elected by house representatives makes recommendations to the head on matters of daily routine. In 1938 the Council met fortnightly and had certain judiciary powers, boys accused of anti-social behaviour sometimes being handed over to it for judgement, but its powers and the use made of the Council have varied a great deal in the last thirty years. It has never been an integral and central part of the organization of the school as it clearly has been at Dartington or Summerhill or King Alfred's. The structure of government at Bryanston is relatively conventional, but based also on a relaxed and informal discipline which gives a quality to the human relationships which minimizes the dominance of masters or prefects and the submission of the rank and file pupil:

> The staff are themselves a community.... They are, in a degree unusual in schools, mutually concerned, loyal, and careful of one another's welfare, as well as of the welfare of the boys.... True teaching can never be mere instruction: it must always be a shared experience.[13]

The school is committed to the Christian revelation of the nature of God and the universe:

> Education must, therefore, be *essentially* religious if it is to fulfil its purpose. This means not only attendance at services and scripture lessons, but the cultivation of the art of look-

---

[13] From 'Et Nova et Vetera', Coade's address on his final Speech Day, June 1959: *The Burning Bow*, pp. 240 and 243.

ing and listening in relation to the activities of the Spirit revealed not only in the Bible or in sacred literature generally, but in the works of artists, musicians and men of letters, as well as in the works of Nature.[14]

In its curriculum Bryanston covers the usual ground but was early in the field with the study of economics and sociology, and the sixth-form humanities course incorporated ethics, philosophy, and the history of science. Spanish, Italian, and Russian were taught at Bryanston when they were seldom known in other schools and scarcely ever all together in one. This has required generous staffing and the ratio from the start in 1928 has been of the order 1 : 11 – favourable, expensive, but probably necessary for the Dalton Plan arrangements and for the exceptional range of teaching offered in a school which now has about four hundred and fifty boys.

In 1942, £30,000 was raised to enable boys from what were then called elementary schools to be educated at Bryanston and the school strongly supported the recommendations of the Fleming Report, which proposed that at least 25 per cent of the entrants to independent schools should come into this category. Certain firms paid the fees for sons of employees to attend the school and at least two local education authorities also sent boys. After ten years the figure of boys at the school in what may be called the Fleming group was just under 10 per cent and it has not climbed higher.

The two most distinctive features of Bryanston are its unequivocally Christian basis and its adherence to the Dalton Plan. Other progressive schools are specific in their Christian claims: the Quaker schools and the Steiner schools, for instance. But Bedales, St. Christopher, Dartington, King Alfred, Summerhill, Frensham Heights are much less explicit on their religious position or are not Christian. Bryanston declares its interest. As for the Dalton Plan, Bryanston is unique in this group of schools in the detail and consistency of its adherence for nearly forty years to the plan as a method of teaching.

In 1934 Coade contributed an article on the school to *The Modern Schools Handbook*, the symposium on radical schools

[14] The 1962 prospectus, p. 24.

to which reference has been made in earlier pages. There is no article from Bryanston in *The Independent Progressive School*, the 1962 sequel to the earlier book, and partly this is because the word 'progressive' has become a less favourable, more presumptuous term, partly because Bryanston would now prefer to see itself on the left of the public schools rather than on the right of the radical schools. Some people will dismiss such a distinction as arbitrary and misleading, but it can be defended as representing a shift which a number of the schools considered have either deliberately made or have found is becoming relevant. In this category might be found some of the Friends' schools, Bembridge, Rendcomb, Claysmore, and certainly Bryanston.

17 The Slackening Tide: the Thirties and Gordonstoun

I

THE LARGE majority of the progressive schools I have named owe their origin not so much to an educational movement as to a person, to an educational individualist and innovator. This is also true of Gordonstoun and its predecessor and progenitor, Salem.

Kurt Hahn was born in 1886 of Jewish parents with Polish ancestry, and he was brought up as a Jew. His middle-class family was prosperous and cultivated, with iron-founders, teachers, musicians, and doctors scattered through the generations. Hahn was educated at the *Wilhelmsgymnasium* in Berlin, where much of the teaching was academic and arid, but to some of it he responded eagerly and carried lasting influences through life from the work he did then and later at the university in the classics and on Plato in particular. A few months before taking his *Abitur* Hahn says he suffered an attack of sunstroke, which was not taken very seriously at the time but which had many and more serious consequences.

In 1904 Hahn's father, who had had some of his own education in England, sent his son to Oxford, where, at Christ Church, he studied classical philology and discovered to his dismay that many of his English classmates were well ahead of him in classical scholarship. He returned disheartened to Germany in 1906 for further study at the Universities of Berlin, Heidelberg, Freiburg, and Göttingen. At the age of twenty-four Hahn returned to Oxford, where he stayed for nearly four years before returning without taking a degree to Germany in 1914 just before the outbreak of war.

In his autobiographical comments Hahn tells how, when he went to Christ Church for the second time in 1910, he saw clearly, in the regime of the university, concern for the body, the mind, and the future career of the undergraduates which he found different from the German assumptions he had been used to. At that time he met J. L. Calder, a bursar at Oxford from the University of Aberdeen. Calder came of farming stock from Morayshire, and as the recurrent aftermath of his earlier attack of sunstroke made it necessary for Hahn to spend the summers away from the heat and glare of Germany, he went with Calder to his home in the north-east of Scotland. Hahn rented a house and was visited at his home in the Findhorn valley by many friends as he lived the summer life of a wealthy young Jew. He felt the integrity and the grace of the Calder family and enjoyed the friendship of others in that area, especially Alastair Cumming and his mother Lady Smith-Cumming, and the editor of the *Inverness Courier*, Evan Barron. At this time Hahn had been giving a great deal of thought to a school which might realize some of his developing ideas and he discussed this with J. A. Stewart, one of his Oxford tutors, Karl Reinhardt, and others, but it had come to nothing by the time war broke out. After the end of the war the sketch plan of 1913 became the Salem reality of 1920.

During the war Hahn was attached to the German Foreign Office and at the end of hostilities he was secretary to Prince Max of Baden, the last imperial chancellor, who had a major responsibility in the negotiation for the peace treaty and the consequent demand for reparations.

In July 1919 Prince Max took up residence again in Baden at his castle in Salem and Hahn began sifting the mass of material for the memoirs which Prince Max ultimately published in 1927. With Prince Max's strong support the *Schule Schloss Salem* was opened in 1920 in the castle of Salem, with which three other satellite schools at Hohenfels, Hermannsberg, and Spetzgart, several miles from one another, were later associated. In the late 1960s there were more than five hundred children in the schools, about one-third of them girls.

The religious history of Baden reveals severe conflicts between the Protestant north and the Catholic south; its political history provides periods of French dominance, of peasant revolt, of alliance with Austria against Prussia, and later alliance with Prussia against France. The proximity to Switzerland, to

Austria, to Bavaria has provided Baden with a history of conflict and also a liberal tradition, both of which appear in the political changes of the nineteenth century. The constitutional form of government of the Grand Duchy later became what it now is, a *Land*, roughly like an English county.

The castle at Salem had been a Cistercian monastery for seven hundred years, and its broad stone corridors and rooms of plain proportions were enriched by the baroque decorations and religious furniture characteristic of southern Germany. In Salem the ruling family maintained the continuity from the monastic beginnings and developed further the beautiful estate the monks had built up over centuries: for the last fifty years the boys and girls in these historic surroundings have been working out what were at first new educational ideas based on the thinking of Kurt Hahn more than of any other of his German colleagues. This is the background of responsible aristocracy in which Hahn must be placed.

When the school started in 1920 Hahn was put in charge of the boarding side with Miss Marina Ewald, who has served Salem for nearly fifty years. The director of studies was Karl Reinhardt, the founder of the Frankfurt Reform Gymnasium, who was over seventy in 1920, but whose experience gave shape to the academic work of Salem. Kurt Hahn was thirty-four when Salem was founded, and he had had no sustained experience of schools or of teaching. With Prince Max he was dismayed at the moral anarchy of Germany at the end of the war and wanted to provide some bulwark against the creeping decay. Salem was their answer. As the principles and the practice of Gordonstoun are in essentials the same as those of Salem, we can examine them in detail later. For the present we can trace the steps which brought Hahn to England in 1933.

Salem started with very few boys and girls and built up its numbers quite quickly. Prince Max's name drew the children of aristocratic families to Salem, and rumours spread that it was 'a school for princes'. Parents who could not afford the fees were encouraged to discuss their situation with the school authorities and were offered some remission. Over a period of forty years about 30 per cent had such financial help.

Hahn has always been concerned with physical fitness and at no time more than in the first years of Salem, when most boys and girls had suffered from malnutrition in the Allied blockade of Germany at the end of the war. By 1930, together with physical fitness, his preoccupation was to train a moral independence devoted to finding 'a moral equivalent to war' (a phrase of William James's which Hahn never tires of quoting). The school by its connections and its twin heredity, on the one hand in the German and English establishment, and on the other in the progressive movement in education, was in an uncommonly strong position even after Prince Max's death in 1929. There were masters and boys and girls from a variety of countries, including England, and Salem had a living quality, according to some a self-sufficiency of purpose, that occasionally strayed over the borders into arrogance. It was and was not of Lietz's *Landerziehungsheime*, it was and was not a relative of the *Wandervögel* movement, it was and was not an English public school, it was and was not like Abbotsholme or Bedales, it was and was not Plato's Athenian Academy transposed to Baden. Hahn, the moving spirit, was of the Jewish middle-class intelligentsia and not an aristocrat, an Anglophile in devastated post-war Germany, an internationalist and liberal whose spirit and whose school and whose ethnic origins could not have been more at variance with Hitler and the Nazi movement which had begun in Bavaria across the borders from Baden and which by the late 1920s was growing in power.

In the autumn of 1932, in the so-called Potempa incident, five of Hitler's S.A. men kicked a young Communist to death at Beuthen before the eyes of his mother. They were tried and sentenced to death, but Hitler intervened and greeted them as 'comrades' in a telegram and sought for their release. In response to this Hahn sent a letter to all old boys and girls of Salem in the following terms:

> By the telegram of Hitler to the 'comrades' of Beuthen a fight has been initiated which goes far beyond politics. Germany is at stake, its Christian way of life, its reputation, the honour of its soldiers; Salem cannot remain neutral. I call upon the members of the Salem association who are engaged on S.A. or S.S. work to break their allegiance either to Hitler or to Salem.

This is the clearest summary of Hahn's personal convictions: his passionate belief in the need for moral independence and for a school that spoke out through its present and past pupils for human values. Erich Meissner, who served Salem and Gordonstoun for nearly thirty years, recalled this period in a speech he gave to the Gordonstoun Society in 1942, and said that many friends of Salem, who were reasonable and brave persons, strongly disapproved of Hahn's letter for they saw that when Hitler came to power there would be revenge. In any case they thought it gratuitous and foolhardy to the point of arrogance to pit the strength of a public school with some two hundred boys and girls in it at the time against the ruthless political power of the Nazi Party. However, Kurt Hahn followed up his letter with two public speeches elaborating his implacable opposition to this degradation of human dignity, the German reputation, and Christian compassion. Of course, Salem was a powerful school at which were the children of some of the leading aristocratic and industrial families in Germany, together with a substantial minority of the sons of influential persons from other countries.

On 30 January 1933 Hitler was appointed chancellor by President Hindenburg after the dismissal of von Schleicher, and charged with forming a national government on a constitutional basis. Hahn knew as well as anyone that his denunciations would not be overlooked, and following on the Reichstag fire of 4 March he was among those arrested in the mass imprisonments of liberals, socialists, and communists. He was placed in Überlingen gaol on 8 March. At once the Margrave of Baden and other German friends and supporters sought for his release, and so too did those in other countries, including Ramsay MacDonald, the British prime minister at that time, whose interest in Bedales will become apparent later. William Temple, the archbishop of York; Geoffrey Bell, the bishop of Chichester; and Geoffrey Winthrop-Young were friends who supported Hahn both then and later. He was released after five days at Überlingen and in July 1933 he left Germany for England.

Prince Max's son, the Margrave of Baden, declared himself responsible for Salem, which almost certainly saved the school from immediate victimization, and a little later Meissner became head for some weeks during a period when the Nazi attack on the school and what it stood for was mounting dangerously. One of the English masters, who later moved to Gordonstoun, took Meissner, who was in personal danger, over the border to Switzerland in 1935, but the school continued. A violent press campaign grew up against Salem and, as Meissner put it, 'the local S.A. formations began to consider Salem as a territory that must be conquered and occupied'. The familiar, vile tactics of intimidation of children and families became more obvious, together with the invitation to serve the Fatherland by informing the police and the party of 'anti-German' behaviour or opinions among the pupils or the masters. By stressing loyalty to the party, the Fatherland, and the Führer the main attack was directed against the Salem idea of citizenship and internationalism.

The Salem principle of physical fitness could be distorted to serve Nazi purposes, and undoubtedly later to some extent it was, but it is significant that only in 1944 did the S.S. take the school over. The resistance which Hahn's 1933 letter encouraged appears to have been maintained to some extent even throughout the war. After 1945 Hahn returned to Salem to help to encourage its revival and he lives for part of each year now in his retirement at Hermannsberg, and part in Britain.

II

When Hahn came to England in July 1933 he was forty-seven years old, a refugee without money, dejected, and apparently defeated. But he had good and influential friends who knew and admired his work in Germany, and the 'Friends of Salem' advised him to start a similar school in this country. William Temple, then archbishop of York, Lord Tweedsmuir, better known as John Buchan the novelist, G. M. Trevelyan the historian, the headmaster of Eton, and Geoffrey Winthrop-Young were among the Friends of Salem. Hahn has always managed to find powerful allies. He returned to Scotland and two months after his arrival was tutoring boys at Doune of Rothiemurchus in Inverness-shire. He met the Cumming family again, and it was from them that the Gordonstoun estate was leased for a very low rental in 1934, the school opening in April of that year. The history of the estate can be traced from the thirteenth century, and the history of the area from farther back still. The house is a mixture of styles and periods and lies above the Moray Firth, with the harbour of Hopeman village a mile or two away in one direction and the small eighteenth-century Michael Kirk a mile in the opposite direction, with the Cairngorm Mountains to the south and the North-west Highlands across the firth in Sutherland and Caithness.

Like Salem, Gordonstoun opened with a few boys but, as Henry Brereton, later the warden, points out, the difficulties were far greater in Scotland than in Baden. The devotion and labour of a Cistercian community had maintained Salem as a beautiful, prosperous, and ordered estate, which the pride and taste of the Grand Dukes enriched still further for the school, but at Gordonstoun everything had suffered from years of neglect and the uninhabited buildings and grounds cried out for capital to be spent on them. In 1934 English and Scottish public schools were going through a bleak period and the competition between them for pupils was sharp. The first Gordonstoun boys came from a small group of parents who knew of Hahn and his work, or were boys who were failures or misfits in their previous schools. After the commanding position of Salem, which could be exclusive in any way it chose, Gordonstoun found itself dealing with a fairly high proportion of frail or difficult or intellectually mediocre boys, which was seen to be a doubtful blessing because success in this field tends to make it more difficult to recruit boys of good ability. However, Hahn tried to add thirty new boys each year and was so successful that by 1939, after five years of edging forward in this way, there were one hundred and thirty-five boys in the school. The guardian, or head boy, in 1939 was Prince Philip of Greece, who had come with a few German boys and others from Salem preparatory school in 1934 to be among the first pupils at Gordonstoun.

The reputation of the school was beginning to offer some prospect of stability in 1939 when war finally came. Despite Hahn's anti-Nazi record, his naturalization as a British subject, his repeated condemnation of Hitler's regime, and his known concern for refugees, he was under a cloud in the early days of the war. There were about a dozen German adults at the school at that time and rather more German boys. The German nationals were interned, and H. L. Brereton recalls with rueful amusement that British masters at Gordonstoun were at first rejected when they volunteered for service with the Local Defence Volunteers. North-east Scotland was no place for a school at that time, and after nine months of confusing and difficult circumstances the school was evacuated in June 1940 to Plas Dinam, the Welsh home of Lord Davies, who had two sons at Gordonstoun and whose sympathy for, and active work in, international causes drew him to the ideals for which Hahn strove.

For Gordonstoun, as for all schools, the war years were exceedingly difficult: the school had to divide into two, the numbers dropped by over one-third, and there was a financial crisis which very nearly finished the school altogether. Yet there were opportunities which Hahn took during those five years which established him and his educational ideas more firmly by the end of the war than in 1939. The beginnings of what has become the Outward Bound movement, of which we shall hear more later, are to be found in the war years, and Hahn's opinions on leadership and training methods were listened to with respect by the Admiralty and the War Office between 1940 and 1945.

When the school returned to Morayshire in 1945 the problem of re-establishment was huge. Military occupation had badly damaged all the buildings and Gordonstoun House had been gutted by fire; the post-war shortages of money and supplies made it seriously possible that the school would not be able to take proper advantage of its new ascendancy. As with other schools, austerity within and outside munificence brought Gordonstoun through this storm, and today it is a school of over four hundred boys and girls with a strong reputation which is no longer dependent on the presence of Hahn, who retired from the headship in 1953. But it is Hahn's ideas that have formed the framework of the school.

Hahn summarized his educational principles and practice in a broadcast talk he gave in 1934:

Nothing was original in Salem. We cribbed and copied from

many sources; from Plato, from Dr. Arnold of Rugby; from Eton, from Abbotsholme, from Hermann Lietz, from Fichte and from Wilhelm Meister. ... We did not believe in originality in education nor in experiments on human beings.[1]

He considered that there were three characteristic approaches to education: the Ionian; the Spartan; and the Platonic. The Ionian view is called after the reputation for self-indulgence and individualism linked with the Ionians of the fifth century B.C., and the modern equivalent for Hahn leads to the child-centred and self-expression theories from which the child never feels the sting of defeat or the hard challenge of painful effort. This is not the way for Salem or Gordonstoun. The second approach he calls the Spartan, where the emphasis is on service to the school and the state, especially through excellence in academic or athletic activities. More ordinary children are rated second best, and everything has to be done for the sake of the school, not by the individual choice of persons. This, too, is not the way for Salem or Gordonstoun. The Platonic view is the answer for Hahn, and he lists six 'Salem laws' which are intended to do justice both to the community and to the individual child. Hahn does not present these laws as abstractions supporting a particular view of man or of education. Instead, he is quite specific and practical.

1. Put all the children in dress which does not hide their limbs and this will encourage a pride in physical fitness. The school uniform at Gordonstoun for normal day wear, as at Abbotsholme, Bryanston, and Claysmore, is an open-necked shirt, pullover, shorts, and stockings.
2. Build up the physical fitness of every child: this should start from the basic skills of running, jumping, and throwing. The formal and more sophisticated skills for specific games can follow later, but a boy should be responsible for his own exercise and it should be part of his routine all the year round four or five times a week and, if he does not take to it at first, it will be accepted in time:

[1] Reprint from *The Listener*, 28 Nov. 1934, p. 10.

I should think as little of asking [boys] whether they want to train as I should think of asking them whether they feel in the mood to brush their teeth.... Self discipline really is the condition of self-expression.[2]

3. Restrict team games to two days a week; they should be compulsory on those two days and should be prohibited on all other days, weekdays and Sundays. In this way Hahn sought to control the games fetish, but to give a place to team competition and skill.

4. Give children genuine opportunity for self-discovery, because in Hahn's view every boy or girl has a *grande passion* (a favourite expression) which too often has not had a chance to express itself. A variety of activities is needed, each a challenge and test of self-reliance and self-expression, and each a vital and dignified part of community life, not put into a pocket of time away from the normal flow of the day and called a hobby. Maybe the *grande passion* (Hahn appears to think of one supreme, and not of many equally absorbing competitors) will be found in playing the trumpet or the cello, in writings plays, in a programme of scientific inquiry, in climbing mountains or sailing boats, in sculpting, in building, painting, or caring for animals. This is Coade's 'creative moment', and in one way or another all radical schools seek to provide a variety of valid experiences, as do most other good schools in these days. For Hahn puberty is a period of 'poisonous passions' and childhood a period of natural reverence: to these romantic and questionable polarities we shall return.

5. Make the children meet with triumph and defeat, at first building carefully on their gifts and potentialities to ensure success, but later teaching them to overcome defeat in harder enterprises.

6. Provide periods of silence, following the precedent both of the Quakers and of the monasteries. To this end, besides rooms for quiet work and reading, boys at Gordonstoun walk the mile to service at Michael Kirk in silence and are encouraged to make space for contemplation and reflection. As the current prospectus puts it:

[2] Ibid., p. 11.

If aloneness means boredom then the intellectual life has been mismanaged or neglected. Therefore care must be taken to see that the variety of occupations does not engulf the individual.[3]

In 1938 Hahn put the same point this way:

Neither the love of Man nor the love of God can take deep root in a child that does not know aloneness.[4]

Gordonstoun is an organized boys' and girls' school having little in common with the permissiveness of Summerhill or Dartington. The physical self-discipline was formulated into a Training Plan which continues now: it establishes a routine of daily habits for which a boy early becomes responsible. The Plan is a chart relating to house regulations, personal habits, and work preparation. As an example, the following headings are included as daily routines: a morning run on rising, two warm washes in the day (soap all over), two cold showers, before breakfast and after afternoon activities (additional showers if other strenuous exercise is taken at another time of the day), two cleanings of teeth, sixty skips, five press-ups, eating is forbidden between meals except at precisely stated times, set duties are recorded, hair is washed once a fortnight, conditions for study are included in the records – and so on.

For the first two terms boys are supervised in filling in their Training Plans, which they have to do daily, recording plus for the tasks completed and minus where they have been left undone. Usually from about his third term at Gordonstoun a boy is left to fill in his Training Plan himself as a daily task, and normally no one checks it because it is regarded as a matter of honour for him to complete it. Hahn and his successors have laid great stress on this principle of trust, which is approached from several points of view and for which deliberate training is needed, the Training Plan being one clear example. At Gordonstoun the point is clearly made that the Training Plan requires no real introspection, for the information is factual and the right answer clear. The habit of providing a

[3] p. 12.
[4] *Education for Leisure*: lecture given in Oxford, Jan. 1938, p. 8.

voluntary, accurate, unflattering record can be salutary self-discipline, and the need to provide a record at all is a steady reminder of the framework of necessary routine.

In addition to the Training Plan, boys keep their own records of school marks on a system borrowed from the Dalton Plan, but whereas the Training Plan becomes a matter of personal information which may be inspected by a housemaster only for some exceptional reason, the work record is checked by a form supervisor each week, and the progress of boys is considered in staff meetings two or three times a term, Gordonstoun boys are trusted when they have been trained to trust themselves, and there is no suggestion that the pupils always know best what is good for them.

When a boy enters the school, usually at thirteen, he is inducted into the arrangements for a time and normally by the end of his first term he is given permission to wear the full school uniform (there are two uniforms, one for the day and the other, the 'school uniform', for the evening). Usually by the end of his third term he has the responsibility for marking his Junior Training Plan himself, and by the beginning of his third year the housemaster changes this to the Senior Training Plan. In the houses certain older boys are recommended for responsible jobs, as is common in any boarding-school, and at Gordonstoun the housemaster recommends to the headmaster that these boys be given a white stripe. Up to this point the transitions from one phase to the next have been in the hands of the housemaster and the headmaster: 'white stripers' can now become eligible, on the basis of responsible work conscientiously carried through, for promotion to colour bearer candidates, and the proposals for these changes come from the body of colour bearers themselves. This gives to the colour bearers, never more than one-tenth of the school, a position of standing without much in the way of privilege. The headmaster selects from the colour bearers a small group to be helpers and one of these to be the guardian or head boy of the school. The helpers are usually in charge of a house, or bear special organizing responsibility for a sector or department in school affairs like health, practical work, seamanship, or expeditions, and they have powers of command. Tasks of lesser responsibility are usually in the hands of colour bearers, who are 'expected to maintain, if necessary to defend, the standard of the School and its written or unwritten laws.' This complex dispersal of responsibility resembles what is done at Abbotsholme and Bryanston, but it has more formality at Gordonstoun.

There is not much to remark in the curriculum at Gordonstoun. It has not departed greatly from a conventional grammar-school range, although a modified Dalton plan has been operated. At the same time the school has not aspired to intensive high-level work for university scholarships. This was Hahn's preference, and it is maintained by the school now:

> The conditions imposed by the present examination system must be accepted but it is often harmful and unwise to force a boy to reach certain academic standards at the cost of his natural mental development. An early scholastic success brought about through undue pressure is often followed by a sad anti-climax because mental resources have been tapped at the wrong moment and in the wrong way.... It is the design of Gordonstoun to stimulate by variety of interests minds that are endowed with the reserves of energy which spring from willing and well-conditioned bodies.[5]

Here the part played by the other features of Gordonstoun life is vital. There is a range of individual projects, the *grandes passions* which have already been commented upon, on which some hours are spent each week, and these can be an extension of some physical pursuit or music, acting, painting, sculpture, craft, or a piece of 'research'. In short, it is one or a number of projects such as we have seen in several of the other innovating schools. Bryanston, Abbotsholme, Bedales, and other schools have followed the same course, but Hahn in his 1938 address gave a special moral colouring to these enterprises:

> ... the building instinct can perhaps protect the biggest proportion of boys; exploration and adventure come next in the wideness of their appeal; music, painting, will protect not many, but those very much worth protecting....

[5] Ibid., p. 10.

Each of these non-poisonous passions may grow to be powerful enough to prevent the sexual impulses that well up during adolescence from absorbing the available emotional energy.[6]

Another part of the Gordonstoun life is physical work, with all the moral significance that it generated in Hahn's scheme of things. All boys undertake training in practical seamanship and the school keeps boats of varying sizes in Hopeman harbour, a mile or two away. There are special courses and more applied training for boys who intend to have careers in the Royal Navy or the Merchant Navy. When Hahn was in Salem, Lake Constance close at hand gave the contact with sailing. The Moray Firth is different, with fishing villages along the rugged coast and a naval base not far away at Lossiemouth.

A second physical activity greatly valued at Gordonstoun is mountaineering, which developed when the school was evacuated to Wales and when, after the war, a branch of the school was housed sixteen miles from Gordonstoun and at a distance from the sea at Altyre. During the war the sea school at Aberdovey in Merioneth in Wales had strengthened the rather limited appeal of the Moray Badge scheme in which Hahn had placed a good deal of faith in 1936 and 1937. Seamanship, and climbing were added to the athletics for which Salem boys had been noted between 1933 and 1938.

Like many innovating schools Gordonstoun has required estate work of its boys from the beginning, partly from financial necessity, partly on educational principle. There is in addition 'the services', which Hahn felt offered deep satisfaction to boys and in which he saw the element of training transformed into pride in responsibility. In 1935 a school coast-guard service was formed and when there is a likelihood of rough weather a Watchers' Corps, trained to handle life-saving apparatus, mans the school lookout point on the rocky coast. In 1940 a school fire service was formed and was incorporated into the war-time Fire Service. It continues now to serve the school as an efficient unit, with mobile pumps and tenders which can be called on in an emergency in the area. Gordonstoun boys have also been trained in mountain rescue, and

[6] Ibid., p. 5.

more recently a surf rescue unit and a ski patrol have been formed. All of these organizations illustrate the concern for life-preservation, for rescue, which Hahn and his successors feel to be affirmative and outward-looking, the antidote to the selfishness and apathy which too often assails adolescents in general, and boarding-schools in particular.

In 1961 Gordonstoun formed a Combined Cadet Force and boys may choose to do their advanced training in the naval or army sections of the Force or in one of the rescue services or may train throughout in the Scout Troop. The C.C.F. is an organization providing the kind of training that most of the other progressive schools rejected in the inter-war period and, in this day of small peace-time forces of professionals and highly technical warfare, they have felt no urge to revise this decision.

Gordonstoun speaks of hardening while sparing, of responsibility to and for the community, of maintaining the spiritual strength of childhood unbroken and undiluted through 'the loutish years', of love of enterprise, love of aloneness, love of skill. The purpose of fitness is, to quote the title of a recent book, the unfolding of character.[7] Hahn attributed much of the proper growth of persons to 'a healthy pasture' and the discipline of increasing responsibility. Greek athletics is a guide to the running, jumping, and throwing that Gordonstoun boys know well. The morning run and the details of the Training Plan have much in common with Reddie's exact regime for Abbotsholmians. The hierarchy leading through an élite to the guardian raises echoes of the Attic *ephebia* and the philosopher-king or guardian of Plato. Gordonstoun has a headmaster, a warden, and a director of studies in its government, a model reminiscent of Eton and Winchester and of the checks and balances of *The Republic*. The director of studies is expected to see that the academic programmes of each boy are suitably planned, and if necessary he has to defend the claims of schoolwork against a head who may take boys out of class for sudden assemblies or for a few days

---

[7] A. Arnold-Brown, *Unfolding of Character: The Impact of Gordonstoun* (London, 1962). Mr. Arnold-Brown was a boy both at Abbotsholme and Gordonstoun. Some of his facts on Abbotsholme (pp. 4–5) are inaccurate but he shows how Gordonstoun has affected one old boy.

in the hills. The warden represents a wise counsellor who is not caught up in the day-to-day administration, 'the philosopher in the watch tower', who can advise in any way that seems appropriate and whose problems relate more to policy and guidance than to precise decision-making.

Hahn spoke often of a responsibility to the community, which led him to forge, or seek to forge, links with the neighbourhood. The Moray Badge became the County Badge scheme, the sea school led to Outward Bound, the Outward Bound scheme leads on to the Duke of Edinburgh Awards, and all of these are linked with the name of Kurt Hahn. Gordonstoun has always welcomed a number of overseas pupils, but this has been usual in many schools. In addition attempts have been made to offer some of the school's facilities, notably the athletics track, for the use of the young people of the neighbourhood, but neither Arnold-Brown nor other sympathetic commentators on Gordonstoun have thought that over the years this has really counted for much. The special nautical course at Gordonstoun from 1941 until 1965 gave a shortened programme for boys going into the Merchant Navy, and a group of fifteen or so were members of the school for this two-year period, all of them unlikely to receive a public school education otherwise.

Hahn began, and the school continues, a graded scheme of fees. An average fee is worked out which must be maintained for each boy, and a minimum fee (usually about half) is fixed which must be paid. The rest is an assessed fee, and from a list of assessed fees, which range from about two-thirds above the average to one-third below, parents are asked to assess their own ability to contribute on the general assumption that anyone making a claim on the Gordonstoun Society's fund must, as far as possible, be balanced by someone else offering a correspondingly larger sum. A recent estimate stated that about one-quarter of the boys are supported by the Gordonstoun Society. In the school's thinking the need for such remissions of fees is as follows:

> The law of deterioration cannot be broken unless children born to wealth or position are placed in an environment that frees them from an enervating sense of privilege. This

environment can be assured by a sufficient admixture of boys drawn from homes where the conditions of life are not only simple but somewhat hard. Upon such a basis alone can a vital and vigorous school society be maintained.[8]

As the fixed fee is in itself now above £350, the number of children from 'simple' or 'hard' homes cannot be high even though at least one-quarter of the families are getting some financial help.

Hahn does not write of child development in psychological terms. His way of thinking is impressionistic and his descriptions have a rather vague, theological content and a literary romantic, moral, unscientific, dogmatic quality. There can be no doubt that as a headmaster he made a very strong impression on many boys and that as a promoter he convinced a great number of shrewd people that his kind of compassionate integrity deserved support. To illustrate these points we can turn to his writings on Gordonstoun which are listed by Arnold-Brown and lodged in the library of Cambridge University; understandably these are not substantial and are mostly talks to conferences, broadcast talks, annual reports to governors, letters to *The Times,* and so on. He is a practitioner and promoter whose theories are more felt and practised than explicated. One of the most developed of his presentations appears in an essay he wrote in 1957 in which he reflects upon the results of Salem and Gordonstoun as a prelude to the Outward Bound developments.[9] He considers that Salem established beyond doubt two principles which were as much matters of health as of education. The first was that purposeful athletic training helps to build vital health and that this has psychological concomitants enabling boys and girls to defeat their own defeatism. The second principle 'deserves the name of a discovery: that the so-called deformity of puberty should not be regarded as a decree of fate'.[10] There is a treasure of childhood in joy of movement, compassion, curiosity, innocence, a spiritual strength, as Hahn saw it, and these things

---

[8] Prospectus, p. 19.
[9] K. Hahn, 'Outward Bound', in *Year Book of Education* (London, 1957), pp. 436–62.
[10] Ibid., p. 436.

can be preserved through the period of the deformity of puberty, 'the loutish years', because each child has 'a guardian angel' capable of protecting the dangerous period of sexual change. Words like these sum up development from childhood into adolescence almost as a morality play, which Hahn, usually a brilliant, fastidious, and dramatic phrase-spinner in English, occasionally takes close to melodrama.

It is not difficult to draw fairly precise Platonic parallels with much of Hahn's theory. Socrates in *The Republic* traces reason, emotion, and basic appetites as the elements of man's responses, and what is found in the individual may also be ound in the state. Plato even goes so far as to equate the Guardians with reason, the Auxiliaries (the executive classes) with the emotions, and the Producers with the appetites. Virtue is a kind of health and good habit of the soul, vice a disease, deformity, and sickness,[11] and when emotion can be diverted as energy on the side of reason, virtue can grow as a habit of the soul. The civic qualities which follow are temperance and justice, and elsewhere Plato indicates that 'children, women, servants, and the vulgar mass' are the readiest victims for wayward and uncontrolled behaviour. The simple and moderate desires which are guided by reason are to be found in men of the best endowment and education, whose influence is acknowledged and accepted by the rest.[12] In the Gordonstoun community everyone was either a silver or a golden citizen, and to be fair to Hahn, he does not accept Plato's tendency to write off the masses.

To Hahn a boy's soul at puberty is in special danger of being led away by the passions of the body. This dualism is at the root of all Hahn's ideas, and he speaks out against current psychological views: 'We feel a certain missionary obligation to unmask the psychologist's dogma as the fallacy which it is.... What they consider a normal development during adolescence is in fact a grave and avoidable malady.'[13] The psychoanalysts are wrong, in Hahn's view, and the ground for his opposition is really a combination of his practical experience with adolescents, his Christian conviction, his platonic inter-

---

[11] *The Republic*, book iv, sec. 444.
[12] Ibid., sec. 431.
[13] *Year Book* (1957), p. 437.

pretations, and his moral fervour. He would not claim much first-hand knowledge of young children, nor would it appear that he has read widely in the psychological literature. He would not claim that he was a classroom teacher of great experience in the sense that Reddie or Badley or Curry or Coade was, for Hahn has been more the director of a school and an inspirational figure to staff and boys. He is not a countryman or a noted climber or a sailor, but he speaks of a love of the high hills and of the sea and this has merged into the ideals of physical striving, self-knowledge, service, rescue, and reverence for life which are part of the Gordonstoun mystique.

Hahn was baptized into the Anglican church in 1945. He had become a believing Christian long before, but had felt that he should continue to ally himself with other Jews in their appalling sufferings after Hitler came to power and during the war. Hahn's opposition to Hitler was from the start on general liberal principles and not particularly because of Nazi anti-Semitism, and this example illustrates two fundamental beliefs which Gordonstoun exists to express. First, that when all philosophical refinements have been permitted, there is discernible right and wrong, sometimes incontestably clear as in the Potempa incident or the mistaken Allied demand for unconditional surrender, sometimes difficult to detect as in the need to be truthful about the errors and deficiencies of others as well as your own. The second fundamental precept is that only persons affirm right and wrong, but they need training for the job. These propositions may be disputed by philosophers on logical grounds, but Hahn is a moralist, interested more in ethics and a kind of metaphysics and believing that a school takes less from logic than from the behaviour and conviction of its founder and his colleagues.

Gordonstoun has its critics, and one of them sums up Hahn's plan as an attempt to keep boys out on the beautiful mountains and on the majestic sea so that they might develop beautiful souls. This, he says, 'is a muddled rehash of the pathetic fallacy and belief in *mens sana in corpore sano* and is typical of Hahn's so-called idealism'.[14] Wilkinson attacks Hahn

---

[14] E. Wilkinson: 'Poisonous Passions', in *Granta*, 1 Dec. 1962, pp. 14–17. Mr. Wilkinson was Guardian at Gordonstoun in 1959 and wrote the article when an undergraduate at Cambridge.

for making extravagant claims for the value of drill routine and physical training in the Gordonstoun services. Physical fitness, says Wilkinson, will not necessarily restore the soul, nor will rescue routines normally enable boys to discover God's purpose in their inner life. He says that so much character training through willing bodies has led to a neglect of exacting intellectual pursuits and points to a percentage of university entrants well below what might be expected. The director of studies, in the *Gordonstoun Record*, has lent colour to this view, although he comments in 1961 that there is an improvement in the academic quality of the entrants which should be reflected in the next few years. Expressing university entrants as a proportion can be misleading, but from figures available it would appear that in the 1950s, of every hundred entrants to Gordonstoun, about twelve to fifteen went on to universities in Great Britain or overseas. This proportion is now changing and in a survey of four hundred and sixteen leavers between 1960 and 1966, 34 per cent went to universities and 19 per cent to other places of higher education.[15] The figures do begin to compare favourably with those of Bryanston or Bedales. Wilkinson makes the point, however, that Gordonstoun is, to quote the director of studies, 'weighted on the less gifted side'. Where character building has been stressed, learning and intellectual rigour, together with artistic achievement, have not been made desirable goals for boys who could have been challenged by them. Wilkinson also doubts very much that the routine honesty of the Training Plan and the other features of the trust system lead to lasting moral qualities because boys are not faced with real moral problems in the school, where the spirit and method offer support in dealing with the relatively simple school situations. A rude shock awaits the Gordonstoun boy who thinks he is well provided for morally when he leaves school and is on his own. Finally, Wilkinson claims that in sexual matters the school is not as balanced and 'healthy' as it claims to be, and this partly because of Hahn's conviction that poisonous passions are released if sexual powers are not diverted to good purposes. To finish the denunciation Wilkinson sums up Hahn's idealized Atlantic Community as jingoistic froth. As Hahn retired from Gordonstoun in 1953

[15] See *Gordonstoun: Some Facts*, produced by the school in March 1967.

when Wilkinson was twelve or thirteen years old, this attack is in one sense an admission of the lasting influence of the founder's ideas and at the same time sharp, if overstated, criticism of some of Hahn's more romantic formulations which are far out of touch with the modern mood. But the structure of the Gordonstoun system stands, and can absorb criticism and modify itself without serious surrender. Its serious concern for moral, physical, religious, and intellectual education is rare, and is explicit in its way of living

Criticisms of a different kind came from a man who, in his fifties, spent nearly two years at Gordonstoun as an adviser on many matters, for which he had the title of research officer.[16] Heckstall-Smith had been a master in a public school, the head of two county grammar schools, and had joined the Society of Friends before the Second World War, having been an officer in the first. He had been a successful farmer on resigning a headship in 1939 a few months before the outbreak of war, and Hahn invited this many-sided man to take a general, constructively critical place at Gordonstoun. In Heckstall-Smith's account there appears a courteous incompatibility with the school's ideas. For him Hahn had immense personal charm and uncomprehendingly patrician ways: 'The Platonic theory of the absolute supremacy of the golden citizen allowed Dr. Hahn to interrupt anything whenever he happened to feel like it ... no teaching arrangement was safe.'[17]

Heckstall-Smith said the trust system generated latent tension which, with 'rather emotional talks to the whole school in assembly' and what he calls a snakes-and-ladders system of promotion and demotion, produced an atmosphere among the boys of mutual sympathy such as might be found in villagers living on the slopes of an active volcano.

Elsewhere Heckstall-Smith speaks of Hahn's wish to have girls as well as boys at Gordonstoun, with a considerable majority in favour of the boys. This never came to anything under Hahn but it leads Heckstall-Smith to say: 'I got the impression that Dr. Hahn regarded the girls as a gymnastic apparatus for improving the character of the boys (the ones who really mattered) by giving them regular practice in chivalry.'[18]

[16] Heckstall-Smith, *Doubtful Schoolmaster*.   [17] Ibid., p. 130.
[18] Ibid., p. 121. Since 1972 girls have been taken as pupils.

Heckstall-Smith believes that constantly present in Hahn's mind was the idea of dramatic rescue – not just rescue, but dramatic rescue, and the fire service, the coastguards, the mountain rescue, and the whole Outward Bound concept spring from this root principle. Certainly Hahn's view of adolescence has this same theme of rescue in it: the non-poisonous passions acting as guardian angels to protect the vitality of boyhood.

Heckstall-Smith left Gordonstoun in 1949 to go to Dartington which, to put it mildly, he preferred. In his book he does not really try to place Hahn in a proper life-context, treating him more as a charming and wrong-headed despot. forgetting the comments that he had made about himself when he was head of a country grammar school: 'Instead of being the expert critic on the side – I was now the Establishment.'[19]

Does Gordonstoun deserve to be considered as a progressive school? Academically, probably not, except that it has not emphasized examination success. In the amount of physical work done in the school day it is unusual and deliberately so, and in the devotion to the sea, the mountains, and the rescue services it has a different emphasis from other schools. In its explicit concern for moral integrity and the emphasis placed on the physical basis for much of this, Gordonstoun is different again. The need for quietness, for aloneness, is part of the discipline of self-knowledge.

Hahn's rejection of psycho-analysis placed him far away from Neill or Curry or Badley or the Russells, and Gordonstoun is conservative on the interpretation of puberty. The conventional criticism of the public school of the 1920s and 1930s was that sexual problems were dealt with by cold baths and team games. Hahn had an answer which was also based on baths and exercise, but with hobbies, idealism based on Christianity, a trust system, the idea of service, and a certain disseminated responsibility to add to the total effect.

Hahn retired in 1953 and the school has now modified itself in many ways, but not in any that are significant. Mr. Chew, who took over from Hahn in 1953, retired in 1968 and died in 1971. He has been succeeded by Mr. Kemp, who earlier in his career had taught at Gordonstoun. The school in 1969 and

[19] Ibid., p. 57.

1970 is notably different, but the Hahn continuity persists. There are about ten schools in this country and overseas following the Gordonstoun pattern, mostly with headmasters who taught or were pupils at the parent school. These schools are all in the public school mould but with a difference, and there has never been a metropolitan Gordonstoun. Perhaps the closest resemblance to the school itself is to be found in the Outward Bound movement, through which Kurt Hahn saw the ideas and practices suitable for a right-wing innovatory public school made available in some measure to working-class city-bred boys.

III

In the 1957 *Year Book* Hahn wrote the essay on Outward Bound enterprises already mentioned,[20] and he refers to his own conviction in the mid-1930s that he had failed to spread the health-giving attitudes of Gordonstoun beyond the limited circle of boarders and day boys in the school. At the end of 1936 Gordonstoun and a large day school, Elgin Academy, combined to start the tests for the Moray Badge: certain standards were required in athletics, life-saving, and cross-country expeditions, and no smoking or drinking was permitted during the training period. The local response was poor in 1937, and the national reaction was negligible to a letter Hahn wrote to *The Times* appealing for help and an extension of the plan. However, by the time of the outbreak of the war in September 1939 the response of schools in Morayshire had greatly improved and during the early part of the war men like Dawson of Penn, Boyd-Orr, Admiral Richmond, and William Temple advocated a wide extension of the Moray Badge training plan. Early in 1940 a County Badge Experimental Committee was formed under the chairmanship of the then master of Balliol, Lord Lindsay, with a membership including the headmasters of Eton and Winchester, the chairman of the University Grants Committee, Julian Huxley, Members of Parliament, and other notables. The County Badge scheme was the Moray Badge programme with improvements and amendments, and this was based upon the Salem

[20] *Year Book* (1957), pp. 436–62.

and Gordonstoun regime of athletics, swimming, testing expeditions, and projects of skill, art, or study. The necessary stages in the scheme were to be covered in part-time courses run under the auspices of certain existing voluntary associations, or else in intensive, residential courses of about a month conducted at Gordonstoun's Welsh war-time base, where many of the visiting boys were found to be healthy but not fit. On the model of this kind of course the War Office set up in Glenfeshie the Highland Field-Craft Centre for young soldiers lacking the skills, confidence, and experience which the Experimental Committee were trying to produce at their intensive courses and which were necessary for officers.[21] The centre remained in being from March 1943 till November 1944, the Normandy invasions having begun in June of that year.

The Experimental Committee did not get the financial support it had hoped for from the Board of Education, the voluntary bodies were not providing much help for the programme, and the first move came from private sources. In 1941 Lawrence Holt of the Blue Funnel Line was able to offer the financial backing necessary to open the Outward Bound sea school at Aberdovey: 'The training ... must be less a training for the sea than a training through the sea, and benefit all walks of life.' The requirements in athletics and land expeditions were maintained and to these were added, but not emphasized, the sea-going enterprises together with rescue training: fire-fighting, resuscitation, and sea rescue. Short courses of four weeks for boys sent by local authorities or by industry were offered at Aberdovey, and boys from Gordonstoun, then about forty miles away at Llandinam, were able to join regularly in this work. The sea school is still in existence and something like twenty-five thousand boys have passed through in groups of about eighty in each month's course.

In 1946 the Outward Bound Trust was founded and the financial burden on Lawrence Holt was shared, enabling the work to extend. By the end of the 1950s the Trust controlled four schools in Britain, two sea schools, one at Aberdovey and a second at Burghead not far from Gordonstoun in Morayshire,

---

[21] An account of this centre and the work done there is to be found in Arnold-Brown, *Unfolding of Character*, pp. 72–110.

and two mountain schools, Eskdale, opened in 1950, and Ullswater in 1955. Courses for girls were started in this country in 1955, and Outward Bound centres for boys have been established in Nigeria, Kenya, Malaya, Australia, Germany, Austria, and elsewhere.

Hahn has been the moving spirit in the start of all this. The inaugural meeting of the Outward Bound Trust was held early in 1946 at Trinity College, Cambridge, with G. M. Trevelyan as host and Geoffrey Winthrop-Young in the chair and Admiral Richmond as a member, all founder-governors at Gordonstoun. Many of those connected with the Moray Badge scheme, with the Experimental Committee, and with the Aberdovey sea school came in to support the new Trust. Arnold-Brown was the first warden of Eskdale in 1950, which, as he says, was to be not a climbing school but a character-training school based on mountaineering.

The objects of the Trust have been set forth in many places and with some minor variations can be summarized as follows: short-term residential schools, normally of twenty-six days' duration, aiming to open to boys and girls, usually aged fourteen and a half to nineteen and a half, a fuller life both for themselves and the community they live in. The young people in these schools are supposed to come from all levels of society, from a wide range of schools and from industry, from a variety of religious backgrounds and, if possible, from many nationalities: this has been of particular importance in multi-racial or tribal societies such as Kenya, Nigeria, and Malaya. The main appeal of the course is adventure and endurance on the sea or in the mountains, and to seek from these experiences new areas of confidence and competence in oneself. Those who know what service and dependability are, are thought to be more likely to show initiative, and to undertake leadership with Christian humility.

All these principles are of the Gordonstoun stamp, and the courses are compressed versions of those to be found at the school. Outward Bound was one of Hahn's means to spread more widely through society an important part of what the Gordonstoun boys receive, although, of course, many others besides him were engaged in its beginnings. The more recent development of the Duke of Edinburgh's Award is another extension of Hahn's work, because this is in direct line with the Moray Badge, the part-time parallel to the full-time arrangements of Outward Bound and Gordonstoun.

IV

Another extension of Hahn's influence and interest can be seen in Atlantic College at St. Donat's in Glamorgan, which began its teaching in 1962. This college is intended to be the first of a number of residential international schools for boys between sixteen and nineteen, usually aiming at university entrance. The first boys at St. Donat's came from the countries of the Western community, including the U.S.A. Later the boys came from a wide variety of countries, always provided that a national group was large enough to have an identity and give variety and tang to the community life. The policy was at first to have 25 per cent of the boys from Great Britain and then to build up seven national groupings, each of about 10 per cent of the total number, which is likely to be four hundred and fifty. Desmond Hoare, the headmaster until 1969, was a retired rear-admiral who not only guided the school for seven years but by 1967 had persuaded the board of Governors to make the school co-educational.

The long-term aim is concerned with social integration, at first in the context of the European and the American peoples and later in the context of the countries behind the Iron Curtain. The short-term aim is to provide an international school for boys (and now girls) who are likely later to be in positions of importance. Such a school will provide courses for entrance to the universities of the country in which it is set, and by arrangement these qualifications are expected to admit each boy or girl to university in his native country if he or she so wishes. Thus German boys educated at St. Donat's will qualify for admission to German universities by taking Advanced level courses in English together with any necessary additions. The teaching of languages is an important feature in this whole enterprise, both as a tool for necessary communication and as a means of deeper understanding of national characteristics and cultural assumptions. These emphases are, of course, acceptable to Hahn, but not specially

The Thirties and Gordonstoun

individual to him. More familiar and characteristic ideas and phrases appear, as exposition of the aims continues:

> The advancing material prosperity of the western world has brought evils in its train. Among these are a decline in the physical fitness of young men, insufficient satisfaction of the youthful interest for adventure and that decline of compassion which is reflected in the plain business of individual unhelpfulness one to another.

Services exist for beach rescue, cliff rescue, canoe lifeguards; and while the college is right on the sea coast it is also a short distance from the Welsh mountains and so all the practices of Gordonstoun in physical endurance, initiative, team work, and individualism can be repeated. During his time at the college each pupil, like boys at Gordonstoun, works on a project which is based on the requirements of the Trevelyan Scholarship for higher education. The courses at the college aim to take each pupil to three A levels and to insist on a breadth of study which includes a common course on philosophy and, for non-scientists, some study of science. The results in the last six years have been markedly better than the English national average. To ensure contact beyond the walls of the castle, youth groups, schools, and conferences are invited to St. Donat's and for British entrants a proportion rather over one-half is aimed at from maintained schools and about one-fifth from private schools, the remainder of the entry being transfers from industry and commerce. In fact in the late 1960s only about 10 per cent were 'private' pupils, the rest being supported mostly by government grants from the variety of countries represented.

Familiar names appeared among the Council from whom the Governing Body was chosen. Air Marshall Sir Lawrence Darvall, formerly of the NATO Defence College in Paris, was a governor of Gordonstoun and chairman of the Council of Atlantic College, Mme. Besse was on the Board at Gordonstoun and her husband on the Council of St. Donat's, and H. L. Brereton, the warden of Gordonstoun, was on both, as was Hahn himself. Hahn's educational specifications are always recognizable, whether seen at Gordonstoun, Outward Bound, or St. Donat's, and it is his achievement that he has left a group of institutions with a similar stamp upon them. In each case his flair for attracting the money and the interest of influential people has marked him out as an educational promoter who has convinced men and women of the desirability of the Gordonstoun product. He is the one educationalist who has helped to found since the 1930s not one but a series of schools, the Outward Bound movement, the Duke of Edinburgh Awards scheme, and Atlantic College. Hahn says his ideas are derivative and he is sincere in thinking so, but his own interpretation and presentation are peculiar to him, not permissive, not Freudian, physically rather than psychologically based, favouring single-sex education rather than co-education (except at Salem and Atlantic College), morally emphatic and not indulgent, both Continental and British in theory and practice, Platonic, romantic, Christian, claiming collective and individualistic response. This is the most pervasive and successful of the new school models in the last thirty years, and even though modifications are taking place at Gordonstoun itself, and elsewhere, Hahn was the innovator.[22]

[22] For two recent assessments, see part iv of R. Skidelsky, *English Progressive Schools* (London, 1969) and part ii of H. L. Brereton, *Gordonstoun* (London, 1968).

18 The Second World War: Wennington

THIS BOOK does not pretend to name every radical school in England. No mention has been made of the Hall School founded at Weybridge by Miss Gilpin and now at Wincanton, or Dauntsey's, which G. W. Olive transformed, or St. Mary's Town and Country School founded in Hampstead in 1937 with a second location in the country, or Monkton Wyld founded in 1940 in Charmouth in Dorset, or the remarkable communities for young delinquents described by David Wills in *The Barns Experiment* and *The Hawkspur Experiment*, or Finchden Manor founded by George Lyward, or Red Hill School founded by Otto Shaw, or many others.

Wennington School, which in 1945 moved from its first home in north Lancashire to its present accommodation in Yorkshire, near Wetherby, may serve as an example of several community schools which were formed in the stress of the Second World War as a gesture both of survival and of idealism. These schools were not a further wave of new foundations corresponding to the first surge of the 1890s and the second of the 1920s. Evacuation and the shock of total mobilization and the whole deployment of world war produced improvisations and a flexibility enforced by events. The war years yielded the last innovatory group we shall consider.

Kenneth and Frances Barnes were both Quakers (Mrs. Barnes died in 1959), and between 1930 and 1940 Barnes, after some years of teaching in grammar schools, was head of the science department at Bedales. He and his wife felt the need to try to affirm in a school human and religious values at a time when a flood of destruction was pouring over the world. In 1940 bombing had started in London, in Bristol, and on Merseyside and the vast human problems of evacuation of children cried out for help. A large guest house, Wennington Hall in north Lancashire, furnished and at nominal rent, was offered as a school, and Kenneth and Frances Barnes gathered round them a few like-minded colleagues and families prepared to set up a community for children as a pacifist counter-statement to destruction. The children came from all over the country and the number of boys and girls grew slowly. There was no endowment for this school and Barnes says that they had the bare necessities for living, no educational equipment, and about £200. For some time there was not sufficient money to pay the staff and during the first term they and their families had to pay for their keep. As the numbers of children increased the teachers were able to draw an equal rate of pay, with additional family allowances, these financial arrangements being arrived at by common consent. The parents of the children paid what they could afford and the school was, for quite a time, close to financial ruin. Only the devotion of staff and the frugality of life tided the school over to more prosperous times.

By 1948 the numbers of pupils and resources were such that the Ministry of Education inspected and recognized the school as efficient, which brought in its train the condition that the Burnham scale be used in salaries and so financial communal egalitarianism disappeared. A trust had been formed in 1942 and a group of governors, with strong professional and academic interests represented, took some of the planning off the shoulders of Mr. and Mrs. Barnes.

It had not been the Barnes's intention that Wennington should be a war-time undertaking only, but, like others who founded schools then which have continued to the present, they found the comprehensive realities of war-time conditions gave a firm and unique quality to the life of the school:

> Personal responsibility, full co-operation in the life of a community, the sharing of every kind of work, domestic, agricultural, constructional, these were not merely ideals but rooted in necessity. Experience of the tradition of 'outdoor work' established by Abbotsholme and Bedales was specially valuable at this point. The one thing we had to spend money on to begin with was equipment for a workshop – for we had to make all the rest of our equipment.[1]

[1] K. C. Barnes, 'Wennington', in *The Independent Progressive School*, ed. Child, p. 157.

In a lecture given by Eleanor Urban on Monkton Wyld a similar point was made. This school was founded near Lyme Regis in Dorset in 1940 by a group of friends, with Carl and Eleanor Urban as leading spirits:

> We had in common several things: a lack of interest in money making as the main motive for work, a dislike of dictatorship, power politics, and militarism.... We wanted to provide something of a microcosm with basic human activities such as farming and building going on.... The origin of the school certainly had something to do with war and peace ... destructive forces in European politics had stimulated us to an attempt to be constructive.[2]

At Wennington, constructional and renovating work is still done, some of it, under expert direction, quite advanced and ambitious, like the laying of hard tennis courts and the concrete constructions for an extended sewage plant. This is a part of the thinking on which the school was founded, although in 1940, without money or equipment, the sheer necessity of economics and physical survival made the work essential in a sense different from the contemporary situation. It has been characteristic of Wennington that boys, girls, and staff have taken part in such work. A good deal of classroom furniture has been built in the workshop, and this has been true of a number of the schools considered so far: Reddie made this a feature of Abbotsholme, Hahn tried to build up working relationships between the boys and girls of Salem and the local workmen and craftsmen, Dewey maintained that work done which was meaningful in terms of the community's needs was significant in a special sense. The arts and crafts, including pottery and music, have always been encouraged at Wennington, as at the other radical schools, because it is believed that they give to a person a means of creating and experiencing which intellectual exercises do not offer.

Experiments in teaching have been tried over the years: the Dalton system was used for some time, but was discontinued when the staff thought that the weaker pupils were finding

[2] From a manuscript sent to the author by Mrs. Urban, who died in 1967, her husband having died some years earlier.

the record-keeping and the self-direction of their time and assignments too complex. The productive relics of the full system can be seen today in time given to 'private' study, in which individual work based on the course has to be done and periodically scrutinized. Such flexibility permits boys and girls to fit in music lessons and extra time on individual projects or corporate activities. While Wennington accepts the need to prepare students for higher education by training on examination courses, it remains critical of specialist sixth formers and is ready to encourage children with the appropriate ability to keep their intellectual frontiers open, to study arts, sciences, and social sciences for their personal enrichment.

At most times the majority of the staff and Governing Body at Wennington have been members of the Society of Friends. The teaching on religious matters aims to provide as sound a knowledge as possible of the development of religion in the Western world so that if commitment to belief follows it should be well informed: 'What we seek is that religion should be regarded as a matter for serious and discriminating discussion, from whatever point of view, and as a significant force in history.'[3]

In 1944 Barnes wrote a review of the first four years in which he said that from the outset one of the chief enemies of the school's progress was idealism, because progressive education was too much influenced by the traditions of Rousseau and too many schools achieved an unreal freedom by an illusory repudiation of the society outside their gates. At Wennington there had been talk about equality between adults and children and this had given rise in practice to mistrust and carping criticism. There was mention of 'a free school' and some members of staff interpreted this as synonymous with independent choice for individuals; it took time to establish that a group the size of a school demanded some structure of authority and some sentiment of loyalty to decisions. Mistakes were made in school government and, writing in 1944, Barnes concluded that it was an error to start off with a school council on formal lines because the children were then too young, too inexperienced and the school too immature for

[3] *The Independent Progressive School*, p. 161.

the idea of self-government to be appropriate in any real sense.[4] He and his colleagues looked forward to the time when a school council could take on real responsibility. Writing nearly twenty years later, he gave an account of the transitions to the present arrangement of counsellors, a Wennington variant on prefects, and an elected Senate, representative of members of the staff and the various forms in the school. This body was arrived at after there had been for a while a full school meeting when numbers were small enough to make this profitable, but this time passed within a few years of the foundation of the school. The Senate now has sub-committees and an established procedure and is an advisory body of weight; however, no attempt is made to evade the fact that final authority for decisions rests with the heads and the staff.[5]

On a number of occasions Barnes has written of the dangers of permissiveness, and of the snares of too little, rather than too much, efficiency in progressive schools. He sees education as being concerned with leading children towards 'the abundant life' which offers opportunity for intensity of effort and feeling and a wide range of knowledge and aspiration:

> The abundant life to the person who lives it is not necessarily happy; it is certainly not continuously happy.... Education is not like taking a child on a journey from town A to town B, deciding on your objective and making sure that you get him there. It is, on the contrary, an adventure [which] ... may alter profoundly your ideas on where you want to go.[6]

One fixed point for Barnes is co-education, and he writes that when he went to Bedales in 1930 after some years of grammar-school teaching he was prepared for shocks:

> What I found seemed to me remarkably wholesome and normal in the best sense of the word. I found an astonishingly high standard of physical vigour and health. When I looked

---

[4] K. C. Barnes, *The First Four Years* (1944), 16 pages. These ideas on the period are taken from the pamphlet *passim*.
[5] *The Independent Progressive School*, p. 162.
[6] Ibid., pp. 164–7.

at the girls and remembered the statement of a certain headmistress that 'co-education took the bloom off the girls', I wondered that anyone could have been so ill-informed and so far from the truth. Equally false seemed the idea that it made boys soft.[7]

Barnes believes that every boy and girl is the better for contact with both men and women and he considers that anyone who regards Plato's *Republic* as a reliable textbook on education should try discussing it with the sixth form of a co-educational boarding-school. Elsewhere Barnes has said that Gordonstoun looks to a training of character rather than to academic achievement, and that it undertakes this training through certain definite procedures associated with physical fitness and resourcefulness. He both accepts and rejects these principles. He rejects the maleness, he accepts the notion of challenge, and envies Gordonstoun the proximity of mountains and sea. But for him the essentials are to be achieved between persons:

> There are no tricks in education; we cannot use physical endeavour, intellectual effort, gamesmanship, musical or artistic experience, nor the outward patterns of religion to 'do things' for us. They cannot take the place of the essential experience – the encounter of person with person.... This encounter must be direct, not mediated by mutual submission to a pattern of thought or a system. It must not be in terms of 'loyalty to the school' or a desirable *type* of character.[8]

Later in the same article he says that he considers, with Suttie in *The Origins of Love and Hate*, that in our patriarchal society thriving on possessions and ownership there is a taboo on tenderness and we are driven by the desire for power and not the impulse to love. Barnes wants Wennington to nourish persons who will be sensitive and will love and who have the steadiness of understanding to detect and to overcome unscrupulousness in all its forms. In 1962, in com-

[7] K. C. Barnes, *The Co-educational Boarding Schools* (1953), p. 2.
[8] The school magazine, *Wennington School 1961–62*, p. 4.

pany with some other members of the Society of Friends, Barnes wrote a pamphlet, *Towards a Quaker View of Sex*, in which, among other things, they drew attention to the fundamental importance of the inner quality of any relationship which was tender, responsible, and enduring. This was more significant to them than codes of behaviour dutifully observed, and Barnes believes that co-education, especially in a boarding-school, gives a special opportunity to seek for and to find the fundamental criteria of moral conduct.

As a Quaker, Kenneth Barnes sees 'that of God in every man', and the co-education at Wennington and his existential awareness suggest that he is somewhat similar to A. S. Neill. However, Barnes maintains the need for authority and community power, and he has beliefs about what, when, and how children should be taught. He is not as permissive, as truly anarchic, as Neill. They both feel keenly the paradox of their exclusive position as heads of independent schools, and try to offer the facilities of their two schools to as wide a range of child and parent as possible.

The problem of weaving principle into practice confronts all schools perennially, but most have recognizably a method, a routine, a structure of authority, a formality which is expected and which they exert. In Wennington these things exist, but in a form which makes them different in so large a degree as almost to be different in kind, and the heart of the matter is in the quality and structure of community life. Teachers at Wennington may be known to children by their Christian names, as might members of any company of friends. While a school is for learning and teaching, the best of this kind is thought to be a by-product of a way of living in which function and responsibility can be seen to come from a mutual respect. The adults decide what is to be offered in teaching, they take the lead in guiding the way of living of the school, but the children are expected to understand what is being offered, to have views on everything, and to come to see what way of living is being required and why. Barnes and his colleagues expect the children to agree with the regime for the most part, because the psychological distance between adults and pupils ought to be small and the common nature of the enterprise in learning ought to be easy to grasp. These generalized ideas are worked out in day-to-day living with children who are expected to comment, to criticize, and not necessarily to submit.

We have already seen that no school can live on its history, and those that began, like Wennington, in the stress of war, have an affluent, egalitarian, disenchanted present to contend with. Wennington was led until 1968 by its founder, who has now been succeeded by his senior colleague Brian Hill, who has served the school for many years. The transition to its second generation of leadership is critical for Wennington's institutional steadiness. At present it can reasonably be placed to the right of Summerhill, and rather less to the right of Dartington, and probably to the left of nearly all the other schools we have considered.

19 The International Movement in Progressive Education

WHILE MOST of the schools and personalities so far considered have been British because the main focus of this book is upon England, schools in Germany, France, Holland, Switzerland, and the United States of America have been mentioned and men and women from many nationalities have rightly come into the foreground at different points. Because educational innovators have been such individualists and because they have been engaged in creating schools by teaching and living with children, they have not had the time, the energy, or the desire to create strong and powerful national and international movements. The New Education Fellowship is the most representative example of the progressive movement in education over a period of nearly fifty years.

I

The loose organization of the Fellowship developed out of the Conference of New Ideals in Education, which had its first meeting in 1914. Within this Conference the Theosophical Fraternity in Education grew large enough to acquire identity, and by 1920, from a meeting at Letchworth of this Fraternity, the New Education Fellowship began to take form.[1]

The Fraternity wished to bring together the efforts of pioneers in education working in both state and independent schools and to emphasize the part to be played by education in winning the peace. Mrs. Beatrice Ensor had started in

[1] Much of the material in this chapter is based upon the manuscripts of the late Dr. William Boyd entitled *The New Education of the Twentieth Century*, which he allowed the author to read. When Dr. Boyd died in 1962 the manuscripts were edited by Wyatt Rawson and published under joint authorship in 1965 with the title *The Story of the New Education*. This book has been called upon *passim* as well as in the passages indicated.

January 1920 a magazine entitled *Education for the New Era, An International Quarterly Journal for the Promotion of Reconstruction in Education* and this was intended to support the outlook and work for peace of the newly formed League of Nations, which was developing political, economic, and social functions but no educational organization. The *Journal* was international and set out to record the growth of experimental education; it envisaged the establishment of an international fellowship of teachers, with an annual conference. The first conference was arranged for Calais in 1921, one of its purposes being to give shape and organization to the proposed society. As the origin of the whole undertaking was the Theosophical Fraternity, it was agreed that to avoid narrowing the appeal of the conference, care should be taken to keep Theosophy in the background. The invitations were sent out in the name of Mrs. Ensor's journal, which by that time had changed its title from *Education for the New Era* to *The New Era in Home and School*, the conception of the new education having by this time widened out beyond schools and teachers. Interested parents, social workers, psychologists, doctors, and administrators were also invited to Calais, to the first New Era International Conference on Education to be held at the Collège Sophie-Berthelot from 30 July to 12 August 1921 on the theme 'The Creative Self Expression of the Child'.

Over one hundred members from fourteen different countries attended. Germans were not admitted to a conference in France at that time and French Catholics were suspicious of the spiritual assumptions of the organizers, but pioneers who had not previously met or who had been separated by war were able for the first time to talk and to exchange information. Reports of the conference show that there were at least three main divergences of view in the opinions on self-expression in children. Robert Nussbaum, a Swiss, called into question the whole idea of creative self-expression on the grounds that children were imitators who drew upon ideas derived from their family and society and that their work should be looked on in this sense. Followers of Dr. Montessori distrusted the whole notion of imaginative activity in children because the learning situations that Madame Montessori advocated were so structured that free-ranging activities were at a minimum and, as we have seen, an environment was provided in which necessary learning (necessary for the ends Dr. Montessori had in mind, that is to say) was willingly undertaken by the children. In different ways Nussbaum and the Montessorians were presenting similar objections. A. S. Neill, on the other hand, wanted even more freedom for self-expression, not so much to achieve new, creditable, and spontaneous learning by children, but to break the shackles of the moralists. His interpretation of freedom in 1921, as in the present day, appeared to many a dangerous doctrine.

While this conference was interesting in itself, there was also the question of the construction of a society. As *The New Era* had officially issued the invitations, it was thought valuable to base any more definite organization upon it:

> It was due to Theosophists that the Fraternity came into being and for the first few years the Fraternity, *The New Era* and the Fellowship were financed by the generosity of two wealthy Theosophists. It was never an aim however to spread the tenets of Theosophy.... The greatest care was taken not to theosophize the schools or the Fellowship.[2]

An international committee proposed the following scheme, which was accepted. Two other publications were to be established comparable to *The New Era*, one in French to be edited by Adolf Ferrière, who, as we have seen, had started the International Bureau of New Schools in Switzerland as far back as 1899, and one in German to be edited by Dr. Elizabeth Rotten, who was born in Germany of Swiss parents but who had worked from England as a Quaker dealing with prisoners of war. These journals gave communication in the three major languages of the Western world, and all subscribers to any of the three were by that fact to be members of the international organization. The English section kept the conference designation of the New Education Fellowship, the French version of which became the *Ligue Internationale pour L'Education Nouvelle* and the German at first *Internationaler Arbeitskreis für Erneuerung der Erziehung* and later the *Weltbund für Erneuerung der Erziehung*.

[2] From notes contributed by Mrs. Ensor to Dr. Boyd's manuscripts.

The principles of the Fellowship, which will be mentioned later, were published in all editions of the three journals, and this was considered sufficient to give the Fellowship identity without recourse to a constitution or rules for the international body. Countries were expected to make their own arrangements for national branches of the movement but it was agreed that the autonomy of the journals, language groups, and countries would be supplemented by the common recognition that *The New Era* would provide the international links. The editors of the three journals, *The New Era*, *Pour L'Ère Nouvelle*, and *Das Werdende Zeitalter* were given the task of calling a conference every two years and, with additional advice as they required, to decide on the programme.

Early in 1922 the three journals appeared with substantially similar statements of the principles of the New Education Fellowship which had been generally agreed at Calais and which appeared in each issue until 1932. I state them in detail so that we can see where later disagreement arose:

1. The essential aim of all education is to prepare the child to seek and realize in his own life the supremacy of the spirit. Whatever other view the educator may take, education should aim at maintaining and increasing spiritual energy in the child.
2. Education should respect the child's individuality. This individuality can only be developed by means of a discipline which sets free the spiritual powers within him.
3. The studies, and indeed the whole training for life, should give free play to the child's innate interests – interests which awaken spontaneously in him and find their expression in various manual, intellectual, aesthetic, social, and other activities.
4. Each age has its own special character. For this reason individual and corporate disciplines need to be organized by the children themselves in collaboration with their teachers. These disciplines should make for a deeper sense of individual and social responsibility.
5. Selfish competition must disappear from education and be replaced by the co-operation which teaches the child to put himself at the service of his community.

6. Co-education – instruction and education in common – does not mean the identical treatment of the two sexes, but a collaboration which allows each sex to exercise a salutary influence on the other.

7. The New Education fits the child to become not only a citizen capable of doing his duties to his neighbours, his nation and humanity at large, but a human being conscious of his personal dignity.[3]

A few moments' scrutiny of these articles will show how vague they are. They are not a creed either in philosophy or in methodology but could be made the sketch for one. Followers of Dewey would probably not agree that all education should prepare the child to seek and realize the supremacy of the spirit, because pragmatists often doubt the validity of the spirit. However the second half of the first article tones down any sharp clash between, say, Theosophists and naturalists. Many of the articles emphasize the uniqueness of a child's individuality and the readiness of children to initiate learning, although this takes different forms at different ages. In the fifth article 'selfish competition' must disappear from education, but this does not exclude the possibility of unselfish competition while it also stresses co-operation. In the sixth article co-education is not actually commended as the right educational organization, but an unexceptionable moral is drawn on the salutary influence of the sexes on one another. Thus Catholic members and single-sex educators in England and elsewhere are not excluded. These seven articles are sufficiently definite by implication to indicate what the New Education is about and sufficiently permissive to avoid offending too much those who have an orthodoxy of their own, whether liberal Catholic like Georges Bertier's of the *École des Roches* or anarchic like A. S. Neill's.

The three editors were virtually directors of the international undertakings of the Fellowship and two-yearly conferences followed at Montreux (1923), Heidelberg (1925), Locarno (1927), Elsinore (1929), Nice (1932), and, after a break of four years, Cheltenham (1936).

[3] Quoted from Boyd and Rawson, *The Story of the New Education*, pp. 73–4.

In August 1939 a European conference was to take place at the Sorbonne, but in the light of events it was postponed *sine die*. The international activities of the Fellowship after the end of the war of 1939-45, with UNESCO in existence, can be mentioned later. Meanwhile the national movements came into existence with varying strength between the wars in Switzerland, France, Holland, Italy, Spain, Belgium, Germany, Austria, Denmark, Sweden, Finland, Russia, Poland, Estonia, Czechoslovakia, Hungary, Bulgaria, Yugoslavia, Egypt, Japan, China, and the United States. Later India, Pakistan, Ceylon, South Africa, Australia, and New Zealand provided numbers of delegates to the international conferences and a national membership which was for example in Australia very strong. The movements in England, Wales, Northern Ireland, and Scotland, which had independent existence from 1928 as the English New Education Fellowship, gave steady support to the international movement, and some branches of the N.E.F. were established in Latin America.

After the 1927 conference at Locarno the international organization was made more definite. As many national sections began to produce Fellowship magazines of their own, subscription to one or other of the original three journals was not considered sufficient as a credential for international membership. National sections had to be formally affiliated to the international movement and represented on an International Council, which in turn came to have an Executive Board which was at first called a Consultative Committee. The days of the scale of organization which could be managed by three largely voluntary editors acting as joint directors from England, Switzerland, and Germany were over.

Voluntary service or work for token payment had enabled the Fellowship to start and to grow, but the size of the enterprise and the conditions of slump in the early 1930s made it necessary to try to provide a more stable financial base for this loose federation of movements. Trusts, foundations, educational research organizations, and private individuals had for more than ten years financed the Fellowship, but as the national sections and branches grew in number and in size they wanted more money for their own undertakings and had less to spare for international costs. A subscription for international work was added to the national subvention and the liaison and administration was carried out from a London centre, but by 1937 the deficit was mounting dangerously and any development of large-scale international work faded. However, the international conferences of the 1920s and 1930s were the only world-wide exchange of ideas on educational innovation by an organization with such coverage. This aspect of the work of the New Education Fellowship continues at the present time in a very different style, and the pre-eminence of these conferences ended with the beginning of the 1939–45 war.

When the first conference took place in Calais in 1921 there were about one hundred participants from fourteen countries and many of them were Theosophists, socialists, or pacifists, according to the recollections of some of the delegates. At Montreux in 1923 over three hundred and seventy attended from at least twenty-two countries and, noticeably, a few Germans were present. More remarkable still, the 1952 conference was held in Heidelberg, in Germany itself, and four hundred and fifty people from twenty-nine countries attended, including government representatives from several of them. At Locarno in 1927 over eleven hundred attended, with about 25 per cent from Germany, about 15 per cent from Great Britain, and slightly fewer from the United States. At Elsinore in 1929 there were about eighteen hundred present, with large numbers coming from the Scandinavian countries, but still with much the same coverage of countries as at Locarno. In 1932 at Nice there were again about eighteen hundred participants, and so great was the demand on the organizers that it was 1936 before what was really the last of these gatherings was arranged in Cheltenham, and here the numbers were noticeably smaller, about one thousand in all. The Russian bloc, the Germans, and the Italians together provided only about 5 per cent of the numbers: the restrictions of totalitarianism had tightened dramatically despite special attempts to invite Communist, Nazi, and Fascist countries to participate. We have already seen that the 1939 conference in Paris was cancelled before it began.

Each of the national movements during the eighteen years before 1939 developed its own programme of activity, and in many cases they were influential in discussions leading to educational legislation and change. Boyd and Rawson in their book report some of the developments in many countries during this period, and a more detailed statement is provided in the successive issues of the three journals in French, German, and English, to which were added, especially in the 1930s, other national publications in new languages: in Scandinavian languages in Sweden and Finland, in Spanish, in Dutch, in Bengali, in Japanese, in Hungarian, in Italian. Many of these publications were reports of conferences within nationalities or with a common language.

To get some feeling of the themes which engaged the attention of the N.E.F. before 1939, we can look at the reports of conferences and the symposia which appeared from time to time in *The New Era, Pour L'Ère Nouvelle,* or *Das Werdende Zeitalter*. At Calais in 1921 the general theme of the lectures and discussions was 'The Creative Self Expression of the Child', and at Montreux two years later it was an education for creative service – this word 'creative' has been from the start one of the hallmarks and danger signals for the N.E.F. At Heidelberg in 1925 the schools of the New Education movement were passed under review, schools like those considered in earlier chapters of this book. In 1927 at Locarno the theme was the meaning of freedom in education; in 1929 at Elsinore it was the relevance of the new psychology of Freud, Adler, Jung, Piaget, of behaviourism and mental measurement, to the curriculum.

These themes were all related to educational and individual salvation by some kind of personal dynamic, they were nearly all critical of the rational in education and were psychological in the sense that they were devoted to personal development through freedom. We have seen earlier that the new psychology achieved at least a European surgence in education in the 1920s, and the N.E.F. was one of the instruments for this. While Montessori's psychology was more restricted in scope and focused more sharply on education than Freud's or Jung's or even Adler's, it was really the thinking of the three dynamic psychologists with its awareness of unconscious factors which had most repercussions in the N.E.F.

The Fellowship had declared itself non-political and uncommitted in religious matters in the 1920s, concerned only with the freedom required for personal development. The slump forced national economic realities into educational discussions. Mussolini, Hitler, and Stalin made it increasingly difficult for liberals to survive, and discussing the personal dynamic in education by itself was seen to be not enough. The conference at Nice in 1932 showed the change of viewpoint and context, for here the delegates discussed education and changing society. In 1921 the N.E.F. had wanted to concentrate into education some of the intense desire for peace and, like many other liberals, to think that boundless disgust with the waste, terror, and degradation of war was enough to stir compassion and steel resolve. The achievements on a fingernail budget over ten years were an encouragement to hope that new men and women were growing for a new world. By 1932 the members knew they had seriously and urgently to think how education could help in preserving peace in the world or, more brutally, in preventing war. The theme was 'Education and Changing Society', and when one reads the report itself the bitter anxieties and premonitions of the early 1930s arise strongly again through one's awareness of the nobility, the sincerity, the importance, and the irrelevance of so much that was talked about. Mrs. Ensor said that human relations needed changing so that we could assent to and accept what living in a world society meant. Dr. Rotten wanted educators to be aware of their own aggressiveness and purge themselves from it, recognizing that it would take decades rather than years to achieve. Van der Leeuw of Holland saw in art a way to equilibrium, and Dr. Montessori wanted to disperse all hostility between adults and children, which could best be done under her system. These may all be called psychological contributions. There were others which may be called, for the present, sociological. Dr. Becker, the Prussian minister of education, asked the N.E.F. to face the fact that there were views on behaviour and education other than those of the Fellowship and that it was a sign of maturity to understand the interpretations of morality and the ways of behaving of nations different from one's own. The French wanted all countries and delegates to extend their knowledge of other cultures and to agree on the basis of a secular humanism which would indicate the values that were supported and commended by believers and secularists alike. Dr. Harold Rugg of the United States put before the delegates the view that educationalists needed to be committed to a reconstruction of society as a whole, with education as one feature in the whole complex structure.

At Cheltenham in 1936 the theme was the educational foundations of freedom in a free community, and in the circumstances it is not surprising that few delegates from Russia or Germany or Italy were present. There was some straight political and social analysis. R. H. Tawney spoke of hardship, deprivation, and privilege in England and repeated some of the powerful arguments he had presented a few years earlier in his Halley–Stewart lectures on equality. Charles Freinet, a French Communist, spoke in the same critical vein on human injustice and hypocrisy. There were contributions designed to clarify the meaning of the term 'freedom' from participants like Sir Sarvepalli Radhakrishnan, Professor Henri Wallon, and Dr. G. P. Gooch. Dr. J. H. Hadfield spoke as a psychiatrist and Dr. Carlton Washburne as a theorist and practitioner in education, and each touched on the theme of indoctrination, teaching, and the encouragement of choice and value-judgement. At Cheltenham many of the discussions were socio-political and controversial, and for the first time the content and significance of religion in the free community came up for open consideration as a restricting or liberating force.

At Nice in 1932 a new statement of principles had been worked out, which replaced the 1921 version and was more precise in its awareness of the threat to free peoples everywhere:

> In twenty years education might transform the social order and establish a spirit of co-operation capable of finding solutions for the problems of our time....
>
> It is only an education which realizes a change of attitude to children ... that can inaugurate an era free from the ruinous rivalries, the prejudices, anxieties, and distress characteristic of our present chaotic, insecure civilization....

1. Education should enable the child to comprehend the complexities of the social and economic life of our times.
2. It should be so planned as to meet the diverse intellectual and emotional need of children of different temperaments....
3. It should help children to adapt themselves with goodwill to the demand of social life by ... a developed sense of personal initiative and responsibility.
4. It should promote co-operation ... by bringing teachers and children to realize the importance of diversity of character and independent thinking.
5. It should lead children to appreciate their national heritage and to welcome gladly the special contribution made to human culture by every other nation.[4]

The 1921 statement spoke of the supremacy of the spirit, setting free spiritual powers, giving free play to a child's innate interests, and the abolition of selfish competition. The 1932 statement is more definite, but whereas in 1921 there was explicit mention of co-education in 1932 there was none.

In 1937 the English section produced a fairly clear programme based on the two principles of co-operation rather than competition and discipline by consent rather than coercion. The authors stated that they wanted to raise the school-leaving age to sixteen with adequate maintenance grants, to adjust education to individual abilities as gauged by modern psychological methods, to give equal status to all kinds of schools, to re-examine the selection and training of teachers, to reconsider the purpose and effectiveness of examinations, to reduce the size of classes, and to increase the numbers of nursery schools. Here again is an example of a greater readiness in the 1930s to make principles match more definite objectives, which in a permissive organization is by no means easy to achieve.

The American Progressive Education Association was, according to Cremin, rather wary of coming into full association with the N.E.F. Although the P.E.A. had been in existence since April 1919, it did not send representatives to an N.E.F. conference until 1925, 'probably fearing the taint of

[4] Translated from the French version.

pedagogical and political radicalism that attached to the
N.E.F.'[5] Some two hundred American delegates attended the
Elsinore conference in 1929, and in 1932 the P.E.A. became the
American branch of the N.E.F. Although the P.E.A., which
changed its name to the American Education Fellowship in
1944 and back to the P.E.A. in 1953, came to a petering end
finally in 1955 because, according to Cremin, 'it simply failed
to comprehend the fundamental forces that move American
education',[6] it produced in 1938 an indictment of Nazi brutality under the title 'For the Understanding and Defense of
Democracy'. This declaration inspired the English section to
state its position in 1939, saying that it regarded with abhor-
rence the deliberate encouragement in the young of racial
prejudice, of totalitarian and militaristic views, the suppres-
sion of information, and the distortions of propaganda, as well
as the distortions of art and science for political ends. They
deplored the use of fear, distrust, and cruelty as instruments
of policy, and the persecution of persons and racial minorities.
They detested the glorification of war and militarism and the
readiness to repudiate international co-operation.

The totalitarian regimes had forced the authors of this statement to confront the belief that 'the fate of Democracy is a first
and immediate concern of educationalists'. This kind of political commitment represents a radical change of outlook from
the earlier belief of the Fellowship in the efficacy of the emancipated school community to transform life. Which is perhaps
another way of saying that three years after the first world
war in history is a more likely time for faith in human
magnanimity than one year before the second.

The Fellowship, over nearly twenty years in the inter-war
period, set up many commissions and published many reports
and symposia on subjects which are commonly thought of as
characteristic of the progressive movement. *The New Era* had
symposia on self-government, free time-tables, new methods of
art teaching, drama in education, psycho-analysis and its
derivatives, youth movements, new schools in England and
other countries, sex education, intelligence and intelligence
testing, examinations, international understanding, the Dal-

[5] Cremin, *Transformation of the School*, p. 248.
[6] Ibid., p. 273.

ton Plan and other special educational systems, and the training of teachers. National and international commissions drew up reports on psychology and education, on reform in the curriculum, on examinations, on education for leisure, on the schools and the state, on co-education. Noticeably less was done in the sciences and mathematics, although, of course, these did appear in places throughout the period.

Probably enough has been said in passing to indicate the distinction and quality of participants in the conferences of the N.E.F. Men and women of the highest repute across the world were invited and this is some indication of the position the Fellowship had established for itself, and of course the standing of the people who accepted the invitations made the reputation of the Fellowship more secure. Men like Baudouin, Coué, Jung, Dalcroze, Michael Sadler, Ballard, Burt, Percy Nunn, Tawney, Buber, Adler, Pierre Bovet, Paul Langevin, Harold Rugg, Carson Ryan, Fred Clarke, Piaget, Robert Ulich, A. D. Lindsay, Radhakrishnan, Gooch were all participants, some of them regularly. Women like Beatrice Ensor, Maria Montessori, Susan Isaacs and Helen Parkhurst added their support. The International Council of the movement consisted of representatives elected by national sections and this Council elected by invitation the Executive Board, consisting of persons distinguished in education and not necessarily directly connected with the N.E.F. Many of the people mentioned above have from time to time been members of the Board. But the burden of the Fellowship's work was borne until well after the end of the war in 1945 by a number of devoted officers all of whom lived long to serve the N.E.F. Beatrice Ensor was the main originator of the Fellowship and served it fully until she went to live in South Africa in the later 1930s, although she continued to work for the N.E.F. Elizabeth Rotten also continued to give similar service and Clare Soper came to London in the early years to help to administer the international work, from which she retired in 1951. J. B. Annand, who combined the international work and the English section secretaryship after Miss Soper retired, himself went into retirement in 1962. Dr. Peggy Volkov, until her retirement in 1962, served as the editor of *The New Era* for nearly thirty years, having taken it over from Mrs. Ensor.

The devotion and energy of this group of persons and of many others in England and all over the world in the inter-war years, during the war, and after gave a remarkable coherence and continuity to an organization which places no great store by its institutional mechanisms. The emphasis on people rather than on precept, we are told in many places in the Fellowship's publications, has been the notable feature of the N.E.F. organization and activity ever since its beginnings. During the inter-war years the Fellowship's activities were at their peak, and it might now be valuable to turn to the war-time and post-war developments.

II

From 1939 to 1945 the national movements in the U.S.A. and in England were able to keep a surprising amount of activity going. Many refugees had fled to both countries in the years before the war, the Allies had their forces in both, and there were exiled Allied governments in London. Obviously the official international work of the N.E.F. was finished for the duration, but in India, Australia, New Zealand, and South Africa there was much N.E.F. activity, the Middle East countries held two regional conferences in Cairo during the war, and in Sweden and Switzerland N.E.F. members worked mainly through child relief organizations to undertake as much welfare and educational activity as possible. Many of the N.E.F. members in German-occupied countries were already marked men as known liberals. In Norway and Denmark, and especially in Norway, teachers, with support from parents and children, tried to resist imposition of educational programmes by the Nazis and any interference with the teaching in schools. N.E.F. members were, of course, only part of this heroic resistance, but for many people reprisals followed in forced labour, imprisonment, and death. In France there was a methodical take-over attempt in Alsace and Lorraine and a consistent Nazi pressure throughout to control schools, training colleges, and universities. N.E.F. leaders like Professor Langevin (who was the post-war minister of education who effected such striking innovations in the French educational system), Professor Wallon, Professor Marcault, and Professor Pieron either escaped to Switzerland or England or hid or fought with Resistance forces.

The American Progressive Education Association took up the responsibility of maintaining some international work after the outbreak of the European war in September 1939, and in July 1941 at the University of Michigan they staged what was called the Eighth International Conference (the abortive Paris conference of 1939 would have been the eighth) on the theme 'Educational Reconstruction'. Mrs. Eleanor Roosevelt was the chairman with John Dewey as the president, and the latter spoke on democracy and civilization. Visitors from abroad who took part at that period of depression for the Allies were Thomas Mann, in self-imposed exile, Laurin Zilliacus from Finland, and Professor Fred Clarke from England. After Pearl Harbor in December 1941 international work for educational innovation ceased for the U.S.A. as it had done for Britain in 1939.

In 1941 there were three N.E.F. conferences in Oxford in eight months at each of which Karl Mannheim took an important part. Mannheim, a Hungarian by birth and a Jew, had built an international reputation for himself in Heidelberg and Frankfurt in the 1920s and early 1930s by his writings. He was listed as an enemy of Nazism because his criticisms of totalitarianism in *Ideology and Utopia* in 1926 and later in *Man and Society* showed the strength and ruthlessness of both Fascism and Nazism on the one hand and Communism on the other. He fled from Hitler in 1933, first to Holland and then to England, where he began to teach at the London School of Economics. He was deeply aware that Germany was inviting another world war and that it might lead to the eclipse of democracy, for democratic countries, as he thought did not have the ruthlessness to organize the affairs of men and the state so as to provide really effective resistance to militant dictators. The Weimar Republic had been so permissive that there was no dynamic purpose or organization of control out of which democratic change could grow. At the beginning of the English version of *Man and Society* published in London in 1940 he wrote that the German version was written in the early 1930s in the conviction that the democratic system had run its course, because the Weimar Republic had revealed the helplessness of the old *laissez-faire* order to deal with modern mass society, either politically or culturally, but that when he had lived for a while in England he had found a much more deeply rooted liberal democracy which tempted him, as he said, to an optimism that hid the profound crisis:

> To the Western countries the collapse of liberalism and democracy and the adoption of a totalitarian system seem to be passing symptoms of a crisis which is confined to a few nations, while those who live within the danger zone experience this transition as a change in the very structure of modern society.

The need for priorities in war-time quickly made the theme of 'planning for freedom' urgent and relevant. Mannheim was not specific about the changes likely or necessary in society in the way that Marx was. Instead, he indicated key points at which diagnosis was needed if social change was to take place cumulatively over society as a whole. He wrote and spoke of economics and economic organization, of property, law, individual and group values, the nature and influence of élites, the meaning of freedom. Inevitably he spoke much of education. In 1940–41 Professor Fred Clarke, Sir Percy Nunn's successor as director of the University of London Institute of Education, invited Mannheim to become a part-time lecturer in the sociology of education and he gave courses there until he was appointed to a chair of education at the Institute in 1946, when he left his general concern with sociology at the London School of Economics to concentrate his energies on educational sociology, a study virtually unknown in England. He held this post for one year only and Mrs. Floud says of him:

> ... the attraction of his mind and personality had us all in his power. As a Professor of Education his success was astonishing and his death in 1947, at the age of 54 ... deprived London of a formidable teacher at the height of his powers.[7]

[7] Mrs. Jean Floud, in an essay on Mannheim in *The Function of Teaching*, ed. A. V. Judges (London, 1959), p. 66. See also K. Mannheim and W. A. C. Stewart, *An Introduction to the Sociology of Education* (London, 1962), pp. 187 and xvii.

Mannheim took part in all three conferences arranged by the N.E.F. in Oxford in 1941 and the themes show the marks of his interests: *The Future of Society, A New Deal for Youth, Towards Education in a Planned Democracy.* Besides his interest in the social context in which schools and colleges grow and take forms of organization which affect the pupils, he considered the relationship between the school and the other institutions of society. While the first of these emphases was related to the N.E.F. interests in child development,[8] the second was new.

In 1942 the N.E.F. held a conference on the educational and social problems of adolescence and later held another on the social aims of post-war European education. One of the participants was Dr. Drzewieskí, who had been secretary before the war of the Polish section of the N.E.F. and who later became head of the Reconstruction Department of UNESCO. In 1942, in relation to this second conference, six commissions were set up to study the kinds of reform needed in English education, and some of this thinking was valuable in the planning which led to the 1944 Act. The commission or working party was a long-established activity of the N.E.F., as shown by its work on examinations begun in 1927, and on teacher training, nursery schools, and curriculum reform begun in 1929. In 1942 a so-called 'children's charter' was drawn up. The N.E.F. took advantage of the presence of Allied governments and other representatives in Britain to call together a conference at which nineteen countries were represented (and this at a time before the war had really turned in the Allies' favour). The president of the Board of Education, Mr. R. A. Butler, gave the opening address, and the charter, with an explication, was issued as an act of faith:

> The Inter-Allied Conference convened by the New Education Fellowship and meeting in London on 11 and 12 April 1942, humbly requested the Governments of the Allied Nations to approve and adopt the following Charter for Children as a statement of the basic and minimum rights of

[8] For further elaboration of this aspect of Mannheim's thinking which came later in his life, see Mannheim and Stewart, *Introduction to Sociology of Education*, particularly ch. x.

children to be secured and guarded, above and beyond all considerations of sex, race, nationality, creed, or social position.

1. The personality of the child is sacred; and the needs of the child must be the foundation of any good educational system.
2. The right of every child to proper food, clothing, and shelter shall be accepted as a first charge on the resources of the nation.
3. For every child there shall always be available medical attention and treatment.
4. All children shall have equal opportunity of access to the nation's stores of knowledge and wisdom.
5. There shall be full-time schooling for every child.
6. Religious training should be available for all children.

The committee which drafted the charter went on to urge that an International Office of Education should be set up in London or Washington or Moscow charged with responsibilities for reconstruction after the war: feeding and caring for children of all nations, ex-enemy and Allied alike; rebuilding schools, re-equipping libraries and laboratories; encouraging international life by exchanging teachers and children; attending to the problem of an international auxiliary language. These aims bear the hallmark of N.E.F. concerns, and this proposal for an international Office of Education reminds one that in 1920 Mrs. Ensor and her colleagues had pointed out that with all the bright promise of the League of Nations and its subsidiary associations, no international bureau of education had been set up and this was a most serious deficiency.

As early as 1942 the Council of Allied Ministers of Education began work on preparing a draft constitution for a new educational and cultural organization, and at the joint invitation of the French and the British, delegates from forty-four countries, with a chair reserved for Russia as a forty-fifth, were called together.

In London in November 1945 the Allied ministers of education together with representatives of the U.S. State Department met to form the preliminary commission from which the

United Nations Educational, Scientific and Cultural Organization (UNESCO) was officially set up in Paris in 1946. It would be foolish to ascribe to the N.E.F. the major initiative for this chapter to show how close to the international aspirations of the fellowship this enterprise was. Indeed, Professor Lauwerys, the then deputy chairman of the International Fellowship, was chairman of the commission of the Conference of Allied Ministers charged with making recommendations on the psychological and political re-education of children in occupied Europe, part of which involved the revision and writing of textbooks. W. B. Curry of Dartington, an active worker for the N.E.F., was specially concerned about the proper teaching of history, and this reappeared in a later UNESCO project on the writing and presentation of a cultural history of mankind.

A further advantage of the Allied presence was the opportunity in 1943 to arrange conferences to enable each country to understand the educational system and problems of the others. The tide of war was beginning clearly to turn for the Allies, and understanding of the problems of occupied Norway, France, Poland, and Czechoslovakia, and of China and Russia and the U.S.A. was compounded with hope and expectation that before long the theoretical grasp was going to be directed on to the practical tasks of actual reconstruction in liberated countries.

Educational reform was also being discussed in and for Britain, and the Executive Committee of the E.N.E.F. submitted a report to the so-called Fleming Committee which in 1942–3 met to make recommendations to the government on the future of the public schools. The E.N.E.F. report recommended that these schools should be taken over into the general provision of national education and made 'to serve a useful purpose', for at that time their favoured position and provision gave them a standing which was no longer suitable for a democratic society. There was still, of course, the difficult problem of the other independent schools, like the progressive group, which had many of the educational virtues which the E.N.E.F. were looking for but which could only admit those who could afford the fees.

In 1943 the E.N.E.F. spent a summer conference discussing the Government White Paper mapping the territory of the

1944 Act, and again the egalitarian, sociological temper was evident. They wanted all fees abolished in maintained schools; equal educational opportunity regardless of income; the extension of maintained nursery-school provision; the reorganization of secondary education on what would now be called the comprehensive principle, or something like it; some residential schooling for all; and non-sectarian religious teaching for all; day-release education, county colleges, educational settlements and adult education, free meals and milk where needed, wider opportunities for higher education. In the atmosphere of reform, the 1944 Act was for the E.N.E.F., as for many people, as much a proposal about the social and economic order as it was about education. The E.N.E.F. had strength from the maintained schools in its membership in 1943, and the independent progressive schools, although they continued to advertise in and give a special flavour to *The New Era*, were less dominant in the Fellowship's discussions.

After the end of the war international conferences were quickly resumed, national sections revived, and a great number of monographs and booklets produced, ranging from summaries of new plans in a variety of countries to guidance on children's communities, fatherless children, psychological services, play, and mental health. Before the war there had been ten or twelve journals in various languages and of these *The New Era* and the American *Progressive Education* continued; *Pour L'Ère Nouvelle*, which had lapsed, was now revived. It is not possible here to speak in detail of the growth of sections picking up the threads again. Political factors were sharper, secular–religious cleavages were deeper, individualist–collectivist dichotomies harsher, with time and opinion more on the egalitarian and collectivist side of the argument. And so it has tended to remain.

By 1955 it had become clear that the pre-war pattern of what might be called the main theme conference addressed by celebrities and accompanied by sessions on sectional specialisms was no longer appropriate. An innovation tried at Chichester in 1951 provided each delegate with time to be spent in one or another of the arts, learning both with others and in a personal way. It proved successful and exciting and came to be a common feature of many succeeding N.E.F. conferences, adopting with adults what had been since the start in 1921 an article of faith in the Fellowship concerning the education of children – that arts like painting, pottery, drama, and music contributed uniquely to the personality and its development.[9]

Once or twice conferences have been arranged since the Utrecht conference of 1956 calling upon the techniques of group dynamics, with lectures on educational topics followed by permissive and wide-ranging small group seminars guided by well-briefed and non-directive chairmen. Such innovations, for example in 1966 at Chichester reiterate the Fellowship's concern for psychological and personal factors and the advantages in self-realization which these are expected to bring to persons both in their own life and in their professional skill and sensitivity.

It might be thought that UNESCO would displace and ultimately destroy the N.E.F., but this has not so far happened, and for some good reasons. Although the N.E.F. has a very loose organization, what there is rests on two complementary principles. Nationally, members of the Fellowship provide a body of opinion and a pressure group dealing first with home problems. Internationally, there is a small permanent secretariat and a large board of consultants who deal with broad policy throughout the world. Because money is always tight, the expectation of financial backing is small and the voluntary participation has to be high. This makes the organization much more varied and more durable, if more liable to breakdown in places. UNESCO can provide money for experts to identify problems and try to deal with them. The national sections and the N.E.F. itself are able to provide valuable information and sometimes the organization through which inquiries may be conducted. Besides, the N.E.F. is a voluntary body with the *esprit de corps* that can go with it, while UNESCO is the mammoth which has to learn to work with those who have lived in the forest for a long time. Correspondingly, the N.E.F. can find the official existence of an enlightened purpose reassuring:

> The purpose of the Organization is to contribute to peace

[9] See Boyd and Rawson, *The Story of the New Education*, ch. x, pp. 166–76.

and security by promoting collaboration among the nations through education, science, and culture, in order to further universal respect for justice, for the rule of law and for the human rights and fundamental freedoms which are affirmed for the peoples of the world ... by the Charter of the United Nations.[10]

Since 1947 the N.E.F. has taken part, in some way or another, in many UNESCO projects, too many to list in detail, but important enough to illustrate by example. First of all factual inquiries, like surveying textbooks; collecting data with bodies like the World Health Organization, the International Labour Office, and the Food and Agriculture Organization on national health statistics, diet, and physical education; bringing together facts for a yearbook in education. Besides the factual inquiries there were early projects on fundamental education, on methods of teaching international understanding. Later the N.E.F. took part in what was called the Tensions Projects, which sought to discover deeper causes of human conflict, the nature of prejudice and stereotyped thinking. The full scale of this very difficult inquiry brought in universities and other bodies, but the N.E.F. tried to understand especially the problems and techniques of attitude change, and about this time began to employ the methods of group dynamics at its conferences, at first with limited success. Other examples of N.E.F. enterprises which were linked to UNESCO were the inquiry into methods of teaching the background to human rights in different countries; or preparing the working papers for a conference on education and the mental health of children in Europe; or the unusual and valuable conference on the role of the inspector in a variety of school systems; or the pilot project in the early 1960s on the relationships between adults and adolescents.

The N.E.F. has had the advantage of some financial support from UNESCO for these and other projects, yet a few of the reports can scarcely be considered as highly successful. However, the Fellowship's undeviating attention to international understanding, to the role of the school and the teacher and the pupil in building a positive world outlook and teaching a

[10] From the *UNESCO Declaration*.

balanced conception of history, has developed alongside a concern for the psychological factors in aggression and fear. Boyd made this point in the unpublished manuscript which he made available to me shortly before his death in 1962:

> The child-centred education of 1921 has been supplemented by the culture-centred education of 1955: the basic idea of freedom was still to the fore but with a greater stress on self-control. The over-emphasis on conscious mentality had been modified by the discoveries of the analytic psychologies and corrected in practice through free creative expression.

Harold Rugg, a leading American participant, said in Germany in 1955 at a conference of the pioneers of the N.E.F. that a much sounder theory of education was now available than in the early days of the movement. This was based on a clearer understanding of the kind of civilization to be striven for; a more comprehensive theory of behaviour based on biology, psychology, and sociology; a grasp of aesthetics as it is related to self-expression; an acceptance of the nature and importance of religious experience. He might also have added a new realism about politics and economics. A more recent example, chosen from many, of the contemporary emphasis is in *Look Out*, written in 1965 and subtitled 'A Contribution to World Studies', by Dr. J. L. Henderson, one of the honorary advisers to the N.E.F.

III

The progressive schools of the first quarter of this century provided many persons who gave the N.E.F. its start. Its early history in the 1920s is very like that of many of the schools we have considered earlier. Some of the leaders were pacifists: Kees Boeke of Holland, for instance, Paul Geheeb and Elizabeth Rotten of Germany and Switzerland; others were socialists or communists. Besides the educators there were psychologists who provided theoretical argument and clinical evidence, and the interpretations of Freud, Jung, Adler, and Rank were well known to members of the N.E.F.

The periodicals and the conferences were concerned with

teaching method and the whole texture of life in a school community. It would probably be fair to say that the progressive schools in England and other countries made the sharpest impact in N.E.F. affairs in the 1920s. The emphasis on the child and his development was accompanied by the belief that he would develop best in a specially prepared community, often co-educational and often residential and usually small. As Boyd put it: 'On this conception of education, the essential thing was not the subjects nor the methods of learning, but right relations between parent and child, and between teacher and pupil.'[11]

For the next decade until 1939 there was a growing tension in the movement between those who continued to want free school communities as an example which might influence more and more people and those who wanted the schools of the innovators to become deliberately aware of conflict and to educate for social reconstruction. From 1933 it became increasingly obvious that Germany was using schools as part of a larger strategy, as Italy and Russia were also doing. Mannheim, Clarke, and others in England made the N.E.F. see how close was the weave in the fabric of society, and that schools were part of it. This affected the movement in two main ways. It began to bring the independent progressive schools more into the public eye as examples not only of freakish behaviour and ideas, but as schools which were trying to think about the part education should play in a world approaching, and later at, war. Secondly, it brought the maintained schools as much into this problem as the independent schools. If most maintained secondary schools in 1939 were not very free in their organization, evacuation and the difficulties of war made it imperative that new and less strictly controlled practices should be adopted and this brought many of them unwillingly, without great experience, and often in conditions of real difficulty, into more permissive ways.

After the war what has often been called democratic planning and the trend to egalitarianism and collectivism have affected the New Education Fellowship as much as any other society. The old days of the spearhead of advance in education

[11] W. Boyd, 'The Basic Faith of the New Education Fellowship', in *Year Book of Education* (1957), pp. 198–9.

being in the progressive school have gone. After 1944 the state became increasingly confident in its assumption that 'privilege' would die and that maintained schools would be able to challenge quality wherever it was found, whether in the public schools or in the progressive schools.

For nearly thirty years N.E.F. principles have influenced the colleges of education and through them a good deal of primary schooling. Now these ideas are beginning to affect the secondary schools, and the influences in this direction come from national and local agencies, through professional associations, and through reports of influential working parties. In England the strongest initiative in curriculum reform is going to come from the Schools Council, the original sponsors of which are the Department of Education and Science and the local education authorities and on which all the leading educational interests, especially the professional associations of teachers, are represented.

The N.E.F. as one of these interests has been active and resilient for nearly fifty years and remains committed to freer ways than yet exist in the majority of England's schools. With new mobilization of power and with influence in education much more starkly related to politics and economics in one direction and to research in another, the future of this permissive organization may be even more difficult, but its vitality and importance to the history of educational innovation in England and in the world cannot be doubted; its confidence can be seen in the fact that in 1966 the New Education Fellowship changed its title to the World Education Fellowship, and when this is being written, in 1971 it continues to seek to initiate research.

20 Three Headmasters: (1) Cecil Reddie and Abbotsholme

ABBOTSHOLME opened its doors in October 1889 and it has continued in unbroken occupation of the same estate ever since, not even being displaced through two world wars. This estate is just within the south-west border of Derbyshire, the river Dove running through it and joining the Churnet not far away. If any one man should be named as the originator of twentieth-century innovation in English education it is Cecil Reddie, the founder of Abbotsholme, but for reasons which will appear he has seldom been given this recognition in England.

I

Cecil Reddie was born on 10 October 1858 in London at Fulham as the sixth child in a family of ten. James Reddie, his father, the son of a Fifeshire landowner, was a Scot who was born near Dunfermline and studied for the Scottish bar at Edinburgh University. He came to England and became a civil servant. Reddie's mother was English, the daughter of a considerable landowner in Norfolk. She died in 1867 after her tenth child had been born, three months before Cecil's ninth birthday. Four years later James Reddie died and the family was scattered into the care of relations. So from the age of twelve and a half Cecil Reddie had no family roots, and throughout the rest of his life we read only of one unmarried sister with any regularity, Miss Florence Reddie. She was at Abbotsholme for many years as a combination of housekeeper and hostess for her brother in a post entitled 'lady superintendent'.

After five years in English schools Cecil was sent by a Scottish uncle as a foundation scholar to Fettes College in

Edinburgh, a boarding-school formed on the English public school pattern in the Scottish academic tradition. He did well there, particularly in classics, mathematics, and science, with creditable performances in German, but he was consistently weak in French. He played rugby for the school's first fifteen in his final year, and in the opinion of Professor J. J. Findlay, who first met Reddie in 1890 and who was for many years the chairman of the school Council at Abbotsholme,

> [Reddie] was shaped for life by his closing years at Fettes. . . . As a Senior Prefect his affections became deeply engaged on behalf of younger boys.[1]

He seemed to want to give them the encouragement and security which he as an orphan at their age had lacked, and Findlay considers that this was at least part of his motivation in a lifework devoted to helping boys of his own class to develop happily and safely through adolescence to young manhood.

Reddie has given an account of his schooling in a paper he read at the Authors' Club in London in 1909[2] which we can compare with Badley's account of his schooling at Rugby. All three of Reddie's schools, Godolphin and Birkenhead in England, and Fettes, in Scotland, were concerned mainly with the classics, and while in two of the three he was taught some English, history, and geography, in none was he taught to speak or write his own language properly. He learned some French and German, some mathematics and natural science, but 'our chief intellectual disciplines were Latin and Greek grammar and composition, with fragments of Greek and Roman history'.[3] They had an hour a week of drawing and two

---

[1] B. M. Ward, *Reddie of Abbotsholme* (London, 1934), introduction by Professor J. J. Findlay, p. 15. A recent assessment of Reddie appears as part ii of Skidelsky, *English Progressive Schools*. The most recent is a doctoral thesis of the University of Nijmegen in Holland by Dr. J. H. G. I. Giesbers. This has been translated into English and is entitled *Cecil Reddie and Abbotsholme* (1970).

[2] 'How Should We Educate Our Directing Classes?': a paper read at the Authors' Club, 5 July 1909. Contained in the records of the Authors' Club and more fully reported in *The Abbotsholmian*, vol. iii, no. 3 (1909) pp. 7–26. This is the school magazine.

[3] *Abbotsholmian*, vol. iii, no. 3, p. 14. Reddie always uses 'we' in his writings where others would use 'I'.

hours a week of singing, which together comprised their aesthetic education. In summer there were twenty-four hours a week of cricket, which for Reddie, with undiscovered astigmatism in both eyes, was, as he called it, purgatory. In winter there were four hours a week of football and cross-country runs, and throughout much of the year swimming. Nevertheless, at the age of fifty, he summed it all up: 'This education was of the best then available. If the program was imperfect, we had plenty of leisure in which to do what we listed and educate ourselves. Best of all, we had lovely scenery, bracing air, magnificent buildings and genial masters.'[4]

He left Fettes when he was nearly twenty, an unusually late age as he admits, and his headmaster said of him:

> He distinguished himself in the classical and mathematical studies of the school and left high in the sixth form. He bore an admirable character in all respects, and though entering fully into the life of the school, was marked by a greater thoughtfulness and spirit of inquiry than is usual with boys at school.[5]

Reddie says he knew nothing about geography or politics or about his own body and mind and lived in a state of massive confusion because of his own inability to co-ordinate what he was being taught in the classroom, the chapel, and the playing fields: 'Education should aim at unity. If it leaves the mind chaotic, it can hardly be commended.'[6] Yet despite this, he said, most boys left their public school full of devotion to their *alma mater*, and in this Reddie included himself, perhaps not surprisingly, for in the introduction to the volume *Abbotsholme* he speaks of the difference between an orphan's view of school and that of boys who could look on it from

> the fixed and secure vantage ground of home: to them school was, at most a second interest. To me, on the contrary, school was home [where I had to] try and find some new object with which to allay the hunger of the heart, increased

---

[4] Ibid.
[5] A testimonial written on 7 March 1888, ten years after Reddie left Fettes, where he had returned to teach 1886–7.
[6] *Abbotsholmian*, vol. iii, no. 3, p. 15.

as it was by a not unnatural idealisation of the scenes and persons which had vanished. [I] had, indeed, as early as I can recall, a bias towards idealising not only the absent but the present ... an olympus of heroes ... objects of reverence and worship.[7]

Reddie admits to periods of bitter disillusion about the age of seventeen with people, and a chaos of principles, ideas, and ideals. By now he was among the most senior boys at Fettes and he found a new enthusiasm for work in 'a friendship with a youngster' whom he wanted to educate. In these disenchanted days this stirs a leaden echo and the reverberations from Homer, Pericles, Plato, and Victorian sex reform are not difficult to hear. Nor are the signs of emotional hunger and intensity in an orphan of high intelligence and principle in a conventional Edinburgh boys' boarding-school where he remained for six years.

II

In 1878, at the age of twenty, Reddie entered the University of Edinburgh, his father's university, as an exhibitioner to undertake the study of medicine, which he had chosen because he hoped it would connect science and human life: at Fettes he had used his free time to do a good deal of experimental work on his own in the laboratories, especially in his last two years. But he reports that he found the aim of the whole training was to cure people when they were ill rather than to keep them healthy, and after a year of satisfactory work as far as his examinations were concerned, Reddie moved from medicine to chemistry. Medicine was 'too material and mechanical to satisfy a nature which was travelling fast towards poetry and metaphysics', and he did not expect a great deal more from the study of natural sciences. He was devouring books in an attempt to gain some understanding of contemporary life, and the university curriculum was incidental: 'Nothing learnt at school seemed to give a clue to the actual life of the city and the big world.'[8]

[7] Reddie, *Abbotsholme* (London, 1900), p. 5.
[8] Ibid., p. 11.

In 1882, when he was nearly twenty-four, Reddie graduated as a bachelor of science, mainly in chemistry but with supporting physics and mathematics. Later he was elected by the Senatus as the Vans Dunlop Scholar in chemistry and chemical pharmacy and given the opportunity to study chemistry for three years in a European university. He chose Göttingen and at the end of his course there in 1884 presented his thesis in German and was awarded the Ph.D. degree *magna cum laude*, the highest degree usually conferred on a foreigner. Undoubtedly a good academic future would have been available to Reddie had he chosen it.

He came to the conclusion very rapidly that the intellectual life and the social order in Germany were incomparably stronger than they were in Britain, and that the quality of the teaching and the level of work done in Göttingen were higher than in Edinburgh, which was better in these things than most universities in Great Britain. 'Every day in Germany one felt the mind expanding and the fog melting away.'[9] In one place Reddie says that, besides his study of science, best of all for him was the chance to study Germany, its people, and its language. This was the resurgent, confident Germany of the 1880s and Reddie's love-affair with its idealized *Zeitgeist*, although shockingly darkened in 1914, lasted through his life.

While in Göttingen, Reddie took the opportunity to attend some university lectures on socialism where, according to him, the facts quoted were largely drawn from British Blue Books; these must have been based on work done by Marx, Engels, and their associates. Reddie already had a high respect for Hyndman, whose work Reddie first met in 1880–1 and who became the best-known interpreter of political Marxism in England.[10] The period 1880–8 was the time during which Reddie was, in Findlay's words, 'a red-hot Socialist'. But it was not Hyndman's Marxism that came to appeal to Reddie when he returned to England in 1884.

[9] Ibid., p. 13.
[10] See *Historical Bases of Socialism* (London, 1883), *Commercial Crises of the Nineteenth Century* (London, 1892), *Economics of Socialism* (London, 1896).

III

There were three men who played an important part in Reddie's life about this time and whom he met in Edinburgh. The first was J. Archibald Campbell of Barbreck in Argyllshire; the second was Patrick Geddes, at first a biochemist, who later became important in the development of sociology in Great Britain; the third was J. Edward Carpenter.

Archibald Campbell aroused Reddie's artistic sensibilities when he was an undergraduate, for Campbell was interested in the visual arts and poetry. He knew Ruskin and was in general accord with Ruskin's social thought, and it was probably through Campbell that Reddie first came across Ruskin's and Carlyle's writing even before he went to Germany. Campbell was also deeply interested in mysticism and seems to have possessed, as some Argyllshire Highlanders are reported to do, psychic powers: it was Campbell who, about 1901, in a trance after one of Reddie's 'great rows' with some of his colleagues, told him what the dismissed masters were like and roughly where they then were, and undoubtedly it was Campbell who started Reddie the scientist on the trail that led to Jakob Böhme, William Blake, Edward Maitland, and Anna Kingsford, the spiritualist borderland, the Theosophical country, and the Eastern religions. These things started in 1880, before Reddie went to Germany in 1882; they were renewed on his return to Edinburgh in 1885, and Reddie shows from his writing at Abbotsholme and from the further meetings with Campbell that the friendship remained.[11] Campbell's name appears in the list of the Advisory Council for Abbotsholme until after the First World War.

Patrick Geddes was the second man who was particularly important at this phase of Reddie's development. Campbell of Barbeck was of the family of Inverary Castle and a relative of the Duke of Argyll; Geddes was the son of a Gaelic-speaking warrant officer from Deeside in Aberdeenshire. The boy had

[11] See *Abbotsholme*, pp. 11 and 13, references in Broadsheets, an early prospectus, confidential documents in the Abbotsholme archives written by Reddie on 'the great rows' and correspondence the author had with the late Dr. G. Lissant Cox, who was a pupil at Abbotsholme from 1892 and who, although he did not meet Campbell, 'heard much about him' from Reddie.

ambitions to be an artist after his schooling at Perth Academy, but they did not mature. He never attended a university as an undergraduate and he was never awarded a degree, but he lived much of his active life in, or connected with, universities. He served T. H. Huxley in London as an apprentice and demonstrator and then was recommended by him to work in Paris and study zoology. Geddes saw Paris in the early 1870s when the reconstruction of France was going on after the shock of defeat. When Geddes returned in 1877 at the age of twenty-three to be senior demonstrator in the zoology department at University College, London, he was already concerned about life-habits, whether of insects or of humans. Frederic Le Play's methods of examining the life of human communities were familiar to Geddes, and he translated the formula *Lieu, Travail, Famille* into the English form which offered a model for investigation to generations of geographers and sociologists: Place, Work, Folk.[12] In 1880 he became senior demonstrator at the University of Edinburgh.

Geddes had become interested in the life and lot of students and began to concern himself with self-governing and self-supporting lodgings for them. By 1892, after his marriage, he had started 'the world's first Sociological Laboratory' in the Outlook Tower in Castlehill. Geddes was also interested in the work of the Fellowship of the New Life, a socialist-utopian society whose importance for the beginnings of Abbotsholme we shall consider later. Many Ruskinians belonged to the Fellowship, and the idea of a wholesome community which emerged in Geddes's building co-operatives and his later work in town and country planning in Great Britain, Cyprus, and India was the expression of the principles of the Fellowship.[13] Reddie says of Geddes: '[His] object appeared to [me] nothing less than the creation of a Synthesis of universal Thought and

---

[12] Geddes widened Le Play's formula from 'family' to 'folk', which enabled him to view towns and cities as living organisms and not only as collections of family units. See S. H. Beaver, 'The Le Play Society and Field Work', in *Geography* (July 1962), p. 230.

[13] Lewis Mumford is probably Geddes's best known disciple. Geddes collaborated with Victor Branford in and after 1902 and when they helped to found the Institute of Sociology in London and to start its periodical *The Sociological Review*. Both Geddes and Branford appear on the list of members of the Advisory Council in Abbotsholme prospectuses for twenty-five years. Geddes accepted a knighthood from a Labour government in 1931.

Action.... [He] aimed mainly at a reorganisation of Knowledge which would enable the human unit to reconstruct society.'[14]

Reddie's re-entry to Scottish society brought him directly under Geddes, in whose laboratory he demonstrated in biological chemistry in 1884–5. Geddes reinforced Reddie's growing understanding of the linkages between the physical and biological sciences, geography, sociology, economics, and politics and his increasing dissatisfaction with what was taught in schools. It was probably as a result of Geddes's influence that Reddie during that year lived in a poor village in the valley of Leith Water below Dean Bridge 'so as to learn how the workers actually existed'.[15]

After a year in Geddes's laboratory Reddie was appointed as a lecturer in chemistry at Fettes, his old school, where he stayed for two years. He spent part of the summer of 1886 visiting schools in Germany and Switzerland, interesting himself in their methods of teaching science and their books on educational theory and practice, for, as he said when he began to teach on his return to Edinburgh in 1884, '[I] entered the scholastic profession without having had an hour's training in it.'

Reddie met Edward Carpenter in Edinburgh in February 1886 when Carpenter lectured on one of his favourite themes, 'private property', and Reddie was captivated by him. Edward Carpenter was born in 1844 at Brighton into a family of established naval connection. He graduated at Cambridge in 1868, took orders a year later, and became a fellow of Trinity Hall. He was for a short while one of J. F. D. Maurice's curates at the University Church before Maurice's death in 1872. By 1874 Carpenter's religious position was so unorthodox that he resigned both his curacy and his fellowship, and until 1881 he lectured in the newly formed University Extension programme in Cambridge, as Reddie did in Edinburgh a few years later. In 1877 Carpenter visited the United States and came to know Walt Whitman, whose writing he greatly admired, as much for its content as for its new style of unfettered dithyrambs which

[14] *Abbotsholme*, p. 14.
[15] From an obituary notice of Edward Carpenter by Reddie in *Everyman*, 11 July 1929.

Carpenter adopted himself for his book *Towards Democracy*. This first appeared in 1883 and he gave an inscribed copy to Reddie at their Edinburgh meeting in February 1886.

In 1881 Carpenter had begun the simple way of living, like Whitman's which he pursued for the rest of his life:

> The two words Freedom and Equality came for the time being to control all my thought and expression. The necessity for space and time to work this out grew so strong in April of this year [1881] I threw up my lecturing employment. Moreover, another necessity had come upon me which demanded the latter step — the necessity, namely for an open-air life and manual work. I could not finally argue with this any more than with the other. I had to give in and obey.[16]

In 1883 he bought a seven-acre small-holding at Millthorpe in Derbyshire, built a house on it, and worked with his labourers to make the holding into a paying proposition as a market garden. He became accustomed to the care of horses and cattle, farm work, and the use of farm tools. Such work became integral to Abbotsholme six years later. Carpenter became the champion of a simple-life socialism, did much street-corner speaking in northern industrial towns, and interested himself in the self-supporting Ruskinian communities at Totley near Sheffield and Norton near Nottingham. He wrote on 1 September 1914 in reply to an address of congratulation for his seventieth birthday:

> I have sometimes been accused of taking to a rather plain and Bohemian kind of life, of associating with manual workers, of speaking at street corners, of growing fruit, making sandals, writing verses, or what not, as at great cost to my own comfort and with some ulterior or artificial purpose — as of reforming the world.... I have done the thing primarily and simply because of the joy I had in doing it, and to please myself. If the world or any part of it should in consequence insist on being reformed, that is not my fault.

---

[16] From a personal note concluding the 1902 edition of *Towards Democracy*.

This was the man whom Reddie first met in Edinburgh in February 1886. In August of the same year he spent some days with him at Millthorpe, Carpenter's Derbyshire house. Reddie left Fettes in the winter of 1886 to take up work as a science master at Clifton, his first and only contact as a master with an English public school. Before he left Scotland, Dr. Potts, the Fettes headmaster, wrote to tell Reddie that he would find 'a well-developed Red element in Bristol'.

After a year of successful teaching, during which he lived not in a poor man's house but in College Gate with six other bachelor masters, Reddie asked Carpenter for advice on his future. Carpenter, who had visited Reddie at Clifton, advised him to leave the school, saying that Reddie had got all he ever would from it and he took Carpenter's advice, the more particularly as Carpenter invited him to Millthorpe to spend time thinking over what to do next. Reddie had just applied unsuccessfully for the headship of a new London day school, St. Dunstan's College, on the suggestion of the Clifton headmaster, the Reverend James Wilson, who wrote in his letter of support:

> He has an unusual degree of originality in educational views, and has to some extent tested them here and elsewhere.
>
> It is by my advice that he is seeking some post where he may have greater freedom for developing his methods than he can have here, where he is not senior in any department and has to work on fixed lines.... [He] would require considerable freedom in the management of detail.[17]

This somewhat equivocal support from Wilson first put the thought into Reddie's head that he might at twenty-nine, with three years of schoolteaching experience, launch out on founding a school of his own to express the educational and social ideas which he discussed with Carpenter so eagerly during the summer of 1888.[18] During the winter of 1888 Reddie lectured for the Scottish Universities Extension Scheme and returned in April 1889 to Millthorpe to work out precise

---

[17] *Abbotsholme*, p. 631.
[18] Ibid., p. 20.

proposals. Edward Carpenter was the man who helped Reddie to discover what his life's work was to be and to begin to make it actual, Carpenter the aristocratic simple-life socialist, who farmed and made sandals, the writer and poet, the admirer of Whitman and the mystical religions of the East, the reformer of heterosexual and homosexual attitudes, the advocate of dress reform, manly love, and comradeship.

Carpenter's name appeared together with Reddie's and two others as one of the founders in the preliminary announcement in the early summer of 1889 of the commencement of Abbotsholme, but he withdrew before the beginning of the school term in October. Although Carpenter is named in 1889 as one of several 'Fellows of Abbotsholme', he is not named as a member of the Advisory Council in 1910 although J. A. Campbell and Patrick Geddes are. In his obituary of Carpenter, Reddie mentions his occasional visits to Abbotsholme up to 1908 but dwells mostly on the period 1888–9, which undoubtedly was the time when Carpenter and Reddie made their deepest impressions on one another:

> It is those six months when I lived close to him that I recall most vividly. I was 29 and he 43. In that quiet valley there was a wonderful peace. Our meals were simple, but marvellously satisfying.... We would go to the little brook at the bottom of his garden for a bathe; but we stripped rather for the sun and airbath.... Edward Carpenter was slightly built, but wiry and very masculine. He believed that mere nudity in sun and air and water was a blessed physician for body, soul, and spirit. He was opposed to excessive intellectuality.... He preferred on the whole to be with handworkers because ... he found talking with them rested his own sensitive brain ... I sometimes, perhaps often, troubled him because of my rather quick brain.
>
> As I look back over all these years, I feel that he was one of the greatest teachers of his time, all the more because he worked quietly and personally with no self-consciousness or desire for publicity and fame.

When Reddie returned to Edinburgh from Germany in 1884 he came into contact with the Fellowship of the New

Life, to which Geddes and Carpenter were attached and probably Campbell too. In 1900 Reddie wrote of Carpenter:

> [He] had developed original but very sane and wholesome views on social questions. If they were tinged, perhaps, with some elements of democratic enthusiasm, they were quite free from anything approaching public theft or violent prescriptions of any kind. They owed their origin, doubtless, to a preformed knowledge of our social chaos, and a powerful sympathy arising from strong affections.[19]

Badley's estimate of Carpenter was almost precisely similar, without the implicit disapproval of democratic enthusiasm. The Fellowship of the New Life was an association for people of such views. Thomas Davidson, the prime mover in founding the Fellowship, was a Scot a few years older than Carpenter. The idea of what could be achieved in and by the life of a community devoted to spiritual values and the workaday needs of living dominated Davidson's thinking. He came to England in 1883 and tried to interest people in setting up a community where everyone could cultivate 'a perfect character'. By the end of 1883 the Fellowship of the New Life had been constituted and the implications were considered of trying to reform society by creating communities which subordinated material to spiritual things. These communities would live simply by the sweat of their brows, would share a liberally conceived religious conviction, and would be committed from the start to providing responsible education.

Some of those who took part in these discussions were very dubious first about the stability of communities of this kind and second about their cathartic effect on mass society in any case. They wanted to form an intellectual pressure group, as Armytage says, rather than a communitarian experiment. So the Fabian Society formed itself and broke away from the Fellowship of the New Life. Bernard Shaw, who joined the Fabian Society in May 1884 soon after it was formed, characterized the communitarian gradualists as 'sitting among the dandelions' and the intellectual gradualists as 'organizing the docks'.[20]

[19] Ibid, p. 14.   [20] Armytage, *Heavens Below*, p. 332.

Reddie had an understanding of both groups but temperamentally he was with Davidson. He wanted 'to help to create a higher type of human being'.[21] When Davidson returned to the United States later in 1884 he said that he had not been in sympathy with the socialist ideology of many members of the English group, as he believed it was only by individual reformation that social and political changes could really be brought about. Such beliefs were shared by Carpenter, Reddie, and Badley. Carpenter's answer was a spiritually based anarchism. Reddie's and Badley's answer was to found schools which were called 'New Schools' and which had an emphasis on community. Before Abbotsholme opened in 1889, *The Sower*, which was the journal of the Fellowship (the title was later changed to *Seed Time*), announced that while the Fellowship itself had not yet had the means to sponsor and open a school based on the principles it had enunciated in 1886,[22] friends and associates were going to establish such a school aiming 'to develop all the faculties of the boy'[23] and to provide a 'new transmissable consecration' which might redeem the ethical and economic confusion of society.[24]

IV

In the second half of 1888 Reddie published a series of articles in a periodical called *Today* under the general title of 'Modern Mis-Education' and in these, while making some approving remarks about the public schools, he developed a fierce critique of their principles and practice. When they speak of industry, he said, all they mean is incitement to compete for academic or athletic success; they have no notion of the virtues of cooperation either for the school or for society which so desperately needs to learn how to develop corporate responsibility. When the public school teaches lessons of restraint it does so by developing a code to which boys conform and not by enabling them to see both the necessity and the satisfaction of social duty and self-control. When the public schools speak of modesty, said Reddie, it is narrowed to false modesty on the one hand and prudishness on the other; they ignore the lusts

[21] *Abbotsholme*, p. 16.
[23] See below, p. 391.
[22] *The Sower* (July 1889).
[24] *Seed Time* (Apr. 1890).

for money, power, and comfort which can corrupt and they ignore modesty as the consequence of genuine humility. Finally, Reddie claimed that when the public schools spoke of purity it became a niggling and debased evasion of their responsibilities for the sexual and moral education of their boys. He wanted schools to help boys to see the debilitations of materialist England on the one hand and on the other to develop a positive morality and an understanding of social responsibility.

This series of articles has in it many of the main themes for Reddie's invective which appear and reappear through his professional life: the lusts for power and wealth, selfishness, prudishness, sexual ignorance, intellectual torpor, contempt for manual work. These state *per contra* what he hoped to find in a school, and each of these themes has less to do with schoolroom practice than with social analysis, with faults outside school which need to be recognized and against which attitudes must be prepared in school. The themes are more in the nature of moral affirmations which could offer a basis for political proposals. They seemed to be in keeping with the radical position of the Fellowship of the New Life, and in 1888 it looked as though the author of 'Mis-Education' was the man to open the New School for the Fellowship. Through Carpenter's good offices two others were drawn into the scheme, and in 1889 Abbotsholme house and estate were found. Reddie had £88 to put into the venture; R. F. Muirhead, an ex-army tutor who was to teach mathematics and be treasurer, put in rather more, and William Cassels, who was a disciple of Ruskin and who was to run the farm, was prepared to put up £2,000. Edward Carpenter lent money free of interest until the estate was bought outright by Reddie in 1894.

Reddie was to be the headmaster of the school and it was he who drew up the details of the prospectus and of the academic planning. Carpenter, Muirhead, and Cassels had hoped that the emphasis on the land and the dignity of labour and Reddie's castigation of the foundation of the public schools would make the New School into an agricultural community for practical socialism, where schoolwork would be related to understanding the economics of living and the equality and brotherhood of man. Instead they found the prospectus stating that Abbotsholme was 'a school for the sons of the Directing Classes' and Reddie thinking in aristocratic terms. He set these down most clearly in a series of lectures which he gave nearly ten years later and which he published in 1901, having delayed the appearance of the book until the South African War was over:

> Our task then is to lay aside the ideas and system which perhaps suited our national childhood and set to work to devise an educational engine suited to our Imperial future.... In particular we need to create a Directing Class. We can create it through sane and wholesome education. We must, however, create also a class trained to obey. And for this I know no better agent than compulsory military service.... It would cure at one stroke our two chief national vices, lack of honourable subordination and lack of unselfish patriotism.[25]

In *John Bull* and other writings Reddie builds up a highly idiosyncratic interpretation of the historical and geographical factors by which Great Britain obtained control of one-fifth of the dry globe during her ascendancy, which she was certainly losing, and which according to Reddie she deserved to lose. Anglo-Celtic civilization was decaying through emigration to the New World, through the exploitation of men and markets after the Industrial Revolution by a new governing class, and through the readiness of our landowning classes to idle and surrender their leadership. The masses, says Reddie, are prepared to do as little as they can and as badly as possible without actually falling into unemployment.

Carpenter and Cassels wanted to build up communities from the bottom and so dissolve class distinction by examples of enriched and unselfish living in self-supporting groups in agricultural surroundings, and Reddie wanted to begin at the top, accepting a hierarchy, and assuming that if the masses had more power they would not know what to do with it. We have to get rid of our 'idiotic idea of democracy', realizing that equality of opportunity is only a half-truth. Democracy needs an aristocracy and without it would perish. By the time

[25] *John Bull: His Origin and Character* (London, 1901), pp. 49 and 53.

Abbotsholme began, Reddie's 'red-hot Socialism' had cooled into something else and we recall his deep respect of Carlyle. In 1894 Reddie, now the sole owner of Abbotsholme estate, wrote: 'If Oxford did her duty, artizans would not want "labour members", nor to substitute for "cultured selfishness" the still worse selfishness of the ignorant.'[26]

V

Reddie was a striking-looking man of immense vitality, just under six feet tall, upright, and military in bearing. Writing of 1900, an Abbotsholmian said:

> During haymaking Dr. Reddie moved with a brisker step, his dark eyes more piercing, his black hair more lustrous, his vivacity more overwhelming, his laughter more compelling, and his whole personality more vivid and dynamic than during the rest of the year.... He was a little terrifying to a small boy and the retreating back was a not unwelcome sight. The retreating back was clothed in a light-grey Norfolk jacket and the muscular legs by which it was borne along in white shorts and neatly fitting grey stockings. The shoes were strong, terribly expensive and beautifully polished.

R. F. Muirhead and William Cassels, as Reddie's partners when Abbotsholme opened in 1889, were prepared to be active workers in the school with Reddie as headmaster. In a few weeks Muirhead and Cassels proposed majority decisions of the triumvirate for school practice and policy and Reddie refused this. He proposed to resign and start up elsewhere, taking the twelve boys whom he had brought to Abbotsholme of the first sixteen who were then there. Muirhead and Cassels decided to resign instead and leave Reddie as sole owner provided he repaid to them their invested capital, which he did in a few years.[27] For thirty-seven years he owned Abbotsholme,

---

[26] *Abbotsholme*, p. 126; from an article comparing conferences at the Universities of Oxford and Edinburgh.

[27] 'We beg to inform you that the partnership between us as proprietors of the New School, Abbotsholme, Rocester, Stafford, was determined (that is,

and it is reported that when he bought the estate 'through the generous assistance of a friend' in 1894, he went out and rolled on the grass for joy.

In 1892 J. H. Badley, who came to the school when it opened, left to marry and to start Bedales. Reddie regarded this as an act of betrayal and in October 1894 he drew up an agreement which each master was requested to sign on appointment. By this Reddie placed his own experience and skill at the disposal of his staff, expecting that they would not use this opportunity and the experimental results which the school was building up for their own private advancement.

> No individual has any legal or moral right to make these results or the methods of obtaining [them] known to outsiders ... nor to allow outsiders, whether visiting the school or not, to get to know these results except as sanctioned expressly by the Head Master in writing.[28]

If a master preferred not to agree to be bound in this way, he was to be regarded as only temporary and would not be permitted to take a full part in the 'advantages which the agreement renders possible'. Reddie wanted to form 'colonies' of Abbotsholme to spread over the whole land the principles and practices peculiar to the school and to provide legitimate promotion chances for capable Abbotsholme-trained masters. He did not want pirate imitators and looked to a federation of like-minded schools resolved to avoid competition and to encourage co-operation.

Bedales was hailed in the *Pall Mall Gazette*[29] as 'an offshoot of Abbotsholme' and Badley was called 'Dr. Reddie's lieutenant' in a later issue.[30] In the course of this interview Badley spoke of the importance of the influence of women in a boys'

---

terminated) on 31 December 1889 and that since that date Dr. Reddie the Head Master has been the sole Proprietor of the School.
> We are,
> Yours faithfully,
> Cecil Reddie
> R. F. Muirhead (Engineering & Maths)
> W. Cassels (Agriculture)'

The letter ending the partnership.
[28] *Abbotsholme*, p. 218.   [29] 22 Aug. 1892.
[30] 5 Oct. 1892.

school and said that he thought the school of the future was probably a mixed day school. Reddie was ferociously opposed to co-education during adolescence; thus although Reddie said he looked for a federation of like-minded schools, the only one which was a brother school was rejected from the start. Many years later, after three or four Abbotsholme masters had left or been dismissed as a consequence of some of 'the great rows' and had gone to Bedales, Reddie wrote an article in *The Abbotsholmian*[31] entitled 'The Relation of Abbotsholme to Bedales' in which the following signally anti-federal sentiments appear:

> Have they not exploited to the full the fact that they originally sprang from Abbotsholme and hoisted our banner ... whenever the connection seemed likely to benefit them?[32]
>
> We have never been intimate with Bedales. Our respective points of view appear to us to be, and to have always been, radically different. It is quite certain we have never adopted anything from Bedales.
>
> We have never been there, never troubled our heads about it, and no-one from there has been invited to visit us....
>
> We wish Mr. Badley a prosperous voyage on his own peculiar course and only beg him to leave us alone and not mislead the public by pretending that he knows anything about our life.[33]

Relationships were much less strained between Reddie and his Continental followers in Germany, Switzerland, France, and elsewhere. But they were farther away, were not Abbotsholme's competitors, and he visited them rarely.

Abbotsholme in the 1890s was an exceedingly stimulating place and many visitors and birds of passage on the staff took away ideas which they did not acknowledge as generously as Badley did. In December 1896, for instance, a book which was well reviewed appeared under the title of *The Foundations of Success: A Plea for a Rational Education*. The author was Stanley de Brath, who was a member of Abbotsholme staff

---

[31] Vol. ii (July 1908), pp. 13–16.
[32] Ibid., p. 14. [33] Ibid., p. 16.

in 1894–5, and in his book, after outlining a number of theoretical approaches to education, he sketched in principles and practices which very closely resembled what Reddie had written and created. But de Brath made no acknowledgement of his indebtedness. Reddie had shattering quarrels with his colleagues in 1900, 1904, and 1906 and he felt that a number of them were vilifying him and Abbotsholme while capitalizing on his ideas in the schools they started, which in no case lasted any length of time.

When all justifiable allowance is made for his feelings that educational plagiarism was being practised all round, there remains Reddie's erratic psychology. He was liable to manic-depressive cycles, recurring paranoia, and an obsessional attention to detail combined with an empyrean of mysticism and symbolism. His violence of temper was known and feared and was matched by his violence of language. Writing in December 1908, he says:

> It seems to us quite clear that the chief impediments to reformed Education are: the stupidity of Parents ... and the treachery of ambitious persons who attach themselves to new movements, like Judas to Jesus ... and who after picking the brains of their Master as well as his pocket, betray him to the Philistines.[34]

There were two 'great rows' in 1900 and 1904. Reddie prepared a fifty-page 'true story of the 1900 episode' which is in the confidential archives at Abbotsholme and which reads at times like something from Strindberg with overtones of Kafka and occasional glimpses of Victorian farce-melodrama and maybe Evelyn Waugh. Dr. Van Eyk, a Dutchman, came to Abbotsholme to teach in 1898 but by 1900 he considered Reddie was 'trying to be like Napoleon and have all your subordinates mere tools'. As a result of the quarrel between Reddie and five of his subordinates, all five were dismissed or left. Van Eyk was dismissed summarily, and characteristically left owing a large sum to the school tailor. In 1901 he set up a new boarding-school on borrowed money within twenty miles

---

[34] From an article, 'Attempts to Wreck Some of the New Schools', in *Abbotsholmian*, vol. iii, no. 1 (Dec. 1908), p. 24.

of Abbotsholme,[35] employing a number of the dismissed staff, but he went bankrupt within a year and fled to France, where he met and married a woman with £300 a year. Van Eyk is admittedly a picaresque figure, but the 1900 quarrels had a seismic effect on Abbotsholme and on Reddie himself. Breakdowns occurred and recurred for the rest of his active life. In 1906, when he went to the United States partly for reasons of health, two of his colleagues wrote to parents alleging that Reddie was 'morally unsuited to be Head'. Some parents came together to examine the charges: Reddie was exonerated from the homosexual innuendoes, and we are told that the two men recanted, but it was nineteen months before he was permitted to return to Abbotsholme. Reddie had his greatest decade in the 1890s and by the turn of the century the school began the decline which only really ended when Reddie retired.

During the First World War the numbers dropped disastrously. This was due partly to the withdrawal of boys who were foreign nationals, partly to the difficulties of staffing in wartime, and partly to Reddie himself. One of his pupils at this time, who became a friend later in Reddie's life, and was with him when he died in 1932, wrote a disturbing account of this war period.

> The war shattered Abbotsholme.... The numbers dropped from 39 in the summer term 1914 to 22 the following term.... The strain of the situation rapidly affected C.R.... His temper was ungovernable. He shouted, stormed and raged. He seldom came into class without a cane. Teaching, what there was of it, was thrown completely to the winds, and instead we suffered tirades against the English, against women and against public schools. Only Germany was extolled, although at that very time German bullets were tearing Old Abbotsholmians to death. His classes became reigns of terror and lay like a lead weight upon the happiness of the boys.... The freedom and gaiety of the school completely disappeared. Instead there was a feeling of oppression and failure.... Each term more boys left. With the school melting away before his eyes, and being powerless to

[35] Imperial School, Hatherton Hall, Cannock, Staffs.

stop it, C.R. was a picture of tragic impotence.... By February 1917 there were only 13 boys.[36]

The man whom Reddie had singled out as his likely successor, Roderick Bemrose, died nearly at the end of the war, and Reddie never really sought for another. There was a temporary resurgence of Abbotsholme's fortunes in the early 1920s as far as numbers went, but looking back, a pupil of that time says that staff problems were constant. He recalls two main types of master, one which wanted to rebuild education on freedom of expression and one which wanted to drown war memories in drink. 'C.R. quarrelled violently with the former and sacked the latter.'[37]

Reddie was prevailed upon to retire in 1927 at the age of sixty-eight, although attempts had been made since 1919 by old boys and friends of the school to bring about the change. They were resolved to save the school despite the impossible old man and their patience and tenacity are a profound tribute to the strength and secret potency of Reddie's magnetism. After negotiating the mine-field of Reddie's resistances, in 1927 they persuaded him to permit Colin Sharp, then reader in English at St. Stephen's College, Delhi, to visit Abbotsholme to study Reddie's methods and ideas with a view to succeeding him. At that time there were two pupils, 'one at first away with a cold'. For ten weeks Colin Sharp lived with Cecil Reddie and listened:

> Nightly he never stopped talking from 6 p.m. to 2 a.m., but when not riding his particular hobbies of ... sex, the inferiority of women and the 'putrid' English character, he talked with humour, decisiveness and a delicacy of sympathy and artistry which provoked a quick and deep affection.... It was a cold January with snow and fog for six weeks, but the only fires in the house were in his study, Miss Gifford's office, the kitchen and the boiler.... The study ... had two armchairs, one with broken springs ... the seat of honour for the listener in his nightly talks.[38]

[36] G. H. Dixon, 'During The War', in *Fifty Years of Abbotsholme 1889–1939*, pp. 37–8.
[37] Geoffrey Peach, 'Post-War Days', ibid., p. 40.
[38] C. H. C. Sharp, 'The Change Over', ibid., p. 44.

Reddie proposed Sharp as his successor in March 1927, and the limited company which took over the school and estate from Reddie was incorporated as Abbotsholme School Ltd. on 20 July 1927 with Reddie as emeritus warden, the only school owned by a company of former pupils.

In 1927 there were two boys. In 1937 there were one hundred and five and in 1969, in substantially similar premises and with the third headmaster after Colin Sharp, who retired in 1949 and died in 1966, there were well over two hundred, the limit of the accommodation at that time. Most notable of all the changes is the move towards co-education for both educational and economic reasons. Abbotsholme admitted girls for the first time in 1969.

VI

When Reddie retired on an annuity in 1927 to Welwyn Garden City he seemed to slough off his past as an educational pioneer and turned to many of the minority interests which he had not fully pursued at Abbotsholme, some of them characteristically idiosyncratic. He read much on the theme of the historicity of Jesus, he played Gregorian melodies on his organ, he joined the Shakespeare Fellowship, which was concerned with establishing the authentic authorship of the works of William Shakespeare. In his years at Abbotsholme he had worked out a new version of writing down musical notation and supported the simplification of spelling and the development of phonetics. He did not use a pen but a kind of quill or reed and this was linked with an interest in print calligraphy and the abolition of capital letters. At Abbotsholme he had also perfected a form of the perpetual calendar and supported the double summer time reform, and these causes he continued to champion. He joined the British Society for the Study of Sex Psychology. He said again and again he was going to write his memoirs but he never managed to start them.

Reddie prided himself on his Scottish or Celtic connection and used language of extravagant ferocity when speaking of England, 'that cesspit and madhouse'. His school in Derbyshire he called a state and said that it was 'half a mile from England'. Germany offered him the pattern of submissive hard work and training and he asserted day in day out that in Germany there was thoroughness, industry, social purpose, and intellectual quality altogether lacking in England. Reddie's maps and diagrams, his furniture design, his Herbartian principles (without, interestingly enough, any trace of Freud or psycho-analysis in his psychological interests), his authoritarianism, his compulsive love of detail were Germanic. His desire to serve as well as dominate his boys and his general temperament were not at all Germanic.

Reddie had not the deep respect for Oxbridge that Badley had by reason of his Rugby and Cambridge background. It was an alien tradition which, with one foot in Edinburgh and the other in Jena, Reddie perpetually trounced. But Abbotsholme could not reasonably expect to survive in England after 1918 on the strength of an idealized German *Zeitgeist*. Reddie's individual conflicts were so great and his range of ideas so intensely personal that he could not take, and certainly did not want to take, realistic sociological stock in England. His assessment was always in terms of moral degeneration and moral renaissance. It was Colin Sharp who with generous patience and insight saw to the heart of Reddie's message and reinterpreted it in such a way that Abbotsholme could survive and prosper in England:

> [Reddie] bristled with inconsistencies. A believer in love, friendship and co-operation as the mainsprings of life, yet impatient, intolerant, even ruthless towards those who opposed him. The creator of the school war memorial 'The Radiant Lover', radiating love from ever inch of his body, yet the man who at one period ordered boys to be publicly flogged. Convinced of the importance of individuality and independence of thought, but an imperious autocrat who sought to crush all resistance to his will both inside and outside the school. A realist who dabbled in the occult and stressed the value of the symbol. Unsentimental to the point of indifference, yet capable of deep and lasting affection for boys, to whom he devoted his life and also for a few specially favoured women. An ascetic who loved flowers, the colour of wine in a wine glass and was never without an abominable cigar.... But whatever his mood he was always the supreme

personality of the place. He created it and it seemed empty without him.[39]

Here we have the inward-looking Reddie, the king of his castle, unable to give to and receive full adult affection from either men or women, proud, orphaned, and didactic. This is not Reddie the socialist who lived in the miner's cottage or who planned for the revolution that would end the injustices of private property. Reddie the opponent of the conventional public school was not greatly sympathetic to, or interested in, popular education and the emerging structure of the local education authorities and the Board of Education in 1902 or the growth of the civic universities. To be sure he had ideas about these things, or some of them, as his evidence to the Bryce Commission clearly shows.[40] But he gave no thought to Abbotsholme in its national educational context.

This man was the progenitor of modern progressive education in this country, the Tory radical, the Platonist who believed in the dignity of labour, the progressive who abhorred co-education for adolescents despite some latter-day qualifications, who slandered England and her public school from 'an educational laboratory' in south-west Derbyshire which during his headship of thirty-eight years only once had more than sixty boys on the roll at the beginning of a term.

[39] G. H. Dixon, 'Cecil Reddie,' ibid., p. 9.
[40] See *Abbotsholme*, pp. 151–92.

21 Three Headmasters: (2) J. H. Badley and Bedales

JOHN HADEN BADLEY was born in Dudley, near Birmingham, in 1865, the youngest in a family of four. His father was a well-respected and comfortably successful doctor who had inherited a prosperous practice from his father.[1] Still earlier generations had been doctors, but more remote ancestors had been Staffordshire farmers and small landowners. Badley remembers his father as a man who spent little time with his children, and whose reserve was somewhat forbidding. At mealtimes and very occasionally at Christmas or some such season they saw him and talked with him: on the occasion that Badley reports his father as going on holiday with the family, he stayed for only two days and 'it was something of a relief when the visit was over'. Recollecting in tranquillity, Badley speaks with affection and respect of the unpretentious goodness of his father in his care of poor patients and his forbearance with his son, who showed no wish to study medicine. When Badley senior died he divided his possessions equally between his four children and J. H. Badley, writing long afterwards, said: 'It was his business ability and the value of the property he left that eventually made possible the building of Bedales.'[2]

Mrs. Badley was a woman of sincere, Evangelical Christian convictions who, in the first ten years in particular of her son's life, gave him and his sisters a secure and reasonable upbringing. The migraines which affected her earlier in life made her into a semi-invalid later, but Badley recalls the contrast between her lively temperament and his father's restraint.

---

[1] Biographical material is based mainly on Badley, *Memories and Reflections*, and on written records provided by Mr. R. A. Wake, H.M.I., who was senior history master at Bedales during the 1950s. In addition the author had a number of conversations with Mr. Badley at Bedales in November 1962 and later. At ninety-seven years of age then, his memory was astonishingly accurate as subsequent checking has revealed.

[2] Badley, *Memories and Reflections*, p. 19.

She introduced the children to painting and sketching, to literature, and to music. Like many families, they acted in charades and made up their own dramatic entertainments, although the theatre for Mrs. Badley was forbidden territory. However, there were family readings of Longfellow, Tennyson, Bunyan, Shakespeare, Dickens, and Scott. All the children were 'great readers' and their father usually gave them well-chosen books as birthday and Christmas presents. On Sundays Mrs. Badley took them to church, but Dr. Badley did not accompany them although he conducted daily family prayers. Writing nearly seventy years later, Badley concluded that his father probably believed in the ethic of Christianity but not in its theology: 'We should now find ourselves much in sympathy.'[3]

As his mother became more of an invalid, nurses and governesses took over the care of the children. John Haden did not go to school until 1878, when he was thirteen years of age. Until that time he was taught the basic skills at home and built up a considerable love for history, literature, and the visual arts, together with the necessary knowledge and accuracy in arithmetic. Rather unexpectedly Dr. Badley and his wife gave their children a sound basis in human and animal physiology, illustrated by the doctor's dissections and instruction from the skeleton. In addition Dr. Badley gave instruction in general science and in astronomy, often choosing his gifts of books in relation to these.

II

After this sheltered childhood young Badley went at the age of thirteen to a preparatory boarding-school, where he had two years which 'were the only period in my life that gives me little or no pleasure to look back upon'. At the age of fifteen he went straight into the upper school at Rugby, and he was head of his house for three years. There were more periods of Greek and Latin in the curriculum than of all the other subjects added together, there was no spoken French, modern history was taught perfunctorily as compared with ancient history, and the science was optional. Art, craft, and music were just

---

[3] Ibid., p. 22.

O

beginning as free time pursuits. Much that Badley experienced at Rugby constricted his interests, and he doubted the wisdom then and later of subjecting average or poor students to the classical routines.

Nevertheless Badley was a good student and did outstandingly well at Rugby. He gained the top leaving exhibition in classics and in 1884 went as a scholar to Trinity College, Cambridge, although the school advised him to go to Oxford. His credentials as a 'swot' at Rugby were therefore unimpeachable, but in addition he gained a football cap as a member of the school rugby fifteen and so he was also a 'swell'. 'For the self-reliant, whether scholarly or athletic, and most of all for those happy few who combined all these qualities, it was a good school, if a hard one.'[4] During his vacations Badley had learned to climb and swim and row and sail. Encouraged by the wise freedom offered by his parents, he travelled round England and the Continent with a tutor and later with his sisters.

Badley read classics for his Tripos and gained a First. He formed the interests in music, the theatre, literature, religion, politics, and travel which were common to an intelligent, enlightened, and comfortably off undergraduate at that time. One of his closest friends was Edmund Garrett, a president of the Union, who interested Badley in politics and social questions generally and whose sister Badley later married. He came to know Roger Fry, Lowes Dickinson, and the writings of Edward Carpenter, whom he afterwards met. In literature Shelley, Tennyson, Browning, Swinburne, Rossetti, Hugo, and Walt Whitman all appealed to him. He once heard Ruskin lecturing at Oxford towards the end of his career there, and although he struck Badley as ranting somewhat, his prose writings on art and social questions greatly impressed the young man. For a while William Morris's poetry engaged Badley's interest, but later it was displaced by his prose writings on socialism and the rediscovery of art and community.

Of his classical training Badley said: 'It was a great experience for its own sake and for the lasting gains that it left ... an experience for which I have always been profoundly thank-

[4] Ibid., p. 48. A full account of his life at Rugby can also be found in his book *A Schoolmaster's Testament* (Oxford, 1937), pp. 12–25.

ful in spite of the cost ... exacted by the classical education of those days.'⁵ It is no surprise, therefore, to find in the first Bedales prospectus:

> We had better give up the idea that Latin is studied at school for the sake of the literature. Not one boy in ten ever reaches at school the point at which it becomes literature to him, or goes on to it afterwards.... For the other nine the main value of Latin is in the process of language-study, and the literary value must be brought to them in readings, stories, translations, plays. This admitted, Latin will hold a much smaller place in school-work [at Bedales] for most boys than hitherto. But it should have a place for all.⁶

Cambridge had greatly changed his outlook upon religion, for instead of the evangelical beliefs of his childhood or the formal Anglicanism of his years at Rugby, 'Henceforward, what I felt to be real and all-important in religion was ... not to be found in the doctrinal framework of the Church.'⁷

The 1892 Bedales prospectus says:

> ... Of religious teaching, if religious teaching means Jewish history, collect-learning, the critical study of a Greek text, or insistence upon certain 'religious' forms, there will be little. If it means all such teaching as may make us understand better and wish and strive more earnestly for what we daily pray for, 'Thy Kingdom come, Thy will be done', there will (it is hoped) be little else.⁸

III

After Badley met Edward Carpenter at Abbotsholme, Carpenter was almost a termly visitor to Bedales for a time, finding what Badley was doing more acceptable than what Reddie was doing:

> Edward Carpenter was at heart an anarchist in the exact meaning of that term, with no connotation of violence.

---

⁵ *Memories and Reflections*, p. 88.   ⁶ (Cambridge, 1892), p. 11.
⁷ *Memories and Reflections*, p. 99.   ⁸ p. 16.

Through him ... I learnt to distrust any system involving more than a minimum of State control to ensure ... freedom, equality of opportunity and treatment and methods of production in which the common benefit should not be subordinated to private profit.[9]

Badley says that, although he consistently voted Labour, he did not join a party 'whose aims in its earlier days seemed limited to furthering a particular class-interest'.[10] Amy Garrett, whom he married in the autumn of 1892, was a champion of women's rights who was later prepared to join the activist wing of the suffragette movement, but her poor health made this impossible. Badley supported his wife in her concern for women's rights, although he did not approve of her becoming a militant. After 1893, when he opened Bedales, he had a public reputation to consider and he maintained that a headmaster aiming at encouraging children to think for themselves should not have a particular political or religious label. Carpenter's community anarchism probably attracted him more as a moral affirmation than as an expression of a well-grounded political and economic theory. Badley decided to make his moral affirmation in terms of a school and so to show what life between persons should or could be like: 'Every school is, consciously or not, an embodiment of social aims, and it was by making Bedales a working model of what a community should be that I thought I could do most to realize mine.'[11]

IV

However, to return to Badley going down from Cambridge in 1888, knowing only that he did not want to be a classics don or a public-school master, feeling intensely moved at leaving the university which had meant so much to him, and without a clear idea of what to do with his life. He says of this period: 'Of all that has been of greatest value in my life – friendships, marriage, an absorbing lifework and the powers and aims that shaped it – there is little that had not its roots in those four years at Cambridge.'[12]

[9] *Memories and Reflections*, p. 306. [10] Ibid., p. 307.
[11] Ibid. [12] Ibid., p. 320.

He spent the winter and spring in Germany developing his knowledge of the language, the literature, and the social and political thought of that country. In the early summer of 1889 his old Cambridge friend Lowes Dickinson wrote to him of a new venture, a school in which he might be interested. Dickinson mentioned that Edward Carpenter was working with others in planning this new venture, and that in itself was an attraction. Badley read the preliminary statements about the school and came hurrying back to consult the new head. He was appointed to teach mainly history and French and later, of course, classics. He was to be given board and lodging and paid 'a living wage', for this was an educational venture supported by impecunious socialists to do unorthodox things. But Badley had his private income and the low pay did not bother him. He spent the summer in France improving his spoken French; and in October 1889 he began to teach in the New School in Derbyshire which at last gave him unwavering assurance of where his career was to be found. Cecil Reddie and Abbotsholme needed a man like Badley to bring boundless energy, academic excellence, and a fresh, critical mind to bear on educational theory and practice. They needed Badley for both the pedigree of Rugby, Cambridge, and classical scholarship, and for his quiet moderation: 'I have an innate distrust of extremes both in ideas and expression of them, which inclines me always to take a middle course.'[13] Equally, Badley needed Reddie and Abbotsholme to launch him on the career that led to his life's work at Bedales: 'Abbotsholme was the most momentous turning point in my life.... But for my marriage I should not have wished to leave the surroundings in which I had first found myself.'[14]

Badley considered Reddie a man of great gifts and originality to whom he owed much, both as a master-craftsman in the classroom and as a daring thinker. In the first Bedales prospectus he acknowledges this:

> The present scheme seeks to embody ideas on which most exponents of the modern scientific view of education are agreed, and to embody these ideas in practical methods suggested by the writer's experience of the New School,

[13] Ibid., p. 318. [14] Ibid., pp. 320–1.

Abbotsholme, at which he has been an Assistant Master from its foundation to the present year, and to which he wishes to acknowledge his deep obligation.[15]

Badley had asked Reddie if he could bring back his wife, whom he proposed to marry in the summer of 1892, to live with him in Abbotsholme, and this Reddie did not want. He had no suitable accommodation and he preferred bachelor masters who could give unstinted service to the school, as he did himself, without the demands made on a man by his wife or by his children. It is probable that by 1892 Badley had gained sufficient confidence and experience to wish to be independent of a despot like Reddie. Badley always maintained that Reddie was right in his educational aims and much of his practice, but wrong in his understanding of the community. For Badley, autocracy in a school, as in a state, stood condemned by its long-term if not also by its short-term results, and he claimed that he had learned from Reddie how to think about and conduct a school and, hardly less, how *not* to.

V

The contrast of temperaments and experience between these two major figures in modern educational radicalism when summed up are striking. Reddie, the sixth of ten children, had lost his mother when he was eight years old and his father when he was twelve, after which the large family had been scattered to relations. He had grown up in a Scottish public school and had a distinguished academic record as a scientist at a Scottish and a German university. After some fumbling he had settled on his career, had been attracted by the same kind of socialism as Badley, had taught briefly in two public schools, and then saw his course clear before him. By dominant energy he brought Abbotsholme into being when he was thirty-one years of age, having very little money of his own, but possessing and publicizing a massive and sometimes comically precise rationale of the theory and practice of education. He remained the owner and head of Abbotsholme, didactic, autocratic, the captain with subordinates. He had a commanding presence

[15] p. 1.

and a strong and attractive personality, apparently confident in all company. He was a bachelor who was courteous to women, but who seldom understood them and later developed some crankish antipathies to them.

Badley was the only son with three elder sisters; and his parents, his sisters, and his wife gave him secure affection throughout, although his mother was a semi-invalid through his late childhood and his father's was not an outgoing temperament. Badley says of himself that he had been plagued by diffidence and shyness and that he inherited his father's intensely reserved nature. We have already commented upon Badley's preference for control and moderation, and one of his earliest pupils gives us a glimpse of this. 'For Mr. Badley I have awe and reverence. To most of the subjects he taught he gave an interest, which, for me, was a kind of suspended excitement; his presence always made me nervous, but often pleasurably so.'[16]

Where Reddie had a fine academic record as a scientist, Badley's distinction was as a classic. Badley remained in politics sympathetic to the left. Reddie, after a decade in contact with the Fellowship of the New Life and the early Fabians, rejected their egalitarian ideas and concentrated on the sons of the directing classes, although he rejected equally the plutocracy. Professor Findlay in his obituary of Reddie said '... for Labour or Liberal politics ... he had no use'.[17]

Badley was comfortably off, although he spent his own money (and more than once supported by the generosity of his sisters) freely on Bedales. Reddie also spent a great deal of his own money on Abbotsholme, but he had no private income to devote to the cause. Each of them was the legal owner of his school, Reddie for thirty-seven years and Badley, later in conjunction with his wife and two sisters, for forty years. Only when Abbotsholme was threatened with extinction in 1927 did Reddie consent to make the school over to a committee of old boys who found a new headmaster, formed a limited company, and saved the school. Badley had resolved to retire in 1935 at the age of seventy; and to prepare for this a limited company, largely made up of Old Bedalians, was formed in

[16] E. L. Grant Watson, 'Pioneers', in *The Old School*, ed. Greene, p. 219.
[17] *Manchester Guardian*, 9 Feb. 1932.

1933 when the school was thriving and had one hundred and fifty pupils.

Badley often asserted that his ideas on the development of Bedales came from the principle of free growth. The first school prospectus suggests, however, that Badley had many clear ideas on what he wanted:

> The first lesson a child must learn is absolute obedience to authority. Then, by calling reason and affection into play, obedience becomes rational and willing, and the learner becomes in some degree a teacher, and can be trusted with a measure of direction. The day must be full of occupation ... but there must also be times without a fixed occupation for individual tastes to assert themselves and for self-development.[18]

Colin Sharp, Reddie's successor, said of him,

> His way was not to state problems and leave them open for the boys' solution, but directly or indirectly to lead the boy to the solution which he himself held and not to tolerate any other.... Opposition made him all the stronger in compelling boys and staff and even parents to conform to the framework of his organization.[19]

This seems to be the universal opinion, together with a general agreement on the magnetism of the man. Badley, in a recorded conversation in 1962, said he thought Reddie was something of a Prussian, and that Abbotsholme was a one-man school in a way that Bedales was not. Abbotsholme found itself associated with an authoritarian and hierarchical political and social ideal, but Bedales aimed at an increasing freedom and equality under Badley; and Alex Devine, the headmaster of Claysmore bore this out when he wrote in 1903:

> The attitude of [Abbotsholme] has always been that of 'the new education'. Its headmaster ... takes his stand on the platform of 'There is but one Education, the new Education, and Reddie is its prophet' ... Badley has a much broader

---

[18] p. 14.
[19] Ward, *Reddie of Abbotsholme*, pp. 309-10.

mind than Reddie can claim, and he has far too sane and comprehensive an outlook to do extravagant things.... I know no school in England so absolutely interesting [as Bedales].[20]

A final point of comparison and contrast between the two men is in their approach to religion. Each was unorthodox in that neither belonged to any branch of the church, though each was Christian in sympathy. Whereas Reddie was interested in symbolism and mysticism, as his appreciation of Blake, Maitland, and the writings of the Eastern religions shows, Badley said, in connection with the Blake studies of his colleague, Joseph Wicksteed, that symbolism, in Blake or elsewhere, had little magic for him.

Yet, when all is said, it was Reddie who focused Badley's ideas, it was Reddie who sparked off the potential in Badley which led to Bedales. It was Badley's more stable temperament and restraint, as well as his originality and determination, that gave Bedales the steady understanding it needed, and it was Reddie's penetrating but imperious cast of mind that created and nearly ruined Abbotsholme.

Reddie regarded the foundation of Bedales in 1893 as an act of betrayal, despite Badley's acknowledgements to him and to Abbotsholme. The two men met only once after that, about thirty years later, at a conference at which they were both speaking, and Badley says that Reddie was then mellow, kind, and courteous. On the occasion of Abbotsholme's fiftieth anniversary in 1939, Badley returned to Abbotsholme and wrote in the jubilee volume:

> ... I can look back as one of those who knew its first beginnings and shared the glad feeling of creative activity under ideal conditions that was to spread so far and open a new era in education.... It was [Reddie's] vision, worked out by one who had something of real genius ... that has made Abbotsholme a model from which so many 'New Schools' of different types have derived their general pattern and their inspiration.[21]

[20] In a letter dated Jan. 1903 to Dr Edward Lyttleton, then head of Haileybury.
[21] *Fifty Years of Abbotsholme 1889–1939*, pp. 56–7.

VI

Although John Haden Badley claimed with justification that throughout his time at Bedales he aimed at continuously increasing the areas of freedom and equality for pupils and staff and that he was not an autocrat, his unofficial title was 'the Chief'. In its practices Bedales contrives to be decentralized, but nevertheless Badley first founded the school and then controlled and ran it for forty-two years of its entire eighty years of existence.

Bedales can point to an extraordinary longevity and stability in a proportion of the teaching staff in the first fifty years. Badley served for over forty years, and his second master Oswald Powell went to the school only a few months after Badley and left in 1933. Basil Gimson taught mathematics and many other things for thirty-three years, Geoffrey Crump taught English for twenty-six years, T. J. Garstang taught mathematics for twenty-five years, Miss Thorp was matron for thirty years, and Mrs. Fish was head of Bedales Junior House at Dunhurst for twenty-two years.

When a man is the first to promote a really lasting co-educational boarding-school in England, when he is regarded from time to time in common gossip as a progenitor of socialism, atheism, unlimited freedom for children, sexual precocity, and the subversion of patriotism, when he is also the owner of the school – when such a man appoints and holds a staff which builds the reputation of the school high in public regard, institutional factors are not enough to account for it all. In 1958 a pupil at Bedales visited Badley when he was ninety-three and her words are a fitting conclusion to this brief sketch of the founder of the school:

> It is hard to realize that this frail but still incredibly active old man ... is entirely responsible for the origin of Bedales. Bedales is not something inevitable in the history of education ... [it] is no longer very revolutionary (because the outside world has caught up with it) but it is still unique.
>
> He is an old man, so old that he seems once more to be young.... The Chief is wearing old, grey flannel trousers,

an open-necked and comfortably crumpled shirt, a tweed jacket and white gym-shoes; by his side is a dark liquorice-brown walking stick which his thin hand grasps firmly. His skin is brown in patches and freckled; his white hair is fine and wispy; a sparse beard decorates with the moth-like touch of an impressionist's brush his mouth and chin. A pair of delicate gold-rimmed spectacles bridges his prominent nose. Superflous flesh has disappeared from his face, leaving the handsome bone-structure visible.[22]

John Haden Badley enabled others to join in building Bedales with him, many of them, as we have seen, going on to membership of other progressive schools, while no one could stay at Abbotsholme with Cecil Reddie for more than a few years.

VII

When Badley retired in 1935 after forty-three years as headmaster, Frederic Alfred Meier was appointed as his successor and remained headmaster until 1946, when he retired at the age of fifty-nine to go to the University of London Institute of Education as a senior lecturer in physical sciences concerned with training teachers of physics. Meier was trained as an engineer, and besides graduating with high distinction at the University of London, served his apprenticeship in 1906-7 in a shipbuilding yard. In 1907 he went on to Cambridge to take mathematics in the first part of his Tripos and natural sciences in the second part, again graduating with distinction. It was in 1910 that his teaching career began, and he served at Glenalmond and Marlborough before going to Badley's old school, Rugby, in 1914. He went to Bedales in 1935 after a career at Rugby as head of the science department which made his name widely known as a teacher of physics.

Badley said that it might appear to be strange to choose a man as headmaster who had no previous experience of a progressive school, and even more odd to choose a public school master who had no personal knowledge of co-education. However, an Old Bedalian had been head of the science department

[22] *Bedales Chronicle*, vol. 42, no. 8 (June 1958), pp. 1-2.

at Rugby before Meier, with whom he worked for some years as a colleague. It was felt by the Bedales governors that the appeal should be spread as widely as possible and that when a good candidate who had no experience of progressive education offered himself he should be asked why he wished to run the possible risk of moving away from the kind of school with which he was familiar and in which he might be expected to rise to the top. In this way the choice was as extended as it could be, and it was seen that Meier well understood what was involved. He and Mrs. Meier served the school well for eleven years.

The same pattern reappeared when Hector Beaumont Jacks was appointed in 1946. Mr. Jacks was an Oxford classic with experience at Wellington College and other public schools and at the junior school of Cheltenham College and another preparatory school. He had no previous direct contact with a progressive or co-educational school. Again the governors looked for the best candidate, satisfying themselves that he understood what he was undertaking and letting Bedales teach him the rest. Mr. Jacks retired in 1962 and his successor, Mr. Timothy Slack, is a Wykehamist who read Modern Greats at Oxford and taught at Repton; but unorthodoxy appears in a period of service at Salem, the German school on which Gordonstoun is modelled, and in another period of work in Burma.

Badley enjoyed his retirement without coming back into school affairs. The confidence and gratitude of the school were such that some years ago, after the death of Mrs. Badley, the Bedales governors provided a flat for Mr. Badley attached to the school sanatorium, where he lived until his death aged one hundred and two early in March 1967, a revered and almost legendary figure whose vast span of experience gave a sense of depth and stability to the first seventy years of the school's existence.

22 Three Headmasters: (3) A. S. Neill and Summerhill

A. S. NEILL had a different start in life from Reddie and Badley and has remained a different kind of influence in progressive education from his first entry. Both the older men had established their reputations as educational radicals by the end of the century and Neill did not start his lifework, for reasons which will appear, until after the end of the First World War. He was twenty-five years younger than Reddie, and he started Summerhill thirty-five years after Abbotsholme, about three years before Reddie's retirement. This third educational innovator comes from a different generation and he has remained for more than forty years true to a set of educational ideas not only much more extreme than Reddie's or Badley's, but more radical than those of any other educator in England at any time.[1]

II

Neill was born near Forfar in the east of Scotland in 1883 in a family of eight surviving children. His father was a village schoolmaster in Kingsmuir on a salary of about £120 a year, and life was very simple and pleasures few. Neill says that the children had no pocket money and on market days they tried to pick up a copper or two by holding farmers' horses. Neill was at this time a poor scholar who could not really bring his mind to bear on classroom tasks, although he enjoyed practical work and mechanical problems. His father cuffed him often because he could not or would not learn, and as the schoolmaster's salary was paid on the basis of 'payment by results',

[1] The account of Neill's life which follows is based on his account 'My Scholastic Life' in the Summerhill periodical *Id*, nos. 2–7, Sept. 1960–Oct. 1961. The author has also drawn on a recorded conversation which he had with Neill (he prefers the plain surname) in October 1962 and on correspondence since then, and on other sources which are acknowledged in the text. A recent account appears as part iii of Skidelsky, *English Progressive Schools*.

his impatience with the only member of his family who did not pass on to Forfar Academy was understandable.

At fourteen years of age Neill started as a clerk in a gas meter factory in Edinburgh, seventy miles from his home, in lodgings and lonely, miserable, and homesick. After pleadings and promise of diligence he returned home to study for the junior grades of the civil service, but he could not keep to his resolve and was sent to work in a Forfar draper's from 8 a.m. to 8 p.m. on week-days and till 10 p.m. on Saturdays. After a period at this job the boy was clearly overtaxed, and his father and mother decided that they had better try to make him a teacher. 'It's about the only thing he's fit for', was his father's comment according to Neill. He started as a pupil-teacher in his father's school and he served the usual period of four years before taking the competitive examination for entry to what was then a normal school and would now be called a college of education. Neill tells us that there were one hundred and four entrants and he came one hundred and third and returned to the ranks of ex-pupil-teachers, as those who failed to enter the normal school were called.

The only way to adequate qualification, as his full-time training at the normal school had been refused, was to study part-time for the Acting Teacher's Certificate while working during the day in school. He says that he had three years in a school in Fife which were, to him, misery, for he did not like his headmaster or his draconian discipline. The village minister taught him Greek and lent him books by the classic authors and poets, and for a variety of reasons Neill developed a burning desire to improve his own education. He had passed the Acting Teacher's Certificate in the third class and found his intellectual ambitions leading him towards the university. By further part-time study he passed the university entrance examination, thereby becoming a fully certificated teacher. After two much happier years in another school, he entered Edinburgh University, starting by studying chemistry and natural philosophy, but changing his course to the honours school of English, working under George Saintsbury and editing the university magazine, although Neill would characteristically reverse the order. He got a Second Class degree in 1912 and declares that he was a conventional young Tory with no convictions about education and no desire to re-enter teaching but rather to become an author. He got a job with an Edinburgh publishing firm and worked as a sub-editor on a one-volume encyclopaedia. Later he transferred to London to write sections on English language and literature and mathematics in another of the firm's publications, *Jack's Self Educator*. In 1913 he was engaged as art editor to a new publication, *The Piccadilly Magazine*, where he enjoyed the whole creative business of producing a new journal. But war broke out, the journal never appeared and the staff was dismissed. At the age of thirty-one Neill returned to Scotland and applied for a post at a school in Gretna Green where he had served as a pupil-teacher. This time he was appointed headmaster and began seriously to think about education.

The boys and girls he was teaching in the village school were mostly destined for farm work or domestic service and the formal curriculum seemed to Neill irrelevant. So began his interest in the kind of thing children ought to be asked to do in school. In the rural setting of the Lowlands, where country conservatism was blended with the Scottish veneration for knowledge and schooling, Neil began to experiment with play methods and says his discipline began to become slack. He sums up the hostility of a number of the parents in the words of one of them: 'I send my laddie to the school to learn, no' to mak' snowmen.'[2]

Neill was and remains a skilled journalist and all the way through his educational life he has written of his experiences in one form or another. He wrote two near-novels about his Scottish experience, the first *A Dominie's Log* and later *A Dominie Dismissed*. The first book is an imagined account of a young graduate teaching in an unorthodox way in a village school, and in *A Dominie Dismissed* the teacher is forced out of his job by dissatisfied parents, seeks to enlist in the army, is found to be unfit and ordered to live an open-air life. The dominie returns as a cattleman to the village where formerly he had been the schoolmaster, witnesses the discomfiture of his successor, a conventional disciplinarian, and finds the friendship and support of the children freely given to him. Finally, he marries Margaret Thomson, a simple, uneducated girl, who

[2] See *Id*, no 2 (Sept. 1960), p. 4.

attended the dominie's evening classes and who is the daughter of the farmer he works for. His fictional account of the Gretna Green freedom is summed up in various parts of the two books, in each of which visitors or natives are tools for the dominie's spate of wisdom and humane speculation and in which the children are natural, shrewd, moving, and impish when given their freedom by the dominie, and lumpish, cowed, and dull when they are with his successor, the well-meaning, efficient disciplinarian Macdonald. The pawky Scots sentimentalism makes these books a plain man's *Émile*, and the didactic destruction of culture, discipline, convention, and timidity make them a *Candide* without style.

After the war Neill produced *A Dominie Abroad* about his school at Hellerau in Austria, and in 1920 *A Dominie in Doubt* appeared, dedicated to Homer Lane, 'whose first lecture convinced me I knew nothing about education'. In the customary expository, humorous, conversational style of the books, the dominie says in *A Dominie in Doubt*:

> As a work on education the *Log* isn't worth a damn.... I say that because when I wrote it I knew nothing about the most important factor in education – the psychology of children ... I was looking at children from a grown-up point of view. I thought of them as they affected me, instead of as they affected themselves.... If your aim is to make boys joiners and girls cooks ... cookery and woodwork ought to be chucked out of schools.... Creation and self-expression are the only things that matter in education. I don't care what a child is doing in the way of creation whether he is making tables, or porridge, or sketches or snowballs.... There is more education in making a snowball than in listening to an hour's lecture on grammar.... Making snowballs is nearer to true education than the spoon-feeding we call education to-day.[3]

To return from this digression on the *Dominie* books to the main biographical line. Even though Neill was not dismissed from Gretna Green, some of the parents were undoubtedly

---

[3] A. S. Neill, *A Dominie in Doubt* (London, 1920), pp. 12–15.

A. S. Neill and Summerhill

hostile to his methods and outlook. In 1915 Neill says that he began to feel guilty about not volunteering for war service and he applied to join the army. As a second lieutenant in the artillery he was posted to Trowbridge, where he instructed gunners in mathematics and did not serve abroad. From Trowbridge, Neill arranged to travel to Cerne Abbas to see Homer Lane and the Little Commonwealth at work, and so began a friendship which Neill acknowledges as one of the most important in his life. Not only did he see a free community at work, he was introduced to psychology by Lane and discovered Freud, and this marks the change between the tone of the first two *Dominie* books and *A Dominie in Doubt* and *A Dominie Abroad*, the two post-war publications.

Before he was demobilized the Little Commonwealth had been closed and Neill's hope of returning to teach there was dashed. By now he was clear that he wanted to devote his energies to educational innovation, and he did not want to return to the restrictions of maintained education or the censoriousness of unsympathetic parents in a village. Neill took up a post at King Alfred School, his first experience of a private progressive school. We have already noted his criticisms of John Russell, the headmaster, who was just reaching the end of his career, 'a kindly, humane soul one could not help loving.' After experience of Homer Lane, Neill found Russell and King Alfred's with its governing committee too constricting, and resigned in 1920 to join Beatrice Ensor as co-editor of *The New Era* at the time of the foundation of the New Education Fellowship:

> I was always critical of this body; to me it seemed too much to sit on the fence, but it had a very difficult task. Its members were of different races and religions and it had to study their feelings, and also it strove, rightly, to make the new education part of the State system. I thought that it gradually became conservative and timid. I attended its international conference at Calais in 1921 and from there went to lecture in Salzburg and thence to stay with friends in Hellerau near Dresden in South-East Germany.[4]

[4] *Id*, no 3 (Oct. 1960), p. 4. For an account of his thinking at the time of the existence of Hellerau, see Neill's *A Dominie Abroad*.

In the aftermath of the war Neill helped Mrs. Ensor to bring refugee children across to Holland and at Hellerau decided to set up an international school in a building which had been built for a Dalcroze establishment. Neill found one section of the building being used as a school for local children, a second as a centre for eurhythmics, and it was the third that the international section was to use. He recalls that he had £400 saved and that this was riches at a time when the value of the mark was desperately low. There were many nationalities in the school and Neill began to put into practice the theories of freedom which he had advocated for so long.

In the evenings the children in his section at Hellerau would dance to gramophone records, while the children under the German staff would be listening to Goethe or Nietzsche (or so Neill reports). While he thought this pitiful, he became very much aware of good music, art, and philosophy, which his cultivated German colleagues took for granted but which had been very little in evidence in Neill's world up to that time. But we shall have more to say later about his attitude to what is loosely called culture.

The political and economic tensions of the early 1920s increased when the French occupied the Ruhr in an attempt to enforce reparation payments, and the United States and Great Britain dissociated themselves from the French policy. In 1923 there was the abortive *putsch* of the National Socialist German Workers Party in Munich and in 1925 shots were fired in the streets of Dresden. In the alarm and chaos which followed, Neill took his small international division to Austria, where they lived in an old monastery up the Sonntagberg mountain in the Tyrol and experienced fierce opposition from the traditional Catholic peasantry, who found the relaxed habits, behaviour, and dress of these youngsters very shocking: 'The Roman Catholic peasants around were the most hateful people I had met; grown up men and women threw broken bottles into the pond we bathed in. To them we were pagan and unwelcome foreigners.'[5]

The Austrian education authorities said that every school had to teach religion and this Neill was determined not to do. The law was difficult also in a number of other ways, and so

[5] *Id*, no. 3, p. 5.

after seven months in Sonntagberg Neill and his wife (he had married an Australian in Dresden) decided to return to England and to continue their freedom school there. Neill became very clearly aware of the direction his educational ideas had to take and his German experience helped him to sharpen the edges of his own position. In general, he concludes, Germans were thinking in terms of conscious abilities of children and teaching them in terms of adult knowledge of what children ought to know and how they ought to behave. Neill says that he wanted to think of the unconscious, the id, and while this position has changed a little over the years, substantially he maintains that viewpoint. Besides the music and the art he had learned about and enjoyed in Germany and Austria, he recollects that most importantly of all he returned to England a convinced internationalist for ever. 'One cannot run an international school and have any trace of racialism and insularity.'[6]

In 1924 the dominie whose first venture out of Britain had been these four years in Europe returned to Lyme Regis, where at short notice he was able to find a house in which he could start with five pupils brought from Austria, three of them on reduced fees and two of them on none. 'Summerhill' was the name given to the house after Mrs. Neill's family house in Australia, and this name was taken to Leiston in Suffolk in 1927, when the present house was bought and the most widely known school of the extreme progressive group came to the location with which it has been associated for forty years. Only at the age of thirty-five, deeply influenced by psycho-analysis, did Neill start at King Alfred's on the path of independent innovation in school, and it was not until he was forty-one that he launched Summerhill.

III

There are as few restrictions as possible on freedom of choice at Summerhill:

> Before the war we had certain out-of-bounds rules made by the staff. Pupils were forbidden to use the front stairs

[6] Ibid.

and the staff lavatory; the round lawn at the front door was out of bounds. The staff room was free from invasion. Gradually these ... have disappeared. Gradually the staff-room furniture goes the dilapidated way of the pupils' sitting room furniture.[7]

As Summerhill has always been badly off, the buildings and equipment have not been lavish, and the treatment they get is evidence of the irresponsibility and destructiveness of children for whom Neill thinks freedom is more important than orderliness or submission.

There are other, more lasting safety-prohibitions: children are not permitted to bathe unless there is a life-saver present for every six others; children under eleven are only allowed to cycle in the street if accompanied by an older person; no airguns are allowed, and no climbing on roofs. Alcohol is forbidden and smoking is actively discouraged.

Moral judgements on children's behaviour are not passed, and discipline is in the hands of the General School Meeting. No religious instruction is given; bad language is not encouraged but is permitted as normal, particularly in newcomers to Summerhill. Children in this co-educational school are expected to accept sexuality as a normal, liberating experience and to anticipate that in the conventional day-to-day world this open-mindedness will not necessarily be shared or understood.

Children have been known to attend no classes for terms, occasionally for years, and no one urges them to do so for they are not ready to respond, or so Neill's interpretation would run. His faith is based on the child's capability for self-direction and on the school as a community in which the tolerance and confidence are available to make this possible. If freedom of this kind, which allows a child to be primitive without censure for as long as he feels he needs to be, is offered it makes possible an education of the feelings which is more fundamental to Neill than an education of the intellect, which can follow. This conception of education as therapy by freedom is profoundly different from most other interpretations we have so far met, though closer to what is done at Dartington

[7] *Id*, no. 7 (Oct. 1961), p. 2.

than to what is done at Gordonstoun. Erich Fromm, in an introduction to the latest symposium from Neill's writings, summarizes Neill's educational principles roughly as follows: [8]

1. Neill maintains a faith in 'the goodness of the child' with full potentialities to love life and be interested in it.
2. The aim of education, as for life, is to work joyfully and to find happiness.
3. Intellectual education is not enough and emotions and feelings are in educational territory.[9]
4. Education should be attuned to the psychic needs and capacities of children and this means accepting their aggression and self-centredness and not expecting maturity and altruism too early. Only so will children build up sincere values and attitudes and avoid hypocrisy.
5. Fear creates hostility, and discipline and punishment create fear. The adult exercising authority and enforcing discipline will distance himself from children.
6. Any respect between teacher and child must be mutual. If a teacher does not use force against a child, the child must learn that he has no right to do violence to the teacher and intrude upon the adult and expect to be attended to just because he is a child. Compassion and sympathy are all very well in Neill's psychological world, but they have to be realistic and two-way, and this is his interpretation of the cliché that freedom does not mean licence.
7. Neill says that in forty years he has never lied to a child, and even if one rephrases this to say that Neill never steps back from telling the truth as he sees it, the claim demands searchingly steady integrity.
8. This sort of education assumes that persons have ultimately to accept their aloneness, their independence and their personal responsibility. To do this the primary ties with father and mother or later social substitutes must eventually be cut. One finds security in accepting the world

---

[8] A. S. Neill, *Summerhill: A Radical Approach to Education* (London, 1962), pp. xii–xv. See also L. R. Perry (ed.), *Bertrand Russell, A. S. Neill, Homer Lane, W. H. Kilpatrick* (London, 1967), *passim*.

[9] While this theme recurs through Neill's writings *passim*, it has a book to itself, *Hearts not Heads in the School* (London, 1945).

intellectually, emotionally, and artistically to the realistic limit of one's abilities.

9. If this is the ultimate assumption, feelings of guilt are an impediment, for the primary function of guilt is to bind children to some form of authority. Fromm claims that in our society guilt is not usually a response to the voice of conscience but far more often an awareness of disobedience to authority and fear of reprisal, whether that reprisal is physical punishment, withdrawal of love, or social ostracism.

10. Summerhill is concerned with basic humanistic values, and Neill has made his opposition quite clear to the Christianity of the churches as he paraphrases it in terms of sin, guilt, repression, and hypocrisy.

Summerhill is intended to be, in the true sense of the terms, an anarchic community in which children may grow up. In that we depend upon one another for survival, Summerhill is part of Leiston, whose tradesmen supply it; of a cash-based society, in that it is kept going by fees from parents who earn a living; and of a nation with a school system which Neill ceaselessly attacks. In most other senses Summerhill opposes the society in which it is set and the values on which it is based and calls itself a freedom school:

> If I tried to reform society *by action* society would kill me as a public danger. If, for example, I tried to form a society in which adolescents would be free to have their own natural love life, I should be ruined if not imprisoned as an immoral seducer of youth. Hating compromise as I do, I have to compromise here, realizing that *my primary job is not the reformation of society, but the bringing of happiness to some few children.*[10]

This school is a form of utopian community similar to the ideal communities which have appeared from time to time in our history, particularly in the nineteenth century.[11] It has a life and purposes of its own but it has the intention to point

---

[10] *Summerhill*, p. 23: italics in the last lines the author's.
[11] See Armytage, *Heavens Below*.

the way to society on how to rear its children and on the values in human relationships on which the life and organization of that society should be based. Summerhill has few sociological pretensions, no sense of the co-existence of institutions, it makes no concessions to history, and has no strategy of continuity; nor does it know how to effect change. It grounds its case on persons and abhors organization in so far as that requires control, foresight, regulation, absence of freedom. Some consequences and by-products of this are that Neill regards the use of force and war as atavism, the power struggles of politics as dirty and evil, the control by the patriarchal society as the castration of the young. When he claims that he refuses to mould character he means that he tries to give the maximum opportunity to his pupils to grow up in a children's society where adults are available but not setting the standards. Summerhillians are obviously bound to be influenced by the presence and ideas of Neill and his colleagues and by the behaviour of the other children and the inevitable dilapidation of the amenities and equipment.

The emphasis on happiness, on the psycho-analytic interpretation of personality development, and the freedom principle leads Fromm to admit to two reservations. The first is that Neill 'underestimates the importance, the pleasure and the authenticity of an intellectual in favour of an artistic and emotional grasp of the world'.[12] The second is that Neill 'overestimates the significance of sex as Freudians tend to do'. Each of these reservations indicates the distance between Summerhill and the intellectual and moral traditions in education. All the progressive schools speak of a concern for the whole personality and an unwillingness to force the intellectual pace, while increasingly coming to terms with examination requirements that lead on to further and higher education or qualify for a career. Summerhill gives no undertaking to prepare anyone for an examination and does not regard this route as a specially commendable one:

[Some parents say], 'If my son cannot read at twelve, what chance has he of success in life? If he cannot pass college entrance exams. at eighteen, what is there for him but an un-

[12] Ibid., p. xv.

skilled job?' But ... I never doubt that in the end, if not molested or damaged, he will succeed in life.

Of course, the philistine can say, 'Humph, so you call a lorry driver a success in life!' My own criterion of success is the ability to work joyfully and to live positively.[13]

For Neill what a pupil learns should be what he wants to learn and Neill has no prescription to offer on basic general education. Besides anything else, he does not present a case logically with arguments, but didactically with anecdotes from which the reader is expected to make generalizations. This matter of basic education is a case in point:

> It is an absurd curriculum that makes a prospective dressmaker study quadratic equations or Boyle's Law....
> Creators learn what they want to learn in order to have the tools that their originality and genius demand. We do not know how much creation is killed in the classroom with its emphasis on learning....
> It is taken for granted that every child should learn mathematics, history, geography, some science, a little art, and certainly literature.... The average young child is not much interested in any of these subjects....
> Parents are slow in realizing how unimportant the learning side of school is. Children, like adults, learn what they want to learn.... Only pedants claim that learning from books is education.[14]

Neill claims that he is not decrying learning but wanting it to follow play. If a child, however, chooses all play and no work, Neill is not prepared to say that this makes him a dull boy. This is what the child wants to do and until his spontaneous motivation changes this is what he should do. Summerhill does not consider knowledge in terms of content, coherence, range, or scholarship. It does not consider learning in terms of habit formation or stimulus-response or association, only in terms of feeling-readiness or of acceptance–rejection. The quality, type, or range of what is accepted or rejected and how it is presented do not often enter into Neill's discussions.

[13] Ibid., p. 29.   [14] Ibid., pp. 24–7.

He says that this is the part of the child that is above the neck, not the emotional, vital part. It also brings up the old question of criteria and evaluation, and this Neill does not answer, saying instead: 'Let the child be himself. Don't force him to do anything.' However, he cannot be himself except in living with others in some kind of culture, influenced by it, forming habits, and making choices. Neill sees this and says that where children are allowed to play for as long as they want or need to, there should ideally be workshops, gymnasia, libraries, playing fields, good teaching to balance the endless repetition of jazz records. He goes on to say wistfully that his library has always been poor, consisting mainly of parents' cast-offs, his playing fields bad, his teachers underpaid and often wrong for the job, working out their own problems and constantly changing. Had he been rich enough he might have had two schools, one with a full range of fine and beautiful things and the other, some distance away, for those who had much hate and antagonism to work out. Most of the time Neill writes as if the fine and beautiful things are not the vital things, because his experience shows that if you give freedom it leads to destruction and the fine things will be spoiled and broken and all will come to dilapidation. Here is a dilemma, and Neill cannot deny that he is opposed to high culture if that requires control and discipline.

Neill may be prepared to admit that high culture has created fine things through dedicated effort of head, hand, and heart, but he is Calvinist enough to say that man is born into social evil, although he has through freedom, Freud, and Reich the chance of salvation. This is not far from Rousseau, although Neill says he does not know enough about Rousseau to be a disciple. Children need to grow in their own way, at their own speed, he says, so that they can enjoy the products of high culture with sincerity if they want to, and will not be looked down on if they do not.

Neill writes out of practical experience, not out of theory. Summerhill started with what Neill calls the problem era when he could not get enough ordinary pupils to make the place pay and took in all kinds of problem children – 'destructive, thieving, hateful brats'. At this time he thought psychology could work miracles and he took in cases of birth injury, the mentally ill, the educationally subnormal, and the strain on the total community was too great. Hence, writing of Summerhill, he has never been able to say how his principles would work with a school of predominantly average children, mentally and socially. His conclusion is, however, that if freedom can succeed to the extent it has with the range of problem children he has had, how much more will it succeed with those who are quicker to benefit and less deeply disturbed.

IV

Neill's lifework has lain in lonely territory. Summerhill is not 'recognized as efficient' by the Department of Education and Science and reports of Her Majesty's Inspectors in 1949 (quoted in full, with Neill's comments, in *Summerhill*) and 1959 indicate that, on the whole, standards of building and equipment, staffing, teaching success, continuity, and learning achievement did not reach a level satisfactory to the visitors.

The School Meeting arises out of Summerhill life and is different from the Moot at Dartington or School Councils in other schools as we have met them in earlier pages. First of all the numbers of children and staff in the school are small enough for everyone to attend it if they wish, and it deals by vote with all social matters. Neill says that the vote of a six-year-old carries as much weight as his own and he gives instances of occasions when he strongly advocated a case which was defeated: forbidding smoking to those under sixteen, suggesting penalties for those who stayed out of bed late, banning indoor football played in a room near to Neill's own which disturbed him when he was working. Some basic matters of school policy and arrangements are not discussed by the School Meeting – bedroom arrangements, payment of school bills, appointment and dismissal of teachers. But the regulation of bullying, of cases of stealing, of inconsiderate behaviour, and so on, come under the care of the School Meeting.

The records of meetings are completely inadequate and precedent is referred to little because any plea can be brought up again and again. 'Laws' are few and kept until changed, 'regulations' are too many to be remembered by all, especially as there are no records of them; *ad hoc* decisions are most frequent and most open to perpetual reconsideration.

Meetings can get disorganized and noisy, and it is not easy to keep to the point. There is monotonously frequent discussion of behaviour at bed-time and keeping of bed-times, of bad behaviour in the dining-room, of taking and interfering with private property, of damage to possessions. The School Meeting is a weekly reminder that the cost paid if there is not even a loose structure of precedent is perpetual repetition, but this, says Neill, is not repetition for the children involved. Talking shows what the community really wants and the children do not want to be against the sense of the meeting; but clearly there are times when the decisions are by no means clear-cut and even if they are some children are not prepared to accept them, and here the resources of reasonable persuasion in the community are sorely taxed.

The position of the adults at Summerhill often causes difficulty for members of the staff, both those who succeed and those who fail. Accommodation is in keeping with the comment in one report: 'living conditions both in the house and in the huts have an austerity usually associated with extreme asceticism ... the main impression is drab, Spartan, and comfortless'. Salary to all staff was for a while at the rate of £20 a month, net income, for the school pays any income tax and national insurance and provides free accommodation throughout the year, vacations included. However, £240 a year with an extra dividend declared in favourable times, in these days of the Burnham scale with a variety of allowances and increments, was so low that only the rich, the devoted, the bird of passage, or the desperate would accept it, and Neill has had them all as colleagues at different times. The pay is now rather higher, but still low by national standards. At Summerhill it is not possible to limit teaching to the areas in which the staff are professionally qualified. A graduate who combines sciences and arts in his degree has taught at different times biology, history, geography (which he had not previously studied), mathematics, general science, and a little Latin. Leaving aside Neill's convictions that schools should be concerned with hearts not heads (significantly, not hearts *and* heads), it is impossible that teachers faced with this variety of demand upon them, as well as the wide age and ability range, could offer the quality of teaching that would attract children consistently. When the children can take it or leave it, it is not surprising that the intellectual achievements are low. Summerhill cannot really offer teaching beyond O level, and Neill says: 'Books are the least important apparatus in a school. All that any child needs is the three R's; the rest should be tools and clay and sports and theatre and freedom.'[15]

This has led some teachers to say that while they got used to becoming subservient to the children and to being out of touch with adult things, they thought that children were being deprived of challenges and intellectual pleasures and were the victims of a misguided philosophy. Readers of *Id* will note that almost every article is about the Summerhill freedom in one form or another. There is nothing about national problems of education, no continuing assessment of how Summerhill methods may or may not have permeated to primary schools, no real discussion of teaching methods, no recognition that there is a crisis in the national supply of teachers. Usually the theme is the creative, courageous minority, the radical right-minded few, and this view, of course, needs to be defended and reaffirmed. However, convincing evidence for particular conclusions is difficult to come by because records have not been kept, neither records of individual pupils nor the customary statistics. The memories of Neill, his wife, and his senior colleagues represent the school archives, and it is virtually impossible to provide a cumulative record of, for instance, the number of children of foreign nationality at Summerhill over the last five years or the number of O level passes since 1960, or the occupational background of the parents of all children since the end of the war. The records are not there because there is no money to pay for a regular school secretary and in any case Neill does not think that kind of record is of any real use. While this may be a rationalization, it is also part of his belief that these data are trivial compared with the chronic, profound, important aspects of a person. While there has been a move recently to keep reports on children, in Neill's mind no worth-while report can be kept, or else it ought to be a considered statement with perspective and therefore so lengthy as to be impracticable. Yet proper

[15] *Summerhill*, p. 25.

research comparing Summerhill performances with those of other schools in a whole range of activities cannot be undertaken until reliable data are available. At present only anecdotes can be obtained, or biased samples where it is difficult to get total figures for the whole group, or statements about the life of the school such as some of those mentioned in this chapter, for and against.[16]

It would be exceptionally difficult to get evidence on which to try to assess the effect and effectiveness of a Summerhill education, and even more difficult to compare it meaningfully with what is achieved in other kinds of schools. As an example, Neill claims, with instances, that a fair proportion of Summerhillians achieve intellectual or professional distinction and that this in large part is due to the chance to play, to be free, without intellectual compulsion in their Summerhill days. For this to be more than a hunch it would be necessary to examine the length of time spent at Summerhill, the age of entry to more ordinary competitive life in school, college, or university, and the proportion of effect of the more orthodox training on the ultimate performance. Equally, comparisons would have to be made with performers of comparable distinction who did not go to Summerhill at any stage. Obviously, social-class background comes into this and the whole undertaking is very complex indeed. But it is now beginning to become possible, as techniques of measurement, assessment, and comparison are more sensitive than even a few years ago. Only in this way can Neill's hunches and claims be substantiated in the disinterested fashion of research. Although he does not think research tools could do justice to the truth of assumptions about freedom and self-regulation, the strategy of trying to show how far his ideas are right will have to lie in this direction.

Neill has said from time to time that he resents and regrets that for the most part only well-to-do parents can send their children to Summerhill. He would like to take boys and girls from homes lying across the class structure, and by cutting

[16] A recent attempt at evaluation is E. Bernstein, 'Summerhill after 50 years; the first follow-up', *The New Era*, vol. 48, no. 2 (1967). The difficulties of sampling and interpreting results are admitted, but the author concludes that Summerhillians on the whole 'adapt successfully to society' and are well able to understand the need for authority, while being critical of it.

costs to the bone and accepting a few children supported by local authorities he has some variety in parental background. For the most part, however, it is the liberal intelligentsia who send their children to Summerhill, both from this country and abroad. A recent group of children among the sixty who were pupils at that time at the school had fathers and mothers who were between them a psychiatrist, a fabric designer, an engineer, an actress, a dramatherapist, an architect, a surgeon, a university lecturer, a jewellery designer, a businessman, a journalist, and a publisher. The Department of Education and Science will not recognize Summerhill as efficient, but they do not try to close the school. Local authorities take up a few places, but very few. Neill's royalties help to keep Summerhill afloat, and the appearance a few years ago of *Summerhill* in America led to an influx of American children and visits from prospectors who planned the American equivalent of the English school. Scandinavia has recognized Neill, so has Japan, and his ideas are known widely in the world. He has recently been awarded honorary degrees by British universities. Yet his school is not widely copied, and his lists of applicants are not solid or reassuring, certainly not with working-class applicants.

V

Neill combines the strong feeling, directness, and dogmatism that characterize many Scots with the moral determination and devotion to purpose that owe more to Calvin than to Freud. He has no party political affiliations and never has had, the nearest being a long membership of the Progressive League, of which he is a former president. The League is a politically independent organization which holds that political and economic problems must be viewed in relation to cultural, sociological, and psychological factors. Its aims include the initiative of action on particular issues and the promotion of co-operation between progressive organizations. He is the most radical of the educational innovators because he is the most radical critic of our society. It is difficult to draw up an ordered statement of the kind of world Neill wants to see or of the steps by which we move from where we are to the transformed social life of the future. Like any religious man, he believes that men need to renew a right spirit within them. But that spirit is to be an affirmation of love which, to use one of his favourite phrases, says yes to life. His notion of love has most of St. Paul's magnificent catalogue of qualities, but with the addition of a special tribute to the pleasures and the rightness of sex. Happiness is a word Neill often uses, and this appears to be difficult to attain in terms of respect for the law, restraint, the clarification of right and wrong, self-denial. Realization of the self is not discussed by Neill in these aspects, though Neill's life and work bear witness to the fact that he understands them and the necessity for them.

Children are, he claims, innately wise and realistic. However, he admits that in some cases their primitivism can make them hateful brats and he has met some with whom even he could do nothing. His assertions about the innate qualities of children are acts of faith in a 'good' force in children and a 'good' force in a certain kind of free society which will enable the 'good' psychological force to express itself in social life and institutions. If the intellect can look after itself, as Neill has said, when men have been thus 'saved', so too can the kind of society good and wise people with a freedom-school background will make. This again is a religious kind of statement: 'except ye be born again ye cannot enter into the Kingdom of heaven.' Neill is under no illusions of the roughness of the road — how could he be after forty-five years of the stresses and anxieties of Summerhill and his place crying at the edge of the wilderness?

When children have been made happier, when their aggressions have been transformed and their fears dispelled, what kind of action will they take? Neill's prescriptions are as full of denunciatory yearnings as those of other radicals, religious or secular, and often as vague. They will denounce force, they will champion honesty and sincerity, they will oppose fear with love, they will have the integrity of self-knowledge, they will not need to delude themselves with religion or symbols of status or cant, they will suffer aggression from others with forbearance, they will challenge shams in hypocritical appearances and in grossly materialist public life. All of these unexceptionable aspirations have been taken from Neill's writings, and as many others could have been chosen.

What of the future? Neill is well into his eighties and there is no one else in Britain quite like him, although some approximate to him or have done so: Aitkenhead of Kilquhanity; East of Burgess Hill, which closed in 1962; Curry of Dartington, who died in 1962; Michael Duane formerly of Risinghill, a London comprehensive school; and on the Continent the late Kees Boeke of Holland and Paul Geheeb of Germany and Switzerland, though neither was a Freudian. Neill has written of the future of Summerhill, and it is best to end with his own words and opinions:

> ... the basic issue is ... to make the home more loving, the child free from inhibitions, the parent free of neurosis.
> The future of Summerhill itself may be of little import. But the future of the Summerhill idea is of the greatest importance to humanity.... The bestowal of freedom is the bestowal of love. And only love can save the world.[17]

[17] *Summerhill*, p. 92.

23 Some Facts, Figures, and Interpretations

I

WHEN THESE unorthodox schools were founded they did not want or expect to have the seal of the central authority's approval. As the years have passed nearly all have come to be 'recognized as efficient' and included in the lists issued from time to time. First, to recall the relationship between the central authority and schools in this country.

It has been possible for independent secondary schools to be inspected by Her Majesty's Inspectors on behalf of the central authority since soon after the formation of the Board of Education in 1902, and many have been recognized as efficient for more than half a century. The option to seek recognition was in the hands of the schools, and as time passed more and more independent schools of all kinds thought the approval desirable. Leighton Park was among those accepted in the early groups in 1906, Bedales followed in 1911, and Badminton in 1919, while public schools also took up the recognition, Harrow in 1910, Rugby in 1913, and Winchester in 1919, but Eton did not consider it necessary until 1936. While all of this relates to secondary schools, there are of course large numbers of independent schools in the nursery, primary, and preparatory sectors and these had a similar option open to them from about 1927. Schools recognized as efficient were inspected at fairly regular intervals and if standards were not maintained recognition could be suspended or withdrawn.

However, it was not compulsory to seek recognition or to invite inspection. There were attempts to introduce powers of inspection by either the Board of Education or the local authority in the Education Act of 1921, but while these were available they were never seriously enforced and by 1944 had become a dead letter. Part III of the 1944 Act provided for the registration of all independent schools, and these are defined

P

briefly as establishments which are not maintained by local authorities or in receipt of grant, in which full-time education is provided for five or more pupils of compulsory school age.[1] Such was the congestion of other educational business following on the passage of the Act that this registration was not enforced until thirteen years later in 1957. In the meantime, however, another clause of the Act was brought into effect which was able to prepare the way for registration. The minister was empowered in part IV of the Act[2] to require inspection by H.M. Inspectors of all educational establishments and so to make compulsory what had been largely ignored after the 1921 Act. The inspectorate was able to take up this work from 1949 and by the time registration was brought into effect on 30 September 1957 much was already known about the independent sector. Six months' grace was offered to schools which had to register and provide the required information, and since 31 March 1958 it has been an offence to conduct an independent school which has not been registered. All the schools which had already been recognized as efficient were accepted on the register and nearly all of the innovating schools considered in earlier pages which were founded before the outbreak of war were already recognized by 1944. Exceptions were Dartington Hall, Summerhill, and the Rudolf Steiner schools.[3]

According to the Department of Education and Science, in January 1965 there were in England and Wales 3,560 independent schools, of which 1,539 were recognized, although the number of pupils in the recognized schools was more than twice the number in the unrecognized schools, 306,638 as against 151,569. To put it another way, about 58 per cent of the registered independent schools were not in 1965 approved as efficient. However, just over 90 per cent of the radical schools considered in this book were so recognized.[4] To mention a few in addition to those already noted: Abbotsholme was accepted in 1933, Claysmore in 1925, Bootham in 1907, Saffron Walden in 1920, St. Christopher in 1929, Frensham

[1] *Education Act 1944*, section 114.   [2] section 77 (2).
[3] Dartington was provisionally recognized in 1959 and this acceptance was later confirmed. Michael Hall was recognized in 1950 and Wynstones in 1952. Summerhill has not yet been accepted, although, of course, it has been inspected more than once.
[4] *Statistics of Education* (H.M.S.O., 1965), part i, table 10 (5), p. 29.

Heights in 1935, Bryanston in 1933, and Wennington in 1948. In other words, during the inter-war period of optional recognition only a very small number of these schools were so much at odds with national standards that they opposed this kind of scrutiny.

Therefore, despite any unorthodoxy, these innovating schools are competent enough for official approval:

> Ministry recognition of independent schools means something more than the arbitrary application of standards. It means that a school has been sifted and tested by experienced men who are genuinely concerned for education.... As a result of visiting a number of unrecognized schools ... I had no difficulty (even in the case of a 'Borderline' school) of seeing why recognition had been refused. Moreover the gap between the best unrecognized school visited and the worst recognized was considerable[5]....

II

Exactly comparable figures for the number of pupils who have attended the progressive schools over the years are not obtainable. The publication *List of Independent Schools*, which early in its history was known as *List 60* and is now *List 70*, presents its data in different styles in different years. From these data, reliable as they are, it is not possible to compare the numbers in schools from thirteen to eighteen, or the proportion staying at school after sixteen, or the proportion of boarders in the secondary age range. In addition, as we have seen, not all the progressive schools are registered as efficient and so included in *List 70*, or where they have been they have been accepted at different times, so that the record stretches back unevenly.

The schools have tried to provide me with figures when they have been asked for them, but complete records have not always been kept and so it has not been possible to fill in the gaps reliably. However, the numbers are so comparatively small in any case that, allowing for the degrees of error, only general kinds of categorization are really possible.

[5] P. Wood, 'What is Ministry Recognition Worth?', in *Where*, 14 (autumn 1963), pp. 5–6. Published for the Advisory Centre for Education.

The rough total in 1965 in the schools considered in earlier chapters was almost exactly 7,000 in all the age groups, with the large preponderance in the secondary group aged eleven to eighteen, although eight of the twenty-five schools take children aged below eleven, mostly in small numbers. If this aggregate is compared with the total of children of secondary age range at maintained schools, some idea of the proportion of children in progressive schools can be obtained. In 1965 there were 2,819,054 in this group, and if the numbers in other secondary schools are added (special schools, direct grant schools, other independent schools), the total comes very close to 3,500,000 in secondary schools. As a percentage of 3,500,000 the total of 7,000 at the innovatory schools comes out at 0·2 per cent.[6]

If we make some comparison with the public schools, these small numbers in the progressive schools may be seen in a different perspective. Kalton has estimated that there were about 86,000 boys from age eleven onwards in the public and direct grant schools of England and Wales at the beginning of 1964.[7] This represents about $2\frac{1}{2}$ per cent of the secondary school aggregate and is more than twelve times the number of pupils in the progressive schools, though it must be admitted that some of those in the progressive group are also counted in Kalton's public school sample: for example, Bootham, Leighton Park, Bryanston, Claysmore. The difference would be much larger if girls' public schools were added.

Educationally, Abbotsholme, Bedales, Rendcomb, St. Christopher, and the rest were established either as correctives to the public schools or else to develop a religious or social principle into practice in a school which bore little educational resemblance to a public school. There is none of the presumed advantage of 'the old boy network' in progressive schools, which are too liberal-anarchic, too small, and too new to have any organizational power, and whose ideas are *ex hypothesi* supposed to run counter to any notions of an establishment. The irony now is that their educational ideas may count for little when integration is in the wind. Their independence

---

[6] Figures for maintained schools may be seen in *Statistics of Education*, part i, table 10 (5), pp. 28–9.

[7] G. Kalton, *The Public Schools* (London, 1966), p. 14.

makes them bedfellows with the public schools where a decade or two ago neither had any desire to breathe the same educational air as the other.

By looking at the size of individual schools at different times we can get an impression of stability or change. The following comparison of twelve schools at periods before and after the war is based on figures provided in *List 60* and *List 70*. Where there are boarders they are given as a total in brackets, and the age range of the schools has not been given because the comparison is made in order to detect growth within schools as distinct from comparison of size between schools. In this matter of increase in numbers much depends, obviously, on the kind of buildings and area of ground available for new building, and on financial backing, whether in endowment or income, but the average increase from 1933 to 1965 in these twelve schools is 133 per cent.

During the same period Gordonstoun grew from about fifty at its beginning in 1934 to over four hundred pupils. The increase in all the schools was fairly steady in the thirty years which straddle the Second World War. The days of the eccentric, when Reddie and Devine nearly ruined their schools financially, were over. Curry ran risks at Dartington but he was backed by sound finance in other Elmhirst enterprises. Barnes had to build from a war-time start and Neill, who is not on this chart, wavered between having forty and sixty pupils during most of this time.

Schools which have a return for 1938 show an increase by 1950 and a steep upward gradient in the 1950s and 1960s corresponding to a period of growth and prosperity in independent schools after the end of the war. During the same period the school-leaving age was raised; school fees in maintained schools were abolished; the early warnings of dissatisfaction with secondary school selection and the beginnings of comprehensive reorganization could be detected; building and rebuilding to deal with the ravages of war and the vast increases in numbers occupied the foreground. The Fleming Report, *The Public Schools and the General Educational System*, appeared in 1944 with its suggestions of a 25 per cent intake of pupils to boarding-schools on bursaries related to a means test. But the many other huge enterprises in education through the

1940s and 1950s left very little time or attention for the independent schools. Reports by all three political parties in the 1950s and 1960s indicated that they had in mind to do something, but only in December 1965 was Sir John Newsom's Public Schools Commission set up.[8]

Only five of the twelve are within striking range of four hundred pupils, and of these five, three have an age range down to junior and infant years. The proportional and aggregate increases are large, but not one of the establishments is large, or even average, by contemporary secondary school sizes. They rank among the smallest secondary schools in the country and this reflects the principle of the extended family from which they began and to which most of them still hold. It also exposes them to criticism on grounds of inequality and the need for social justice.

In the post-war atmosphere of planning, with education considered nationally as a social investment both in terms of money and manpower and the sequence of input, throughput, and output, many of the educational principles and practices of progressive, as of other, schools are being seen in the framework of viable educational units, of minimum economic size, of cost-creep, and Burnham salary reviews. Of course, these features were there at all times and no school can run without realistic financial control and hard-headed accounting. But between the wars the institution and its legitimate demands were subordinated to the care of the child and his personal growth and development. This led to consideration of individual objectives and the school had to be relatively small to encompass these purposes. As the pressure of state rationalization at that time was not great the innovatory schools relied upon *laissez-faire* market competition to enable them to produce a minority educational product. Now the institutional and organizational pressures are much tighter on each of the schools and on all of them as a body, and at this point we can look at the financial situation.

[8] See Public Schools Commission First Report, vol. i (H.M.S.O., 1968). See also R. Lambert, *The State and Boarding Education* (London, 1966). A very different book is R. Lambert and S. Millham; *The Hothouse Society* (London, 1968). This has as its subtitle 'An explanation of boarding-school life through the boys' and girls' own writings'.

III

Some broad indications of progressive school fees have been obtained from *List 60* and *List 70* for the same years as for the numbers of pupils at the range of schools shown in Table 1. At the same time figures were obtained for a matching number of public schools, and these were chosen for the most part from the same county area as the progressive school. In a very approximate way some comparisons between the two groups of schools can be made. The recent work by Kalton gives a much more comprehensive range of data on the public schools.[9] Where a range of fees has been quoted in one or another source of data for any one year, I have based my statements on the mid-point between the two figures given.

For this group of progressive schools the average fee charged in 1933 was £153, although the fluctuations were wide: Saffron Walden cost parents 55 per cent of the charges at Bedales, which were the highest. By 1965 the Saffron Walden fees were only about 5 per cent less than those at Bedales, and as the column shows, the discrepancies between fees in different schools narrowed dramatically over the thirty-three years between. The highest fee in 1965 was charged by Bryanston (£540) and the lowest by Michael Hall (an average of £405) and Saffron Walden (£417). This puts Michael Hall at exactly 75 per cent of the Bryanston charge and Saffron Walden at about 80 per cent, a very different position from 1933 when the Essex school, as I said above, was charging 55 per cent of the Bedales fee. In 1965 the average for this whole group of schools was £456, almost exactly three times the 1933 average of £153.

Three general comments can be made from these figures. First, and obviously, the narrower margins in 1965 indicate an evening up of charges which is likely to be due to a more comparable range of facilities, for it is improbable that schools which have a poorer staff–student ratio, a narrower curriculum, and inferior equipment and accommodation could compete on equal financial terms with schools which offered a notably better standard for the money, or with well-equipped

[9] Kalton, *The Public Schools*.

TABLE 1
Number of boys and girls at schools named on dates shown

Name of school	1933	1938	1950	1957	1965	Increase 1933–65 as a percentage
Abbotsholme	78 B (78)	81 B (81)	108 B (108)	145 B (145)	193 B (193)	140
Bedales	201 B+G (161)	174 B+G (c. 130)	202 B+G (194)	261 B+G (c. 200)	389 B+G (295)	94
Clayesmore	70 B (70)	211 B (207)	199 B (199)	210 B (209)	216 B (216)	205
Saffron Walden	157 B+G (132)	187 B+G (171)	272 B+G (c. 200)	334 B+G (228)	365 B+G (238)	140
Leighton Park	129 B (114)	156 B (121)	267 B (c. 150)	278 B (c. 168)	292 B (273)	124
Badminton	150 G (97)	119 G (c. 75)	187 G (c. 110)	225 G (132)	342 G (229)	112
St. Christopher	183 B+G (54)	155 (c. 70)	206 B+G (c. 120)	260 B+G (c. 160)	380 B+G (221)	110
Michael Hall*	—	—	—	270 B+G (c. 90)	393 B+G (101)	44
Frensham Heights	—	100 B+G (c. 70)	182 B+G (c. 145)	197 B+G (c. 150)	222 B+G (161)	122
Bryanston	198 B (198)	291 B (291)	326 B (325)	424 B (424)	445 B (445)	120
Dartington Hall*	—	—	—	—	256 B+G (150)	—
Wennington*	—	—	87 B+G (85)	86 B+G (c. 80)	119 B+G (111)	38

* Entry on the table is shown after the school was first recognized as efficient.

maintained schools which offered it for nothing. The second comment is that the period during which the gap was closed between the most expensive and the cheapest schools was in the post-war years. The differences were as wide in 1938 as they were in 1933, but by 1950 they were shrinking. The post-war boom in independent education gave the poorer schools a chance to face the reality of competition with others and the means to strengthen their own offerings.

The third comment relates to the changing value of money. It is notoriously difficult for economists to make valid comparisons between the pre-war and post-war periods because the data on which calculations have been made have differed. However, leaving out all technical explanations, in the statements which follow 1958 is taken as 100.[10] On this rating 1964 is returned as 115·4; 1957 as 97·1; 1950 as 68; 1938 as 37; 1933 as 33. These are the years on which I have made the financial readings indicated in Table 2.

If we work in averages for this group of schools we find that the average fee of 1950 at £197 is only 3 per cent below the 1958 figure of £293, if we make appropriate allowances for the value of money. The average fee for the pre-war years of £153 is proportionately a much higher charge. The 1933 equivalent of £293 in 1958 is rather under the £99, which as we have seen was the lowest fee in this group, charged by Saffron Walden. However, if we move on to 1964 when the average fee was £455 and the retail price index was just over 115, the fee which would have matched the 1958 charge would have been about £350.

These comparisons show that the radical schools were charging comparatively high fees before the war by 1958 standards and that the level climbed steeply again between 1958 and 1964; this trend has continued till now. Small schools which maintain a staff-pupil ratio of 1 : 11 or so are likely to be expensive, especially at a time when teachers' salaries and allowances have been increased. Equally, the cost of secondary education has mounted sharply as a range of new equipment and materials and developed facilities in many subjects from craft to science have come into use. Nearly all the innovating schools have been involved in large building programmes since the

[10] *British Economy: Key Statistics 1900–1964.*

TABLE 2
Fees of progressive and public schools in £s

Name of school	1933	1938	1950	1957	1965	Increase 1933–65 as a percentage
Abbotsholme	144/180	144/180	198/252	302	474/513	205
Denstone	120	120	180	270/300	472	290
Bedales	180	155/170	231	225/360	390/490	145
Rugby	201	201	270	411	537	168
Clayesmore	157–10	157–10	192	279	420	173
Canford	157–10	170	225	345	462	134
Saffron Walden	99	99	174	267	417	315
Felsted	95/123	140/150	210	324	435/498	325
Leighton Park	157–10/189	157–10/189	171/255	231/315	459	185
Radley	185	185	240	330	552	198
Badminton	126/157–10	121/157–10	144/189	204/300	390/480	207
Cheltenham Ladies' College	126/157–10	150/162	210	300	459	226
St. Christopher	150	150	185/200	240/326	417/519	212
Aldenham	90/115	90/115	165	351	522	410
Michael Hall	—	—	—	218/312	366/444	54
Eastbourne				252/325	510	73
Frensham Heights	—	151	180	264/330	510	240
Cranleigh		130/150	195/216	273/318	543	290
Bryanston	168	180	210	360	540	220
Sherborne	165	165	225	336	474	187
Dartington	—	—	—	—	405/504	—
Kelly College, Tavistock					441	
Wennington	—	—	180	300	417/435	136
Giggleswick	—	—	174/190	294	360/405	91

end of the war. The cost per place in any secondary school, maintained or independent, is much higher now, even allowing for the changing value of money, than it was only ten years ago, and there is no sign of the end of this climbing graph.

If we turn to the public schools whose fees were listed in the earlier table, we find that the average fee in 1933, which in the innovating schools was £153, was in the public schools £169, or about 11 per cent higher, the lowest fee and the highest being about that distance above the corresponding fees in the progressive schools. In 1965 the difference has been halved and the progressive school average is £456 while the public school figure is £483, or about 6 per cent higher. The difference between the averages of both groups in 1950 is about $7\frac{1}{2}$ per cent and in 1957 about 8 per cent, the public schools still the higher in each case. Kalton's more comprehensive data place the public school average fee a bit higher, but not significantly so.

Whatever educational differences there may be between these two groups of independent schools, the income level to which they must direct themselves is similar. One of the named objectives of Sir John Newsom's Commission was to ensure that increasingly the public schools should be open to boys and girls irrespective of the income of their parents. At this stage all that need be said is that parents sending their children to progressive schools have to make inroads into their incomes very similar to those made by parents of public school boys and girls.

In boarding-schools masters and mistresses take on many additional duties and the supervision and general care in out-of-school hours inevitably go further in claiming time. Some consequence of this is seen in the apparently more generous staffing ratios, where, as has been mentioned, 1 : 11 or 1 : 12 is not uncommon. The 1965 returns state the ratio in direct grant schools as 1 : 16·8; in independent schools as 1 : 12·8; and in maintained secondary schools as 1 : 18·7.[11] A ratio weighted for sixth form and residential duties makes the proportions look much less uneven.

A further consequence of the demands of boarding-schools is often seen in the salary scale. The days of pecuniary sacrifice

[11] *Statistics of Education*, part i, pp. 61 and 50.

by devoted teachers in pioneer schools are finished in the recognized progressive schools: they cannot gain recognition until the salary and superannuation structure compares with the national scales and provisions. In a number of the progressive schools the scale starts at a point or so above the comparable Burnham scale and keeps this position: generous responsibility allowances, living accommodation on favourable terms, occasionally children's allowances, reduced fees for children attending the school – these and other inducements are available. It would not be fair to suggest that all of these are found together or can be gathered by all teachers as a matter of course, but a scrutiny of the salaries and emoluments available to the staff of these schools indicates that they are on average more favourable than the Burnham scale, although not more than might be expected as a return for boarding duties and the consequences of a residential community life.

This favourable position has been reached in the majority of the schools only in the last twenty years. In the 1930s and the 1920s equal subsistence-level salaries were not uncommon, the adherence to Burnham scales where they were applied was strictly interpreted, and allowances were few and competitive. This was true of the country as a whole, of course, but in most cases the unorthodox schools had no solid financial backing to sustain a generous allowance policy. Since the end of the war the schools have recognized the stronger bargaining position of teachers and have had the confidence to raise the fees to meet the mounting costs.[12]

IV

Some statements can be made about the career patterns of former pupils from progressive schools on the basis of an inquiry conducted to collect necessary data. As in most investigations of this kind, a deceptively simple account can be given of the purpose, the strategy, and the procedure. The practical problems that arose in this case are very familiar to all social investigators, and I must underline that the comments from this part of the whole inquiry are presented as impressions

---

[12] These conclusions are based on salary statements provided for the author by the schools for the years mentioned in the table of fees used earlier in this chapter.

rather than as authenticated conclusions.[13] Many of the technical details have been omitted so that the argument can be more simply presented.

In earlier pages of this book at least twenty-six schools have received substantial mention and sixteen of them were visited in 1963–4 in order to compile lists of names and addresses of all pupils who left the schools in the years 1933, 1938, 1943, 1948, 1953, and 1958: the choice of years was related to the extraordinary war-time conditions between 1939 and 1945. Old pupils who were known to have died in the intervening years were excluded from the lists and additional information on the remaining persons was obtained: the length of time they were at school, the age at which they left, further education and choice of career, if these were known, and so on.[14] The schools chosen were co-educational and single-sex day and boarding and covered the spectrum of unorthodoxy which we have already noted. A questionnaire with a covering letter was sent by post to every person whose name and address had been obtained, with appropriate follow-up to those who did not at first respond. There were in all 1,535 persons on our lists.

The questionnaire asked for factual data: period spent at the progressive school, with dates; examinations taken, with results; further and higher education, if any, with relevant qualifications or experience; marital status (particularly important in relation to women's careers); military service or its equivalent; career and experience, with dates; a statement of present salary within broad markers in eight categories ranging from 'under 500' to 'over £5,000', together with any fringe benefits. Another question was aimed to discover whether respondent who had children would consider, or had already arranged for, attendance at a progressive school for their sons and daughters. The occupations of fathers and guardians when the respondents were at school were asked for and this enabled us to establish a rough social-class position for the school

[13] The author was helped in this part of the study first by Miss Margaret Thomas and later by Mr. Colin Creighton. A more detailed account of the work on which this section of this chapter is based appears in *The Educational Innovators*, vol. ii (London, 1968).

[14] The author would like here to express gratitude to the heads of these sixteen schools for their readiness to make records available and to offer time and help to enable these lists to be made up.

leavers by classifying these occupations according to the 1951 categories of the Registrar-General, which fall into five groups ranging from professional and higher administrative grades in group I through lower grade non-manual workers and skilled manual workers in group III to unskilled workers in Group V.

Of the 1,535 people to whom questionnaires were sent 798 responded, i.e. about 54 per cent. This is not a high proportion, but represents a very respectable sample of the total. In the statements which follow based on the 798 replies I have tried to make such allowance as I can for various differences and we have often analysed the results by treating the Quaker schools and the 'unattached' schools as two separate groups, as the response from the Quaker schools was proportionately higher.

Looking first at the social-class background of fathers of the respondents, using the Registrar-General's 1951 categories, the results come out as follows over the whole sample:

TABLE 3
Social-class background of fathers of respondents as a percentage

R-G's group	I	II	III	IV	V	Retired, don't know, etc.
	38	43	11	0.3	—	7.7

If we break this formulation down into the response for Friends' schools and for those I have called 'unattached' because they are separate institutions, the results are as follows:

TABLE 4
Social-class background by social grouping

R-G's group	I	II	III	IV	V	Retired, don't know, etc.
Friends' schools	34	45	12.5	—	—	8.5
Unattached schools	45	38	7.5	0.7	—	8.5

The fathers of 81 per cent of the children at these progressive schools fall into social classes I and II as compared with 19 per cent of 'the economically active and retired males in England

and Wales, 1961'.[15] Whereas 11 per cent of the fathers in our sample fall in to group III (lower grade non-manual workers and skilled occupations), 51 per cent of the male population comes into this category. Only 0·3 per cent of our sample comes into groups IV and V combined, whereas the national figure is 30 per cent. The larger proportion of Quaker boys in group III of our sample is probably accounted for by the fairly generous provisions of scholarships and bursaries at Friends' schools either from the Friends' Education Council or other Quaker sources or through special arrangements with local education authorities. However, there is a large predominance from upper income and social groupings in Friend's schools and this in its turn is likely to influence the career patterns of the children.

If we compare these figures with those provided by Kalton for the public school,[16] we find that 84 per cent of fathers in these schools fall into groups I and II as compared with 81 per cent in our sample.

I examined the age at which our sample left school and found that 70 per cent of them stayed until they were at least coming up to seventeen.

TABLE 5
Percentage of 798 respondents leaving progressive schools at different ages

Age	14–15	15–16	16–17	17–18	18–19	19+
	1·9	6·0	22·2	42·5	25·9	1·4

Kalton collected the figures for public schools, direct grant schools, and maintained grammar schools. He also provides data on the percentage of boy leavers at all maintained secondary schools in the country. Figures are set down in Table 6 below so that rough comparisons may be made. The figures in Table 5 above are for both boys and girls while Kalton's figures are for boys only. The figures have been conflated here to give one reading in each cell, where Kalton gives separate readings for day pupils only, day and boarding pupils mixed, and boarding pupils only.[17]

[15] *Census 1961, England and Wales, Occupation Tables* (H.M.S.O., 1966).
[16] Kalton, *The Public Schools*, pp. 35–6.
[17] Ibid., p. 81.

TABLE 6
Percentage of leavers from different kinds of secondary school by ages

Type of school	14–15/15–16	16–17	17–18	18–19	19+
Progressive	7.9	22.2	42.5	25.9	1.4
Independent	2	12	28	50	8
Direct grant	3	14.3	26.3	45.3	11
Maintained grammar	7	36	18	29	9
All secondary	67	20	5	6	2

The proportion of leavers between fourteen and sixteen from the grammar schools is not very different from the figure for the unorthodox schools. It is known from our data that about 53 per cent of the 7.9 per cent who left their progressive school under the age of sixteen went on to another school and do not represent a loss to full-time education. This is much less true of the grammar school sector. Parents of some children at the radical schools clearly thought that their sons and daughters stood a better chance in examinations and careers if they moved at this stage to more conventional schools. The percentage loss at this point from the independent or direct grant school is between a half and a quarter of that from the other schools.

A second matter of note is the loss after O level at sixteen and seventeen from the grammar school and the progressive school. If eighteen is taken as the usual age at which Advanced level examinations in the General Certificate of Education are taken, something like 61 per cent of grammar school pupils have left at or by that stage while the figure for the progressive schools is over 72 per cent. Only 42 per cent from the public schools leave by or at the age of eighteen and about 44 per cent from the direct grant schools. However, it should be remembered that our sample for the progressive schools covers a period in the 1930s when the statutory minimum leaving age was fourteen and when the school-leaving pattern in the country as a whole was not as it was in 1962–3 when Kalton's figures were obtained. The picture at the present time is likely to be very different and much more broadly similar over all types of school, with far higher percentages staying on into the sixth form.

I broke down these data on school leaving in progressive schools by social class and between Friends' schools and unattached schools. The most striking thing here was that there was no sign of early leaving across the five class groupings, or to put it another way, roughly the same percentage in all classes stayed up to sixteen to seventeen years of age, up to seventeen to eighteen, and up to eighteen plus. Children whose parents were dead or retired, or not in an active, earning job, often stayed on until eighteen plus – the figure was just above 42 per cent of this rather special group. There is a high percentage of late leaving in Friends' schools among those who were not getting much financial support from the family. Perhaps again the generous scholarship and bursary position in Friends' schools helped this situation.

Of the 798 there were 509 who were married – about 64 per cent; 427, or about 84 per cent, of this group had children. Of these parents as a group, about 79 per cent said they would arrange or had arranged a progressive school education for their children and just under 20 per cent said they would not send their children to a progressive school. Many of these rejected the proposal because they thought they could not afford it, and some thought a day school more important than anything else but would have liked to find one run on unorthodox lines although they usually could not. The parents often claimed that the family upbringing would be permissive and in line with progressive school practice even if they could not afford to send their children to such an establishment – they had come to value it for what it had done for them.

I examined the record of those who went on from unorthodox schools to get further qualifications whether by full-time or part-time study. Some of these qualifications required study at a university, others at a college of education or a technical college, others through professional associations, and so on. Of the 798 respondents at least 84 per cent gained one additional qualification by further study and a sizeable proportion took still higher qualifications in addition. About 36 per cent of these qualifications were degrees or diplomas in technology and this is almost exactly the same as the proportion for boys quoted by Kalton as going from the public schools to the universities in 1962–3.[18] About 16 per cent of the progressive group qualified as doctors or dentists. These figures should be read against the relatively high proportions leaving their progressive school by or at an age earlier than eighteen. About 19 per cent of maintained grammar school boys at that time went from school to university or college of advanced technology.

About 14 per cent of the progressive school sample gained teachers' certificates in education, roughly 9 per cent through colleges of education, or training colleges as they used to be called, the remaining 5 per cent as graduates in university departments of education. About 2 per cent of the boys in the independent and direct grant schools went to colleges of education in 1962–3, and from the grammar schools about 4 per cent. The interest in teaching of former pupils of progressive schools is noticeably high and will be detailed later.

In our sample something over 5 per cent from Friends' schools took additional entry qualifications after leaving school, like the former Higher Schools Certificate or Advanced level subjects in the present General Certificate of Education or the Ordinary National Certificate or Diploma. The comparable figure from the unattached progressive schools was above 11 per cent. For the moment it is enough to say that a high proportion of pupils got necessary qualifications either at their progressive school or after leaving it, which adds a dimension to the conclusion already arrived at, that there were quite a number leaving progressive schools at or before the age of eighteen.

Many of these schools have junior sections, or eleven plus as well as thirteen plus entries, and it is not uncommon for pupils to enter at the sixth form level. Of those who left by the age of sixteen, 35 per cent had been at the school for five years or longer, while of those who left at eighteen or over, some 25 per cent had been at the school for less than five years. (See table 7).

This distribution indicates the difficulty of relating career choice to the influence of the progressive school, for many pupils in the sample will have spent at least as long at other schools. But some differences there clearly are.

First of all it is not unexpected, when 81 per cent of the

[18] Ibid., p. 95.

TABLE 7
Length of time spent at progressive school by percentage of age group

Age of leaving school	Under 5 years	5 years and over	Don't know
14–16	65·1	34·9	—
16–17	47·5	52·5	—
17–18	35·7	63·7	0·6
18+	24·8	75·2	—

fathers of the sample are in groups I and II of the distribution of occupations, to find that much the same percentage of the respondents themselves were in these groups – about 80 per cent. The breakdown within this large proportion yields some interesting variations and these are set out in tabular form, following the model given first in 1951 by Roe.[19] She distinguished eight categories of occupation and plotted against these five levels of responsibility and class positions. This work was done in America but it has provided a useful structure on which, with few modifications, we can establish a sketch of the distribution of occupations reported by our sample.

The largest proportion of occupations is to be found in the 'service' group (column 1), where, of 24·9 per cent of the total, 18·5 per cent were teachers, which is a notable proportion by any standards, especially when one remembers again that this sample stretches over twenty-five years from 1933 to 1958. Teachers who are graduates are not even required to take a teaching qualification, hence the difference from the 14 per cent who did so quoted above. When we differentiate between the group from Friends' schools and those from unattached progressive schools we find that the Quaker group are about 28 per cent higher as compared with the unattached group in the proportion of the sample under this heading of service. Neill claims in a number of places that scarcely any Summerhillians are teachers: they are too free for positions involving authority.

The second largest group has to do with organization, and it is mainly business, industry, trading, or administration that are involved. Even if the business contact group is added, the proportion is still smaller than the service group, and there is

[19] Anne Roe, *The Psychology of Occupations* (New York, 1956).

TABLE 8

Percentages of the sample by groups of occupations with examples

Registrar-General's group	1 Service	2 Business contact	3 Organization	4 Technology	5 Outdoor	6 Science	7 General culture	8 Art and Entertainment	Total
I	0·1 (clergyman, psychiatrist)	—	3·3 (director, company secretary, chief accountant, higher civil servant, actuary)	4·9 (engineer, surveyor)	—	8·0 (doctor, dentist, research scientist, statistician)	3·9 (lawyer, journalist, economist)	3·3 (architect, writer, producer)	23·5
II	21·9 (teacher, social worker, inspector, educational therapist)	0·3 (auctioneer, public relations officer)	9·4 (manager, administrator, local government official, buyer, shop assistant)	4·4 (technical manager, draughtsman, ship's officer)	4·3 (farmer, smallholder, agricultural development officer)	9·0 (nurse, optician, veterinary surgeon, physiotherapist)	3·6 (lecturer, translator, publisher, bookseller)	3·9 (lecturer, artist, TV or film director, teacher of the arts)	56·8
III	2·0 (nursery nurse, chef, hairdresser, home help)	0·8 (sales representative, market research interviewer)	9·0 (secretary, clerk, shop assistant)	1·6 (skilled manual worker, technical assistant)	0·3 (forester, technical worker)	2·7 (laboratory technician, chiropodist, auxiliary nurse)	—	1·1 (actor, musician, model, photographer)	17·5
IV & V	0·9 (receptionist, domestic servant)	—	—	0·7 (semi-skilled and unskilled worker)	0·7 (labourer)	—	—	—	2·3
Total	24·9	1·1	21·7	11·6	5·3	19·7	7·5	8·3	100·1

no real difference between the Quaker and unattached samples under this heading.

The science category (column 6) provides us with nearly 20 per cent of the sample, and here again those from Friends' schools are about 28 per cent more numerous than the unattached respondents. What this seems to suggest is not very surprising: pupils from Friends' schools find themselves drawn to careers of service and to careers in science, by far the largest proportion of which are in medicine and might, in a different cross-classification, be allied to the service category. But it should not be thought that the response from the unattached schools under this heading is negligible – it is not. In technology (column 4) the Quaker respondents are over 25 per cent fewer than the unattached respondents, which may appear surprising. In art and entertainment (column 8) the unattached return is about 60 per cent higher than that from the Friends' schools, which with the rather more conservative Quaker tradition is not unexpected, but anyone knowing the Friends' schools today would not find the gap now as wide as all that. A rather smaller discrepancy, but still a significant one, is to be found in the higher number of respondents from the unattached schools under the heading of general culture (column 7).

Without trying to lean too heavily on these figures, we can see a broad distribution of careers with teaching and service highest of all, organization and science close behind, and Quaker patterns of service revealing themselves predictably. Again the arts have a higher place than is usual, especially for the unattached schools.

Two professions do not appear, except marginally, and these might also be predictable. The first is the church, and as Friends have no order of priesthood this is likely, although about half of the pupils attending Friends' schools do not come from Quaker families. We have noticed elsewhere that in the unattached schools the approach to religious teaching is not usually aligned to any ecclesiastical position, and of course the women in the sample are more or less excluded from this profession. The second low-scoring profession is a career in the armed forces, and this again might be expected for both groups of schools. Friends are committed as a body to pacifism, and the unattached group of schools have no sympathy for military organizations. At least 6 per cent of public school leavers in Kalton's sample joined the forces, and this relates to the proportion of parents who are in the forces.[20] There is, however, a proportion of public school leavers going into farming which compares well with the 5·3 per cent in the progressive group (column 5).

We classified the occupations of the parents of the respondents on the Roe model as above: they gave this information on the questionnaire.

TABLE 9

Percentage of parents by occupational group

1	2	3	4	5	6	7	8
13	1	41	15	6	11	9	4

The dominance of the organizational group (column 3) is surprisingly heavy, followed by technology (column 4) a long way behind, with the service category (column 1) lying a very close third, and a scientific career (column 6) coming next, where most of the sample are doctors.

As we now know the occupational distribution for the children of the sample mentioned above, we can compare this with the distribution for their fathers: it would be best to compare only the returns for the males of our sample for obvious reasons. Taking the whole male sample, we find that only half as many of the sons went into organizational jobs compared with the fathers and this means that the distribution to categories other than organizational does not drop as steeply as with the fathers. The shortest and clearest way to make the comparison is to state it in tabular form.

Some influence in the changes between fathers and sons must be ascribed to the changes in national opportunity. For instance, the number of openings in science and technology has greatly increased. The highest proportion here is in the unattached sons, and this has something to do with the school. However, the percentages of fathers and sons in the unattached group concerned with entertainment (column 8) are com-

[20] Kalton, *The Public Schools*, pp. 96–7.

TABLE 10

Percentage distribution of occupations of fathers and sons

	1 Service	2 Business contact	3 Organization	4 Technology	5 Outdoor	6 Science	7 General culture	8 Art and entertainment
Total male sample								
Fathers	10·5	1·7	42·0	16·0	4·7	8·7	10·2	6·1
Sons	12·8	1·6	21·5	22·0	6·8	13·6	14·1	7·6
Quaker sample								
Fathers	10·5	2·7	45·2	16·4	5·5	7·8	9·6	2·3
Sons	15·6	1·7	24·9	19·8	6·3	13·9	12·7	5·1
Unattached sample								
Fathers	10·5	—	36·3	15·3	3·2	10·6	11·3	12·9
Sons	7·6	1·5	15·3	26·0	7·6	13·0	16·8	12·2

parable and significantly high as compared with the Quaker return, and here both school and parental influence have been almost equally at work, as a further breakdown of parent–child occupation showed. The highest percentage in the service grouping (column 1) is to be found in the Quaker sons, where 15·6 per cent of the sample are. In general, the move away from the high preponderance of organizational jobs in the fathers to service, technology, science, and general cultural work for the sons, together with a relatively high return from both the unattached fathers and sons in art and entertainment, indicates the interest in individualistic and socially useful work that characterizes the progressive group as a whole through the schools. If anything, the unattached group shows up somewhat more often in the individualistic categories and the Quaker group under the socially useful headings – and this we might expect.

Although scarcely any men and women in the sample had entered upon a career in the armed forces, 58 per cent of the men and 9 per cent of the women had undergone national service. Sixty-four per cent of the Quaker men and 48 per cent of the unattached men had served, together with 10 per cent of the Quaker women and 9 per cent of the unattached women. We have included under this heading, mostly an adult wartime and early post-war generation, those who were conscientious objectors, who usually had some form of alternative service to perform.

TABLE 11

Percentage and form of military service

	All men	Quaker men	Unattached men
Army	35·1	26·8	55·4
Navy	11·7	10·2	15·4
R.A.F.	23·0	24·8	18·5
Merchant Navy	1·4	1·9	—
Conscientious objectors	28·8	36·3	10·8

The proportion of conscientious objectors is high, predictably so in the products of Friends' schools, but also much above the average in unattached schools. When asked if they could name benefits they thought the various forms of service might have offered for their career, nearly 70 per cent of the Quaker sample and over 50 per cent of the unattached said that they had gained in self-assurance or experience in authority. About 12 per cent claimed the practical experience was of value for their career and almost none said they had learned habits of discipline. Forty-nine per cent of all those who had undergone service said it had no value at all.

Of the 798 respondents, 527 were in employment at the receipt of the questionnaire. Of the 267 not in employment about 65 per cent were housewives, another 18 per cent were in full-time study, about 12 per cent were doing unpaid work, a few were unemployed or sick, and a similar fraction had either retired or had never worked because they did not need to. Those in employment were asked about their present gross salary, and 94 per cent answered the questions.

TABLE 12
Percentage earning salaries at various levels in £s

Below 500	501– 750	751– 1,000	1,001– 1,500	1,501– 2,000	2,001– 3,000	3,001– 5,000	Over 5,000
8·7	16·5	19·0	23·6	10·5	11·7	7·1	3·0

The median income falls in the £1,001–1,500 category, but there is a fairly wide dispersal over the whole range. On the whole, the earnings of the Quaker sample were higher than those of the unattached: 65 per cent of the Quaker earnings fall below £1,500 and 35 per cent above; the figures for the unattached are 74 and 26 per cent. If we take the total numbers of men and women and analyse them in the same way we find that 45 per cent of men earn over £1,500 and only 7 per cent of the women. About 21 per cent of the women earn less than £500, though some of these are in part-time jobs. It would appear, however, that the women from the unattached schools have a higher average income than the Quaker women – it is the Quaker men who earn more than their counterparts.

Naturally the average income is higher the older the age group, and this can be shown in tabular form:

TABLE 13
Average income by percentage and year of sample

Year of leaving	£1,500 and under	Over £1,500
1933	19·2	80·8
1938	23·8	76·2
1943	26·7	73·3
1948	51·5	48·5
1953	76·5	23·5
1958	95·4	4·6

A fuller version of this table shows more clearly the kind of development that has taken place.

TABLE 14
Percentage of men in salary groupings by year of sample in £s

Year of leaving	750 and under	751–1,500	1,501–3,000	3,000 and above
1933	—	19·2	30·8	*50·0*
1938	4·8	19·0	*50·0*	26·2
1943	6·7	20·0	*50·0*	23·3
1948	3·0	*48·5*	33·3	15·2
1953	4·4	*72·1*	20·6	2·9
1958	*50·8*	44·1	4·6	—

The italic figures show where the large groups in each year's sample are to be found, and the table represents a flight of steps so that more than half of those who left in 1958 were earning less than £750 and half of those who left in 1933 were earning over £3,000, with correspondingly ascending steps in the intervening years. The figures were obtained in 1963, so that the large proportion of the 1958 sample who went on to a university or some other form of higher education had just started on their careers. If we recall that 84 per cent of the 798 respondents gained at least one further qualification after leaving school, that over 38 per cent took a university degree or the equivalent, and that most courses take three years, the picture of more than half the 1958 sample earning less than £750 is to be expected. Obviously the progressive schools would not consider earnings by themselves as a measure of educational success. However, the figures in this table show that, while children in progressive schools come from families where over 80 per cent of the fathers are in occupational groups I and II, the education given by the schools has not been so unworldly that it has hampered pupils in their careers. Nevertheless, because a large proportion of our sample have entered teaching or other social welfare professions, the average income is lower than, say, a comparable sample of boys from public schools, both because the latter have gone into the better paid professions, the armed forces, the higher civil service, or industry, and because there are women in the progressive sample, which in itself brings a lower average.[21] Without taking time on detail, 79 per cent of the men and women teachers were earning under £1,500 and if this was limited to men teachers only, 58 per cent of those were under £1,500. On the other hand the same proportion of lawyers (58 per cent) were earning over £1,500, and the majority of this group were above the £3,000 mark; much the same pertained for the group of architects, and all those in television, film, or radio work earned over £1,500.

The age at which the respondents first took up permanent paid employment is a useful index of their social and educational standing:

TABLE 15

Age on commencement of permanent paid employment as a percentage

Age	15–16	17–18	19–20	21+
	6	24	21	49

If the parents of these children were predominantly members of the liberal middle class, the children themselves follow in their fathers' footsteps with a wider spread of professions and occupations to show for it.

We were not able to make a comparison between this pattern of results, with readings across twenty-five years, and a similar maintained school sample, for the data do not exist. The best we could do was to make a comparison between the

[21] See I. Weinberg, 'The Occupational Aspirations of British Public Schoolboys', in *The School Review* (University of Chicago), vol. 74, no. 3 (1966), pp. 265–82; J. Wakeford. 'The Cloistered Elite' (London, 1969).

1958 returns for the progressive schools and the national survey of twenty-one-year olds carried out in that year. We chose those educated at maintained grammar schools whose parents were placed in social classes I and II since more than 80 per cent of the children in the progressive schools had parents in these groupings, as we have seen. The grammar school leavers and the progressive school leavers were compared on the Roe classification (see Table 8 above). There were certain occupational groups in which there was no significant difference in the frequency distribution between the two samples, for instance in the readings for the business contact occupations. There were some headings under which there were significant differences, and as the statistical analysis is too detailed for verbal description, those categories are set down in tabular form. Subdivisions for the two social classes have been made and for the two groups of progressive schools.

TABLE 16

*Comparison of progressive school leavers and grammar school leavers in 1958 according to Roe categories**

	1	2	3	4	5	6	7	8
Registrar-General's group I								
Friends' schools	+		—	—				
Unattached				—		—	+	+
Registrar-General's group II								
Friends' schools					—		+	
Unattached	—	—				—	+	+

* A higher proportion is shown (+) and a lower is shown (—).

The Quaker service category in group I is significantly larger than the grammar school return, and a large part of this can be ascribed to the proportion of those in what might be called the medical helping professions. In no other category in group I do the Quaker schools by themselves produce a higher proportion than the grammar schools; in organizational jobs and careers in technology they produce a lower proportion and in the rest break fairly even. The unattached schools have a much higher proportion than the grammar schools in the general cultural and art and entertainment categories and a lower proportion in the organizational and scientific categories. In the

Registrar-General's group II the Friends' schools score high in the general cultural category, as do the unattached schools once again, and again the Quaker leavers score low in technology, with all the rest breaking fairly even. It is surprising that the proportion of teachers does not bring the Quaker schools higher in the service category. In group II the unattached schools score high in general culture and in art and entertainment and are once again lower in science and organization, with another low rating in the service category. Group II teachers in grammar schools and Friends' schools are relatively of the same high proportion and both are significantly higher than in the unattached schools.

These are rough assessments, and if the progressive schools are bulked as a single return they score higher than the maintained schools in the service category, in the outdoor category, and in the science, general culture, and art and entertainment groupings. In other words, out of the eight categories in the Roe table, there is a detectable difference in five of them in the proportion of alumni from progressive schools as compared with those from maintained schools. In business contacts the score is even, and the high score moves to the maintained schools under the heading of organization and to a lesser degree in technology. Substantially, the picture that has already been sketched continues in the comparison with the maintained schools: service, culture, the arts, science, outdoor pursuits are leading categories of employment for the progressive schools. As compared with maintained schools, they score lower in business contacts and technology, and to some extent in organization.

V

In this chapter on facts and figures an attempt has been made to review the growth of the radical schools from four points of view. Recognition by the Board or Ministry of Education is a sign of standards of provision, of facilities and staffing, of educational achievement, and nearly all of the schools have aimed for this and obtained it. Those who have not are now under scrutiny and pressure will be upon them. The progressive schools cannot now be as defiant as they used to be, or to put it another way, the Department of Education and Science now has more experience of permissive education on which to base its recommendations.

The second topic was numbers, growth, expansion. Numbers show a relatively slow growth and a strong attachment to a small school community, the upper limits at Bryanston and Gordonstoun, the biggest schools, still being under five hundred. Here, in the dawn of the comprehensive school, is a sharp difference from current thought in the maintained sector.

Third, there is the theme of cost, of fees, salaries, economic survival. Fourth is the sketch of the career pattern of former pupils to see what effect the education provided by these schools has produced and to chart any preferences that have appeared over the years.

The story of the development of the schools, the ideas of the founders, and the educational principles of a loosely connected movement have been set down in earlier chapters. The facts, figures, and suggested interpretations in this chapter have sought to add data and perspective to the record.

24 Conclusion

I

WHILE ONLY Abbotsholme claimed in 1890 to be providing an education for the sons of the directing classes who might ordinarily go to public schools, the other schools had the same clientele in mind – daughters as well as sons at Bedales and King Alfred's. These schools in the 1890s provided between them a curriculum such as we find in many schools today: English, modern languages, mathematics, sciences (including geology, physics, chemistry, biology), history, geography, some economics, and social studies. Physical education included walking, climbing, swimming, cycling, canoeing, and, to a limited degree, gymnastics and the usual school games. Work on the land and in the daily routine of the home was related to physical fitness, and was intended to lead to an understanding of basic crafts and skills and a deeply woven awareness of the interdependence of a human community. Boys and girls painted, sculpted, worked in wood, and made music as part of normal life. None of this kind of thinking was found to any notable degree in the public or maintained schools at the time.

Reddie and Badley were concerned for mental health and wanted to be explicit about this rather than to accept the unspoken attitudes and disapprobations implicit in public school good form. Frankness, and a reasonable enthusiasm for the good name and good behaviour of the school were encouraged among the pupils at Abbotsholme and Bedales. At the public schools, sex, religion, and politics were not discussed as part of the open exchange of ideas between masters and boys. At Abbotsholme, Bedales, King Alfred's, and Claysmore, particularly at the first three, education was concerned with such matters. King Alfred's was even so unusual as to base its case on humanism, and this rationalism appeared all the more extreme and objectionable to public school religion.

The new schools were opposed, root and branch, to the

hierarchy of the public school. Fagging and privilege were replaced by the ideal of the school family, although even in these radical schools caning was retained; but the relationships of teachers and pupils were supposed to be informal – distressingly casual as some critics said. Even though Reddie was an autocrat and Badley remained sufficiently aloof to be called the Chief throughout his time at Bedales, their involvement in the life of the boys was far more comprehensive than the formalities of the public schools in the 1890s allowed to their heads. Reddie and Badley went cycling and camping and walking and climbing with their boys, and at Bedales after 1898 girls joined the parties. The assistant masters and mistresses also entered into this spirit in the schools, but it was not common in other schools of the time.

Reddie, Badley, and Devine sought to reform all sides of school life. The boys' clothes at Abbotsholme and Bedales were far more comfortable and practical than at Eton, Harrow, Winchester, or Westminster. Chapel services at the innovating schools had no historic liturgy or established form of service. Worship gathered together prayers, invocations, and hymns from the Bible, from sacred literature in many lands and religions, from poetry and prose. Music both sacred and secular was part of the worship and of the daily life in a way unique to schools of the time, but much more generally frequent in the last twenty years.

The heads of these new schools were at one time allied to the radical left, but later they addressed themselves directly to the middle classes. The schools were communities set in the country and many of their ideas are to be found in the same family of thought as those of Ruskin or Edward Carpenter. Whereas earlier in the century Robert Owen had ventured into industrial and urban renewal, as the Fabians and the Independent Labour Party did at the turn of this century, the radical schools of the 1890s, indeed progressive schools generally from that time, have not made an impact on education in the city. The school set in the country, and therefore usually a boarding establishment, makes its appeal to the intellectuals of the left and the liberal intelligentsia. It is highy significant that all four of the protest schools of the 1890s made no common cause with new state schools. The Balfour

Act of 1902 called out little answering approach from these four. There was simply no mutual recognition because maintained schools were not aiming at the same things or the same income groups as the progressive schools.

The innovators were not social revolutionaries, prepared to start a political organization. I have emphasized more than once that no corporate movement was shaped in radical education, and I have said that the strength of this group of schools has been their individual identity, their family life, and the assumption that parents of the real families of the pupils would be prepared to join the school family in a shared enterprise. Before 1914 the public schools ridiculed this liberal individualism, while the new state grammar schools were too preoccupied with their own identity to be much concerned about anyone else's, and inevitably found respectability more enticing than innovation. But until the beginning of the Second World War the progressive schools were crusading to reform the whole of secondary education.

Reddie and Badley and Devine laid out their educational beliefs and practices and waited for takers. Parents were choosing and buying what they had to offer and in the first forty years what they provided was risky. Unlike the local authority foundations these schools could never have a guaranteed supply of pupils, and if the ideas were too extreme, the cost too high, or the organization faulty the venture would end in bankruptcy, and there have been times when all three schools have been perilously near it.

The Quaker schools took the hint and moved in the same direction as these three, rather more moderately and rather less far, as might be expected. Because the centre of gravity of the Society of Friends is not one man and his conviction and energy, but a committee of a dispersed, national, religious movement, their stability has been in some ways the greater.

After the First World War the target for criticism was still the public schools, but England was a different place in the 1920s. The internationalism of these pioneer schools and of the New Education Fellowship grew in the years following the establishment of the League of Nations. Rendcomb, Dartington, Summerhill, the Malting House, Beacon Hill were all founded in a fresh, post-war conviction that much needed changing. The public schools were also exposed to new and savage attacks from within in books like Alec Waugh's *Loom of Youth*, Robert Graves's *Goodbye to All That*, and Lytton Strachey's onslaught on Thomas Arnold in *Eminent Victorians*. This mood of disenchantment and intellectual and moral emancipation was right for the new schools, and they showed a strong desire to influence state schools, public schools, and training colleges, these sympathies leading to active political participation by a number of former pupils of progressive schools in the late 1920s and 30s. Schools like Eton and Haileybury and Berkhamsted and Rugby and Winchester produced Orwell and John Strachey and Connolly and Attlee and Graham Greene and William Plomer and Hugh Gaitskell, but these were the known rebels, exceptions and *francs tireurs*. Former pupils of the progressive schools were, on the other hand, expected to be radicals, and if one of them was a political or cultural conservative he was looked upon as a rare specimen.

Educational theory in the radical schools was taken very seriously indeed in the 1920s and 30s, and the three points of emphasis were the importance of freedom rather than restraint in infancy; the importance of spontaneity and expressiveness with the consequence that play and exploration and the child's initiative, especially in the arts, were stressed; the importance of positive attitudes and the primacy of emotions rather than intellect in education. Freud and sex, Adler and the will to power, McDougall and the instincts, Jung and individuation all had a major place in progressive educational theory and practice of the time. Perhaps most important of all was the pervading acceptance in these circles of the unconscious mind and its educational significance. For the bulk of ordinary people education was pre-eminently concerned with intellectual, moral, and spiritual training, with premeditated and selected goals and practices, with curricula, subjects, and explicit methods, with teachers teaching and pupils learning, with lessons understood and examinations passed. Neill, the Russells, Susan Isaacs, Curry, and Rudolf Steiner were committed to something very different.

In the later 1920s and early 1930s, when Bryanston and Gordonstoun were founded, politics and economics had broken the social vacuum that surrounded psycho-analysis and its derivatives. The depression around 1930 brought the misery and poverty of millions before the public eye and conscience, and an empty stomach and unemployment were seen to disturb psychological equilibrium just as surely as infantile frustration or inhibition. The growing political burden of Communism and Nazism, and more particularly the second, became heavier and its consequence in the flood of refugees pressed heavily on the internationally minded progressive schools. Psycho-analysis and free discipline appeared to be socially and politically misdirected to many men and women whose relatives and friends had died in gas-chambers or who had left possessions and position to escape alive with their children from Germany. But the liberals in the progressive schools extended a welcome as far as they could and they were obvious enemies of Fascism and Nazism, many of them meeting the totalitarian threat as convinced pacifists. Monkton Wyld and Wennington were founded in 1940 to reassert these values to refugees and evacuated children even in war-time. There have been no new progressive schools of this kind founded since 1945 except Atlantic College and a few other schools of the Gordonstoun stamp.

II

The preceding section was an historical retrospect. Now I turn to a number of conceptual points arising from the progressive tradition.

The radical schools have been much concerned with the unique life of the school community. In so far as a school can be said to have a purpose which the teachers and the pupils together realize, the innovators have been fairly explicit in stating their general intentions and shaping the means. Perry has made a valuable analysis of what he calls 'the child-centred model', from which some of the following points are taken.[1] Using such a model the knowledge dimension in school is reduced and the role of the teacher as intellectual authority is diminished. The fact that curricula abridge and compress

[1] L. R. Perry, 'What is an Educational Situation?', in *Philosophical Analysis and Education*, ed. R. D. Archambault (London, 1965), pp. 59–86. See also his editorial comments *passim* in *Bertrand Russell, A. S. Neill, Homer Lane, W. H. Kilpatrick*.

knowledge for coherence and mastery is played down: pupils are expected to look after the knowledge aspect for themselves far more than in the traditional school situation. In the personality dimension the child-centred teacher is not expected to instruct the pupil in what to believe, but to lead him by discussion and by example to accept worthy, but not very well-defined, objectives, and discussion is seen as a good instrument in itself. Essentially the teacher is a guide, a therapist, a psychologist more than an instructor and the assumption is that the pupil will come to see this and co-operate in the whole process. If the response of the pupil in the knowledge dimension or in the personality dimension is not co-operative, the child-centred teacher tends to see this in terms of breakdown in personal relationships, whereas to the traditional teacher it tends to appear as laziness or incomprehension or moral weakness on the part of the pupil. A major part of the responsibility for conducting pupil-teacher relationships in the child-centred mode of thinking is placed on the child, although in another area of the theory it is assumed that there is a developmental sequence whereby children's problems lead into and become adult problems. Here is a dilemma in child-centred thinking – the encouragement of spontaneity on the one hand, and the expectation of maturity beyond a child's years on the other. Traditionalists emphasize the secondary-school age range and are less sure of what to do with young children; the child-centred supporters stress the development of younger children, and their interest-based principles of self-regulation are more difficult to maintain with the standard of knowledge required for older adolescents.

These broad categories form a sketched recapitulation of many beliefs and practices instanced in the schools we have considered earlier. I now turn to some rather different conceptual points.

Education may be seen as a deliberate attempt to induct younger members of a society into ideas, skills, and attitudes which arise from the past or are intended to be of use in dealing with the present and the future. It would be possible to trace this argument through a very broad social context, but for the moment I wish to keep it within the school. In general terms school education has to do with teachers, pupils, knowledge, and the institutions within which the transaction of education takes place. The teachers and the pupils can be grouped together as persons, but this would be to overlook the relationship between them that the existence of a school presupposes. The school is in business to teach and to enable children to learn, whether by traditional or child-centred methods. Ross Finney put the matter like this: 'The [primary] purpose of school is to pass on cognitive capital. Only secondarily is it for getting young people together.'[2]

Of course, because they *are* together the young people and their elders do in fact strike up human relationships of all kinds, and the progressive schools regard this as a prime necessity, but the classroom and the school present a pattern of relationships in which a leader is needed whose institutional function to instruct has already been decided. The teacher is not the 'natural' leader of the group: only a child in the group or some older person, spontaneously chosen either by election or by acceptance of his superiority, can be that. Personal or natural leadership arises when somebody leads spontaneously, being readier to act, more unexpected and complex, maybe more ruthless, than the led. An 'institutional' leader may not do this because he has an expected pattern of behaviour to follow and a conventional framework in which to operate: as one writer has it, his personal influence must be strained through the sieve of formality.[3]

The teacher is, in the first place, an institutional leader. Prestige attaches to the office and authority rests, at the beginning, in the laws and traditions of the office and only later on the teacher as a person. Willard Waller in *The Sociology of Teaching* puts this point trenchantly: 'Until the teacher's definition of the situation has been accepted he cannot relax. Friendly attitudes must spring up only in a situation defined in terms of teacher domination.'[4] So bald a statement may perturb many people and it appears to be the antithesis of the principles of Homer Lane, Neill, and Curry, but Waller is only stating what happens in most schools. In any case the

---

[2] R. L. Finney, *A Sociological Philosophy of Education* (New York, 1928). For a recent contribution to the discussion of this whole issue, see Elizabeth Richardson, *The Environment of Learning* (London, 1967).

[3] The late Sir Fred Clarke, in a letter to the author.

[4] W. Waller, *The Sociology of Teaching* (New York, 1932), p. 297.

statement offers wide variations of interpretation and indicates simply that the teacher has the training and the responsibility for planning how to communicate knowledge to a group of children who may not wish to learn what he presents. If this is so, some kind of final authority and incentive has to be available within the structure of the group and, according to Waller, it is vested in the teacher. This dominance–submission aspect is a basic condition of the relationship between the teacher and his pupils, whether it is arrived at by the traditionalist's method or by Neill's method of waiting for inner development in the child. The final recognition by the child is that this adult has something to give for which his pupils must accept conditions which will allow him to teach them.

In this area of leadership, authority, dominance, and submission, one is constantly moving between psychological and sociological interpretations. The psychological interpretation is concerned with the content of, the changes and motives in, human experience. Sociology is concerned far more with the structure of the groupings in which the content, changes, and motives express themselves. The territory of institutional and personal relationships between teachers and pupils is a borderland because from one point of view we are concerned with the content of human attitudes and experience and from another we are interested in the kind of grouping and organization which gives direction to these psychological processes. The progressive schools are committed to a psychological emphasis in the relationship between teacher and pupil and seek to accept only the necessary minimum of dominance–submission structure, a sociological emphasis, to make this possible. The traditional model would reverse the order and this is a very important distinction in trying to understand the difference of ethos between a grammar or public school and a progressive school.

It was said earlier that school education has to do with teachers, pupils, knowledge, and the institutions within which the transaction of education takes place. Enough has just been said on teachers and pupils to show the importance progressive schools attach to the personal part of the teacher's relationship. Earlier still in this chapter, I mentioned the tendency in these schools to diminish the importance of the factual side of knowledge. In the past the evidence for this is seen in the readiness to wait until a child wants to learn; in giving initiative to the pupil in the project method; in avoiding a stereotyped examination objective; in new methods of teaching such as those advocated by Montessori, Dalcroze, Cizek, Caldwell Cook, Dewey, and seen in Helen Parkhurst's Dalton plan, Gordonstoun's training plan and rescue services, and the three phases of growth in Steiner's methodology. However, since the end of the Second World War new initiatives in educational methods have come from sources outside the progressive movement, notably in curriculum reorganization: the New Mathematics, Nuffield Science, French in primary schools, programmed instruction, the Schools Council's School Leaving Age Project and its many other undertakings now being developed. These are the new experts who are experimental and test out ideas and methods.

So far in this consideration of conceptual points arising from school education I have looked at teachers, pupils, and knowledge. Now I turn to the institutions within which the transaction of education takes place, and at this point the argument moves back into the mainstream of historical and social analysis.

III

A school cannot maintain existence for long without stable financial backing: it needs pupils, teachers, and equipment and in England, as we have seen, it has to be recognized as efficient by the central authority. If the school is part of the national provision its building and upkeep are, within broad limits, the responsibility of the local education authority and the Department of Education and Science. Many schools were originally, and still are, religious foundations, supported as to a small part from church funds and as to a much larger part from local authority and central sources. Education has become a social service which has to compete for its share of the gross national product with the other services, like health, housing, foreign commitments, and defence, and there is a tendency for the interests of the local areas and regions, which have administered education since 1902, to detect and combat increasing control from the centre. The Royal Commission on Local Government recently redrew the present map of over one hundred and forty authorities to form a much smaller number of regions, with the obvious redistribution between local and national taxation and political and administrative power if these recommendations are accepted.[5]

With an expanding education service like ours a vast amount of central financial planning is necessary. The planning has to include forecasting the number of school places needed for children of different ages and a long-range provision of the facilities for the training of teachers in corresponding numbers. A consequence of this decentralized organization with ultimate responsibility at the centre in the hands of the secretary of state for education and science is that he can insist upon equality of standard throughout the country. The spurs that prick him to maintain this could be political expediency as well as humane concern and the professional conscience of his permanent civil servants and Her Majesty's Inspectorate.

Political policy and calculation are bound to appear in many government decisions on educational matters. Economic decisions are obviously made on political grounds as well, but recently political policy is even more obvious. The recent Labour government decided that in one form or another secondary education should be comprehensive in form. Where in 1962 about a dozen local authorities operated comprehensive schools, in 1970 the application by all one hundred and forty-six authorities of the comprehensive principle remained to be worked out following upon the central requirement in Circular 10/65 to draw up plans. There are, of course, strictly educational arguments for comprehensive education, but there are many political ones too, and many of them have to do with making life chances more equal, with reducing middle- and upper-class privilege. The Conservative government elected in June 1970 has now modified the requirements of Circular 10/65 and political influences are once more apparent.

[5] *Report of the Royal Commission on Local Government in England 1966–69*, vol. i (Command 4040). The main recommendations propose sixty-one new local government areas, grouped, with Greater London, into eight provinces. The present Government has modified these proposals and changes are planned for 1974.

Secondary education is expensive and the country has a right to expect efficiency and value for money. Implicit in this economic argument is a concern for as fair a distribution of manpower and equipment as possible, and so there is talk of a proper use of plant, rationalization of teacher supply, the minimum size for an economic unit in secondary education, the use of mechanical aids of all kinds, the problems of man management in large-scale organization. The crest of the wave of the social sciences in British educational thinking broke with great power in the 1960s.

Richard Peters speaks of some of these features as extrinsic to education:

> Some politicians whose noses quiver at the scent of any sort of under-privilege have found in education a quarry that they think they may more safely run to earth than the ferocious old foxes of private ownership and disparity of income. Others, with nervous eyes on the technical achievements of the U.S.A. and U.S.S.R., gladly listen to economists who assure them that education is a commodity in which it is profitable for a community to invest. Sociologists tell teachers that they have a role of acting as a socializing agency in the community.... In all the hubbub about plant, supply of teachers, shortage of provision, streaming and selection too little attention is paid to what it is that so many are deemed to be without.[6]

The 1944 Act stated that secondary education in its totality, for the whole range of pupils, would be available according to age, ability, and aptitude, and no longer on the basis of ability to pay. The first step in organization was the so-called tripartite plan in which 'parity of esteem' was looked for as between grammar, technical high, and secondary modern schools, and the latest step in this progression is the policy of comprehensive schools. But schools persisted which admitted children whose parents could pay and the teachers continued to say that they wanted to provide education for these pupils. We have seen earlier how these schools have come under the

[6] R. S. Peters, *Education as Initiation: an Inaugural Lecture*, University of London, pp. 9 and 11.

professional eye of the central authority and have to be recognized as efficient, and few of those I have dealt with in this book are not regarded as being well-run educational establishments. The three principal criticisms of independent schools are that they provide teaching conditions which demand a larger proportion of trained staff than the maintained schools; that they take a sector of the child population which comes from affluent homes and so they act as a socially divisive group; that, in the case of the public schools, former pupils are at a position of advantage in entry particularly to the older universities and in careers by reason of their school education – what is often called 'the old boy network'.

The maintained, tripartite, secondary system was considered by the recent Labour government as an historic blunder in social administration and they undertook in a very clear way to reshape educational organization as part of political strategy. Sociologists, economists, and social theorists have perspectives for society as a whole in which education is seen as an instrument for self-preservation or prosperity, for conservation or change. They are not primarily concerned with a person being educated, still less with the liberal or the progressive tradition, and here lies the cause of a good deal of recrimination between the teacher, the administrator, the economist, and the politician. Each adopts a different viewpoint or emphasis on education with variable attempts at comprehending one another.

The progressive schools were founded by teachers who had ideas of what should be taught and how it should be taught. Each school was to be a place in its own right, sufficient for the children and parents who supported it, and the foundation owed nothing to local or national administration, it was not thought of as an economic or political agency in any direct sense, and history has not given these unorthodox schools any disproportionate influence in entry to higher education or to certain careers.

The National Union of Teachers, in numbers and influence by far the greatest of the teachers' associations, in its evidence to the Newsom Committee on the independent schools demanded the complete integration into the maintained system not only of the public schools but of all other independent education, largely on the principle that fee-paying education is inconsistent with an egalitarian democracy and a range of maintained schools of the highest quality. A number of other bodies submitted evidence of a similar kind, and writing on this Kenneth Barnes, the head of Wennington, said:

> Can anyone be so complacent about mass-organized education as to believe that it needs no more shocks from independent innovators? Is it certain that in large-scale organization the odd-man-out on the school staff, the chap with the queer ideas, will some day be given a headship to show whether he is a creator or only mad? ... Because my school is independent I can say frankly to parents that I put personal development before academic success, that I value maturity, originality, resourcefulness, love, and generosity before examination results.... There are many State-school teachers, especially in the primary schools, whose convictions are similar, but my independence makes it possible to stand out firmly and to get all-round support for a thorough-going project.... Does the N.U.T. wish to deny the right of Wennington School to exist, to take away its independence with that of Summerhill and Eton?[7]

Barnes goes on to ask what kind of legislation would be necessary to take away the independence that already exists and to prevent the future establishment of schools, and concludes that legislation no less venomous than that of the Conventicle Act of 1662, which forbade the religious meetings of Dissenters under mounting penalties, would be required. He does not believe that any British government would be so stupid or so totalitarian as to try.

IV

Dr. Pedley, writing of comprehensive schools, has said:

> It would seem more difficult for the head of a school with over 1,000 pupils effectively to carry out a radically pro-

[7] K. Barnes, 'Do they know what they want?', in *The Guardian*, 29 Mar. 1967.

gressive policy. Such a policy depends for success upon the faith of the teachers that it is right: preferably the faith of all the teachers and certainly the great majority. A head can only work through his staff. He can inspire them, encourage them, set them his own example – but he cannot expect always to convert them.... Is it likely that fifty teachers could be found to staff one local school who believed, for example, in more self-government for the pupils; who were prepared to abjure the convenience of routine control of young children by prefects, prepared to share in these chores themselves and to share out the sense of power which comes from taking decisions that really matter; who were prepared to renounce the aids of orthodox rewards and punishments? And even if it were likely, would not such a large team of individualists tend always to diverge? It is significant that all our really progressive schools are small schools.[8]

It is undoubtedly hard for a maintained day secondary school, part of the provision for compulsory schooling between certain ages, to be noticeably unorthodox because of parental misgivings in the area which it serves and the pull of the norm of the other schools of a particular local authority. Yet there have been exceptions. Two which are often quoted are Prestolee Elementary School near Farnworth in Lancashire, whose headmaster was Edward O'Neill, and St. George-in-the-East in London's East End, with Alexander Bloom as head. O'Neill went to Prestolee in 1918 after service in two or three schools of legendary ferocity elsewhere. He had himself come through a harsh childhood in a Salford slum, where he lived with his mother and sister in an off-licence, his father being a drunkard. O'Neill's scholastic career was not good, and after service as a pupil-teacher, he went to Crewe Training College, from which he qualified in 1913. At Prestolee, between Bolton and Manchester, for a long time he encountered hostility from teachers, managers, and parents as he revolutionized the curriculum and the conduct of the school. There were the usual letters in local papers about children doing what they liked, without a time-table. We have seen this kind

---

[8] See R. Pedley, *The Comprehensive School* (London, 1963). Quoted here from 'Comprehensive Schools', in *Anarchy* (Aug. 1962), p. 231.

of thing in the independent progressive schools. O'Neill and the pupils made furniture, set up aquaria, produced self-written books, built gardens, mounted exhibitions, decorated the school. Many of the children when he first went were half-timers in the mills and he fought the mill-owners, some of the parents and managers, and the children themselves to do away with part-time earning.

O'Neill addressed the Conference of New Ideals in Education and was known to all the leaders of the progressive movement during his headship of over thirty years at Prestolee. During that time he won substantial support from parents, the Lancashire authority, and in the area at large. As teachers came to know the kind of school Prestolee was, most of those who joined the staff were prepared to sympathize with the aims and methods.[9] But when O'Neill retired the L.E.A. or the governors or succeeding heads were not expected to continue his ideas and methods.

Alexander Bloom was appointed to the derelict St. George-in-the-East in Cable Street, Stepney, at the end of the Second World War, and before his death ten years later he had conducted a school on free lines. When he began there was no careful selection of colleagues by the head and no consultation between parents and the school. Bloom was given two hundred and sixty boys and girls from local primary schools and ten teachers mostly strangers to one another and to him. He had close knowledge of war-time and post-war Stepney with its babel of tongues and desert of bomb ruins. He started a community rather than a school and the style was alien to Stepney. As with O'Neill, his ideas drove away many of his teachers and led to public criticism of him and his work in the local juvenile court. A. S. Neill and others praised Bloom's work and the L.C.C. later on sent especially difficult children to him from outside the vicinity of his school, recognizing worth in his unorthodoxy. But again, after his death there was no educational policy that guaranteed continuity of his ideas and methods. The same can be said for Mr. Mackenzie's innovations at Braehead in the Lowlands of Scotland.

Mention has already been made of Mr. Duane, the former head of Risinghill, an L.C.C. comprehensive school in Fins-

[9] For details, see G. Holmes, *The Idiot Teacher* (London, 1952).

bury. Duane went there in 1960 and adopted a permissive discipline in an area which was described as having 'some of the worst slums, brothels, and clubs in North London and being opposite a market from which a constant stream of rubbish is blown into the school grounds'.[10] As with St. George-in-the-East children were collected from four other schools to start it off, with the obvious results at the beginning of gang conflict, destructiveness, and obscenities. About one hundred pupils were on probation and in three years children from Risinghill appeared in the juvenile court over two hundred and forty times. Mr. Duane would not use corporal punishment and claimed that after a few years the pupils on probation were less than one-tenth of what they had been, and that many of the juvenile court cases were not due to delinquency by the children but to gross neglect by the parents so that the children were appearing before the magistrates as in need of care and protection. The comprehensive nature of the school presupposed a proportionate spread of intellectual ability from high to low. At Risinghill at first the lower end of the ability range was very heavily weighted: many parents and teachers of children of ability did not choose the school for their boys and girls. There were many immigrants in Islington, especially Cypriots and West Indians, and Mr. Duane had members of staff who spoke Greek and Turkish as well as other languages to help with this kind of assimilation. He declared himself a humanist and antagonized many people thereby. Gossip, press reports, some bad behaviour by pupils tended to obscure the increasing academic and social success the school appeared to be having.

In January 1965 the L.C.C. produced a statement that acute accommodation pressure in other nearby schools made it necessary to rearrange premises. Risinghill in 1960 and soon after had over fourteen hundred pupils on the roll and the new intake at eleven plus had nearly all put the new school as their first choice. In 1965 there were two hundred and forty first year places but only one hundred and fifty-two boys and girls

[10] From an article by M. Hamlyn in *The Sunday Times*, 10 Jan. 1965. An extended consideration of this school is to be found in Leila Berg, *Risinghill: Death of a Comprehensive School* (London, 1968). Mrs. Berg is highly critical of the L.C.C. and favourable to the continuation of Mr. Duane's work at Risinghill, which after his departure was renamed Starcross School.

actually started at the school and of those only a half had made the school their first choice and only one fifth made it their second choice. In 1964 the numbers at the school had fallen from over fourteen hundred four years before to about eight hundred and fifty, and the L.C.C. report says:

> There is substantial evidence of increasing parental preference for single-sex schools in the area. The Council must take these considerations into account if its arrangements for secondary education are to be based on the best interests of the pupils and parental wishes, as they must be.

The claims of other schools for greater space were real enough and in 1965 Risinghill was closed, amid loud protests from the progressives, to make way for another secondary school. Mr. Duane believed that Risinghill had just reached its turning-point. He considered that parents and local primary schools were seeing that the pupils were by no means only wild and in a short while the school would have got its proper, first-choice share of children of good ability. However, the school was closed and Mr. Duane was displaced, but to him 'the Council's long-established practice of safeguarding such head teachers' salaries, and so far as possible, their status, will apply'.

Very many articles and news reports were written on the subject. One of these expressed the hope that if the recommendation in *Half Our Future* to found an experimental school were carried out, it might be Risinghill:

> If the L.C.C. doesn't appreciate Risinghill there are plenty of people who do. It has received petitions from the staff, from the Islington probation officers, from the parents and from several groups of children. As *Freedom* puts it ... 'When kids march through the streets demanding that their headmaster should not be sacked, that headmaster has made a breakthrough in education.'[11]

It would appear that the points made by Pedley have been borne out at Risinghill. Comparing it with some of the schools

[11] J. Ellerby, 'Mr. Duane of Risinghill', in *Anarchy* (Feb. 1965), p. 56.

considered in earlier chapters of this book, of course the community advantages are with Ackworth with nearly five hundred pupils and Bedales with less than three hundred pupils as compared with Risinghill's fourteen hundred. Of course the two progressive schools have boys and girls from homes whose parents have selected these schools because they want their children to live in that kind of educational atmosphere. Of course the physical surroundings in Yorkshire and Hampshire are startlingly different from those in Finsbury. Of course the staff are hand-picked and have voluntarily become a part of the educational enterprise at Ackworth and Bedales. Of course even if all local education authorities were as good as the best, they must safeguard public money and see that justice is done as between schools and as between parents. Clearly if a particular approach to schooling is so unorthodox as to unsettle many parents in a neighbourhood and lead to falling numbers, the local education authority cannot be required to sustain the experiment within the framework of zoning and compulsory schooling for the years necessary for the idea to be tested and accepted. Perhaps, however, it will now be possible for at least some local education authorities to take the risks involved, and to invest in a Reddie or a Neill or a Barnes or a Bloom, and try to assess the results with a hope of continuity. The recommendations of Dr. Lambert on the foundation of local authority boarding-schools, of which there are at present only a few, may help in this direction.

V

In curricular matters there are growing-points in schools of all kinds and these have come through original teachers like Cizek or Caldwell Cook or Armstrong or in our own day Gerd Sommerhoff; or through psychological thinking as in Piaget or Skinner or Bruner; or through sociological thinking as with Willard Waller, Bernstein, or Mannheim; or by academic revaluations as with Dienes in mathematics or I. A. Richards or F. R. Leavis in English or Namier in history; or in group rethinking of which good examples are the Nuffield Science curricula, the American ventures in physics, chemistry, and biology, and the Schools Council enterprises in the social sciences and the humanities in this country. The progressive schools cannot any longer claim that they are in any special sense educational laboratories. They have no particular likelihood of being uniquely original now that many others are actively engaged in giving their best efforts to academic and curricular reconstruction on the basis of what expert knowledge in subject matter, sociological context, and learning theory can provide.

Sevenoaks, a fifteenth-century grammar school, became a public school about twenty years ago, and its work in art, mathematics, technical activities, and English is original by any standard, as is the social outlook in its voluntary service unit and the international centre. Experience of Dartington as well as Repton is represented on the staff and the combination of ancient and modern may account in part for the quality and vitality of the whole curriculum there.[12] Other examples could be quoted to show that in the field of curriculum the progressive schools are not likely to be the lone pioneers any more. In art, drama, mathematics, modern languages, music, and science, good and original teaching can be found in many maintained and public schools as well as in the innovatory schools we have considered.

VI

Progressive schools have a belief that education is made for man and not man for education. Uniformly they have a fundamentally religious, if not always a Christian, view of the worth of persons: knowledge and competition are subordinate to the ideal of relationship; intellectual achievement is ultimately part of your way of living with yourself and others, and even if you cannot grasp this until much later, your school should so balance your learning and living that you are on the way to seeing that this is a real issue. This demands a proper respect for a range of experience – intellectual, aesthetic, religious, moral, social, physical, emotional, and expressive. It also requires a comprehensive view of what the curriculum provides and what the rest of school life is directed towards.

[12] L. C. Taylor (ed.), *Experiments in Education at Sevenoaks* (London, 1965).

The progressive schools see the economic framework in which schools are set, they see the sociological, political, and administrative structure, but for them all real life is meeting. A secular society concerned with parity of esteem, an equitable system of school provision, and a rationalized distribution of facilities in the context of planning and social engineering will settle a number of economic and structural questions and will probably provide a social service to which society is entitled in terms of efficiency. But what then? The innovators have been teachers with a conviction that what they taught was a symbol, an excuse, for something more profound and personal – a relationship of the kind indicated in earlier pages. They have set up independent schools to bring together others of like mind to help in this, however imperfectly. Where secular maintained schools provide the places and the amenities as a social service and where research has improved and refined the instruments of teaching, a school can be a humane, intellectually lively, well-organized, and efficient organization. While it may have, it need not have a declared set of principles and values which teachers and parents voluntarily select for themselves and their children.

Perhaps at the end we may now have to say that what has been called progressive in relation to the world between 1750 and 1970 no longer signifies. To meet a new challenge of size, mechanization, rationalized manpower, and the transformation of work and leisure, a different kind of progressive school must arise to correct the social and economic inequalities which history has provided, and to take opportunity by the forelock. Here large, comprehensive schools are tending to become the norm and mechanical aids the necessary supplement to teachers. The simulations of mental processes which have been applied in programmed instruction and the computer provide a new dimension and may enforce a revaluation of the school as a social community. Here the notion of the school as an extended family is not only not progressive any more, it may be an anachronism. This is a field of comparison rich in research possibilities which this book as a study of a movement has not explored. Such an investigation would be very complex indeed, but more sensitive techniques of inquiry now make it almost feasible.

VII

In most cases progressive schools over the years have shown a gradual regression in educational practice towards an imaginary average, but even now they are still recognizably unique as communities, as Caroline Nicholson found when she visited them in 1963 and thought them freer, more receptive, more informal, more permissive than other secondary schools and as Edward Blishen corroborated in 1966: 'There seemed to me to be a dignity [at Dartington] that arose from the agreeableness and frankness of the relationships.'[13] So far I have not found evidence that such continuity in local authority schools exists, though the gap is narrow at some points and young people as a whole now appear more ready for this kind of educational ethos.[14]

If the progressive schools have been mainly the preserve of the liberal intelligentsia it is because they have represented a minority product in which such groups are interested. The implied assumptions are that the child should be an initiator who accepts only necessary, minimal submission to his adult teacher so that, as a consequence, he is not overawed by adult life when he attains to it. His habits of relationship to adults and his self-concept are expected to lead to an open-minded confidence and readiness to question. Alongside this scepticism, however, he is supposed to realize the need for mutual understanding and the acceptance of responsibility. This is part of a kind of adult life-view which has usually been found in the past in certain parts of the upper-middle reaches of the class structure: detachment, insight, and confidence in the ability to influence or change the situation are all necessary for it. If this is so the political criticism of progressive education, that it is an example of privilege, is shallow. Admittedly, the schools charge higher fees and have the advantages of smaller classes, but if the kind of education offered by Bedales

[13] E. Blishen, 'Experiments in Education', in *The Daily Telegraph*, 22 Apr. 1966, p. 19.
[14] E. Blishen (ed.), *The School That I'd Like* (London, 1969). See also the impact of Ivan Illich, *Deschooling Society* (London, 1971) and *Celebration of Awareness* (London, 1971) and the writings of Paul Goodman.

and Summerhill were open to all, would many parents find it easy to share the educational and cultural assumptions of these schools and others like them? Will the L.E.A. take the risk and provide it? If so it will have to be as an unusual commodity, and not as the ordinary school provision. And if they will not provide it at all, will they then say that future Badleys and Neills will not be allowed to start such schools privately and take their chance of public support? This is what Barnes is talking about when he speaks in terms of a new Conventicle Act. It is in this context that Illich's 'deschooling' should be seen.

Richard Peters makes two points which can bring the long recapitulation of this final chapter to a point of rest:

> Education, then, can have no ends beyond itself.... To be educated is not to have arrived at a destination; it is to travel with a different view.... 'There is a quality of life which lies always beyond the mere fact of life' [as Whitehead said]. The great teacher is he who can convey this sense of quality to another, so that it haunts his every endeavour and makes him sweat and yearn to fix what he thinks and feels in a fitting form.... It is education that provides that touch of eternity, under the aspect of which endurance can pass into dignified, wry acceptance and animal enjoyment into a quality of living.[15]

Many teachers as persons have this in mind and so do schools of many kinds. The innovators of the last two centuries whom I have presented in this book have in addition tried to build a place and a community which they thought was nearer to this heart's desire.

[15] Peters, *Education as Initiation*, pp. 47–8.

Bibliography

Books

Acland, T. D., *The Education of the Farmer, Viewed in Connection with that of the Middle Classes in General*, London, 1857.
Archambault, R. D. (ed.), *Philosophical Analysis and Education*, London, 1965.
Armytage, W. H. G., *Heavens Below*, London, 1961.
— *Four Hundred Years of English Education*, Cambridge, 1964.
Arnold, M., *A French Eton; or, Middle Class Education and the State*, London, 1864.
Arnold-Brown, A., *Unfolding of Character: The Impact of Gordonstoun*, London, 1962.
Attersoll, J., *Translation of the Reports of M. le Comte de Capo D'Istria and M. Rengger upon the Principles and Progress of the Establishment of M. de Fellenberg at Hofwyl, Switzerland*, London, 1820.
Badley, J. H., *A Schoolmaster's Testament*, Oxford, 1937.
— *Memories and Reflections*, London, 1955.
— *Bedales: A Pioneer School*, London, 1923.
Barbier, A., *Éducation Internationale*, Paris, 1862.
Barbier, C. P., *William Gilpin, his Drawings, Teaching and Theory of the Picturesque*, Oxford, 1963.
Bazeley, E. T., *Homer Lane and the Little Commonwealth*, London, 1928 and 1948.
Beer, M. (ed.), *The Life of Robert Owen by Himself*, London, 1920.
Bell, A., *An Experiment in Education, Made at the Male Asylum of Madras*, London, 1797.
— *An Experiment in Education, Made at the Male Asylum at Egmore, near Madras*, London, 1805.
— *An Analysis of the Experiment in Education, Made at Egmore, near Madras*, London, 1807.
Bennett, C. A., *History of Manual and Industrial Education up to 1870*, Peoria, Ill., 1926.

Bentham, J., *Chrestomathia*, in J. Bowring (ed.), *The Works of Jeremy Bentham*, 11 vols., Edinburgh, 1838–43.
Berg, Leila, *Risinghill: Death of a Comprehensive School*, London, 1968.
Besant, Annie, *Gospel of Atheism*, 1877.
Blavatsky, Helena, *The Secret Doctrine*, London, 1931.
Blewitt, T. (ed.), *The Modern Schools Handbook*, London, 1934.
Blishen, E. (ed.), *The School that I'd Like*, London, 1969.
Blyth, E. K., *Life of William Ellis*, London, 1889.
Body, A. H., *John Wesley and Education*, London, 1936.
Bonham-Carter, V., *Dartington Hall*, London, 1958.
History of Bootham School, 1823–1923, London, 1926.
Boring, E. G., *A History of Experimental Psychology*, New York, 2nd ed., 1950.
Bowring, J. (ed.), *The Works of Jeremy Bentham*, 11 vols., Edinburgh, 1838–43.
Boyd, W., and Rawson, W., *The Story of the New Education*, London, 1965.
Brath, S. de, *The Foundations of Success: a Plea for a Rational Education*, 1896.
Brereton, H. L., *Gordonstoun*, London, 1968.
Bright, J., and Rogers, J. E. T. (eds.), *Speeches on Questions of Public Policy by Richard Cobden, M.P.*, 2 vols., London, 1870.
British Economy: Key Statistics 1900–1964, Cambridge.
Brooke, H., *The Fool of Quality*, 4 vols., London, 1766.
Brown, J., *Sermons on Various Subjects*, London, 1764.
Brown, W. H., *Brighton's Co-operative Advance*, Manchester (n.d.).
Bryson, Gladys, *Man and Society: The Scottish Inquiry of the Eighteenth Century*, Princeton, 1945.
Buchanan, B. I., *Buchanan Family Records*, Cape Town, 1923.
Burton, Hester, *Barbara Bodichon*, London, 1949.
Byron, Lady Noel, *What Fellenberg has Done for Education*, London, 1839.
Carpenter, E., *Towards Democracy*, 1883 and 1902.
Carpenter, L., *Principles of Education: Intellectual, Moral and Physical*, London, 1820.

Castle, E. B., *Moral Education in Christian Times*, London, 1958.
Child, H. A. T. (ed.), *The Independent Progressive School*, London, 1962.
Coade, T., *The Burning Bow*, London, 1966.
Combe, G., *Essays on Phrenology*, Edinburgh, 1819.
   Elements of Phrenology, Edinburgh, 1824.
   A System of Phrenology, Edinburgh, 1825.
   The Constitution of Man, Edinburgh, 1828.
   Moral Philosophy, or, the duties of man considered in his individual, domestic, social and religious capacities, Edinburgh, 1840.
   Discussions on Education, in *Select Works of George Combe*, 5 vols., London, 1893.
Comenius, J. A., *The Great Didactic*, trans. M. W. Keatinge, London, 1896.
Cook, E. T., and Wedderburn, A., *The Works of John Ruskin*, London, 1905.
Cremin, L. A., *Transformation of the School*, New York, 1961.
Cresswell, D., *Margaret McMillan: A Memoir*, London, 1948.
Cullen, A., *Adventures in Socialism*, Glasgow, 1910.
Culverwell, E. P., *Montessori Principles and Practice*, London, 1913.
Curry, W. B., *The School*, London, 1934.
   Education for Sanity, London, 1947.
   'Dartington Hall', in *Modern Schools Handbook*, London, 1934.
Davenport-Hill, R. and F., *The Recorder of Birmingham: A Memoir of Matthew Davenport-Hill*, London, 1878.
Davies, J. D., *Phrenology: Fad and Science*, New Haven, Conn., 1955.
Dawes, R., *Remarks Occasioned by the Present Crusade against the Educational Plans of the Committee of Council on Education*, London, 1850.
   Hints on an Improved and Self-Paying System of National Education, Suggested from the Working of the Village School of King's Somborne in Hampshire, London, 5th ed., 1855.
   Effective Primary Instruction, London, 1857.

Schools and Other Similar Institutions for the Industrial Classes, London, 1853.
Suggestive Hints towards Improved Secular Instruction, Making it bear on Practical Life, London, 6th ed., 1953.
Observations on the Working of the Government Scheme of Education and on School Inspection, London, 1849.
Day, T., *The History of Sandford and Merton*, 3 vols., London, 1783–9.
Demolins, E., *Anglo-Saxon Superiority: To What Is It due?*, London, 1898.
L'Éducation Nouvelle, Paris, 1901.
Dewey, Evelyn, *The Dalton Laboratory Plan*, London, 1924.
Dewey, J., *The School and Society*, New York, 1899.
Moral Principles in Education, New York, 1909.
How We Think, New York, 1910.
Interest and Effort in Education, New York, 1913.
Democracy and Education, New York, 1916.
My Pedagogic Creed, New York, 1897.
The Child and the Curriculum, New York, 1902.
Dictionary of National Biography.
Dowling, P. J., *The Hedge Schools of Ireland*, Dublin (n.d.).
Edgeworth, Maria, *Harry and Lucy*, London, 1778.
Edgeworth, R. L., *Memoirs*, 2 vols., London, 1820.
Edmunds, L. F., *Rudolf Steiner Education*, London, 1962.
Eliot, G., *Romola*, 3 vols., London, 1863.
Ellis, E. E., *Memoir of William Ellis*, London, 1888.
Ellis, J., *Songs for Children*,
The Human Body Described,
Lessons on Objects,
Ellis W., *Thoughts on the Future of the Human Race*, London, 1866.
Elmhirst, L. (ed.), *Rabindranath Tagore, Pioneer in Education*, London, 1961.
Fairchild, H. N., *The Noble Savage*, New York, 1928.
Farrar, F. W. (ed.), *Essays on a Liberal Education*, London, 1867.
Fichte, J. G., *Wissenschaftslehre*, 1795.
Finney, R. L., *A Sociological Philosophy of Education*, New York, 1928.

Bibliography

Flexner, A., *A Modern College and a Modern School*, New York, 1923.
Fortescue, Hugh (3rd Earl Fortescue), *Public Schools for the Middle Classes*, London, 1864.
Freud, S., *The Interpretation of Dreams*, London, 1900.
The Psycho-Pathology of Everyday Life, London, 1904.
Three Essays on the Theory of Sexuality, London, 1905.
Totem and Taboo, London, 1912.
Introductory Lectures on Psycho-Aanalysis, London, 1915–17.
de Genlis, Stephanie Félicité (Marchioness de Sittery), *Adèle et Théodore*, 3 vols., London, 1783.
Gaskell, E. C., *The Life of Charlotte Bronte*, 2 vols., London, 1857.
George, W. R., *Citizens Made and Remade*, New York, 1913.
The Junior Republic: Its History and Ideals, New York, 1910.
Gibbon, C., *The Life of George Combe*, 2 vols., London, 1878.
Giesbers, J. H. G. I., *Cecil Reddie and Abbotsholme*, Nijmegen, 1970.
Gilpin, W., *Memoirs of Dr. Richard Gilpin*, London, 1879.
Godwin, W., *An Account of the Seminary ... at Epsom in Surrey for the Instruction of Twelve Pupils...*, London, 1783.
An Enquiry Concerning Political Justice, and its Influence on General Virtue and Happiness, 2 vols., London, 1793.
Graham, Patricia A., *Progressive Education: From Arcady to Academe*, New York, 1967.
Graves, R., *Good-bye to All That*, London, 1929.
Greene, Graham (ed.), *The Old School*, London, 1934.
Greville, C. C., *A Journal of the Reign of Queen Victoria from 1837 to 1852*, 3 vols., London, 1885.
Grove, W. H., *A Memoir of the Late Rev. William Gilpin, MA.*, Lymington, 1851.
Guggisberg, K., *Philipp Emanuel von Fellenberg und sein Erziehungsstaat*, 2 vols., Berne, 1953.
Haight, G. S., *George Eliot and John Chapman*, New Haven, Conn., 1940.
Harrison, J. F. C., *Learning and Living, 1790–1960*, London, 1961.

Harwood, A. C. (ed.), *The Faithful Thinker*, London, 1961.
Heckstall-Smith, H., *Doubtful Schoolmaster*, London, 1962.
Henderson, J. L., *Look Out*, 1965.
Hennell, Mary, *An Outline of the Various Social Systems and Communities Which Have Been Founded on the Principle of Co-operation*, London, 1844.
Henry, W. C., *A Biographical Notice of the Late Richard Dawes, M.A., Dean of Hereford*, London, 1867.
Hill, Matthew Davenport, *Public Education: Plans for the Government and Liberal Instruction of Boys, in Large Numbers; as Practised at Hazelwood School*, London, 2nd ed., 1825.
Hill, A., *Sketch of the System of Education, Moral and Intellectual, in Practice at the Schools of Bruce Castle, Tottenham, and Hazelwood, Near Birmingham*, London, 1833.
— (ed.) *Essays Upon Educational Subjects Read at the Educational Conference of June 1857*, London, 1857.
Hill, R. and F. (eds.), *Laws of Hazelwood School*, London, 1827.
Hodgson, G. E., *Rationalist English Educators*, London, 1912.
Holmes, E., *What Is and What Might Be*, London, 1911.
— *In Quest of an Ideal*, London, 1920.
Holmes, G., *The Idiot Teacher*, London, 1952.
Hyndman, H. M., *Historical Bases of Socialism*, London, 1883.
— *Commercial Crises of the Nineteenth Century*, London, 1892.
— *Economics of Socialism*, London, 1896.
Isaacs, Susan, *Intellectual Growth in Young Children*, London, 1930.
— *Social Development in Young Children*, London, 1933.
Itard, J. E. M. G., *An Historical Account of the Discovery and Education of a Savage Man*, trans. 1802.
Jolly, W., *Education, Its Principles and Practice as Developed by George Combe*, London, 1879.
Jones, E., *The Life and Work of Sigmund Freud*, 3 vols., London, 1953, 1955, 1957.
Judges, A. V. (ed.), *The Function of Teaching*, London, 1959.
Kalton, G., *The Public Schools*, London, 1966.
Kamm, Josephine, *Hope Deferred: Girls' Education in English History*, London, 1965.

Kant, I., *Critique of Pure Reason.*
Kay-Shuttleworth, J., *Four Periods of Public Education*, London, 1862.
Knox, V., *Liberal Education; or, A Practical Treatise on the Methods of Acquiring Useful and Polite Learning*, London, 1781.
Laborde, E. D. (ed.), *Education of Today*, Cambridge, 1935.
Lambert, R., *The State and Boarding Education*, London, 1966.
Lambert, R. and Millham, S., *The Hothouse Society*, London, 1968.
Lampe, D., *Pyke the Unknown Genius*, London, 1959.
Lancaster, J., *Improvements in Education, as it Respects the Industrious Classes of the Community*, London, 3rd ed., 1805.
Lawrence, E. (ed.), *Friedrich Froebel and English Education*, London, 1952.
Légouis, E., *The Early Life of William Wordsworth*, trans. J. W. Matthews, London, 1897.
Lilley, Irene M., *Friedrich Froebel: A Selection from His Writings*, Cambridge, 1967.
Loukes, H., *Friends and Their Children*, London, 1958.
Lovett, W., *Elementary Anatomy and Physiology*, London, 1851.
  The Life and Struggles of William Lovett, London, 1876.
Lowndes, G. A. N., *The Silent Social Revolution*, Oxford, 1937.
  (ed.) *Margaret McMillan*, Nursery Schools Association, London, 1960.
Lynch, A. J., *Individual Work and the Dalton Plan*, London, 1924.
McCallister, W. J., *The Growth of Freedom in Education*, London, 1931.
McMillan, M., *Early Childhood*, 1900.
  The Life of Rachel McMillan, London, 1927.
  Labour and Childhood, London, 1907.
  Education Through the Imagination, 1904.
MacMunn, N., *A Path to Freedom in the School*, London, 1914.

Differential Partnership Method of French Conversation, London (n.d.).

The MacMunn Differentialism: A New Method of Class Self-Teaching, London (n.d.).

The Child's Path to Freedom, London, 1926.

MacNab, H. G., *The New Views of Mr. Owen of Lanark Impartially Examined*, London, 1819.

Mack, E. C., *Public Schools and British Opinion, 1780–1860*, London, 1938.

The Public Schools and British Opinion since 1860, New York, 1941.

Malleson, E., *Autobiographical Notes and Letters*, London, 1926.

Mallinson, V. (ed.), *Adolescent at School*, London, 1949.

Mannheim, K., *Ideology and Utopia*, London, 1926.

Man and Society, London, 1940.

Mannheim, K. and Stewart, W. A. C., *An Introduction to the Sociology of Education*, London, 1962.

Manson, D., *New Pocket Dictionary*, 1762.

Mayhew, K. C. and Edwards, A. C., *The Dewey School*, New York, 1936.

Mayne, E. C., *The Life and Letters of Anne Isabella, Lady Noel Byron*, London, 1929.

Mayo, C. H., *A Genealogical Account of the Mayo and Elton Families*, London, 2nd ed., 1908.

Mayo, E., *Lessons on Objects*, London, 1831.

Lessons on Shells, 1831.

Analysis of History, 1835.

Mill, J. S., *Autobiography*, London, 1873.

Molesworth, J. N., *The Great Importance of an Improved System of Education*, 1867.

Montessori, Maria, *The Discovery of the Child*, 3rd ed., Adyar, Madras.

The Secret of Childhood, Calcutta, 1936.

More, Hannah, *Strictures on the Modern System of Female Education*, 2 vols., London, 1799.

Morley, J., *The Life of Richard Cobden*, 2 vols., London, 1881.

Morris, T., *General View of the Life and Writings of the Rev. David Williams*, London, 1792.

Neill, A. S., *A Dominie in Doubt*, London, 1920.
A Dominie Abroad (n.d.).
Summerhill: A Radical Approach to Education, London, 1962.
Hearts not Heads in the School, London, 1945.
A Dominie's Log (n.d.).
A Dominie Dismissed (n.d.).
Nunn, T. P., *Education: Its Data and First Principles*, London, 1920.
Owen, R., *A New View of Society; or, Essays on the Principles of the Formation of the Human Character*, London, 1813–14.
Report of the Proceedings at the Several Public Meetings held in Dublin, Dublin, 1823.
Observations on the Effects of the Manufacturing System, London, 1815.
Report to the County of Lanark of a Plan for Relieving Public Distress, Glasgow, 1821.
The Life of Robert Owen, 2 vols., London, 1857.
A Statement Regarding the New Lanark Establishment, Edinburgh, 1812.
The New Existence of Man upon the Earth, London, 1854.
Owen correspondence.
Owen, R. D., *An Outline of the System of Education at New Lanark*, Glasgow, 1824.
Threading My Way, London, 1874.
Parkhurst, H., *Education on the Dalton Plan*, London, 1923.
Pedley, R., *The Comprehensive School*, London, 1963.
Pemberton, R., *The Attributes of the Soul from the Cradle*, London, 1849.
The Happy Colony, London, 1854.
An Address to the People, on the Necessity of Popular Education, in Conjunction With Emigration as a Remedy for All our Social Evils, London, 1859.
The Science of Mind Formation, London, 1858.
An Address to the Bishops and Clergy of All Denominations, London, 1855.
Pemberton, R. C. B., *Pemberton Pedigrees*, Bedford, 1923.
Perry, L. R. (ed.), *Bertrand Russell, A. S. Neill, Homer Lane, W. H. Kilpatrick*, London, 1967.

Pestalozzi, J. H., *How Gertrude Teaches Her Children*, trans. L. E. Holland and E. C. Turner, London, 1894.
Leonard and Gertrude, 4 vols., Frankfurt and Leipzig, 1781–7.
Plato, *The Republic*, book iv.
Pollard, H. M., *Pioneers of Popular Education 1760–1850*, London, 1956.
The Public and Preparatory Schools Yearbook, London, 1937 and 1964.
Reddie, C., *Abbotsholme*, London, 1900.
John Bull: His Origin and Character, London, 1901.
Rich, R. W., *The Training of Teachers in England and Wales during the Nineteenth Century*, London, 1933.
Richardson, Elizabeth, *The Environment of Learning*, London, 1967.
Roe, Anne, *The Psychology of Occupations*, New York, 1956.
Rousseau, Jean-Jacques, *Émile*, 1762, trans. Barbara Foxley, London, 1961.
Russell, B., *Principles of Social Reconstruction*, London, 1916.
Autobiography, 1872–1914, London, 1967.
Autobiography, 1914–1944, London, 1968.
On Education, London, 1926.
The Practice and Theory of Bolshevism, London, 1920.
Russell, Dora (ed.), *Thinking in Front of Yourself*, London, 1934.
Sargant, W. L., *Essays of a Birmingham Manufacturer*, London, 4 vols., 1869–72.
Seguin, E., *Idiocy and its Treatment by the Physiological Method*, 1866.
Traitement, Moral, Hygiène et Éducation des Idiots, 1846.
New Facts and Remarks on Idiocy, 1870.
Report on Education, 1876.
Silber, K., *Pestalozzi: The Man and His Work*, London, 1960.
Silver, H., *The Concept of Popular Education*, London, 1965.
(ed.) *Robert Owen on Education*, Cambridge, 1969.
Simon, B., *Studies in the History of Education, 1780–1870*, London, 1960.
Education and the Labour Movement, 1870–1918, London, 1965.
Simpson, J. H., *Howson of Holt*, London, 1925.

Schoolmaster's Harvest, London, 1954.
An Adventure in Education, London, 1917.
The Future of Public Schools, Rugby, 1943.
Sane Schooling, London, 1936.
Skidelsky, R., *English Progressive Schools*, London, 1969.
Smith, Barbara Leigh (later Bodichon), *A Brief Summary in Plain Language of the Most Important Laws Concerning Women*, London, 1854.
Women and Work, London, 1857.
Smith, F., *The Life and Work of Sir James Kay-Shuttleworth*, London, 1923.
Smith, P. Woodham, 'History of the Froebel Movement in England', in E. Lawrence (ed.), *Friedrich Froebel and English Education*, London, 1952.
Spencer, H., *An Autobiography*, 2 vols., London, 1904.
Educational: Intellectual, Moral and Physical, London, 1861.
Spurzheim, J. G., *A View of the Elementary Principles of Education*, Edinburgh, 1821.
Steiner, R., *The Story of My Life*, London, 1928.
The Philosophy of Spiritual Activity, 1916.
Mysticism (n.d.).
The Education of the Child in the Light of Anthroposophy, 1922.
The Spiritual Ground of Education, 1947.
Education and Modern Spiritual Life, 1954.
Stevens, H. W. Pettit, *Downing College*, London, 1899.
Stewart, W. A. C., *Quakers and Education*, London, 1953.
The Educational Innovators, vol. ii: *Progressive Schools 1881–1967*, London, 1968.
Stewart, W. A. C. and McCann, W. P., *The Educational Innovators 1750–1880*, London, 1967.
Stewart, W. A. C. and Mannheim, K., *An Introduction to the Sociology of Education*, London, 1962.
Strachey, L., *Eminent Victorians*, London, 1918.
Suttie, I., *Origins of Love and Hate*, London, 1935.
Sturge, H. W. and Clark, T., *The Mount School, York, 1785–1814, 1831–1931*, London, 1931.
Taine, H. A., *The Ancient Regime*, trans, J. Durand, London, 1876.

Taylor, C., and Matern, J., *Institutiones Pietatis*, 1676.
Templeman, W. D., *The Life and Work of William Gilpin*, Urbana, Ill., 1939.
Tinker, C. B., *Nature's Simple Plan*, Princeton, 1922.
Trimmer, Sarah (Mrs), *An Easy Introduction to the Knowledge of Nature, and Reading the Holy Scriptures*, London, 1780.
Turner, D. M., *A History of Science Teaching in England*, London, 1927.
Unwin, Stanley, *The Truth about a Publisher*, London, 1961.
de Villevielle, Count Louis, *The Establishment of M. Emmanuel de Fellenberg at Hofwyl*, London, 1820.
Wade, J., *A History of the Middle and Working Classes*, London, 1833.
Wakeford, J., *The Cloistered Elite*, London, 1969.
Waller, W., *The Sociology of Teaching*, New York, 1932.
Ward, B. M., *Reddie of Abbotsholme*, London, 1934.
Warner, R., *Miscellanies*, 2 vols., Bath, 1819.
Waugh, A., *The Loom of Youth*, London, 1917.
Whale, J. S., *Christian Doctrine*, London, 1942.
Whitbourn, F., *Lex: Alexander Devine Founder of Clayesmore School*, London, 1937.
Whitehouse, J. H., *Creative Education at an English School*, Cambridge, 1928.
   America and Our Schools, Oxford, 1938.
   'Ideals and Methods in Education' in a *Boy's Symposium*, London, 1932.
   The School Base, Oxford, 1943.
Williams, David, *Lectures on the Universal Principles and Duties of Religion and Morality*, 2 vols., London, 1779.
   A Treatise on Education, London, 1774.
   Lectures on Education, 3 vols., London, 1789.
   History of Philo and Amelia, 1774.
Wills, W. D., *Homer Lane*, London, 1964.
   The Barns Experiment, London, 1945.
   The Hawkspur Experiment, London, 1941.
Wood, A., *Bertrand Russell: The Passionate Sceptic*, London, 1957.
Woodbridge, M. C., 'Sketches of Hofwyl', in *Letters from*

Hofwyl by a Parent, on the Educational Institutions of de Fellenberg, London, 1842.

Wyse, T., *Education Reform; or, the Necessity of a National System of Education*, London, 1836.

Year Book of Education, London, 1935: H. R. Hamley, 'The Testing of Intelligence'.

Year Book of Education, London, 1957: W. Boyd, 'The Basic Faith of the New Education Fellowship'.

Year Book of Education, London, 1957: K. Hahn, 'Outward Bound'.

Year Book of Education, London, 1957: Mario M. Montessori and C. A. Claremont, 'Montessori and the Deeper Freedom'.

Unpublished Material

Black, A., 'Early Co-operative Education, 1830–36', dissertation, University of Manchester, 1951.

Gray, E. M., 'The Educational Work of Emanuel von Fellenberg 1771–1884', M.A. thesis, University of Belfast, 1952.

Hey, C. G., 'The History of Hazelwood School, Birmingham, and its influence on Educational Developments in the Nineteenth Century', M.A. thesis, Wales, 1954.

Hubbard, D. G. B., 'Early Quaker Education 1650–1780', M.A. thesis, University of London, 1939.

Jusmani, A. A., 'The Attitude to the Child in Progressive Educational Theory and Practice in England since 1890', M.Ed. thesis, University of Leicester, 1961.

Williams, David, 'Incidents in My Life', MS. autobiography.

Parliamentary Papers and Official Publications

Board of Education Reports:
  Inspection of Friends' Boarding Schools by the Board of Education, 1905.
  Report by H.M. Inspectors on Bryanston School, Blandford, 1933.

Ministry of Education:
  Education Act, 1944.
  Statistics of Education, part i, table (10)5, 1965.
  Report of the Working Party on Assistance with the Cost of Boarding Education, 1960 (Martin Report).

List of Independent Schools: List 60 or *List 70*.
The Public Schools and the General Educational System, 1944 (Fleming Report).
Half our Future, 1963 (Newsom Report).
Census 1961, England and Wales, Occupation Tables.
Minutes of the Committee of Council on Education:
    1842–3: Rev. J. Allen, 'Report on the Battersea Training School and the Battersea Village School for Boys', P.P. (1843), xl.
    1843–4: R. Dawes to Rev. J. Allen, P.P. (1845), xxxv.
    1845: Rev. H. Moseley, 'Report on the Battersea Training School and the Battersea Village School for Boys', P.P. (1846), xxxii.
    1847–8: Rev. H. Moseley, 'Report for the Year 1847 on Schools Inspected in the Southern District'. P.P. (1847–8).
    1850–1: W. H. Brookfield, 'General Report for the Year 1850', P.P. (1851), xliv(2).
Parliamentary Debates, 3rd ser., cxcix (17 February 1870).
Poor Law Commissioners for England and Wales, Fourth Annual Report, P.P. (1837–8), xxviii, appendix B, no. 3: J. P. Kay, 'Report on the Training of Pauper Children'.
Report of the Commissioners Appointed to Inquire into the State of Popular Education in England, P.P. (1861), xxi(5) (Newcastle Commission).
Report of the Endowed Schools Inquiry Commission, P.P. (1867–8), xxviii.
Report of the Endowed Schools Inquiry Commission, vol. xii: *Special Report of South Counties*, P.P. (1867–8), xxviii(10).
Report from the Select Committee on the Education of the Lower Orders in the Metropolis, P.P. (1816), iv.
Report from the Select Committee on the Education of the Poorer Classes, P.P. (1838), vii.
Report from the Select Committee on the State of the Children Employed in the Manufactories of the United Kingdom, P.P. (1816), iii.
Report of the Royal Commission on Local Government in England 1966–69, vol. i, Command 4040 (Maud Report).

Articles, Periodicals, Pamphlets

A New School, published April 1889 to introduce Abbotsholme School.

Fifty Years of Abbotsholme, 1889–1939.

The Abbotsholmian, magazine of Abbotsholme School:
  vol. ii, no. 3, 1908, 'The Relation of Abbotsholme to Bedales'.
  vol. iii, no. 1, December 1908, 'Attempts to Wreck Some of the New Schools'.
  vol. iii, no. 3, 1909: Report of paper 'How Should We Educate our Directing Classes?', read by C. Reddie at the Authors' Club, 5 July 1909.

Academy, 24 September 1898.

All the Year Round, no. 281, 10 September 1864: 'International Education'.

American Historical Review, vol. xliii, July 1938: D. Williams, 'More Light on Franklin's Religious Ideas'.

Anarchy:
  August 1962: R. Pedley, 'The Comprehensive School'.
  February 1965: J. Ellerby, 'Mr. Duane of Risinghill.'
  January 1967: D. Russell, 'What Beacon Hill Stood For'.

Annual Biography and Obituary for the Year 1818, London, 1818.

Badminton School 1858–1958, published by the school.

Barnes, K. C., *The First Four Years*, 1944.
  The Co-educational Boarding Schools, 1953.
  et al., *Towards a Quaker View of Sex*, 1962.

Bedales (Haywards Heath, Sussex). A School for Boys: Outline of its Aims and System, 1892.

Bedales Chronicle:
  vol. 42, no. 8, June 1958.
  vol. 44, no. 2, spring 1960.
  vol. 45, no. 1, 1960.

Bedales School Roll, 1952, ed. B. Gimson.

Bernard, Sir Thomas (ed.), *Of the Education of the Poor: Being the First Part of a Digest of the Reports of the Society for Bettering the Condition and Increasing the Comforts of the Poor, etc.*, London, 1809.

Brief Statement of the Proposed Plan for International Schools, London, 1863.
British Journal of Educational Studies:
   vol. v, no. 1, November 1956: C. Bibby, 'A Victorian Experiment in International Education: The College at Spring Grove'. vol. xiv, no. 1, November 1965: C. Duke, 'Robert Lowe – A Reappraisal'.
Child and Man, periodical of the Anthroposophical Society, Summer 1964.
Child Study Society, London, *Journal of Proceedings*, vol. vi, 1926: Margaret McMillan, 'The Nursery School'.
The Christian Scientist, 1889.
The Clarion.
The Book of Clayesmore School (n.d.).
The Constitution and Laws of the Universal Community Society of Rational Religionists, London, 1839.
Co-operative News, 5 October 1878.
Crisis, vol. iii, nos. 7 and 8, 19 October 1833.
The Daily Telegraph, 22 April 1966: E. Blishen, 'The Lessons are Now Compulsory', and 'Experiments in Education'.
Dawes, R., *The Teaching of Common Things*, London, 1854.
Durham Research Review:
   no. 10, September 1959: J. L. Dobson, 'The Hill Family and Educational Change in the Nineteenth Century. I: Thomas Wright Hill and the School at Hill Top, Birmingham'.
   no. 12, September 1961: J. L. Dobson, 'Bruce Castle School at Tottenham and the Hills' Part in the Work of the Society for the Diffusion of Useful Knowledge'.
Education, London, 1854.
Educational Review:
   vol. 12, no. 3, 1960: A. Price, 'A Pioneer of Scientific Education: George Combe (1788–1858)'.
   vol. 14, no. 2, February 1962: A. Price, 'Herbert Spencer and the Apotheosis of Science: I'.
   vol. 17, no. 1, November 1964: N. Ball, 'Richard Dawes and the Teaching of Common Things'.
The English Review, June 1924.
Ellis, William, *A Few Words on Board School*, 1875.

Everyman, 11 July 1929: obituary notice of Edward Carpenter by C. Reddie.
Forum of Education, vol. v.
Fraser's Magazine, n.s., vol. xxv, February 1852: Florence Fenwick Miller, 'William Ellis and his Work as an Educationist'.
Friends' Quarterly Examiner, vol. 70, 1936: E. B. Castle, 'The Position of Friends' Schools'.
National Froebel Foundation Bulletin, February 1949.
Gentleman's Magazine, May 1867.
Geography, July 1962: S. H. Beaver, 'The Le Play Society and Field Work'.
Glasgow Herald, 14 September 1957: C. P. Barbier, 'Gilpin, Master of Cheam'.
Good Words, vol. 22, 1881: W. Jolly, 'William Ellis, Educacationalist and Philanthropist'.
The Gordonstoun Record, 1961.
Gordonstoun: Some Facts, produced by the school, March 1967.
The Guardian, 29 March 1967: K. Barnes, 'Do they know what they want?'
Hahn, K., *Education for Leisure*: lecture given in Oxford, January 1938.
History of Education Journal, vol. x, 1959: S. E. Ballinger, 'The Idea of Social Progress through Education in the French Enlightenment Period: Helvétius and Condorcet'.
Id, Journal of the Summerhill Society, nos. 2–7: Neill A. S., 'My Scholastic Life', September 1960–October 1961.
Illustrated London News, 20 July 1867.
Journal of Education, n.s., vol. ii, 1877: E. C. Tufnell, 'Sir James Kay-Shuttleworth'.
Journal of the Society of Arts:
  vol. ii, no. 91, 18 August 1854: W. Ellis, 'On Economic Science'.
  vol. xi, no. 540, 27 March 1863: 'Proposed International Schools'.
Lane, Homer, *Four Lectures on Childhood: The Age of Loyalty*, ed. Rev. H. H. Symonds.
The Listener, 28 November 1934.

Lloyd's Weekly London Newspaper, 7 January 1855.
The London Echo.
London Magazine, vol. ix, 1824: T. de Quincey, 'Plans for the Instruction of Boys in Large Numbers'.
McMillan, Margaret, 'Citizens of Tomorrow', 1906.
   'The Child and the State', 1907.
   'London Children: How to Feed Them and How Not to Feed Them', 1907.
   'Schools of Tomorrow', 1908.
Mason, Charlotte, 'A Short Synopsis of the Educational Philosophy Advanced by the Founder of the Parents' National Educational Union' (n.d.).
Manchester Guardian, 11 May 1897 and 9 February 1932.
Modern Language Notes, vol. lv, no. 4, April 1940: J. H. Warner. 'The Basis of J. J. Rousseau's Contemporaneous Reputation in England'.
Museum (Edinburgh):
   no. 1, April 1861: J. Lorimer, 'Reciprocal Naturalisation. I: International Education'.
   no. 2, July 1861: J. Lorimer, 'II: The International School the Complement of the International Exhibition'.
Museum and English Journal of Education, vol. ii, no. 8, June 1865: W. Ellis, 'Combinations and Strikes from the Teacher's Point of View'.
Education for the New Era: an International Quarterly Journal for the Promotion of Reconstruction in Education, January 1920. Title changed to *The New Era in Home and School.*
The New Era, 1920s.
Pour l'Ère Nouvelle, 1920s.
Das Werdende Zeitalter.
New Moral World, passim, 1840–2.
The Discipline of Freedom, Conference of New Ideals in Education, 1923.
New Ideals Quarterly.
The New Statesman.
Owen, Robert, *Address Delivered at the Meeting in St. Martin's Hall, Long Acre, London, on the 1st January, 1855*, London, 1855.
Pall Mall Gazette, 22 August and 5 October 1892.

Pendle Hill Pamphlet, no. 9, 1940: H. H. Brinton, 'Quaker Education in Theory and Practice'.

Peters, R., *Education as Initiation: An Inaugural Lecture*, University of London.

Philanthropic Society, *An Address to the Public*, London, 1790.

Philanthropic Society, *First Report*, London (n.d. but 1789).

Phrenological Journal, vol. ix, n.s., no. lxxxvii, 1846.

Proceedings of the American Philosophical Society, vol. 98, no. 6, 1954: N. Hans, 'Franklin, Jefferson, and the English Radicals at the End of the Eighteenth Century'.

Proceedings of a Conference called by the Committee on Education of New York Yearly Meeting, 1881: J. Wood, 'Education among Friends in England'.

Proceedings of the Second Co-operative Congress, Birmingham, 1831.

Proceedings of the Third Co-operative Congress, London, 1832.

Progress Today, vol. xvii, no. 1: L. B. Pekin, 'The Way of Life at St. Christopher School, Letchworth'.

Progressive Education, U.S.A.

Prospectus for Dartington Hall, 1954.

Prospectus for Bryanston School, 1962.

Prospectus for Gordonstoun, 1967.

Prospectus entitled 'École Internationale de Saint-Germain-en-Laye', February 1867.

Reader, vol. v, no. 129, 17 June 1865, 'International Education'.

Report of the Committee on the Closing of the Little Commonwealth, July 1918.

Report of the First Summer Conference of the New Education Fellowship in Calais, 1921, *The Creative Self Expression of the Child:* H. Baillie-Weaver, 'La Co-éducation'.

Report of the Educational Conference of the Society of Friends, 1879.

Researches and Studies, University of Leeds Institute of Education, no. ii, January 1955: A. A. Evans, 'The Impact of Rousseau on English Education'.

Review of Reviews, 15 November 1893.

Saga, Bryanston School magazine.

Anniversary Saga, 1928–1948 (symposium).

Grant, C., 'St George's School: A Retrospect': address to St. George's Parents' Association, 5 July 1941.

The School Review, University of Chicago, vol. 74, no. 3, 1966: I. Weinberg, 'The Occupational Aspirations of British Public Schoolboys'.

The Sower, later *Seed Time*, journal of the Fellowship of New Life.

Spectator, 18 September 1897.

Star in the East, 17 August 1839.

The Sunday Times, 10 January 1965: article by M. Hamlyn.

Surrey Archaeological Transactions, xxv, 1924: Sir H. C. M. Lambert, 'A Cheam School Bill in 1766'.

The Theosophical Educational Trust, Second Annual Report, November 1918.

The Times, 13 November 1877 and 30 September 1955.

The Times Educational Supplement:
    6 May 1920: letter from Belle Rennie.
    no. 2226, 17 January 1958: C. P. Barbier, 'Submerged by Dr. Syntax: William Gilpin of Cheam'.
    2 August 1963: 'The Dalton Plan'.

The Toynbee Record, magazine of Toynbee Hall.

Ulster Journal of Archaeology, vol. xiv, 1908: J. J. Marshall, 'David Manson, Schoolmaster in Belfast'.

Union, vol. 9, no. 1, 1 December 1842.

University of London Institute of Education, Education Libraries Bulletin, Supplement 7, London, 1964: B. C. Bloomfield (ed.), 'The Autobiography of Sir James Kay-Shuttleworth'.

Wennington School, 1961–2, the school magazine.

Westminster and Foreign Quarterly Review:
    vol. liii, July 1850: W. Ellis, 'Classical Education'.
    vol. liv, January 1851: W. E. Hickson, 'Educational Movements'.

The Westminster Gazette, 15 November 1897 and 30 September 1898.

Where?, Autumn 1963 (A. C. E.): P. Wood, 'What is Ministry Recognition Worth?.

Wigram, D. R., *The System of Work at Bryanston School*, 1947.

Supplementary Bibliography

Goodman, Paul, *Compulsory Miseducation*, New York, 1966.
  The Community of Scholars, New York, 1966.
Illich, Ivan, *Deschooling Society*, London, 1971.
  Celebration of Awareness, London, 1971.
Taylor, L. C. (ed.), *Experiments in Education at Sevenoaks*, London, 1965.

Index

Page references in *italics* indicate the main treatment of the subject

A Quoi Tient la Superiorité des Anglo-Saxons? (Demolins), 208, 210
Abbotsholme School, xiii, 93, 140, *146–8*, 171, 173, 231, 347, 378, 388, *391–401*
   opening of, 145–6
   principles of, 146–8, 151–2
   decline of, 148
   Badley and, 149–50, 394, 407–11
   and Clayesmore, 157, 160
   and German and Swiss schools, 202–7, 209–10
   and *École des Roches*, 209–10
   co-educational, 313
   and Bedales, 349–53
   'recognised as efficient', 436
   growth rate, 442
   fees, 444
   See also Reddie, Cecil
Aberdovey sea school, 340
Ackworth School, 91, 174, 177, 178, 179, 180, 182, 482
Acland, T. D., 104
Address to the Bishops and Clergy of All Denominations (Pemberton), 51
Adèle et Théodore (de Genlis), 13
Adler, Alfred, 246, 360, 365, 375, 468
adolescence:
   Steiner's view of, 196–7
   Hahn's view of, 326, 333–4
adult education, at Dartington, 265, 268
Adventure in Education, An (Simpson), 239
Adventures in Socialism (Cullen), 37
agricultural schools, 93
   Fellenberg and, 79–80, 84
   Lady Byron and Craig, 84–5
agriculture in curriculum:
   at Abbotsholme, 147
   in Lietz schools, 203
Aitkenhead, John, 434
Alcott House School, Ham Common, 81
All the Year Round, 108, 111, 124
Allen, William:
   and New Lanark, 40–1
   and agricultural school, 93
Almack, Rev. William, 65

Almond, Hely Hutchinson, 147*n*
Alpha Union, 196
American history, at Bembridge, 236
American Progressive Education Association (American Education Fellowship), 212, 363–4, 367
American schools, 212, 221–2
Analysis of History (Mayo), 81
Andressen, Alfred, 202*n*, 203, 204
Annand, J. B., 365
Anthroposophical Society, 196, 291
Anthroposophy, 291–302. *See also* Steiner, Rudolf
Arnold, Matthew, 103, 104, 133
Arnold, Thomas, xiii, 325, 468
Arnold-Brown, A., 331*n*, 332, 333, 341
arts in curriculum:
   at Badminton, 187
   at Bembridge, 235
   at Bryanston, 307
   at Clayesmore, 157
   at Dartington, 265, 277
   at Steiner schools, 297
Arundale, George, 192, 196
Arundale School, 196
Ashton Rational school, 47
assignments, in Dalton Plan, 309, 311–12
Association of All Classes and All Nations, 44
Association School (Ronge), 112
Atkins, Thomas, 51, 53
Atlantic College, St. Donat's, 342–4, 469
attendance:
   Hazelwood insistence on, 58
   prize schemes for, 99
attendance at lessons, voluntary:
   at Beacon Hill, 284
   at Summerhill, 422
Attributes of the Soul from the Cradle (Pemberton), 50, 51

Bacon, Sir Francis, 27
Baden, Prince Max of, 318, 319, 320
Baden, Margrave of, 321
Baden-Powell, Lord, 234

Badley, Mrs. Amy (*née* Garrett), 404, 406, 408, 414
Badley, John Haden, 144n, *149–53*, 171–2, 209, 228, 233, 236, 247, 269, 307, 335, *401–14*, 415
  early life and education, 149, 401–5, 408
  at Abbotsholme, 149–50, 394, 407–11
  and Bedales, 150–3, 164, 165, 210, 212, 390, 394, 395, 405–6, *410–13*, 465, 466, 467
  compared with Reddie, 152–3, 172, 394–5, *407–11*
  and A. Devine, 154, 155, 157, 161, 410
  and King Alfred's, 163
  influence of, 212, 271, 412, 414
  and Carpenter, 389, 404, 405
Badminton School, *184–8*, 198, 210, 218
  'recognised as efficient', 435
  growth rate, 442
  fees, 444
Badock, Mrs., and Badminton, 184
Baillie-Weaver, H., 195
Baker, Miss B. M., 188
  and Badminton, 185, 186, 187
Balfour Education Act (1902), 174
Ballard, P. B., 365
Barbier, Aristide, and international education, 119–20
Barbier, Edmond, 120–1
Barclay, David, 177
Barnes, Frances, 345–6
Barnes, Kenneth, 345–52, 477
  and Wennington, 345–6, 348–52, 439
Barns Experiment, The (Wills), 345
Barron, Evan, 318
Bartlett, Miss, and Badminton, 184
Barwell, Louisa, 80
Basedow, Johann Bernhard, 91
baths, school, 251
Battersea Normal College, 86, 87–9
Baudouin, Charles, 365
Bazeley, E. T., 223, 225
Beacon Hill School, 280–6
Beale, Dorothea, 186
Becker, Dr., Prussian Minister of Education, 361
Bedales, 164, 166, 345, 482
  Badley and, *149–53*, 390, 395, 405–6, *410–13*, 465, 466, 467
  and Claysmore, 157, 160
  and King Alfred's, 164–5
  and Frensham Heights, 200
  and *École des Roches*, 209–10
  international renown, 212
  Montessori school at, 218
  Curry at, 270–1
  estate work, 312
  co-education, 349
  later heads, 413–14
  'recognised as efficient', 435
  growth rate, 442
  fees, 441, 444
Bedford College, 185
Beer, Max, 33
Belfast Play School, 3, 8–11
Bell, Dr. Andrew, 8, 35, 36, 56, 60
  monitorial system, 27, 34, 95–6
  rewards and punishments, 96–7
Bell, Geoffrey, bishop of Chichester, 321
Bembridge School, *234–8*, 312. *See also* Whitehouse, John Howard
Bemrose, Roderick, 398
Bentham, Jeremy, 56, 67, 100, 137, 138, 140
Berg, Leila, 480n
Bergson, Henri, 246
Berlin, 120
Bernard, Sir Thomas, 36, 92
Bernstein, E., 431n
Bertier, Georges, 357
Besant, Mrs. Annie, 250
  and Theosophical movement, 189–90, 192, 195, 290, 291
Besse, Mme., 343
Beveridge, Sir William, 233
Bieberstein, 203, 204, 212
Birkbeck schools, 117, *127–31*
  Socratic teaching methods, 128
  utilitarian principles, 129
Birkett, H. de P., 168
Birmingham Lunar Society, 18
Black, Aubrey, 43
Blackheath School, 103
Blake, William, 190, 383, 411
Blavatsky, Helena Petrovna, and Theosophical Society, 189, 190, 191, 290
Blishen, Edward, 277–8, 485
Bloom, Alexander, 478, 479
boarding schools, 243–5
Bodichon, Barbara, 104, 109, *113–18*, 129, 134, 135
  and Portman Hall School, 113–14, 117
  early life, 114–15
  model for Romola, 115

Index

educational influences on, 117
and co-education, 136
radical views on religion, 136–7
Bodichon, Eugène, 116, 118
Boeke, Kees, 375, 434
Böhme, Jakob, 191, 383
Bonser, Dr., 267, 273
Bootham School, 63, 64, 178, 179, 182
sister school of The Mount, 312
'recognised as efficient', 436
Borough Road School, 99
Borough Road Training College, 124
Boulton, Matthew, 18
Bovet, Pierre, 365
Boy Scout movement, 207, 234
Boyd, Dr. William, 353n, 375, 376
Boyd-Orr, Lord, 339
Bradford School Board, 251
Bradlaugh, Charles, 189
Braehead School, 479
Brandt, Jules, 120
Branford, Victor, 384n
Brath, Stanley de, 395–6
Bray, Charles, 109
Brayley, Edward Westlake, 63, 64
Brenton Asylum, Hackney, 93
Brereton, Henry L., 323, 324, 343
Brief Summary in Plain Language of the Most Important Laws Concerning Women (Bodichon), 116
Bristol, Hilda, 268n
British and Foreign Schools Society, 132, 180
British and National schools, 84, 99, 128
British Psycho-Analytical Society, 246
Brooke, Henry, 13
Brougham, Henry, 115
Brown, John, on child nature, 19
Bruce Castle School, 55, 56, 63, 64–6, 114
self-government by pupils, 57, 64–5
science teaching, 63–4
Bryanston School, *303–16*
alignment to public schools, 303–4
under Jeffreys, 303–5, 308
discipline, 304, 314
seminar and tutorial system, 304, 309
Dalton Plan, 305, 308–12, 315
under Coade, 305–8
art and craft tradition, 307, 313
Sea Cadets and Pioneers, 312–13
clubs and societies, 313
sister school of Cranborne Chase, 313
Christian basis, 314–15

curriculum, 315
'recognised as efficient', 437
fees, 441, 444
growth rate, 442, 464
Buber, Martin, 365
Buchan, John, 322
Buchanan, James, 89, 112, 115, 117, 137, 138, 261
and New Lanark Infant School, 37–8
Buchenau, 204
Buckingham, James Silk, 52
Burgdorf, 76
Burgess Hill School, 434
Burnham scale, 429, 440, 446
Burt, Sir Cyril, 276, 365
Buss, Frances Mary, 185
Butler, R. A. (now Lord), 369
Butler, Samuel, head of Shrewsbury, xiii
Byron, Lady Noel, 89, 100, 115, 139
and Fellenberg, 80, 82–4
and Ealing Grove School, 82, 84–5, 93
and Co-operative movement, 82
Byron, Lord, 82

Calder, J. L., 318
Cambridgeshire Village Colleges, 237
Campbell, J. Archibald, 383, 388, 389
Canadian schools, 212
career patterns, 451–63
social class, 448–9
leaving age, 449–51
further education, 451
choice of career, 452–9
high proportion of teachers and service group, 453, 455
few in church or armed forces, 456
salaries, 459–61
Carlyle, Thomas, 109, 144, 190, 393
Carpenter, Edward, 149, 466
and Badley, 389, 404, 405
and Abbotsholme, 391, 392, 407
and Reddie, 144, 146, 147, *385–90*, 391, 392
Carpenter, Rev. Lant, 62
Cassels, William, 146, 391, 392, 393
Castle, Professor E. B., 183
Cave, Sir George, 226
Central Poor Law Board, 86
Central Society of Education, 81
Chambers's Educational Course, 49
Chapman, John, 109, 115, 116
Charterhouse School, 132

Chartism, 90
Cheam School:
  Gilpin and, 3–7
  commercial principles, 4, 5–6
  Mayo and, 47, 81–2, 85, 137
  'new scheme' of laws and punishments, 4–5, 25
  self-government, 4
  curriculum, 5–7
Cheltenham Ladies' College, 186
Chevalier, Michel, 119
Chew, F. R. G., 338
Child, Hubert and Lois, at Dartington, 276–8, 279
child:
  18th-c. views on, 14–17, 19–21
  perfectibility, 15–16, 21, 23
  'artificial', 17
  depravity, 19–21
  psychology of, 23–5, 35–6, 107, 224, 259–60, 286, 294, 350, 422, 433
Child and the Curriculum, The (Dewey), 255n
Child and the State, The (McMillan), 252
Child's Path to Freedom, The (MacMunn), 227
child-centred education, *471–3*
  18th-c. move towards, 17, 21–2
  Froebel and Ronge, 111–12
Children's Councils, 169, 183. *See also* self-government
Christian Brothers school, Paris, 87, 88
Christian Commonwealth (Morgan), 51
Christian Socialist, The, 250, 252
Christianity as Mystical Fact (Steiner), 289
church hostility to innovators, 45, 137
Citizens of Tomorrow (McMillan), 252
civics in curriculum:
  at Badminton, 188
  at Bembridge, 235
  at Bryanston, 310
  in Theosophical schools, 198
Clarendon Commission (1861–4), 132, 134
Clarion, 252
Clarisegg, 205
Clark, Thomas, 55
Clarke, Sir Fred, 365, 367, 368, 471n
Clarke, Miss, of Dunhurst, Bedales, 218
classical-Christian ideal of education, 21–2

19th-c. distrust of, 110
classics in curriculum:
  Gilpin's attitude to, 6
  defence of, 20
  Spencer's criticism of, 105
  Combe's subordination of, 107
  at Isleworth College, 122, 124
  none in Birkbeck schools, 128
  in Quaker schools, 175, 182
  at Rendcomb, 241
Clayesmore School, *154–60*, 312
  'recognised as efficient', 436
  growth rate, 442
  fees, 444
Clifton College, 144, 387
clothes – *see* dress reform
Club of Thirteen, 19
co-education, 136
  Portman Hall, 113
  in Quaker schools, 177, 182
  at Dartington, 272, 275, 278
  in E.N.E.F. aims, 357
  See also Atlantic College; Beacon Hill; Bedales; Frensham Heights; King Alfred's; Little Commonwealth; Michael Hall; Saffron Walden; St. Christopher; St. George's, Harpenden; Salem; Steiner schools; Summerhill; Wennington; Wickersdorf
Co-operative movement, *42–6*, 82, 84
Co-operative schools, 42–4, 45
Coade, Thorold F., 193, 335
  and Bryanston, *305–8*, 311, 312, 313, 315
Cobden, Richard, 115
  and international education, 118, 119, 120
Coleridge, Samuel Taylor, 13
Colonial College, Hollesley Bay, 208
Colquhoun, Patrick, 36
Combe, George, 121, 130, 138
  and phrenology, 105–6
  educational views, 107–8, 109, 117
  proposed curriculum, 108, 114
  and population restraint, 127
Combined Cadet Force, Gordonstoun, 331
Comenius, J. A., 9, 10
commercial principles in curriculum, 4, 5–6
  at Hazelwood, 61–2, 66
Committee of Council on Education, 74, 87, 89

communism – *see* socialism and communism
community ideal, 465, 467, *469–73*
  at Abbotsholme, 145
  at Beacon Hill, 282–3
  at Bedales, 406
  at Bryanston, 306, 312
  at Dartington, 271, 274–5
  at Dewey's Laboratory School, 255
  in Junior Republics, 221–2
  in Little Commonwealth, 222–6
  at Summerhill, 378, 422–3
  in Theosophical schools, 197
  at Wennington, 346–7
comprehensive schools, 474, 475, 477–82
concentric system, 28–9
Constitution of Man, The (Combe), 107, 127
Cook, Captain James, 18
Cook, Caldwell, 247, 473
Cook, E. T., 233
Corn Laws, 89, 114
corporal punishment – *see* punishment, corporal
Coué, Émile, 365
Country Boarding School movement (*Landerziehungsheime*), 202–6, 212
County Badge scheme, 339
County Councils Act (1888), 134
Cox, Dr. G. Lissant, 383n
Craig, E. T., 46, 84–5, 134
'cramming' and examination pressure, reaction against:
  at Abbotsholme, 147, 152
  at Badminton, 187
  at Bedales, 152
  at Claysmore, 157
  at Dartington, 275, 278
  at Gordonstoun, 338
  at King Alfred's, 162, 164
  in Theosophical schools, 198
  at Wennington, 348
Cranborne Chase School, 313
Crane, Mrs. Murray, 308
Creighton, Colin, 447n
Cropper, James, 93
Crump, Geoffrey, 412
Cullen, A., 37
Culverwell, E. P., 217
Cumming, Alastair, 318, 322
current affairs – *see* civics
curriculum, innovations in, xii–xiii
  by Gilpin, 3, 5–7

commercial principles, 4, 5–6, 61–2, 66
gymnastics, 62
  by Combe, 107–8
social science, 109, 110, 125, 127–31
  at Abbotsholme, 146–7
  at Badminton, 187–8
  at Beacon Hill, 283–4
  at Bedales, 151–2
  at Belfast Play School, 9–11
  at Bembridge, 235
  at Bryanston, 307, 309, 315
  at Claysmore, 157, 159
  at Dartington, 277
  at Hazelwood, 62
  at King Alfred's, 162–3
  at King's Somborne, 71–2
  at Laurence Street Academy, 27–31
  in Lietz schools, 203
  at Malting House, 256–7
  at New Lanark, 39–40
  in Quaker schools, 175
  in Steiner schools, 294–9
Curry, William Burnlee, *268–77*, 335, 434, 468, 471
  early life, 268–9
  and B. Russell, 269–70, 285
  at Bedales, 270–1
  at Oak Lane, 271–2
  at Dartington, 272–6, 278, 439
  and New Education Fellowship, 371

Dalcroze, E. J., 365, 473
Dalcroze School, Dresden, 220
Dale, David, 33, 36–7
Dalton Plan, 169, 236, 305, 306, 328, 329, 347
  at Bryanston, 308–11, 315
Dancy, J. C., xiii
Daniel, John, 41
Dartington and Dartington Hall Trust, 262, *264–79*
  purchase by Elmhirsts, 264
  establishment of Trust, 265
  commercial enterprises, 265–6, 267
  non-commercial enterprises, 265
  co-education, 266, 272, 275, 278
  tutor system, 267, 275
  criticisms of school, 267, 277–8
  reorganization, 267–8
  appointment of Curry as head, 268, 272
  discipline and self-government, 273–5, 278

Dartington and Dartington Hall Trust, *Contd.*
  inspection and recognition, 276, 436n
  H. and L. Child as heads, 276
  no set religious instruction, 277
  Dr. R. Lambert as head, 279
  growth rate, 442
  fees, 444
Darvall, Air Marshal Sir Lawrence, 343
Darwin, Charles, 138
Darwin, Erasmus, 18
Dauntsey's School, 345
David, Dr. A. A., 229
Davidson, Thomas, 389, 390
Davies, Lord, 324
Davies, Emily, 104
Davies, J. D., 107
Davies, Sir Thomas, 242
Davis, William, 93
Dawes, Rev. Richard, 68, 75, 137
  educational views, 69-74
  belief in school books, 73
Dawson of Penn, Lord, 339
Day, Thomas, 13, 18, 19, 100
De Morgan, William, 114
De Quincey, Thomas, 55
Delius, Frederick, 122
Democracy and Education (Dewey), 255n
Demolins, Edmond, 207-9, 210, 212
Demolins, Joseph Jules, 209
Deptford, McMillan nursery school at, 219, 252-3, 261
Devine, Alexander, *153-61*, 172, 236
  early career and work with delinquents, 153-4
  and Clayesmore, *154-60*, 466, 467
  and J. H. Badley, 154, 155, 157, 161, 410
  and C. Reddie, 155, 156-7, 161, 410
Dewey, John, xii, 201, 246, 264, 266, 271, 367, 473
  influence on S. Isaacs, 255-6, 258, 260
Dickens, Charles, 108, 109, 111, 124, 138
Dickinson, G. Lowes, 404, 407
Diderot, Denis, 18
diet in schools, 197, 285
Dijon, 87
discipline and authority:
  denounced by Montessori, 215-16
  in Steiner schools, 299
  at Bryanston, 314

discipline and authority, relaxation of:
  at Dartington, 273-5
  at Beacon Hill, 285
  at Wennington, 348, 351
  See also attendance; punishment; self-government
Discovery of the Child, The (Montessori), 215n
Dodge, Miss, American heiress, 195, 200
domestic science, in Quaker schools, 182
Dominie books (Neill), 230, 417-19
Douglas-Hamilton, Mrs., 195, 196, 199, 242
Douglas-Hamilton Educational Trust, 200
Downing College, Cambridge, 68
drama in curriculum:
  at Beacon Hill, 283
  at Bryanston, 313
  in Steiner schools, 298
  in Theosophical schools, 198
dress reform, 466
  at Abbotsholme, 147
  at Badminton, 185
  at Bryanston, 304
  at Clayesmore, 157
  at Dartington, 185
  at Gordonstoun, 325
  at King Alfred's, 170
Duane, Michael, 434, 479-81
Duppa, B. F., 80

Ealing Grove School, 82, 84, 85, 88, 93
Early Childhood (McMillan), 251
East, James, 434
École des Roches, 209-10, 212, 357
École de l'Humanité, 205
École Nouvelle de la Suisse Romande, 205
Edgeworth, Maria, 13, 21, 39, 55, 60, 63, 67, 100
Edgeworth, Richard Lovell, 14, 18, 19, 35, 55, 60, 67, 89, 100
Edgeworth, Richard Lovell jr., 14
Edinburgh, Philip, Duke of, 323
  Awards, 332, 341
Edinburgh, University of, 144, 381-2, 384
Edinburgh Secular School, 130
Education Acts:
  (1870) 85, 133, 135
  (1902) 174
  (1921) 435
  (1944) 435-6, 475

Index

Education (Administrative Provisions) Act (1907), 252
Education (Provision of Meals) Act (1906), 252
Education, Board of, 133, 171, 181, 182, 238, 435
Education and Science, Department of, 436, 463
Education: Intellectual, Moral, and Physical (Spencer), 104
Education: Its Data and First Principles (Nunn), 246
Education of the Child in the Light of Anthroposophy (Steiner), 291
Education of the Farmer, Viewed in Connection with that of the Middle Classes in General (Acland), 104
Education through the Imagination (McMillan), 252
Education and Modern Spiritual Life (Steiner), 293
Education for the New Era, 354
Education Nouvelle, L' (Demolins), 209
Eldon Judgement (1805), 103
elementary and primary schools, 54
  early 19th-c., 69–70, 84, 85–6
  prize schemes in, 99
  late 19th-c., 132–5
  state provision of, 139, 143
  effect of Revised Code on, 171, 172
  Whitehouse's ideas on, 237
  influence on J. Simpson, 238
Elgin Academy, 339
Eliot, George, 109, 115
Ellis, John, 48–9
Ellis, William, 109, 114, 136, 138, 139
  and international schools, 121, 130, 134, 135
  early career, 125–6
  religious, political and social views, 126–7, 137
  his influence, 130–1
  and Birkbeck schools, 117, *125–31*
Elmhirst, Dorothy (*née* Whitney, then Straight), 264–6, 268, 272, 280
Elmhirst, Leonard:
  and Tagore, 262–4
  and Dartington, *264–8*, 272, 279, 280
Émile (Rousseau), 76
  influence in England, 12–13
  leading ideas of, 15–17, 91
  critics of, 19–20, 23
Eminent Victorians (Strachey), 468
Emlohstobba (Lietz), 202, 203, 206, 210

Endowed Schools Act (1869), 133, 143
Endowed Schools Inquiry Commission (1864–8), 133
Engels, Friedrich, 289
English in curriculum:
  at Abbotsholme, 147
  at Badminton, 187
  in Quaker schools, 175
English New Education Fellowship, 358, 363, 371–2
English Review, The, 242
English Woman's Journal, The, 116
Enlightenment:
  European, 22, 34, 51, 100
  French, 20, 32, 75, 137
Ensor, Mrs. Beatrice, 163, 248, 353
  and Theosophical Educational Trust, 193–6, 199
  and Frensham Heights, 199, 200
  and Montessori system, 217, 218
  and New Education Fellowship, 361, 365, 370, 419
Ethical Society, 251
Eton College, 132, 331, 435
Ettersburg, 204
European Association for International Education, 120
eurhythmics, in Theosophical schools, 198
eurhythmy, in Steiner schools, 294, 298
Everett, Ernest, 269
Ewald, Marina, 319
examination pressure – *see* 'cramming'
Examiner, The, 111
Experimental School of Industry, Westminster, 93
Eyk, Dr. Van, 396

Fabian Society, 389–90, 409
fagging, abolition of, 466
fees:
  19th-c. at King's Somborne, 69–70
  in progressive and public schools, 441–5
Fellenberg, Philipp Emanuel von, xii, 89, 163
  and Pestalozzi, 77–8
  and agricultural and manual education, 78–9, 91
  educational establishments, 79–80
  influence of, 80–1, 82–5, 86, 87, 100, 137, 139, 201
Fellowship of the New Life, 144–5, 148, 196, 199, 384, 388–90, 391, 409

Fels, Joseph, 252
Ferguson, Adam, 34
Fernhead, 93
Ferrière, Adolf, 210–11, 212, 355
Fettes College, 144, 378–80, 385
Few Words on Board Schools, A (Ellis), 130
Fichte, J. G., 78, 288, 289, 325
Finchden Manor, 345
Findlay, J. J., 202, 379, 382, 409
Finney, Ross, 471
Fish, Mrs., of Dunhurst, Bedales, 218, 412
Fisher, H. A. L., 253
Fleming Report, 245, 315, 439
Flexner, Abraham, 266
Florence, 120
Fool of Quality, The (Brooke), 13
Ford Junior Republic, 221, 223
Forster, W. E., 85, 133, 179
Fortescue, Earl, 104
Foster, Joseph, 40
Fothergill, John, 177
Foundations of Success, The (de Brath), 395
Fox, William Johnson, 117
Franchise Act (1867), 135
Franklin, Benjamin, 19, 78
Free School Community, Wickersdorf, 205, 206
Freideutsche Jugend-Bewegung, 207
Freie Waldorfschule, 292
Freinet, Charles, 362
French in curriculum:
  at Abbotsholme, 147
  at Beacon Hill, 284
  in primary schools, 473
French Eton, A (Arnold), 104
French Revolution, 78, 83, 115
Frensham Heights School, 199–200
  'recognised as efficient', 436
  growth rate, 442
  fees, 444
Freud, Sigmund, influence of, 221, 247–8, 360, 375, 468
  on A. S. Neill, 248, 419, 434
  on S. Isaacs, 259, 260, 261
Friends, Society of (Quakers), 92, *174–83*, 187, 236, 348, 351, 449, 467. *See also* Quaker schools
Friends Public School Society, 179
Froebel, Friedrich, 75, 163, 201
  kindergarten, 111–12, 137
  influence of, 137, 138, 221
Fromm, Erich, 423, 425

Froude, J. A., 109
Fruits of Philosophy (Knowlton), 189
Fry, Roger, 404

Gall, F. J., 105
games, fetish, reaction against:
  at Abbotsholme, 146
  at Clayesmore, 157
  at Gordonstoun, 326
Garden City movement, 145, 165, 192
Garden City Theosophical School (Arundale), 196
garden schools, Theosophist schools as, 198
gardens, school:
  at Abbotsholme, 147
  at Battersea College, 88
  at Cheam, 6, 88
Garibaldi, Ricciotti, 114
Garrett, Edward, 404
Garstang, T. J., 412
Gaskell, Elizabeth C., 15, 109
Gebesee, 204
Geddes, Sir Patrick, 207, 233, 389
  and Reddie, 383–5, 388
Geheeb, Edith, 205
Geheeb, Paul, 205, 375, 434
General Schools Certificate, 168
Genlis, Mme. de, 13
George, W. R., and Junior Republic, 221–3
German in curriculum:
  at Abbotsholme, 147
  at Beacon Hill, 284
German schools based on Abbotsholme, 202–7
Gibbs, Michael, 40
Gilbert, W. S., 105
Gilpin, Eva M., 345
Gilpin, William, 12, 71, 100
  at Cheam School, 3, 4–7
Gimson, Basil, 412
Girard, Père, 87
Girls' Public Day School Trust, 185–6
girls' schools, 178, 179, 182, *184–8*, 312, 313
Gladstone, W. E., 234
Glasgow Secular Society, 130
Godolphin School, 185, 379
Godwin, William, 13, 18
Goethe, 288–9, 297
Gooch, Dr. G. P., 365
Goodbye to All That (Graves), 468
Goodman, Paul, 485*n*

Index

Gordonstoun, 312, *322–39*
  opened, 323
  war years in Wales, 324
  re-established, 324
  Platonic approach, 325, 331, 334, 337
  'Salem laws', 325–7
  self-discipline, 327–9, 337
  Training Plan, 327–8, 336
  dispersal of responsibility, 328–9
  curriculum, 329–32
  projects and physical work, 329–31, 335, 338
  'services', 330–1
  links with neighbourhood, 332
  fees, 332
  criticisms of, 335–8
  influence of, 339
  growth rate, 439, 464
Gorst, Sir John, 252
Gospel of Atheism (Besant), 189
Göttingen University, 382
grammar, teaching of, 39
grammar schools, 133, 139, 172, 467, 472
  aping of public schools, 143
Grammar Schools Act (1840), 103
Grant, Rev. Cecil, 200, 217, 219, 234
Graves, Robert, 468
Great Ayton School, 179, 182
Great Importance of an Improved System of Education, The (Molesworth), 104
Greaves, J. P., 81
Greek – see classics in curriculum
Gresham's School, Holt, 228, 238, 270
Grote, George, 126
group dynamics, at N.E.F. conferences, 373, 374
Grovesmühle, 204
'guardian angel', Hahn's idea of, 334, 338
guardians, pupils as, 59, 65
Guild of St. George, 233

Hadfield, Dr. J. H., 362
Haeckel, Ernst, 289
Hahn, Kurt, 124, 278, 307, 312, *317–44*
  in Germany, 204, 205–6, 318–21, 335
  and Salem, 318–21, 347
  influenced by Reddie, 206
  in England, 318, 321, 322–4, 332, 339–44
  and Gordonstoun, *322–39*, 343–4
  and Outward Bound, 332, 338, 339–42, 344

  criticisms of, 335–9
  and Atlantic College, 336, 342–4
Hall School, Weybridge, 345
handicapped children, Steiner homes and schools for, 292, 300
handicrafts in curriculum:
  at Abbotsholme, 146, 147
  at Badminton, 187
  at Bembridge, 235
  at Bryanston, 307
  at Dartington, 277
  at King Alfred's, 164
  in Lietz schools, 203
  in Quaker schools, 182
Happy Colony, The (Pemberton), 51
Hardie, Keir, 250
Harley, Winifred, 268, 272
Harris, Mr. and Mrs. Lyn, 198, 200–1, 218
Harris, N. K., 201
Harrison, J. F. C., 44
Harrow Lectures on Education, 306
Harrow School, 132, 143, 305, 306, 435
Harry and Lucy (Edgeworth), 13
Hartley, David, 126
Harvey, T. E., 233
Hastings, George, 104
Haubinda, 203, 204, 210, 212
Hawkesworth's Voyages, 18
Hawkspur Experiment, The (Wills), 345
Hazelwood School, xiii, 8, 28, 41, *54–67*, 95, 97, 99, 100
  objects and principles, 56–8, 65–7
  punctuality, attendance, and silence, 58
  self-government by pupils, 59
  rewards and punishments, 59
  rank, 59
  motivation of pupils, 60–1
  curriculum and teaching methods, 61–3
  science teaching, 63–4
Hazlitt, William, 13
Heckstall-Smith, H., 278, 337–8
hedge schools, 8
Hellerau international school, 420
Helvetic Society, 75
Henderson, Dr. J. L., 375
Herbart, Johann Friedrich, 80, 163, 212, 289
Hermannsberg, 318
Hermetic Society, 192
Hewlett, Maurice, 122
Hickson, J. Godfrey, 164

Hickson, W. E., 89
Highland Field Craft Centre, 340
Hill, Arthur, 55, 56, 58, 64
Hill, Brian, 352
Hill, Edwin, 55
Hill, Frederic, 55
Hill, George Birkbeck, 57, 64–5
Hill, Matthew Davenport, 41, 55, 56, 116
Hill, Miranda, 113
Hill, Octavia, 113
Hill, Rowland, 55, 57, 62, 64
Hill, Thomas Wright, 55, 56, 62
Hill family, xiii, 4, 8, 28, *54–67*, 71, 75, 89, 100, 134, 139
  and Bruce Castle School, 55, 56, 63–6
  and Hazelwood School, 54–67
  and Hill Top School, 55
Hill Top School, 55
history in curriculum:
  American, at Bembridge, 236
  at Badminton, 186, 188
  in Steiner schools, 296
History of the Fairchild Family (Sherwood), 94
History of Philo and Amelia (Williams), 13
Hitler, Adolf, 320, 321
Hoare, Desmond, 342
Hodgson, W. B., 106, 109, 120, 127
Hof Oberkirch, 205
Hofwyl, 77, 79–81, 82, 91
Hohenfels, 318
Hohenwerda, 204
Holmes, Edmund, 192, 194, 217
Holt, Lawrence, 340
Holyoake, George Jacob, 41, 47
Home and Colonial School Society, 112
Hooker, Charles, 123
Household Words, 108, 111
How Gertrude Teaches Her Children (Pestalozzi), 76
How We Think (Dewey), 255n
Howson, G. W. S., 238, 270
Human Body Described, The (Ellis), 49
humanism and rationalism:
  at Beacon Hill, 285
  at Dartington, 278
  at King Alfred's, 162, 165, 168, 465
Humanistic schools (Ronge), 112, 136
Hume, David, 34
Hunt, Thornton, 109
Huxley, Julian, 339

Huxley, Thomas Henry, 120, 123, 138, 207, 384
Hyde rational school, 47, 48–9
Hyett, Sir Francis, 243n
Hyett, Miss V. A., at King Alfred's, 168, 170–1
hygiene in curriculum:
  at Abbotsholme, 147
  at Beacon Hill, 285
Hyndman, H. M., 144, 250, 382

Ideology and Utopia (Mannheim), 367
Illich, Ivan, 485n, 486
Ilsenburg, 202, 203, 204, 210, 212
imagination, child's, emphasis on:
  by S. Isaacs, 257
  by M. McMillan, 219
  by R. Steiner, 299
In Quest of an Ideal (Holmes), 193
Independent Labour Party, 251
individual teaching and work:
  at Dartington, 271
  in Lietz schools, 203
  in Theosophical schools, 198
  at Wennington, 348
Industrial Revolution, 33, 92, 99
industry, schools of, 7, 86, 87, 91–3, 95
Ingénu, L' (Voltaire), 18
Inner Light, Quaker belief in, 175–6, 183
inspectors, H.M., and inspections, 435–7
  introduction of, 85, 90
  at Bryanston, 305, 307, 311, 437
  at Dartington, 276, 436
  at King Alfred's, 168
  at Michael Hall, 301, 436n
  at Quaker schools, 182
  at Steiner schools, 436
  at Summerhill, 428, 436
  at Wennington, 346
Institut Jean-Jacques Rousseau, 211
Institutiones Pietatis (Matern), 175
Intellectual Growth in Young Children (Isaacs), 256n
Interest and Effort in Education (Dewey), 255n
International Bureau of Education, 211
International Bureau of New Schools, 211, 212, 355
International Exhibition (1862), 119
International School, Isleworth, 121–4, 130, 135

Index

international schools, *118–24*, 130, 134, 135
international studies and internationalism:
  at Atlantic College, 342
  at Badminton, 186, 188, 210
  at Beacon Hill, 283
  at Outward Bound schools, 341
  at Quaker and Theosophical schools, 210
  at Salem, 320, 322
Isaacs, Susan, 248–9, 251, 269, 280, 468
  and Malting House School, 254–60
  influence of Dewey, 255–6, 258, 260
  and M. Montessori, 258, 259, 260
  and Freud, 259, 260, 261
  and the Russells, 283, 285–6
  and New Education Fellowship, 365
Isleworth, 121, 130, 135
Italian in curriculum, at Bryanston, 315
Itard, J. E. M. G., 213

Jacks, H. B., 414
Jackson, Sir Cyril, 252
James, William, 320
Jardine, Professor George, 34
Jefferson, Thomas, 19, 78
Jeffreys, J. Graham, and Bryanston, 303–5, 307, 308
Johnson, Miss Finlay, 217
Jones, Ernest, 246
Journal of Education, 208
Judge, William Quan, 190, 192
Jung, Carl Gustav, 246, 297, 360, 365, 375, 468
Junior Republics, 221–3
juries and jury courts, school, 95, 96
  Bell and, 96–7
  at Cheam, 4
  at Hazelwood, 59
  at Laurence Street Academy, 25
Jusmani, A. A., 278

Kalton, G., 438, 441, 445, 449, 450, 451, 456
Kant, Emanuel, 78, 288, 289
Kay-Shuttleworth, Sir James, 74, *85–90*, 111, 119, 137, 139
  interest in Pestalozzi and Fellenberg, 85–6, 88, 89
  and education of pauper children, 86–7, 100
  and Battersea Normal College, 87–9
  and punishment, 94

Kempe, J. W. R., 338
Kent Education Committee, 251
Kenworthy, J. C., 145
Kilpatrick, W. H., xii
Kilquhanity School, 434
kindergarten movement, 111–12
King, Miss:
  at St. Christopher, 198, 199
  and Frensham, 199, 200
King Alfred School, *164–71*, 188, 201, 247
  'recognised as efficient', 168
  Children's Council, 169
  Montessori department, 218
  Neill at, 419, 421
King Alfred School Society, 163–4, 165, 167, 170
King's College School, 103
King's Somborne School, 69–74, 137
  'comprehensive' basis of, 69–70
  curriculum and teaching methods, 71–3
  attendance, 73
Kingsford, Anna, 192, 383
Kirchberg, 76
knowledge, role in education, 107, 470–2
Knowlton, Charles, 189
Knox, Vicesimus, on child nature, 19, 20
Kreutzlingen, 87
Krishnamurti, 291

Laboratory School, University of Chicago, 255, 256
Labour and Childhood (McMillan), 252
Ladell, H. R., 124
Ladies' College, Bedford Square, 115
Lamb, Charles, 13
Lambert, Dr. Royston, 279, 482
Lancaster, Joseph, 8, 35, 41, 56, 60
  and rewards and punishments, 9, 97–9
  monitorial system, 27, 34, 95
Landerziehungsheime, Lietz and, 202–6, 212, 320
Landschulheime, 205
Lane, Homer, 194, 213, *221–31*, 244, 247, 259, 471
  and Little Commonwealth, 221–7
  followers of, 227–30
  compared with Montessori, 231
Langevin, Paul, 365, 366

520 *Index*

language teaching, natural method of, 28
Large, Harold, 221
Latin – *see* classics in curriculum
Laurence Street Academy, 25–31
    fees, 23
    discipline, 25
    remedial methods, 25–6
    'reciprocal assistance', 26–7
    reforms in curriculum, 27–31
    attitude to learning languages, 28
    introduction of political economy and sociology, 30–1
Lauwerys, Joseph, 371
Lawrence, Evelyn, 260*n*, 261*n*
Le Play, Frederick, 384
Leader, The, 109
leadership principle, 57, 341
Lean, Dr. Bevan, 182
Lectures on Education (Williams), 23–31
Leeuw, G. van der, 361
Leeds Grammar School, 103
Leigh Smith, Anne, 113
Leigh Smith, Barbara – *see* Bodichon, Barbara
Leigh Smith, Benjamin, 114–15
Leigh Smith, Isabella, 113
Leighton Park School, 179, 181, 182, 183, 198, 312
    'recognised as efficient', 435
    growth rate, 442
    fees, 444
Leonard and Gertrude (Pestalozzi), 76
Lessons on Objects (Ellis), 49
Lessons on Objects (Mayo), 81
Lessons on Shells (Mayo), 81
Letchworth, 194–5, *196–201*, 353. See also St. Christopher
Letters from Hofwyl (Barwell), 80
Lewes, G. H., 109
Liberal Education (Knox), 20
Lietz, Dr. Hermann, 210, 325
    and his schools, 202–6, 212, 320
Ligue Internationale pour l'Education Nouvelle, 355
Lincoln School, New York, 266
Lindfield, 93
Lindsay of Birker, Lord, 339, 365
List of Independent Schools (*List 60*; *List 70*), 437, 439, 441
Little Commonwealth, 194, *223–6*, 228–30, 238, 240, 247, 419
Liverpool Rational school, 46–7
Lloyd George, David, 234

Local Government Act (1894), 134
Locke, John, xii, 9
London Children: how to feed them and how not to feed them (McMillan), 252
London County Council, 479–81
London College of the International Education Society (International School), 120, 121–4, 130, 135, 137
London Echo, 252
Loom of Youth, The (Waugh), 468
Lorimer, James, 119, 120, 135
love, importance of, emphasis on:
    by K. Barnes, 350
    by H. Lane, 224
    by A. S. Neill, 433
    by B. Russell, 286
    by R. Steiner, 294
Lovelace, Lord, 93
Lovett, William, 125, 130
Lyttelton, Edward, 155, 156
Lytton, Lord, 224, 225*n*
Lyward, George, 345

Maberly, Gerald C., 164
McCallister, W. J., 220, 222
MacDonald, Ramsay, 321
McDougall, William, 468
Mack, E. C., xiii, 152
Mackay, R. W., 109
Mackenzie, Mr., of Braehead, 479
Mackintosh, Sir James, 32
McMillan, Margaret, *249–54*, 282, 283
    and Séguin, 213
    and M. Montessori, 219, 252
    work in Bradford, 251
    with Rachel in London, 251–3
    on aims of Nursery Schools Association, 253
    compared with S. Isaacs, 260, 261
    and R. Steiner, 293
McMillan, Rachel, 249–53, 260
MacMunn, Norman, 217, 227–8, 229
MacNab, H. G., 41
Madras Asylum, 97
Maitland, Edward, 192, 383, 411
Malting House School, 249, *255–61*, 280, 283
    and Beacon Hill, 285–6
Man and Society (Mannheim), 367
Manchester, 86, 110, 130, 153
    influence on Owen, 33
Manchester Committee for the Extension of the Kindergarten System, 112

Index

Manchester Froebel Society, 112, 138
Manchester Literary and Philosophical Society, 18, 34
Manchester University Settlement, Ancoats, 234, 237
Mann, Thomas, 367
Mannheim, Karl, 367-9
Manson, David, 3, 71, 100
  early life, 8-9
  as hedge schoolmaster, 8
  and Belfast Play School, 9-11
  as social reformer, 12
manual work in curriculum, 91-3, 465
  at Abbotsholme, 146, 346, 391
  at Bedales, 346
  at Clayesmore, 157, 159
  in Lietz schools, 203
  in Quaker schools, 176, 182
  at Wennington, 346
Marcault, Émile, 306, 365
mark system, 56, 59
Married Women's Property Acts, 116
Martineau, Harriet, 109, 115
Marx, Karl, 289
Mason, Charlotte, 218-19
Matern, John, 175
Mathematics, New, 473
Maurice, F. D., 113, 385
Mayo, Dr. Charles, 47, 81-2, 89, 137, 139
Mayo, Elizabeth, 81, 139
meals, school, 251
Mechanics' Institutes, 49, 127
medical inspection and treatment, 162, 251, 252, 260
Meier, Frederic Alfred, 413-14
Meissner, Dr. Erich, 203-4, 321-2
Merchant Taylors' School, 132
merit tickets, 95, 96-7, 99
Meux, Lady, 250
Miall, F. W., 164, 165
Miall, Louis Compton, 163
Michael Hall School, 293, 301
  'recognised as efficient', 436n
  growth rate, 442
  fees, 444
middle classes:
  alternatives to public school, 56, 66
  and late 19th-c. innovators, 103-5, 109-10, 135, 139
Mill, James, 100, 125, 126
Mill, Sir John, 68
Mill, John Stuart, 126, 129, 137, 138, 140

Mill Hill School, 64
Mitford, Colonel William, 7
Modern School, Letchworth – *see* St. Christopher
Molesworth, J. N., 104
Molt, Emil, 291
monitorial system:
  Manson's anticipation of, 5
  Williams's form of, 27
  Bell and Lancaster, 5, 27, 34, 95-8
Monckton Wyld School, 345, 347, 469
Montagu, George, later Earl of Sandwich, 221, 226
Montesquieu, Baron de La Brède et de, 76
Montessori, Maria, 193, *213-21*, 228, 308, 360, 473
  early years and work, 213-15
  and M. McMillan, 219, 252
  compared with Lane, 231
  and S. Isaacs, 258, 259, 260
  and New Education Fellowship, 354-5, 361, 365
Montessori Method:
  at Bedales, 218
  and Mrs. Ensor, 194
  at King Alfred's, 166, 218
  and New Ideals in Education, 193
  in Quaker schools, 218
  at St. Christopher, 196, 218
  at St. George's, Harpenden, 218
Montessori Method, The (Montessori), 215
Montgomery, B. H., 169
moral education, Hahn's and Reddie's emphasis on, 320, 335-6, 390-1
Moral Philosophy (Combe), 109, 117
Moral Principles in Education (Dewey), 255n
Moray Badge scheme, 330, 332, 339, 341
More, Hannah, 20-1, 26
More, Sir Thomas, 51
Morgan, John Minter, 42, 51
Morley, Henry, 110-11, 129, 134, 135, 136, 137, 138, 139
Morris, William, 93, 144, 199, 235, 250, 404
Moseley, Rev. Henry, 73
Mount School, The, York, 178, 179, 182, 185, 312
mountaineering, 330, 341, 343
Muirhead, R. F., 146, 391, 393
Müller, Friedrich Max, 188, 190

Index

Mullins, Alice, 164
Mumford, Lewis, 384n
Münchenbuchsee, 76, 77
Murray, Gilbert, 188
Museum, 119
music in curriculum:
  at Abbotsholme, 147
  at Bryanston, 307, 310, 313
  at Clayesmore, 157
  in Quaker schools, 182
  in Steiner schools, 294, 298
My Pedagogic Creed (Dewey), 255n
Mylne, Professor James, 34
Mysticism (Steiner), 289

Naples, 130
National Association for the Promotion of Social Science, 104
National Community Friendly Society, 44
National Froebel Union, 112, 138
National Hall School, 130
National Society, 74, 88, 132
National Union of Teachers, 476
'natural' education, 15–18, 23–5, 34
'negative' education, 14
Neill, A. S., 274, 278, 280, 357, *415–34*, 439, 468, 479
  at King Alfred's, 166, 167, 419, 421
  and H. Lane, 167, 230, 247, 418, 419
  and Montessori system, 220
  and psychoanalysis, 247–8, 421
  similarities with K. Barnes, 351
  and New Education Fellowship, 355, 419
  early years and journalism, 415–18
  attitude to 'culture', 420, 426–7
  international school in Austria, 420
  and Summerhill, 421–34
  educational principles, *423–8*, 471, 472
New Education Fellowship, 211, 212, *353–77*, 419, 467
  Theosophical origins, 167, 194–5, 196, 201, 306, 353–4
  first conference (1921), 354–5, 359
  statement of principles, 356–7, 363
  organisation and membership, 357–60
  themes and conferences, 360–5
  1932 statement of principles, 362–3
  individual participants, 365–6
  wartime developments, 366–72
  Inter-Allied conference (1942), 369–70
  and UNESCO, 371, 373–5
  E.N.E.F. and 1944 Act, 371–2
  post-war egalitarian trend, 372–3, 376
  achievement and influence, 375–7
New Era in Home and School, 211, 217, 220, 248, 354, 355–7, 360, 364, 365, 372, 419
New Era International Conferences, 354–5, 359–63
New Ideals in Education, 193, 194, 196, 305
New Ideals Quarterly, 193, 306
New Lanark, 33, 34, 36, 38, 43
New Lanark Day School, 37–42, 47
New Lanark Infant School, 39–42, 47
New Moral World, 45, 46, 49
New School, Streatham – *see* Michael Hall
New Schools and New School movement, 155, 160, 161, 171–2, 173–4, 205, 210–12, 233
Newcastle Commission (1861), 113, 132, 134
Newsom, Sir John, Public School Commission, 440, 445, 476
Nicholson, Caroline, 485
Nietzsche, Friedrich, 289
Nightingale, Florence, 125
'noble savage', 14
  cult of, 18
normal schools, 86, 87
North of England Agricultural School (now Great Ayton), 179
North London Collegiate School, 185
Norwood School of Industry, 86, 87
Nunn, Sir Percy, 217, 246–7, 365, 368
nursery and infant schools and groups:
  at Badminton, 218
  at Beacon Hill, 282–3
  at Dartington, 268
  at King Alfred's, 165, 218
  McMillan sisters and, 219, 251, 253–4
  at St. Christopher, 218
  in Steiner schools, 294
Nursery Schools Association, 219, 253
Nussbaum, Robert, 354

O'Neill, Edward, 478–9
Oak Lane County Day School, Philadelphia, 271
object method, 77
  in Owenite and Rational schools, 39, 47–8

Index

Ockham, 93
Odenwald, 205, 212
Of the Education of the Poor (Bernard), 92
Olcott, Colonel H. S., 189, 190
Olive, G. W., 345
On Education (Russell), 280
open air, McMillan sisters' emphasis on, 253
Opie, Mrs., 115
Origins of Love and Hate, The (Suttie), 350
Orthophrenic School, Rome, 214
Osborne, C. H., 240*n*
Outward Bound movement, 312, 324, 332, 339–41
Owen, Robert, xi, 18, *33–42*, 71, 75, 80, 93, 100, 134, 138, 261, 466
  and Industrial Revolution, 33
  influences of Manchester and Scotland, 33–4
  educational theories, 34–6
  his ten innovations, 40
  and New Lanark Day School, 39–42
  followers of, *42–54*, 117
  and Co-operative schools, 43
  and Rational Religionists, 44
  utopian schemes, 50–1, 52
Owen, Robert Dale, 38, 55, 60, 80

pacifism:
  influence at Beacon Hill, 281
  in New Education Fellowship, 375
  at Wennington, 346
  among former pupils, 458–9
Pädagogik im Grundriss (Rein), 202
Pall Mall Gazette, 394
parents:
  participation of, at King Alfred's, 167, 170
  occupations of, 447, 456
  social class, 448–9
Parents' National Educational Union, 218
Paris, 87, 120
Parker, Barry, 168
Parkhurst, Helen, xii, 365, 473
  and Dalton Plan, 305, 306, 308–9
Parks, Bessie, 115
Paul-Jones, Mrs., 170
pauper children, 86–7
'payment by results' – *see* Revised Code
Peckham, 117
Pedley, Dr. R., 477, 481
Pemberton, Robert, 42
  influenced by Owen, 50–1
  utopian schemes, 51–3, 54
  language teaching experiments, 53
Percival, Dr. Thomas, 18, 34
Pereire, J. R., 213
Perry, L. R., 469
Pestalozzi, Johann Heinrich, xii, 35, 51, 67, 111, 163
  life of, 75–6
  educational theories, 76–7
  and Fellenberg, 77–8
  effects of, 81, 85, 86, 100, 137, 139, 201, 221
  and manual education, 91
Pestalozzian method:
  at Owenite schools, 47, 48, 51
  in Britain generally, 75, 81–4, 86–9
Peters, Richard, 475, 486
Philanthropic Society, 95, 96, 97
Phillips, M. P., 303*n*
philosophical societies, 18
philosophy in curriculum, at Bryanston, 315
Philosophy of Spiritual Activity, The (Steiner), 289
phrenology, 105–7, 109
physical fitness, Hahn's emphasis on, 319, 322, 325, 329, 339, 343
Piaget, Jean, 261, 360, 365
Pieron, H., 365
Pioneers, at Bryanston, 312
Plato and his *Republic*, influence on Hahn, 320, 325, 331, 334, 337, 344
play methods, 417, 468
playing-cards, teaching by, 11
political economy, at Laurence Street Academy, 30. *See also* social science
Poole, Thomas, 13
Poor Law Amendment Act (1834), 86
Poor School, Hofwyl, 79, 80
Portman Hall School, 113–18
Potempa incident, 320, 335
Pour L'Ere Nouvelle, 211, 356, 360, 372
Powell, Oswald, 412
Practice and Theory of Bolshevism, The (Russell), 282
Praetorius, Rosalie and Mina, 112
Prestolee Elementary School, 478–9
Priestley, Joseph, 18, 19, 32, 56, 115
primary schools – *see* elementary and primary schools
Principles of Education: Intellectual, Moral and Physical (L. Carpenter), 62
Principles of Social Reconstruction (Russell), 269

Printing School, Whitechapel, 93
programmed learning, 301, 473, 484
Progressive Education, 372
projects, 203, 329–30, 339, 473
psychoanalytical movement, 246–8, 254, 259, 360, 375, 468
Public Education (Hill), 56–62, 63, 67
public schools, 186
  in 18th century, 3–4
  in 19th century, 66
  reform of, 132, 139
  grammar schools modelled on, 143
  in relation to Abbotsholme, 146, 172, 390
    to Bedales, 151, 172
    to Bembridge, 234–7
    to Rendcomb, 238–45
  attendance figures, 437–8
  post-war attacks on, 439–40, 467, 476
  fees, 441–5
  social class of pupils, 449
  further education, 451
  professions, 456, 461
Public Schools Act (1868), 132, 143
Public Schools for the Middle Classes (Fortescue), 104
Public Schools and Public Opinion, The (Mack), 152*n*
punctuality, at Hazelwood, 58, 60
punishment, 94–9
  in Steiner schools, 299
punishment, corporal, 94
punishment, corporal, abolition of:
  at Belfast Play School, 8
  at Bryanston, 307
  in George Junior Republic, 222
  at Laurence Street Academy, 25
  at Morley's school, 110
  at New Lanark, 38, 39–40
  in Quaker schools, 183
  in Steiner schools, 299
  in Theosophical schools, 197
punishment, unorthodox:
  at Belfast Play School, 9
  at Cheam, 4–5
  at Hazelwood, 56, 59, 60
  in Lancaster's monitorial schools, 97–9
pupil-teachers, 86, 90
Pyke, Geoffrey, 254, 258, 260, 280, 285–6

Quaker schools, 91, 98, 173, *174–83*, 210, 315, 467
  founding of, 177–9
  co-education, 177, 182–3
  only girls' school, 178, 182
  for 'disowned', 178–9
  non-Friends as pupils and teachers, 180
  curriculum, 182
  Children's Councils, 183
  Montessori methods in, 218
  social class of pupils, 448–9
  leaving age, 451
  choice of career, 453–9
  occupational groups, 462–3
Queen's College, London, 185
Queen's Scholarships, 90
Queenwood Agricultural College, 72
Quick, A. O. H., 240*n*

Rachel McMillan Training College, 253
Radhakrishnan, Sir Sarvepalli, 362, 365
Raikes, Robert, 95, 97
Ralahine agricultural colony, 84
Randall, Miss, at Badminton, 185
rank in schools, 95
  at Belfast Play School, 8, 10–11
  at Hazelwood, 59, 61
Rational Religionists, Universal Community Society of, 44–5, 49, 54
Rational schools, 44–8
rationalism – *see* humanism and rationalism
Rawlinson, J. F. P., 226
Rawson, Wyatt, 193, 353*n*
'reciprocal assistance' method, 27
records of children:
  at Bryanston, 309–10
  at King Alfred's, 162
  at Wennington, 348
  See also Dalton Plan
Red Hill School, 345
Reddie, Cecil, 93, 124, *144–51*, 171–2, 236, 269, 307, 335, *378–401*, 415
  early life and education, 144–5, 378–82, 408
  influence of Ruskin, 144, 147, 233, 383
  and Fellowship of New Life, 144–5, 148, 388–90, 409
  and Abbotsholme, *145–51*, 173, 202, 206, 210, 212, 347, 387–8, *391–9*, 407, 408, 409, 439, 465, 466, 467
  and Badley, 149–53, 394–5, 407–11
  and Devine, 155, 156–7, 161

Index

and Lietz, 202-3, 206
and Hahn, 206, 331
and Scout movement, 207
and Demolins, 207-8
and Ferrière, 210
achievement, 212, 400-1
admiration of Germany, 382, 397, 399, 400
influence of Campbell and Geddes, 383-5
influence of Carpenter, 385-90
Reddie, Florence, 378
Rein, Wilhelm, 202, 203, 212
Reiner, Charles, 81, 82
Reinhardt, Kurt, 318, 319
religion, radical views on, 136-7
religious instruction:
  non-sectarian at Abbotsholme, 147
  none at Beacon Hill, 283
  none in Birkbeck schools, 128, 137
  at Bryanston, 310
  at Dartington, 277
  at Isleworth College, 123, 137
  none at King Alfred's, 163
  at Laurence Street Academy, 31
  in Lietz schools, 203
  by Rational Religionists, 45-6, 48
  non-sectarian at St. Christopher, 198
  none at Summerhill, 422
  at Wennington, 348
Rendcomb College, 152n, 229, *238-45*, 312
Rendu, Eugène, 119, 120
Rennie, Belle, 193, 308-9
Republic, The – see Plato
Research in Education, Society for, 236
Revised Code (1862), 90, 99, 128, 132, 171, 172
rewards, 95, 97-8, 99
Rham, Rev. W. L., 93
Ricardo, David, 126
Rice, Charles E., 164-6
Richmond, Admiral, 339, 341
Risinghill Comprehensive School, 434, 479-82
Roberts, Paul, 200
Roe, Anne, 453, 463
Rogers, Rev. William, 130
Ronge, Bertha, 111-12, 134, 138
Ronge, Johannes, 111-12, 134, 136, 138, 139
Roosevelt, Eleanor, 367
Roscoe, William, 18
Rotten, Dr. Elizabeth, 355, 361, 365, 375

Rousseau, Jean-Jacques, xi, xii, 3, 35, 39, 51, 89, 100, 111
  effect on English educational thought, *12-22*, 67, 137, 139, 201
  ideal of 'negative education', 14, 15
  and natural education, 15-18
  and four periods of educative process, 15-17, 24
  opposition to, 19-21
  influence on Pestalozzi, 75, 77, 78
  and manual education, 91
Royal Society, 29
Rugby School, 63, 132, 143, 228, 229, 239, 403-4
Rugg, Dr. Harold, 362, 365, 375
Ruskin, John, 93, 130, 190, 199, 466
  influence on Badley, 404
  on Reddie, 144, 147, 233, 383
  on Whitehouse, 234, 235, 237
Russell, Bertrand, *279-86*, 468
  Curry and, 269-70, 285
  political and social views, 280-2
  educational theories and experiments, 280-6
  and Beacon Hill, 280, 282-6
Russell, Dora, 280-6
Russell, James Earl, 264
Russell, John, and King Alfred's, 166-7, 419
Russian in curriculum, 284, 315
Ryan, Carson, 365

Sacred Books of the East, The (ed. Müller), 189
Sadler, Michael, 365
Saffron Walden School, 152n, 178, 179, 182
  'recognised as efficient', 436
  fees, 441, 443, 444
  growth rate, 442
St. Brandon's School, 185
St. Christopher School, Letchworth, 196-201
  Theosophical origin, 196-7
  co-education and community aims, 197
  Montessori school at, 196, 218
  curriculum, 197-8
  non-sectarian religious teaching, 198
  re-organization, 200-1
  'recognised as efficient', 436
  growth rate, 442
  fees, 444
St. Elphin's School, 185

St. George-in-the-East School, 479
St. George's School, Harpenden, 200, 217, 218, 234
Saint-Germain-en-Laye, 120
St. Mary's Town and Country School, 345
St. Paul's School, 132
St. Thomas's, Charterhouse, 130
salaries, 445-6
Salem group of schools, 204, 206, 307, 312, *318-22*, 324, 333, 347
'Salem laws', 325-7
Salford Co-operative school, 43
Sanderson, Miss B. M., 187, 188
Sandford and Merton (Day), 13-14, 15
Sane Schooling (Simpson), 152n, 240n
Santiniketan, 199, 262
Sargant, William, 62, 67
Schmitz, Dr. Leonard, 121, 124, 134, 135
School, The (Curry), 271n, 272
School and Society, The (Dewey), 255
school-leaving age, 449-51
School Leaving Age Project, 473
School Meeting, at Summerhill, 428
Schools Council, 377, 473, 483
Schools Inquiry Commission (1868), 57, 64, 122
Schools of Tomorrow (McMillan), 252
Schwabe, Mme. Salis, 130
science in curriculum, 105, 108-10
  at Badminton, 187
  at Beacon Hill, 284
  in Birkbeck schools, 128
  at Bryanston, 315
  at Clifton, 144
  at Hazelwood and Bruce Castle, 63-4, 66
  at Isleworth College, 123, 124
  at King's Somborne, 72
  in Lietz schools, 203
  at Malting House, 257
  at New Lanark, 39
  Nuffield Science, 473
  in Quaker schools, 176, 182
Scientific Educational Institution for the Higher Social Classes (Hofwyl), 79-80
Scott, Sir Walter, 80
Sea Cadet Corps, 312-13
seamanship in curriculum:
  at Bryanston, 312-13
  at Gordonstoun, 330, 332
  at Outward Bound schools, 340-1

Secret Doctrine, The (Blavatsky), 189
Seed Time, 145, 390
Séguin, E., 213-14
self-expression as educational concept:
  in work of S. Isaacs, 257
  at first New Era International Conference, 354, 360
  in Neill's work, 418
self-government:
  at Badminton, 186, 188
  at Beacon Hill, 284
  at Clayesmore, 158
  at Dartington, 271, 273-5
  in George Junior Republic, 222
  at Gordonstoun, 328-9
  at Hazelwood, 56, 59
  at King Alfred's, 166, 169
  at Laurence Street Academy, 25, 26
  in Little Commonwealth, 225-6
  in Quaker schools, 183
  at Rendcomb, 240, 243-4
  at Rugby, 229, 239
  at Salford Co-operative school, 43
  at Summerhill, 422, 428-9
  in Theosophical schools, 197
  at Tiptree Hall, 228
  at Wennington, 348-9
  at Wickersdorf, 205
  See also discipline and authority; teacher-pupil relationship
seminar and discussion method, 304
Sergi, Giuseppe, 213
'setting', at Bryanston, 310
Sevenoaks School, 483
sex instruction, at Abbotsholme, 147
sexuality, acceptance of:
  at Dartington, 275
  at Malting House, 259-60
  at Summerhill, 422, 433
'shaming' as punishment 9, 98
Sharp, Cecil J., 164, 165
Sharp, Colin:
  and Abbotsholme, 148-9, 307, 398-9
  on Reddie, 398, 400, 410
Shaw, George Bernard, 250, 389
Shaw, Otto, 345
Sheffield Rational school, 47
Sherwood, Mrs., 94
Shrewsbury School, 132
Sibford School, 152n, 179, 182
Sidcot Quaker school, 91, 152n, 177, 179
silence:
  at Hazelwood, 58

Index

Hahn's emphasis on, 326, 338
Simon, B., 135
Simpson, J. H., 152n, 193, 247, 269
   and Lane, 229–30, 244
   at Rendcomb, 229, *238–44*
   early career, 238, 270
Sinnett, A. P., 189, 192
Slack, Timothy, 414
Slavson, Richard, 258, 260
Smith, Adam, 34
Smith, William, 115
Smith-Cumming, Lady, 318
social class of pupils, 448–9
Social Development in Young Children (Isaacs), 256n, 259
social sciences in curriculum, 109, 110
   at Badminton, 186, 188
   in Birkbeck schools, 125, 127–31
   at Bryanston, 315
   at St. Christopher, 198.
   See also civics
social work by schoolchildren:
   at Atlantic College, 343
   at Badminton, 186, 187
   at Bryanston, 312
   at Gordonstoun, 330
socialism and communism, influence of, 171
   on Badley, 406
   on Miss Hyett, 168
   on McMillan sisters, 250
   on Reddie, 144
   on Russells, 281
Sociology of Teaching, The (Waller), 471
Somerville, Mrs., 115
Songs for Children (Ellis), 49
Soper, Clare, 365
Sower, The (later *Seed Time*), 145, 390
Spanish in curriculum, at Bryanston, 315
Spencer, Herbert, 104, 109, 138, 140, 163, 247
Spetzgert, 318
Spiekeroog, 204
Spiritual Ground of Education, The (Steiner), 292
Spurzheim, J. G., 105, 107, 109
Sriniketan, 263
Star in the East, 46
State and Boarding Education, The (Lambert), 279
Steiner, Rudolf, 190, 192, *287–302*, 468
   and Anthroposophy, 288–302
   rift with Theosophical Society, 290–1
   educational theories, 291–302

schools 'recognised as efficient', 436n
Stekel, Wilhelm, 248
Stewart, Dugald, 34
Stewart, J. A., 318
Stow, David, 105
Strachey, Lytton, 468
Straight, Willard, 264
Suggestive Hints towards Improved Secular Instruction (Dawes), 72
Summerhill School, xiii, 230, 231, 248, 278, *421–32*
   few restrictions, 421–2
   co-education, 422
   anarchic community, 422, 424–5
   neglect of intellect, 425–8, 430
   problem children at, 427–8
   not 'recognised as efficient', 428, 432, 436
   School Meeting, 428–9
   staff, 429–30
   lack of records, 430–1
   few former pupils as teachers, 453
   See also Neill
Sunday schools, 95
   of Rational Religionists, 45
Suttie, I., 350
Swedenborg, Emanuel, 190
Swiss schools based on Abbotsholme, 205
Synge, J. H., 81

Tagore, Rabindranath, 199, 262–4
Taine, H. A., 17
Taunton Commission (1868), 134, 143, 178, 180, 186
Tawney, R. H., 362, 365
Taylor, Christopher, 175
teacher–pupil relationship, 135–6, 466, 470–2
   at Abbotsholme, 147, 170, 381
   at Badminton, 184, 187
   at Bedales, 170
   at Claysmore, 170
   at King Alfred's, 170
   at Laurence Street Academy, 26–7
   Owenite schools, 40, 43
   at Wennington, 351
   at Wickersdorf, 205
teacher training, 86, 87–90, 128
Teaching of Common Things, The (Dawes), 72
teaching machines, 307
Temple, William, Archbishop of York, 321, 322, 339
Tensions Project, 374

Thackeray, W. M., 109
Theosophical Educational Trust, 167, 173, 195, *196–201*, 218, 242
Theosophical Fraternity in Education, 167, *192–6*, 218, 353, 354
Theosophical schools, 194–201, 210
Theosophical Society, 167, 189, 190–2, 290–1
Theosophists and education, 188–201, 287
Thomas, Margaret, 447n
Thorndike, Edward Lee, 264
Thornycroft, Hans, 164
Thorp, Miss, matron of Bedales, 412
Thring, Edward, 147
ticket system of discipline, 95, 96–7, 99
Tiptree Hall School, 227
Tobler, Herman, 205
Today, 390
Tolstoy, Leo, 199
Tonbridge School, 20
Towards Democracy (Carpenter), 386
Towards a Quaker View of Sex (Barnes), 351
Toynbee, Arnold, 233
Toynbee Hall, 233–4, 237
Training Plan, at Gordonstoun, 327–8, 331, 336, 473
Trevelyan, G. M., 341
Trevelyan Scholarships, 343
Trimmer, Mrs. Sarah, 15
Tschiffelli's experimental farm, Kirchberg, 76
Tuckfield, Mrs., 93
Tufnell, Carleton, 86
Tuke, William, 177
tutorials, at Bryanston, 304, 309
Twining, Thomas, 120
Tyndall, John, 120

Ulich, Robert, 365
Underhill, Evelyn, 306
UNESCO, 371, 373–4
Union, 44
Universal Brotherhood and Theosophical Society, 190
University College, London, 111
University College School, 103
Uppingham School, 143
Urban, Carl and Eleanor, 347
Utilitarians, 129, 138
Utopia (More), 51

Vandeleur, J. S., 84

Versailles, 87
View of the Elementary Principles of Education, A (Spurzheim), 107
Village Colleges, 237
Volkov, Dr. Peggy, 365
Voltaire, 18

Wade, John, 127
Walker, Charles, 40
Wallasey, 110
Waller, Willard, 471, 472
Wallis, Isabel White, 164
Wallon, Henri, 362, 366
Wandervögel, 206–7
Washburne, Dr. Carlton, 362
Washington, George, 78
Watt, James, 18
Waugh, Alec, 468
Weardale, 99
Wedgwood, Josiah, 18
Wehrli, Jacob, 80, 87, 89
Weltbund für Erneuerung der Erziehung, 355
Wennington School, *345–52*, 469
'recognised as efficient', 437
growth rate, 442
fees, 444
Werdende Zeitalter, Das, 211, 356, 360
Wesley, John, on child nature, 20
Westminster Infant School, 115
Westminster Review, 109
Westminster School, 93, 132
What is and What Might Be (Holmes), 192
Whitechapel, 93
Whitehead, Alfred North, 273
Whitehead, Elizabeth (Mrs. F. Malleson), 113, 114, 117, 118, 130
Whitehouse, George, 232
Whitehouse, John Howard, 232–8
Liberalism and Quakerism, 232, 234, 236
influence of Ruskin, 233–4, 235
at Toynbee Hall, 233
at Bembridge, 234–8
idea of School Base, 237
Whitman, Walt, 144, 385
Whitwell, Miss, at New Lanark, 41
Whynstones School, 293
'recognised as efficient', 436n
Wickersdorf, 205, 206, 212
Wicksteed, J. H., 411
and King Alfred's, 165, 167–8
Wicksteed, Philip, 167